MODALITY IN GRAMMAR AND DISCOURSE

TYPOLOGICAL STUDIES IN LANGUAGE (TSL)

A companion series to the journal "STUDIES IN LANGUAGE"

Volumes in this series will be functionally and typologically oriented, covering specific topics in language by collecting together data from a wide variety of languages and language typologies. The orientation of the volumes will be substantive rather than formal, with the aim of investigating universals of human language via as broadly defined a data base as possible, leaning toward cross-linguistic, diachronic, developmental and live-discourse data. The series is, in spirit as well as in fact, a continuation of the tradition initiated by C. Li (*Word Order and Word Order Change, Subject and Topic, Mechanisms for Syntactic Change*) and continued by T. Givón (*Discourse and Syntax*) and P. Hopper (*Tense-Aspect: Between Semantics and Pragmatics*).

Volume 32

Joan Bybee and Suzanne Fleischman (eds)

Modality in Grammar and Discourse

MODALITY IN GRAMMAR AND DISCOURSE

Edited by

JOAN BYBEE
University of New Mexico
SUZANNE FLEISCHMAN
University of California, Berkeley

JOHN BENJAMINS PUBLISHING COMPANY
AMSTERDAM/PHILADELPHIA

The paper used in this publication meets the minimum requirements of American National Standard for Information Sciences — Permanence of Paper for Printed Library Materials, ANSI Z39.48-1984.

Library of Congress Cataloging-in-Publication Data

Modality in grammar and discourse / edited by Joan Bybee, Suzanne Fleischman.
p. cm. -- (Typological studies in language, ISSN 0167-7373; v. 32)
Papers from a symposium on Mood and Modality held at the University of New Mexico in 1992.
Includes bibliographical references and index.
1. Modality (Linguistics)--Congresses. 2. Grammar, Comparative and general--Mood--Congresses. I. Bybee, Joan L. II. Fleischman, Suzarne. III. Series.
P299.M6M64 1995
415--dc20 95-17034
ISBN 90 272 2925 2 (hb.) / 90 272 2926 0 (pb.) (European; alk. paper) CIP
ISBN 1-55619-639-3 (hb.) / 1-55619-640-7 (pb.) (U.S.; alk. paper)

John Benjamins Publishing Co. • P.O.Box 75577 • 1070 AN Amsterdam • The Netherlands
John Benjamins North America • P.O.Box 27519 • Philadelphia PA 19118-0519 • USA

To the memory of Dwight Bolinger

Contents

Modality in Grammar and Discourse
An Introductory Essay*

Joan Bybee
University of New Mexico

Suzanne Fleischman
University of California, Berkeley

This volume is the result of a symposium on Mood and Modality held at the University of New Mexico in 1992, the goal of which was to bring together linguists whose research has targeted this area of grammar but whose approaches to it reflect differing perspectives on functional linguistics. The symposium was planned so as to include a diversity of languages, of foci (synchronic and diachronic), and of theoretical orientations, especially with regard to the interaction of morphosyntactic, semantic and discourse-pragmatic factors.

Given the complexity of this linguistic domain, the many and diverse ways it comes to be expressed in different languages, and the tendency of researchers to work narrowly within the confines of their own theoretical and methodological frameworks, there was reason to fear that symposium participants might not find adequate common ground nor a sufficiently common metalanguage to be able to communicate with one another. However, just as a similar symposium on tense and aspect a decade earlier (Hopper 1982) confirmed the status of those categories as valid cross-language categories of grammar—what we refer to, following Bybee & Dahl (1989), as 'gram types'—, so too the current symposium succeeded in demonstrating that despite differences in terminology, language areas, and theoretical perspectives, we were in effect all examining similar phenomena and could participate in meaningful dialogue about our data and analyses. Thus while the papers in this volume present a wide range of topics and perspectives, they nonetheless converge around a number of key issues, and in the aggregate seem to have succeeded in moving us toward a better understanding of the functions of modality and its forms of expression in natural language.

In the course of the symposium several essential issues came up repeatedly regarding both the categories in question and the levels of linguistic analysis at which they operate. One of the most basic of these issues concerns the relationship between 'mood' and 'modality'.

Mood and modality

As used here, **mood** refers to a formally grammaticalized category of the verb which has a **modal** function. Moods are expressed inflectionally, generally in distinct sets of verbal paradigms, e.g. indicative, subjunctive, optative, imperative, conditional, etc., which vary from one language to another in respect to number as well as to the semantic distinctions they mark. **Modality**, on the other hand, is the semantic domain pertaining to elements of meaning that languages express. It covers a broad range of semantic nuances—jussive, desiderative, intentive, hypothetical, potential, obligative, dubitative, hortatory, exclamative, etc.—whose common denominator is the addition of a supplement or overlay of meaning to the most neutral semantic value of the proposition of an utterance, namely factual and declarative.[1]

In the terms of the framework set forth in Bybee and Dahl (1989), modality is a *semantic domain*, while moods, as formal categories of grammar, can be either cross-language *gram types* (e.g. conditional or subjunctive) or *language-specific categories* (e.g. the Delayed Imperative in Buriat, an Altaic language; note that we distinguish these two levels by use of an initial upper case letter to signal language- or family-specific categories, retaining lower case for cross-language gram types.)

Modality is expressed in language in a variety of ways: morphological, lexical, syntactic, or via intonation. These are not mutually exclusive. Thus in the Spanish sentence *dudo que haya ganado el premio* 'I doubt (that) he won the prize', the 'dubitative' modality is conveyed redundantly by both the lexical meaning of the main verb and the subjunctive mood of the subordinate-clause verb. In this volume we will be concerned primarily with grammatical (morphological and syntactic) expressions of modality, including forms that may be currently undergoing grammaticalization.

Function and its relation to linguistic form

A second issue we wish to clarify at the outset of our discussion concerns the relationship between domains of modality and their expression in natural languages. In some approaches to modality, function is studied for its own sake. In this volume we take the position that analysis of function should explain distribution of form. That is, the modal categories we operate with do not lead an autonomous existence in some abstract logical or semantic space; rather, they correspond to—indeed are determined by—(a) the formal distinctions made in particular languages, (b) documented pathways of language change, and (c) prominent cross-language patterns of form-function correlation.

In the area of modality, however, cross-language comparison has been a difficult task, for several reasons. First, because the semantic/functional domain of modality is so broad; second, because modality, as we have discovered, lends itself best to investigation in social, interactive contexts (elaborated below); third, and conceivably most important, because of the extent to which languages differ in their mapping of the relevant semantic content onto linguistic form. A case in point that came up repeatedly in the course of our discussions concerns the category **irrealis** and the nature of the realis/irrealis distinction. The languages that came under our scrutiny differed in terms of what they classify as realis and what they classify as irrealis, prompting us to question whether the distinction is cross-linguistically valid at all, and if so, whether it corresponds to a gram-type distinction, such as perfective/imperfective, or whether it more closely resembles a supercategory such as mood.

As noted above, it also became clear over the course of our discussions at the symposium that many of the functions of modality are inextricably embedded in contexts of social interaction and, consequently, cannot be described adequately apart from their contextual moorings in interactive discourse. Several papers in this volume explore particular modalities specifically as they occur in contexts of face-to-face communication. But even in those that do not make explicit reference to contexts of social interaction, this factor is nonetheless in evidence.

Modal categories and their associated nomenclature

Our linguistic understanding of modality has its roots in modal logic (a branch of philosophy of language) and in particular in the distinction between 'deontic' and 'epistemic' modality. Modal logic has to do with the notions of possibility and necessity, and its categories epistemic and deontic concern themselves with these notions in two different domains. Epistemic modality has to do with the possibility or necessity of *the truth of propositions*, and is thus involved with knowledge and belief (Lyons 1977:793). Deontic modality, on the other hand, is concerned with the necessity or possibility of acts performed by morally responsible agents (Lyons 1977: 823), and is thus associated with the *social functions of permission and obligation.*

The epistemic notion is of considerable use to linguists, given that many languages have grammatical markers which function explicitly to express an evaluation of the truth of a proposition. Accordingly, most linguists understand epistemic modality as expressing the degree of a speaker's commitment to the truth of the proposition contained in an utterance. Thus, one way epistemic possibility is expressed in English is by *may* and *might* (*we may/ might lose the election*), while epistemic necessity is expressed by *must* (*they must have won the election*). However, as applied to natural language, there is no reason to restrict the epistemic notion just to necessity and possibility, as is traditional in philosophy of language. For one thing, commitment to the truth of a proposition is often a matter of degree. For another, epistemic modality can be seen as overlapping with, or even encompassing, another grammatical category, namely evidentiality.[2] For our purpose, the former expansion of the epistemic notion will be adhered to (i.e. construal along a continuum) but not the latter. The symposium from which this volume emerges deliberately excluded the study of evidentials, which were the subject of an earlier meeting in this same series (see Chafe and Nichols 1986).

Deontic modality has also proven to be a useful concept for linguists; however, its translation into linguistic categories has not been as smooth as in the case of epistemic modality (cf. Bybee 1985, Bybee, Pagliuca and Perkins 1991). As understood in philosophy of language, deontic modality focuses on the notions of obligation and permission. It is found in directives that grant permission (*you may go now*) or impose obligations (*eat your vegetables!*), as well as in statements that report deontic conditions (*Yeltsin should slow down reforms in Russia*; *graduate students can check out books for the whole semester*).

A problem with the deontic notion for linguists, however, is the imperfect nature of its fit with the corresponding linguistic categories that we encounter in the world's languages as well as in language change: i.e., it is at once too broad and too narrow. For one thing, unlike 'agent-oriented' modality—a supercategory label that will be used by most papers in this volume in preference to 'deontic'[3]—deontic modality fails to distinguish subcategories that are expressed *inflectionally* (i.e. as grammaticalized moods), such as imperative, from *lexical* or *periphrastic* (i.e. auxiliary) expressions of obligation or permission. Furthermore, deontic modality as traditionally understood excludes certain semantically related notions such as ability (physical and mental) and desire that have linguistic expression similar to that of permission and obligation. While one argument for the category 'deontic' might be the well-documented pathway of change whereby deontic modals over time come to acquire epistemic functions, in actual fact this change affects a broader range of meanings than the term 'deontic' indicates.

The traditional division of modality into epistemic and deontic reveals some interesting cases of polysemy in which the same form can be used for both types of modality. Thus English *may* can express either deontic permission (*you may come in now*) or epistemic possibility (*this may be your lucky day!*), while *must* can express deontic obligation (*you must be here by seven*) as well as inferred probability (*that must be the mailman at the door*). A diachronic view of this polysemy yields the observation, documented in many languages, that so-called deontic meanings typically evolve into epistemic meanings.[4]

With regard to the difficulties attaching to 'deontic' as a supercategory label, even this change from deontic to epistemic meaning in fact affects a broader range of categories. While it is true that obligation markers may come to be used for epistemic functions such as probability or inference, in the case of permission markers it is not 'permission' per se that licenses a meaning of epistemic possibility (e.g. in the case of *may*). Virtually all *permission* markers can be traced back to expressions of *ability*, permission being just one sense of a more generalized 'root-possibility' meaning that arises from ability (Bybee, Perkins and Pagliuca 1994). Root possibility predicates general enabling conditions (e.g. *it can take three hours to get there*). These include permission, which is a *social* enabling condition. Bybee (1988) has shown that it is the root possibility sense that gives rise to epistemic possibility.

A second instance of categories other than narrowly-defined deontic categories developing epistemic meanings is that of verbs indicating desire (and obligation) evolving into futures. This development parallels the deontic to epistemic shift in that a change occurs from a modal expression predicating conditions on an agent—an 'agent-oriented' modality—to a modal expression that has an entire proposition in its scope and communicates the speaker's stance with regard to the truth of that proposition—a 'speaker-oriented' modality.

For the reasons suggested above, Bybee (1985) proposed a change in the categorial nomenclature of modals as follows: **Agent-oriented modality** encompasses all modal meanings that predicate conditions on an agent with regard to the completion of an action referred to by the main predicate, e.g. obligation, desire, ability, permission and root possibility. **Epistemic modality** retains its traditional definition: epistemics are clausal-scope indicators of a speaker's commitment to the truth of a proposition. Markers of directives, such as imperatives, optatives or permissives, which represent speech acts through which a speaker attempts to move an addressee to action, are called **speaker-oriented.**

It will be observed that the distinction between agent-oriented and speaker-oriented modalities cross-cuts the traditional category of deontic modality. Agent-oriented modals include deontic statements (statements that describe obligations and permission), while speaker-oriented modals include speech-act types such as imperatives that impose conditions of obligation. A prime motive for replacing the deontic category by an agent-oriented category is that the latter better reflects general morphosyntactic trends in expression type: i.e., there is a strong, quasi-universal tendency for agent-oriented modality to be expressed by verbs, auxiliaries or non-bound particles, whereas the remaining two types (speaker-oriented and epistemic) are often expressed inflectionally (Bybee 1985). A second universal pattern is diachronic, namely the tendency referred to above whereby the agent-oriented modalities develop predictably into the other two types (Bybee, Perkins and Pagliuca 1994).

Agent-oriented and epistemic modality

As noted above, many modal forms exhibit a systematic polysemy between agent-oriented and epistemic meanings. The theoretical issue raised by such polysemy is whether a form should be regarded as having a single underlying basic meaning (a so-called invariant meaning) that combines with contextual factors to yield differing interpretations for individual tokens, or whether, alternatively, it has a complex set of semantic properties that by definition incorporate meanings derived from context. A more specific issue that this polysemy raises is that of targeting the particular contextual factors that favor one interpretation over the other. In this regard, **Bernd Heine**'s paper focuses on agent-oriented modals that can also express epistemic meanings, using data from German. His analysis isolates contextual factors as well as conceptual properties resident in the meanings of the modals that operate together to enable addressees to correctly choose an agent-oriented or an epistemic reading. **Jennifer Coates**' contribution builds on Heine's analysis and discusses the particular case of root possibility (in English). Applying the conceptual properties Heine proposes to contrast agent-oriented and epistemic interpretations of modals, Coates shows that this distinction is weaker with respect to the modal domain of possibility than with respect to other areas of modal meaning.

Analyzing the Spanish modals *poder* 'can' and *deber* 'ought to,' **Carmen Silva-Corvalán** also argues for the importance of context in the interpretation of modal meanings. However, she rejects the idea that these modals are inherently polysemous, positing instead an invariant meaning for each one: 'does not preclude X' for *poder* and 'favors, requires or entails X' for *deber*. These invariant meanings are more generalized than the agent-oriented meanings and require supplementation from context to produce their actual interpretations in particular utterances. Many of the contextual factors Silva-Corvalán points to resemble those proposed by Heine.

Edith Bavin takes a diachronic and comparative approach to some of these same issues, examining the development of obligation markers in Western Nilotic languages. While obligation markers in these languages have developed from sources different from those found in European languages (i.e. from impersonal constructions rather than from agent-oriented modal verbs), the same sorts of contextual factors influence addressees' interpretations of them as agent-oriented or epistemic.

Sherman and **Phyllis Wilcox** present one of the first analyses of modality in American Sign Language, showing once again the familiar pathway of change whereby agent-oriented modals eventually acquire epistemic meanings. The Wilcoxes also isolate a set of linguistic parameters that distinguish the meanings of ASL modals, and describe further a set of *gestural* parameters that iconically mirror the semantic properties of the modal markers.

The interactional basis of modality

In recent years, an increased understanding of many grammatical categories has come about through examination of these categories in the actual contexts in which they are used—what is referred to as 'discourse' or 'situation' context. Whereas for the analysis of tense, aspect, transitivity, ergativity, reference, etc., linguists have looked for the most part at narrative discourse, and with good result, modality cannot be studied solely with respect to narrative, since many modal functions surface only in face-to-face interactive discourse. That is, they typically depend not just on a monologic speaker (the narrator in narrative discourse), but on a dialogic (explicitly or by implication) speaker-addressee interaction. This is the case in the imposing of obligations (through statements or through directives), in the giving and receiving of permission, and in exchanges of information, with appropriate expressions of commitment to the truth of that information. In fact, modals can be viewed as strategic linguistic tools for the construction of social reality, as demonstrated by Julie Gerhardt (1985, 1990) in detailed studies of the use of modals in child language.

Two papers in this second section of the volume highlight the social functions of modality by analyzing chronologically the development of the functions to which children put modal forms. **Soonja Choi**'s paper on sentence-ending particles in Korean shows how children learn to integrate information they have to offer into the aggregate of information shared by speaker and addressee. Because of the strong interactive function of the Korean particles and the way they figure in the construction of appropriate discourse, these particles are acquired earlier by Korean children than are the more purely epistemic markers of languages such as English. **Jiansheng Guo**'s study of the acquisition of Mandarin *neng* (roughly 'can') emphasizes that children's command of a modality marker depends on their association of that marker with particular contexts of interaction. The meanings of modals in general, Guo argues, are rooted in the social, interactional functions of language; and in the case of *neng*, which he interprets as functioning in various ways as a challenge to the addressee, the information-exchanging function is clearly subordinate to the interactive function.

The interactional functions of modals can also be observed in adult language. Using texts that represent interactive discourse in written form (i.e., conversations in written texts of several different genres), **John Myhill** and

Laura Ann Smith undertake to make cross-linguistic comparisons of the use of obligation markers in languages of different types (English, Mandarin, Biblical Hebrew and Hopi). An important finding of their study is that obligation expressions can carry a range of subtle nuances that render them appropriate for carrying out speech-acts other than simply imposing obligations or making reference to obligations already in force. These include evaluating the effects of actions, explaining actions that might be construed as impolite, expressing lack of sympathy, and persuading one's conversational partner to do something.

Also included in this section is **Frantisek Lichtenberk**'s comparative study of the functions of the 'apprehensional epistemic' modality found in various Austronesian languages. While the methodology of his study differs from that of the three preceding papers in this section in not being based on a data corpus of explicitly interactive discourse, the forms Lichtenberk investigates—whose functions include issuing a warning to the addressee ('watch out! you may get sick') as well as conveying the speaker's apprehension about something that might happen to the addressee—are clearly suited to negotiatory discourse. Moreover, the changes they undergo in certain of the languages investigated clearly demonstrate their dependence on speaker-addressee interaction.

We also include in this section a highly original—and unorthodox (in the context of traditional analyses of modality)—paper by **John Haiman** that helps delimit the range of grammaticalizable modalities by targeting a set of speaker attitudes (the 'sarcastive', the 'guiltive', the 'mass-productive') that as far as we know have never become grammaticalized as moods. Although sarcasm functions like a mood, insofar as it expresses a speaker's attitude toward the proposition of an utterance produced in a dialogic exchange, its formal markers (segmental or suprasegmental) never seem to make it into the service sector of natural languages, i.e. they never become grammatical. Haiman speculates on why this is the case.

Irrealis modality and subjunctive

A term widely used in discussions of modality, especially with respect to Native American and Indo-Pacific languages, is 'irrealis', often contrasted with 'realis.' Irrealis refers to a very broad conceptual category that covers a wide range of **non-assertive** modal meanings and receives formal expression in certain languages. Unfortunately, it is difficult to determine in many instances whether the modal meaning of an utterance is contributed specifically by the so-called Irrealis marker or by some other element (lexical or morphosyntactic) of the discourse context, in which case the Irrealis marker is functionally redundant. This ambiguity calls into question the labeling of certain language-specific forms as Irrealis markers. A similar problem arises in the description of Subjunctives in European languages; like Irrealis markers, Subjunctives occur in a wide range of non-assertive contexts, and the status of their semantic content is very much in question.

A second and not insignificant problem with irrealis as a cross-language gram-type is the degree to which languages vary in their assignment of notional categories to the grammatical category Irrealis. Each language that operates with this category seems to make its own determination as to which notional categories will be considered irrealis. Thus, for both irrealis and subjunctive, it is difficult to circumscribe a focal meaning for the gram-type. Several approaches to the latter problem are demonstrated in the papers of our third section.

For **Wallace Chafe**, the realis/irrealis distinction is based on a fundamental assumption on the part of language users—an assumption which presumably operates in the same way for users of any given language—that some of their ideas belong to the domain of objective reality while others have their source in the imagination. This basic cognitive principle of judged reality vs. unreality is expressed formally by the Realis/Irrealis distinction in Caddo and the Northern Iroquoian languages, albeit in slightly differing contexts and through the use of different formal devices. Chafe sees another instantiation of this distinction in English speakers' judgments about the referentiality or non-referentiality of indefinite arguments.

Marianne Mithun also treats Irrealis categories in Native American languages in a paper that foregrounds the theoretical problem of the cross-language variability of irrealis as a gram-type. Appealing to the same underlying distinction as that described by Chafe, Mithun argues that this common cognitive distinction gets applied in different ways in different languages, a state of affairs which accounts for the fact that Irrealis functions vary so widely across languages. She insists, however, that this cross-linguistic variation is not random, and explains the different language-specific construals of irrealis described in her paper as the respective outcomes of differing diachronic developments.

The paper by **Suzanne Romaine** takes a diachronic look at the Tok Pisin particle *bai*, which now functions primarily as a future marker but which also has a variety of modal functions (as do most future markers). Drawing on an extensive corpus of data (synchronic and diachronic, spoken as well as written), Romaine traces the stages through which the clause-initial time adverb *baimbai* 'by and by' grammaticalizes into the reduced pre-verbal marker *bai* and in the process acquires a set of future and 'irrealis' functions. Her study also points out the striking conformity of these developments to cross-linguistically established trends.

Irrealis modality is also a primary focus of **Suzanne Fleischman**'s paper, summarized in the section below on the interaction of modality with other categories of grammar.

As noted above, there are certain similarities between Irrealis categories and the Subjunctives of European languages. **Patricia Lunn**'s paper is representative of recent work on the Spanish Subjunctive in its appeal to pragmatic considerations—contextual and interactional factors—to account for the use of Subjunctive vs. Indicative forms in several varieties of discourse. Lunn shows that Subjunctive coding is not limited to unreal and non-assertive propositions, as suggested in traditional accounts of the Spanish Subjunctive; this mood can also be used to signal background information in literary texts, and in journalistic discourse to mark particular information as 'common knowledge'.

Modality and other categories of grammar

In the final section of this volume we group together four papers that in different ways explore the interaction between modality and other domains of grammar, specifically: negation, complementizers, past tense, and imperfective aspect. In these papers we see once again the crucial role that interactive contexts play in shaping the meanings that result from the combinations of grammatical categories.

Frank Palmer's contribution investigates the systematic irregularity (this is not an oxymoron) that we find across languages in the behavior of modals and in the meanings that emerge when modals appear under the scope of negation. A particularly widespread irregularity involves the strategies languages use to express the semantic notions of 'necessary-not' and 'not-necessary'. This may involve use of a different verb altogether from the one normally used in affirmative contexts, as in English *mustn't* vs. *needn't*, or a 'displacement' of the negative marker for 'necessary-not' to a syntactic position that corresponds formally to 'not-necessary', as in French and Italian (Fr. *il **ne** faut pas partir*, It. ***non** deve venire*).

Zygmunt Frajzyngier's paper advances the claim that in various unrelated languages modality appears to be expressed by complementizers, which function to code the modality of embedded clauses. More specifically, he links the presence of one or more complementizers (treated as a parametric variation within the GB framework), as well as their syntactic position in embedded clauses, to the presence or absence (synchronic or diachronic) of certain modalities in the sentence as a whole. Of particular interest in this paper are cases of clauses with multiple complementizers expressing different types of modality, e.g. agent-oriented and epistemic. The paper also has implications for formal syntactic theories that posit COMP as a component of the sentence.

When agent-oriented modals combine with past tense the resulting unit often undergoes a meaning change, losing the past-tense component of its meaning and coming to signal a weakened version of its original modal meaning in the present tense. **Joan Bybee**'s paper explores the reasons for this development by studying the uses of *would* and *should* in texts from Middle English and Early Modern English. Bybee argues that these modals lose their past sense because of the implication that a modal condition in past tense continues into present time, pointing to the conclusion that modal meaning is heavily influenced by the interactive contexts in which it is used.

The last paper in the volume, by **Suzanne Fleischman**, surveys a wide range of evidence pointing to an overlap (synchronic and diachronic) between the aspectual gram-type imperfective and irrealis modality, and poses the question of why, in so many unrelated languages, verb forms marked for imperfective aspect come to acquire meanings subsumable under the broad modal heading of irrealis. Since none of the languages Fleischman refers to has a formally grammaticalized Irrealis category, and in light of the notorious elusiveness of irrealis pointed out above, her definition of irrealis is worth noting here. She characterizes 'irrealis' as prototype category, at the semantic level, expressing a spectrum of meanings that signal a speaker's lack of belief in or lack of commitment to any of the following: the reality or referentiality of a situation; the possibility that an agent's wishes, hopes or intentions will effectively be realized; the authenticity of an utterance or a chunk of discourse; or the normalcy of a discourse or of a communicative situation. These parameters are illustrated with data from various languages and discourse genres.

So, here goes, readers. We hope you enjoy the papers. And don't be put off by the realization that mood is a grammatical category with an attitude! We'll get it straightened out one of these days.

NOTES

* We are grateful to Greg Thomson for assisting the editors and authors in manuscript preparation and copy editing. The indexes were prepared by Lisa Dasinger and Jacki Trademan.

1 In this volume we avoid the term 'mode' because of the problematic ambiguities it presents, being used with widely different meanings in the grammars of different languages. In many European languages it translates what is here referred to as 'mood', while in the grammars of certain non-European languages it is used to label categories whose meanings fall under the headings of tense and aspect. We are aware, of course, that languages often bundle tense, aspect, and mood information into portmanteau morphology, thereby making it difficult to decide how to label such categories.

2 The term 'evidential' was first introduced by Jakobson (1957) as a tentative label for a verbal category that indicates the source of the information on which a speaker's statement is based. As currently understood, evidentiality covers a range of distinctions involved in the identification of the source of one's knowledge. Various languages have grammaticalized evidential markers indicating whether or not the speaker vouches personally for the information contained in a statement. (See Chafe and Nichols 1986, Willett 1988).

3 In place of the traditional distinction of linguistically relevant modals into 'epistemic' and 'deontic', Bybee (1985) recategorizes the modals into 'agent-oriented,' 'speaker-oriented', and 'epistemic'. These categories will be defined and elaborated on below. Other categories distinguished in modal logic, e.g. 'dynamic' and 'alethic' modalities (cf. Lyons 1977:791, Palmer 1986:102-103), will not be discussed here, being less germane to the analysis of modality in natural language.

4 The earlier 'deontic' meanings may or may not be preserved. English *must*, for example, retains its obligative meaning, whereas *might* has lost its earlier abilitative meaning.

REFERENCES

Bybee, Joan L. 1985. *Morphology: A Study of the Relation between Meaning and Form (=Typological Studies in Language,* 9) Amsterdam & Philadelphia: John Benjamins.

Bybee, Joan L. 1988. "Semantic Substance vs. Contrast in the Development of Grammatical Meaning." *Proceedings of the Berkeley Linguistic Society.* 14.247-264.

Bybee, Joan & Östen Dahl. 1989. "The Creation of Tense and Aspect Systems in the Languages of the World". *Studies in Language* 13.51-103

Bybee, Joan L., William Pagliuca, & Revere D. Perkins. 1991. "Back to the Future". *Approaches to Grammaticalization.* ed. by E. C. Traugott &. B. Heine, vol. 2, 17-58. Amsterdam & Philadelphia: John Benjamins.

Bybee, Joan L., Revere D. Perkins & William Pagliuca. 1994. *The Evolution of Grammar: Tense, Aspect and Modality in the Languages of the World.* Chicago: University of Chicago Press.

Chafe, Wallace L., & Johanna Nichols. 1986. *Evidentiality: The Coding of Epistemology in Language.* Norwood, N.J.: Ablex.

Gerhardt, Julie. 1985. "On the Use of *will* and *gonna*: Toward a Description of Activity Types for Child Language". *Discourse Processes* 8.143-75.

Gerhardt, Julie. 1990. "The Relation of Language to Context in Children's Speech: The Role of *hafta* Statements in Structuring 3-Year-Old's Discourse". *IPrA Papers in Pragmatics* 4. 1-57.

Hopper, Paul, ed. 1982. *Tense-Aspect: Between Semantics and Pragmatics.* Amsterdam: John Benjamins.

Jakobson, Roman. 1957. *Shifters, Verbal Categories, and the Russian Verb.* Cambridge, Mass: Russian Language Project, Department of Slavic Languages and Literatures, Harvard University. (Repr. *The Selected Writings of Roman Jakobson.* Vol 2.130-147 [1971] The Hague: Mouton.)

Lyons, John. 1977. *Semantics* , vol. 2. Cambridge: Cambridge University Press.

Palmer, Frank R. 1986. *Mood and Modality.* Cambridge: Cambridge University Press.

Willett, T. 1988. "A Cross-Linguistic Survey of the Grammaticization of Evidentiality". *Studies in Language.* 12.51-97.

I
Agent-Oriented and Epistemic Modality

Agent-Oriented vs. Epistemic Modality
Some Observations on German Modals[1]

Bernd Heine
University of Cologne

1. Introduction

Recent research on the domain of modality has focussed in particular on the nature of one basic distinction, that between what has variously been referred to as deontic, root, objective, pragmatic or agent-oriented modality on the one hand and subjective, hypothetical, or epistemic modality on the other.[2] A number of generalizations have been proposed about the nature of agent-oriented as opposed to epistemic modality, such as the following:

a. In many languages, agent-oriented and epistemic meanings are expressed by means of one and the same expression.
b. Wherever there is adequate historical evidence available on the evolution of a language, agent-oriented meanings have been shown to be older than epistemic ones (Shepherd 1982, Bybee and Pagliuca 1985, Traugott 1989).
c. Epistemic meanings are said to be more strongly subjective than agent-oriented ones, and the transition from agent-oriented to epistemic uses of a given linguistic expression has been described as involving subjectification (cf. Langacker 1985), whereby meanings tend to become increasingly based in the speaker's subjective belief state/attitude toward the proposition (Traugott 1989:35).
d. In the ontogenesis of language, agent-oriented modality develops prior to epistemic modality (but see Soonja Choi, this volume for different observations). For example, for both English and German

children, modal verbs at first serve agent-oriented rather than epistemic functions (Stephany 1989:4).

e. Similarly, in second language acquisition, agent-oriented uses of modal elements tend to appear earlier than epistemic ones (Ramat 1992).

There are a number of questions that the study of these two kinds of modality raises, such as the following:

(i) What factors can be held responsible for the fact that linguistic expressions for agent-oriented modality are extended to also express epistemic modality?

(ii) If a linguistic item is used for the expression of both agent-oriented and epistemic modality, are we dealing with an instance of homonymy or of polysemy, that is, does that item simultaneously belong to two different categories or only to one? The former view is favored by Coates (1983), Palmer (1986), as well as a number of other authors, while the latter is argued for by Sweetser (1982), Traugott (1989) and others.

(iii) Is the transition from one kind of modality to another discrete/discontinuous or gradual/continuous?

(iv) How can the shift from agent-oriented to epistemic modality be described in a model based on grammaticalization theory?

While these questions have been addressed in a good deal of research over the past decade, none has been answered satisfactorily, nor will the present paper attempt to provide conclusive answers. Most discussions relating to these questions have centered around modality in English. This paper will focus on a language different from but closely related to English, and its aim is to provide some fresh data that might be relevant to answering the above questions.

2. German modals

2.1 *German and English modals compared*

A number of authors have pointed out that German modals differ from their English counterparts essentially in being more verb-like (Abraham

1989:357); some (cf. Jenkins 1972:9-12; Steele et al. 1981; Abraham 1992) go so far as to argue that a categorial boundary separates German and English modals, the latter belonging to a category called AUX and the former to that of Verb. German modals such as *können* 'can' or *müssen* 'must', etc. differ from their English counterparts, e.g., in the following ways:

a. They exhibit inflections (e.g., *ich kann* 'I can', *du kannst* 'you can').[3]
b. They may appear in non-finite constructions (e.g., *um kommen zu können* 'in order to be able to come').
c. They may iterate (e.g., *er will arbeiten können* 'he claims that he can work').
d. They are not restricted to any fixed order with respect to each other or to the perfect auxiliary *haben* 'have' (e.g., *er hat arbeiten gekonnt* 'he has been able to work' vs. *er kann gearbeitet haben* 'he may have worked').
e. They may also occur in certain constructions without any other verb in the same clause (e.g., *er kann Handstand* 'he can do a handstand').
f. "Auxiliary reduction" does not apply to them.[4]

There are, however, a number of properties that German modals share with their English counterparts, e.g. (cf. Helbig and Buscha 1988:107ff.; 123ff.):

(i) They express a restricted range of grammatical functions.
(ii) They form a closed set of entities.
(iii) They normally do not passivize.
(iv) They do not form imperatives.
(v) They typically require main verbs, rather than noun phrases or adverbial phrases, as complements.
(vi) In their presence, main verbs are used in a non-finite (infinitival) form.
(vii) They lack a present tense 3 sg. inflection (*-s* in English and *-t* in German).
(viii) They do not take the infinitive marker (*zu*) to introduce the main verb.
(ix) Finally, and most importantly in this context, German and English modals are both used to express agent-oriented as well as epistemic meanings.

What this suggests is that we are dealing with a difference in degree rather than in kind: while German modals are more verb-like than their English cognates, the two are similar enough to be comparable. For more details, see Heine (1993).

2.2. *A survey*

In the present section, eight German modals are looked at with a view to determining how and to what extent they are associated with agent-oriented/deontic and epistemic modality, respectively, or, to use the terminology of German grammarians, with "objective" and "subjective" modality. The modals in question are:

müssen	'must'
sollen	'should'
können	'can'
wollen	'want, will'
mögen	'like, may'
dürfen	'be allowed to, may'
möchten	'want to, would like to'
werden	'will'

One may wonder what justification there is to include *werden*, essentially a future tense marker, within the paradigm of modal auxiliaries. While I do not wish to argue that *werden* is a modal, as has been done elsewhere (see especially Vater 1970), the main reason for including it here is that like "true modals" it exhibits a distinction between non-epistemic and epistemic uses. Note furthermore that *können*, like English *can*, has two non-epistemic senses: root possibility and permission (cf. Bybee, Perkins, and Pagliuca 1994). These two senses will not be distinguished in the quantitative analysis that follows; our concern will be essentially with the distinction between non-epistemic and epistemic modality, rather than between agent-oriented and epistemic modality. These distinctions will be clarified below.

In the association of the eight modals with these two categories of modality in given utterances, the following three situations will be distinguished, where "A" stands for agent-oriented and "E" for epistemic modality:

A, E: The relevant utterance is automatically associated with either an A or an E interpretation, with no further contextual clues required, i.e., either A or E constitutes the "basic meaning" or *focal sense* (see Heine, Claudi and Hünnemeyer 1991) of the utterance concerned.

A1, E1: The relevant utterance does not have a focal sense of A or E, but is associated with specific linguistic or extra-linguistic contexts that are suggestive of either an A or an E interpretation. We may say that in such cases A or E constitutes a *non-focal sense.*

A2, E2: The relevant utterance is not automatically associated with either A or E. There are, however, highly specific contexts where an A or an E interpretation is conceivable. In such cases, A or E will be said to constitute a *marginal sense.*

This threefold classification is somewhat crude; a more fine-grained typology would be desirable. For the present analysis, however, this classification is sufficient to study the problems at issue here. I illustrate the three situations with two examples.[5]

(1) *Er muß mindestens 1,80 m sein.*
he must at.least 1.80 metres be
'He must be at least six foot.'

a. [E: "On the basis of the evidence available I am led to conclude that ..."]
b. [A: "They are looking for a new goal-keeper (he has to be at least six foot)"]

The most likely reading of *muß* in (1) is the epistemic one (cf. (1a), hence (1) is said to have a focal epistemic sense (E). (1) has, however, a non-focal agent-oriented sense (A1) in addition, which is foregrounded, e.g., in a context like (1b).

An example of a marginal sense is provided by the utterance in (2) below. While (2) has a focal A sense ("He is obliged to come"), contexts can be conceived of that would invite an E2 interpretation. A context like (2a), for example, calls up the marginal epistemic sense, conveying the meaning: "I have every reason to conclude that he is coming".

(2) *Er muß kommen.*
he must come
'He has to come.'

a. ["I can already hear his voice (so he must be coming)"]

In what follows, quantitative data are presented that bear on the question of whether and to what extent certain standardized utterances are associated with the two kinds of modality. To this end, index values are calculated on the basis of the three-fold classification proposed above: a value of 1.00 is given to an utterance whenever a focal sense is involved, 0.66 in the case of a non-focal sense, and 0.33 in the case of a marginal sense. I illustrate this procedure with reference to examples (1) and (2) above: the utterance in (1) (*Er muß mindestens 1.80 m sein*) would receive an index value of 1.00 for its focal epistemic sense and of 0.66 for its non-focal agent-oriented sense. Utterance (2), on the other hand, would have an index value of 1.00 for its focal agent-oriented sense and of 0.33 for its marginal epistemic sense. Values are calculated for declarative (e.g., *Er muß kommen* 'He must come'), interrogative (*Muß er kommen?* 'Does he need to come?'), and negative utterances (*Er muß nicht kommen* 'He need not come'), for main verb perfect forms (*Er muß gekommen sein* 'He must have come'), auxiliary past tense forms (*Er mußte kommen* 'He had to come'), as well as for first- (*Ich muß kommen* 'I must come'), second- (*Du mußt kommen* 'You must come'), and third-person subject utterances (*Er muß kommen* 'He must come'). The sum totals are divided by the total number of utterances considered, thereby establishing average index values for agent-oriented and epistemic modalities. The maximum value attainable is 1.00, the minimum value 0 (zero). For example, a modal will receive the maximum value of agent-oriented modality if in all utterances considered it has a focal agent-oriented sense, and the minimum value if it has neither focal, non-focal or marginal agent-oriented senses; see APPENDIX for details.[6]

A number of calculations have been carried out on the basis of selected parameters; the results obtained are summarized in Tables 1 through 4. In Table 1 the eight modals are compared in terms of the degree to which they correlate with each of the two kinds of modality. As the index values suggest, the modals can be arranged along a scale for each of the two modalities. At

Table 1. *Index of modality of eight German modals (Affirmative/negative, declarative/ interrogative, present/past tense uses; see* APPENDIX*)*

	Index value of modality	
	Agent-oriented	Epistemic
Möchten	0.92	0
Dürfen	0.74	0
Wollen	0.75	0.15
Müssen	0.51	0.37
Mögen	0.47	0.37
Werden	0.59	0.46
Können	0.46	0.50
Sollen	0.44	0.50

one end of the scale are *möchten* and *dürfen*, which have the highest values for agent-oriented modality and exhibit no epistemic uses, at least not in the corpus considered. [FN 7] At the other end we find *können* and *sollen*, which have the lowest values for agent-oriented and the highest values for epistemic modality.

The extent to which these modals are associated with agent-oriented and epistemic modality appears to correlate with their relative degree of grammaticalization in general and with prototypical 'verbiness' in particular: thus, the highest A values and the lowest E values are found with the items most prototypically verb-like. *Wollen* 'will', for instance, is more verbal (has more verbal properties) than modals like *müssen* 'must', *können* 'can', or *sollen* 'should', in that it can still take subordinate clauses introduced by *daß* 'that' as complements and, accordingly, does not require subject identity between the auxiliary and the main verb, as in (3). Also it can be passivized, as in (4) (Vater 1970).

(3) *Hans will, daß Anna zu Hause bleibt.*
Hans wants that Anna at home stays
'Hans wants Anna to stay home.'

(4) *Von Hans wird gewollt, daß Anna zu Hause bleibt.*
by Hans is wanted that Anna at home stays
'Hans is requested to leave Anna at home.'

Table 2. *Index of modality of four German expressions (on the basis of eight German modals; see Appendix)*

			Index value of modality	
			Agent-oriented	Epistemic
a.	Sie kommt.	'She is coming.'	0.87	0.02
b.	Sie weiß es.	'She knows it.'	0.77	0.32
c.	Sie hat viel Geld.	'She has a lot of money.'	0.67	0.27
d.	Sie kennt ihn.	'She knows him.'	0.37	0.59

Table 3. *Index of modality of eight German modals according to various grammatical distinctions (see Appendix)*

	Type of proposition	Index value of modality	
		Agent-oriented	Epistemic
a.	Perfect (e.g., Er hat kommen müssen. 'He had to come.')	0.75	0
b.	Interrogative (e.g., Muß er kommen? 'Does he need to come?')	0.72	0.11
c.	Negative (e.g., Er muß nicht kommen. 'He need not come.')	0.74	0.26
d.	Past (e.g., Er mußte kommen. 'He had to come.')	0.62	0.20
e.	Present (e.g., Er muß kommen. 'He must come.')	0.60	0.43
f.	Main verb perfect (e.g., Er muß gekommen sein. 'He must have come.')	0.19	0.55
g.	Main verb progressive (e.g., Er muß am Kommen sein. 'He must be coming.')	0.02	0.64

Table 4. *Index of modality of eight German modals according to grammatical person of the sentence subject (Affirmative/negative, declarative/interrogative, present/past uses; see Appendix)*

	Index value of modality	
	Agent-oriented	Epistemic
1st person subject	0.70	0.18
2nd person subject	0.69	0.25
3rd person subject	0.57	0.35

The behavior of the modals also differs greatly in accordance with the type of main verb figuring in the utterances. Thus, verbs of action and telic verbs associate predominantly with agent-oriented modality; cf. utterance (a) in Table 2, involving the motion verb *kommen* 'come'. The situation is more complicated in the case of stative verbs: while some, like *wissen* 'know (information)' and *haben* 'have', gravitate toward agent-oriented uses, *kennen* 'know, be acquainted with', has a majority of epistemic uses.

The modal behavior of the eight items considered also varies in accordance with the type of proposition and the tense and aspect in which the modals occur, as can be seen in Table 3. According to this table, in Perfect constructions the modals are confined to agent-oriented uses (a). Even with verbs such as *kennen*, which generally associate strongly with epistemic modality, an epistemic reading is unlikely once the modal auxiliary has a Perfect form.

Furthermore, in Interrogative (b) and Negative (c) propositions and in the Past tense (d) the modals correlate primarily with agent-oriented rather than with epistemic modality. Epistemic uses prevail, however, if the main verb is in the Perfect (f), and Progressive constructions[8] are almost entirely associated with epistemic modality (g).

Finally, the interpretation of an utterance is also affected by the grammatical person of the subject. As Table 4 suggests, an utterance is most likely to have an agent-oriented interpretation when the subject referent is first-person and least likely when it is third-person; conversely, epistemic modality correlates most strongly with third-person and least strongly with first-person subjects.

3. Context

3.1 *The linguistic context*

The quantitative data on German modals presented in the preceding section allow us to isolate several linguistic factors that appear to be relevant for characterizing the uses of the two kinds of modality. These data suggest that an utterance is very likely to have a focal agent-oriented sense if:

a. any of the modals *möchten*, *dürfen* or *wollen* is involved;
b. the main verb is an action or a terminative verb;
c. the modal is in the perfect or past tense.

Furthermore, a modal is more likely to have agent-oriented than epistemic modality as its focal sense if:

d. it occurs in interrogative rather than in declarative utterances;
e. it occurs in negative rather than in affirmative utterances;
f. the subject is first or second (rather than a third) person.

Thus, the more of the linguistic properties (a) through (f) an utterance has, the more likely it is to express agent-oriented rather than epistemic modality. Conversely, a focal epistemic sense is more likely if the main verb is in a progressive or perfect form or is stative.

What these observations suggest is that the agent-oriented vs. epistemic distinction works in roughly the same way with German as with English modals. For example, according to the findings on English modals presented by Coates, the following associations can be observed: (a) All agent-oriented modals can occur in interrogative constructions where epistemic modals are not normally found (1983:244-245). (b) Epistemic but not agent-oriented uses are associated with the progressive aspect (1983:246). (c) The core meanings of agent-oriented modals are crucially associated with agentivity, that is, the action referred to in the main predication is carried out by someone (or something) using their own energy (Coates 1983:245). (d) Epistemic meaning is typically associated with existential subjects and stative verbs (1983:245; see also Bybee, Perkins, and Pagliuca 1994). We will return to these cross-linguistic observations below.

3.2 *Contextual frames*

While the above linguistic characterization allows us to predict within limits whether a given utterance will receive an agent-oriented or an epistemic interpretation, it does not account for a considerable number of actual uses of German modals. Many times, when queried whether a given utterance was suggestive of agent-oriented or epistemic modality, an informant's reaction was to search for a relevant context based on past experience. If the informant could remember a context that matched the utterance in question, then he or she would answer the question with reference to that experience. If not, then he or she would be likely to declare the utterance unacceptable. Thus, rather than semantic, syntactic or other rule-governed behavior, it was the presence or absence of a cluster of related experiences, let us call it the contextual frame, that seemed to be crucial in deciding between the two modalities. Consider the utterance in (5):

(5) *Das Bier sollte kalt sein.*
the beer should cold be
'The beer should be cold.'

In accordance with the observations made in 3.1, (5) is strongly suggestive of a focal epistemic sense since there is an inanimate subject and a stative main verb. Nevertheless, the majority of our informants, all native speakers of High German, described (5) as having a focal agent-oriented sense. What appears to account for the agent-oriented interpretation of (5) is its association with a contextual frame like a party situation where someone is offered a warm beer. One possible reaction would be to answer with (5), and in such a case, (5) can only receive an agent-oriented interpretation. In accordance with the terminology introduced in Section 2, the contextual information just presented may be said to constitute the *focal* contextual frame for (5). A non-focal frame would be provided, e.g., by (5a) which triggers an epistemic interpretation of (5).

5a ["I put the drinks into the fridge more than two hours ago
(so the beer should be cold by now)"]

Coates (1983:233) notes that the interpretation of English modals as agent-oriented (that is, "root" in her terminology) depends in most cases on the presence of agentivity. This also applies to a large extent to German modals, though agentivity need not be, and frequently is not, explicitly expressed; what matters is the contextual frame associated with the use of the modal. The utterance in (5) has no formally expressed agent; its association with focal agent-oriented modality derives from contextually recoverable agentivity, i.e., the speaker wishes to urge someone to put the beer into the fridge, or to replace the bottle of warm beer by a bottle of cold beer. What this suggests is that any attempt at characterizing the relationship between the two types of modality strictly in terms of the linguistic categories that typically correlate with each one is likely to achieve little more than probabilistic approximations; it is unlikely to explain the relationship.

The notion of a contextual frame is similar to what others have called an 'inferential schema', or simply a 'frame', i.e. a body of knowledge evoked by the language user in order to provide an inferential basis for the understanding of an utterance (cf. Levinson 1983:281). It is beyond the scope of the present paper to define the parameters that are relevant for classifying contextual frames as either focal or non-focal; presumably they have to do with factors such as the following:

a. Contextual clues: Focal frames require a minimum of contextual clues, they are triggered spontaneously without involving major mental effort or imagination. Non-focal frames, on the other hand, require a certain amount of mental energy.
b. Knowledge of the world: An example like (6) has a focal epistemic sense, since we cannot manipulate time in such a way as to license an agent-oriented interpretation.

(6) *Es muß drei Uhr sein.*
it must three o'clock be
'It must be three o'clock.'

c. Social norms: We believe in a positive world and expect other people to behave in a socially acceptable way. Therefore, while (7a) may receive either an agent-oriented or an epistemic interpretation, (7b) receives only an epistemic sense, since we do not expect someone to want someone else to behave in a socially disapproved way.

(7) a *Er muß tapfer sein.*
he must brave be
(i) 'He has to be brave.'
(ii) 'He must be brave.'

b *Er muß feige sein.*
he must cowardly be
'He must be a coward.'

Conversely, utterances having human agents as subjects and action verbs as predicates, that is, structures typically associated with agent-oriented modality, trigger a focal epistemic meaning if they are associated with contextual frames that discourage an agent-oriented interpretation, as in (8).

(8) *Er muß seine Frau schlagen.*
he must his wife beat
'He is said to beat his wife.'

These are but a few of the factors that may be relevant to the evocation of contextual frames, possible additional factors being frequency and/or intensity of experience, perceptual salience, propensity for memory storage, or the stereotypes an utterance tends to evoke.

3.3 *Conceptual properties*

In addition to contextual frames, the choice between the two kinds of modality depends crucially on certain conceptual properties. Agent-oriented uses of German modals are associated with the following properties:

a. There is some force (**F**) that is characterized by an "element of will" (Jespersen 1924:320-1), i.e., that has an interest in an event either occurring or not occurring.[9]
b. The event is to be performed typically by a controlling agent (**C**).
c. The event is dynamic (**D**), i.e., it involves the manipulation of a situation and is conceived of typically as leading to a change of state.
d. The event has not yet taken place at reference time, i.e., its occurrence, if it does in fact take place (see (e) below), will be *later than the reference time* (**L**).
e. The event is non-factual (Palmer 1986:96), though there is a certain *degree of probability* that it will occur (**P**).

Take utterance (9), for example, where F is the speaker (9a) or some other force the speaker has in mind (9b), and C is the sentence subject *er*. The event is dynamic (D), as can be concluded from the use of the action verb *kommen*, and is supposed to take place later than at reference time (L). Finally, the modal *muß* expresses a high degree of probability (= strong obligation) that the event will in fact take place (P).

(9) *Er muß kommen.*
he must come
'He has to come.'

a. [A: "I insist that he comes"]
b. [A: "His boss insists that he comes"]

Differences between the various modals exist with regard to the degree of probability that the event will take place: the probability is low in the case of *können* and *dürfen* (permission) but high in the case of *müssen* (strong obligation), with the remaining modals being intermediate. But the modals differ also in other respects. There are essentially three kinds of relevant participants: the speaker (S), the modal force (F), and the agent (C), the last of these being typically, though not necessarily, coded as the sentence subject. While F is different from C in the case of modals such as *müssen* 'must', *sollen* 'shall, should' or *können* 'can' (= "subject-external modality"), as can be seen, e.g., in (9), it is identical with C in the case of the modals *wollen*, *mögen*, and *möchten* (= "subject-internal modality"), as in (10), where the subject *ich* 'I' is both the modal force F and the agent C, and in this instance also S.

(10) *Ich möchte kommen.*
I want. to come
'I would like to come.'

F can refer to either the speaker or to some other human being, or even to a non-human entity. Thus, in (11), F may be either a human authority, e.g., the speaker, or a non-human (e.g., religious, institutional, or moral) power.

(11) *Du darfst nicht stehlen.*
you may not steal
'Thou shalt not steal.'

There is no necessary relationship between F and C on the one hand, and certain kinds of nominal referents on the other. For example, in the agent-oriented reading of (5), repeated below for convenience, it remains unclear, in the absence of additional contextual clues, whether F refers to the speaker or to some other force, or whether C refers to the hearer, to another agent, or to no explicit agent at all.

(5) *Das Bier sollte kalt sein.*
the beer should cold be
'The beer should be cold.'

While there are no compelling clues as to the referential identity of F in (5), nevertheless, some kind of F is implied, as can be derived, e.g., from the fact that a possible response to (5) would be to inquire about the referent of F by asking: *Wér möchte, daß das Bier kalt ist?* '*Who* wants the beer to be cold?'

While prototypical instances of agent-oriented modality are characterized by the presence of the properties listed above, prototypical instances of epistemic modality lack all properties except P. Thus, in the epistemic reading of (5), there is neither F nor C, no D is involved, and the later-than-reference-time constraint (L) does not apply (see (14) below).
Since P is shared by the two kinds of modality, it will not be considered in the remainder of this paper.

3.4 *On the transition from agent-oriented to epistemic meanings*

While we can distinguish the two kinds of modality on the basis of the conceptual properties C, F, D and L, these properties are not of equal importance. Consider, for example, utterance (12b). The use of *muß* does not entail L; that is, there is no later-than-reference-time constraint involved: the action of *schlafen* can be assumed to take place over an interval that includes reference time, yet (12b) has a focal agent-oriented sense.

(12) a. *Warum ist Klaus nicht hier?*
why is Klaus not here
'Why is Klaus not here?'

b. *Er muß schlafen.*
he must sleep
'He has to sleep.'

It might seem as if F is also irrelevant in (12b) since no explicit force is mentioned. Yet one could inquire about a possible F by asking: *Wér ist dafür verantwortlich, daß er schlafen muß?* '*Who* is responsible for the fact that he has to sleep?' Thus, F may be said to be potentially present in (12b), albeit backgrounded.

In examples like (12b), where L does not apply, the difference between agent-oriented and epistemic modality becomes minimal: While (12b) has a focal sense of agent-oriented modality, it may also be understood to convey an epistemic meaning, i.e. 'he must be sleeping.' In such cases we are dealing with what Coates refers to as merger: the agent-oriented and the epistemic senses of (12b) are in a *both/and* relationship, they are mutually compatible; in order to understand (12b) it is therefore not necessary to decide which of the two senses is intended since they are not mutually exclusive (see Section 4).

Furthermore, there are contexts in the use of *müssen* 'must' where both C and L are absent and D is largely irrelevant, as in (13). Verbs that behave in a similar way to *frieren* 'freeze, be cold' are *leiden* 'suffer', *weinen* 'cry', or *gähnen* 'yawn'.

(13) *Er muß frieren.*
he must freeze
'He is freezing/feeling cold.'

In examples like (13), F is some unidentified force, and we are dealing with an instance of focal agent-oriented and non-focal epistemic modality. Once F is eliminated, however, an agent-oriented interpretation is ruled out: no F is implied in (14), which therefore expresses exclusively epistemic modality.

(14) *Ihn muß frieren.*
him must freeze
'He must be freezing/cold.'

What the observations made in this section suggest is that of the four properties considered, only F is obligatorily connected with agent-oriented modality: modal utterances that lack F lack the "element of will" to which Jespersen (1924:320-21) referred. In such cases we are dealing with an epistemic rather than an agent-oriented sense.

Typically, the lack of F will leave all other components of the modal concept unaffected. Thus, P remains the same whether or not F is present: the degree of probability that the situation described in the utterance will obtain is high in the case of *müssen* 'must' and low in the case of *können* 'can', irrespective of F. Take, for example, the modal *sollen* 'shall, should': in the agent-oriented interpretation of (15), F may refer either to the speaker (15a) or to another person (15b), while in the epistemic interpretation of (15), the speaker is excluded as source of the modal force (15c); the modal source is associated with someone other than the speaker, as suggested by the fact that (15d) would not be an appropriate paraphrase of (15).

(15) *Sie soll heute zu Hause sein.*
she should today at home be
'She should be at home today.'

a. [A: "I want her to be at home today"]
b. [A: "Someone wants her to be at home today"]
c. [E: "Someone claims that she is at home today"]
d. [*"I claim that she is at home today"]

In many of its agent-oriented uses, *sollen* excludes the speaker as a source of F, as can be seen in (16), where the subject is a first-person referent.

(16) *Ich soll kommen.*
I should come
'I should come.'

[A: "Someone wants me to come"; *"I want to come"]

3.5 *Discussion*

The distinction between the two categories of modality has been associated with a number of factors. First, as pointed out above, one major distinguishing property is that agent-oriented senses are likely to refer to situations that are supposed to obtain later than at reference time (= property L). Thus, an utterance like (17) (= (5)) has future reference when used in its agent-oriented sense (17a) but present reference when used epistemically (17b).

(17) *Das Bier sollte kalt sein.*
the beer should cold be
'The beer should be cold.'

a [A: "I want the beer to be cold (so you'd better put it into the fridge again")]
b [E: "I have reason to assume that the beer (standing in front of me) is cold"]

Similar observations have been made for English modals. Coates (1983:235), for example, notes that, with the exception of root *can*, English modals in their agent-oriented uses always have future reference (see also Palmer 1986:97; Bybee, Perkins, and Pagliuca 1994):

> [...] one of the conditions of using Root MUST, SHOULD or OUGHT (= 'Obligation') or Root MAY or CAN (= 'Permission') is that the speaker believes that the action referred to in the main predication has not already been achieved. In other words, commands, recommendations and permission-granting utterances all refer to an action which will be carried out at a time subsequent to the utterance (Coates 1983:233).

As noted in 3.4, the association of agent-oriented modality with deictic time is not as rigid in the case of German modals as Coates suggests it is for English modals. Note further that there are contexts where the later-than-reference-time constraint does not apply, e.g., in the case of modals used in the past tense, as in (18), where exclusively agent-oriented modality is involved.

(18) a *Er mußte es tun.*
he had.to it do
'He had to do it.'

b *Er wollte zu Hause sein.*
he wanted at home be
'He had intended to be at home.'

What this suggests is that the later-than-reference-time constraint is a concomitant, rather than a defining, property of agent-oriented modality.

Furthermore, Bybee, Perkins and Pagliuca (1994) observe that the two modalities expressed by English *must* correlate with mutually exclusive linguistic environments: in the Past tense, in the Present tense with a stative verb, and in the Progressive, *must* can only have an epistemic ("inferred certainty") reading, while in the non-past with dynamic verbs, *must* is only agent-oriented and refers to the future. Apart from the strong correlation between progressive aspect and epistemic modality observed in Section 2 (Table 4), the German cognate *müssen* does not exhibit a similarly rigid distinction: for example, dynamic verbs may have a focal epistemic meaning and stative verbs a focal agent-oriented meaning in the present tense, as the following examples show, respectively:

(19) *Er muß kommen; ich höre schon seine Stimme.*
he must come I hear already his voice
'He must be coming; I hear his voice already.'

(20) *Er muß heute nachmittag unbedingt zu Hause sein.*
he must today afternoon by.all.means at home be
'He definitely has to be at home this afternoon.'

Even in English, the distinction is not as clear-cut as Bybee, Perkins and Pagliuca (1994) suggest. Consider an utterance like (21), where *must* may have either an agent-oriented (21a) or an epistemic interpretation (21b) (Perlmutter 1970:115; Calbert 1973:7); see also (26) below.

(21) *Clyde must work hard.*

a [A: "Clyde is obliged to work hard"]
b [E: "It must be the case that Clyde works hard"]

Second, with reference to property C, Coates (1983:245) observes that the core meanings of agent-oriented modals in English are crucially associated with agentivity. This applies to German modals as well, as we saw in Section 2, where action verbs, which typically require an agent, were shown to trigger an agent-oriented interpretation of modals in the majority of examples. At the same time, however, agentivity is not decisive for defining agent-oriented modality in German, as (17) illustrates. The same may be said for property D, also demonstrated by (17), which contains neither a dynamic predicate nor an agent-like participant. This raises the following question: If agent-oriented modality can be defined with reference to one property only, namely F, what accounts for its strong association with properties C, D, and L?

There appears to be a straightforward answer: since the presence of F implies that an event may, should or must happen, this entails that the event will occur later than now, and more often than not an event that happens will involve agents and actions, less typically also inanimate forces. Thus, the presence of F suggests that we are dealing with a kind of utterance that tends to be associated with agents and dynamic processes typically leading to changes of state. If, however, a modal utterance lacks F, i.e., if it expresses epistemic modality, it is likely to be associated with states and time-stable situations. It is not surprising therefore that epistemic modality is closely associated with utterances involving existential subjects and stative verbs, or verbs in the progressive and perfect aspects.

That existential subjects, impersonal subjects and dummy subjects are strongly associated with epistemic, rather than with agent-oriented modality, has been argued repeatedly in the literature on English modality (Coates 1983; Bybee, Perkins, and Pagliuca forthc.). Bybee, Perkins, and Pagliuca (1994) in fact observe that the presence of a dummy subject precludes an agent-oriented reading in cases like (22):

(22) *It should take me about four hours to get there.*

While we have not been able to make corresponding observations about German, there are contextual frames where the presence of a dummy subject does favor an epistemic reading. Thus, while (23) is associated equally with an agent-oriented and an epistemic interpretation, (24) may be said to have a focal epistemic reading (24b), but only a non-focal agent-oriented reading (24a).

(23) *Der Brief muß in zwei Tagen da sein.*
the letter must in two days there be
'The letter must be there in two days.'

(24) *Es muß zwei Tage dauern, bis der Brief da ist.*
it must two days last until the letter there is
'It must take two days until the letter is there.'

a. [A: "... I'll be in trouble if the letter arrives earlier"]
b. [E: "... since it is a long way to get there"]

Yet even in the presence of existential/dummy subjects and durative verbs like *dauern* 'last', an agent-oriented sense is possible (24a). What might account for the stronger epistemic force in the case of contextual frames like (24) is the fact that the absence of a human or animate subject is also likely to suggest absence of a manipulating force F and, hence, to favor an epistemic interpretation. Note, however, that German has a paradigm instance of an impersonal marker, which is *man* 'one', and this marker is almost exclusively associated with agent-oriented modality. Thus, even in utterances with a main verb *kennen* 'know' as their predicate, which strongly correlates with epistemic modality (as we saw in Section 2.2, Table 2), there is a focal agent-oriented sense if the sentence subject is *man*, as in (25).

(25) Man muß sie kennen.
one must her know
'You have to know her.'

There appears to be an obvious reason for this: *man* only occurs as a subject, refers exclusively to human referents, is associated with human activities, and tends to imply some manipulating force. It is therefore not surprising that it promotes agent-oriented, rather than epistemic, interpretations.

4. On models

4.1 *Metaphor model vs. context model*

A number of studies of grammaticalization have claimed that the development of grammatical categories involves a metaphorical process (see especially Claudi and Heine 1986; Sweetser 1988; Heine, Claudi and Hünnemeyer 1991; Stolz 1991; see also Bybee and Pagliuca 1985:73). For example, there are good reasons to argue that the shift of the English *be going to*-construction from a concrete/lexical meaning to the abstract/grammatical meaning of future tense has a metaphorical base. First, this shift involves a transfer from the "real-world", the world of referential entities and kinetic activities, to the world of discourse, to entities that exist in acts of speech or, e.g. with reference to the development of modal auxiliaries, a transfer from the socio-physical world to the world of reason and belief (Sweetser 1984:24). Thus, we are dealing with a transfer from one domain of human conceptualization to another. Second, the metaphoric nature of this transfer can also be derived from the fact that our *be going to*-example meets the criteria commonly applied to define metaphor, e.g., that the statement, if taken literally, is false. While in the sentence *Sally is going to town* the phrase *is going to* has its literal meaning of motion in space, it has a "transferred sense" in sentences like *Sally is going to wake up in a minute*, where the literal meaning is ruled out.[9]

Essentially the same kind of metaphorical transfer can be observed in other instances of grammaticalization: they involve a transfer from one cognitive domain to another, with the effect that, from a certain stage onwards, an expression undergoing this shift becomes false or meaningless if taken literally, that is, if interpreted as designating its original meaning. A number of such source domains and their corresponding target domains are discussed in Heine, Claudi and Hünnemeyer (1991). It goes without saying that we are dealing here with a specific kind of metaphorical transfer that has been described as "emerging metaphor" (Heine, Claudi and Hünnemeyer 1991:60-62).

There is, however, at least one problem with this metaphorical model. This problem concerns the continuous nature of grammaticalization. Metaphor is commonly assumed to involve a discrete "jump" from one domain to another - a process that is hard to reconcile with the gradient nature of grammaticalization chains (Heine 1992). In the case of *be going to*, the shift from physical motion to grammatical function proceeded in a chain-like manner. This is suggested on the one hand by historical evidence (cf. Pérez 1990) and on the other hand, by the present use patterns of the construction.

That conceptual shift in the process of grammaticalization is chain-like and continuous is due to the particular circumstances giving rise to new grammatical meanings: such meanings are derived from existing meanings via context extension (Aijmer 1985), and through the conventionalization of invited inferences or conversational implicatures (Traugott and König 1991). This reasoning has been advanced with reference to the transition from agent-oriented to epistemic meanings. Thus, Traugott (1989:50-51) argues that from 'permission' one can implicate 'expectation': thus, if I say *You may go*, I may, in the right circumstances, implicate that I want you to go, from which you may infer that you have some obligation to go. With reference to the modality of obligation, Traugott and König observe:

> [...] *must* in the epistemic sense of 'I conclude that' derived from the obligative sense of 'ought to' by strengthening of conversational inferences and subjectification. If I say *She must be married* in the obligation sense, I invite the inference that she will indeed get married. This inference is of course epistemic, pertaining to a state of affairs that is anticipated to be true at some later time (Traugott and König 1991:209).

This overall process, of which pragmatic strengthening appears to be a part, is called 'context-induced reinterpretation' by Heine, Claudi and Hünnemeyer (1991, Chapter 3), because it is specific contexts (or "circumstances") that invite new inferences and ultimately lead to the emergence of (new) grammatical meanings.

To summarize, in order to account for the conceptual shift from concrete/lexical to abstract/grammatical meaning we have two main models at our disposal: one that rests on a metaphorical interpretation of the process and may therefore be called the metaphor model, and another relying on context-induced reinterpretation, which I call the context model. While in the past, scholars have argued in favor of either one or the other, more recent investigations suggest that both models are required to understand the process concerned.

There are, however, two contrasting positions with regard to the role these models should play in a theory of grammaticalization. On the one hand, there is the position of Traugott (1989), Traugott and König (1991), and of

Bybee, Perkins and Pagliuca (1994.), according to which different kinds of grammaticalization have to be distinguished; and while some kinds are handled best in terms of the metaphor model, others have to be accounted for in terms of the context model. Among these authors again, there are differing views as to where exactly the models apply. While all agree that the metaphor model typically applies in the case of concrete/lexical structures and the context model in the case of more strongly grammaticalized structures, disagreement exists as to where to draw the boundary between the two. For Traugott (1989) and Traugott and König (1991), the transfer from concrete source propositions to auxiliary functions of tense and aspect is metaphorically structured[11] while the transfer from agent-oriented (deontic) to epistemic meanings is not:

> But the shift to epistemics of conclusion, belief, knowledge, hear-say, hypothetical conditionality, and so forth has little of the analogical mapping from one conceptual domain onto another that is characteristic of metaphor (Traugott 1989:50).

Sweetser (1982) on the other hand suggests that the conceptual shift from the agent-oriented to the epistemic domain is a clear instance of a metaphorical process. Bybee, Pagliuca and Perkins (forthc.) again argue that the English modal auxiliaries *must* and *should* both have experienced an extension from agent-oriented to epistemic modality, but whereas the extension of *must* is suggestive of metaphorical transfer, that of *should* might be due to the conventionalization of implicature and, hence, would have to be dealt with in terms of the context model.

The different behavior of *must* and *should* had already been pointed out by Coates (1983:14ff.). In her work on English modal auxiliaries, she observed that in the transition from one kind of modality to another there are three types of indeterminacy, which she refers to, respectively, as gradience, ambiguity, and merger. Gradience concerns the nature of the continuum of meaning, e.g., in the transition from the core of ABILITY to the periphery of POSSIBILITY of English *can*. Ambiguity may be described in terms of the following properties (cf. Coates 1983:15-16):

a. A given expression has two senses and it is not possible to decide from the immediate context which of these is intended.
b. The two senses are in an *either/or* kind of indeterminacy since either of them may be chosen.

c. These senses belong to different categories, viz. the categories of agent-oriented (= root) and of epistemic modality, respectively.
d. The categories concerned are discrete.

The only example of ambiguity in Coates' work on English modal auxiliaries involves *must*, which is ambiguous between an agent-oriented (26a) and an epistemic sense (26b).

(26) *He must understand that we mean business.*

a. [A: "It is essential that he understand that we mean business"]
b. [E: "Surely he understands that we mean business"]

Merger shares with ambiguity properties (a) and (d). Instead of properties (b) and (c), however, it has (b') and (c'), respectively:

b'. The two senses are in a *both/and* relationship, i.e., they are mutually compatible. In order to understand the relevant expression, it is not necessary to decide which of the two senses is intended.
c'. In certain contexts, the two senses are "neutralized", i.e., they are not mutually exclusive.

As examples of merger, Coates (1983:17) cites English *should* and *ought to*, as in (27):

(27) a. A: *Newcastle Brown is a jolly good beer.*
B: *Is it?*
C: *Well it ought to be at that price.*
b. [A: Obligation of the maker to provide a good beer]
c. [E: Logical assumption - "the beer costs a lot, therefore it is good"]

According to Heine, Claudi and Hünnemeyer (1991) on the other hand, for all instances of grammaticalization analyzed so far, both the metaphor and the context models are required, each relating to a different level: the context model to the micro-level and the metaphor model to the macro-level of conceptual shift. The former perspectivizes the continuous nature of conceptual shift, that is, the fact that this shift proceeds in a series of overlapping, contextually defined extensions, while the macro-level perspectivizes the fact that, given enough micro-level extensions, conceptual shift will cross boundaries between cognitive domains, like that between the domain of concrete, "real-world" phenomena and that of abstract grammatical functions. In the case of the *be going to*-example alluded to above, the context model takes care of the many micro-level extensions to be observed both in the historical and the present uses of this construction, including the numerous situations of ambiguity between physical motion and intention, or between intention and prediction, or even among all three senses. The metaphor model, on the other hand, is concerned with and accounts for the macro-level shift from a concrete source proposition to an abstract grammatical function.[12]

The data considered in the previous sections suggest that the distinction between agent-oriented and epistemic modality is of a discrete nature in the case of German modals, being based on presence vs. absence of the modal force F. It was noted, however, that three additional properties tend to be associated with this distinction, namely presence vs. absence of a controlling agent (C), of a dynamic event (D), and of the later-than-reference-time constraint (L). The more of these properties are present, the more pronounced the semantic contrast between the two interpretations is likely to be and the more likely it is that we are dealing with instances of ambiguity; conversely, the more of these properties that are absent, the more we approach what Coates refers to as merger. Take, for example, utterance (13), repeated here as (28):

(28) Er muß frieren.
he must freeze
'He is freezing/feeling cold.'
('They let him freeze.')

Muß in (28) is likely to involve a modal force F, hence, its focal sense is an agent-oriented one, although apart from F, none of the properties normally accompanying agent-oriented uses, i.e. C, D or L, is clearly present. There is, however, an almost equally pronounced epistemic sense ["He must be freezing"], and the two senses can be said to be suggestive of merger, in that they satisfy criteria (b') and (c') mentioned above: given the right context, there is not much of a difference whether the hearer interprets (28) in its agent-oriented or in its epistemic sense. (28a) below would be an example of such a context: the contextual information *Er hat keinen Mantel an* ("He isn't wearing a coat") may be interpreted alternatively as the force that is responsible for the content expressed by (28) or else as a presupposition leading to the logical assumption underlying the epistemic interpretation of (28).

(28) a. ["Er hat keinen Mantel an; ..."]
'He isn't wearing a coat; ...'

It is in utterances like (28), used in contexts like (28a), that an inferential mechanism could have been at work (Bybee, Pagliuca and Perkins 1994) whereby an agent-oriented sense of obligation gives rise to an epistemic sense of inferred certainty.

What this would seem to suggest is that the transition from the agent-oriented to the epistemic sense of (28) involves both discontinuity and continuity; discontinuity because even in a context like (28a), the two modalities can clearly be distinguished, and continuity because, given the right context, it does not matter which of the two senses is intended by the speaker and selected by the hearer: the information value remains essentially the same. A similar situation is found in the case of modals other than *müssen*, which means that, for all modals considered, the same descriptive framework can be employed. [13]

To summarize, the fact that there is only one criterial property that distinguishes the two kinds of modality in German modals would seem to suggest, first, that an element of discreteness separates the two modalities. Second, it suggests that the transition from agent-oriented to epistemic modality may be regarded as an instance of semantic bleaching in that it involves the "bleaching out" of property F, i.e., of Jespersen's "element of will" (1924:320-1). At the same time, however, there are also gains: with the elimination of F, the modals acquire new senses that are characterized by what Traugott (1989:49) calls the "strengthening of focus on knowledge, belief, and the speaker's attitude toward the proposition".

Third, such observations suggest that there are reasons to regard the transition from agent-oriented to epistemic concepts as being metaphorically structured, as has been argued for independently by Sweetser (1982; 1988), Bybee and Pagliuca (1985), and Heine, Claudi and Hünnemeyer (1991): it involves a transfer from one domain of human experience to another, from the sociophysical world to the epistemic world (Sweetser 1982:492-5), the former being a dynamic world of willful human beings who act and are capable of imposing their will on other agents, the latter essentially a static world, one that may but need not be associated with human participants (Heine, Claudi and Hünnemeyer 1991:176-178).

4.2 *Another example*

In a paper on "Temporal distance: a basic linguistic metaphor", Fleischman (1989) observes that distance in the past frequently serves to move a real event from actuality to a hypothetical world, and that expressions for temporal distance are often pressed into service to express, *inter alia*, social distance and politeness, as in (29):

(29) *I thought/was thinking* about asking you to dinner.

In this way, Past tense forms referring to a present situation are "felt to be less assertive, more deferential, whence more polite" than corresponding Present-tense forms:

> The risk of a possible negative reply is reduced since no invitation has actually been issued. Use of the PAST tense in speech acts of this type serves to cancel - or at least attenuate - their illocutionary force [...] (Fleischman 1989:9).

The result is that temporal distance serves as a metaphorical vehicle for social/ interpersonal distance as well as for a number of other notions relating to evidentiality, speaker subjectivity, etc.

A different explanation is volunteered by Bybee (This volume) with regard to English modal verbs used in the Past tense. She discusses some of the same evidence adduced by Fleischman but describes the phenomenon without reference to metaphor; rather, her parameters are the particular semantics characterizing modals on the one hand, and the use of past tense on the other:

> [...] the use of *wanted to* in present time in Modern English is possible because it implies that certain conditions on carrying out the wanted predicate may not be met. The so-called polite or remote uses of Past tense as in
>
> (21) *I wanted to ask you a question.*
>
> arise in the same way. That is, (21) implies that there might be conditions that are unmet. Among these implied conditions is the question of whether the addressee wants to be asked a question — thus the deferential use of the Past. (Bybee, this volume).

According to Bybee, a series of factors work together to produce the deferential or polite senses apparent in the two English examples presented above:

a. First is the fact that modal verbs are stative verbs. When modals are used in the Past what is asserted is that a state existed before the moment of speech, but not that the state necessarily still exists in the present.

b. Since the state may still exist in the present, a modal in the Past tense may be used in contexts where it has present relevance: it may receive the interpretation "that the modality is still in effect, and [that] the predicate action will be carried out if the right conditions are met" (Bybee, this volume).

c. The combination of the modal sense and the Past sense is said to produce a hypothetical reading; compared to Present tense modals, modals in the Past tense may then express hypothetical situations in conditional apodosis, as can be seen in (30a), as opposed to (30b):

(30) a. If I saw Judy, I would tell her the news.
b. If I see Judy, I will tell her the news.

d. In the context of a dialogic discourse (typically involving first and second person referents), the hypothetical sense may then be exploited to express a deferential or polite sense, as in (29) above, e.g., to tone down or weaken the illocutionary force of an otherwise assertive speech act, as described in the above quotation by Fleischman.

As is to be expected in such processes of grammaticalization, with the development of new senses, old uses may gradually lose in significance. For example, the more the hypothetical sense gains ground, the more the past sense disappears. Stage (a) is no longer relevant for English Past tense modals such as *would* and *could*; for *should*, Bybee (This volume) adds that "one could argue that there are no past uses at all".

I do not wish to delve into the question as to whether the development sketched in (a) through (d) is appropriate only to languages with a fuzzy/overlapping zone between the morphological categories of past tense and subjunctive, or to languages lacking a subjunctive category altogether. In German, for example, Bybee's scenario does not seem to apply in cases where there is a well marked formal distinction between Past tense and Subjunctive:

the role of a hypothetical or deferential sense is invariably assumed by the Subjunctive rather than the Past tense, as can be seen in (31).

(31) *Ich kann Ihnen helfen.*
'I can help you.' PRESENT

Ich könnte Ihnen helfen. SUBJUNCTIVE
(Similar meaning, but more hypothetical, or polite, deferential)

Ich konnte Ihnen helfen.
'I was able to help you.' PAST
(Past significance only)

It would seem, however, that this question does not touch the main point made by Bybee. What is obvious, is that Bybee's account offers a legitimate alternative to that of Fleischman, one that rests on a series of inferences that can be described in terms of context-induced reinterpretation (Heine, Claudi and Hünnemeyer 1991, Ch. 3).

Bybee (this volume) argues that Fleischman's metaphorical explanation of a transfer from temporal distance to social distance in certain politeness forms does not account for the fact that it is always modal verbs that are involved in this transfer. Yet Bybee's account does not explain how it is that modals which express a situation involving unmet conditions are also used for marking a certain kind of social relationship (politeness). What I wish to argue here again (cf. Heine, Claudi and Hünnemeyer 1991), is that an explanation for a conceptual shift in the process of grammaticalization must have two components: one relates to the macro-effects of the process which are suggestive of a shift from one domain of human conceptualization to another, in this case from the domain of time to that of social relations; the other relates to the micro-effects which are suggestive of a gradient sequence of contextual and inferential extensions leading to the emergence of chain-like use patterns of the linguistic items concerned.

While Fleischman's analysis highlights the macro-level of the process, Bybee's approach perspectivizes the micro-level. The way in which the two models are interrelated is sketched graphically in Figure 1 (cf. Heine, Claudi and Hünnemeyer 1991, Ch. 4). Thus, rather than contradicting or excluding one another, the two models complement each other and are both required for a better understanding of grammaticalization.

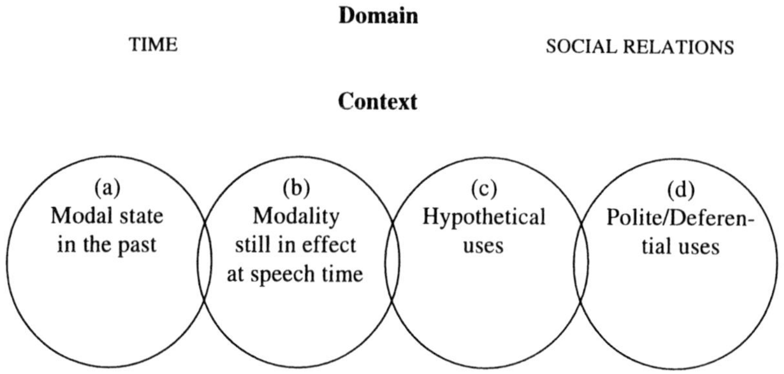

Figure 1. *A metaphor-and-context model for some of the senses of English* would *and* should.

5. Conclusions

In previous research it has been established that epistemic uses of modals tend to develop out of agent-oriented uses; that is, the latter are older than the former (see especially Shepherd 1982; Bybee and Pagliuca 1985; Traugott 1989; Bybee, Pagliuca and Perkins 1994.). From this it follows that contexts associated with agent-oriented modality reflect more conservative or less grammaticalized use patterns than contexts associated with epistemic modality. While there may be exceptions, this conclusion seems to hold true for most of the data considered here; it is also confirmed by diachronic analysis.[14] With reference to German this would mean in particular that the most conservative behavior is encountered if

a. modals such as *möchten* 'would like to', *dürfen* 'be allowed to, may', or *wollen* 'want', rather than modals like *sollen* 'should' or *können* 'can' are involved,
b. the main verb is an action verb like *kommen* 'come',
c. the modal is used in the perfect or the past tense,
d. the modal occurs in interrogative rather than in declarative utterances,
e. the modal occurs in negative rather than in affirmative utterances, or
f. if the subject is a first or second person, rather than a third person referent.

Some related observations have also been made for English modals. Traugott (1989:52), for example, notes that older meanings tend to be maintained longer in negative environments, and draws attention to the relative paucity of epistemic (as opposed to agent-oriented) uses of *must not* and *mustn't* in British English and to the maintenance of the volitional sense of *will* in *We won't go*.

One main claim made in this paper is that it is not possible to describe the transition between agent-oriented and epistemic modality in German modals exclusively in terms of linguistic categorization. What has to be taken into consideration in addition are the contextual frames with which particular uses of a modal are associated. Utterances having human agents as their subject and dynamic main verbs may still have a focal epistemic sense if associated with a contextual frame that discourages an agent-oriented interpretation. More important, however, is the presence vs. absence of the modal force F in determining which variety of modality a given modal utterance receives.

Finally, as we saw in Section 4, the transition from one kind of modality to another has elements of discontinuity as well as continuity, and can thus be accounted for by appeal to both the metaphor model and the context model of grammaticalization. In this respect, the problem looked at in this paper does not differ significantly from other instances of grammaticalization studied so far.

NOTES

1 I wish to express my gratitude to Werner Abraham, Joan Bybee, Eithne Carlin, Wallace Chafe, Ulrike Claudi, Zygmunt Frajzyngier, Tom Givón, Christa Kilian-Hatz, Christa König, Andreas "Donald" Lessau, Frank Lichtenberk, Franz Potyka, Heinz Roberg, Dan Slobin, Thomas Stolz, Eve Sweetser, as well as a number of other participants of the Albuquerque symposium on Mood and Modality for valuable discussions on this paper, most of all to Suzanne Fleischman. I am also indebted to the Deutsche Forschungsgemeinschaft (German Research Society) for its financial support.

2 In the following, y will use the terms "agent-oriented" and "deontic" as defined by Bybee, Pagliuca and Perkins (1991, 1994), with slight modifications to be specified below. Note that the distinctions referred to above are not only terminological; for Coates (1983), for example, "root modality" embraces "deontic" and "dynamic categories", and "epistemic modality" also includes "alethic" modality.

3 See Steele et al. (1981:260-264) and Heine (1993) for additional exemplification.

4. Note, however, that, compared to full-fledged verbs, they have a reduced paradigm of personal inflections, lacking e.g. the present tense 3sg. suffix *-t*; see below.

5 Square brackets "[]" are used in this paper for contextual information relevant for the semantic interpretation of an utterance.

6 While it is hoped that the observations made in the course of the survey will reveal some salient semantic characteristics of German modals, the survey is biased in several ways. For example, the three informants, all students of the University of Cologne having some acquaintance with linguistics, had to take the three-fold classification proposed here for granted in their responses.

7. The situation would be different if subjunctive uses of modals were included.

8 I am referring to the non-standard progressive of the form *Er ist am Essen* 'He is eating' which, although not acceptable in High German, is nevertheless found in some form or other in many modern German dialects.

9 Cf. the notion of *preference* as defined by Givón (1990:529).

10. For further evidence on the metaphorical nature of conceptual shift in grammaticalization, see Heine, Claudi and Hünnemeyer 1991.

11 The examples provided by Traugott (1989:207) involve such developments as that from GO to future, from COME to perfect, or from BE AT/IN to progressive. The process concerned is described by Traugott as one involving "spatio-temporal metaphors".

12 In addition to these two models, a third model has to be distinguished, namely the bleaching or containment model (Tom Givón, p.c.; see Heine, Claudi and Hünnemeyer 1991:108ff.). We will not further deal with this model here, essentially since it is confined to semantic substance while our primary concern is with the cognitive and pragmatic strategies underlying the process of grammaticalization (but see below).

13 As noted above, this does not necessarily apply to *werden*, whose status as a modal is controversial.

14 The present paper is based exclusively on synchronic findings.

REFERENCES

Abraham, Werner 1989. "Futur-Typologie in den germanischen Sprachen." Abraham and Janssen 1989. Pp. 345-369.

Abraham, Werner 1992. The Aspectual Source of the Epistemic-Root Distinction of Modal Verbs. Paper presented at the Symposium on Mood and Modality, Albuquerque, University of New Mexico, May 8-10, 1992.

Abraham, Werner and Theo Janssen 1989. *Tempus - Aspekt - Modus: Die lexikalischen und grammatischen Formen in den germanischen Sprachen.* Tübingen: Max Niemeyer Verlag.

Ahlqvist, Anders ed. 1982. *Paper from the Fifth International Conference on Historical Linguistics.* Amsterdam: John Benjamins.

Aijmer, Karin 1985. The semantic development of *will.* Fisiak 1985. Pp. 11-21.

Bybee, Joan L. and William Pagliuca 1985. Cross Linguistic Comparison and the Development of Grammatical Meaning. Fišiak, J. 1985. Pp. 59-83.

Bybee, Joan L., William Pagliuca, and Revere D. Perkins 1991. *Back to the Future.* Traugott, Elizabeth C. and Bernd Heine 1991.2. Pp. 17-58.

Bybee, Joan L., Revere D. Perkins, and William Pagliuca forthc. *The Grammaticization of Tense, Aspect, and Modality in the Languages of the World.* Chicago, London: University of Chicago Press.

Bybee, Joan L. This volume. The Semantic Development of Past Tense Modals in English. Paper prepared for the Symposium on Mood and Modality, University of New Mexico, Albuquerque, 8 - 10 May, 1992.

Calbert, Joseph P. 1971. "Modality and Case Grammar." *Working Papers in Linguistics* (Ohio State University), August 1971:85-132.

Claudi, Ulrike and Bernd Heine 1986. "On the Metaphorical Base of Grammar." *Studies in Language* 10,2:297-335

Coates, Jennifer 1983. *The Semantics of the Modal Auxiliaries.* London/Canberra: Croom Helm.

Fišiak, Jacek, ed. 1985. *Historical Semantics, Historical Word Formation.* Berlin: Mouton de Gruyter.

Fleischman, Suzanne 1989. "Temporal Distance: A Basic Linguistic Metaphor." *Studies in Language* 13,1:1-50.

Givón, T. 1990. *Syntax: A Functional-Typological Introduction.* Volume II. Amsterdam/ Philadelphia: John Benjamins.

Haiman, John 1985. *Iconicity in Syntax.* (Typological Studies in Language, 6.) Amsterdam/Philadelphia: John Benjamins.

Heine, Bernd 1992. "Grammaticalization Chains." *Studies in Language* 16,2:335-68.

Heine, Bernd 1993. *Auxiliaries.* New York: Oxford University Press.

Heine, Bernd, Ulrike Claudi and Friederike Hünnemeyer 1991. *Grammaticalization: A Conceptual Framework.* Chicago: University of Chicago Press.

Helbig, Gerhard and Joachim Buscha 1988. *Deutsche Grammatik.* Ein Handbuch für den Ausländerunterricht. Eleventh edition. Leipzig: VEB Enzyklopädie.

Jacobs, R. and P. Rosenbaum. eds 1970. *Readings in English Transformational Grammar.* Waltham, Mass.: Ginn and Co.

Jenkins, L. 1972. *Modality in English Syntax.* Indiana University Linguistics Club: Mimeograph.

Jespersen, Otto 1924. *The philosophy of grammar.* London: Allen and Unwin.

Lakoff, George & Mark Johnson 1980. *Metaphors We Live by.* Chicago/London: University of Chicago Press.

Langacker, Ronald W. 1985. "Observations and Speculations on subjectivity." In Haiman 1985. Pp. 109-150.

Levinson, Stephen C. 1983. *Pragmatics.* Cambridge: Cambridge University Press.

Palmer, Frank R. 1986. *Mood and Modality.* Cambridge: Cambridge University Press.

Pérez, Aveline 1990. "Time in Motion: Grammaticalisation of the *Be Going to* Construction in English." *La Trobe University Working Papers in Linguistics* 3:49-64.

Perlmutter, D. M. 1970. "The Two Verbs 'Begin'." In Jacobs, R. and P. Rosenbaum 1970. Pp. 107-119.

Ramat, Anna Giacalone 1991. "Grammaticalization Processes in the Area of Temporal and Modal Relations." To appear *Studies in Second Language Acquisition* 14 (1992).

Shepherd, Susan C. 1982. "From Deontic to Epistemic: An Analysis of Modals in the History of English, Creoles, and Language Acquisition." In: Ahlqvist, Anders 1982. Pp. 316-323.

Steele, Susan M., Adrian Akmajian, Richard Demers, Eloise Jelinek, Chisato Kitagawa, Richard Oehrle, and Thomas Wasow 1981. *An Encyclopedia of AUX: A study in Cross-Linguistic Equivalence.* (Linguistic Inquiry Monographs, 5.) Cambridge, Mass./London: MIT Press.
Stephany, Ursula 1989. "Modality in First Language Acquisition: The State of the Art." To appear in *Proceedings of the Symposium on Modality in Language Acquisition, Berlin, Free University, 1-3 May, 1989.*
Stolz, Thomas 1991. *Von der Grammatikalisierbarkeit des Körpers.* I: Vorbereitung. Typescript, University of Bochum.
Sweetser, Eve Eliot 1982. Root and Epistemic Modals: Causality in Two Worlds." *Berkeley Linguistics Society* 8: 484-507.
Sweetser, Eve Eliot 1984. *Semantic Structure and Semantic Change: A Cognitive Linguistic Study of Modality, Perception, Speech Acts, and Logical Relations.* Ph. D. dissertation, University of California at Berkeley.
Sweetser, Eve Eliot 1988. Grammaticalization and Semantic Bleaching. *Berkeley Linguistics Society* 14:389-405.
Traugott, Elizabeth C. 1989. "On the Rise of Epistemic Meanings in English: An Example of Subjectification in Semantic Change." *Language* 65,1:31-55.
Traugott, Elizabeth C. & Bernd Heine, eds 1991.1, 1991.2. *Approaches to Grammaticalization.* 2 volumes. Amsterdam/Philadelphia: John Benjamins.
Traugott, Elizabeth C. and Ekkehard König 1991. "The Semantics-Pragmatics of Grammaticalization Revisited." Traugott, E. C. and B. Heine 1991.1. Pp. 189-218.
Vater, Heinz 1970. On the Generation of Modal Verbs. Paper read at the Ethno-Linguistic Seminar, Bloomington, Indiana.

ABBREVIATIONS

A/E = focal agent-oriented/epistemic sense
A1/E1 = non-focal agent-oriented/epistemic sense
A2/E2 = marginal agent-oriented/epistemic sense

APPENDIX

Agent-oriented vs. epistemic modality of eight German modals

The data presented below have been elicited from three native speakers of High German. While a number of discrepancies were noted among these informants, the overall ratios turned out to be essentially the same.

A. Linguistic data

1. Present

Er muß kommen	A	E2	*Er muß Geld haben*		E	*Er muß sie kennen*		E
Er soll kommen	A	E	*Er soll G. haben*		E	*Er soll sie kennen*		E
Er kann kommen	A	E2	*Er kann G. haben*	A	E	*Er kann sie kennen*		E
Er will kommen	A		*Er will G. haben*	A	E	*Er will sie kennen*		E
Er mag kommen	A	E2	*Er mag G. haben*	A2	E	*Er mag sie kennen*		E
Er darf kommen	A		*Er darf G. haben*	A		*Er darf s. kennen*		
Er möchte kommen	A		*Er möchte G. haben*	A		*Er möchte s. kennen*	A	
Er wird kommen	A	E2	*Er wird G. haben*	A2	E	*Er wird sie kennen*	A2	E

2. Past

Er mußte kommen.	A		*Er mußte Geld haben.*			*Er mußte sie kennen.*		
sollte	A	E	*sollte*		E	*sollte*		E
konnte	A		*konnte*	A		*konnte*		
wollte	A		*wollte*	A		*wollte*		E2
mochte	A		*mochte*	A2		*mochte*		
durfte	A		*durfte*	A		*durfte*	A	
-			-			-		
-			-			-		

3. Perfect

Er hat kommen		*Er hat Geld haben*		*Er hat ihn kennen*	
müssen.	A	*müssen.*	A2	*müssen.*	A2
sollen.	A	*sollen.*	A2	*sollen.*	A2
können.	A	*können.*		*können.*	A2
wollen.	A	*wollen.*	A	*wollen.*	A2
-		-	-		
-		-	-		
-		-	-		
-		-	-		

4. Negation

Er muß nicht kommen.	A		*Er muß kein Geld haben.*			*Er muß sie nicht kennen.*	A2	E
soll	A		*soll*	A		*soll*	A1	E
kann	A		*kann*	A1	E	*kann*		E
will	A		*will*	A		*will*	A	E
mag	A		*mag*	A2		*mag*	A	E1
darf	A		*darf*	A		*darf*	A	
möchte	A		*möchte*	A		*möchte*	A	
wird	A		*wird*	A1	E	*wird*		E

5. Question

Muß er kommen?	A		*Muß er Geld haben?*	A2		*Muß er sie kennen?*	A	E
Soll	A		*Soll*	A1		*Soll*		
Kann	A		*Kann*	A	E1	*Kann*		E
Will	A		*Will*	A		*Will*		E1
Mag	A		*Mag*	A1		*Mag*		
Darf	A		*Darf*	A		*Darf*	A	
Möchte	A		*Möchte*	A		*Möchte*	A	
Wird	A		*Wird*	A1		*Wird*		E2

6. Main verb in perfect

Er muß gekommen sein.		E	*Er muß Geld gehabt haben.*		E	*Er muß sie gekannt haben.*		E
soll		E	*soll*		E	*soll*		E
kann		E	*kann*		E1	*kann*		E
will		E	*will*		E	*will*		E
mag		E	*mag*		E	*mag*		E
darf			*darf*			*darf*	A2	
möchte			*möchte*		E2	*möchte*	A2	
wird		E	*wird*		E	*wird*		E

7. Second person subject

Du mußt kommen.	A		*Du mußt Geld haben.*		E	*Du mußt sie kennen.*		E
sollst	A		*sollst*		E	*sollst*		E
kannst	A		*kannst*	A	E2	*kannst*		E2
willst	A		*willst*	A	E2	*willst*		E2
magst			*magst*		E2	*magst*		E
darfst	A		*darfst*	A		*darfst*	A2	
möchtest			*möchtest*	A		*möchtest*	A2	
wirst	A1		*wirst*	A1	E	*wirst*		E

8. First person subject

Ich muß kommen.	A		*Ich muß Geld haben.*	A		*Ich muß sie kennen.*		E
soll	A		*soll*		E2	*soll*		E
kann	A		*kann*	A1		*kann*		E1
will	A		*will*	A		*will*	A2	
mag	A		*mag*		E2	*mag*		E
darf	A		*darf*	A2		*darf*	A1	
möchte	A		*möchte*	A		*möchte*	A	
werde	A		*werde*	A		*werde*		E

B Quantitative data (Based on A above)

Kind of proposition	Value of modality: Agent-oriented	Value of modality: Epistemic	Number of instances	Maximum number of points	Index of modality (1.00 = maximal, 0 = minimal value): Agent-oriented	Index of modality: Epistemic
1 Present (3rd person subject)	41	43	24	72	0.57	0.60
2 Past	33	10	18	54	0.61	0.19
3 Perfect	21	0	12	36	0.58	0
4 Negation	56	23	24	72	0.78	0.32
5 Question	52	11	24	72	0.72	0.15
6 Main verb in perf.	2	54	24	72	0.03	0.75
7 2nd p. subject	33	26	24	72	0.46	0.36
8 1st p. subject	39	16	24	72	0.54	0.22
Kind of expression						
Er kommt.	137	28	58	174	0.79	0.16
Er hat Geld.	94	61	58	174	0.54	0.35
Er kennt sie.	46	94	58	174	0.26	0.54
Kind of modal						
Dürfen	47	0	7	63	0.75	0
Möchten	41	1	6	54	0.76	0.18
Wollen	48	23	8	72	0.67	0.32
Können	38	30	8	72	0.53	0.42
Müssen	31	31	8	72	0.43	0.43
Mögen	23	25	7	63	0.37	0.40
Werden	25	32	6	54	0.46	0.59
Sollen	30	40	8	72	0.42	0.56

The Expression of Root and Epistemic Possibility in English[1]

Jennifer Coates
Roehampton Institute

1. The root/epistemic distinction

The distinction between root (or agent-oriented or deontic) modality and epistemic modality has proved enormously useful to those attempting to describe the modal systems obtaining in the world's languages. The analysis of English is no exception (see Coates 1983; Haegeman 1983; Palmer 1990). Moreover, there is general agreement on the definition of these terms. Epistemic modality is concerned with the speaker's assumptions or assessment of possibilities, and in most cases it indicates the speaker's confidence or lack of confidence in the truth of the proposition expressed. Root modality encompasses meanings such as permission and obligation, and also possibility and necessity. This means that the root/epistemic distinction cuts across the necessity/obligation and possibility/permission distinctions (see diagram below). As in many languages, in English the same linguistic forms express both root and epistemic meanings. So, for example, *may* can express both root and epistemic possibility; *must* can express both root and epistemic necessity.

	Root		Epistemic	
CAN *MAY*	permission	possibility ←——————→	possibility	*MAY*
MUST *HAVE TO*	obligation	necessity ←——————→	necessity	*MUST* *HAVE TO*

Figure 1. *Meaning and the root/epistemic distinction*

As far as the expression of necessity is concerned, this polysemy is unproblematic: the root/epistemic distinction remains distinct, as the following examples illustrate. *Must*, in (1a), expresses the root meaning of obligation, in (1b) it expresses the (weaker) root meaning of necessity, and in (1c) it expresses epistemic necessity.

(1)	a.	*You must finish this before dinner*	ROOT
	b.	*All students must obtain the consent of the Dean*	ROOT
	c.	*I must have a temperature*	EPISTEMIC

It is my impression, however, that there is some confusion about the root/epistemic distinction when it is applied to possibility. In this paper, I want to re-examine this area of modality, and will argue that: (i) the semantic contrast between root and epistemic possibility is considerably weaker than in other root/epistemic pairs; (ii) where the same linguistic form expresses both root and epistemic possibility, instances of **merger** (see Coates 1983:17) are common (*may*); (iii) where a linguistic form expresses predominantly root possibility, epistemic readings are likely to develop (*can*).

2. Root and epistemic possibility

In order to discuss the root/epistemic contrast in relation to the expression of possibility in English, I shall make use of the set of properties developed by Heine (this volume) in his analysis of the German modals. Heine argues that the following properties are criterial:

a. There is some force **F** that has an interest in an event either occurring or not occurring (Heine comments that **F** "is characterised by some 'element of will', to use the wording of Jespersen (1924:320-1)". (Heine this volume)
b. That event is to be performed by some agent **A**.
c. The event is dynamic (**D**).
d. The event has not yet taken place at reference time and, if it does take place, that will be at a time *later* than reference time (**L**).
e. The event is non-factual, but there is a certain degree of *probability* that it will occur (**P**).

In an utterance such as *she must go to bed now*, **F** may refer to the speaker ('I insist that she goes to bed now') or to an absent parent ('her mother insists that she goes to bed at this time') or to any other source of power the speaker may have in mind. The pronoun *she* is the agent (**A**), the event — *go* — is dynamic (**D**), the event has not yet taken place at the moment the utterance is produced (**L**), and there is a high probability (**P**) that the event referred to will take place.

As Heine (this volume) says: "While prototypical instances of agent-oriented modality are characterised by the presence of the properties [i.e. **F**, **A**, **D**, **L** and **P**], prototypical instances of epistemic modality lack all properties except **P**". This means that the fewer of these properties there are in any given instance, the weaker will be the semantic contrast between the two interpretations of these sentences. If we look at the examples given in (1) above, we can justify the claim that the semantic contrast between root and epistemic meaning is strong here by applying Heine's criteria. In (1a) and (1b) **all** of the properties are present, while only **P** is present in (1c). In other words, examples of root *must* in English would normally be classified as prototypical examples of agent-oriented modality, while examples of epistemic *must* would be classified as prototypically epistemic.

Let's turn to the contrast between root and epistemic possibility. Examples (2) and (3) below are typical instances of the expression of root possibility.[2]

(2) *well I think there is a place where I can get a cheap kettle* (S.1.4.62)

(3) *I am afraid this is the bank's final word. I tell you so that you may make arrangements elsewhere.* (W.7.9.37)

Can (see example 2) is the normal exponent of root possibility in English, while *may*, as illustrated in example (3), is the exponent of root possibility in more formal contexts (in this case, a letter from a Bank Manager). Properties **A**, **D**, and **L** are present in both (2) and (3), but **F** (force) is absent.

In everyday discourse, *can* expressing root possibility is most commonly found in examples like (4) and (5) below, general statements of possibilities with impersonal subjects.

(4) *certain things can be sex-linked to the Y chromosome* (S.5b.2.54)

(5) *first thing in the morning they come, you can hear the whistle* (S.1.14A.43)

These two examples display *none* of Heine's properties apart from **P**. Even more perplexing are archetypal examples of *can* such as (6) below, which Palmer (1990:152-4) describes as 'existential':

(6) *Lions can be dangerous*

Palmer justifies his use of the term 'existential' by claiming that paraphrases involving 'some' (*some lions are dangerous*) or 'sometimes' (*lions are sometimes dangerous*) are more appropriate than paraphrases using 'possible for'. What is intriguing about examples like (6) is that, besides lacking **F**, **A**, **D**, and **L** (the properties associated with non-epistemic modality), they also lack **P**. In other words, some examples of *can* lack all the properties which Heine claims are normally associated with modal meaning.

Although we have seen that examples of root possibility vary in the number of properties associated with them (examples (2) and (3) are associated with properties **A**, **D**, **L** and **P**, examples (4) and (5) are associated only with **P**, while example (6) is associated with none of the properties), they all share one characteristic: absence of **F**. In his analysis of German modals, Heine argues that only **F** is obligatorily connected with root modality: "once the use of a modal is characterised by a lack of **F** then it lacks that 'element of will' that Jespersen (1924:320-1) referred to, and we are dealing with an epistemic rather than an agent-oriented sense" (Heine, this volume). On the basis of this argument, (2), (3), (4), (5) and (6) all fail as instances of root modality.

Let's look now at the expression of epistemic possibility in English. Epistemic possibility has many exponents, notably *maybe*, *perhaps*, *I think*, *possibly*, *probably* and the modal auxiliaries *may*, *might* and *could*. Examples are given in (7), (8), (9) and (10) below.

(7) *that may be yellow fever, I'm not sure* (S.4.2.65)
(8) *I may be a few minutes late, but don't know* (S.7.3E.6)
(9) *I think it's unlikely actually but he might do it today* (S.8.1A.18)
(10) *The only snag is that it has been raining ... and I could get held up for anything up to a week.* (W.7.2.29)

These examples are not associated with **F**. However, examples (8), (9) and (10) are associated with **L** (since they refer to events that are to occur later than reference time), and example (9) is also associated with **A** and **D**. Thus, only (7) is prototypically epistemic in Heine's sense.

Example	Properties					Type of modality
	F	A	D	L	P	
1a	+	+	+	+	+	root obligation
1b	+	+	+	+	+	root necessity
1c	–	–	–	–	+	epistemic necessity
2/3	–	+	+	+	+	root possibility
4/5	–	–	–	–	+	root possibility
6	–	–	–	–	–	'existential'
7	–	–	–	–	+	epistemic possibility
8	–	–	–	+	+	epistemic possibility
9	–	+	+	+	+	epistemic possibility

Figure 2. *Matrix showing presence or absence of Heine's properties*

A summary of the properties associated with examples given so far is presented in the figure above. This shows that, using Heine's criteria alone, we are unable to distinguish clearly between instances of root and epistemic possibility in English. This figure includes examples (1a), (1b) and (1c) to show how clearly Heine's properties distinguish between root and epistemic necessity. But in the case of examples of root and epistemic possibility in English, this table would force us to conclude that there is often no difference (cf. examples (2) and (9) which share four properties; examples (4) and (7) which both have one property, **P**). While the use of these criteria has helped to demonstrate that the distinction between root and epistemic possibility is weak, it is not the case that examples are indistinguishable. So what distinguishes root from epistemic possibility?

The crucial distinction between forms expressing root possibility in English and forms expressing epistemic possibility in English is that the latter involve **Subjectivity** (which I shall refer to as **S**). Forms involving **S** can be defined as 'devices whereby the speaker, in making an utterance, simultaneously comments upon that utterance and expresses his attitude to what he is saying' (Lyons 1977:739). As examples (7), (8), (9) and (10) above illustrate, **S** is an integral component of the expression of epistemic possibility. The speakers in (7), (8), and (9) and the letter-writer in (10) are not only making statements but are simultaneously expressing their lack of confidence in the propositions expressed in these utterances. In every case here, speaker's uncertainty is encoded in an accompanying phrase which reinforces the modal: *I'm not sure* in (7), *don't know* in (8), *I think it's unlikely* in (9), and *the only snag is* in (10). (We can compare earlier examples of root possibility: *I can get a cheap kettle* (2) and *you can hear the whistle* (5). Both are statements of fact; subjectivity is not involved. The difference between *I can get a kettle* and *I may get a kettle* is that in the latter the speaker's uncertainty is encoded too.)

We therefore need to add **S** to the matrix to show that this acts as the criterial property where the expression of possibility is concerned. (see Figure 3)

If we ignore **P**, which is common to both root and epistemic modality (except in unusual cases like (6)), we can see that the reason for the weakness of the root/epistemic distinction in the expression of possibility is the absence, in utterances involving root possibility, of properties normally associated with root meaning. Exponents of root necessity (e.g. 1b) differ from exponents of epistemic necessity (e.g. 1c) on five measures, whereas exponents of root possibility (e.g. 2/3) may differ from exponents of epistemic possibility (e.g. 9) by as little as one property (presence or absence of **S**).

One of the reasons that the weakness of this distinction has been unproblematic for speakers of English is that root and epistemic possibility are, by and large, expressed by *different* linguistic forms. *May* is the only modal form which regularly expresses both root and epistemic possibility, and when expressing root possibility it is restricted to the most formal contexts (as in (3) above). The extent of overlap between the two forms is small, as the following statistics show (these record my analysis of a representative sample of 200 cases of *can* and 200 cases of *may*, all examples of spoken British English taken from *the Survey of English Usage*):

Example	Properties						Type of modality
	F	A	D	L	P	S	
1a	+	+	+	+	+	–	root obligation
1b	+	+	+	+	+	–	root necessity
2/3	–	+	+	+	+	–	root possibility
4/5	–	–	–	–	+	–	root possibility
6	–	–	–	–	–	–	'existential'
1c	–	–	–	–	+	+	epistemic necessity
7	–	–	–	–	+	+	epistemic possibility
8	–	–	–	+	+	+	epistemic possibility
9	–	+	+	+	+	+	epistemic possibility

Figure 3. *Matrix to show the distinction between root and epistemic meanings in English*

Table 1. *The use of* can *and* may *in contemporary spoken English*

can:	Root Possibility	129	*may*:	Epistemic Possibility	147
	Ability	41		Permission	32
	Permission	10		Root Possibility	7
	Undecidable	20		Valediction	1
	TOTAL	200		Undecidable	13
				TOTAL	200

As these figures demonstrate, each linguistic form is overwhelmingly associated with one particular meaning (*can* with root possibility, *may* with epistemic possibility). The category 'undecidable' refers to those examples which I could not assign unproblematically to one meaning rather than another. Often, this was because there was not enough contextual evidence to permit a definite reading; in the case of *may*, however, some examples exhibit 'merger', that is, the phenomenon whereby utterances containing *may* combine elements of *both* root and epistemic meaning (see 3.1 below).

3. The linguistic consequences of a weak root/epistemic contrast

In the previous section, I have demonstrated the weakness of the root/epistemic distinction in the expression of possibility. As I have argued, the blurring of the root/epistemic boundary in this semantic area is not often problematic in English, given the use of different linguistic forms. However, there are certain interesting linguistic developments in this area which are a direct result, I would argue, of the weakness of the distinction. One involves the growing instances of merger with *may*. The other is the development of epistemic readings for *can* in contemporary spoken American English.

3.1 *May and merger*

Merger, as I have explained elsewhere (see Coates 1983; Leech and Coates 1980), refers to instances where two meanings co-exist in a both/and relationship. In other words, two readings are available for a given utterance, but instead of having to choose one meaning and discard the other (as with ambiguous examples), the hearer is able to process *both* meanings. Merger occurs quite frequently in more formal texts (example 11) and is becoming endemic in academic writing (as example (12) illustrates):

(11) *or the pollen may be taken from the stamens of one rose and transferred to the stigma of another* (W.10.3.27)

(12) *... the process of simplification ... through which even forms and distinctions present in all the contributory dialects may be lost* (Trudgill 1986:126)

In both these examples, the only property clearly present is **P**. Properties associated with root meaning (**F**, **A**, and **D**) are absent, while **S**, normally criterial for *epistemic* meaning, is not typically associated with this kind of formal style with its passives and inanimate subjects. So instances such as these lack clear markers of either root or epistemic meaning. The two meanings merge, and the reader is not required to choose one or the other:[3]

(11') Root: 'it's possible for the pollen to be taken ...'
Epistemic: 'it's possible that the pollen will be taken ...'

(12') Root: 'it's possible for forms and distinctions ... to be lost'
Epistemic: 'it's possible that forms and distinctions ... will be lost'

It is significant that such examples of merger come typically from the (formal) written domain. In spoken language, exponents of root and epistemic possibility are normally distinguished prosodically: for example, *may* and *can* do not receive stress when expressing root possibility, but *may*, when it expresses epistemic possibility, *is* normally stressed. Epistemic *may* is also typically associated with fall-rise intonation (see example (13) below):

(13) *I may* be wrong (S1.2.38)

While *writers* can exploit the both/and relationship of root and epistemic meanings when talking about possibilities, *speakers* are constrained by prosodic factors to choose one or the other. If a speaker uttered example (11) with a fall-rise nucleus on *may*, for example, the only interpretation available to hearers would be epistemic.

3.2 *The development of epistemic* can

Given the historical pattern of epistemic meanings developing from root meanings (Bybee & Pagliucca 1985; Traugott 1989), it would not be surprising if *can* were to develop an epistemic reading. Moreover, the homogeneous picture of *can* given so far in this paper is not the whole truth: *can* does have some well-established specialised epistemic uses.

First, it provides the missing negative form in the epistemic *must* paradigm (see Palmer, this volume). The invariant form *can't* (not *cannot* or *can not*) expresses 'it's necessarily the case that ... not ...' (nec ~ p) or 'it's not possibly the case that' (~ poss p) in examples such as (14). (Note the stress on *can't* and the fall-rise intonation contour.)

(14) [speaker describes friends arriving early]
I almost phoned them up and said come a bit later — and then I thought oh they've probably left by now — so I didn't and — twelve thirty, now that ... căn't be them, and it was (S.2.7.6)

Second, *can* is used in interrogative constructions to express epistemic *possibility*. Example (15) is a cliché of pop music and Hollywood-style films, but it makes the point clear:

(15) *Can it be true?*
['Is it possible that this is true? that she loves me?']

Such examples have a clear relationship with the use of *can't* discussed above, in that (15) could be glossed *it can't be true! (it must be false)*. Example (16) comes from a radio discussion of Government policy on pensions:

(16) *Can that be sensible?*
['Is it possibly the case that that is sensible?']

The speaker was clearly trying to make the point *That can't be sensible!*

In British English, these are still the only contexts in which a form of *can* is used with epistemic meaning (though *could* is making headway as an alternative to *might* in the expression of tentativeness — see example 10). But in American English, *can* is starting to appear in other contexts. The following example occurred during the Symposium on Mood and Modality (held at the University of New Mexico in May, 1992) as a participant finished her presentation:

(17) *we hope this coding system can be useful* [to other linguists working in the field]

This utterance meant something like 'we hope there's a chance that this system will be useful'. For British speakers, this utterance is not possible: a British speaker would have to say 'we hope this coding system *will* be useful', thereby losing the subjective force. As the person who uttered (17) commented to me afterwards, *can* in this utterance is 'a sort of hedge'. American speakers seem to have no problems with utterances of this kind.

So if *can* is developing an epistemic meaning in the United States but not in Britain, what is different in the linguistic environment in the United States? I would like to suggest three factors:

a. *can* is less commonly used to express permission in American English; *may* is the normal exponent of permission (Coates & Leech 1980);
b. the 'bleaching' of root *can* is further advanced in American English, with the majority of examples not associated with **F**, **A**, **D** or **L**;
c. *may* is the chief exponent of epistemic possibility in British English, but is less common in American English, where *may* has connotations of formality.

More generally, there are many reasons why we would expect *can* to develop epistemic possibility readings. First, all the other modal auxiliaries in English express both root and epistemic meaning. Second, it seems to be the case that epistemic meanings derive from earlier, non-epistemic meanings (Traugott 1989:52). Third, the evidence from child acquisition research is suggestive: children develop deontic meaning much earlier than epistemic meaning (Stephany 1986); Guo (this volume) claims that the Mandarin form *neng* (*can*) is starting to be used to express epistemic possibility in children's speech. Fourth, the occurrence of merger with examples of *may* (illustrated in Section 3.1) illustrates the fuzziness of the root/epistemic boundary in the expression of possibility. Fifth, as this paper has attempted to demonstrate, root and epistemic possibility are only weakly distinguished.

Given these circumstances, and a historic pattern in the development of *can* from ability meanings to permission meanings to root possibility meanings (Bybee 1988), I would predict that initially examples of epistemic *can* will co-occur with syntactic features such as inanimate subject and stative verb, and in contexts where accompanying words support an epistemic reading. Example (17) is of this type, with an inanimate subject *this coding system*, and the phrase *I hope* introducing subjectivity to the utterance. However, it is difficult to imagine *can* becoming a serious contender in the expression of epistemic possibility unless it can develop a stressed alternative to the usual [kən]; until that happens, utterances like *I can come* will be processed as root.

4. Conclusions

In this paper, I have argued that the distinction between root and epistemic meanings is much weaker in the case of possibility than in other areas of modal meaning. I have demonstrated that the weakness of this distinction arises from the nature of root possibility, typical examples of which are not associated with Heine's properties **F**, **A**, **D** and **L** (normally criterial for root meaning). As a direct consequence of the weakness of the root/epistemic distinction, instances of merger are common (in the case of *may*), and epistemic readings are beginning to occur in declaratives with *can*. Speakers will exploit the potentialities of the English modal system to say the things they need to say. Whether this means that *can*, like the other English modal auxiliaries, will develop the full range of epistemic meanings remains to be seen.

NOTES

1 I would like to record my gratitude to Bas Aarts, Joan Bybee, Suzanne Fleischmann, Talmy Givón, Bernd Heine and Charles Meyer for their comments on earlier drafts of this paper.

2 Examples from this point onwards will be taken from the Survey of English Usage, University College, London (prosodic information omitted).

3 *Can* is also beginning to be involved in merger, in contexts where the speaker/writer wishes to hedge what they are saying. A nice example occurs on Inland Revenue (UK) Tax Forms: *False statements can result in prosecution.*

REFERENCES

Bybee, Joan. 1988. "Semantic Substance Versus Contrast in the Development of Grammatical Meaning". *Proceedings of the Fourteenth Berkeley Linguistic Society* 247-279.

Bybee, Joan & William Pagliuca. 1985. "Cross-Linguistic Comparisons and the Development of Grammatical Meaning". *Historical Semantics and Historical Word Formation* ed. by J. Fisiak, 59-84. The Hague: Mouton.

Coates, Jennifer. 1983. *The Semantics of the Modal Auxiliaries.* London: Croom Helm.

Coates, Jennifer & Geoffrey Leech. 1980. "The Meanings of the Modals in Modern British and American English". *York Papers in Linguistics* 8.23-34.

Guo, Jiansheng. This volume. "The Interactional Stucturing of Meaning: Children's Use and Development of the Mandarin Modal *neng* 'can'".

Haegeman, Liliane. 1983. *The Semantics of Will in Present-day British English.* Brussels: Paleis der Academiën.
Heine, Bernd. This volume. "Agent-Oriented vs. Epistemic Modality — Some Observations on German Modals".
Jespersen, Otto. 1924. *The Philosophy of Grammar.* London: Allen & Unwin.
Leech, Geoffrey & Jennifer Coates. 1980. "Semantic Indeterminacy and the Modals". *Studies in English Linguistics* ed. by Sidney Greenbaum, Geoffrey Leech & Jan Svartvik, 79-90. London: Longman.
Lyons, John. 1977. *Semantics.* Cambridge: Cambridge University Press.
Palmer, Frank. 1990. *Modality and the English Modals.* (2nd edition). London: Longman.
Stephany, Ursula. 1986. "Modality". *Language Acquisition* ed. by Paul Fletcher & Michael Garman. (2nd edition) 375-400. Cambridge: Cambridge University Press.
Traugott, Elizabeth Close. 1989. "On the Rise of Epistemic Meanings in English: An Example of Subjectification in Semantic Change". *Language* 65.31-55.
Trudgill, Peter. 1986. *Dialects in Context.* Oxford: Blackwell.

Contextual Conditions for the Interpretation of 'poder' and 'deber' in Spanish*

Carmen Silva-Corvalán
University of Southern California

1. Introduction

This study deals with some aspects of the grammar of *poder* 'can, may' and *deber* 'must' in Spanish. *Poder* and *deber* are considered to be *modal verbs* or *modal auxiliaries* both on syntactic and semantic grounds (see, among others, Marcos Marín 1975:211; Narbona 1989; Rivero 1977).[1] Many grammars of Spanish (e.g. Gili Gaya 1976; Hernández 1986; Real Academia Española 1973) include *querer* 'want', *saber* 'know', *osar* 'dare', *soler* 'be used to', etc. as 'modal verbs' as well. Syntactically, however, *poder*, *deber*, *osar* and *soler* are different in that they share the requirement to occur exclusively in construction with an Infinitive with an equivalent subject, a constraint which does not apply to *querer* and *saber* (see Narbona 1989, and Rivero 1977 for further discussion of the syntax and semantics of these and other periphrastic verbal constructions). Semantically, *poder* and *deber* stand apart as the only modals that can make a statement, in at least one interpretation, about the possibility of p, as the paraphrases of examples (1 a-b), given in (2 a-b), show.

(1) a. *Jon puede/debe tocar el clarinete.*
b. *Jon quiere/sabe/osa/suele tocar el clarinete.*
a. 'Jon may/must play the clarinet'
b. 'Jon wants to/knows how to/dares to/is in the habit of playing the clarinet'

(2) a. It is possible/very likely that Jon plays the clarinet.
b. It is the case that Jon wants/knows how to/dares to play/often plays the clarinet.

There are, then, syntactic and semantic arguments for treating *poder* and *deber* as a class in Spanish. In contrast to modal verbs in English, whose syntactic and semantic characteristics have been studied in depth (see Coates 1983, Perkins 1982 & 1983, Palmer 1977 & 1979, Halliday 1970, and numerous references in these studies and in the present volume), Spanish modals have received little attention, perhaps due to the fact that their syntactic characteristics have not appeared to be as distinct as those of the English modals when compared with other verbs which may occur in auxiliary position in verbal periphrases.

Note, however, that *poder* and *deber* pose a number of special syntactic and semantic questions of general and specific interest: What syntactic constraints apply to these modal verbs? What is the most adequate way to describe their semantics? Can a monosemantic approach account for the various uses of *poder* and *deber*? What is the relation between the messages conveyed by *poder* and by *deber* (as in examples 3-4)? What role do the linguistic and extra-linguistic contexts play in the interpretation of the meaning of these forms? Indeed, as can be seen in the suggested readings of the following examples, *poder* and *deber* can convey different messages, which include such notions as ability, permission, possibility, and necessity.

(3) *Juan puede venir.*
'John can/may come.'

Possible paraphrases:
a. John is able to come.
b. John is allowed to come.
c. It is possible for John to come/that John will come.

(4) *Juan debe venir.*
'John must come.'

Possible paraphrases:
a. John has the obligation to come.
b. It is very likely/I can confidently infer that John will come.

In addition, *poder* and *deber* cannot be interpreted to convey possibility in their non-finite forms, as the unacceptability of the paraphrases in (5 b) and (6 b) indicate.

(5) a. *Juan va a poder cruzar el río.*
'John's going to be able/be allowed to cross the river.'

Unacceptable reading:
b. **Va a ser posible que Juan cruce el río.*
'It may be the case that John will cross the river'

(6) a. *Juan va a deber cruzar el río.*
'John's going to have to cross the river.'

Unacceptable reading:
b. **Es muy posible que Juan vaya a cruzar el río*
'It's very likely that John's going to cross the river'

By contrast, when combined with conditional verb morphology, *poder* is interpreted to convey possibility (ex. 7), while *deber* can only convey (weak) obligation, as in example (8).

(7) *Juan podría hacerlo.*
'John could do it'

Possible reading:
It may be possible for John to do it.

(8) *Juan debería hacerlo.*
'John should do it'

Unacceptable reading:
*'It's very likely that John would do it'

In this essay I examine the factors that determine the different interpretations of *poder* and *deber* in different contexts, and argue for the adequacy of a monosemantic approach in the analysis of the semantics of these verbs. I propose to show that the 'modal verbs' each have an invariant meaning (IM), but are interpreted to convey different contextual meanings (CM) as a consequence of their interaction with other elements in the context (e.g. animacy of NPs, aspect, tense).

I approach the problem mainly through an examination of examples of *poder* and *deber* in actual language use.[2] My analysis suggests that a monosemantic approach is more appropriate for Spanish on at least two grounds: (1) The different meanings proposed (ability, possibility, permission, politeness) are shown to be a function of the interaction between the modal and other elements (linguistic and extra-linguistic) in the discourse. (2) A monosemantic perspective, which admits the possibility of synonymy in context, can account for the choice of one "synonymous expression" over another on the basis of their different basic meanings. The invariant meanings proposed for *poder* and for *deber* justify the choice of one modal over the other in a particular utterance where both may be interpreted to convey, for instance, epistemic possibility (more strictly 'epistemic necessity' in the case of *deber*, but I will not make a difference between possibility and necessity here). While the analysis of the data allows me to argue against a polysemantic approach to the meaning of modals, it also leads me to propose that their contexts of occurrence may be polysemantic, i.e., at times more than one interpretation of the meaning of a given modalized utterance is possible. Thus, the inclusion of a specific context (defined by a combination of features, e.g. animacy and agentivity of entities) in one or another set of contexts associated with the inference of different messages (e.g. possibility, permission) is in some cases fuzzy.

2. Theoretical frameworks

Linguistic studies of modality in natural languages differ at least in three respects: (1) the definition and types of modality identified; (2) the establishment of what constitutes 'true' modality; and (3) the theoretical approach used in accounting for the semantics of modality.

Thus, Palmer (1979), for instance, uses modality to refer to the meanings of the English modal verbs, classified on the basis of their formal features. By contrast, Halliday (1970) considers modalities to be only those meanings related to the assessment of probability. A modality is expressed by a form which represents "the speaker's assessment of the probability of what he is saying, or the extent to which he regards it as self-evident" (p. 328). Therefore, though all modal verbs in English may express modalities, in Halliday's view they are not modality when they express permission, volition, ability, obligation, etc.[3]

Bybee (1985:169) explicitly establishes a more sensible and appropriate difference between *mood*, a verbal category which has also been considered to represent the speaker's assessment of the degree of factuality of the proposition, and *modality* in the following terms: *modality* is "a conceptual domain [including root and epistemic meanings] which may take various types of linguistic expression," while *mood* refers to a subdivision of this conceptual domain and is realized as "a marker on the verb that signals how the speaker chooses to put the proposition into the discourse context." (165) That is, mood, a grammatical category signalled by verbal affixes, is one among several means of expressing modalities.

Different theoretical models have been adopted in studies of modality in English (Coates 1983; Haegeman 1983; Kratzer 1977; Perkins 1983; Sweetser 1982). Haegeman, Kratzer and Perkins propose a basic or core-meaning approach to account for the meaning of modals,[4] arguing that this core meaning is present in all their uses and is compatible in different contexts with the various notions which have been associated with the modals (e.g. necessity, permission). Out of context, however, i.e. in their lexical entry form, only the basic meaning is present.

Coates rejects both a purely monosemantic and a purely polysemantic approach: the former, she insists, fails to deal with the problem of indeterminacy in real language, while the latter has to assume discrete categories of meaning in a semantic field characterized precisely by indeterminacy. Instead, she seeks to reconcile the two approaches observing, on the one hand, that the root/epistemic distinction is discrete,[5] but on the other, that examples assigned to the two categories are indeterminate inasmuch as they cover a range of possible meanings. Quite naturally, then, Coates directs her attention to 'fuzzy set' theory (Zadeh 1965, 1972), a model which allows her to account for clearly classifiable discrete cases as belonging to the *core* of the set, as well as for various degrees of indeterminacy or gradience as belonging to the *skirt* or the *periphery*.

In contrast, Sweetser views the 'possibility' use of modals as a metaphorical extension of root meaning. Adopting the 'force dynamics' semantics of Talmy (1982, cited in Sweetser 1982), she argues that the reasoning processes underlying epistemic meanings are "subject to compulsions, obligations, and other modalities, just as our real-world actions are subject to modalities of the same sort" (484), i.e. to those modalities (ability, necessity, permission) considered to convey root or deontic meanings. Accordingly, an understanding of the epistemic world of possibilities and logical conclusions in terms of the sociophysical world explains quite naturally the connection between, for instance, epistemic *may* as the absence of a barrier to the speaker's conclusions about the truth of the proposition, and permission -granting (i.e. root) *may* as the absence of a potential barrier for the truth of the proposition in the sociophysical world.

Sweetser further agrees with the observation made by other linguists (e.g. Coates, Kratzer, Perkins) that pragmatic factors will determine which world the modal is taken as operating in. Thus, the identification of a real-world cause will determine a root reading, while the identification of a body of premises will determine an epistemic one.[6] In either case, the contextual interpretation of such modals as *can* and *may* (as well as of verbs like *let* and *allow*) appears to be that of "taking away a potential barrier" (485). Sweetser acknowledges that there may be ambiguity between real-world force and epistemic force, which in turn implies contextual ambiguity, but she leaves open the question of the basic meaning or basic contribution that different modals make to the interpretation of an utterance.

Like Coates, I feel that "the imprecision of our knowledge of the world might be inherent" (p.11), and that fuzzy set theory may be of use in the analysis of modality (cf. Sweetser on contextual ambiguity). Contrary to Coates (and perhaps also to Sweetser), however, I argue that modals have basic, core meanings along the lines of the definitions proposed by Perkins (1983), while fuzziness applies rather to the contexts, linguistic and extra -linguistic, in which modals are used. Fuzziness or graded membership of contexts allows for various interpretations of modalized propositions, and the precise point at which one interpretation is no longer possible is usually difficult to establish. Contextually inferred messages (e.g. ability, possibility), in principle infinite, have been mistakenly considered to be the, or part of the, meaning of the modal.[7]

The question of the basic meanings conveyed by linguistic expressions, as opposed to the meanings, messages or pragmatic implicatures which these forms appear to have in specific contexts of use, is a recurrent theme in semantic-pragmatic studies. With particular respect to closed grammatical systems (e.g. pronouns, verbal affixes), there seems to be general agreement that a distinction between basic, invariant, or systemic meaning, and secondary, implicated, or non-systemic meanings or functions must be made (Bello 1977; Bull 1971; García 1975; King 1992; Silva-Corvalán 1991). By contrast, there is little agreement as to what exactly constitutes the semantic substance of the linguistic units under analysis.

With respect to *poder* and *deber*, I propose that these modals may be characterized as having invariant meanings which account for the use of the modal instead of a non-modalized verb, or for the choice of one modal over the other in particular discourse contexts. *Poder* and *deber* interact with other linguistic and extra-linguistic elements that contribute to producing the multiple sentential and/or discourse meanings that are compatible with the semantics of the modals.

I am suggesting, then, the existence of three meaning components or types of meaning in language: (1) de-contextualized, systemic invariant meaning; (2) contextualized meaning; and (3) prototypical discourse meaning.[8] These meaning components are not specific to modals, but characterize all linguistic elements; contextualized and prototypical meanings are related to decontextualized invariant meanings in systematic, principled ways which need to be empirically ascertained.

Invariant meaning (IM) refers to the meaning which underlies, or is present in, all uses of a modal; *contextualized meaning* (CM) is the message which the modal conveys, or the analyst infers that the modal conveys in a specific context. Contextualized meanings derive from the interaction of the modal verb with morphosyntactic, semantic, prosodic, and pragmatic factors which constitute its context of use. Thus, every linguistic element contributes a specific meaning to the total, but the CM goes beyond the sum of these meanings because it incorporates pragmatic factors that may not be context -independent as the IMs of grammatical forms (as opposed to lexical forms) appear to be. *Prototypical discourse meaning* (PM) refers to the most frequent message (contextualized meaning) that the modal conveys in a corpus of language data.

A PM tends to correspond to the meaning that most language users (and sometimes even linguists) assign to a form. This confusion arises from the fact that the inferred message is so frequent that speakers assume it is part of the meaning of the form (cf. Faltz 1989, cited in Bybee, Perkins & Pagliuca 1994: Ch. 6).

IMs and CMs correspond in part to what Bosch (1985) calls 'context independent lexical meaning' and 'context dependent contextual notions', respectively. Contextual notions are in principle infinite and unique for each new context, an observation which leads Bosch to propose that "we should give up the notion of the meaning or interpretation of a sentence or utterance as an identifiable unit or thing altogether" (257). By contrast, it seems to me that there is reason to propose an intermediate level of contextual meanings which are associated with or derived from classes or types of contexts, rather along the lines of what García (1975:276-7) discusses in terms of "the chief uses of the meaning" of a form or "great classes of messages", all of which are characterized by the same common reason for using one form rather than another. Thus, though there is in principle no end to the messages that may be postulated, I would like to propose that CMs may cluster into "great classes of messages" (the most frequent ones becoming the PMs) that underlie groups of utterances where the modal is inferred to convey the same or similar meanings.

The term 'modality', as the expression of speaker attitude towards the contents of a proposition, is a semantic notion covering a range of meanings: certainty, probability, possibility, belief, obligation, necessity, permission, volition, intention, doubt, prediction, and denial. The speaker's attitude may be conveyed through verb morphology (mood), lexically, syntactically, prosodically, or by a combination of these linguistic devices. Here, I focus on lexical and affixal manifestations of epistemic and root modalities. For example, the proposition *Juan viene mañana* 'John is coming tomorrow' can be modalized to express speaker uncertainty or prediction about the probability of actualization of the event encoded in the proposition (henceforth p) by using the modal verbs (henceforth m) *poder* or *deber*. Thus, *Juan puede/debe venir mañana*, may be paraphrased, for instance, as 'Speaker believes that it is possible for Juan to come/that it is very likely that Juan will come tomorrow'. Marked with Future morphology, on the other hand, these modals may not convey possibility, but rather dynamic or deontic modalities: *Juan podrá/deberá venir mañana* 'Juan will be able to/will have to come tomorrow'.

I distinguish between *epistemic* (EP) and *root possibility* (RP) contextual meanings (cf. Coates 1983). Epistemic and root possibility are concerned with the speaker's assessment of or assumptions about the likelihood that the content of a proposition is or may become true. EP and RP differ in that the former involves the speaker in logical inference and has p and m in its scope, while the latter has only p in its scope and is *agent/event oriented*, i.e., the subject of the modalized infinitive is normally a willful agent and/or the infinitive is a dynamic verb.[9] This difference has consequences for negation, such that negation affects p in the case of epistemic sense, but m and p in the case of root sense. When an affirmative modal (example 9) interpreted to convey RP is negated, the negative form is interpreted as a negative fact (example 10).[10] To preserve the possibility interpretation, therefore, root modality must be negated on p (example 11), while epistemic modality may be negated on m, as example (12) shows.

(9) *Ahí pueden fumar.* *Root possibility*
'They may smoke there'
Paraphrase:
It's possible for them to smoke there.

(10) *Ahí no pueden fumar.* *Permission negated.*
'They can't smoke there.'
Paraphrase:
It is the case that they are not allowed to smoke there.

(11) *Ahí pueden no fumar.* *Epistemic possibility*
'They may not smoke there.'
Paraphrase:
It is possible that they do not smoke there.

(12) *Juan no debe estar en casa.* *Epistemic possibility*[11]
'John must not be home.'
Paraphrase:
It is very likely/I confidently infer that John is *not* home.

I further use the term *root modality* to encompass both the deontic and dynamic categories of modal logic, namely obligation, necessity, permission (see examples 13-14), and ability (example 15), noting that though ability is not usually considered to be truly a modality, it is relatable to deontic modality, and at times may be indistinguishable from RP, as Bybee, Perkins & Pagliuca (1994) note to be the case in a large number of languages.

(13) *Debes comer para sobrevivir.* *Obligation*
'You must eat to survive.'

(14) [Father to young son]
Puedes hablar cuando yo me calle. *Permission*
'You can speak when I stop talking.'

(15) *Juan puede andar en bicicleta; aprendió de pequeño.* *Ability*
'John can ride a bicycle; he learnt when he was a child.'

The invariant meanings (IM) for *poder* and *deber* that I propose here are approximately those that Perkins (1982) postulates for the English modals *can* and *must*.[12] The definition of modals is formulated with variables ranging over different systems of laws and principles and different sets of circumstances or contexts of use. It incorporates four elements: 1) the invariant or basic meaning of the modal, which relates the variables C and X (defined below); 2) K, representing one of various systems of laws or principles (e.g. social, magic, natural, rational laws, which embody our knowledge of the world, including those principles which regulate linguistic interaction) according to which the modalized proposition can be interpreted; (3) X, the third element, represents the event, state of affairs, etc. referred to in the proposition; and (4) C, which stands for a set of circumstances, presupposed or explicitly identified, under which K is relevant.

The circumstances include the structure of p, which may consist of an n-place predicate (y,z), where y = subject, z = predicate. This interpretation of C differs from that of Perkins, for whom C is a variable which may represent such notions as 'personal interactions', 'deontic source', 'subject-oriented'. The problem is that it is not clear how Perkins's definition accounts for the role of linguistic characteristics of p, including mood for instance, in the interpretation of the meaning of modalized p.

The various elements that bear upon the interpretation of a modal are summarized in the following formula: K (C..[IM]..X), which I illustrate below. The ensuing sections study uses of *poder* and *deber* and focus on C and X in order to examine the interaction between these variables and the specific semantic contribution proposed for the modals.

3. Poder

I assume that the formula proposed by Perkins (1982) for *can* captures the meaning of *poder*: K (C *does not preclude* X). This formula incorporates both the IM and the elements that contribute to the CM. Thus, *poder* presents the IM 'does not preclude' and it relates actualization of X to a set of circumstances C, such that with reference to a set of principles K, the circumstances C do not preclude X. The values of K and C are recognized (and specified by the analyst) in context; these variables (which include morphosyntactic, semantic and prosodic features) plus the modal chosen determine whether X is interpreted under a dynamic, deontic or epistemic modality (Heine (this volume) proposes similar variables in his stimulating account of German modals).

Interestingly, the specific semantic contribution proposed for *poder*, 'does not preclude', appears to agree with the meaning postulated for *can* by

Bybee, Perkins & Pagliuca (1994: Ch. 6), i.e., 'enabling conditions exist', as well as with the meaning suggested by Sweetser (1982) in terms of the presence or absence of 'barriers'. The question might arise why I agree with Perkins in assigning a negative meaning to *poder*. This is because it seems to me that a negative meaning captures more appropriately than a positive meaning (such as 'enables' or 'makes possible') the sense of 'difficulty overcome' which appears to be incorporated in most of the CMs of *poder*. This is taken up again later in this essay.

Example 16 illustrates how the definition of *poder* would lead to an interpretation of *ability* assuming certain values for K and C. Different values for K and C would obviously lead to different interpretations.

(16) *Mi hija puede contar hasta diez.*
'My daughter can count up to ten'

IM: K (C *does not preclude* X)

(i) K: natural/biological laws (e.g. learning capacity)
(ii) C: (a) speaker's previous experience of p (empirical circumstances, i.e. speaker's evidence that p is true)
(b) y = agent ('my daughter'); z = event ('count up to 10'); time orientation: generic (i.e. valid for an unspecified past, present and future time)
(iii) X: my daughter counts up to 10

CM: given humans' learning capacity and the circumstances in C, addressee interprets that speaker intends to convey the message that y (his/her daughter) *has the ability* for z ('count up to ten').

Given an affirmative sentence, the elements in C that appear to bear upon the CM include (cf. Heine, this volume):

(i) the presence or absence of a deontic source,
(ii) evidentiality or previous experience of p (cf. Givón 1982, Wright 1990),
(iii) degree of agentivity of the subject,
(iv) aspect of the situation (stative, dynamic, etc.),
(v) morphological aspect and mood,

such that various combinations of these elements account for the meanings traditionally associated with *poder*, 'ability, permission, possibility', i.e. these so-called meanings are indeed contextual inferences.

Pottier (1976) discusses the same three meanings for *pouvoir* 'can' in terms of 'pouvoir physique/possibilité interne', 'pouvoir par autorisation/ possibilité externe', and 'probabilité/possibilité neutre' (pp.39-41). In addition, Palmer (1977:2) observes that epistemic modality should be seen as a more basic concept "since what is (epistemically) possible includes what can (dynamically) be done". This led me to think, for a while, that the IM of *poder* should explicitly include 'possibility'. It became obvious to me later, however, that 'possibility' is a CM which may be derived from 'does not preclude', since not precluding X in fact implies (though not equivalently) making X possible.

3.1 ***Poder*** *in Present tense form.*

The data examined indicate that examples of *poder* in Present tense affirmative form group into five sets of CMs (or "great classes of messages"), discussed below, with the following readings: permission, ability, mitigation, root possibility, and epistemic possibility. It is in principle possible, however, that other sets of CMs might be identified in a much larger corpus of data.

It must be emphasized that many cases are not easy to fit neatly into one of these five CMs. The indeterminacy of many cases may be viewed as stemming from possible indeterminacies of K and C in natural language use, e.g. the strength of the deontic source, weak indication of evidentiality. Analogous observations made by Coates in regard to the meaning of English modals led her to develop a prototype model of analysis. As in her English data, my data contain a number of examples with contexts which appear to represent the core set of features associated with a certain CM, but many examples fall somewhere in the skirt or towards the periphery of the set.

Let us look now at examples of *poder* in contexts whose features have led me to propose five different modalities (sets of CMs).

3.1.1 *Permission.*

Whenever a strong deontic source, i.e. some person or institution that clearly creates obligation or permission (Lyons 1977:843), is identified either explicitly or implicitly, the CM inferred is *permission*, as in example (14). The most clearly identifiable context for permission, then, includes a strong deontic source, an agentive subject, and future time orientation. The transcribed conversations examined do not offer these clearly identifiable contexts. This is most likely due to the nature of the data, which do not contain pragmatic situations that would elicit the granting of permission. Example (17) is representative: it seems to assume a deontic source, but its non-specific agent and the generic rather than future time orientation make our interpretation move in the direction of root possibility.

(17) *En España a los dieciocho años ya puedes votar.* (M18,p34)[13]
'In Spain you can vote when you're eighteen.'

(i) K: social laws (governments have authority over citizens)
(ii) C: (a) deontic source implied (legal code of laws)
(b) y = agent; z = event; time orientation: generic
(iii) X: y,z

CM: y is allowed to z
(Possible CM: it is possible for y to z)

Both deontic source and set of laws under which a specific example is to be interpreted may lead to indeterminacy. On the one hand, written codes of laws (e.g. traffic regulations, state laws) constitute strong deontic sources and contribute to a more clearly identifiable CM of permission. On the other hand, ethical principles may be somewhat weaker sources of obligation, and a parent to a child, or a teacher to a student, may or may not constitute a strong deontic source. Weaker deontic sources (e.g. people at the same authority level, abstract entities, such natural phenomena as river currents) determine contextual meanings which move away from permission towards interpretations of ability or possibility, as in example (18).

(18) *Creo que ésta es una democracia y que uno puede hacer lo que quiera.* (M25,p.6)
'I think that this is a democracy and one can do what one wants.'

In example (18) the deontic source is an abstract entity, 'democracy' (as opposed to Franco's dictatorship), and X is not a specific event. In addition, time orientation is generic. Given these values for C and X, example (18) may lend itself to an interpretation of root possibility as well as permission.

That these inferred meanings are contextually determined is supported by the fact that a change in the environment of the modal has consequences on its interpretation, as shown in (19).

(19) [Father responding to son's request for permission to go out]
Confío en ti, puedes hacer lo que quieras.
'I trust you, you can/may do what you want.'

A specific animate deontic source, a specific agent, and the pragmatics of the interaction (request for permission) make the permission CM of *poder* much less peripheral.

3.1.2 *Ability.*

The IM 'does not preclude' is interpreted as 'ability' when the following contextual factors obtain: (a) K: natural or rational principles that permit us to infer either innate or learned capacities to do z. (b) C: (i) the speaker has evidence that X has been previously actualized, or that at least z has been, and the circumstances are such that z may be valid also for a 'new' y; (ii) y is animate, agentive, and specific; z is an event; core time orientation is generic or present; if y is 'new', it is future.

Examples (20) and (21) illustrate contextual conditions for the CM 'ability':

(20) *Ella os puede decir todo, todo referente a la droga.* (M11,p39)
'She can tell you everything, everything about drugs.'

(21) *El árabe y el ruso, pues, no los ha llegado a hablar, pero vamos, para conversación puede defenderse.* (M26)
'Arabic and Russian, well, she hasn't managed to speak them, but, in conversation she can get by.'

Note that *saber* 'to know' may also convey 'ability for z', as in *Yo sé nadar* 'I know how to swim'. *Saber*, however, simply asserts knowledge or ability for; it does not implicate precluding circumstances as *poder* does. Therefore, *saber* is not compatible with circumstances that imply that X is somewhat surprising or that it involves effort. Thus, when y performs an event that involves effort, or the overcoming of a given barrier, or a certain degree of difficulty, p may be modalized with *poder* (ex. 22) but not with *saber* (example. 23):

(22) *Juan puede nadar mariposa por horas.*
'John can swim the butterfly (stroke) for hours.'

(23) **Juan sabe nadar mariposa por horas.*
*'John knows how to swim the butterfly (stroke) for hours.'

Further evidence for the implication of 'overcoming difficulty' is provided by a comparison of example (21) with its non-modalized version in (24).

(24) *El árabe y el ruso, pues, no los ha llegado a hablar, pero vamos,* para conversación se defiende.
'Arabic and Russian, well, she hasn't managed to speak them, but,in conversation she gets by.'

Without *poder*, example (24) says that the subject referent (the speaker's daughter) does well in conversation, a statement which is too assertive precisely because it does not convey the idea that this person encounters a certain amount of difficulty in speaking Arabic and Russian. Example (25) is also illustrative.

(25) *No, no claro, vamos, de hecho esas voces que se graban, tú con tu oído no las escuchas...solamente las puedes escuchar cuando rebobinas la cinta y escuchas lo que se grabó.* (M5,585)
'No, no, well, in fact some of those voices which you record you can't hear with your naked ear...you can only hear them when you rewind the tape and listen to what was recorded.'

From example (25) one infers that a certain amount of difficulty has to be overcome for the modalized event to take place. In fact, the speaker explicitly states that only after rewinding the tape can certain voices be heard. The implication of the existence of precluding cirsumstances derived from the IM of *poder* weakens the strength of the assertion.

3.1.3 *Mitigation.*

By weakening the assertiveness of utterances, the use of *poder* may be said to convey a CM of *mitigation*, which may at times be interpreted as *politeness*. This is clearly seen in utterances containing a *verbum dicendi*, especially with a first person subject. The fixed conversational expression *puedo/podemos decir* 'I/we might say', shown in example (26), constitutes a typical example of mitigated assertiveness.

(26) *Pero en la vida social, podemos decir, no nota diferencias con, con las gentes que están en cualquier barrio madrileño.* (M26,212)
'But in social life, we might say, you don't notice differences among people who live in any *barrio* in Madrid.'

3.1.4 *Root possibility.*
The clearest context for the interpretation of root possibility includes (a) a non-agentive, non-volitional, non-specific subject (y); (b) a stative verb (i.e., z is not an event); (c) no evidence of previous actualization of p; (d) non-past time orientation. Thus, the only CM that may be inferred for examples (27) & (28) is RP.

(27) *Ya puede tener todos los millones que quiera [la persona sigue siendo buena, si es buena por naturaleza].* (M9,p.7)
'(S)he may have all the millions (s)he wants [the person continues to be good, if (s)he's good by nature].'

(28) *Una música diferente, a, digamos, a la música que tú* (non-specific) *puedes escuchar de un piano, de un violín, etc.* (M5,663)
'Music which is different, shall we say, from the music you (non-specific) might hear from a piano, a violin, etc.'

Many examples, however, with animate subjects and more or less dynamic verbs may be interpreted to convey both ability and RP (ex. 29), or to be closer to an ability reading (ex. 30a) or to an RP interpretation (ex. 31).

(29) *Argentina puede salir muy bien del paso, en cinco o seis años.* (M9,A464)
'Argentina can/may very well solve its problems, in five or six years'

(30) *No se dan cuenta que salen estos militares y creo xx, entonces como son unos bestias, pues pueden xx unas matanzas (a) y pueden hacer cosas mhm tremendas.* (M10,p13)
'They don't realize that these military men go out into the streets and I think xx, then since they are like animals, well they can xx killings (a) and they can do mhmm terrible things.'

(31) *El colegio está cerquísima. Puede ir andando.* (M11,p9)
'The school is very near. You may/can walk there'

3.1.5 *Epistemic possibility.*
EP involves the speaker's logical inference and lack of confidence about the possibility of actualization of p. There are a number of clear examples of EP interpretation in the data examined. In these clear cases, C includes one or

more of the following elements: (a) inanimate, non-specific subjects, or obligatory subjectless sentences; (b) a stative verb (e.g. *ser* 'to be', *estar* 'to be', *querer* 'to want', *saber* 'to know'); (c) negative consequences of z for y. Further, when a negated Infinitive is modalized by affirmative *poder*, an epistemic sense must be inferred (as in example 11). Examples (32-33) illustrate.

(32) *...que si hoy se cierra el plazo, dentro de tres meses ya puede ser el examen.* (M5,135)
'...if the deadline is today, then the exam may be within three months.'
CM: Based on previous experience, given that today is the deadline to register for the exam, I infer that it is possible that the exam may be given in three months.

(33) *Puede ser ésa una diferencia respecto a otros regímenes totalitarios.* (M5,250)
'That may be a difference with respect to other totalitarian regimes.'

In the case of epistemic possibility, K includes rational laws (people can make predictions, deduce, infer, etc.). As for C, lack of evidentiality and stative aspect are indeed crucial. If evidentiality exists, an example may then be interpreted as conveying RP, as in (34) and (35):

(34) *No es un clima muy estándar. Efectivamente, te puede llover y al día siguiente hacer un sol espléndido.* (M6,p2)
'It's not an even climate. In fact, it can rain one day and the following day the sun may be shining brightly'
CM: I have evidence that the climate is not even. I may infer with confidence that it is possible for it to rain one day and the following day be sunny.

(35) *Luisa puede ser la Decana de Filosofía, porque ha renunciado a su otro cargo.*
'Louise can be the Dean of Philosophy because she has resigned her other job.'
CM: Now that she has resigned her other job, I infer that it is possible for Louise to be the Dean of Philosophy.

Example (35) appears to be indeterminate between a RP and an ability CM. This is to be expected when the context does not offer core contextual conditions because it seems rather clear that CMs are all related through the assumption of ability for z existing: if y is assumed to have ability for z, then z is possible in a given world and y may be allowed, advised, etc. to z.

Poder has become lexicalized in the expressions *puede que* 'maybe' and *puede ser que* 'it may be that', which can only convey EP, as illustrated in examples (36) & (37).

(36) *Pero ya eso la policía no te explica nada. Si alguna vez coincides con algún amigo, amigo te hablo que lo has visto dos o tres veces - entonces puede que a lo mejor te cuente algo.* (M24,p10)
'But the police don't explain anything to you. If you happen to run into a friend, friend I mean someone you've seen two or three times - then he *may* perhaps tell you something.'

(37) *Pues aquí ese coche* puede ser que *sobre el setenta y dos al setenta y cuatro como mucho dejaron de fabricarlo.* (M9,A353)
'Well here, that car, *maybe* they stopped making it around seventy two or seventy four at the latest.'

Support for the lexicalized status of *puede que* and *puede ser que* is offered by the fact that they may only have third person singular morphology, and that they are subjectless. With respect to negation, only *puede ser que* may be negated and, as it is epistemic possibility, negation affects only p. Examples (38-39) are illustrative.

(38) a. ****No** puede que Juan lo engañe.*
b. *Puede que Juan* no *lo engañe.*
'It is possible that John is not cheating him'

(39) a. ***No** puede ser que Juan lo engañe.*
b. *Puede ser que Juan* no *lo engañe.*
a. 'It can't be possible that John is cheating him'
b. 'It is possible that John is not cheating him'

3.2 *Conclusion*

The data examined indicate that the most frequent CM of *poder* when used in Present tense form is root possibility (58 of 110 cases studied). Ability, EP, and mitigation account for 9%, 8%, and 4%, respectively. Furthermore, 9 examples are indeterminate between ability and RP, and 20 examples are indeterminate between permission and RP.

Two further points must be emphasized: (1) Some of the 58 cases of RP are in the periphery of this CM, close to readings of permission or ability; and (2) The nature of the data (conversational discourse) must have consequences on the frequency of occurrence of the CMs identified, such that other discourse genres would most likely yield different percentages of distribution of CMs.

It is clear that we are dealing with intersecting contextual sets. On the other hand, it is not clear to me that a strict prototype approach is the most appropriate one to account for the facts. Indeed, a prototype model does not acknowledge the relevance or validity of necessary or sufficient conditions in the interpretation of CMs. Nevertheless, there do appear to be certain necessary contextual features in every CM, and there are cases when the necessary conditions are also sufficient to identify a CM as, for instance, 'permission': a specific strong deontic source, a specific agent, direct speech, a dynamic situation, positive consequences of p (ex. 40); or 'epistemic possibility': non-agentive, non-intentional 'doer', stative situation, negative consequences of p (ex. 41).

(40) [Teacher to child]
Puedes salir de la sala ahora.
'You may leave the room now'

(41) *El mundo puede estar al borde de una crisis nuclear.*
'The world may be about to suffer a nuclear disaster'

What happens to be the case is that these sets of contextual conditions are frequently not a question of plus or minus in conversation, but of more or less. It seems that the contextual features which are necessary conditions in the permission and ability sets --deontic source and evidentiality-- are precisely the fuzzy ones. The fuzziness of contexts plus the logical relations between ability, necessity, mitigation, permission, RP and EP often lead to intersecting CMs.

4. Deber

Like *must* in English, *deber* can be used in either an epistemic or a deontic sense, as shown in examples (42-43). An example of the type of (42) involves 'epistemic necessity', while an example of the type of (41) (with *poder*) involves 'epistemic possibility' (cf. Lyons 1977: 791). However, given that necessity and possibility are related notions, I have chosen to use the term epistemic possibility in the semantic analysis of *deber* as well.

(42) [Loud car engine noises]
Ese debe ser Fernando. Epistemic possibility
'That must be Fernando.'
Interpretation:
On the basis of frequent previous associations between loud engine noises and Fernando's car, speaker confidently infers that the person in the loud car is Fernando.

(43) *Debes estudiar para aprobar el examen. Deontic obligation/necessity*
'You must study to pass the exam.'
Interpretation:
Common knowledge indicates that it is required/necessary to study in order to pass an exam.

The IM of *deber* has some points of overlap with that of *poder*, but while *poder* 'does not preclude X', *deber* 'favors X', 'requires X', or 'entails X'. That is, while *poder* communicates the speaker's lack of strong belief in the possibility of actualization of p, *deber* communicates confidence in the realization of p; it has connotations of 'very likely', 'necessary', and 'appropriate'. The contribution of *deber* to the meaning of modalized p appears to be, then, to require X as essential in the light of a set of circumstances C, interpreted under a system of laws K, as represented in the formula: K (C requires X).

This definition is slightly different from the one proposed by Perkins (1982:255) for the core meaning of *must*: K (C entails X). I have substituted the term 'requires' for 'entails' in order to avoid misunderstanding due to a reading of 'entails' in its strict logical sense. I use 'requires' in the sense of 'demanding as necessary or essential'. Thus, *deber* presents the IM 'requires' and it relates actualization of X to a set of circumstances C, such that with reference to a set of principles K, the circumstances C require X. As in the case of *poder*, the values of K and C are recognized in context; these variables (which include morphosyntactic, semantic and prosodic features) plus the modal chosen determine whether X is interpreted under a dynamic, deontic or epistemic modality.

Example (44) illustrates how the definition of *deber* would lead to an interpretation of epistemic possibility assuming certain values for K and C.

(44) *Tener un coche allí [en USA] debe ser algo alucinante.* (M25,p5)
'To have a car there [in the USA] must be out of this world.'

IM: K (C *requires* X)
(i) K: rational laws (capacity to infer from available evidence)
(ii) C: (a) absence of deontic source
(b) preceding discourse gives some indication that p is true
(c) y = inanimate subject; z = stative; time orientation: generic
(iii) X: having a car in the USA is out of this world
CM: given humans' rational capacity to infer the likelihood of p from available evidence, I interpret that the speaker intends to convey the message that y ('to have a car in the USA') *is very probably* z (' be out of this world'). (*Epistemic possibility* sense).

By postulating for *deber* a core meaning of 'requirement of X', it is possible to account for such CMs as obligation, advice, and probability, depending on whether a number of contextual circumstances prompt a reading of more or less forcible requirement. These circumstances include: (1) Animacy and agentivity of y; (2) Nature of the deontic source, if any; (3) Speaker approving or disapproving attitude towards p; (4) Adverse or positive consequences of p.

4.1 ***Deber*** *in Present tense form*

Deber occurs infrequently in the data examined. Epistemic possibility seems to be more frequently expressed by the lexicalized expression *puede que*, while the auxiliary *tener que* 'to have to' is more commonly used to convey deontic necessity. Only 26 cases of Present tense affirmative *deber* (*de*), plus 6 negative examples are attested in the data. The CMs of the 26 positive examples range from 'high likelihood' (24 examples) to 'obligation/necessity' (2 examples). The negative examples range from 'obligation/necessity' to 'advice.'

4.1.1 *Epistemic possibility to necessity*
Spanish grammars note a difference between *deber* 'must' (obligation) and *deber de* 'must' (possibility), but at the same time acknowledge that this lexical opposition is being lost. The data examined support this observation (cf. Sirbu 1988). The opposition *deber* - *deber de* is disappearing in the

Present tense, but appears to be more stable in other tenses (see Section 5 on tense and modality). *Deber de* occurs in only 4 of the 24 examples of epistemic possibility (see example 45). Furthermore, two examples with *deber de* in the Imperfect Indicative do not convey possibility but rather advice or obligation, as shown in (46).

(45) A: *Es que se para [el coche] y luego-*
B: xxx (incomprehensible)
A: *Sí. Es que* debe de *estar estropeado el freno.* (M24,p27)
A: 'It's that it stalls [the car] and then-'
B: xxx (unintelligible)
A: 'Yes. It's that the brake *must* be broken.'

(46) *Yo exactamente no lo sé. Tendría que ser [el referendum] a primeros del año que viene o algo así. Debían de solucionarlo antes de terminar la jefatura de ellos [los socialistas].*(M24,p29)
'I don't know exactly. It [the referendum] would have to be at the beginning of next year or something like that. They [the socialists] *should* resolve this question before the end of their term in office.'

Deber is more strictly modal in its semantics than *poder* in that it is in all contexts non-factual, i.e., propositions modalized by *deber* cannot be interpreted as 'actualized'.[15] This semantic difference accounts for the fact that one of *deber*'s CMs is EP, but not RP, which is related to ability and evidentiality. In its EP contexts, *deber* may be preceded by negation but is not affected by it. Examples (47) a-c are illustrative (see note 11).

(47) a. *El alto debe ser Pepe.*
b. *El alto no debe ser Pepe.*
c. **El alto debe no ser Pepe.*
a. 'The tall one must be Pepe.'
b. 'The tall one can't be Pepe.'
c. *'The tall one must not be Pepe.'

The core contextual features associated with epistemic possibility are as follows:

(i) K: rational laws
(ii) C: (a) evidence that p may be true
(b) absence of deontic source

(c) speaker attitude towards p is neutral
(d) adverse consequences of p
(e) y = inanimate; z = stative; time orientation: non-past

A human subject, a non-stative situation, speaker disapproval of not-p, and adverse consequences of not-p determine readings which move away from assessment of epistemic possibility towards the necessity end of the CM continuum. examples (48a) and (48b) illustrate such a case.

(48) A: a. *Porque se estropean las construcciones de agua [en La Granja]. Por lo visto ya están muy pasadas de agua y pues se deben estropear. Entonces las cuidan.*
B: *Las están arreglando.*
A: b. *Exactamente, las* deben *cuidar.* (M24,p34)
A: a. 'Because the fountains break [at La Granja]. It's obvious that they're too old (oversaturated) and so, of course they (*must*) break. So they take care of them.'
B: 'They're fixing them.'
A: b. 'Exactly, they have to (*must*) take care of them.'

In (48a), a combination of core factors: inanimate subject, speaker neutral attitude (i.e. neither approval nor disapproval) towards p, adverse consequences of p, and evidence favoring the truth of p, determine a CM of epistemic possibility. In (48b), on the other hand, C (human subject, non -stative situation, adverse consequences of not p) allows an interpretation of necessity.

4.1.2 *Mitigation*

Changes in the contextual circumstances of *deber* in (48b): animate and agentive subject, a possible though weak deontic source, strong evidence that p is true, adverse consequences of not-p, bring about a CM which is indeterminate between high likelihood, categorical necessity or requirement, and mitigation.

Note that example (48) illustrates intriguing uses of *deber* in utterances which repeat the content of an immediately preceding non-modalized p. This appears to indicate that in certain cases *deber* is used to convey a degree of speaker uncertainty in the truth of p as a pragmatic strategy for mitigating the degree of assertiveness of the utterance. The communicative purposes which motivate the use of this strategy need to be further investigated. The choice of *deber* over *poder*, which may also be interpreted to convey 'mitigation', appears to be related to the higher degree of certainty implied by the IM of *deber*.

4.1.3 *Obligation to advice*

The six negative constructions with *deber* in the data all express weak obligation or advice:

(49) *Nadie debe pensar por ti, ni nadie debe decidir por ti nunca, en ninguna circunstancia.* (M18,p27)
'No one should think for you, and no one should decide for you ever, under no circumstances.'

I will not say much here about the expression of deontic obligation. I would like to point out, however, that *haber que* 'to be necessary' and *tener que* 'to have to' typically express necessity and obligation in affirmative constructions in Present tense, as in (50) (cf. Sirbu 1988).

(50) *Por ejemplo, hay que dar tres pagas al año, que dice el gobierno, pues tres pagas al año se tienen que dar. Que hay que dar un mes de permiso, pues un mes de permiso se tiene que dar.* (M9,p17)
'For instance, it is necessary to give three extra paychecks every year, the government says, well then three extra paychecks have to be given. And it's necessary to give one month of leave, well then one month of leave has to be given.'

What is relevant, however, is that *tener que* also occurs, albeit quite infrequently, in possibility contexts, as seen in (51):

(51) *Y me pasó. Me pegó una pasada un 600, que yo digo, 'Pero la madre del cordero, ese tío tiene que llevar un turbo ahí detrás.'* (M9,p3)
'And he passed me. A 600 passed me so fast, that I go, "Good heavens, that guy must have a turbo behind".'

There are several indications that the use of *tener que* in possibility contexts may be a recent development in Spanish: (a) The fact that neither *tener que* nor the main verb Infinitive can be negated (exx. 52a-b); (b) Infrequent occurrence of *tener que* in contexts of possibility; and (c) This 'meaning' of possibility is not acknowledged in current grammars and dictionaries.[16]

(52) a. **Ese tío va tan lento que no tiene que sentirse muy bien.*
b. **Ese tío va tan lento que tiene que no sentirse muy bien.*
a. 'That guy's going so slowly that he doesn't have to be feeling well'
b. 'That guy's going so slowly that he has to **not** be feeling well'

4.2 *Summary*

There appear to be a number of contextual sets of circumstances associated with different CMs of *deber.* It seems possible to identify core contextual circumstances invariably associated with epistemic possibility. By contrast, fuzzy contexts make obligation, advice, and mitigation not always easy to differentiate. As in the case of *poder*, agentivity, evidentiality, and the possible consequences of p play an important part in the establishment of CMs. Furthermore, ex. 46 suggests how verb morphology interacts with lexical modalities. The next section explores this question further.

5. Modality and tense mood aspect

This section discusses the co-occurrence of *poder* and *deber* with verbal markers of tense, mood and aspect other than 'Present tense'. Proposing IMs for these verbal affixes is beyond the scope of this study. Therefore, my analysis will consider only what appears to be their contextual contribution.

5.1 *Non-finite forms and Imperative*

I have observed in the introductory section that EP and RP are not possible CMs when the modals are in Infinitive form (ex. 53). This restriction extends to the Present Participle (ex. 54). Furthermore, neither modal is interpretable in the Imperative (ex. 55). Thus, one might say that, like English modals, *poder* and *deber* are 'defective' in this respect: they lack CMs of possibility in the Infinitive and the Present Participle, and lack the Imperative altogether. In the Infinitive (53) and the Present Participle (54) only root modality CMs are inferred (e.g. obligation, ability). With regard to the Past Participle, the behavior of *poder* and *deber* differs: while *deber* appears to retain many of its possible CMs, including EP (56), *poder* in the Past Participle may convey ability (57), but cannot be interpreted to convey RP (58) nor permission.

(53) *Juan quiere deber/poder hacerlo.*
'John wants to have the obligation/be able to do it.'

(54) *Juan está debiendo/pudiendo hacerlo hace tiempo.*
'John is having to/being able to do it for a long time now.'

(55) **Debe/puede hacerlo*!.
*'Have to (must)/be able to (can) do it!'

(56) *El árbol ha debido caerse con la lluvia.*
lit: the tree has had to fall because of the rain
'The tree must have fallen because of the rain.'

(57) *Juan ha podido irse.*
'John has been able to leave.'

(58) **El árbol ha podido caerse con la lluvia.*
*'The tree has had the ability to fall because of the rain.'
Not a possible CM: The tree must have fallen because of the rain.

Verb morphology has been shown to be modal in that it can contribute to the proposition the meaning of 'more or less assertiveness', where *assertiveness* is defined as speaker belief or confidence in the truth of the proposition. Degrees of assertiveness are pragmatically inferred to convey degrees of hypotheticality. These two notions correlate with verb morphology roughly as in the scale below (cf. Fleischman 1989; Klein-Andreu 1986; Silva-Corvalán 1989).

Greatest assertiveness	
factual	Preterite Indicative
	Present indicative
least hypothetical	Future indicative
	Imperfect indicative
	Present subjunctive
most hypothetical	Conditional Indicative
	Imperfect subjunctive
Least assertiveness	

In addition, verb morphology expresses tense and aspect oppositions, roughly as follows: past time perspective (Preterite, Imperfect), omni-temporal or atemporal time perspective (Present), future time perspective (Future, Conditional, and perhaps also the Subjunctive forms). In regard to morphological aspect, it may be argued that Preterite and Future are perfective,[17] Imperfect and Conditional Indicative, and Subjunctive forms are Imperfective, and Present Indicative seems to be unmarked for aspect (cf. Silva-Corvalán 1991).

Let us now examine examples of *poder* and *deber* in non-Present form.

5.2 *Imperfect and Preterite Indicative*

31 examples of *poder* in Imperfect Indicative were examined: 6 are non-past time oriented and exhibit desiderative (ex. 59) and RP CMs (cf. Bybee, this volume); the rest have past time orientation and convey CMs of ability, permission, RP (ex. 60), and obligation or advisability (this last one only in one negative example, 61).

(59) *Nos podíamos parecer a Argentina y, nosotros, a Estados Unidos en eso, en eso, ¡en el dinero!* (M9,A446)
'I wish we were (lit: we could be) like Argentine and, we, like the United States, in that, in that, with respect to money!'

(60) *Y estaba - todo la ca-, las calles estaban heladas. Y teníamos que dar saltos, porque nos escurríamos y nos podíamos matar, ¿comprendes?* (M10,p6)
'And it was - the whole st- the streets were icy. And we had to jump around, because it was slippery and we could kill ourselves, you see?'

(61) *Y cuando llegué a Madrid, ya definitivamente pues me planteé el problema que yo no podía estar mirando al techo. Tenía que hacer algo, ¿no?* (M10,p3)
'And when I returned to Madrid, I definitely faced the question that I couldn't just stare at the ceiling. I had to do something, right?'

Example (59) is interesting in that it has a CM not identified for *poder* in Present tense, namely desiderative, in contexts with future time orientation. This CM is inferred when the speaker's attitude is clearly approving of p. If speaker attitude is neutral, however, the CM of *podía* with future time orientation is simply possibility, as in (62).

(62) *Si estás aburrido podías ir al cine.*
'If you're bored you could go to the movies.'

Although it appears as if in Spanish root possibility in the past is marked by the Imperfect morpheme (*-ba/-ía*), this is not so. Past time orientation is inferred from other signals in the context, as illustrated by the minimal pair sentences in (63), where (63 a) has a future time orientation (signalled by *el próximo año* 'next year'), while (63 b) may only be past (signalled by *antes* 'before, in the past').

(63) a. *Si te apoyaba la ITT, podías ser Presidente el próximo año.*
'If ITT supported you, you could be President next year.'
b. *Si antes te apoyaba la ITT, podías ser Presidente, pero ahora ya ese apoyo no sirve.*
'If in the past ITT supported you, you could be President, but now their support is useless.'

Halliday (1970:337) notes that "modality itself is not subject to variation in tense". Contrary to Halliday, Coates (1983:107) discusses, for instance, *could* as expressing, among other meanings, root possibility in the past, i.e., as 'past' of *can*. Example (64) is from Coates (ex. ii, p. 108).

(64) Past of *can* = Root Possibility
With all but one of the cookers the grid of the grill pan *could* be at one of two possible distances from the heat. The exception was the Cannon, which had four available positions.
'Exceptuando una de las cocinas, la rejilla del grill podía estar en una de dos posibles distancias del calor. La excepción era la Cannon, que tenía cuatro posiciones posibles.'

It seems to me that it is more appropriate to state that *could* is **compatible with** past time contexts, just as *podía* is in Spanish, since past time in (64) is indeed indicated by the verb forms *was* and *had* in the second sentence.

In Spanish, however, *poder* may occur with Preterite morphology and unambiguously refer to **past** root possibility in certain contexts which do not contain any other time reference (cf. Bybee's (this volume) interesting study of the development of the hypothetical senses of past modals in English). Compare examples (65) & (66) (fuller contexts are given in examples 69-70).

(65) *Pudo marcharse.*
could-3psg leave
'He was able to leave'

(66) *Pudo pasar algo terrible.*
might happen something terrible
'Something terrible might've happened.'

Example (65) conveys factuality of the event. By contrast, contextual features, namely inanimate subject, stative verb, adverse consequences of p, and speaker disapproval of p, determine a root possibility interpretation of example (66), which is counter-factual; the Preterite suffix indicates that this is root possibility in the past.

I have proposed that the IM of *poder* implies that a certain amount of effort must be expended in 'not precluding X'. The relation between this IM and the CM of (66) is, then, easy to establish: speakers do not assume that entities may spend effort in the actualization of an event whose consequences are adverse, so the only possible reading for (66) is of non-actualization or non-factuality. Thus, this CM does not appear to be fuzzy, but rather a category with clear boundaries defined by three features: adverse consequences of p, speaker's disapproval of p, Preterite morphology. This analysis is confirmed by the acceptability of (67) and (68 a), and the unacceptability (under 'normal circumstances') of (68 b).

(67) *Con esfuerzo, pudo marcharse finalmente.*
'After trying hard, he was finally able to leave.'

(68) a. *Estoy contenta, porque pudo pasar algo terrible, pero no pasó.*
'I'm happy because something terrible might've happened, but it didn't.'

b. **Estoy contenta porque pudo pasar algo terrible.*
*'I'm happy because something terrible could happen'

I have excerpted the modalized propositions in (65-66) from actual occurrences in the corpus (exx. 69 & 70) in order to contrast them in minimal contexts, thus highlighting the contribution of adverse vs. neutral consequences of p.

(69) *Tuvo esa suerte y se pudo marchar. Le dieron un lectorado.* (M10,p3)
'He was lucky and managed to leave. They gave him a lectureship.'

(70) *Fue muy grave aquello. Pudo pasar algo terrible, porque si los militares se echan a la calle - con seguridad ocurría una masacre. Yo no sé qué hubiera ocurrido.* (M10,p13)
'That was really a critical situation. Something terrible could've happened, because if the military get onto the streets - surely there would've been a massacre. I don't know what would've happened.'

Adverse consequences of p is a crucial feature for CM root possibility with Preterite *poder*. Despite the animacy of the subject, while example (71) allows the inference that the situation did occur, (72) can only convey possibility (unless, of course, the speaker had wanted to become extremely poor, but I would not consider this to be a 'normal social circumstance').

(71) *Pudimos quedarnos en Inglaterra.*
'We could stay in England.'

(72) *Pudimos quedarnos en la miseria. [La situación estaba muy mala.]*
could-we stay-us in the poverty
'We could've gone broke.' [The situation was bad.]

In its actual, more extended context of occurrence, example (71) in fact conveys root possibility: staying in England was possible but not actualized. However, this has to be made explicit by the speaker (*pero él no quiso* 'but he didn't want to'), as shown in the actual utterance (73).

(73) *Pero pudimos quedarnos en Inglaterra, porque le ofrecieron una permanencia, pero él no quiso.* (M10,p4)
'But we could have stayed (lit: could stay) in England, because they offered him a permanent position, but he didn't want to.'

Otherwise, possibility with Preterite *poder* may be expressed if the modal is combined with the Perfect Infinitive, as in English, such that example (74) does not then require any further context to be interpreted as a possibility which existed in the past, i.e. as counterfactual in the present.[18]

(74) *Pudimos habernos quedado.*
'We could have stayed.'

There are no examples with Preterite *poder* plus Perfect Infinitive in the data from Madrid. I note, however, that in my variety of Chilean Spanish, this tense combination is required in examples (66), (70), (72), & (73). My intuitions in this respect are confirmed by the responses of four native speakers from Chile and Argentina to an elicitation test given to determine the meanings associated with *poder* and *deber* in various tense forms. This may reflect a difference between Madrid and Latin American Spanish, but conversational data from this latter variety must be examined before any further proposals can be made in this respect.

The Perfect Infinitive does occur, however, with Present, Imperfect, and Conditional forms of *poder*. All examples have past time orientation and stress the non-factuality or hypotheticality of p. This higher degree of hypotheticality becomes more evident through a comparison of examples (60) and (75).

(75) *Tenía yo esto aquí que se podía haber utilizado.*
'I had this here that could've been used.'

Imperfective aspect in example (60) allows the interpretation that 'killing ourselves' is omnitemporally possible if the contextual circumstances referred to in the example obtain. By contrast, Perfective aspect of modalized p in (75) conveys that the possibility of p existed but is no longer available.

Examples with *deber* in Preterite and Imperfect are scarce (19 cases). It is marked for tense only when combined with *ser* 'to be' in contexts which explicitly indicate uncertainty about p (ex. 76).

(76) *Debió ser eso de las 10 u 11 de la noche [cuando empezaron los dolores del parto]. Y, no sé si nació a las 8 de la mañana.* (M24,p18)
'It must've been at around ten or eleven at night [when labor pains started]. And, I think she was born at eight in the morning.'

All other cases of Preterite and Imperfect *deber* convey obligation or advice, even when combined with Perfect Infinitive, as shown in (77). Otherwise, they are lexically differentiated (i.e. by using *deber de*) in contexts of possibility, as illustrated by (78) and (79).[19]

(77) *Por eso a mí me parece que debiste haber grabado a personas muy jóvenes porque tienen el lenguaje* cheli.(M10,p15)
'That's why it seems to me that you should've recorded very young people - because they speak this *cheli* language.'

(78) *Y mi madre debió* de *nacer en el año once o doce, porque tiene 75 o 74 años.* (M10,p2)
'And my mother must have been born in 1911 or 1912, because she's 75 or 74 years old.'

(79) *Y la cogieron en el aeropuerto justo al llegar a Las Palmas. Entonces allí debía, debía* de *haberlo llevado [la droga]. No sé cómo funciona esto.* (M24,p9)
'And they caught her at the airport just when she was arriving at Las Palmas. So she must have taken it [the drug] there. I don't know how that works.'

In regard to the Preterite/Imperfect opposition, I can only suggest at this point that they reflect two different degrees of speaker assertiveness: stronger and weaker, respectively. Thus, *mutatis mutandis*, in the case of *deber*, Preterite morphology turns the IM requirement into obligation, while Imperfect morphology makes it less assertive and allows a peripheral reading of weak obligation.

In my variety of Spanish, where opposition with *deber de* has disappeared, the expression of epistemic possibility in the past retains *deber* in the Present and marks tense with the Perfect Infinitive. Thus, examples (78) & (79) are rendered as in (80) & (81), respectively.

(80) *Debe haber sido eso de las 10 u 11 de la noche ...*
must-Pres. have been at around ...

(81) *Y mi madre debe haber nacido en el ...*
must-Pres. have been born in ...

5.3 *Conditional and Future*

There are no occurrences of *deber* with future morphology in the data, and only one of *poder*, with CM permission:

(82) *Entonces esa persona que quiera abortar - podrá abortar siempre que esto lo diga en las primeras semanas de su embarazo.* (M10,p7)
'So a person who may want to have an abortion - will be able to have one provided she requests it during the first weeks of pregnancy.'

In example (82), permission is associated with future time orientation and identification of a deontic source (the law). If time orientation is present, Future morphology independently conveys possibility, i.e. when combined with non-modal verbs (see note 17), and it does so with *poder* as well. Consider examples (83) a-b.

(83) a. *Si tú lo dices, será* (be-Fut.) *cierto.*
'If you say so, it must be true.'

b. *Si tú lo dices, podrá ser cierto.*
poder-Fut. be true
'If you say so, it may be true.'

The translations provided for examples (83) a-b are intended to capture the fact that *poder*, because it incorporates the notion of effort, makes p more hypothetical than when it is modalized simply by Future morphology.

By contrast, *deber* in the Future does not appear to be compatible with an epistemic modality context, as I show in (84). Only root modality CMs may be inferred for *deber* with Future morphology (85).

(84) a. ?*Si tú lo dices, deberá ser cierto.*
b. *Si tú lo dices, será cierto.*
'If you say so, it must-fut be true.'

(85) *La inauguración deberá ser mañana.*
'The inauguration will have to be tomorrow'

There are 6 examples with *poder* in Conditional form; they all occur in root possibility contexts. Indeed, since Conditional morphology conveys very weak assertiveness, it is not surprising that in every case it communicates probability of p, regardless of the context. That is, non-modal verbs modalized by Conditional morphology are interpreted to refer to hypothetical events as well. Example (86) illustrates.

(86) *Podrían hacerme una virguería - se suele decir una virguería, o sea una cosa bonita -, arreglarme los dientes, quedarían perfectos.* (M11,p27)
'They could do me a 'virguería' - they usually say 'virguería', you know, something pretty , fix my teeth, they would look perfect.'

On the other hand, *deber* in the Conditional may receive a deontic or an epistemic interpretation depending on the same contextual features established for Present *deber*. The contribution of Conditional morphology is that of adding weak speaker assertiveness which, in a deontic context, creates a CM of mitigated obligation or advice (ex. 87), and in an epistemic context, a CM of weaker confidence in the truth of p (ex. 88).[20]

(87) *El gobierno debería dar una explicación.* (M5,p21)
'The government should give an explanation.'

(88) *No vamos a saber exactamente las consecuencias, ¿no? [de entrar al Mercado Común Europeo] En principio, debería de ser bueno.* (M18,p15)
'We won't know exactly what the consequences will be, right? [of entering the Common Market] In theory, it should be good.'

5. Conclusions

It seems to me that an intriguing conclusion of this study is that, contrary to what is usually believed about the determining and specifying effect of context on the meaning of linguistic elements, a number of examples of *poder* and *deber* have proved to have indeterminate CMs precisely because their context of use makes them so. Assuming, then, basic IMs for these modals, one may conclude that indeterminacy is a consequence of the fuzziness of contexts (including such extra-linguistic factors as systems of beliefs, assumed shared knowledge, interpersonal relations, etc.). I have focused on this phenomenon from the point of view of the hearer/analyst. However, there is no a priori reason to deny that this would be valid for speakers as well, i.e., speakers themselves may not intend to communicate one message to the exclusion of all other possible ones compatible with a given context of occurrence. A number of examples in the data could be not only cases in which there are no striking differences between two interpretations of an utterance, but ones in which a speaker may either intend two interpretations to be drawn, or not be aware of or concerned about indeterminacies or ambiguities.

I have argued that contextual indeterminacy rather than indeterminate modal meaning accounts for the fuzzy membership of modalized propositions in one or another 'meaning category.' I would like to propose that this is valid for all Romance languages and also for English. With respect to English, for instance, Coates (p. 31) states that *must* has two main meanings (both constituting fuzzy sets): root (obligation/necessity) and epistemic (logical necessity/ confident inference), which she illustrates with the following examples:

(89) 'You *must* play this ten times over,' Miss Jarrova would say, pointing with relentless fingers to a jumble of crotchets and quavers.

(90) That place *must* make quite a profit for it was packed out and has been all week.

My proposal of monosemanticity and contextual fuzziness predicts that changing the contextual environment of *must* in (89) and (90) may cause indeterminate interpretations of the CM of *must*. This is precisely what examples (89 a) and (90 a) show:

(89) a. 'You must play this often,' Miss Jarrova would say when she heard her play it so beautifully.

(90) a. That place *must* make a good profit. They'll close it down if it doesn't.

Contextual modification of (89) and (90) leads to indeterminacy between root and epistemic interpretations of (89a) and (90a), i.e. to fuzzy CM of *must*. Admittedly, Coates's analysis may in essence be the same as mine. Yet, it seems to me more appropriate to acknowledge explicitly that certain forms at least do not have multiple meanings. Rather, they have basic meanings which make them compatible with a number of contexts; this form-context interaction may bring about different *interpretations* of the meaning of the form, which I have referred to as CMs.

In regard to the questions posed at the start, I hope to have shown that a monosemantic approach which goes beyond a level of IM and studies linguistic forms in specific contexts of use adequately captures the relation between IM and CMs of modals, and indeed reflects this interrelatedness more appropriately than a polysemantic analysis, which does not necessarily imply affinity between various meanings. Given my view of language as a system of communication and a particular instance of human behavior, I have sought answers to linguistic questions within and beyond the specific linguistic system under examination. Thus, crucial external factors which have relevance to the interpretation of modalized utterances have been identified: identification and strength of deontic sources, evidentiality, negative consequences of propositions (which are likely to be culture specific), and speaker attitude towards the content of propositions. This appears to be conclusive evidence in support of a non-autonomous semantic approach to the study of meaning.

NOTES

* I would like to thank Joan Bybee, Jenny Coates and Erica García for their extensive comments and insightful criticism of an earlier version of this paper. My thanks as well to Franco D'Introno, Wolfgang Klein, and Michael Perkins, who have contributed helpful observations. Improvements in this present version also owe much to Erica, and, likewise, to Flora Klein-Andreu, Roger Wright and especially to the editors of this volume. I am grateful to all of them for their careful reading of my work and for their penetrating comments. Errors and misinterpretations remain my sole responsibility.

1 Grammars note a difference between *deber* 'must' (obligation) and *deber de* 'must' (possibility), but at the same time acknowledge that this opposition is being lost as the form without the preposition *de* has extended to contexts of epistemic modality. I refer to this change later.

I do not examine here the transitive verb *deber* 'to owe' (*Te debo $1* 'I owe you $1'), because at this synchronic stage of the language it clearly is a different lexical item from modal *deber*.

2 The corpus of spoken data consists of approximately six hours of recorded conversations with seven speakers from Madrid. The data were collected by me and a group of graduate students participating in a seminar which I conducted in Madrid in the summer of 1985. I would like to thank my students for sharing their data with me. Included in this study are three adult women and four adult men. They are all middle class 'madrileños', except one man (M9), who works as a handyman in one of the Colegios Mayores of the University.

3 Halliday refers to these as *modulations* and notes that though modalities and modulations are not identical, they are semantically related, such that their partial reduction to a single network "expresses the closeness of fit of the two systems" (347)] i.e. when they do not convey the meaning of probability.

4 Haegeman deals only with *will*, and Kratzer with *can* and *must*, while Perkins examines a wide range of modal expressions.

5 Coates includes the deontic and dynamic categories of modal logic in a root category, and epistemic and alethic modalities in an epistemic one.

6 This analysis is similar to Lyons's (1977:843) proposal that the identification of a deontic source (an entity with authority) is a prerequisite to the interpretation of a modal as conveying obligation or necessity.

7 In his analysis of *poder* 'can, may', for instance, Narbona (1989:88) appears to identify two verbs *poder*. a modal that does not occur with a compound Infinitive (no example is offered), and a non-modal with the meaning of possibility that does admit this construction (*Puede habérselo prestado* '(He) may have lent it to him). It seems to me that Narbona's proposition that there is a dichotomous modal/non-modal opposition identified by the possibility of co-occurrence with a compound Infinitive is not correct; suggesting the existence of two verbs *poder* would force him to create at least two lexical entries for this verb, a solution that he criticizes elsewhere in his work. Pottier (1976:39) adopts a similar position when he argues that *pouvoir* 'can, may' and *devoir* 'must' clearly represent a case of multiple polysemy. Likewise, Huot (1974, cited in Thibault 1991) states that there are two different auxiliary verbs *devoir* in French.

8 There is at least one other type of meaning which is also conveyed linguistically, namely social meaning. I am not concerned with social meaning here.

9 'Agent-oriented' is here used in a similar, though not identical, way in which Bybee & Pagliuca (1985) have used the term. Indeed, they propose to refer to the notions of *ability*, *obligation*, *desire* and *intention* as 'agent-oriented modalities' because they "predicate conditions of either an internal or external nature on a willful agent" (p. 63).

10 Miller and Kwilosz (1981) investigate the interaction of modality and negation in English through a study of speakers' judgements of the meaning of sentences. Their experiments show that "There is apparently a tendency for verbs of necessity to take *de re* negation [i.e. only p is negated], and for verbs of possibility to take *de dicto* negation [i.e. m and p are negated], but there are exceptions in both cases." This tendency also seems to apply to *poder* and *deber*, but I do not examine this question in depth here.

11 For the EP reading to obtain, the Infinitive must receive stronger stress than the modal.

12 Perkins's definition is in turn modelled on Miller's (1978) discussion of Wertheimer's (1972) characterization of the meaning of OUGHT.

13 Information given in parentheses identifies the tape and either page of the transcription or tape counter number where example is located. Examples without this information are made up by the author.

14 By 'new' y I mean a subject referent for whom the speaker infers that z is valid, as in *M. va a poder caminar después de la operación* 'M. will be able to walk after the operation', on the basis of the speaker's previous evidence that z has been valid for a different subject referent under similar circumstances.

15 Compare *poder* and *deber* in the Preterite: *Pudo cruzar el río* 'He was able to [and did] cross the river' (situation occurred in the past); *Debió cruzar el río* 'He must have crossed the river' (the situation most likely occurred in the past).

16 Moliner (1981), for instance, notes that *tener que* may express necessity, obligation, and strong resolution, but does not include 'possibility.'

17 The perfectivity of the Future (*-rá*) in Spanish is debatable, but there is evidence that supports this analysis whenever this form fulfills its 'tense' function (Silva-Corvalán 1991). By contrast, in contexts where the Future is used to express hypotheticality in *the present*, its aspect seems to be Imperfective. Note, however, that the expression of hypotheticality is subject to some intriguing restrictions with dynamic verbs, as illustrated in (i) and (ii):

(i) A: *¿Por qué no vino Pepe?*
'Why didn't Pepe come?'
B: *Estará enfermo*
'He may be/is probably ill'
(ii) A: *¿Por qué no está Pepe aquí?*
'Why isn't Pepe here?'
B: **Trabajará hoy.*
*'He'll work today.'
Estará trabajando hoy.
'He may be working today.'

18 The Perfect Infinitive by itself expresses conditionality (counterfactual protasis) in certain special constructions of the type of (i) B:
(i) A: *Me habría gustado ir contigo a Chile.*
B: *Haberlo dicho antes, te habría invitado.*
have-it said before,
'Had you said it before, I would've invited you.'

19 This fact poses a challenging question in regard to the process of loss of *deber de* from the system. The observation that past morphology appears to favor its retention, especially with non-stative verbs, needs to be examined statistically in a larger corpus of data. See, also, examples 46, 87, and 88, which give evidence of insecurity in the use of *deber de*.

20 Note that in example 88 the speaker uses *deber de*, but in Chilean Spanish *deber* alone would also be interpreted to convey EP.

REFERENCES

Bello, Andrés. 1977. *Gramática de la lengua castellana* (With notes from Rufino J. Cuervo). 10th edition. Buenos Aires: Sopena.
Bosch, Peter. 1985. Lexical Meaning Contextualized. *Meaning and the Lexicon.* ed. by G.Hoppenbrouwers, P. Seuren & A. Weijters, 251-258. Dordrecht: Foris.
Bull, William E. 1971. *Time, Tense, and the Verb.* 4th printing. Berkeley: University of California Press.
Bybee, Joan. 1985. *Morphology.* Amsterdam: John Benjamins.
Bybee, Joan. (This volume). "The Semantic Development of Past Tense Modals in English."
Bybee, Joan & William Pagliuca. 1985. "Cross-Linguistic Comparison and the Development of Grammatical Meaning." *Historical Semantics. Historical Word Formation,* ed. by Jacek Fisiak, 59-83. Berlin: Mouton.
Bybee, Joan, Revere Perkins & William Pagliuca. 1994. *The Evolution of Grammar: Tense, Aspect and Modality in the Languages of the World.* Chicago: University of Chicago Press.
Coates, Jennifer. 1983. *The Semantics of the Modal Auxiliaries.* London: Croom Helm.
Fleischman, Suzanne. 1989. "Temporal Distance: A Basic Linguistic Metaphor." *Studies in Language* 13.1-50.
García, Erica C. 1975. *The Role of Theory in Linguistic Analysis: The Spanish Pronoun System.* Amsterdam: North- Holland.
Gili Gaya, Samuel. 1976. *Curso superior de sintaxis española.* Barcelona: Biblograf.
Givón, Talmy. 1982. "Evidentiality and Epistemic Space." *Studies in Language* 6.23-49
Haegeman, Liliane M.V. 1983. *The Semantics of Will in Present-day British English: A Unified Account.* Brussels: Verhandeling Letteren, 45.103.
Halliday, M.A.K. 1970. "Functional Diversity in Language as Seen from a Consideration of Modality and Mood in English. *Foundations of Language* 6.322-361.
Heine, Berndt. (This volume). "Agent-Oriented vs. Epistemic Modality: Some Observations on German Modals."
Hernández, César. 1986. *Gramática funcional del español.* Madrid: Gredos
King, Larry D. 1992. *The Semantic Structure of Spanish.* Amsterdam: John Benjamins.
Klein-Andreu, Flora. 1986. "Speaker-Based and Reference-Based Factors in Language: Non-past Conditional Sentences in Spanish." *Studies in Romance Linguistics,* ed. by Osvaldo Jaeggli, & Carmen Silva-Corvalán, 99-119. Amsterdam: Foris.
Kratzer, Angelika. 1977. "What 'Must' and 'Can' Must and Can Mean. *Linguistics and Philosophy* 1.337-355.
Lyons, John. 1977. *Semantics.* Cambridge: Cambridge University Press.
Marcos Marín, Francisco. 1975. *Aproximación a la gramática española.* 3rd edition. Madrid: Cincel.
Miller, George A. 1978. "Semantic Relations Among Words." *Linguistic Theory and Psychological Reality,* ed. by M. Halle, J. Bresnan, & G.A. Miller, 60-118. Cambridge, Mass.: MIT Press.
Miller, George A., & Donna M. Kwilosz. 1981. "Interactions of Modality and Negation in English." *Elements of Discourse Understanding,* ed. by Aravind Joshi, Bonnie Webber, & Ivan Sag, 201-216. Cambridge: Cambridge University Press.

Moliner, María. 1981. *Diccionario de uso del español.* Madrid: Gredos.

Narbona, Antonio. 1989. *Sintaxis española: nuevos y viejos enfoques.* Barcelona: Ariel.

Palmer, F.R. 1977. "Modals and Actuality." *Journal of Linguistics* 13.1-23.

Palmer, F.R. 1979. *Modality and the English Modals.* London: Longman.

Perkins, Michael R. 1982. The Core Meanings of the English Modals. *Journal of Linguistics* 18.245-273.

Perkins, Michael R. 1983. *Modal Expressions in English.* Norwood, N.J.: Ablex.

Pottier, Bernard. 1976. Sur la Formulation des Modalités en Linguistique. *Modalités. Langages,* special issue No 43.39-46.

Real Academia Española. 1973. *Esbozo de una nueva gramática de la lengua española.* Madrid: Espasa-Calpe.

Rivero, María Luisa. 1977. *Estudios de gramática generativa del español.* Madrid: Cátedra.

Silva-Corvalán, Carmen. 1985. "Modality and Semantic Change." *Historical Semantics. Historical Word Formation,* ed. by Jacek Fisiak, 547-572. Berlin: Mouton.

Silva-Corvalán, Carmen. 1989. "The Pragmastylistics of Hypothetical Discourse." *The Pragmatics of Style,* ed. by Leo Hickey, 87-105. London & New York: Routledge.

Silva-Corvalán, Carmen. 1991. "Invariant Meanings and Context-Bound Functions of Tense in Spanish." *The Function of Tense in Texts,* ed. by J. Gvozdanovic & T. Janssen, in collaboration with Östen Dahl, 255-270. Amsterdam: North- Holland.

Sirbu Dumitrescu, Domnita. 1988. "Contribución al estudio de los verbos modales en español." *Hispania* 71.139-147.

Sweetser, Eve. 1982. "Root and Epistemic Modals: Causality in two Worlds." *Proceedings of the Eighth Annual Meeting of the Berkeley Linguistics Society,* ed. by Macaulay, Monica, Orin Gensler, et al., 484-507. Berkeley: Berkeley Linguistics Society.

Thibault, Pierrette. 1991. "Semantic Overlaps of French Modal Expressions." *Language Variation and Change* 3.191- 222.

Wertheimer, R. 1972. *The Significance of Sense: Meaning, Modality and Morality.* Ithaca: Cornell University Press.

Wright, Roger. 1990. "Fact and Fiction in Language and Literature." *Liverpool Papers in Language and Discourse* 3.1-37.

Zadeh, L.A. 1965. "Fuzzy sets." *Information and Control* 8.338-353.

Zadeh, L.A. 1972. "A Fuzzy-Set-Theoretic Interpretation of Linguistic Hedges." *Journal of Cybernetics* 2.4-34.

The Obligation Modality in Western Nilotic Languages

Edith L. Bavin
La Trobe University

1. Introduction

Bybee (1985) includes obligation and necessity in the category of agent-oriented modality which reports the existence of internal and external conditions on an agent with respect to the completion of the action expressed in the main predicate (Bybee, Perkins & Pagliuca 1994:195). Strong obligation ('must') and weak obligation ('should') involve external pressures; in contrast, necessity usually involves some physical conditions (Bybee et al. 1994).

This paper examines the forms, uses and diachronic development of the markers of obligation in Lango and Acholi, two Western Nilotic languages. In addition, some data from three other languages in this group are presented for comparison purposes.[1] The source for the gram which typically marks obligation and necessity in Lango and Acholi is an impersonal form of the verb 'to be fitting, to be suitable'. Lexical items with these meanings have been documented as the sources of obligation grams in other languages in other parts of the world, as reported in Bybee et al. (1994). What is of particular interest are the semantic and syntactic changes required for a third person form of the verb to become a marker of agent-oriented modality, which attributes modality to the subject of the clause. These changes involve extending the syntactic context in which the verb is used.

Grams which mark modalities often have different interpretations depending on the context. For instance, the examples to be discussed below illustrate that the obligation markers in Lango and Acholi may be interpreted with a strong or weak obligation sense, or as marking the intention of the speaker, or with an epistemic function. One way to handle such synchronic variability is to view each interpretation as a different meaning, that is to allow polysemy since polysemy can be viewed as comprising a set of overlapping senses, as in Coates (1983). However, the view taken in this paper is that interpretations are derived from context. When there is synchronic variation in the interpretation of a form, this can be indicative of gradual change in progress. Over time, implications made from the context may become part of the meaning of the form; thus, diachronic extensions can be viewed as grammaticalizations of what were once synchronic extensions of basic meanings, as argued by Fleischman (1989).

There is other support for explaining synchronic variation from a diachronic perspective. For example, Bybee (1985: 191-196) argues that the category of mood is best viewed as a set of diachronically related functions, and Traugott (1989:49) discusses diachronic changes from nonepistemic to epistemic meanings for modal markers, attributing the changes to an increase in subjectivity: as there is an increase in the coding of speaker informativeness about his or her attitude, this is reflected in changes from nonepistemic to epistemic meanings.

The forms most usually used to mark obligation in five Western Nilotic languages are discussed in the next section. The morpho-syntactic properties of the obligation constructions in Lango and Acholi and the lexical sources of these obligation particles are discussed in Section 3. Different contextual interpretations for the particles are illustrated in Section 4, while the sources for other grammatical markers in the languages are discusssed in Section 5. Following this, the use of the verb meaning 'to want' as another marker of agent-oriented modalities is illustrated in Section 6.

2. The Western Nilotic languages

2.1 *Introduction*

There are five languages in the Western Nilotic group: Acholi, Lango, Dhopadhola, Alur and DhoLuo. With the exception of DhoLuo, the languages are spoken in Uganda, with Acholi extending into the Sudan. DhoLuo is spoken in Western Kenya, so it is separated physically from the other four languages. The languages share a high percentage of vocabulary items. Based on a survey of vocabulary items in Ugandan languages, Ladefoged, Glick & Criper (1968) report the number of vocabulary items shared between Acholi and Lango is the same as that between Acholi and Alur (89%). The number of vocabulary items shared between Acholi and Dhopadhola is reported to be 76%. However between Lango and Alur it is 84%, between Lango and Dhopadhola 73%, and between Alur and Dhopadhola, 73%.

All five languages are often claimed to be mutually intelligible, and are referred to collectively as Luo. However, there are significant differences in the grammatical categories. (See Bavin 1982, 1990 for discussion on some of the grammatical categories in Lango and Acholi). In addition, there are phonological differences. For example, Dhopadhola, Alur and Dholuo have a series of dental stops and a number of fricatives, but Lango and Acholi do not.

2.2 *Obligation markers*

2.2.1 *The forms*

Lango and Acholi are similar in the way the modality of obligation is encoded. In Lango (example 1) the particle *myero* is used and in Acholi (example 2), the form is *omyero* or *myero*. Some speakers use one form, other speakers use the other and another group of speakers use both forms. In Alur (example 3) *mako* is the obligation marker, and in Dholuo (example 4) obligation is expressed with *nyaka*. In contrast, Dhopadhola (example 5), makes use of a verbal affix *ripo* which appears between the Subject Prefix and the verb stem. Thus the marking of obligation is one area of difference among the languages.

(1) a. *Myero a-ngol pii*
must 1:SG-cross water
'I must cross the water.'

b. *Dako-ni myero nen-a oyotoyot*
woman-DET must see-1:SG quickly
'This woman should see me immediately.'

(2) a. *Omyero i-tim*
must 2:SG do
'You must do it.'

b. *Omyero doki a-wil ngom*
must again 1:SG-buy land
'I must buy more land.'

(3) a. *Omako a-cith-i kawoni*
must 1:SG-go-SUBJ now
'I must leave now.'

b. *Ka i-mito cam omako i-bed ku cente*
if 2:SG-want food must 2:SG-stay with money
'If you want food, you must have money.'

(4) a. *Nyaka i-chiem mos*
must 2:SG-eat slowly
'You must eat more slowly.'

b. *Nyaka wa-kony-e*
Must 1:PL-help-REF
'We must help each other.'

(5) a. *A-ripo-woth*
1:SG-must-go
'I must go.'

b. *I-ripo-woth*
2:SG-must-go
'You must go.'

The verb in all five languages carries a Subject Prefix to agree with the person and number of the subject, as illustrated in the sentences above and in (6) from Lango. The Subject Prefix is generally a short form of the free pronoun. Dhopadhola is distinct from the other four languages in using *go* as the Third Person Singular pronoun and *jo* as the Third Plural form; *en* 'Singular' and *gin* 'Plural' are used in the other languages.

The Subject Prefix appears on the lexical verb following *myero* in Lango, *(o)myero* in Acholi, *omako* in Alur and *nyaka* in Dholuo. In sentences with a pronominal subject, it is optional to include the free pronoun, but the Subject Prefix is required, as illustrated in (6). The particles themselves do not change in form when the subject changes. Note in (6b) that both the auxiliary *tye* 'to be (locative)' and the main verb carry a Subject Prefix, but the Obligation marker *myero* does not.

(6) *Lango*

a. *(An) a-ngweco*
I 1:SG-run
'I ran.'

b. *A-tye a-ngweco*
1:SG-be 1:SG-run
'I am running.'

c. *Myero onwongo dong a-ngwec oko*
must PI then 1:SG-run already
'I should have run.'

2.2.2 *Other properties*

Other syntactic properties associated with the obligation construction are the position of the subject noun or pronoun, the position of the Negative, the form of the lexical verb following the obligation particle, and changes in interpretation when the particle follows an aspect marker. These properties are discussed below.

In all the languages except Dhopadhola, in which the obligation gram is affixed to the verb, an overt subject can appear either before or after the obligation particle. For example, in (7) from Alur, the subject noun could be placed following *omako*. The subject pronoun in (8), from Lango, could also appear in sentence initial position, but most speakers seem to place a subject pronoun, if used, following *myero,* (recall that subject pronouns are optional).[2] Other grammatical morphemes can seperate the obligation marker from the lexical verb, as indicated in (6c) in which *onwongo* 'Past Imperfective' and *dong* 'then' seperate the particle from the lexical verb. The Negative marker *pe* may appear between the particle and the lexical verb in Lango and Acholi, as in (9c) from Acholi, but it generally appears at the beginning of a subordinate clause, as in (9a) and (9b), without a difference in interpretation.

(7) *Alur*

Awiya omako o-dik-i i-paco tin
children must 3:SG-return-SUBJ LOC-home today
'The children must go home today.'

(8) *Lango*

Onwongo	*gin*	*myero*	*o-bol*	*odilo*
PI	they	must	3:SG-throw	ball

'They would have thrown the ball.'

(9) a. *Lango*

Te	*bedo*	*kobo*	*atin*	*gwok-ere*	*ca*	*ni*	*pe*
NARR	stay	talk	child	dog-POSS	DET	COMP	NEG
dong	*myero*	*gwee*					
then	must	bark					

'He then told his puppy that he mustn't bark.'

b. *Lango*

Onwongo	*o-punyo-wa*	*ni*	*pe*	*myero*	*o-mede*
PI	3:PL-teach-1:PL	COMP	not	must	1:PL-continue
kede	*kodi*	*luwenyi*			
with	way	fighting			

'We were being taught that we shouldn't fight.'

c. *Acholi*

Myero	*pe*	*o-bol*	*odilo*
Must	NEG	3:SG-throw	ball

'He shouldn't have thrown the ball.'

Another property of the obligation construction concerns the shape of the lexical verb following the particle. In all five languages, the Subjunctive form of the verb is used. Most indicative verbs in the Western Nilotic languages are disyllabic and end with a final vowel *o* (e.g. from Acholi and Lango: *neno* 'see', *miyo* 'give', *ryemo* 'chase', *keto* 'put, *bino* 'come', *camo* 'eat', *mito* 'want', *ringo* 'run'). There is also a small set of mono-syllabic verbs in each language (e.g. from Acholi: *coo* 'wake up', *aa* start from', and *oo* 'arrive'). For the disyllabic verbs, the Subjunctive form that follows *(o)myero* is formed by omitting the final vowel (e.g. *nen* from *neno* 'see'), and for some verbs a final vowel *i* replaces the *o*. Driberg (1923) discussing Lango, and Crazzolara (1955) discussing Acholi, specify that the Subjunctive verbs which add a final *i* in place of the *o* are phonologically determined; however this is no longer true as speakers now use the suffix *i* only on motion verbs, or not at all.[3] For example, Acholi speakers vary as to whether they use *i* on the verb *ngwec* 'run' and *dok* 'return', but they do not use a final *i* on non-motion verbs.

The Subjunctive form also follows *wek* 'let, allow', and *gwok* 'prohibition'. Crazzolara (1955:17) describes its function as hortative, and lists the following meanings for the form: wish, invitation, exhortation, command, prohibition. However, there are other uses. For example, in Lango and Acholi, *nen* is used with the meaning 'to be seen'. The form is also used for the imperative; in this function, also, there is variability in the use of the suffix *i* (e.g. *ngweci* or *ngwec* 'run!'), although more Lango speakers than Acholi tend to use the suffix.

Note that in (10) the Acholi speaker uses a final vowel *i* on the verb following *myero*; he also produced (11), in which *bed* does not have a suffix. A few verbs in each language are idiosyncratic since they always appear in the Reflexive form, no matter what the context (e.g. *medde* 'continue, which is illustrated in (12)).

(10) *Myero a-ngwec-i*
must 1:SG-run-SUBJ
'I must run.'

(11) *Myero a-bed piny*
must 1:SG-sit down
'I must sit down.'

(12) *Myero a-med-de i-kwan iyonge mwaka aryo*
should 1:SG-continue-REF with-study after year two
'I must continue studying in two years/I intend to continue studying in two years.'

In examples (1)-(5), the lexical verbs following the Obligation markers are *ngol* 'cross' and *nen* 'see' from Lango, *tim* 'do' and *wil* 'buy' from Acholi, *cithi* 'go' and *bed* 'stay' from Alur, *chiem* 'eat' and *kony* 'help' from Dholuo, and *woth* 'go' from Dhopadhola. These are all Subjunctive forms of the respective verbs, and all have a Subject Prefix. In contrast, verb complements of equi-verbs do not appear in the Subjunctive form, and it is the matrix verb that carries the Subject Prefix, not the complement. For example, *amito neno* means 'I want to see' in both Acholi and Lango. *Mito* has the Subject Prefix, not *neno*. There are two modal verbs in Lango and Acholi (*romo* 'can', and *twero* 'to be able') which behave like equi-verbs; they carry the Subject Prefix and are followed by the Infinitive form of the verb, not the Subjunctive. These properties are illustrated with *romo* in (13).

(13) *Acholi*

Ka	*i-tye*	*i-peko*	*i-romo*	*penyo*	*ngati-mo*
if	2:SG-be	with-problem	2:SG-can	ask	person-some

'If you have a problem, you can ask anyone.'

The position of the Negative *pe* shows up another difference between a complement-taking verb and the modal particle *(o)myero*. As illustrated above, *pe* usually appears between *myero* and the lexical verb. However, *pe* precedes an equi-verb or a modal verb, as in the second clause of (14).

(14) *Acholi*

Gu-yabo	*wang*	*ot*	*ka*	*ngiyo*	*ka*	*kwene*	*ma*
3:PL-open	eye	house	PROG	look	place	where	REL
ogwalpok	*tye*	*iye;*	*pe*	*gi-romo*	*neno-ne*		
frog	be	LOC	NEG	3:PL-can	see-3 SG		

'They opened the window looking for the frog to see where it was; they couldn't see it.'

A change in interpretation is made in both Lango and Acholi when the Past Imperfective marker precedes the obligation marker. For example, in (15) the Acholi speaker is indicating that while there was some obligation for them to play ball they did not, whereas in (16), he is indicating that because it is the most likely situation, he believes they did play ball. That is, when the aspect marker follows the obligation marker, there is an epistemic interpretation. Other interpretations for the obligation constructions will be discussed in Section 4.

(15)

Gin	*onongo*	*myero*	*gu-tuk*	*odilo* [4]
They	PI	must	3:SG-play	ball

'They should/would have played ball.'

(16)

Gin	*myero*	*onongo*	*gu-tuk*	*odilo*
They	must	PI	3:PL-play	ball

'They must have played ball.'

3. Lexical sources

3.1 *Introduction*

The source for the Dhopadhola obligation affix is not evident. *Ripo* is not a lexical verb in the language group and it will not be considered further. However, the lexical sources of the obligation markers in the other four languages are evident.

3.2 *Lango and Acholi*

The lexical verb *myero* is listed by Driberg (1923) in an early description of Lango with the meaning 'to be fitting for, suitable for, a match for'. Crazzolara (1955), writing about Acholi, lists *myero* with the meanings 'to be suitable, fit, becoming, tolerable' while Kitching (1907), also writing about Acholi, lists its meaning as 'to be fit', right, worthy' as well as the obligation meaning 'ought', 'must'. This lexical source is compatible with sources listed for obligation in Bybee et al. (1994) who list 'be fitting' and 'be proper' as possible sources. Clearly, *myero* was a lexical verb in the early part of the century, given the meanings listed by both Driberg and Kitching; Driberg also uses one example, which is given in (17). In both Lango and Acholi the lexical semantics have now been been lost since *myero* is now used only as a modal particle, not a verb.

(17) *Lango*

Oluk	*o-myer-e*	*jobi*
Oluk	3:SG-match-REF	buffalo

'Oluk was a match for the buffalo.' [Driberg, 1923: 391]

In form, *omyero* is the Past Third Person Singular of the verb *myero*. Given that Acholi uses *omyero* or *myero*, it is hypothesized that that both Lango and Acholi started with *omyero*, but Lango has dropped the prefix. This seems the most likely direction of change, since forms generally become reduced in form as they become grammaticized (Bybee 1985) .

Assuming the Third Singular Past form is the source for the obligation particle, one change to be accounted for is the change in the function of the prefix *o*. In *omyero* 'obligation', *o* does not refer to a particular entity, and thus the form *omyero* is impersonal in interpretation. That is, a Third Singular form with past reference was reinterpreted as impersonal and as an on-going state or condition ('It is fitting'). As discussed by Bybee (this volume), a change from past form to present interpretation is common for modals. The impersonal sense of 'It is fitting' indicates that it is desirable for an existing situation to be maintained, that is, certain conditions that hold are appropriate according to the current views of the community, the authority that determines what is fitting or necessary. To maintain the values of this society, a person is obliged to conform to these views.

Since 'It is fitting/suitable' has a non-agentive, intransitive meaning, it is feasible that the short form of *myero* was first used with the impersonal meaning. Recall that a distinction is made for a few verbs in the languages between a short (intransitive) form and a long, transitive form which is marked with the *o* suffix. The distinction might have been more common in earlier stages of the languages, with the *o* suffix being added to the short stem of verbs to mark transitivity. Since this is the same form as the Third Person Subject prefix *o*, the most likely development is that *o* was used to mark a third Person Object but was reinterpreted as a marker of transitivity, and later as part of the verb stem for all but a few verbs. However, this development could have taken place prior to *myero* becoming used as a modal particle.

The impersonal form ('It is fitting') would have propositional scope with the source of the modality being society in general. However, changes have taken place to allow the form to become a clause-internal grammatical marker which predicates the modality onto the agent of a particular activity. One necessary change is that the impersonal verb takes a verbal complement, as in 'It is fitting to run'. In this way, the impersonal lexical item becomes part of a larger construction.

In order to personalize an utterance containing *omyero* and a verbal complement, the speaker must direct the message to or about a particular individual. This would necessitate adding a Subject Prefix. Because Lango and Acholi are pro-drop languages, an overt subject nominal is not required, but the bound form is. The fact that the Subject Prefix did not replace *o* on *myero* indicates the shift was already in progress, with the complement being analyzed as the main predicate. Thus there was a change from a propositional scope lexical modality to a specific predication of the modality onto an agent, the subject of the new predicate.

There is no evidence for discrete stages in the shift, either semantic or syntactic, and it is likely that there was synchronic variability as the changes took place. Thus the following list does not represent distinct stages in the path of change. Rather it illustrates the starting point and the current construction. *Myero* started as a lexical verb but it can no longer be used as a lexical verb, only as a modal particle in a clause which has an inflected predicate.

(18)	*o-myero*	'He/ she/ it fits/matches X'	(transitive)
(OR	*o-myer*	'It fits'	(intransitive))
	omyero	'It is fitting/suitable/appropriate'	(impersonal)
	omyero + verb	'It is appropriate to V'	
	omyero prefix+V	'It is appropriate/ necessary for X to V'	

One further development has occurred. The prefix on *omyero* serves no purpose as a subject marker and has been dropped in Lango, and also by some Acholi speakers. For some of those Acholi speakers who use both forms, the forms have developed different functions. For example, one male who used both *myero* and *omyero* explained the difference as follows: *omyero* has more force, but with *myero* the speaker is just telling someone what they must do. This suggests that *omyero* is more formal, and this would fit in with the hypothesis that it is the older of the two forms. Lango, then, is slightly more ahead in the grammaticalization of the obligation marker in that no speakers have been found to use the *o* prefix. Lango also shows more change in the forms of verb prefixes generally, since *o* is used for third singular and all plural persons.

3.3 *Alur*

The source for the Alur particle *omako* is the lexical verb *mako* 'hold, catch'. The verb form *mako* is currently a lexical verb with the meaning 'to hold, catch' in all five languages under discussion. In addition to its active meaning with an agent subject, it is also used in Acholi in expressions showing a situation has arisen in which a non-animate is the cause of a current state. For example, 'He is mad' is literally 'madness holds/ captures him'. In Alur, the meaning has been extended to the current meaning of obligation.

What is of interest is the form of the verb. As with *omyero, omako* has the *o* prefix, but because the prefix does not refer to a particular person but society at large, it is an impersonal form. Similar developments seem to have occurred with this verb as with *omyero* in Acholi and Lango, in that a verbal complement with Subject Prefix must have been added, and the form *omako* reinterpreted as a clause-internal grammatical marker, which shifts from having propositional scope to predicating the modality onto the subject of the predicate. In its lexical use, *mako* takes a nominal complement; for example, *omako winyo* means 'He/she caught/held a bird'. But the verb *mako* does not take a verbal complement, as is possible with English 'caught'. Consider the sentence 'He/she caught a fish swimming in the river'; here 'fish' could be analyzed as the object of 'caught' as well as the subject of 'swimming'. However, in the Western Nilotic languages, *mako* would not be used here; the verb *gwok* 'constrain' would be used instead.

The fact that *mako* (as a lexical verb) does not take a verbal complement suggests the personal meaning of *omako* was not used as the source for the shift to a modal meaning. It is likely that an impersonal meaning developed for *omako*, as with *omyero*, and that as the semantic changes took place so did the syntactic. Just as with *omyero*, *omako* is a Past form of a verb, and its impersonal meaning 'It was held' has been extended to non-past contexts.

While physical contact is part of meaning of the lexical verb *mako*, 'catch/hold', the modal meaning of *omako* implies social constraints, which are the views held by society as to what is appropriate. For example, the literal interpretation of (3b) is 'If you want food, it is held you stay with money'. *Omako* here does not convey any sense of physical constraint or support; however it does convey the sense of social constraint. That is, a concrete lexical item has been used to express a more abstract notion of constraint. A similar extension has been discussed for English 'have', which once meant 'to hold in one's hand', the meaning has changed so that the notion of physical presence of a possession has been lost, although one can have an abstract possession (Bybee and Pagliuca (1985:72). In Alur, the meaning of *omako* 'hold' has been metaphorically extended so that one may hold ideas as well as physical objects. However, the interpretation is not associated with the personal form of the verb. Since it is the impersonal form which has been grammaticalized with a modality function, it is through this form that the semantic change has spread.

3.4 *Dholuo*

For DhoLuo, Stafford (1967) lists the meaning of the form *nyaka* as 'compulsion/ necessity'. Huntingford (1959), Omondi (1982), Gregerson (1962), and

Malo (1952) also cite the form *nyaka,* although they differ in the senses listed. While Huntingford enters meanings of 'must', 'from' and 'since', Omondi gives only 'must'. The form *nyaka* is also currently used in DhoLuo with a spatial meaning 'up to' and this is a cognate of *naka* 'up to' in Acholi as in example (19).

(19) *Acholi*
Gu-ci-kwalo dyangi naka Patongo
3:PL-go-steal cows up to Patongo
'They went to steal cows as far as Patongo.'

In discussing Lango, not DhoLuo, Driberg (1923) lists *nak* as the stem for 'to bear fruit' with *nyal* or *nywalo* as 'to be fruitful'. In the related language, Dhopadhola, *nyalo* is currently used for the epistemic modality of Possibility ('might'). While it is beyond the scope of this paper to speculate the possible relationship between the Dhopadhola form for 'might' and the DhuLuo form for 'must' and the relationship to a verb meaning 'to be fruitful', it is conceivable that there is one.

While *nyaka* is the form generally used in DhoLuo to mark the modality of obligation, there are alternatives. Malo (1952) gives *onego*, *owinjore* and *oromo*. Omondi (1982) lists both *onego* and *owinjore* with the meaning 'should', while Stafford (1967) lists *onego* and *owinjore* as meaning both 'should' and 'ought'. For the Reflexive verb *winjore*, he gives the meaning 'It is convenient, fitting'. Thus the lexical source for *winjore* is similar in meaning to the source which has developed into the Lango and Acholi markers of obligation.

Omondi argues that while *nego* and *winjo* in DhoLuo are interchangeable, with the meaning 'fits into', there must be a meaning difference since only *winjo* can be substituted by *romo* 'to deserve'. Writing on Alur, Ringe (1948) lists the meaning of *romo* as 'fit'. However, in Lango and Acholi, *romo* does not have either meaning ('deserve' or 'fit'); it functions as a verb in these languages with the meaning 'to be enough, sufficient, equal', and it is also used as a marker of epistemic modality with the meaning 'can'. This is not a function for *romo* in the other three languages in the group.

Although there are alternative forms for marking obligation, one consultant pointed out that he interprets *nyaka* as more 'forceful' than *nego*, and *winjore* as the least strong, being used in the sense 'It is sensible, reasonable' or, 'You the listener should see the sense of what I'm saying'.

3.5 *Similarities among the languages*

In summary, there are some similarities across the languages in the meanings of the lexical sources for the obligation markers, even though the forms are different. These similarities support the notion of a conceptual basis for diachronic changes. For example, *omyero*, the impersonal of 'to be fitting' is the source for the obligation marker in Lango and Acholi. For DhoLuo, Stafford gives the meaning for *winjore*, a weak obligation marker, as the impersonal 'It is fitting', although Omondi lists 'fits into'. The lexical meaning is retained alongside the obligation meaning in Dholuo, unlike the situation in Lango and Acholi, where the lexical meaning has been lost.

Another form used in DhoLuo as a marker of obligation, *romo*, is listed by Ringe (1948) with the meaning of 'fit' for a related language, Alur. This form has developed into the marker of another modality in Lango and Acholi, the epistemic modality of Possibility which, in contrast to the agent-oriented modalities, has scope over the whole proposition.

4. Semantics of the Obligation marker in Lango and Acholi

4.1 *Introduction*

As is documented in several sources, markers of obligation and necessity in a language can be extended to other contexts (e.g. Bybee 1985, Traugott 1989). One often-cited example is the extension of English 'shall', from a meaning of obligation to a meaning of intention when used with first person. In this section I examine some of the interpretations of *(o)myero* in Lango and Acholi. In addition to the obligation meaning (weak and strong), *(o)myero* can also be interpreted as a marker of Necessity, depending on whether the constraints are social or physical. The relationship between the speaker and hearer also affects the interpretation; when an authority figure uses *(o)myero* in an utterance directed to a younger person, it is the obligation sense that is interpreted. Another interpretation is that sentences with *(o)myero* express the speaker's own attitude, rather than society's in general, and this may reflect the speaker's desire for a particular outcome. The form has an epistemic function also. Some of these uses have already been illustrated, and other examples are discussed below.

4.2 *Uses of the Obligation marker for Necessity and Obligation*

In (11), the Lango speaker is tired and wants to sit, so her physical condition motivates the use of *myero*; the form here is interpreted as Necessity, as it is in (20). Necessity 'reports the existence of physical conditions compelling an agent to complete the predicate action' (Bybee et al. 1994). In (20) the children need to lift up their clothes so they don't get wet; the motivation to lift them is created by an external factor, the physical conditions.

(20) *Ma peya wa-oo i-school omyero wa-ngol kulu,*
REL not yet 1:PL-arrived LOC-school must 1:PL-cross river
ma peya wa-ngolo kulu omyero wa-lung bongo-wa
REL not yet 1:PL-cross river must 1:PL-lift clothes-1:PL
'Before we reached the school we had to cross a river; before we crossed the river we had to lift up our clothes.'

Examples (21) and (22), from Acholi, are extracts from a riddle. The listener is told that a man has some obligation to get his things across the river. He has to take three things, a lion, a chicken and some seed, but he can only take one thing at a time because the boat is too small to take them all. If he leaves the lion with the chicken, it will it eat the chicken, and if he leaves the chicken with the seeds, it will eat the seeds. Thus the items must be transported in a particular order. Here the physical conditions create the necessity to take the items in a particular order.

(21) *Ci omyero en o-cwal jami-ni weng loka kulu*
and must he 3 SG-take thing-DEM all across river
'And he needed to take all these things across the river.'

(22) *Omyero o-te mene wiati*
must 3:SG-take which first
'Which one must he take first?'

However, example (23), from Acholi, expresses an obligation; there are strong social constraints concerning choosing a wife.

(23) *Ma peya dako o-bino bot-i omyero i-cul lim*
REL not yet woman 3:SG-come to-2:SG must 2:SG-pay money
'Before the woman comes to you, you have to pay some money.'

Context affects the interpretation of *(o)myero*. It is used, together with the Negative marker, with a sense of strong obligation when a social more is being violated (as in (24)). There is also an obligation interpretation when a person of authority speaks, particularly to a child. This is illustrated in examples (25) - (27) which I have extracted from Alerotek's (1972) Acholi book about a boy named Kidega. (Glosses have been added to the original.) The two forms of the particle (*myero* and *omyero*) are used interchangeably in the text: both appear with verbs with singular or plural subjects, and both appear clause-initially as well as following some other words(s). In the examples, the school headmaster is addressing Kidega and his father. Kidega understands the headmaster's language, but his father does not.

In (25), the headmaster warns the family that they must save so there is enough money to pay the school fees. In (26), the headmaster is directing Kidega to explain to his father; both instances of *myero* in this example are interpreted as markers of obligation; the boy is obliged to translate because his father does not speak the language. In (27), the boy is being warned; if he does not improve his behavior he will not be allowed to continue with his studies.

(24) *Acholi*
In omyero i-cam mot
You(SG) must 2:SG-eat slowly
'You should eat slowly.'

(25) *Edimacta lacen o-tito ni pic myero gi-gwok*
headmaster elder 3:SG-say COMP schoolfees must 3:PL-keep
pien kare me cul pud tye anyim, wa i-nino
because time for school still be ahead, up to LOC-day
dwe 27 me Janwari
month 27 for January
'The headmaster said that they must save their money because school (and school fees) were due on January 27th.' [p. 12]

(26) *A-mito ni myero i-ti ki woru myero en*
1:SG-want COMP must 2:SG-tell to father must he
o-gwok cente pic maber in i-bi-kelo ne i-nino
3:SG-keep money fees properly you 2:SG-FUT-put this LOC-day

dwe *27* *me* *dwe* *man*
month 27 for month this
'I want you to tell your father that he must keep the money properly; you will bring it on the 27th.' [p. 12]

(27) *In Kidega myero i-lub cik me cukul ka i-mito wan.*
you Kidega must 2:SG-follow rules for school if 2:SG-want study
'You, Kidega, must follow the school rules if you want to stay in school.' [p. 13]

4.3 *Obligation particle used to express speaker's attitude or speaker's intention*

Sentences with *(o)myero* often express something about the attitude of the speaker. In (1b), the Lango speaker wants the listener to convey a message to someone else; she is really indicating that it would be more convenient for the other person to travel than her. In the negative sentence (9a), the child's decision is imposed on the dog; the child has heard a noise and wants to investigate the source. And in (28), the speaker is letting us know her disappointment with the non-runner. She could have added the equivalent of 'So why didn't you?'

(28) *Lango*
Myero onwongo i-ngweci
must PI 2:SG-run
'You (SG) should have run.'

Thus *(o)myero)* can be interpreted in many contexts as the speaker's attitude to a particular situation or a desire for a particular outcome. It can also be used to mark the intention of the speaker, as in (12). The intention reading is most common when an *(o)myero* clause is embedded in a matrix clause with the verb *tamo* 'think' and a First Person Singular subject, as in (29); the interpretation is that the predication expressed in the subordinate clause is what the speaker intends to do, not what he must do.

Example (29) is taken from a passage in which an Acholi man is talking about his plans for the future. In terms of cultural expectations he should own land. Because he does not have any land, he intends to acquire it. Comparisons can be made here with English 'have to'. As discussed in Bybee et al. (1994), the obligation expression 'have to' may be interpreted as 'intention'. Here *omyero* is interpretated as 'intention'.

(29) *A-tamo ni omyero a-nong kaka-mo ma-ber*
1:SG-think COMP must 1:SG-find land-some REL-good
ma-ayela o-bi-bedo peke
REL-trouble *3-SG*-FUT-stay not
'I intend to find some good land where there is no trouble (i.e. no war).'

In (30), the speaker's intention is conveyed with an embedded *omyero* clause, but here the nominal *tam* 'idea' is used in the matrix clause rather than the verb *tamo*. The speaker produced the utterance in answer to a question as to whether he would accompany an acquaintance to a social function.

(30) *Onongo a-bedo ki tam ni omyero a-cit ki jo*
PI 1:SG-stay with idea that must 1:SG-go with people
ma a-bedo kwed-gi i-floor-na-ni
REL 1:SG-stay with- 3:PL LOC-floor-1:SG-DET
'I think I should go with the people from my floor.'
(='I intend to go with the people from my floor, not you')

4.4 *Epistemic interpretation of the obligation marker*

obligation modals in English can be used with epistemic functions, as discussed in, for example, Coates (1983). The form *(o)myero* may also be interpreted as having an epistemic function, indicating a qualification on the part of the speaker to the truth of the proposition. That is, it has the whole proposition in its scope. For example, an Acholi speaker answered a question about some people's location with (31), which states the most likely location for the people. The interpretation of o*myero* here is probability, and this is a similar interpretation to that of the English sentence 'The room must be empty' (Coates 1983), in which the speaker is noting the most likely condition of the room.

(31) *Omyero gin gu-cit ka-dwar*
must they 3:PL-go PROG-hunt
'They must have gone hunting.'

In Section 2, we discussed the fact that the speakers of Lango and Acholi may vary the word order of the modality particle and Past Imperfective marker to mark the speaker's commitment to the proposition. That is, the order with the Modal Particle following the Aspect marker is used when the speaker is commenting on the most likely outcome. In English, 'You must have done it' could be used if the speaker sees evidence that it has been done already, or if this is the most likely situation (as in 'The room must be empty'). With emphasis on 'must', it could express a sense of disbelief that you did not do it. In contrast, 'You should have done it' implies you did not, so has a counter-factual interpretation. In Lango and Acholi, the difference between expressing what the most likely situation is and what should have been done (but was not) is marked by the position of the Aspect marker, and listeners use this variation in ordering to interpret the intended message. Thus linguistic context affects the interpretation of the form *(o)myero*.

5. Verb sources for grammatical categories in the languages

Western Nilotic languages frequently use erstwhile verbal forms to mark grammatical categories. This can be observed in changes that have resulted in verbal affixes, as well as in constructions which reflect change in progress as one of the verbs in a combination takes on grammatical functions. The following examples illustrate some of the grammatical forms which have lexical verb sources

In Acholi , Lango and Alur *bi* 'future' is derived from the verb *bino* 'come' which retains its lexical meaning. The form *bi* appears between the subject pronoun and the lexical verb (e.g. *a-bi-camo* 'I will eat' from *a-bino camo* 'I come to eat'). In Lango, the long form, *bino,* can also be used as a future marker. As illustrated in (5), *ripo* 'obligation' is used between the lexical verb stem and the Subject Prefix in Alur. It could well have originated as a verb, as did *bi* 'future', but the verb is no longer in use, unlike *bino* 'come'.

Another example from Lango, Acholi and Alur is the morpheme *be,* used to indicate duration of an event; it is derived from *bedo* 'to stay, sit'. In Lango and Acholi, both the form *be* and the long form *bedo* are used, but in Alur the difference between *bedo* and *be* has been grammaticalized, so that the long form used in past contexts with an anterior function now contrasts with the short, which is used in present time contexts with a Durative function, as in the following examples.

(32) *Alur*

a. *A-be-sayo* *gwok* *para*
1:SG-DUR-look-for dog my
'I am looking for my dog'

b. *A-bedo* *ka-sayo* *gwok* *para*
1:SG-stay PROG-look for dog my
'I have been looking for my dog.'

These examples illustrate that the lexical semantics of a verb may change over time and the form may become re-interpreted as a marker of a grammatical category. The grammaticalized forms may become reduced (e.g. *bi* from *bino*, *be* from *bedo*, and, in Lango, *te* 'narrative marker' from *teko* 'to initiate'). Bybee (1985) and Bybee and Pagliuca (1985) discuss both phonetic erosion and fusion as features of the grammaticalization process. In Lango, Acholi and Alur, the forms *bi* and *be* are clearly well established as grams; not only do they have a grammatical function, they are also reduced in form and are affixed to the verb stem.

There is a difference, however, between developments which result in reduced verb forms as affixes and the development of *(o)myero* as a marker of modality. It is the impersonal form of *omyero* that is grammaticalized, whereas in the other examples cited the grammaticalized verb form appears following a Subject Prefix which varies according to the person and number of the subject of the clause. When a second verb is added to a prefix + verb combination, no major change is needed for the structure to develop into one form: prefix-gram-verb. However, for *omyero* to have become a grammatical marker, the following modifications had to be made: the prefix *o* lost its meaning as a subject marker, a verbal complement was added, and that verb carried a Subject Prefix.

A form which functions both as a gram and a lexical verb in Lango and Acholi is *onwongo* in Lango and *(o)nongo* in Acholi. (The cognate for the lexical verb is *nwango* 'find' in both Dhopadhola and Alur.)[5] There are some parallels between the development of *onwongo* as a grammatical marker and *omyero* as a modality marker. The form *onwongo* is the Third Person Singular Past form of 'find', but it is impersonal in use. It is used in past contexts and functions as a (past) imperfective aspect marker, marking on-going states or activities.

In (33), only the lexical meaning appears, but one sentence may include both meanings, aspectual and lexical, as in (34) and (35). Note that *nwongo* 'find' in both (33) and (35) lacks a Subject Prefix because it follows the narrative linker *te*; no verb following *te* has a Subject Prefix. *(O)nwongo* is similar to *omyero* in that it always precedes the lexical verb. However, there is a difference: while *(o)myero* has lost its lexical meaning, *(o)nwongo* has not. *Myero* has lost its prefix for Lango speakers and also for some Acholi speakers, but o*nwongo* has retained the *o* prefix in Lango and its presence is variable in Acholi.

(33) *Te-nwongo wi nyinyang iyi pii*
NAR-find head crocodile in water
'Then he found the head of a crocodile in the water.'

(34) *Ikare-moro onwongo tye awobi-moro ame*
time-some PI be boy-some REL
onwongo tye kede ogwalogwal-ere a gwok-o o-nwongo
PI be with frog POSS REL dog-DET 3:SG-find
'Once there was a boy who was with his frog that the dog found.'

(35) *Bongi ame onwongo tye idi ot o-bobolo tende me*
clothes REL PI be middle house 3:SG-throw far for
neno ka ogwalogwal-ca nyo tye i-te-re, ento
see if frog-DET maybe be LOC-under-3SG, but
te-nwongo-ni pe
NAR-found-3:SG NEG
'He threw the clothes that were on the floor to see if the frog was under them, but he (the boy) did not find it (the frog).'

To summarize, we have given a number of examples to illustrate that Western Nilotic languages commonly use lexical verbs as the sources for grammatical markers. However, the sources become reinterpreted in one of two types of constructions, one with two verbs with the same subject, and the other an impersonal construction. Sometimes the lexical meaning is retained and sometimes lost. Both of these possibilities have been discussed as possible outcomes in grammaticalization processes. Traugott (1989), for example, argues that when a new function develops, it may exist alongside the old. Another possible outcome is that the new function takes over and the old function is lost.

6. Use of the lexical verb for 'want' for agent-oriented modalities

As discussed in Section 4, *(o)myero* 'must' may also be interpreted as 'need to'. However, another verb which may be used to express obligation or necessity is *mito* 'want', as illustrated in (36). The context for this example is that the speaker has been told he has to cross the river, so he is not expressing an internal desire; rather, the speaker is obliged to get to the other side.[6] Note that *mito*, like *myero* 'must', does not carry a Subject Prefix in Lango.

(36) *Mito nen ni a-ngola kulu*
must see COMP 1:SG-cross river
'It seems I have to/must cross the river.'

Similarly, in Alur, which marks obligation with *omako*, the verb for 'want' is used for 'need to', in the impersonal form *omito*. Consider the following Alur sentences in which the use of the lexical verb *mito* 'want' is illustrated as well as the modal use of *omito*. The modal form *omito* appears in front of a lexical verb which carries a Subject Prefix. However, as a lexical verb *mito* carries a subject pronoun, as in (c). The contrast between (c) and (d) captures the difference in meaning between the two functions: in (c), the speaker desires to run, but in (d) there is a need to run (so that he is not late for class); time is the physical constraint here. In comparison, in (a) the need to work is motivated by the rewards that will follow.

(37) *Alur*

a. *Omito a-tim matek*
need 1:SG-work hard
'I need to work hard'.

b. *Omito nango a-cam*
need PAST 1:SG-eat
'I should have eaten.'

c. *A-mito ringo*
1:SG-want run
'I want to run.'

d. *Omito a-ringo*
need 1:SG-run
'I need to run.'

In DhoLuo, *dwaro* is the lexical verb for 'want', not *mito*, and *dwaro* can also be used to express Necessity, but it is not grammaticalized for this function, as in Lango and Alur, in which the impersonal form is used. The context alone determines whether the interpretation is 'want' or 'need' since the verb carries a Subject Prefix for both interpretations, as illustrated in (a) and (b); the prefix is determined by the person and number of the subject of the predication. In (a), the speaker is not reporting what his friend desires; he is giving his own view that his friend has few possessions and needs to obtain a few more basic necessities to improve his quality of life. The speaker in (b) is not reporting what he wants to do; he has to tell a story because I asked him to. This was part of a session for which the speaker would be paid for his time; he had indicated that he did not want to tell a story since he couldn't remember one.

Note that with both senses (want and need) the verb can have either a nominal or a verbal complement. In (38a), a nominal complement is used, while (b) contains a verbal complement. In other contexts, the verb in each sentence could be interpreted as 'want'.

(38) a. *O-dwaro gik mangeny*
3:SG-need thing many
'He needs many things.'

b. *A-dwaro gano-nu sigana moro ka*
1:SG-need tell-2:SG story certain here
'I need to tell you this story.'

We can compare the use of English 'want' to express what someone needs to do. For example, in 'You want to go to the next counter', which is a response that could be made when someone asks for a particular service at the wrong counter, the interpretation is that you need to go to the next counter. Another context in which 'want' is used with the interpretation 'need to' is a school report on which a teacher might write that a student wants to work harder, meaning that the student needs to. Similarly, when someone says 'I want a pen', it would be interpreted as 'I have need of a pen' in a context in which that person is required to sign a form. It is context which determines whether there are physical conditions present which lead to the 'need' interpretation of 'want', or whether the utterance expresses someone's desire and, perhaps, intention (see Bybee et al. 1994, chapter 6).

As illustrated above, in the Western Nilotic languages there is evidence of grammaticalization for the 'need to' sense in two of the languages, Lango and Alur, but not DhuLuo, in which context alone determines which interpretation to make. This suggests that the 'need to' interpretation has been derived from 'want', following a regular pattern of change in the language group, a pattern of deriving grams from lexical verbs (often impersonal in form). The 'want' interpretation might be newer than that of necessity, but there is no clear evidence which is the older meaning. If 'want' is the newer meaning, it is the newer meaning which is retained in the lexical verb, while the older meaning has been grammaticized in two of the languages. Both senses are retained, but they are formally distinguished.

7. Conclusions

It can be fruitful in a study of grammaticalization to examine diachronic developments in related languages since changes in meaning and functions for lexical items and their cognates can be compared. While languages may be closely related and share a very high percentage of vocabulary items, they may develop different forms for marking grammatical categories although there may be similarities in the semantics of the lexical sources for these categories.

The only languages in the Western Nilotic group to have a verbal affix to express the modality of obligation is Dhophadola. Three of the other five use particles which have developed from lexical verbs, while DhoLuo uses a number of forms which have developed from lexical verbs. In fact, lexical verbs seem to be the predominant source of grams relating to tense/aspect/modality systems in the five Western Nilotic languages.

There is common development in Lango and Acholi of the impersonal form of the verb 'to be fitting, suitable' into a marker of obligation, with the loss of the lexical semantics of the verb. However, the form is more grammaticized in Lango since the impersonal prefix has been dropped, while it is variable in Acholi. In contrast, the impersonal form of the verb 'to hold, catch' has developed into a obligation marker in Alur, but its function as a lexical verb is retained.

The contexts of use for *(o)myero* reveal that it does not always carry a Strong obligation sense. It is in those contexts in which an authority figure is speaking to a subordinate, or when social customs are being discussed that the obligation interpretation is made. In some contexts, the form is interpreted as a marker of Necessity or of Intention, and it can also have an epistemic interpretation. Such synchronic variation is indicative of change in progress with the obligation marker gradually taking on other functions as its meaning generalizes.

Bybee et al. (1994) discuss four semantic notions in the set of agent-oriented modality: obligation, necessity, ability and desire. In the Western Nilotic languages there is a close connection between the notions of obligation, necessity and desire in terms of the forms used to express them. However, the forms used to express ability in the languages are distinct. In Lango and Acholi, ability is currently expressed with a subject-inflected verb which takes an Infinitive complement, as illustrated in (13) and 14), unlike the obligation marker, which is derived from an impersonal construction.

As illustrated above, several paths of development in a language may result in different forms having interpretations associated with agent-oriented modality. The lexical verb for 'want' is also used to express necessity or obligation in three of the languages. While two of the languages use the impersonal form, DhoLuo uses a verb inflected with Subject Prefix, and it is the context alone that determines whether the verb is to be interpreted as desire or necessity.

Language-specific patterns can be detected in the paths of development. For example, the grammaticalization of particles is more advanced in Lango, in that both *mito* and *myero* lack prefixes, although the former is still a lexical verb when used with Subject Prefixes while *myero* is not.

ABBREVIATIONS

NAR	narrative marker	PL	plural
DEM	demonstrative	POSS	possessive
DET	determiner	PROG	progressive
COMP	complementizer	REF	reflexive
DUR	durative	REL	relative marker
LOC	locative	SG	singular
NEG	negative	SUBJ	subjunctive
PI	past imperfective		

NOTES

1 Unless otherwise stated, the data reported in this paper were collected from native speakers of the languages. Many of the examples are taken from discourse, rather than from elicited sentences. The data were collected in Uganda in 1992, in Kenya in 1990, and between 1981 and 1992 from students who have been studying in Australia for short periods. Speakers have ranged in age from 20-38 years. Funding for the research has been from an Australian Research Council grant.

2. Note that the Plural forms of the verb in Lango take *o* as the subject prefix (as does the third singular) rather than *wa* '1 PL', *wu* '2 PL' and *gi* '3 PL' as used in Acholi. Thus there is potential ambiguity if there is no overt subject, and Lango speakers often add a third person plural pronoun plus a definite suffix ('this') *following* the verb as in the examples given below. Thus a third option for sentence (8) is given in (c) below:

a. *Ka o-poto gin-i i-pii-ni*
when 3:PL-fal they-DET LOC-water-DET
'When they fell into the water.'

b. *O-tye o-neno gin-i i-wang dirija*
3:PL-be 3 PL-see they-DET LOC-eye window
'They were looking out of the window.'

c. *Onwongo myero o-bol gin-i odilo*
PI must 3:SG-throw they-DET ball
'They would have thrown the ball.'

The prefix *o* has generally replaced *e* as the form for third singular in Acholi and Lango for past contexts (currently *e* is optionally used in non-switch-reference contexts only). Non-past has a zero prefix in Acholi, but *a* is used in Lango. In *past* contexts, the form *gu* is used for Third Plural in Acholi. This is derived from *gi+o*. For some Acholi speakers, when the overt third plural pronoun (*gin*) is used, there is the option of using the prefix *o* on the verb instead of *gu*.

3. Use of the Subjunctive form depends on the syntactic and semantic context. For a number of lexical items the Subjunctive is used for resulting states (such as 'is stuck', 'is dry' and 'is broken'), and for others, the short form is used as the intransitive. It can also function as a nominal, so it is ambiguous as to whether *amito cam* is 'I want to eat' or I want food'. For most verbs the long form is used for both transitive and intransitive sentences. The final *o* is most likely an old marker of transitivity since it can be analyzed, diachronically, as an object marker. Note that it takes the pronominal object position. Synchronically, however, its function is a verbal marker, and is not restricted to transitivity.

4. The anterior aspect marker is *onwongo* in Lango but *onongo* or *nongo* in Acholi. Past tense is marked by three low tones on the verb in both languages.

5. In Dhopadhola *nwango* is used with past reference, and in Alur, *nwango* 'find' contrasts with *nango* which has past reference. Compare (a) and (b) from Alur:

a. *Koth o-daro bino*
rain 3:SG-finish come
'The rain has come.'

b. *Nango koth o-daro bino*
past rain 3:SG-finish come
'The rain had already come.'

6. Bybee et al. (1994, chapter 6) discuss problems with having both a 'must' and a 'want to' reading for one form since their hypothesis predicts that no gram should display obligation and desire as alternative uses.

REFERENCES

Bavin, E.L. 1982. "Aspects of Morphological and Syntactic Divergence in Lango and Acholi". *Studies in African Linguistics* 13 (3).231-248

Bavin, E.L. 1990. "The ki-V Construction: Development of a Resultative". *La Trobe University Working Papers* 2.29-42

Bybee, J. 1985. *Morphology: A Study of the Relation between Meaning and Form.* Amsterdam & Philadelphia: John Benjamins

Bybee, J. & Pagliuca, W. 1985. "Cross-Linguistic Comparison and the Development of Grammatical Meaning". *Historical Semantics, Historical Word Formation* ed. by J. Fisiak. Berlin: Mouton.

Bybee, J., R. Perkins & W. Pagliuca 1994. *The Evolution of Grammar: Tense , Aspect & Modality*, Ch. 6. Chicago: University of Chicago Press.

Coates, J. 1983. *The Semantics of Modal Auxiliaries.* London: Croom Helm

Crazzolara, J.P. 1955, [c 1938]. *Acholi Grammar.* Oxford: Oxford University Press.

Driberg, J.H. 1923. *The Lango, a Nilotic Tribe of Uganda.* London: J. Fischer Unwin.

Fleischman, S. 1989. "Temporal Distance: A Basic Linguistic Metaphor". *Studies in Language* 13.1-50.

Gregerson, E.A. 1962. "Luo: a Grammar". Yale University PhD dissertation.

Huntingford, G.W.B.1959. *Elementary Lessons in Dho-Luo.* London: School of Oriental and African Studies.

Kitching, Rev. A.L. 1907. *An Outline Grammar of the Gang Language.* London: Society for the Promotion of Christian Knowledge.

Ladefoged, P., R. Grick & C. Criper 1968. *Language in Uganda*, Oxford: Oxford University Press.

Malo, S. 1952. *Dholuo Without Tears.* Kisumu: Anyange Press.

Omondi, L. Ndong'a. 1982. *The Major Syntactic Structures of DhoLuo.* Berlin: Dietrich Reimer Verlag.

Ringe, P.C.1948, *A Simple Alur Grammar.* Eagle Language Study Series.

Stafford, R.L. 1967. *An Elementary Luo Grammar.* Nairobi: Oxford University Press.

Traugott, E. 1989. "On the Rise of Epistemic Meaning in English: An Example of Subjectification in Semantic Change". *Language* 65.31-55.

The Gestural Expression of Modality in ASL

Sherman Wilcox and Phyllis Wilcox
University of New Mexico

...The essence of language is human activity — activity on the part of one individual to make himself understood by another, and activity on the part of that other to understand what was in the mind of the first ...

O. Jespersen, The Philosophy of Grammar (1924: 17)

1. Issues in the linguistic description of ASL

For the most part, modern linguistic descriptions of American Sign Language (ASL) have relied on formalist linguistic theories. The predominant effort has been to demonstrate that ASL is indeed a language and can be described using theories developed for spoken languages. Further, it is typically claimed that the findings of ASL linguistic research lend support to these theories of language.

These theories incorporate several powerful assumptions about the goals and expectations of linguistic investigation (cf. Langacker 1991: 507–514). One assumption is that grammar is independent of meaning. From this assumption follows what Givón (1989: 94–95) calls three "pre-empirical postulates":

(1) Language is a separate module of the mind/brain, not part of 'general cognition';
(2) Structuralism in the analysis of language; that is, language structure can be analyzed independently of its communicative function;
(3) The sign-relation between the linguistic code and its mental designatum is arbitrary, unlike the obvious iconicity seen in pre-human communication.

Another assumption is that the mental is independent from the physical. This leads to the view that linguistic units are mental things that cannot be identified with a set of articulatory, physical characteristics (Fowler 1986: 9). This view is stated by Givón (1989: 95) as another pre-empirical postulate:

(4) Some abstract, idealized entity — be it langue or competence — is the 'object' of linguistic analysis.

Little effort has been expended by signed language linguists in questioning the underlying assumptions of these linguistic theories (S. Wilcox 1990). This seems especially unfortunate because signed languages would appear to be unique, natural "laboratories" for testing the validity of these assumptions, e.g., the obvious presence of iconicity in signed languages needs to be examined. We will suggest in Section 3 that the predominant strategy has been either to ignore iconicity in signed languages or to explain it away. The functional significance of iconicity in ASL has received little if any attention.

The only way for signed and spoken languages to be compared is by positing structures and rules separate from their physical implementation. Indeed, a major premise of those who embrace formalist linguistic theories, such as Poizner, Klima and Bellugi (1987), is that "language is amodal, taking a form which is independent of channel or of behavioral system" (Kimura 1988: 375). Thus, they conclude that "language, independent of its transmission mechanisms, emerges in a ... linguistically driven manner" (Poizner, Klima, & Bellugi, 1987: 23).

One problem with this position, as noted by Kimura (1988), is that it assumes that the organization of language is independent of its motor programming. Another is that it ignores the deep historical and neurological linkages between oral and manual gestures (cf. Kimura 1976, 1979), and between human movement, cognition, and language (Edelman 1987, 1989). Finally, it is difficult to understand how language under such a view — whether spoken or signed — could have ever developed in the human species. For example, commenting on the notion that language can be separated from behavioral systems and transmission mechanisms, Studdert-Kennedy (1986: 101–102) remarks:

> Characteristic motor systems have evolved for locomotion, predation, consumption, mating. Matching perceptual systems have evolved to guide the animal in these activities. The selection pressures shaping each species' perceptuomotor capacities have come, in the first instance, from physical

> properties of the world. By contrast, these perceptuomotor capacities themselves must have played a crucial role in the form of a social species' communication system. [...] Certainly, specialized neuroanatomical signaling devices have often evolved, but they have typically done so by modifying pre-existing structures just enough for them to perform their new function without appreciable loss of their old. [...] Language has evolved within the constraints of pre-existing perceptual and motor systems. We surrender much of our power to understand that evolution, if we disregard the properties of those systems.

The viability of approaches which take into consideration language's physical substance, as constrained by its implementation in human perceptual and motor systems, has been demonstrated for spoken languages (Browman & Goldstein 1990; Bybee 1985, 1994; Fowler 1986; Givón 1984; Mowrey & Pagliuca 1988). We believe such approaches also will prove fruitful in understanding signed languages, and ultimately will be a key link in unifying theories of signed and spoken language on a substantive, i.e. non-formalist, foundation.

It seems to us that language is not dualistically separated from its physical realization, but deeply rooted in its bodily basis.[1] Neither is grammar independent of meaning. Such a view is compatible with cognitive or functional theories of language developed in works such as Bybee (1985), Deane (1991, 1993), Givón (1989), Lakoff (1987), and Langacker (1987, 1991).

For example, Deane (1991) argues for a cognitive, nonmodular theory of language based on an elaboration of George Lakoff's (1987: 283) Spatialization of Form Hypothesis. Deane suggests that several predictions regarding the relation between grammar and cognition follow from the Spatialization of Form Hypothesis (363–64):

(i) According to the hypothesis, the acquisition of grammatical competence occurs when linguistic information is routed to and processed by spatial centers in the brain.

(ii) Specifically, it is claimed that linguistic expressions are processed as if they were objects with internal structural configurations. That is, they are processed in terms of certain basic image schemas, namely part-whole and linkage schemas critical to the recognition of the configurations which define complex physical objects.

(iii) But as Johnson (1987) argues at length, image schemas are basically embodied schemas, high level schemas which function as cognitive models of the body and its interaction with the environment.

In other words, the Spatialization of Form hypothesis treats grammar as a form of image-schematic thought in which words, phrases, and sentences are endowed with an abstract structure grounded in immediate bodily experience of physical objects. It therefore predicts an association between grammar and such cognitive abilities as object recognition, spatial structure, and body awareness, especially modeling bodily movement and position in space.

Stokoe (1991), reacting to current formalist approaches to ASL phonology, has proposed a view of signed language phonological structure which he calls semantic phonology.

> [Semantic phonology] invites one to look at a sign — i.e., a word of a primary sign language — as a marriage of a noun and a verb. In semantic terminology, appropriate here, the sign is an agent-verb construction. The agent is so called because it is what acts (in signing as in generative semantics), and the verb is what the agent does. [...] Semantic-phonological, or s-p, verbs are, like common verbs, transitive or intransitive. For example: when a signer of American Sign Language signifies 'yes', the sign agent (i.e. the signer's active arm including the hand) flexes at the wrist; it is intransitive, it has no object, it acts on no patient. But if the signer signifies 'stupid', the agent action continues until it strikes the forehead; the s-p verb in this sign is thus transitive: it has an object (the grammatical term); or it takes a patient (the semantic term).

Integrating the proposals of Deane and Stokoe, we suggest that human arms and hands are — both phylogenetically and ontogenetically — prototypical and embodied complex objects. Semantic phonology describes the "internal structural configurations" of these objects as they are used to produce a natural language — in this case, American Sign Language.

Thus, by using the phrase "gestural expression" in our title, we wish to propose a theoretical position which makes the following assumptions:

(1) Physical gestures are the means by which all languages are realized — the substance of both signed and spoken languages lies in their gestural expression;

(2) Linguistic theory must acknowledge the physically embodied grounding of linguistic competence — in a very real sense, the body is in the mind (Johnson, 1987), the essence of language is bodily activity;

(3) When physical gestures are used to represent mental designata, there is the likelihood that an iconic or isomorphic relationship will exist between the two — not only at the lexical level, but also at the propositional and pragmatic/discourse levels.

In the next section, we will examine several modal verbs in ASL. In section 3, we will tentatively explore the iconic relationship between ASL modals and their gestural expression.

2. Modality in ASL[2]

The expression of mood and modality has not been extensively explored in ASL. Long (1918) in his chapter on auxiliary verbs briefly describes the production and semantics of the following modals: CAN; CAN'T; MAY (MAYBE, PERHAPS); MAY; SHOULD (OUGHT); MUST (NEED, HAVE TO); HAVE (FINISHED); WILL (SHALL); WON'T.[3]

Fischer and Gough (1978) briefly mention modals in their discussion of ASL verbs, but do not deal with them semantically. Padden (1988) also briefly mentions the modals CAN, WILL, SHOULD, and MUST, but likewise does not discuss in any depth the semantics of these words, focussing instead on what types of nominals may precede modals. Finally, the semantics of modals is typically dealt with in only a cursory way in most ASL textbooks. Questions of strength, of which modals can express deontic and which can express epistemic modality, and other subtle semantic and pragmatic factors are left to students to discover on their own.

2.1. *Root modality*

Strong obligation in ASL is expressed with the lexical modal MUST (Figure 1a). Weak obligation is expressed with the lexical modal SHOULD (Figure 2b).

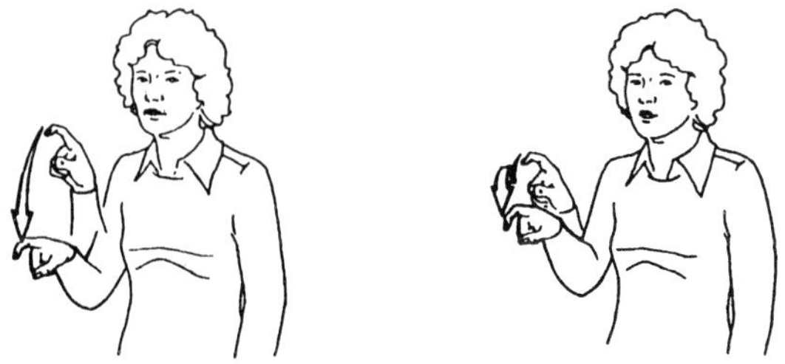

(a) MUST (b) SHOULD

Figure 1: *Modals of obligation*

Long (1918) describes the meanings and production of several ASL words. This text is a rich source of etymological and historical information about ASL (cf. Frishberg, 1975). We will cite Long throughout this paper, primarily as evidence for phonological change.

Long (1918: 26) offers the following descriptions of SHOULD and MUST:

> **Should, Ought,** indicating duty.— Press the crooked forefinger of the right "G" hand against the lips and then move toward side and downward as in "must" (see below). Or,
> (2) Indicate by the signs "better" and "must." Better is signed as follows: Place the end of the right open hand pointing toward the left, palm against the mouth; draw away toward the side, assuming the position of "A" and lifting it to a level with the head. "Must," see below.
> **Must, Need, Have to.** — Crook the forefinger of the right "G" hand, pointing it downward, and press the hand down some distance with more or less force. Sometimes the motion is repeated several times.

The forms described by Long for SHOULD are no longer used. While MUST is essentially unchanged from this earlier form, SHOULD is now made with reduplicated flexion and extension of the wrist. This phonological relationship (single, punctual movement versus reduplicated, cyclic movement) will reappear in other modals and will be explored in more detail in section 3.

According to Boyes-Braem (1981), the forms MUST and SHOULD are related to the Old French Sign Language[4] form of NECESSARY (IL FAUT), in which a G hand (extended index finger) pointed firmly down toward the ground in front of the signer. This could also mean ICI (RIGHT-HERE) or THIS-GROUND. Boyes-Braem argues that the more abstract concept 'necessary' is assigned an abstract deictic handshape (the X, or bent index finger) in ASL.

Modals can occur in three positions: at the end of the verb phrase[5] as in (1), preceding the verb as in (2), or preceding and at the end of the verb phrase as in (3) (Humphries, Padden & O'Rourke, 1980).

(1) $\overline{\text{TELEPHONE NUMBER}}^{t}$, WOMAN SHE-GIVE-ME SHOULD SHE
'The woman should give me the telephone number.'

(2) $\overline{\text{TELEPHONE NUMBER}}^{t}$, WOMAN SHOULD SHE-GIVE-ME SHE
'The woman should give me the telephone number.'

(3) I MUST WIN RACE MUST I
'I must win the race.'

Necessity is indicated in ASL with the use of the word MUST.[6]

Figure 2: CAN

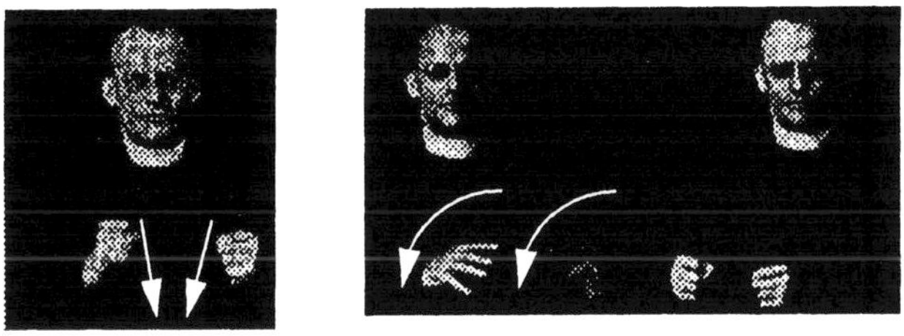

Figure 3: *Old ASL* CAN *and* STRONG

(4) I MUST BOOK I
'I need a book.'

Ability is indicated by the word CAN (Figure 2). CAN is historically related to STRONG as demonstrated in Figure 3 (Higgins, 1923). Long's (1918: 25) description of CAN is the same:

> **Can**, expressing possibility, power, etc.— Hold the "S" hands out in front, elbows against sides, and let the hands drop a little way with a jerk.

CAN can indicate either physical or mental ability:

t
(5) RIDE BICYCLE, I CAN I.
'I can ride a bicycle.'

q
(6) UNDERSTAND ME, CAN YOU HUH?
'Can you understand me?'

Figure 4: CAN'T

CAN is also used to indicate root possibility in ASL:

(7) ___q___
TOMORROW YOU CAN DRIVE YOU?
'Can you drive tomorrow?'
___y___
I CAN I.
'Sure, I can do that.'

Example (8) below shows MUST and CAN being used in these more generalized root senses.

(8) CULTURE MUST HAVE FIVE ...
'Culture must exhibit five [characteristics]'
___cond___
HAVE ALL CULTURE CAN CALL INDEX
'If something possesses all of these characteristics, then we can call it culture.'

CAN is negated either with NOT and negative markers as described above, or with the suppletive form CAN'T (Figure 4).

2.2. *Epistemic modality*

Epistemic possibility can be indicated in ASL with the lexical items POSSIBLE (Figure 5a) and MAYBE (Figure 5b). Long (1918) related the word MAYBE ('may,' 'maybe,' or 'perhaps') to the physical act of comparing weights by using the hands as a balance scale:

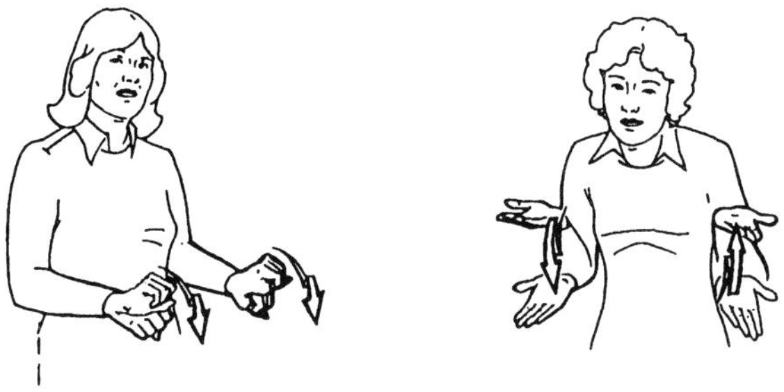

(a) POSSIBLE (b) MAYBE

Figure 5: *Modals of weak inference*

> **May, Maybe, Perhaps**, indicating probability.— Hold out both open hands in front straight from the sides, palms up; balance the hands up and down alternately several times like the balances of a pair of scales.

POSSIBLE is related to CAN; the phonological relationship parallels that of MUST and SHOULD. MUST and CAN are articulated with strong, single movements; POSSIBLE and SHOULD are articulated with weaker, reduplicated movements. Example (9) demonstrates the use of POSSIBLE and MAYBE.

cond q

(9) HE STUDY "over & over again", PASS TEST WILL HE?
'If he studies really hard will he pass the test?'
POSSIBLE.
'It's possible.'

Example (9) could also be answered with MAYBE: 'He might pass the test.'

The modal MAYBE is negated by using NOT accompanied by the negative marker, a set of facial expressions or Non-Manual Signals (NMSs) including a negative (side-to-side) headshake and squeezing the eyebrows together; the negative marker can also be used alone to negate MAYBE. Thus, the answer to example (9) above could be either of the following:

n

(10) MAYBE NOT
'He might not.'

n

(11) NOT POSSIBLE
'It's really not possible.'

Figure 6: IMPOSSEBLE

In addition, there is the single lexical item IMPOSSIBLE (Figure 6). IMPOSSIBLE is a stronger negation than NOT POSSIBLE; it indicates that the proposition is not only not very likely but absolutely impossible.

There is also a variant of CAN'T (Figure 4) that means 'impossible'. It is signed with two small, repeated movements. IMPOSSIBLE (Figure 6) is much more commonly seen.

Epistemic modalities in ASL are expressed with lexical items such as FEEL, SEEM and OBVIOUS (Figure 7)[7], in other constructions such as questions, and with particular NMSs. For example, in discussing a missing item in one's apartment, the dialogue in example (12) could occur (from Cokely & Baker 1980).

(12)
gaze lf ——— q
FEEL SOMEONE 1-CL-rt 'person walks by' NOTICE-TO GO-INTO SWIPE YOU[8]
'Do you suppose someone walked by, noticed it, and just went in and stole it?'

n ——— nodding
NOT-KNOW SEEM+
'I don't know, apparently that's what happened.'

FEEL in the epistemic sense is related to the word FEEL used for the physical sense. Typically, the latter is produced with a single upward movement, while the former uses shorter movements, often reduplicated, and a distinct set of NMSs (this relationship is discussed in more detail in section 3).

SEEM is historically related to the words MIRROR and COMPARE, words related to physical resemblance. In its old form SEEM retained some of its "traditional" or lexical iconicity: "Bring the open right hand up in front toward one side with the thumb edge toward self; turn the hand so as to

(a) FEEL (b) SEEM (c) OBVIOUS

Figure 7: *Modals of inference*

present the palm toward self and *fix the eyes upon it*" (Long, 1918: 63, our italics). Compare this description of SEEM to Higgins' (1923: 92) almost identical description of MIRROR: "vertical palm held at side of face and is gazed into as if into a mirror." As we will see below, Frishberg (1975) claims that this type of iconicity is eroding.

OBVIOUS is related to the ASL word BRIGHT ('bright' or 'light'). Compared to BRIGHT it is made with less stressed, reduced movement. In its epistemic sense it appears in constructions such as:

(13) HE RICH, OBVIOUS

It is worth noting that all of these modals are related to ASL words which denote physical activity and perception:

(i) physical strength (CAN)
(ii) judging the physical weight of an object (MAYBE)
(iii) the physical sense of feeling (FEEL)
(iv) physical resemblance, as reflected in a mirror (SEEM)
(v) the bright light needed for clear visual perception (OBVIOUS)

This relationship has been noted by others (Sweetser 1990), and clearly relies on a metaphorical mapping between embodied, physically-grounded source domains and mental, abstract target domains. The widespread use of conceptual and experiential metaphor in ASL grammar is explored more fully in P. Wilcox (1993).

Finally, we should point out that the deontic modals MUST and SHOULD are not used epistemically in ASL. Thus, the sentence:

(14) *YOU MUST TIRED YOU

cannot mean 'You must be tired' in the epistemic sense. Likewise, the sentence, "We should be finished by 5 PM" in ASL would not use the lexical item SHOULD.

ASL epistemic sentences may also be produced without any of the lexical items discussed above. One way in which this may be accomplished is with tag questions:

q

(15) YOU WORK HARD, YOU TIRED YOU, RIGHT?

In (15), the word RIGHT is accompanied by NMSs which indicate more than a yes/no question. They carry the implication, "Judging by the fact that worked so hard, you must be tired now — I am correct in making that inference, am I not?"

A similar construction can use a generalized tag question marker:

(16) [Two people are looking at a person passing by wearing expensive clothes.]

wh+y

HE RICH, HUH?

'He must be rich.'

Example (16) is accompanied by at least two distinct NMSs: (1) continual head nodding, and (2) a set of NMSs similar to those used as the WH marker, which includes squinting the eyes and squeezing the eyebrows together.[9] Such constructions are like those presented by Givón (1989: 147) in his discussion of non-discreteness in assertions. He notes that "various tags may be used to temper the strength of R-assertions. Such tags are often augmented with intonation, as well as with various irrealis operators."

It may also be possible for epistemic modality to be indicated without any lexical marker. In such instances, the NMSs used in conjunction with the epistemics are enough to convey degree of confidence in an asserted proposition. For example, consider the following situation.

(17) [Two people enter a meeting in a basement room early in the morning. It is cloudy and cold. At lunch, person A turns to person B and says, "Do you think it's raining outside?" Person B answers:]

wh+y
RAIN
'Surely it's raining.'
NMSs (head nodding, eyes squinting, eyebrows squeezed together)

The NMSs that accompany (16) and (17) are quite similar to those that accompany imperative sentences. For example, consider example (18) in Figure 8. The imperative NMSs that accompany the verb GIVE include a sharp head nod, a slight leaning forward of the torso, squinting the eyes, and squeezing the eyebrow together (Humphries, Padden, & O'Rourke 1980). We

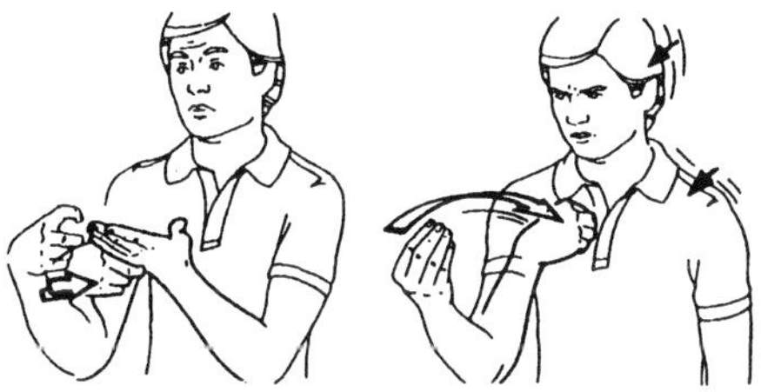

t
(18) TICKET, YOU-GIVE-ME!
'Give me the ticket!'

Figure 8: NMS's *in imperatives*

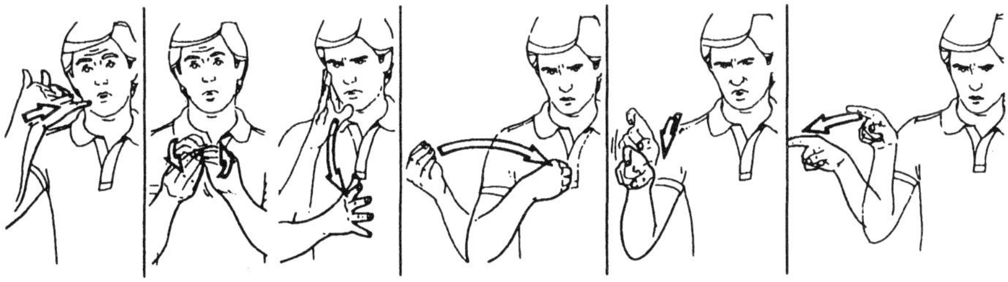

t
(19) TELEPHONE NUMBER, WOMAN SHE-GIVE-ME, SHOULD SHE.
'The woman should give me the telephone number.'

Figure 9: NMS's *in deontic modality*

(20) $\overline{\text{YOUR CAR, WHERE?}}^{\text{whq}}$
'Where is your car?'

Figure 10: NMS's *in WH-questions*

also see similar NMSs in the expression of deontic modalities such as example (19) in Figure 9. Clearly related are the NMSs that accompany WH-questions (see example (20) in Figure 10).

Thus, we find quite similar NMSs used in the expression of the following functions in ASL:

(A) imperative; obligation; request for information; epistemic probability

In the first two (imperative and obligation), the NMSs must accompany lexical material (in imperatives the focus of the NMSs is on the imperative verb; in deontic modals the entire phrase). In WH-questions, the NMSs may accompany a phrase containing a WH-word, as in (20), or a generalized question word usually glossed as "WHAT" (it can mean 'what', 'where', 'who', 'huh' etc.) Given the proper context, NMSs alone (i.e. without a wh-word) can signal a WH-question (21). As we have seen above, in the expression of epistemic probability, these NMSs may be used with modals or alone.

(21) A: YESTERDAY ME BUY TICKET ME.
'Yesterday I bought tickets.'
B: TICKET?
'What tickets ... for what?'

We suggest that the relationships described in (A) are an expression of *interpersonal transitivity*. This in turn is related to the grammatical expression

Figure 11: WILL

of certainty, power, and politeness (Givón 1989; Brown & Levinson 1978). Parallel to (A), the scale of interpersonal transitivity runs from (i) to (iv) below:[10]

(i) I command you to do something: "Sit down!"
(ii) I obligate you to do something: "You must sit down."
(iii) I make a polite request (this indirect speech act is accomplished by means of a request for information in form): "Why don't you sit down?"
(iv) I infer something about you: "You must be tired."

2.3. *Intention, prediction, and volition*

The final modal we will discuss is WILL. Long (1918: 27) attributes only a future sense to WILL:

Will and **Shall**, indicating future.— Hold the right open hand pointing straight out and elevated to a level with the **should**, and push it straight forward the length of the arm.

WILL can also be used in intentional (22), predictive (23), and volitional senses[11] (24):

(22) SEND-YOU LETTER, WILL ME.
'I will send you the letter.'
(23) HE RECOVER WILL HE.
'He will get well.'
(24) HE ACCEPT RESPONSIBILITY WILL HE.
'He will accept responsibility.'

Figure 12: Modern WON'T

Negation of WILL depends on the sense. The intentional and predictive senses can be negated with the ASL negation markers described above, or with expressions of speaker uncertainty or doubt. Thus, negative versions of (23) are:

(25) HE RECOVER, NOT.

(26) HE RECOVER, DOUBT ME.

The negation of a volitional such as (24), however, requires WON'T:

(27) HE ACCEPT RESPONSIBILITY WON'T HE.

WON'T has undergone extensive phonological restructuring since it was described by Long (1918: 27):

> **Won't.**— Hold the right "S" hand out in front from the side, jerk the hand back, doubling the elbow.

In 1918, WON'T was clearly related to CAN (see Figure 3). The upward motion of WON'T was the result of forearm flexion (the strong contraction of the bicep muscles) — the opposite motion from that used in CAN (forearm extension). Today, WON'T is signed with a different handshape and in a different location, beginning with the hand in upper neutral space in front of the signer's face and ending with the hand over the shoulder (Figure 12).

The change in handshape (from "S" to "open A") has brought modern WON'T into a set of relations with other words denoting negation. Thus, the open-A handshape of modern WON'T parallels the open-A of NOT and DENY/TURN-DOWN.[12]

The change in location has brought modern WON'T into a set of relations with words which use the time line in ASL (Frishberg & Gough, 1973). The time line is a line along the horizontal plane near the signer's ear and cheek used consistently for many signs indicating time other than the present. WILL and TOMORROW move forward along the time line (see Figure 11); YESTERDAY, BEFORE, LONG-AGO are examples of signs that move toward the signer's back.[13] This is not to say that WON'T has acquired a temporal sense. It has resulted, however, in WILL and WON'T taking part in a nicely iconic relationship: volitional WILL moves forward (as does future WILL) while WON'T jerks backward.

Finally, it should be noted that the gestural component of old WON'T and modern WON'T are the same, even though the change in location has resulted in a change from upward movement to backward movement: both are produced with forearm flexion (bicep contraction).[14]

3. Iconicity in ASL

Judging from the literature on ASL, the existence of iconicity in this language has been viewed as something of an embarrassment to ASL linguists. This is not hard to understand, given that from Saussure to Chomsky, formal linguistics has maintained that to the extent that a communication system exhibits iconicity, it is less a human language. More recently, Givón (1984, 1989) and Haiman (1984) argue against this position for spoken languages, suggesting instead that linguistic form is often motivated by iconic principles. For example, Haiman (1984: 1) writes, "linguistic forms are frequently the way they are because, like diagrams, they resemble the conceptual structures they are used to convey."

It is difficult to deny the existence of iconicity in signed languages. Few sign language linguists would, however, ascribe the deeply significant role to iconicity that functional and cognitive linguists have in spoken languages. Rather, many ASL linguists have taken a different approach, the intent of which appears to be to explain away iconicity in ASL. They claim that although iconicity may be present in ASL, it is eroding over time; it plays no role in the acquisition, processing, or storage of language; and grammatical processes routinely act to override and submerge it.

Frishberg (1975) argues that historical change acts to diminish iconicity and heighten the arbitrary nature of ASL. We would point out, however, that Frishberg's study deals primarily with iconicity at the lexical level. Meier

(1981; 1991) and Klima & Bellugi (1979) argue that iconicity plays an insignificant role in the acquisition of ASL by deaf children. In Meier's study, two models of iconicity are proposed. One assumes that deaf children are attuned to verbs that happen to be enactments, or mimes, of an action, the other that deaf children are attuned to verbs that map the spatial relations of the actors. It turns out that deaf children follow neither model; deaf children in Meier's study showed no tendency to use iconic verb forms earlier than arbitrary verb forms.

It is interesting to note that Meier's second iconic model was tested using the so-called directional, or person-agreement forms. In ASL, person-agreement in these verb forms is indicated by incorporating spatial loci (which have typically been assigned to a previously mentioned nominal) into the verb. Other verb inflections in ASL, such as aspect, involve changes in the temporal/kinematic structure of the verb's movement. Thus, even if we accept Meier's conclusions about the influence of iconicity vs. arbitrariness in language acquisition, it is worth noting that these verb forms do, nevertheless, incorporate iconicity: "Prototypically and phylogenetically/ontologically, topic/participant deixis tends to be spatial, while propositional deixis tends to be temporal" (Givón, 1984:270). In ASL, this type of deixis is coded by indexing spatial locations. Coding of information about the temporal structure of a verb's meaning, however, is accomplished by modifying the verb's movement (which necessarily involves the sign's temporal structure). There is no evidence that ASL is becoming more arbitrary in this regard — that is, ASL is not beginning to code topic/participant deixis in the kinematics of the verb's movement and aspectual information as spatial locations.

Klima & Bellugi (1979) further claim that iconicity is not relevant in encoding and remembering processes. Such a claim is at odds with Givón's (1989: 97) **iconic imperative**:

> All other things being equal, a coded experience is easier to store, retrieve and communicate if the code is **maximally isomorphic** to the experience.

Finally, Klima & Bellugi (1979) argue that the grammatical processes of ASL function to suppress whatever iconicity may exist: "One of the most striking effects of regular morphological operations on signs is the distortion of their forms so that iconic aspects of the signs are overridden and submerged" (1979: 30). As an example, they describe the morphological process which may be added to a signed word to indicate intensity. This process consists of the addition of an initial hold on the sign followed by a sudden

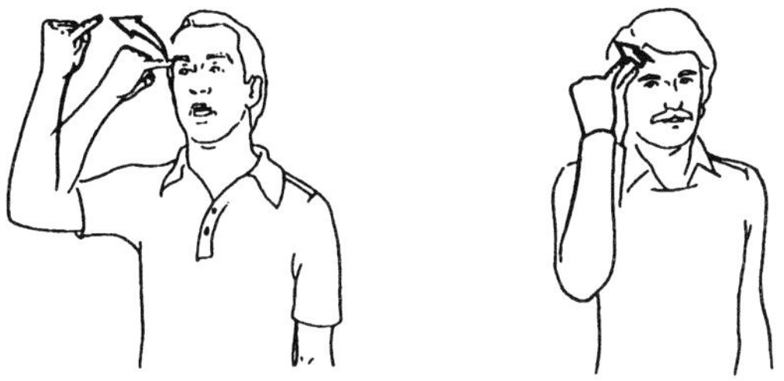

(a) IDEA (b) SUPPOSE

Figure 13: IDEA *and* SUPPOSE

release.[15] When applied to the sign SLOW, the resulting sign means 'very slow.' Klima and Bellugi's point is that the sign VERY-SLOW is made with a very fast movement: "Thus the form of 'very slow' is incongruent with the meaning of the basic sign" (30). The grammar of ASL seems to have submerged the iconicity of VERY-SLOW.

But if this is true, it is only because iconicity has re-emerged in the new form. VERY-SLOW has not overridden the iconicity, it has merely shifted it to the morpheme meaning 'very.' 'Very' can be understood metaphorically in terms of the build up of pressure (intensity). As pressure increases so does intensity, until it is suddenly released. In the ASL morpheme 'very' this build up of intensity is iconically signalled by a build up muscular or gestural energy. Finally, the metaphoric pressure is released — as is the gestural energy in the sudden release into a short, rapid movement. It is an iconic process, and one which, we would suggest, is not unlike a similar process at work in spoken language when, for example, teenagers say, "That's bad." Typically, 'bad' will be pronounced with an extended hold on the bilabial, followed by a sudden release. Of course, the meaning is the same as the ASL example — 'very' (how 'very bad' came to mean 'very good' is another story).

3.1. *Iconicity in the expression of modality in ASL*

A number of facts about the expression of modality lend themselves to a discussion of iconicity in ASL. First, we have already noted the relation between pairs of modals: MUST and SHOULD (Figure 1), CAN and POSSIBLE (Figure 2 and Figure 5a). Other words discussed above also take part in this relationship: FEEL, SEEM, and MAYBE. The relationship can be described in terms of stress and reduplication.[16] MUST is stressed and unreduplicated;

Table 1. *Transitivity Parameters*

	HIGH	LOW
Participants	2 or more participants, A and O[a]	1 participant
Kinesis	action	non-action
Aspect	telic	non-telic
Punctuality	punctual	non-punctual
Agency	A high in potency	A low in potency
Affectedness of O	O totally affected	O not affected
Individuation of O	O highly individuated	O non-individuated

a. 'A' = Agent and 'O' = Object

SHOULD is unstressed and reduplicated. The same holds true for CAN and POSSIBLE.

For FEEL, the relevant feature for the present discussion is reduplication. When FEEL is produced using a single, upward movement it refers to the physical sense of feeling. When it is produced with multiple, reduplicated movements (and the appropriate NMSs discussed above) it acquires the epistemic meaning described above.

The same phonological relationships are seen between the forms for BRIGHT/OBVIOUS described above, and for IDEA and SUPPOSE (Figure 13). SUPPOSE can be used to express hypotheticals ("Suppose you and I drive to California?") and to mark conditionals:[17]

(28) SUPPOSE TOMORROW SNOW, I GO-AWAY SKIING.
'If it snows tomorrow, I'll go skiing.'

In order to describe how these forms are iconic, we must return to Stokoe's semantic phonology and propose the notion of *phonological transitivity*. By phonological transitivity, we mean simply that ASL signs *in their production* can be described as phonologically transitive (an agent, a hand, performs a punctual action on and significantly changes a passive patient, the other hand) or phonologically intransitive (a single patient acts, non-punctually). We are intentionally using semantic terms for phonological, or formational, characteristics of a sign, to bring out the close relation between meaning and form — the iconic relation.

To further elaborate the concept of phonological transitivity we can invoke several of the parameters proposed by Hopper and Thompson (1980: 252) for understanding the notion of semantic transitivity. The parameters listed in Table 1 seem especially pertinent to phonological transitivity.

Many of the modals discussed in this paper have only one participant (even when two hands are forming the words, it is not the case that one is acting on the other). Reduplication affects a sign's formational characteristics on the kinesis, aspect, and punctuality parameters: reduplicated signs are less active, nontelic, and have no obvious transitional phase between inception and completion (i.e., they are cyclic as opposed to punctual).[18] Finally, note that phonological transitivity is an expression of phonetic or gestural substance (this will be elaborated further below).

The iconicity principle at work in these modals can now be summarized as follows:

(A) Senses which are more physically or interpersonally grounded, or semantically less abstract, are expressed with more gestural substance; the more epistemic or semantically abstract senses are expressed with reduced gestural substance.

Ferreira Brito (1990: 255) comments on the same relationship between deontic and epistemic modals in Brazilian Cities Sign Language (BCSL). Deontic modals are expressed with "simple and energetic movements" which, she suggests, is related to an underlying metaphor of obligation for something to be done as actions or events in the real world. Epistemics are distinguished by nonenergetic movement of the hands.

SEEM is more complex. Consider the following: In a discussion of which of two possible translations would be more appropriate for a particular ASL utterance, the following conversation took place:

(29) Speaker A: 'Which do you think she said, this [index$_i$] or that [index$_j$]?'
Speaker B: SEEM++ INDEX$_i$
'She probably said this ...'
(The two study the videotape of the utterance under discussion some more.)
Speaker B: SEEM INDEX$_i$!
'Yes, this has to be what she said.'

In example (29), the first occurrence of SEEM is slowly reduplicated; the second is signed once with emphatic stress. The first expresses weak epistemic probability, the second stronger epistemic certainty. The iconicity principle in operation here seems to be:

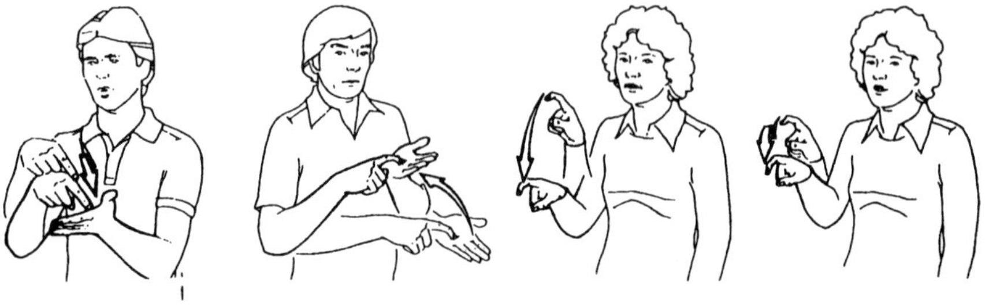

(a) OWE (b) DEMAND/REQUIRE (c) MUST (d) SHOULD

Figure 14

(B) In epistemics, possibility is expressed with reduced gestural substance; probability or certainty is expressed with strong gestural substance.[19]

The iconicity principle (B) appears to be confirmed by the fact that the same relationship holds between other related forms in ASL. Thus, MAYBE may be signed with slow, unstressed, long movements or with stressed, faster, shorter movements. The former means 'maybe, but barely possible;' the latter means 'maybe, probably true'.

This relationship extends to MUST/SHOULD, CAN'T/IMPOSSIBLE, and IDEA/SUPPOSE, and thus, across this limited set of words, we can generalize (B) to the following:

(C) Words with more semantic substance, or less lexical generality (cf. Bybee, 1985: 16), are expressed with more gestural substance; words with less semantic substance and more lexical generality are expressed with less gestural substance.

Finally, the notions of semantic phonology and phonological transitivity expressed in (C) can be used to explore the relationships among four semantically-related ASL words: OWE, DEMAND/REQUIRE, MUST, and SHOULD (Figure 14).[20]

The phonological transitivity of these words is summarized in Table 2. Note that as the words become semantically less substantive (i.e., OWE > DEMAND > MUST > SHOULD) they are expressed with less gestural substance. This process of parallel reduction in the semantic and phonological substance of words has been reported to extensively occur across the world's spoken languages (Bybee, Perkins, & Pagliuca, 1994).

Table 2. *Relation of gestural and semantic substance*

Parameter	OWE	DEMAND	MUST	SHOULD
Participants	+	+	–	–
Kinesis	+	+	+	–
Aspect	+	+	+	–
Punctuality	+	+	+	–
Agency	+	–	–	–
Affectedness of O	+	–	–	–
	6	4	3	0

Of course, many other phonological, morphological, historical, and processing factors have an impact on the changing forms of ASL words. These iconic principles cannot be expected to operate in a totally predictive way. As Givón (1989: 90) notes, however, the lack of total iconic systematicity in no way implies a total lack of such systematicity.

Nor should the extensive presence of iconicity be considered in conflict with conventionalization. Clearly there is a range of iconicity displayed in ASL, from the lexical iconicity explored by Frishberg (1974) to the grammatical iconicity discussed above. Conventionality is at work across this range.

4. Conclusion

Much ASL linguistic research has found itself in an unusual, symbiotic relationship with formalist approaches to linguistics. For many years ASL was considered to be merely pantomime, and it was quite common to "explain" ASL words on the basis of speculation about their purely nonlinguistic origins. This naturally led ASL researchers to distrust any attempt at studying the historical process of how lexemes come into existence in ASL or how lexical material is grammaticized. Also, for many years ASL was haunted by the "spectre of iconicity" (McDonald 1982: vi). Studies which examined iconicity in ASL were seen as calling into question its status as a "true" language as opposed to primitive or pre-human communication, and thus were viewed with suspicion.

It is little wonder, then, that many ASL linguists have been drawn to formalist theories, which by their nature are ahistorical. The symbiosis is further fostered by the fact that formalist approaches assume that language structure can be understood apart from the bodily-based sources of linguistic structure such as gesture and object manipulation, vision, force dynamics, metaphor, and so forth.

In turn, ASL research has done its part in furthering this symbiosis. If the formalist approach merely assumes that it is possible to view some abstract, idealized entity as the true object of linguistic analysis for spoken languages, signed languages seem positively to demand this stance. How else, the reasoning would suggest, could a unified linguistic theory be developed across such radically different substances as light and sound? Having made such an assumption, the conclusion from ASL research that language emerges in a linguistically driven manner (Poizner, Klima and Bellugi 1987: 23) is taken as support, and the symbiotic cycle is completed.

Because of these conditions, and because ASL is an unwritten language which was not seriously described and studied until the late 1950s (Stokoe 1960), there have been few studies of grammatization in this language. We believe we have shown here, however, that when such studies are attempted, they demonstrate that the same processes at work in other languages (Fleischman 1982; Heine et al. 1991; Sweetser 1990) — semantic extension from concrete to abstract senses, reemergence of iconicity between cognitive and linguistic patterning, the use of physical world vocabulary to talk about the mental world — are operating in ASL.

NOTES

1 This view is more fully described in Armstrong, Stokoe and Wilcox (in press).

2 We want to gratefully acknowledge the assistance of our consultants, whose expert intuitions were invaluable: Dennis Cokely, Antoinette Eidson, Betsy McDonald, Jenny Singleton, and Anna Witter-Merithew. Figures are reproduced from Baker and Cokely (1980) and Humphries et al. (1980).

3 ASL words will be glossed in English with small capital letters. The plus symbol (+) is used to indicate reduplication.

4 It is well-attested that ASL is historically related to French Sign Language.

5 Humphries, Padden, & O'Rourke (1980) state that the modal occurs at the end of the sentence, but their example #1 (p. 98, given above as example (1)) suggests that our characterization is more accurate. These examples and many others in this paper are from the exercises in Humphries et al.

6 Actually, there are four related words: MUST, NEED, HAVE-TO, and SHOULD, distinguished by changes in stress and repetition. They are commonly grouped by repetition (cf. Humphries et al.): MUST/HAVE-TO (+stress, –repetition/–stress, –repetition) and NEED/SHOULD (+stress, +repetition/–stress,+repetition). See Section 3 for further discussion.

7 Figure 7c is actually the word BRIGHT; OBVIOUS is made with less stressed, reduced movement

8 In example (12), FEEL SOMEONE ... is signed with the dominant hand, YOU is signed simultaneously with the non-dominant hand.

9 Of course it must be noted that this does not signal a wh-question.Still, it is interesting that Givón (1989: 156) notes that "the use of WH forms to code epistemic uncertainty is wide-spread."

10 The use of these expressions to convey the same speech act is not universal; thus, ASL cannot use the request of information (#3) to indirectly convey a command.

11 Example (24) can have both predictive and volitional readings

12 There is another word using the "S" handshape which includes the notion of denial or negation: REBEL (Long (1918: 16) glosses this as DISOBEY).

13 Although TOMORROW and YESTERDAY also use the open-A handshape, they are not related to the negative signs WON'T, NOT, and DENY. Rather, this handshape is a remnant of French Sign Language (FSL) forms. In FSL, counting starts with the extended thumb as '1'. In ASL, '1' is represented with the extended index finger. Thus, TOMORROW and YESTERDAY appear to be complex forms representing 'one day in the future' and 'one day in the past' respectively. This also reflects the different ways Americans and Europeans count on their fingers.

14 Mowrey & Pagliuca (1988) discuss the same predicament for autosegmental versus gestural phonologies in terms of the features [coronal] and [anterior]; Bybee (1992) for 'plural' and [coronal] in her discussion of formal/structural versus functional/substantive phonology.

15 Klima & Bellugi (1979:30) describe only the change in movement: "an extremely short, rapid movement." Also note that by characterizing the process in terms of addition of an initial hold, we are not implying an analysis based on the Movement-Hold phonology of Liddell and Johnson (1989).

16 Wilbur & Schick (1987) describe several features associated with stress, including non-manual behaviors, sharp sign boundaries, higher placement in the signing space, faster movement, and repetition.

17 Conditionals need not be marked with SUPPOSE; a NMS (raised eyebrows) is enough to signal the protasis. It is interesting that this NMS is also used to mark topics (cf. Haiman 1978).

18 It may seem that reduplicated signs are more, not less active. Note, however, that as a sign such as MUST is repeated, especially if it is also unstressed, the result is to change it from a punctual event to a cyclic state.

19 Although we leave the question unexplored at present, we believe that this is an instance of the iconic expression of force-dynamics in ASL modals (cf. Talmy 1985).

20 Bybee, Perkins, & Pagliuca (1994) note that a common source for obligation are forms meaning 'owe'. The relationship between the forms in Figure 14 would suggest that they too are historically related. We have no evidence that they are (and indeed Boyes-Braem suggests a different lexical source for MUST, as we noted above). Note also that OWE is used almost exclusively with a financial connotation.

REFERENCES

Armstrong, D.F., W.C. Stokoe & S.E. Wilcox. 1995. *Gesture and the Nature of Language*. Cambridge: Cambridge University Press.

Browman, C. & L. Goldstein. 1990. "Tiers in Articulatory Phonology, with Some Implications for Casual Speech." In J. Kingston & M.E. Beckman (Eds.), *Papers in Laboratory Phonology I: Between the Grammar and Physics of Speech*. Cambridge: Cambridge University Press.

Brown, P. & S. Levinson. 1978. "Universals in language usage: Politeness Phenomena." In E.N. Goody (Ed.), Questions and Politeness: Strategies in Social Interaction. Cambridge: Cambridge University Press.

Bybee, J.L. 1985. *Morphology: A Study of the Relation Between Meaning and Form*. Amsterdam: John Benjamins.

Bybee, J. 1994. "A View of Phonology from a Cognitive and Functional Perspective." *Cognitive Linguistics*, 5-4, 285-305.

Bybee, J., Perkins, W.D. & W. Pagliuca. 1994. *The Evolution of Grammar: Tense, Aspect and Modality in the Languages of the World.* Chicago: University of Chicago Press.

Boyes-Braem, P. 1981. Features of the Handshape in American Sign Language. Unpublished doctoral dissertation, University of California, Berkeley.

Cokely, D. & C. Baker. 1980. *American Sign Language: A Student Text (units 1–9)*. Silver Spring, MD: TJ Publishers.

Deane, P.D. 1991. "Syntax and the Brain: Neurological Evidence for the Spatialization of form Hypothesis." *Cognitive Linguistics*, 2(4), 361–367.

Deane, P.D. 1993. *Grammar in Mind and Brain: Explorations in Cognitive Syntax*. Berlin/New York: Mouton de Gruyter.

Edelman, G.M. 1987. *Neural Darwinism: The Theory of Neuronal Group Selection*. NY: Basic Books.

Edelman, G.M. 1989. *The Remembered Present: A Biological Theory of Consciousness*. NY: Basic Books.

Ferreira Brito, L. 1990. "Epistemic, Alethic, and Deontic Modalities in a Brazilian Sign Language." In S.D. Fischer & P. Siple (Eds.), *Theoretical Issues in Sign Language research*. Chicago: University of Chicago Press.

Fischer, S.D. & B. Gough. 1978. Verbs in American Sign Language. *Sign Language Studies*, 18, 17–48.

Fleischman, S. 1982. *The Future in Thought and Language: Diachronic Evidence from Romance*. Cambridge: Cambridge University Press.

Fowler, C.A. 1986. "An Event Approach to the Study of Speech Perception from a Direct-realist Perspective." *Journal of Phonetics*, 14, 3–28.

Frishberg, N. 1975. "Arbitrariness and Iconicity: Historical Change in American Sign Language." *Language*, 51, 676–710.

Frishberg, N. & B. Gough. 1973. Morphology in American Sign Language. Manuscript, The Salk Institute for Biological Studies, La Jolla, Calif.

Givón, T. 1984. *Syntax: A Functional–Typological Introduction Volume I.* Amsterdam: John Benjamins.

Givón, T. 1989. *Mind, Code and Context: Essays in Pragmatics*. Hillsdale, NJ: Lawrence Erlbaum.

Goody, E. 1978. *Questions and Politeness: Strategies in Social Interaction*. Cambridge: Cambridge University Press.
Haiman, J. 1978. "Conditionals are Topics." *Language*, 54, 564–89.
Haiman, J. 1984. *Iconicity in Syntax*. Amsterdam: John Benjamins.
Heine, B., Claudi, U., & F. Hünnemeyer. 1991. *Grammaticalization: A Conceptual Framework*. Chicago: University of Chicago Press.
Higgins, D.D. 1923. *How to Talk to the Deaf*. St. Louis, MO.
Hopper, P.J. & S.A. Thompson. 1980 Transitivity in grammar and discourse. *Language*, 56(2), 251–299.
Humphries, T., Padden, C. & T.J. O'Rourke. 1980. *A Basic Course in American Sign Language*. Silver Spring, MD: TJ Publishers.
Jespersen, O. 1924. *The Philosophy of Grammar*. NY: Norton [1965 edition].
Johnson, M. 1987. *The Body in the Mind: The Bodily Basis of Meaning, Imagination and Reason*. Chicago: University of Chicago Press.
Kimura, D. 1976. "The Neural Basis of Language Qua Gesture." In H.Whitaker & H. Whitaker (eds.), *Studies in Neurolinguistics*. NY: Academic Press.
Kimura, D. 1979. "Neuromotor Mechanisms in the Evolution of Human Communication." In H.D. Steklis & M.J. Raleigh (eds.), *Neurobiology of Social Communication in Primates*. NY: Academic Press.
Kimura, D. 1988. Book review of *What the Hands Reveal about the Brain*, by H. Poizner, E.S. Klima, and U. Bellugi, Cambridge: MIT Press, 1987. *Language and Speech*, 31(4), 375–378.
Klima, E.S. & U. Bellugi. 1979. *The Signs of Language*. Cambridge, MA: Harvard University Press.
Lakoff, G. 1987. *Women, Fire, and Dangerous Things: What Categories Reveal about the Mind*. Chicago: University of Chicago Press.
Langacker, R. 1987. *Foundations of Cognitive Grammar Volume I: Theoretical prerequisites*. Stanford: Stanford University Press.
Langacker, R. 1991. *Foundations of Cognitive Grammar Volume II*. Stanford: Stanford University Press.
Liddell, S.K. & R.E. Johnson. 1989. "American Sign Language: The Phonological Base." *Sign Language Studies*, 64, 195–277.
Long, J.S. 1918. *The sign language: A manual of signs*. Washington, DC: Gallaudet College Press.
McDonald, B. H. 1982. Aspects of the American Sign Language Predicate System. Unpublished doctoral dissertation, University of Buffalo.
Meier, R.P. 1981. "Icons and morphemes: Models of the acquisition of verb agreement in ASL." *Papers and Reports on Child Language Development*, 20, 92–99.
Meier, R.P. 1991. Language acquisition by deaf children. *American Scientist*, 79, 60–70.
Mowrey, R. & W. Pagliuca. 1988. The Reductive Character of Phonetic Evolution. MS.
Padden, C.A. 1988. *Interaction of Morphology and Syntax in American Sign Language*. NY: Garland Publishing.
Poizner, H., Klima, E.S., and U. Bellugi. 1987. *What the Hands Reveal about the Brain*. Cambridge: MIT Press.
Stokoe, W.C. 1960. "Sign language structure: An Outline of the Visual Communication Systems of the American Deaf." *Studies in Linguistics*, Occasional Papers: 8. Buffalo, NY.

Stokoe, W.C. 1991. "Semantic Phonology." *Sign Language Studies*, 71, 107–114.

Studdert-Kennedy, M. 1986. "Two Cheers for Direct Realism." *Journal of Phonetics*, 14, 99–104.

Sweetser, E. 1990. *From Etymology to Pragmatics: Metaphorical and Cultural Aspects of Semantic Structure*. Cambridge: Cambridge University Press.

Talmy, L. 1985. "Force Dynamics in Language and Thought." In Papers from the Parasession on Causitives and Agentivity, 1, 293–337. Chicago: Chicago Linguistic Society.

Wilbur, R.B. & B.S. Schick. 1987. "The Effects of Linguistic Stress on ASL Signs." *Language and Speech*, 30(4), 301–323.

Wilcox, P. 1993. Metaphorical Mapping in American Sign Language. Unpublished dissertation, University of New Mexico.

Wilcox, S. 1990. "The Structure of Signed and Spoken Languages." *Sign Language Studies*, 67, 141–151.

II
The Interaction Basis of Modality

The Development of Epistemic Sentence-ending Modal Forms and Functions in Korean Children

Soonja Choi
San Diego State University

Modality is the linguistic domain that covers the speaker's attitudes and opinions about a proposition (Palmer 1986), and it can be divided into at least two semantic types: agent-oriented modality and epistemic modality (Bybee 1985). Agent-oriented modality, which includes deontic modality, expresses various conditions on the agent, such as ability and obligation, with regard to a proposition. For example, in the sentence 'John can (or must) lift this stone', the auxiliary verbs, *can* and *must*, express the ability and obligation respectively of the agent toward the predicate. Agent-oriented modality also includes desire and intention of the agent as well as permission. On the other hand, the central function of epistemic modality is to express the degree of the speaker's commitment to the truth of a proposition. For example, in 'John should (or may) be home by 5 o'clock', the speaker expresses certainty (or possibility) about the truth of a proposition. Palmer (1986) and others (Bybee 1985, Chafe & Nichols 1986) include evidentiality as a type of epistemic modality, one which specifies the source of information, e.g., hearsay, direct experience, inference. By specifying how the information is obtained, the speaker conveys the kind of warrant he/she has about the proposition, and therefore, the degree to which the proposition is likely to be true. Thus, broadly defined, epistemic modality refers to 'the status of the speaker's understanding or knowledge' of a proposition (Palmer 1986:51).

The semantic distinction between agent-oriented and epistemic modality often parallels a morphological distinction. In an extensive cross-linguistic study of morphology, Bybee (1985) calls attention to a strong tendency for epistemic modality to be expressed inflectionally in bound forms (i.e. morpho-phonologically fused with the verb stem), whereas agent-oriented modality is frequently expressed in non-bound lexical forms, e.g., auxiliary verbs. Bybee (1985:169) gives a historical explanation for this phenomenon: as the meaning of a modal form becomes more abstract over time, from agent-oriented to epistemic, the form itself often reduces phonologically, i.e. from a free lexical form to a bound inflectional form.

In the area of language acquisition, which is the major focus of this paper, children's modal expressions have been reported to develop also from agent-oriented to epistemic modality: Studies of the acquisition of modality in English (Wells 1979, 1985) and other languages (Stephany 1986; Aksu-Koç 1988) have suggested that agent-oriented modality is universally acquired earlier than epistemic modality. Specifically, Stephany (1986) reports that the agent-oriented meaning of desire, e.g., 'I want to/wanna', is the earliest indirect request to develop for English-speaking children, and 'can/can't' also develops early to express ability and permission. In contrast, epistemic meanings related to degrees of certainty about propositions (e.g., possibility, probability) are developed much later in children's language. In her survey, Stephany found that the development of epistemic modality occurs in large part between 3 and 5 years.

Stephany discusses an interesting difference between acquisition in Greek and in English. She notes that her Greek subjects make morphological distinctions of moods — Imperative, Indicative, and Subjunctive — using different inflections at around 1;9 (one year; nine months). On the other hand, in English no such distinctions are apparent at this early stage, partly because the English-speaking children delete the subject in both imperative and declarative sentence and because English does not have modal inflections. Stephany suggests that inflectional languages, such as Greek, may facilitate the acquisition of modal forms because inflections are 'a part of tightly knit lexical forms' (Stephany 1986:398).

In this study of the Korean modal system and its acquisition by children, epistemic modality will be the focus. Although there are only a few studies on Korean acquisition, those studies reported an early emergence of an obligatory class of verbal inflections called sentence-ending suffixes (Zoh 1981; Choi 1991; Kim 1992). These inflections, which are used in informal interactions, include a number of modal forms that relate particularly to the status of the speaker's knowledge and evidentiality. In Zoh's study (1981) of the morphological development of five Korean children, he found that sentence-ending (hereafter SE) suffixes are the first productive morphological category to be acquired by Korean children. Both Kim (1992) and Choi (1991) have shown that productive uses of SE suffixes begin at around 1;9, i.e., *before* 2 years.

In an earlier study (Choi 1991), I analyzed the semantic functions of the first three suffixes, *-ta*, *-e*, and *-ci*, acquired by three Korean children. The data showed that, between 1;8 and 2;2, the children acquired the suffixes in a consistent order, and with clear semantic distinctions that relate to old and newly-acquired knowledge (expressed by *-e* and *-ta* respectively) and to certainty of information (*-ci*). As a first step toward understanding such an early acquisition of modality, I examined the frequency of the suffixes in caregivers' speech to the children. The result showed that the order of acquisition correlated only partially with the input frequency. The study, therefore, suggested that the acquisition of the modal suffixes in Korean is the result of an interaction between the child's cognitive development and the language-specific input.

The present study investigates what roles caregiver-child interactions and the child's cognitive capacity play in the acquisition of Korean modal suffixes. The study analyzes discourse interactions between the caregiver and child, paying attention to both linguistic and extralinguistic contexts in which the child produces a given suffix. The analysis shows that a given suffix is consistently used by all three children in specific types of discourse-pragmatic context. The present study attempts to characterize these types in a systematic way. This discourse approach to data not only enables us to discover the modal meanings acquired by the children, but also gives us insight into how caregiver-child interactions contribute to the child's development of modal meanings. In fact, it will be argued that the discourse-interactional component embedded in the modal meaning enhances acquisition, and that this explains the difference between the early acquisition of modal suffixes in Korean and the relatively late acquisition of epistemic modality reported for other languages. To investigate the cognitive aspects of the acquisition, the kinds of verbs the children use with each suffix will be analyzed, as children's lexical development often gives us insight into their cognitive development (Gopnik & Meltzoff 1984; Tomasello 1992). The study will show that both the child's cognitive understanding of the world and the discourse-interactional aspects of contexts play an important role in children's early acquisition of modal suffixes. The analysis of the present paper includes five modal suffixes acquired between 1;8 and 3;0 by the three children.

The organization of the paper is as follows: First, the kinds of evidential meanings and status of knowledge discussed in recent studies of epistemic modality will be presented. This will be followed by an overview of the Korean modal system. In the remaining part of the paper, the acquisition of modal suffixes by three Korean children will be analyzed.

2. Linguistic coding of evidentiality and knowledge status

A number of studies on epistemic modality have shown that in many languages there are systematic morphological distinctions corresponding to what Palmer (1986:51) describes as "the kind of warrant [the speaker] has for what he says". One type of distinction reported in several studies is the degree to which knowledge has been integrated in the speaker's mind. In particular, epistemic modals in some languages express the difference between what the speaker already knows (e.g., from past experience) and information that the speaker has just acquired from the present context. DeLancey (1986) and Akatsuka (1985) note that this type of epistemic modality distinguishes between old and new knowledge. Specifically, DeLancey (1986) shows that in Lhasa Tibetan, two suffixes contrast in this way *'dug* is used to express newly perceived information, not yet an "integrated part of the speaker's knowledge", while *yod* is used when the speaker expresses old information which has become part of his or her knowledge system. For example, when the speaker unexpectedly finds a strange cat wandering around, *'dug* is used as in *ŋa'i k'a ŋla si-mi 'dug* 'There's a cat in my house'. However, if the speaker owns a cat, and seeing the cat is expected and is part of already established knowledge, *yod* is used instead (i.e. *ŋa'i k'a ŋla si-mi yod* 'There is a cat in my house') (DeLancey 1986:212).

Expressions of the source of information, i.e. evidential markers, are closely related to the distinction between old and new knowledge (Chafe & Nichols 1986). In Turkish, for example, there are two evidential markers distinguishing between witnessed and non-witnessed events: *-dı* is used to report past events that have been directly experienced by the speaker (*Ahmet gel-dı* 'Ahmed came'), whereas *-mıs* is used to express inference or hearsay (*Ahmet gel-mıs* 'he/she/it came (apparently, reportedly) (Aksu-Koç & Slobin 1986). What is interesting is that the functions of the two markers are extended to the expression of old and new knowledge: *-dı* is used for information that is expected from some background knowledge (i.e. old knowledge), but *-mıs* is used for an unexpected event (i.e. new knowledge). Although languages are not identical in terms of how different degrees of integration of knowledge are semantically categorized and how they relate to specific types of evidentiality, these studies and others suggest that the old and new knowledge distinction is an important basis for the evidential/epistemic system in many languages, particularly Asian languages, e.g., Sherpa (Woodbury 1986), Chinese pidgin Russian (Nichols 1986), Korean (H. Lee 1991).

The meanings related to the status of knowledge in this way are often interrelated with discourse pragmatics. Palmer (1986) notes that, in several languages, expressions of status of knowledge depend on what the speaker thinks the listener knows. For example, in Kogi, *ni-* is used when the speaker reminds the listener of information that the latter presumably knows already (e.g., *ni-gu-ku-á* 'I did it just a while ago, as you know'), but *na-* is used when the speaker informs the listener of an ostensibly new proposition, (e.g., *na-gu-ŋgú* 'I tell you he did it some time ago') (Palmer 1986: 76). Palmer goes on to note that, in these cases, it is hard to distinguish between modality and discourse interactional features, since the latter is an integral part of the expression of the speaker's knowledge status.

> It is not easy to draw a clear distinction semantically between discourse features and modality. For in discourse we often express opinion, draw conclusions, etc.; and no doubt, in 'evidential' language [sic] speakers regularly indicate in their conversations and arguments the evidential basis for what they are saying. [...] what are clearly systems of epistemic modality may contain some terms that belong more to discourse (Palmer 1986: 91ff.)

These markers, then, form a distinct type of epistemic modality in which discourse-pragmatics plays an important role.

The old vs. new knowledge distinction discussed by DeLancey and others, and discourse pragmatic functions of epistemic modality discussed in Palmer's work, relate closely to the functions of the morphological class in Korean to be studied in this paper. The sentence-ending modals in Korean are always used in interactive discourse, and, as will be shown below, their meanings relate to the distinctions between old and new knowledge, sources of information, and different assumptions by the speaker about what the listener knows.

3. The modal system in Korean

Korean has two types of modal forms: sentence-ending (SE) modal suffixes and auxiliary verbs. Table 1 shows a list of modal forms in the two categories with approximate meanings in English. SE suffixes occur typically at the end of the sentence, as in (1) with the suffix *-e*. Korean is a verb final (SOV) language, and SE suffixes occupy the final position among the inflections on the predicate: verb or adjective[1].

(1) *Younghi-ka* *Seoul-ul* *ttena-ss-e.*
Younghi-SUBJ Seoul-OBJ leave-PAST-SE
'Younghi left Seoul.'

On the other hand, auxiliary modal verbs are free morphemes which can occur after the main verb. An auxiliary verb must be connected to the main verb by a specific connecting suffix (= connective) on the latter to express a given modal meaning. For example, the connective *-ya* followed by the auxiliary verb *tway-ta*, i.e. *-ya tway-ta* (*-ta* is the citation form), expresses obligation, whereas the connective *-to* with *tway-ta* expresses permission.

(2) *Younghi-ka* *Seoul-ey* *ka-ya/to* *tway-e.*
Younghi-SUBJ Seoul-to go-CONN AUX-SE.
'Younghi must/can go to Seoul.'

Other examples include the connective *-ko* and the auxiliary *siph-ta* expressing desire, and *-swu iss-ta* expressing ability. Thus, connectives are an integral part of the whole auxiliary modal system in Korean. A list of combinations of frequently used connectives and auxiliary verbs in Korean is shown in Table 1B.

All of the auxiliary verbs can be used as main verbs except *-ko siph-ta*, which occurs only as an auxiliary. The meanings of these verbs in the main verb position are as follows: *molu-ta* 'not to know', *kath-ta* 'to be the same', *ha-ta* 'to do', *i-ta* 'to be (Copula)', *po-ta* 'to see', *iss-ta* 'to exist', *tway-ta* 'to become'. As shown in Table 1, when these verbs are used as auxiliaries, some denote epistemic meanings (i.e. *kath-ta*, *molu-ta*, *i-ta*, *po-ta*), and others agent-oriented meanings (i.e. *iss-ta*, *tway-ta*, *ha-ta*). However, note that each form denotes either agent-oriented or epistemic meaning, and there is no overlap of the two types of modality on the same verb, except the verb *hata* 'to do'.

Table 1. *Form and meaning of modality in Korean*

A. Sentence-ending (SE) suffixes

Canonical structure: Verb stem-tense/aspect-SE suffix.

Form	Meaning
EPISTEMIC	
-ta (Type 1)	newly perceived information for the speaker
-ta (Type 2)	new information to the listener
-e	assimilated information, unmarked form
*-ci/-cyana**	certainty of proposition, shared information
-kwun	newly made inference
-tay	reported speech, hearsay/ story-telling
-ney	Information based on factual evidence
-ni	uncertainty and negative bias of proposition
DEONTIC/EPISTEMIC	
-llay	future, desire
-kkey	future, intention, prediction

Note: I have listed those that are relatively frequent in the adult speech and which children acquire early.

* *-cyana* is the suffix *-ci* followed by the negative marker *-ana.* The two morphemes, when combined, express a stronger commitment to the truth of the proposition than *-ci.*

B. Modal auxiliaries

Canonical structure: Main verb-Connective Auxiliary-tense/aspect-SE.

Form		Meaning
EPISTEMIC		
informal	(infinitive)	
-ci molla	(*moluta*)	possibility (weak)
-kes kathay	(*katha*)	possibility (strong)
-tus hay	(*hata*)	possibility (strong)
-n/l kkeya	(*kesita*)	probability
-na pwa	(*pota*)	inference
DEONTIC		
-su isse	(*issta*)	ability
-to tway	(*twayta*)	permission
-ya hay/tway	(*hata/twayta*)	obligation
-ko siphe	(*siphta*)	desire
mos + Verb		negation of ability
-myen an tway	(*twayta*)	negation of permission, negation of obligation
-ki silhe	(*silhta*)	negation of desire

In contrast to the auxiliary verbs, SE suffixes have more abstract meaning, and their semantic functions have been an area of investigation in recent studies of Korean linguistics. Several studies (Choi 1991; H. Lee 1991; K. Lee 1986) have suggested that many of the SE suffixes code the differential status of information in the speaker's knowledge system. H. Lee (1991) states the functions of SE suffixes as follows:

> What is differentiated by sentence-terminal suffixes is various epistemic modality categories, including the speaker's knowledge status, background expectation, evidentiary sources of the information conveyed, and the speaker's assumption about the addressee's point of view. (H. Lee 1991:471)

Several SE suffixes code degrees of integration of information in the speaker's mind. The contrasts among the three suffixes *-ta*, *-kwun*, and *-e* illustrate this point. The suffix *-ta* is often used by the speaker, when he/she has just perceived something noteworthy in the present context, "either because it is about the accomplishment of awaited events or states of affairs at the very moment of speaking" (H. Lee 1993). Consider the following context: John and his wife are waiting for a friend at a restaurant. Their friend is late. Upon seeing the friend finally appear at the restaurant door, John would say:

o-ass-ta
come-PAST-SE
'(He) has come.'

The use of *-ta* is appropriate in this context in which John has just seen the friend and registers the information in his mind for the first time. Comments made with *-ta* may not be directed to the listener; they can be noteworthy remarks to the speaker himself. Once the speaker has registered this new information, in subsequent mentions, e.g., when the speaker repeats the information again to his wife, or when he tells this experience later to another friend, he would use the SE form *-e*:

o-ass-e
come-PAST-SE
'(He) came.'

In this latter context, the use of *-ta*, i.e. **o-ass-ta* is ungrammatical. The use of *-ta* is not restricted to perception of the outside world. It can also occur with an internal state of mind. For example, adult Koreans often say *al-ass-ta* (know-PAST-SE) '(I)'ve got (it)' when they have just come to an understanding of something. (It should be noted that *-ta* is not an aspectual marker denoting perfective aspect. One can use *-ta* when describing a state of affairs as well as an on-going activity if it draws the speaker's attention for the first time, e.g., *ippu-ta* [pretty-SE] '(she's) pretty', or *no-n-ta* [play-PRES-SE] '(They) are playing').

The suffix *-kwun* is similar to *-ta* in that it is also used for newly acquired information. However, the information marked by *-kwun* is often an *inference* based on what the speaker has just seen, as in example (3).

(3) (The mother, upon arriving home, sees her children's school bags lying around. She says to herself,)
ai-tul-i *tolao-ass-kwun.*
child-PL-SUBJ return-PAST-SE
'The children have returned (home).'

By using *-kwun*, the mother indicates that the proposition 'the children returned' is inferred from seeing their school bags. As H. Lee (1985, 1993) argues, both *-ta* and *-kwun* are used for knowledge that has not yet been assimilated into the speaker's knowledge system. The difference between the two suffixes is that *-ta* is used with knowledge obtained through direct experiences, whereas *-kwun* is often used with knowledge obtained through inference.

In contrast to *-ta* and *-kwun*, *-e* is used when the information has already been assimilated into the speaker's knowledge system: the speaker acquired the information in the past, therefore has known it for some time. As mentioned above, once newly perceived information is encoded with *-ta* or *-kwun*, in subsequent mentions *-e* must be used. In H. Lee's survey (1991), *-e* is the most frequent suffix (58%) in spontaneous discourse interactions. This is not surprising, since in conversations participants often contribute to the topic by offering information that they already have about the topic. Indeed, one can conclude that *-e* is the unmarked suffix in conversations.

In discussing *-kwun* above, we have seen how a particular status of knowledge is related to an evidentiary source, e.g., inference. There are a few other suffixes that differentiate evidential sources in Korean. The difference between *-tay* and *-ney* is a case in point. Whereas *-tay* marks hearsay or reported speech, *-ney* signals that the event was directly witnessed by the speaker.

All of these suffixes are used only in informal conversational interactions where participants, familiar to one another, freely and spontaneously exchange information about the current topic. Probably due to this characteristic, the meanings of many suffixes incorporate the speaker's assumption about how much the listener knows. That is, the speaker's choice of a specific SE suffix reflects his or her assumption about status of the listener's knowledge about the proposition (H. Lee 1991). For example, the suffix *-ci* (or *-cyana*) is used when the speaker commits him/herself to the truth of the proposition; it therefore expresses certainty (*-cyana* expresses a stronger commitment than *-ci*). At the same time, *-ci* denotes that the information is also known to the listener or can be readily inferred by the listener. This is confirmed by the use of *-ci* in questions. The suffix *-ci*? is used in a question when the speaker is committed to the truth of the proposition and at the same time wants to confirm that the listener shares this commitment. This is shown in (4). Considering the context of (4), the meaning conveyed by *-ci* is that the speaker is certain that Mary is pretty and also believes that the listener has the same opinion. The speaker expects agreement from the listener. Compare this with the suffix *-ni*? in (5). When *-ni*? is used, it conveys the speaker's assumption that the listener knows more than the speaker about the matter (since only the latter saw Mary). By using *-ni* the speaker expresses a desire to know what the listener knows to be the true.

(4) (Possible context: Both speaker and listener saw Mary and both liked her. The speaker later asks,)
Mary-ka *ippu-ci*?
Mary-SUBJ pretty-SE?
'Isn't Mary pretty?'

(5) (Possible context: The speaker heard from someone that Mary was pretty. The speaker asks the listener, who has seen Mary,)
Mary-ka *ippu-ni*?
Mary-SUBJ pretty-SE?
'Is Mary pretty?'

Thus, *-ci* and *-ni* express different degrees of certainty which also relate to what the speaker assumes about the listener's knowledge. To this category, the suffix *-ta* (Type 2) should be added. This suffix is used when the speaker has assimilated the information conveyed in the proposition but believes that the information is new and noteworthy to the listener. In this case, *-ta* (Type 2) is typically used with a high pitch (see the acquisition section below). For example, when the speaker but not the listener has seen Mary, and the speaker wants to convey this information that is unknown to the listener, the speaker may say *Mary-ka ippu-ta* (*-ta* with a high pitch).

In summary, I have discussed several examples to show that a number of SE modal suffixes in Korean express evidentiality and the different status of knowledge on the part of the speaker and the listener concerning an event or state. These suffixes are used only in informal interactive contexts (e.g., a conversation, or personal letter to a friend). They are not used in formal situations (e.g., a formal speech), nor in contexts where the speaker/writer does not have a particular listener/reader in mind, e.g., written reports. The present study will suggest that such discourse-interactional features and non-verbal contextual cues that accompany them facilitate and enhance the acquisition of epistemic modal suffixes.

How often do adults use these various SE suffixes? As noted above, one can always use the unmarked form *-e*, which simply denotes propositions that are established in the speaker's mind. However, H. Lee (1991) found in his informal conversation data that, although *-e* is used most frequently, it occurs only in just over half of the utterances (58%). For the remaining utterances (42%), 21 different SE suffixes are used, with varying degrees of frequency. Among these, *-ci* was most frequent (15%) followed by *-ta*, *-kwun*, *-ney*, and *-tay*, used at roughly equal frequency of 2%. (*-ni* was used only 1%). Thus, although Korean speakers use *-e* most of the time, they use other SE suffixes spontaneously to express different degrees of certainty about a proposition, about the source of the information, and/or to check the status of knowledge of the listener.

4. Development of SE suffixes in Korean children

As mentioned earlier, research on the acquisition of modality in spontaneous speech has shown that epistemic modality is acquired later than agent-oriented modality (Stephany 1986). In addition, a number of experimental studies have shown that an understanding of different degrees of certainty about a proposition develops only after 3 years (Byrnes & Duff 1989; Hirst & Weil 1982; Moore, Pure & Furrow 1990). It is important to note here that the epistemic meanings in these studies relate to the status of knowledge that results from reasoning by the child which is relatively independent of a particular discourse-interactional context. For example, the distinction between *must* and *may* in English in 'He must/may be home by 5 o'clock' has little to do with the speaker's assumption about how much other participants know about the proposition. Also, in most of the experimental studies on the acquisition of epistemic modality, tests have been designed to understand such context-independent reasoning. For example, in Moore et al. (1990), children (between 3 and 6 years of age) were asked to guess the location of an object hidden in a box solely on the basis of one sentence cues which varied in epistemic modal auxiliaries, e.g, "It must be in the red box" or "it might be in the blue box." Moore et al. found that ability to find the hidden object on the basis of the modal meaning was shown only in children older than four years. However, the results of these studies give little indication of how and when children understand modal forms that incorporate discourse-interactional meanings.

A growing body of research on communicative competence in children shows that children learn to be good participants in conversations from a young age. Several studies (Shatz 1983, 1984; Pellegrini, Brody & Stoneman 1987) have shown that even two-year-olds are capable of giving enough information and keeping their linguistic contributions truthful and relevant to the topic of discourse. Bloom, Rocissano & Hood (1976) have also shown that before children reach two years, they have learned a basic rule of discourse, that of conversational turns, and that between two and three years, children increase the amount of information they contribute to the shared topic.

These studies suggest that the modal functions of SE suffixes in Korean which relate to discourse interactions may be within children's cognitive grasp and linguistic capacity from an early age. Furthermore, there are several characteristic morphological features of SE suffixes that may facilitate early acquisition of SE suffixes in Korean, particularly when we consider Slobin's operating principles (1973). First, SE suffixes occur at the ends of sentences (most often with one syllable consisting of a consonant and a vowel), and therefore are perceptually salient. Second, the SE suffixes constitute an obligatory category in that all sentences in discourse interactions must end with a SE suffix. During interactions with children, the caregiver provides a variety of SE suffixes appropriate to specific discourse contexts. From the acquisition perspective, this means that children hear different SE suffixes frequently from their caregivers. Third, there is a relatively high degree of semantic transparency in that agent-oriented and epistemic meanings are distinguished morphologically, and SE suffixes denote epistemic meanings most of the time. (Table

1 shows that all SE forms in Korean carry the type of epistemic meanings discussed above, except *-llay* and *-kkey* which denote desire and intention respectively. It should be noted, however, that, as discussed in a number of studies, constructions that express desire and intention often develop a use for prediction, which can be considered epistemic (Bybee 1985; Bybee & Pagliuca 1985; H. Lee 1991). In fact, the two SE suffixes are always preceded by the future tense marker *-l*.) Agent-oriented meanings are expressed predominantly by auxiliary verbs, which require children to use two verbs in the sentence, i.e. a main verb and an auxiliary. Also, the SE suffixes have only modal meanings; they incorporate neither tense nor aspectual meanings. All of these morphological characteristics, along with the discourse pragmatic functions of SE suffixes, may enhance children's acquisition of SE suffixes.

4.1 *Data*

I have examined the development of SE modal suffixes in three children, HS, PL, and TJ[2]. The present analysis is based on the children's spontaneous conversations with their caregivers and/or the investigator during the following periods: HS, from 1 (year);8 (months) till 2;8; PL, from 1;8 till 3;0; TJ, from 1;9 till 4;0. All three children are girls.

Table 2 shows the onset of productivity of modal suffixes and auxiliary forms that the three children used during the study period. In this analysis, productivity is determined by counting the number of different verbs (i.e. types, not tokens) used with a given modal suffix. The first session in which the child has produced the suffix with more than three different verb stems is considered to be the onset of productivity. Once the child's production of a given suffix reached this threshold, it was generally the case that the child continued to use the suffix regularly in subsequent sessions. Another important criterion for the analysis is that only spontaneous combinations of verbs and suffixes by the child are considered in this study. If the child's production is an exact imitation of the immediately preceding utterance by the caregiver, it is excluded from analysis. In other words, the data only include verb plus suffix combinations that are different from the ones used by the caregiver in the immediately preceding discourse. For example, if the caregiver asks *mek-ess-e?* (eat-PAST-SE? 'did (you) eat?) and the child answers with the same verb and suffix, i.e. *mek-ess-e* ('(I) ate.'), the child's use of the suffix *-e* is considered an imitation and therefore is not included in the analysis. However, if the child answers with either a different verb (e.g., *hay-ss-e* do-PAST-SE '(I) did') or a different suffix (e.g., *mek-ess-ci* eat-PAST-SE '(I) ate'), or both (e.g., *hay-ss-ci* do-PAST-SE '(I) did') the child's utterance is included in the data.

As can be seen from Table 2, the order of acquisition of the modal suffixes is strikingly similar across the three children. First, note that several SE suffixes are productive in the children's speech before auxiliary verbs appear. Second, we also see a consistent pattern across the three children in the order of acquisition among the SE modals: *-ta* (Type 1), *-e* , *-ci*, *-tay*, and *-ta* (Type 2), in the order mentioned. The two agent-oriented SE modals with future meaning, *-llay* and *-kkey*, are both acquired after *-ta*, *-e* and *-ci* have been acquired.

The general developmental pattern is that the children acquire the suffixes *-ta* (Type 1), *-e*, and *-ci* before the suffixes indicating future, and then the other two epistemic suffixes, *-tay*, and *-ta* (Type 2) are acquired along with some agent-oriented modal auxiliaries. These five SE suffixes are acquired *before* 3 years in all three children. In what follows, I analyze the modal meanings encoded by these suffixes in the children's speech.

In order to identify the meanings of these suffixes in the children's speech, I have examined the linguistic as well as nonlinguistic contexts in which the suffixes are used. Concerning the linguistic context, I have analyzed the structure of discourse interactions between the child and the caregiver. This includes an analysis of discourse contingency (i.e. whether or not the child's utterance maintains the shared topic) and the effect of preceding utterances on the child's selection of a particular SE suffix. Since the children's lexicon is rather limited at this early stage, I have also examined the kinds of verbs to which a particular suffix is attached. As for nonlinguistic contexts, I have analyzed the events, states, and entities that the children refer to in their propositions. I have also examined the types of context which provide the child with particular information, i.e. the source of information.

4.1.1 Acquisition of the suffixes -ta *and* -e*: distinction between unassimilated and assimilated knowledge.*

The first two suffixes to appear in all three children's discourse were *-ta* (Type 1) and *-e*. These two suffixes were acquired at around the same time, i.e. during the first month of study in all three children. HS used the two suffixes productively from the first session (1;10). PL acquired *-ta* at 1;8 and *-e* one

Table 2. *Onset of productivity of modal forms in three Korean children*

Form	HS Age*	PL Age*	TJ Age*
SE suffixes			
EPISTEMIC			
-ta (Type 1)	1;10	1;8	1;9
-e	1;10	1;9	1;11
-ci/cyana	2;1	1;11	2;2
-tay	2;5	2;1	2;3
-ta (Type 2)	2;5	2;9	3;0
DEONTIC/EPISTEMIC			
-kkey	2;1	2;1	2;7
-llay	2;3	2;0	2;6
Modal auxiliaries			
EPISTEMIC			
-na pwa (inference)	2;8	-	3;0
DEONTIC			
-ya tway (obligation)	2;7	2;6	3;1
-ko siphe (desire)	2;6	3;0	3;4
-su isse (ability)	-	2;6	3;6
-to tway (permission)	2;7	2;6	3;1
-mos + Verb (Neg + ability)	2;4	2;6	2;9
-myen an tway (Neg + obligation)	2;7	2;3	3;1

* Ages are in years;months.

month later (1;9), and TJ acquired *-e* at 1;9 and *-ta* three weeks later. Whatever the order of acquisition of the two suffixes was, the two forms served distinct functions in the speech of all three children, who used them to make the same distinctions. The distinction between *-ta* and *-e* went through two phases. During the first phase, *-e* was restricted to requests. Examples are shown in (6) and (7).

(6) HS (1;10)
(Mother and HS open the refrigerator in the kitchen)
→ HS: *uyu cw-e.*
milk give-SE
'Give (me) milk.'

(7) TJ (1;9)
(TJ says to a friend)
→ TJ: *ilwu* *o-a*[3].
here come-SE
'Come here.'

In (6), HS asks her mother to give her some milk, and in (7), TJ asks her friend to come closer. These are appropriate uses of *-e* in that in the Korean adult grammar, *-e* is used for imperative as well as declarative sentences. On the other hand, the children used *-ta* in all statement sentences as illustrated in (8) and (9).

(8) TJ (1;9)
(TJ putting one lego block on top of another)
→ TJ: *olla* *ka-ss-ta.*
up go-PAST-SE
'(It) went up.'

(9) TJ (1;9)
(TJ looks inside her doll house and sees that it's empty.)
→ TJ: *eps-ta.*
not-exist-SE
'There is nothing.'

As shown in (8) and (9), *-ta* was used in statements to describe events (example (8)) as well as states of affairs (example (9)). The contrastive use of the two suffixes, *-ta* for statements and *-e* for requests, was shown by all three children during the first phase. The distinction between statements and requests is parallel to the mood distinction between declarative and imperative: *-ta* for the declarative mood, which expresses the speaker's assertion of propositions, and *-e* for the imperative mood, which directs the listener to do something. It seems therefore that at the beginning the two suffixes distinguish mood in the children's speech. This supports Stephany's finding (1986) that mood distinctions occur early.

At this early period of language development, verbs attached to *-ta* were limited in number and were restricted to those that reflected the child's cognitive interests in trying to understand the world. That is, the kinds of events and states of affairs that the children described (all with *-ta*) were closely related to cognitive concepts that children develop universally at this developmental stage, e.g., existence of an entity, success/failure, and change of state/location (Gopnik & Meltzoff 1984; Slobin 1985; Gopnik & Choi 1990). Furthermore, all of the contexts commented on by the children were in the here and now (see examples (8) and (9), also (10) - (13) below.) The following types of events/states as well as specific verbs, were used by at least two children at this period:

- verbs denoting (non-)existence: *iss-ta* 'exist', *eps-ta* 'not-exist'.
- verbs denoting success: *twayss-ta* 'have become',
- verbs denoting particular states: *can-ta* 'sleeping', *kath-ta* 'be same'
- verbs marking perfective aspect: *hayss-ta* 'done', *olla kass-ta* 'went up'

The three children expressed all four types of events/states with the suffix *-ta* repeatedly (whenever these contexts occurred) during the first few weeks, typically using the specific verbs noted above. This suggests that statements made by the children with the suffix *-ta* at this stage reflect the kinds of concepts they are trying to assimilate into their general cognitive system.

The distinction of mood by the two suffixes, *-ta* for statements and *-e* for requests, lasted only a brief period, however (1 week for HS, 4 weeks for PL, 6 weeks fo TJ). Within 1 to 6 weeks from the time *-e* was first used for requests, both *-ta* and *-e* were used in declarative statements. (The children also began to use *-e* appropriately in questions.) The question then is what specific functions within the declarative sentences the two suffixes serve, if any. The following analyses suggest that the two suffixes systematically contrast different degrees to which a proposition (i.e. event or state to be encoded in language) is assimilated into the child's knowledge system. Specifically, I will argue that the children use *-ta* for newly perceived information which is not fully assimilated into their knowledge system, whereas they use *-e* for information that has been integrated into their body of knowledge.

First, we will discuss the use of *-ta*. The functions of *-ta* in the second phase were similar to those of the first phase. Observe examples from (10) - (13).

(10) (TJ 2;0)
(Looking at the picture of Mr. Bump fallen down on the ground)
→ TJ: *nemecye-ss-ta.*
fall-PAST-SE
'(He) fell down.'

(11) PL (1;9)
(Seeing grandfather's glasses)
→ PL: *apuci-kke-ta.*
grandpa-POSS-SE
'(They're) grandpa's.'

(12) HS (1;10)
(HS puts a lego person in a chair.)
→ HS: *tway-ss-ta.*
become-PAST-SE
'done'

(13) (TJ 1;11)
M: *Mickey eti iss-ni?*
Mickey where exist-SE?
'Where is Mickey?'
(TJ pointing to the picture of a Mickey Mouse on her doll house)
→ TJ: *Mickey yeki iss-ta.*
Mickey here exist-SE.
'Mickey is here.'

The events described in (10)-(13) above occur in the children's immediate context, and are newly registered in their mind. In (10), TJ describes the scene which has drawn her attention, and in (11), PL points out that the glasses belong to her grandpa. In (12), HS marks the completion of her goal as the action was just accomplished, and in (13) TJ has just found the picture of Mickey. These examples illustrate typical contexts in which *-ta* is used, and they can be categorized as follows:

(a) describing a scene in a picture;
(b) describing events/states that the child has just observed:
  i. a perfective aspect which results in a particular state, e.g., *nemecy-ess-ta* 'fallen down', *ollaka-ss-ta*, 'went up',
  ii. an ongoing event/state e.g., *can-ta* 'sleeping',
  iii. naming a referent, *appa-(i)-ta* [4] 'daddy'
(c) commenting on the existence or non-existence of an event/object.

These three types were the dominant types of contexts for *-ta* from the first phase (i.e. when all statements ended with the suffix *-ta*), and continued to be the dominant types after *-e* was also used for declaratives. Table 3 shows the

Table 3. *Context analysis of* -ta *during the first six months of its contrastive use of with* -e.

	HS (1;10-2;4) % (N)	PL (1;10-2;4) % (N)	TJ (1;11-2;5) % (N)
a. picture scene	5 (14)	19 (23)	29 (32)
b. present event/state	45 (116)	28 (34)	49 (55)
c. (non-)existence	46 (119)	17 (20)	18 (29)
Subtotal (a-c):	96(249)	64(77)	96(116)
d. past event/state	2 (5)	1 (1)	1 (2)
e. non-realized event*	2 (6)	0	1 (1)
f. request for information	0	35 (42) **	2 (2)
Subtotal (d-f):	4 (11)	36 (43)	4 (5)
TOTAL:	100 (299)	100 (120)	100 (112)

* Pretend play, negation, make-believe, intention.
** The use of *-ta* in questions by PL was idiosyncratic. This is an overextension in that the adult speaker's use of *-ta* is restricted to assertions. Apparently, PL used *-ta* in this way to check with the caregiver the truth of the newly perceived information (Choi 1990). This use was most extensive from 1;8 till 1;10, and disappeared completely from 2;0.

Table 4. *Context analysis of* -e *during the first six months of its contrastive use with* -ta.

	HS (1;10-2;4) % (N)	PL (1;10-2;4) % (N)	TJ (1;11-2;5) % (N)
a. picture scene	5 (8)	19 (22)	27 (28)
b. present event/state	25 (40)	5 (6)	12 (13)
c. (non-)existence	4 (7)	5 (6)	7 (7)
Subtotal (a-c):	34 (55)	29(34)	46(48)
d. past event/state	17 (26)	42 (50)	32 (33)
e. non-realized event	18 (29)	11 (13)	10 (11)
f. request for information	31 (48)	18 (22)	12 (12)
Subtotal (d-f):	66 (103)	71 (85)	54 (56)
TOTAL:	100 (158)	100 (119)	100 (104)

frequency of *-ta* used in these three types during the first six months from the time *-ta* and *-e* were both used for declarative sentences. As Table 3 shows, the children used *-ta* most frequently in the three types of context (a), (b) and (c). (Further categories (d)-(f) will be introduced below.) This suggests that the semantic content of propositions with *-ta* was something that the children had just perceived through direct experience. The children seemed to describe the events as they became aware of them.

Table 4 shows the frequency of *-e* in different types of contexts. The distribution of *-e* in these contexts is clearly different from that of *-ta*. Although *-e* is used in categories (a)-(c), these amount to fewer than 50% of all the uses of *-e*. (The contrastive uses of *-ta* and *-e* in (a) - (c) will be discussed later.) The majority of the *-e* uses occur in categories (d)-(f):

(d) to give information about a past event/state;

(e) to convince the listener of an event/state of affairs, or to talk about an event/state which was not occurring at the time of speech (e.g., negation, actions which the child was about to perform, make-believe events while playing with a doll or a toy), and;

(f) in questions to verify the truth of a proposition (see Table 4).

These types are illustrated in examples (14) - (17).

(14) PL (1;11)
(Grandmother talks to another adult about the hair salon where PL has recently had her hair cut. PL, hearing all this conversation, says)
→ PL: *polami meli ippukey hay-ss-e.*
PL hair prettily do-PAST-SE.
'PL had (her) hair done. It was pretty.'

(15) TJ (2;2)
(TJ is in the middle of a book, but doesn't want to read anymore. TJ closes the book.)
→ TJ: *eps-e*
not-exist-SE.
'no more.'

(16) TJ (1;11)
(TJ is in another room. M asks TJ to bring a color book.)
M: *ppalli kacko o-a. illwuo-a.*
quickly take come-SE here come-SE
'Bring (it) quickly. Come here.'

→ TJ: *an ka-a*
not go-SE
'(I'm) not going.'

(17) HS (2;0)
(HS gives a piece of apple to the Investigator (Inv). Inv. doesn't want any more. HS holding the apple,)
→ HS: *yoke-nun acci-kke nwu-ka hay(-e)*[5]?
this-TOP uncle-POSS who-SUBJ do(-SE)?
'Who will do (=eat) uncle's apple?'

(By this question, HS implies that it is she who wants to eat the apple. In other words, in her mind 'who' refers to HS herself, and she asks the question to get permission from the investigator.)

In (14), PL states a past event that is well known to her, and in (15) the child creates a desired state (i.e. because the book is closed, reading is finished) and describes it to convince the adult of its truth. In both (14) and (15), the information that the child conveys has been established in her mind before actually saying it. Examples (16) and (17) show that *-e* is used also for negations and questions. In (16), M has asked TJ to come back to the living room, and TJ negates the proposition. In (17), the child asks about a proposition that is on her mind, i.e. she wants to eat the apple. In both cases, the proposition negated or questioned has already been established in the child's knowledge system.

Among the categories (d)-(f), there were, however, individual differences in frequency: HS used *-e* most frequently in wh-questions, whereas PL and TJ used it most frequently for past events/states. Nevertheless, the categories (d)-(f) taken together constitute more than 50% of all the *-e* uses in all three children's speech. This is different from the uses of *-ta* which was rarely produced in these contexts.

Several further analyses support the interpretation that *-ta* and *-e* are used for unassimilated/new and assimilated/old knowledge, respectively. In Table 4, one notices that, although *-e* is used in categories (d)-(f) more than half of the time, it is also used in categories (a)-(c) quite often. Specifically, HS used *-e* for picture scenes (category (b)) 25% of the time, PL and TJ used it for present events/states (category (a)) 19% and 27% of the time, respectively. Thus, both *-ta* and *-e* were used for describing present situations. However, the two suffixes contrasted in a systematic way. One contrast was related to the way the two suffixes were used in repetitions of a proposition. When *-ta* and *-e* occurred within one conversational turn, the first mention of the proposition was marked by *-ta*, and subsequent repetitions then switched to *-e*. This is shown in the following examples:

(18) PL (2;0)
(PL finds the balloon she has been looking for.)
PL: *yeki iss-ta.* *yeki iss-e.* *yeki iss-e.*
here exist-SE. here exist-SE. here exist-SE.
'Here (it) is. Here (it) is. Here (it) is.'

(19) TJ (2;3)
(The picture of an elephant in a book and the elephant design on her pants are similar.)
TJ: *ike ttokkath-ta.* *ike* *ttokkath-e.*
this same-SE this same-SE
'These are the same. These are the same.'

In (18), PL finds the balloon unexpectedly. She gets excited and describes the event with *-ta* first. However, at the second mention of the same proposition, she switches to *-e*. A similar explanation can be given to TJ's utterance in (19). As TJ recognizes that the two pictures are the same, she uses *-ta* (the concept of sameness interested TJ greatly at this period). But once the information has been registered in her mind, she switches to *-e*. This sequence of *-ta* followed by *-e* occurred a number of times in the speech of all three children. The reverse order never occurred. Such a fixed order of *-ta* and *-e* within one conversational unit also occurs in adult speech, and apparently the children learned this order without errors.

Another distinction between *-ta* and *-e* had to do with verb types. As noted above, at the beginning, verbs attached to *-ta* were limited in number and restricted to those that reflected the cognitive concepts that the child was developing at the period of time in question. Most notable verbs were: *iss-ta* 'exist', *ep-ta* 'not-exist', *tway-ss-ta* 'become', *kath-ta* 'same', *ollaka-ss-ta* 'went up'. In addition, *-ta* was also used frequently after a noun to label entities (e.g., *appa-ta* '(It's) daddy'). These verbs were used with high frequency and co-occurred only with the suffix *-ta* during the first few months. Gradually however, propositions about existence, success, change of location, or names of things involved in the here and now were encoded with *-e*, particularly when an event or state was expected by the child (see examples (15), (18), and (19) above, also (20) below). As the children's cognitive

Table 5. *Frequency of occurrence of* -ta *and* -e *in relation to the discourse topic during the first six months. (from Choi 1991)*

	-ta		*-e*	
	Related*	Unrelated**	Related	Unrelated
HS	9%	91%	65%	35%
PL	19%	81%	57%	43%
TJ	24%	76%	64%	36%

*Related to the immediately preceding utterance, or to the current topic.
**Unrelated to the topic, introduction of a new topic.

development advanced, those cognitive concepts seemed to be well established in their knowledge structure. The use of both *-ta* and *-e* for the same verbs occurred at 2;1 for HS, 2;0 for PL, and 2;1 for TJ. From this period, *-ta* was used for new information that relates to a specific discourse context.

(20) TJ (2;1)
(A game of ducks catching fish. TJ is familiar with this game. TJ pointing to one fish)
TJ: *yeki mwulkoki iss-e.*
here fish exist-SE
'Here is a fish.'

Another systematic difference between *-ta* and *-e* that the children show relates to discourse contingency, i.e. whether or not the utterance maintains the current topic and adds new information to it (Bloom et al. 1976). If the function of *-ta* is to register a new and noteworthy event/state in the child's own mind as she begins to understand it, the form would tend to be used in monologue situations where the child tells herself about the meaning of the event. (As mentioned earlier, adult speakers also show this phenomenon.) On the other hand, as H. Lee (1985) notes, *-e* would be used to exchange information since the information has become part of the speaker's knowledge system. The analysis of discourse contingency is shown in Table 5.

In the data, the children used *-e* much more often than *-ta* as they responded to adult utterances giving more information about the topic. Table 5 shows that the proposition with *-ta* was often not related (i.e. non-contingent) to the current topic, but instead, shifted to a different topic that drew the child's attention. As a consequence, the information which co-occurred with *-ta* abruptly interrupted the current topic and often initiated a new topic which the adult then commented on. An example is (21).

(21) TJ (2;0)
(Investigator points to the girl that she colored)
Inv.: *i salam ippu-ci?*
this person pretty-SE?
'Isn't this person pretty?'
TJ: *ippu-ci.*
pretty-SE
'pretty.'
Inv.: *i salam ippu-ci?*
this person pretty-SE?
'Isn't this person pretty?'
(TJ hears a baby cry upstairs.)
→ TJ: *aka wu-n-ta.*
baby cry-PRES-SE.
'A baby is crying.'
Inv.: *aka wul-e?*
baby cry-SE
'Is baby crying?'

In (21), as TJ hears a baby cry, she comments on this, abruptly interrupting the topic of coloring. This non-contingency occurred in 83% (on average) of the children's *-ta* uses. In contrast, the propositions with *-e* showed a much lower frequency of non-contingency (39% on average). In fact, more than half of the time, the propositions with *-e* maintained the current topic. More specifially, *-e* was used to respond to or comment on the preceding adult utterance. PL's utterance in (14) above is a good example of providing more information on the current topic (i.e. about PL's hair).

In summary, several types of analyis have shown that the children in the present study used the modal suffixes *-ta* and *-e* for distinct functions. *-Ta* was used to encode a new and noteworthy proposition as the child became aware of its meaning. At the beginning, propositions with *-ta* also reflected cognitive concepts that the children were developing. At a later stage, *-ta* encoded new/unassimilated information that the child experienced directly in the here and now. In both cases, *-ta* was often used to introduce a new topic during interaction. In contrast, *-e* was used for propositions that were already established in the child's knowledge system, and its function in discourse was to contribute more information to the current topic.

4.1.2 *Acquisition of* -ci*: shared knowledge and certainty of the truth of the proposition*

The third modal suffix to be acquired by the children was *-ci*. (The children also acquired *-cyana* around the same time, and the data in this section include both *-ci* and *-cyana*.) With the use of *-ci*, the interactional function of modal suffixes becomes even clearer. Initially, *-ci* was used in the following contexts: (a) when reiterating a proposition in the preceding utterances produced either by the child herself or by the interactant (example 22), or (b) when redescribing an event or state which had been described several times before (example 23).

(22) PL (1;11)
(PL pointing to Grandmother's hairpin)
PL: *ike hammwuni kke-ya?*
this grandma POSS-SE
'Is this grandma's?'
GM: *ung, hammwuni kke-ya.*
yes, grandma POSS-SE.
'Yes, grandma's.'
→ PL: *hammwuni kke-ci?*
grandma POSS-SE
'Grandma's?'
GM: *ung, hammwuni kke-ci.*
yes, grandma POSS-SE
'Yes, grandma's.'

(23) PL (2;2)
(PL remembers seeing a monster on TV.)
PL: *kweymwul an mwusew-e?*
monster NEG scary-SE
'Monster is not scary?'
GM: *kweymwul eps-e.*
monster not-exist-SE
'There's no monster.'
→ PL: *kweymwul Tibi-ey-na iss-ci?*
monster tv-LOC-only exist-SE?
'Monsters exist only on TV?'

Table 6. *Number of* -ci *utterances in different types of context.*

Age period:	1;10-2;0			2;1-2;6			2;7-3;0		
	HS	PL	TJ	HS	PL	TJ	HS	PL	TJ
a. reiteration of adult's preceding utterance	1	-	1	5	1	1	3	2	-
b. frequent occurrence	-	6	-	-	4	2	-	7	5
c. perceptual evidence in here and now	1	1	-	8	8	1	32	16	18
d. certainty developed through discourse	2	1	-	11	7	2	24	4	7
e. shared past event	-	-	-	-	1	-	1	5	5
f. in wh-questions-	-	-	-	2	-	-	18	5	2
g. cooccurrence with obligation marker	-	-	-	-	8	-	27	4	2
h. other	-	-	-	-	-	-	-	28*	1*
Total *-ci* utterances:	4	8	1	26	29	6	105	71	40

* PL and TJ used *-ci* in the question, *al-ass-ci*?, know-PAST-SE, to mean '(you) got (=understood) (it)?'

In (22), *-ci* is used when PL repeats the grandmother's preceding assertion that the hairpin belongs to her, and in (23) it is used for information which has been given several times before during the session. This characteristic use suggests that at this time children pay attention to large stretches of discourse, i.e. several turns of conversation, and also remember conversations which took place in the past. The repetition of the proposition with *-ci* in this way allows the child to be certain that the information contained in proposition is shared with the caregiver.

Table 6 shows an analysis of the contexts of all *-ci* utterances between two and three years. As Table 6 shows, reiteration of the preceding proposition with *-ci* (example 23) marks the beginning of the development. Between 2;2 and 2;4, the three children begin to use *-ci* in the following contexts: when the child is certain about a proposition based on some perceptual support (category c), and when the conversation progresses in such a way that the child becomes certain of the proposition (category d).

The following examples illustrate these categories:

(24) PL (2;6)
(PL and Mother talk about whether neighbor houses have their lights on or not.)

PL: *emma. ce cip-ey-nun pwul-i kke-ss-e*
mommy. that house-LOC-TOP light-SUBJ turn off-PAST-SE.
'Mommy. Lights are off in that house.'

M: *eti?*
where
'where?'

PL: *yeki*
here
'here.'

M: *ung, ce wuit cip-ey.*
yes that above house-LOC
'Yes, that house on top.'

PL: *ung, wuit cip-ey.*
yes above house-LOC
'Yes, the house on top.'

M: *ung, ung.*
yes yes
'Yes, yes.'

→ PL: *ce alay cip-un pwul khye-cye iss-ci.*
that below house-TOP turn-on-PASS be-SE.
'Lights are on in that house below.'

M: kule-kwuna.
SO-SE
'It is so.'

(25) HS (2;9)
(One coin chip is stuck in toy cash register)

Inv.: *kelye-ss-cyana*
stuck-PAST-SE
'(It's) stuck.'

HS: *kelye-ss-e?*
stuck-PAST-SE
'(It's) stuck?'

Inv.: *ung.*
yes
'Yes.'

HS: *ike kocang na-ss-nunka pwa.*
this obstacle arise-PAST-CONN seem
'This seems to be broken.'

Inv.: *kocang an na-ss-e*
obstacle NEG arise-PAST-SE.
'(It) isn't broken.'

HS: *kocang na-ss-e.*
obstacle arise-PAST-SE
'(It)'s broken.'

Inv.: *tasi ha-l-kkey.*
again do-FUT-SE
'(I')ll do it again.'

(Inv. tries but it still gets stuck)

HS: *an tway.*
NEG become
'(It) doesn't work.'

Inv.: *an tway.*
NEG become
'(It) doesn't work.'

→ HS: *kocang na-ss-ci.*
obstacle arise-PAST-SE
'(It)'s broken.'

In (24), the child maintains the current topic, and tells whether the lights are on or off on the basis of what she sees, i.e. perceptual evidence. In this example, PL first confirms with her mother that the lights are on in the upper apartment. This discussion leads PL to draw the conclusion that the lights in the lower apartment are off by contrast, and PL marks her certainty of this knowledge by *-ci*. In example (25), being broken becomes more and more certain to HS as the coin keeps getting stuck. Also, in (25), the meaning *kocang na-ta* 'be broken' is expressed several times by the child herself before marking it with the suffix *-ci*. This use of *-ci* is analyzed as certainty developed through discourse (category d in Table 6). At this developmental stage, certainty constructed through discourse is often accompanied by perceptual evidence, as shown in (25). At a later time, *-ci* begins to be used in another type of context (from 2;2 for PL and from 2;9 for HS and TJ): it co-occurs with the obligation connective *-ya* or with the nominalizer *ke*, as in (26) and (27).

(26) HS (2;9)
(HS putting coins one by one into the toy cash register.)
→ HS: *yoke ha-ko yoke ha-ya-ci.*
this do-then this do-must-SE
'(I) do this, then (I) must do this.'

(27) PL (2;2)
(PL playing doctor.)
→ PL: *cinchal ha-myen ei wul-myen nappen ke-ci.*
examine do-then ei cry-if bad NOMINAL-SE.
'It is a bad thing to cry *ei* (sound of crying) when (the doctor's) examining.'

This represents category (g) in Table 6. The obligation connective and the nominalizer in Korean denote obligation and normativity, respectively. This is interesting because the two meanings are closely related in that when one is obligated to do something or when one normally does something in a given situation, the predicated event acquires a degree of certainty. In other words, obligation and normativity often lead to certainty of an event occurring. Studies of modality in adult language show that there is a close relationship between obligation and certainty (Bybee 1985). Also, Steele (1975), in a cross-linguistic study of modality, argues that for a systematic relation between deontic and epistemic modality. In particular, Steele's data show that in many languages obligation and certainty of information are expressed by the same morpheme. In Korean, modal forms for obligation and certainty are distinct; however, the two forms frequently co-occur. The three children acquired such co-occurrences from an early stage.

As in adult speech, the suffix *-ci* was frequently used in yes/no questions asking the caregiver to confirm the truth of a proposition: yes/no questions comprised 35% of *-ci* utterances in HS's speech, 25% in PL's speech, and 38% in TJ's speech (these are incorporated in the appropriate pragmatic categories in Table 6). In addition, *-ci* was used in wh- questions. Initially, this is suprising because wh- questions are asked when some particular informa-

Table 7. *Number of* -tay *utterances in different types of context from its acquisition till 3;0.*

	HS (2;5-3;0)	PL (2;1-3;0)	TJ (2;3-3;0)
a. what X would say or feel	3	44	7
b. reported speech	3	10	7
c. during storytelling	-	9	9
d. errors with 1st person	1	1	1
Total *-tay* utterances:	7	64	24

tion is unknown. However, an analysis of the kinds of information requested in wh- questions with *-ci* shows that they are based on certainty of some relevant information. For example, when HS played an alphabet puzzle game and was looking for certain letters, she routinely asked the question *eti ka-ss-ci?* where go-PAST-SE 'Where did (it) go?'. In this context, she knew that a particular letter existed and the question was built on the certainty of its existence, and of finding it.

4.1.3 *Acquisition of* -tay *and* -ta *(Type 2): source of information*

The three children used *-ci* to express shared information which led to the expression of certainty. In the next phase of the development of modality, children acquire modal forms whose primary function is to *inform* the listener of something that the latter does not seem to know. The acquisition of two new modal forms, *-tay* and *-ta* (Type 2), shows this further development.

In the adult grammar, the function of *-tay* is described as reporting hearsay information or indirect speech (H. Lee 1985). For example, when a speaker reports information indirectly obtained (e.g., heard from another person, or read in a newspaper), the suffix *-tay* is used to mark the indirect source of the information.

The children used *-tay* much less frequently than the three suffixes analyzed above. Although the sample size is small, the data show a consistent pattern. As Table 7 shows, *-tay* was used primarily in contexts where the children relayed information whose source was a third party: (a) telling the listener what the child believed the third party said or felt, or (b) reporting what a third party just said. All three children used *-tay* in these contexts. In both contexts, the child gives the listener information that the child assumes the listener may not know. For example, in (28), PL engages in a pretend play with a doll as a baby, and reports what the baby might feel. Obviously, the baby (i.e. the doll) said nothing, but PL infers that the baby felt sick and reports this to her mother, who may not share this information. A similar explanation can be offered for (29): TJ infers that Ernie might hurt his feet by jumping many times. In (30), HS reports to the investigator what her sister has just said, appropriately with the suffix *-tay*.

(28) PL (2;1)
(PL plays with a doll with her Mother.)
→ PL: *aka-ka* *aphu-tay.*
baby-SUBJ sick-SE.
'The baby is sick.'

(29) TJ (2;4)
(TJ looking at a picture of Ernie jumping)
Inv.: *jumphu-ha-e?*
jump-do-SE?
'(Is he) jumping?'
→ TJ: *pal* *ayaya* *ha-n-tay.*
foot ayaya (typical sound made when one is hurt) do-PRES-SE
'He says his feet are hurt.'
Inv.: *ung.*
yes
'Oh, I see.'

(30) HS (2;5)
(HS and her older sister are coloring.)
HS's sister: *nayka* *saykchil* *hay* *cwu-kkey.*
I-SUBJ coloring do give-SE.
'I will color (it) for you.'
(HS immediately reports to Inv.)
→ HS: *enni-ka* *saykchil* *hay* *cwu-n-tay.*
sister-SUBJ coloring do give-PRES-SE.
'(My) sister says that she will color (it) for me.'

As shown in the above examples, all of the utterances with *-tay* were reports about what a third party was feeling or had said. That is, the information with *-tay* did not come from direct experience but from inference or other indirect sources (except for one error in each child's sample which was about the child herself). In addition, PL and TJ sometimes used *-tay* in narrating a story from a picture book. This is partly due to the input. PL's and TJ's caregivers spent much time reading picture books with the children, and they often used *-tay* in telling stories.

When the information to be conveyed was about the child herself, another suffix was used, the suffix *-ta* with a high pitch. *-ta* was used when the information was already known to the child by direct experience, i.e. old information for the child, but new for the listener. This use of *-ta* always carried a high pitch (marked by ↑ in the transcript).

(31) TJ (3;0)
(TJ showing the Investigator her new bracelet on the wrist.)
→ TJ: *na phalci iss-ta*↑
I bracelet exist-SE
'I have a bracelet!'
Inv.: *TJ, phalci iss-e?*
TJ, bracelet exist-SE
'TJ has a bracelet?'
TJ: *ung.*
yes
'Yes.'

(32) TJ (3;0)
(TJ tells the Investigator what she did before the Inv. came.)
→ TJ: *akka-nun Cwunwu-lang pizza mek-ess-ta*↑.
before-Top Cwunwu (TJ's friend)-with pizza eat-PAST-SE
'I ate pizza with Cwunu awhile ago!'
Inv.: *kula-e?*
SO-SE
'Is that so?'

(33) HS (2;9)
(HS putting her sunglasses in her pocket, tells the Inv.)
→ HS: *nay kyowhay ka-lttay yoke kac-ko ka-nunke-ta*↑
I church go-when this take-CONN go-NOMIN-SE.
'This is something that I take to church!'

In all three examples above, the information that the child gave to the investigator was new to the latter. The child marked this assumed knowledge gap in the listener's mind with the suffix *-ta*. It should be noted that the information with *-ta* (Type 2) was often something the child wanted to brag about to the adult, thus it carried a certain affective component.

In summary, both *-tay* and *-ta* convey information the child believes the listener doesn't have. The suffix *-tay* marks information that comes from an indirect source: either inference about what another person would say or would feel or a report of indirect speech. The suffix *-ta* (Type 2) with a high pitch expresses something that the child experienced directly and which the listener might not know. It is interesting to note that the productive uses of the two suffixes, *-tay* and *-ta* (Type 2) all occurred later than *-ci*. This suggests that an understanding of differences in knowledge between the child and the listener develops after the child learns to express shared knowledge.

4.2 *Mechanisms for the early acquisition of SE epistemic suffixes*

The data of this study have shown that Korean children acquire and use several epistemic SE suffixes appropriately at an early stage. Specifically, between 1;9 and 3;0 the three children in the study acquired five SE suffixes to mark distinct meanings. The meanings were distinguished in terms of the following features: degrees of integration of a proposition in the child's knowledge system, source of information, and the child's belief about what the listener knows. In particular, the children in this study distinguished between newly perceived information that was not yet assimilated into their knowledge system and old/assimilated information (*-ta* (Type 1) vs. *-e*); between knowledge shared vs. not-shared with the listener (*-ci* vs. *-tay*/*-ta*), and between direct and indirect sources of information (*-ta* (Type 2) vs. *-tay*). The data suggest that these oppositions are acquired in a consistent order. Figure 1 attempts to illustrate this development. First, *-ta* is acquired to denote newly perceived information that attracts the child's interest at the time of speech. Then, *-e* is acquired to contrast the new knowledge with old/assimilated knowledge. The new vs. old knowledge distinction is related to the child's own knowledge system and does not seem to be related to whether or not the knowledge is shared with the listener. However, as *-ci* is acquired, a new component, the feature of shared knowledge, is added to the SE modal system. The propositions with *-ci* in the children's speech predominently contain information related to the shared topic: 85% of the *-ci* uses have discourse contingency. In addition, *-ci* expresses knowledge shared by the

Form:	*-ta*(Type 1)	→	*-e*	→	*-ci*	→	*-tay*	→	*-ta*(Type 2)
Meaning:	new / unassimilated knowledge		old/ assimilated knowledge		shared knowledge/ certainty		non-shared knowledge/ indirect evidence		non-shared knowledge/ direct evidence

Development of Modal meaning:

|———→ Degree of assimilation of knowledge in the speaker's mind

|———→ Listener's status of knowledge about a proposition

|———→ Source of information

Figure 1. *Development of epistemic functions*

child and the listener. The nature of this shared knowledge is based on discourse or perceptual evidence. This function of *-ci* leads to marking proposition as certain. Later, as *-tay* is acquired, shared knowledge comes to be differentiated from non-shared knowledge, i.e. the child informs the listener of a proposition the latter may not know. Furthermore, *-tay* denotes information that comes from an indirect source. Lastly, *-ta* contrasts with *-tay* in marking a proposition as reflecting the child's direct experience. This developmental order suggests that as each new modal form and its corresponding function are acquired, a new domain of epistemic modality is added to the existing one(s), as shown in Figure 1.

One explanation for these results has to do with children's general cognitive development and capacity at this stage. We have seen that the three children acquired their first SE suffixes to express their own knowledge status, and subsequently to incorporate the listener's knowledge status. This conforms to the general view that children's use of language develops from egocentric to decentered (Piaget 1955). Also, a closer look at the contexts in which particular propositions were expressed suggests that at the earliest stage in the children's development of SE modals, propositions were related to the information in the immediate context. In particular, information with the suffix *-ta* (Type 1) was closely tied to what was going on at the time of speech. Then, the children acquired *-e* and *-ci* to convey information about past events. This parallels the pattern of a child's general cognitive development, which proceeds from an understanding of present events to an understanding of events removed from the present (i.e. past or future). Not only across suffixes, but also with respect to a single suffix, the development of functions reflects underlying cognitive capacity at the time of acquisition. For example, the use of *-ci* was first limited to repetitions of the preceding propositions and later expanded to include past events.

Overall, the perceptual context provided an important basis for the children's acquisition of epistemic meaning of SE suffixes. For example, *-ta* was used with situations that the child experienced at the time of speech, and *-ci* was often used when the evidence was clearly present in the extralinguistic context. Also, *-tay* was used to relay information about a referent that was present in the immediate context. Such an evidential component which is related to the here and now probably influenced the early acquisition of these forms.

During the period of the study, not all SE suffixes were acquired by the children. For example, they did not produce *-kwun* (unassimilated inference based on newly perceived information). Furthermore, for those suffixes that the children did acquire, not all the functions expressed in the adult grammar were present. For example, *-ci*, which in adult grammar also expresses certainty of a proposition based on inference, did not appear often in the children's data with this function. The indirect speech function of *-tay* was not fully developed in the children's speech. Again, these limitations reflect children's cognitive constraints at this developmental stage.

Within these limitations, however, the children acquired a variety of epistemic meanings relating to different degrees of assimilation of knowledge in their minds, different sources of information, and the knowledge status of the listener. As shown in the present analyses, the contrasts at issue were made systematically by the children. Such early acquisition of modality may be due to the morphological saliency referred to above. But more interestingly, it is argued here that the discourse interactional functions of the suffixes play an important role in the early acquisition of epistemic modality. That is, understanding that the modal suffixes mark contrast concerning the exchange of information and the construction of shared knowledge among conversation participants may have enhanced the children's sensitivity to and acquisition of different kinds of information. In particular, we have seen that the distinction between new and old knowledge is related to discourse contingency. Also, the notion of certainty of information is embedded in the expression of shared knowledge. Example (24'), a fuller version of (24), illustrates clearly how the functions of three SE suffixes, *-ta*, *-e*, and *-ci*, are related to the way discourse interaction progresses.

(24') PL (2;6)

(PL and Mother have been engaged in a pretend play for awhile. PL plays a student who came to study in Boston.)

M: *kongpwuha-le o-si-ess-eyo.*
study-CONN come-HON-PAST-SE.
'(You) came (here) to study.'

PL: *ney.*
yes
'Yes'

(PL sees a light in a neighboring house.)

→ PL: *emma, ce, ceki yep cip-ey pwul khye-cye-iss-ta.*
mommy there there side house-LOC turn on-PASS-be-SE
'Mommy, the light is on in that neighbor's house.'

M: *ung. ce cip pwul khye-iss-kwuna.*
yes. that house light turn on-be-SE.
'Yes, the light is on in that house.'

→ PL: *emma. ce cip-ey-nun pwul-i kke-ss-e.*
mommy. that house-LOC-TOP light-SUBJ turn off-PAST-SE.
'Mommy. Lights are off in that house.'

M: *eti?*
where
'where?'

PL: *yeki*
here
'here.'

M: *ung, ce wuit cip-ey.*
yes that above house-LOC
'Yes, that house on top.'

PL: *ung, wuit cip-ey.*
yes above house-LOC
'Yes, the house on top.'

M: *ung, ung.*
yes yes
'Yes, yes.'

→ PL: *ce alay cip-un pwul khye-cye iss-ci.*
that below house-TOP turn-on-PASS be-SE.
'Lights are on in that house below.'

M: *kule-kwuna.*
so-SE
'It is so.'

In this example, as PL sees the light, she gets excited and describes what she sees, abruptly changing the topic from the pretend play to lights in the neighbors' houses. PL encodes this newly perceived information with *-ta.* Once the topic is established and the information registered in her mind, the child describes other houses with the suffix *-e.* As the exchange of information on lights being on or off progresses, PL changes to *-ci* to encode shared information and its certainty. The three suffixes thus mark various types of knowledge status that develop within a particular discourse interaction.

Early sensitivity to the discourse functions of SE suffixes in Korean correlates well with the findings on the acquisition of discourse-pragmatic phenomena for English-speaking children: children use language in requesting information and answering questions from the one-word period (Dore 1974; Shatz 1983). Several studies on discourse contingency between caregiver and child have shown that children imitate caregivers' utterances from early on. One function of imitation is maintaining a shared topic. Bloom et al. (1976) shows that imitation is crucial to the development of the discourse skill of contributing new information to a shared topic. Also, Pellegrini et al. (1987) demonstrate that two-year-old children show signs of observing the cooperative principles, e.g., giving informative and truthful information to construct shared knowledge relevant to the topic of discourse. The present study suggests that such an ability to follow the progression of discourse toward more and more shared knowledge between the speaker and the listener is instrumental to the early acquisition of SE modal suffixes. This would also explain the late acquisition of pure epistemic modal forms whose meanings are relatively context-independent (e.g., English epistemic modal auxiliaries).

Essential to children's sensitivity to discourse interactions is the affective component that exists between the caregiver and the child. First, all of the SE suffixes are used in informal conversations between participants who are intimate with one another. For example, by repeating shared information using *-ci*, and by checking and making sure that it is shared with the caregiver, the child builds a bond between herself and the caregiver. Also, the suffix *-ta* (Type 2) is used when the child wants to brag about something to the adult. Such an affective component may enhance the acquisition of abstract concepts in ways similar to what Akatsuka and Clancy (1991) describe in relation to the early acquisition of conditionals in Korean children. Thus, when the epistemic modal system is deeply embedded in the protocols of discourse interaction, which, moreover, contains an affective component, children may grasp abstract concepts of modality from an early stage. The question still remains, however, whether children learning languages other than Korean spontaneouly make similar distinctions in their own way, and if so, to what extent do children learning different languages systematically express the distinctions we have seen in this paper. In order to answer this question, we need to look at the acquisition of several different languages, focusing on how children express different types of knowledge within discourse interactions.

ABBREVIATIONS

ADV - adverbial suffix
FUT - future
LOC - locative
NEG - negative
PAST - past tense
POSS -possessive
SE - sentence-ending suffix
TOP - topic
CONN - connecting suffix
HON - honorific suffix
NOMIN - Nominalizer
OBJ - object
PL - plural
PRES - present
SUBJ - subject

NOTES

1. In colloquial speech, SOV order is not always observed. In consequence, SE suffixes may occur in the middle of the sentence, as in the following example.

kho	*ca-n-ta*	*thokki-ka.*
well	sleep-Present-SE	rabbit-SUBJ

'The rabbit is sleeping soundly.'

2. I am very grateful to Pat Clancy and Youngjoo Kim for allowing me to analyze HS's and PL's data respectively.
3. *-e* and *-(y)a* are allomorphs. *-e* occurs after high and mid-high vowels and after all consonants. *-(y)a* occurs following low and mid-low vowels.
4. In this case, the full form is *appa-i-ta* (daddy-COP-SE), however, the copula verb *i* 'be' is often deleted after a vowel.
5. *-e* is deleted after a vowel.

REFERENCES

Akatsuka, Noriko. 1985. "Conditionals and the Epistemic Scale". *Language* 61.625-639.

Akatsuka, Noriko & Patricia Clancy. 1991. "Conditionality and Deontic Modality in Japanese and Korean". Paper presented at *The Second Southern California Conference on Japanese/Korean Linguistics*. Santa Barbara, California.

Aksu-Koç, Ayhan. 1988. *The Acquisition of Aspect and Modality: The Case of Past Reference in Turkish*. Cambridge, England: Cambridge University Press.

Aksu-Koç, Ayhan & Dan Slobin. 1986. "A Psychological Account of the Development and Use of Evidential in Turkish". Chafe & Nichols. 1986. 159-167.

Bloom, Lois, L. Rocissano & L. Hood. 1976. "Adult-Child Discourse: Developmental Interaction between Information Processing and Linguistic Knowledge". *Cognitive Psychology* 8.521-552

Brown, Roger. 1973. *A First Language*. Cambridge, Mass.: Harvard University Press.

Bybee, Joan. 1985. *Morphology: A Study of the Relation between Meaning and Form*. Amsterdam: John Benjamins.

Bybee, Joan. & William Pagliuca. 1985. "Cross-Linguistic Comparison and the Development of Grammatical Meaning". *Historical Semantics and Historical Word Formation* ed. by J. Fisiak, 59-83. The Hague: Mouton.

Byrnes, James P. & Michelle A. Duff. 1989. "Young Children's Comprehension of Modal Expressions" *Cognitive Development* 4.369-387.

Chafe, Wallace & Johanna Nichols "eds." 1986. *Evidentiality: The Linguistic Coding of Epistemology*. New Jersey: Ablex.

Choi, Soonja. 1991. "Early Acquisition of Epistemic Meanings in Korean: A Study of Sentence-Ending Suffixes in the Spontaneous Speech of Three Children". *First Language* 11.93-119

DeLancey, Scott. 1986. "Evidentiality and Volitionality in Tibetan". Chafe & Nichols. 1986. 203-213.

Dore, John. 1974. "A Pragmatic Description of Early Language Development". *Journal of Psycholinguistic Research* 3.343-350.

Gopnik, Alison & Soonja Choi. 1990. "Do Linguistic Differences Lead to Cognitive Differences? A Cross-Linguistic Study of Semantic and Cognitive Development". *First Language* 10.199-215.

Gopnik, Alison & Andrew Meltzoff. 1984. "Semantic and Cognitive Development in 15 to 21 Months-Old Children". *Journal of Child Language* 11.594-513.

Hirst, William & Joyce Weil. 1982. "Acquisition of Epistemic and Deontic Meaning of Modals". *Journal of Child Language* 9.659-666.

Kim, Young-joo. 1992. "The Acquisition of Korean". Unpublished manuscript.

Lee, Hyo Sang. 1985. "Consciously Known but Unassimilated Information: A Pragmatic Analysis of the Epistemic Modal Suffix "-kun" in Korean". Paper presented at *The First Pacific Linguistics Conference*, University of Oregon.

Lee, Hyo Sang. 1991. "Tense, Aspect, and Modality: a Discourse-Pragmatic Analysis of Verbal Affixes in Korean from a Typological Perspective." Doctoral dissertation, University of California at Los Angeles.

Lee, Hyo Sang. 1993. "Cognitive Constraints on Expressing Newly Perceived Information: With Reference to Epistemic Modal Suffixes in Korean. *Cognitive Linguistics* 4.135-167.
Lee, Keedong. 1986. "Pragmatic Function of Sentence Enders". *Inmunkwahak (Humanities)* 56.41-59.
Moore, Chris, Kiran Pure & David Furrow. 1990. "Children's Understanding of the Modal Expression of Speaker Certainty and Uncertainty and Its Relation to the Development of a Representational Theory of Mind". *Child Development* 61.722-730.
Nichols, Johanna. 1986. "The Bottom Line: Chinese-Pidgin Russian". Chafe & Nichols 1986.239-257.
Palmer, F. R. 1986. *Mood and Modality*. Cambridge, England: Cambridge University Press.
Pellegrini, Anthony, Gene Brody & Zolinda Stoneman. 1987. "Children's Conversational Competence with Their Parents". *Discourse Processes* 10.93-106.
Piaget, Jean. 1955. *The Language and Thought of the Child*. New York: Meridian Books.
Shatz, Marilyn. 1983. "Communication." *Handbook of Child Psychology*, *Vol 3*, ed. by John Flavell & Ellen Markman, 841-890.
Shatz, Marilyn. 1984. "Answering Appropriately: A Developmental Perspective on Conversational Knowledge". *Discourse Development* ed. by Stan Kuczaj. New York: Springer-Verlag.
Slobin, Dan I. 1973. "Cognitive Prerequisites for the Acquisition of Grammar". *Studies of Child Language Development* ed. by Charles A. Ferguson & Dan I. Slobin, 175-208. New York: Holt, Rinehart & Winston.
Slobin, Dan I. 1985. "Crosslinguistic Evidence for the Language Making Capacity". *The Crosslinguistic Study of Language Acquisition, Volume 2: Theoretical Issues*. ed. by Dan I. Slobin, 1157-1256. Hillsdale, NH: Lawrence Erlbaum.
Steele, Susan. 1975. "Is it Possible?" *Working Papers on Language Universals*. Stanford University. 18:35-58.
Stephany, Ursula. 1986. "Modality". *Language Acquisition* (2nd Edition), ed. by Paul Fletcher & Michael Garman. Cambridge, Mass.: Cambridge University Press.
Tomasello, Michael. 1992. *First Verbs*. Cambridge, England: Cambridge University Press.
Traugott, Elizabeth. 1989. "On the Rise of Epistemic Meanings in English: An Example of Subjectification in Semantic Change". *Language* 65.31-55.
Wells, Gordon. 1979. "Learning and Using the Auxiliary Verb in English". *Language Development*, ed. by Victor Lee. New York: John, Wiley and Sons.
Wells, Gordon. 1985. *Language Development in the Preschool Years*. Cambridge, England: Cambridge University Press.
Woodbury, Anthony. 1986. "Interactions of Tense and Evidentiality: A Study of Sherpa and English". Chafe & Nichols. 1986. 188-202.
Zoh, Myeong-Han. 1981. *Hankwuk Atong-uy Ene Whoyktuk Yenkwu* [A Study of Language Acquisision in Korean Children] Seoul: Seoul National University Press.

The Interactional Basis of the Mandarin Modal *néng* 'CAN'*

Jiansheng Guo
University of California, Berkeley

1. Introduction

The paper explores the relationship between the interpersonal/discourse functions of the Mandarin modal *néng* 'can' and its semantic meanings from a functional perspective. The following statement by M.A.K. Halliday succinctly conveys the essence of functionalism:

> A functional approach to language means, first of all, investigating how language is used: trying to find out what are the purposes that language serves for us, and how we are able to achieve these purposes through speaking and listening, reading and writing. But it also means more than this. It means seeking to explain the nature of language in functional terms: seeing whether language itself has been shaped by use, and if so, in what ways — how the form of language has been determined by the functions it has evolved to serve. (Halliday 1973:7)

Pursuing the program outlined by Halliday, this paper attempts to elucidate how communicative function helps structure the semantic content and influences the semantic change of a grammatical morpheme. Specifically, the development of the Mandarin modal auxiliary *néng* in child speech shows that the interpersonal function constitutes a crucial part of the meaning of the word and has played an important role in changing its semantic content. In this paper, I propose to demonstrate that in child discourse the basic function of the modal *néng* is not merely to express notions such as ability, permission, and epistemic possibility. Rather, its most important function is an interpersonal one, namely to index the speaker's attempt to challenge the addressee. At the first stage of development in child speech, each of this modal's meanings — abilitative, permissive, and epistemic — is deeply embedded in the interpersonal tension between the speaker and the addressee. With respect to dynamic modality, *néng* signals contested ability[1]; it is used to challenge the assumptions the speaker attributes to the addressee about the speaker's ability. With respect to deontic modality, *néng* primarily codes prohibitions, challenging the addressee's actions. And with respect to epistemic modality, *néng* figures prominently in argumentation, challenging the propositional content of the addressee's previous statement. Thus, from the child speaker's point of view, this interpersonal meaning of challenge constitutes an essential, inalienable part of the meaning of the modal.

Previous studies on the semantics of modal auxiliaries have concentrated on their referential meanings (Lyons, 1977; Palmer, 1990; Perkins, 1983).[2] This tendency is representative of studies of the English modal *can*. The meanings of *can*, notoriously elusive and controversial, are traditionally incorporated under the three conventional modal rubrics: ability, permission, and possibility (e.g. Palmer 1990; Lyons 1977, Coates 1983)[3], roughly corresponding to the domains of dynamic, deontic, and epistemic modality (Palmer, 1990). Perkins (1983:35) proposes unified core meanings for the English modals and defines *can* as 'C does not preclude X'. This is roughly interpreted as: 'certain circumstances (C) exist that do not preclude the occurrence of the event predicated by the main verb or the truth validity of the proposition (X)'. This is essentially equivalent to the gloss 'it is possible that'. According to Perkins, this core meaning determines the dynamic, deontic, or epistemic readings, depending on whether it is applied to natural, social, or rational laws. However, both the traditional notions 'ability', 'permission', 'possibility' (including derivatives such as 'it is permitted' or 'it is possible') and the unified meaning proposed by Perkins, have in my opinion, obscured the interpersonal dynamics essential to the meaning of *can*.

Researchers in cognitive linguistics point out the unique force-dynamic nature of modals such as *can*. Talmy (1988) argues in detail that modals in their core meanings contain intrinsic force dynamics, i.e., interactions between barriers and exertions of force. For example, *can't* in the sentence *He can't move* indicates that the subject has a tendency toward moving, but some factor opposes that tendency. Applying the force-dynamics analysis to modals, Sweetser (1982) construes the basic meaning of *can* as 'enablement against some potential resisting force'.

However, these researchers have not gone far enough in specifying the nature of the force dynamics of modals. They elaborate on the the forces that are exerted, e.g. physical, social, or rational enablement. But they do not clarify what kinds of counter forces are exerted. Sweetser (1982) says nothing about the nature of the opposing force, while Talmy (1988) says only that the opposing force is backgrounded. Yet, the very essence of force dynamics is the tension between the two forces. I will argue that the opposing force is as important as the initial force. However, the opposing force is more likely to be found in discourse interactions than in semantic content. The tendency to consider only the semantic content of the modals may be one reason why the opposing force is hard to specify or regarded merely as backgrounded. I suggest that only by considering discourse function as well as semantic content can we fully understand the force dynamics of modals. Using the example of children's use of Mandarin *néng*, I will argue in this paper that the force dynamics of modals is motivated primarily by interpersonal tension in interactional contexts.

The paper is organized in three parts. First, it will give a distributional description of the meanings of *néng* across three different age groups, 3, 5, and 7 year olds. The order of development of the different meanings of *néng* will be shown to be:

physical ability → permission → epistemic uses

Second, it will show that all three meanings serve a common interpersonal function in dialogic discourse: challenge to the addressee. Third, it will argue that change in the meaning of *néng* is primarily motivated by this interpersonal function of challenge. The permission and epistemic meanings emerge as a result of the absorption of this interpersonal function into the semantics of *néng*.

2. Data

Mandarin Chinese *néng* translates into English roughly as 'can'. Syntactically, it is a modal auxiliary, distinct from main verbs.[4] Semantically, it is similar to its English counterpart *can*, in that it is used both in a physical sense, as in (1):

(1) *wǒ **néng** cóng zhèr tiào guò lái.*
'I **can** jump over from here.'

or in a social, permission sense, as in (2):

(2) *zhèi shì dàifu de dōngxi. nǐ bù **néng** dòng dàifu de dōngxi.*
'This is the doctor's thing. You **can't** take the doctor's thing.'

The epistemic meaning of *néng* is marginal compared with that of its English counterpart.[5] It is primarily used in rhetorical questions with sentence -final question markers (e.g. *ma*, or *ba*), as shown in (3):

(3) *gǎngtíng **néng** zài jiā lǐ ma?*
'**Can** a police station be in a home?' (as a rhetorical question)

In (3), it is difficult to distinguish the epistemic meaning from the root possibility meaning.[6]

Néng shares elements of meaning with certain other Mandarin forms. The modal *kěyǐ* 'permitted, allowed' can be used to express the same physical abilitative and social permission meanings as *néng*, but *kěyǐ* is used only in the positive form, not in the negative[7] or V-not-V question form.[8] Only *néng* can express negative physical ability meaning. The negative social permission meaning can be expressed by the modal *xǔ* 'allowed', but *xǔ* has a strong performative sense which marks the speaker as the deontic source. Thus it is often used by adults to give prohibitions to children but is rarely used by children. There are two Mandarin modal adverbs that can express so-called epistemic possibility, *kěnéng* 'possibly' and *yěxǔ* 'maybe'. But these have a specific function of hedging asserted propositions, which is different from the meaning and function of *néng*.

The data used for this paper were collected in a full-time preschool and an elementary school in Beijing, China. Subjects were three 3-year old, three 5-year old, and three 7-year old Mandarin-speaking children. In each age group, the teacher helped to select three children who were regarded as natural playmates. The children were of both sexes. The experimenter took each group to a separate room in the school and instructed the children to play together with toys provided by the experimenter. The children were engaged in four different activities: lego construction, doll play, playdough, and puzzle solving. Each visit lasted about one hour. The data consist of 5 hours of video recording for each age group.

Table 1. *Frequeny of* néng *utterances by age group*

Age	3	5	7
Frequenty	92	74	90

The recordings were transcribed, and all utterances by children containing *néng* identified for analysis. Table 1 gives the frequency in *néng* utterances in each age group.

Four uses of *néng* have been identified according to the semantics of the word in utterances: (1) unambiguous physical meaning referring to physical abilities and characteristics; (2) unambiguous social meaning referring to social permissions; (3) cases ambiguous between physical and social meaning; and (4) epistemic-like meaning. The physical meaning category includes uses traditionally subsumed under dynamic modality, i.e. uses referring to the physical ability or conditions enabling an agent to perform certain acts, or to the physical characteristics that enable an object to have certain functions in specific tasks. The social meaning category includes uses traditionally classified under deontic modality; the source of modality is of a social nature, either the existing social conventions or the participant's authority or wish. The ambiguous meaning category includes uses in which the modality could be interpreted as either physical or social. In the epistemic-like category are uses involving what we generally think of as epistemic modality; the *-like* suffix is added to show that this is not a robust or well-established category (see Section 6 for details). Further elaboration and examples will be given in Sections 3 through 6. Table 2 gives a breakdown of the different meaning categories by age.

From this breakdown we see that about two thirds of the 3 year olds' uses exhibit pure physical meaning, while social meaning is sporadic. In contrast,

Table 2. *Breakdown of semantic categories of* néng *by age*

Age	Physical meaning	Ambiguous meaning	Social meaning	Epistemic-like meaning	N
3	72%	19%	9%	–	92
5	45%	12%	43%	–	74
7	52%	11%	26%	12%	90

Note: The total percentage exceeds 100 due to rounding in calculation.

the social meaning in the 5 year olds' uses shows a much higher frequency, making up 43% of total uses. This indicates that by age 5, *néng* has acquired a new meaning of social permission. The 7 year olds' uses of *néng* are comparable to those of the 5 year olds in the physical and ambiguous categories, but social meaning is used significantly less than among 5 year olds. But the 7 year olds seem to be developing a new meaning, the epistemic-like meaning.

In the next section, I will discuss in detail the discourse functions and semantic content of each category, and argue for a functionalist explanation of the semantic changes of the modal in child development. I will focus on how *néng* is used in interaction, and on the discourse functions this morpheme is intended to serve. For this purpose, the *néng* utterances within each meaning category will be further categorized according to discourse functions.

3. The physical meaning category

I have divided the physical meaning category into three functional sub-categories: (1) challenge to the addressee's assumptions, (2) justification for prohibitions, and (3) reportive uses. In what follows, I will focus on the first two sub-categories to illustrate the challenge function of *néng* and then contrast these with the third sub-category, reportive uses, which does not serve this function. In consideration of space, only one example will be presented and discussed for each sub-category, which, nevertheless, are representative of other utterances in the sub-category in question.

3.1. *Challenge to the addressee's assumptions*

The challenge to the addressee's assumptions category may be further classified into three sub-categories: boasting, new discoveries, and problem reporting.

3.1.1. *Boasting* Examples of boasting may serve as prototypical examples to illustrate the challenge function of *néng* in discourse. In boasting, the child speaker tries to show off to the addressee (primarily the adult experimenter) special abilities that adults do not usually expect children to have. A typical boasting use is shown in (4), where adult experimenter Guo's lack of confidence in the children's abilities, as indicated by his question 'What else can you make?', prompts a series of boasts from the 3 year olds (C1, C2, and C3):

(4) C1: (holds up a lego construction and shows Guo)
zhèige shì wǒ dā de .
'It is me who built this one.'
GU: *shì ma?*
'Is that right?'
C1: *shì.*
'Yes.'
GU: *nǐ hái **néng** dā shénme?*
you still can build what?
'What else can you build?'
C1: *wǒ hái **néng** dā bǐnggān ne.*
I still can build biscuits PRTCL [9]
'I can even build biscuits.'
GU: *ao!*
'Oh, I see.'
C3: *wǒ hái **néng** dā miàntiáo ne.*
I still can build noodles PRTCL
'I can even build noodles.'
GU: *zhēnde a ?*
'Really?'
C2: *wǒ **néng** dā lóufáng.*
I can build buildings
'I can build buildings.'
GU: *zhēnde a?*
'Is it really?'
C1: *wǒ hái **néng** dā jīdàn ne. nǐ kàn, shūshū.*
I still can build eggs PRTCL. you look, uncle
'I can even build eggs. Look, uncle.'
C1: (shows lego construction to Guo)

In order to tease out the meaning and function of *néng* in these utterances, it is appropriate at this point to define my use of certain terminology. I use the term 'semantic meaning' or 'propositional meaning' in the sense of Lyons' *descriptive meaning*, which carries 'factual information' that 'purports to describe some state-of-affairs' (Lyons 1977:50), or Ogden and Richards' (1923) *referential meaning*, as presented by Lyons (1977:175), which identifies 'any object or state-of-affairs in the external world'. In this sense, the

Table 3. *Features of challenge to assumption uses of* néng

Predicated situation:	jump over microphone wire jump from high above by parachute build a big truck with lego build biscuits with lego etc.	
Special markers:	emphatic adverbs:	*hái* (even)
	attention getters:	*nǐ kàn*! (Look); *shūshū* (Uncle)
gestural indicator:	long eye engagement	
Speaker action:	act out or bring about the predicated situation	
Challenging intonation:	high-pitched level intonation over the whole utterance. (vs. the normal falling intonation at the end of the utterance)	

semantic meaning of *néng* in the above utterances evidently refers to the physical ability of the speaker to perform predicated actions.

The above characterization of the semantic meaning of *néng* in these utterances coincides precisely with traditional accounts of the semantics of the Mandarin *néng* and English 'can'. Indeed, if the utterances were extracted from their discourse contexts, nothing more could be said about their meaning. However, in interactive discourse, *néng* has another layer of signification at the interpersonal level. The speakers of these utterances are not merely presenting a neutral claim about their abilities; rather, they are trying to convince the addressee that they are much more competent than the addressee thinks. In other words, they are trying to challenge the addressee's assumption about their abilities. This challenge constitutes the discourse function of *néng* and the utterances that contain it. I use the term 'discourse function' in the sense of *interpersonal* or *affective function*, as discussed by Lyons (1977:50-51), i.e. how the speaker intends to influence the mental state or behavior of the addressee.

What empirical evidence is there that utterances like (4) indeed contain challenges of this nature? A *challenge* implies intense interpersonal interaction and conflicting beliefs. And in effect, there are various indicators in the *néng* utterances in my corpus of intense interpersonal engagement and contest. Table 3 lists several linguistic, para-linguistic, and behavioral features associated with the *néng* utterances to substantiate this claim.

First, the utterances refer to situations that are surprising, i.e. accomplishments not usually assumed of children, such as 'jumping over a microphone wire', or 'parachute jumping from high above'. In addition, many of these utterances contain the adverb *hái*, roughly translated as 'even', indicating that the designated ability is beyond normal expectations, and in particular the addressee's expectation. Third, the speakers always try to fully engage the addressee, using attention getters, such as 'uncle' or 'look' to secure the addressee's attention before making the utterance. Furthermore, the speakers consistently perform the actions in question while making the *néng* utterances, as if to give evidence for the claim. In addition, these utterances are all made using a sustained high-pitch intonation contour over the whole utterance that indicates challenge or contest. Examples in (5) schematically contrast the challenging intonation contour to the normal stative intonation contour without affect.

(5) a. Challenging intonation: *wǒ hái néng tiào shéng ne.*
'I can even jump rope.'
b. Stative intonation: *wǒ néng tiào shéng.*
'I can jump rope.'

All the above indicators suggest that these utterances fulfill a specific discourse function of challenging an assumption of the addressee. But in order to validate this claim, one more question needs to be answered: 'What evidence is there of an assumption on the part of the addressee that the child speaker deems challenge-worthy?' This challenge-worthiness may sometimes surface in the discourse context, as shown in (6):

(6) GU: (instructs C2, who does not know what to do next)
nǐ kěyǐ bāng zhe biérén.
'You can help others.'
C1: *wǒ bù yòng biérén bāng zhe, wǒ jiù* ***néng***
I not need others help PROG I even can
pīn chū lái.
piece-together out come
'I can simply piece (them) together without the help of others.'

In this example, C2 finished her portion of the puzzle quickly. Guo then told her that she could help the other children finish theirs. C1 heard this as an underestimation of his ability to put together puzzles, and produced the *néng* utterance to counter that underestimation. Whether Guo intended his utterance as C1 perceived it is not an issue here; all that matters is that the child speaker interpreted it that way. More often, however, the challenged assumption is not explicitly verbalized. But the speaker believes that the addressee holds the assumption. When children say that they *can* do X with the focus on ability, they believe that their ability is at issue. In general, these beliefs do fit with adult expectations of children's abilities. Most cultures regard children as weak, not fully competent, fragile, and in need of adult protection; and this view of children inheres in the belief structure underlying the *néng* utterances produced by the Mandarin-speaking children in this study.[10] *Néng* utterances provide a strategy for signaling contradiction of the assumed adult beliefs, thereby constituting an explicit situation of force dynamics. The presupposed addressee's assumption constitutes the force that will presumably continue if it encounters no obstacle; the *néng* utterance constitutes the counter-force that challenges and seeks to block that assumption. I gloss this discourse function as 'Do not assume X', thereby emphasizing that it is highly dynamic and transitive at the interpersonal level.

While I am convinced that the discourse function of *néng* is to challenge the addressee's assumptions, I am not claiming that this is also its semantic meaning (in the sense discussed earlier). In (6), a clear sense of physical ability is referred to by *néng*, which serves as the focus of the interpersonal force dynamics. Following Lyons' definition of semantic meaning (his descriptive meaning) as referring to an event or state of affairs in the external world, I take the semantic meaning of *néng* in the category of boasting to be physical ability.

Although the discourse function and the semantic meaning of *néng* are separate components, the two are closely interrelated. The obstacle, in the semantic meaning, does not merely exist in the objective world, but has a deeper social and psychological origin in the presupposed addressee's expectations, which the child speaker seeks to challenge. It is here that the abilitative meaning and the discourse function of challenge find their connection.

In summary, the semantic meaning of *néng* in boasting utterances is that the doer has the ability to overcome an obstacle. In contrast, its discourse function is to counteract the addressee's assumption concerning this ability. At the semantic level, force dynamics operates between ability and a difficulty in the physical domain. At the pragmatic level, it operates between the addressee's expectation and the speaker's challenge to that expectation in the interpersonal domain. The meanings at the two levels are intrinsically connected. The physical obstacle has social and psychological origins in the presupposed assumption of the addressee(s). Thus the use of *néng* has to be understood in terms of both its referential content and its interpersonal function.

3.1.2. *New discoveries* The second subcategory of challenge to the addressee's assumptions is new discoveries. (7) is a typical example of this use:

(7) C1: (holds up lego car to Guo and rotates wheel)
nǐkàn, wǒ lúnzi ***néng*** *zhuàn ne.*
you look, my wheel can turn PRTCL(=even)
'Look, my wheel can even turn.'
(rotates wheel again and then gives it to C3)

This subcategory is similar to boasting in both semantic meaning and pragmatic function. But here the focus is on the patient, namely the toys the child is playing with, rather than on his or her ability. A typical situation is one in which the speaker plays with a toy, and suddenly discovers an unexpected feature or an innovative way to play. The speaker then shows off this newly discovered feature. Thus, the discourse function of these utterances is to challenge, and consequently change, the addressee's expectations about the toys.

3.1.3. *Problem reporting.* The third subcategory under challenge to the addressee's assumptions is problem reporting. Here, the child reports to the adult addressee on a problem in the current activity. This may be a negative statement, as in (8):

(8) C1: (tries to make a lego figure stand; it falls; looks at Guo and shows lego figure)
zhè yàngzi bù ***néng*** *zhàn zhe*
this manner not can stand PROG
'(It) can't stand like this.'

or a question about the characteristics of the object, as in (9):

(9) C2: (doesn't know how to open cotton bundle, holds it up to Guo)
zhè ***néng*** *dǎ kāi ma?*
this can make open Q
'Can this (be) opened?'

These utterances are not made merely to report a problem. Their goal is to solicit the addressee's help. And help will be forthcoming only after a change in the addressee's knowledge about the toys. Thus, utterances in this subtype have a double discourse function: (1) to change the addressee's assumptions about the object, and (2) to get help.

At least two pieces of evidence point to this double function. First, the children produce these utterances in a matter-of-fact manner while showing the objects to the addressee, as if to say 'Look, this toy is not working as you expect. So help me get it to work.' Then, they simply wait for help. Second, the sorts of problems reported in these utterances always relate to a normally expected function of the toys in question. Since the toys are provided by the experimenter, the children naturally hold the latter responsible for the failure of these normal functions to occur. For the same reason, they assume that the experimenter expects the toys to function normally. Thus, a challenge to that assumption is a prerequisite for soliciting help.

I emphasize that these uses are not plain statements or questions; children use a different construction when they encounter difficulties with their own possessions. E.g., if they have difficulty untying their shoe laces, they will produce utterances like (10):

(10) *wǒ jiě bù kāi zhèi xiédài.*
I untie not open this shoe-lace
'I can't untie this shoe lace.'

In (10), the subject is the agent (the speaker), and a Verb+Resultative -complement construction is used instead of *néng*. This construction attributes the failure entirely to the inability of the agent.

3.2. *Justification for prohibition*

The second physical meaning category is justification for prohibition. A typical example is shown in (11):

(11) (C3 puts toy banana into mouth and pretends to eat)
GU: *bié bǎ zhège fàng zuǐ lǐ, hǎo ma?*
'Don't put this into your mouth, OK?'
C1: *yào zhèyàngfàng zuǐ lǐ jiù bù* ***néng*** *wár le*
if (it) is put into mouth like that, then not can play PRTCL
'If you put it in your mouth like that, it can't be played with any more.'

Uses of this type always occur where the adult forbids one child to do something, and then another child makes a *néng* utterance to justify the adult's prohibition. In this category, the *néng* utterance is always negative and always refers to an undesirable state (e.g. loss of an existing ability) that the prohibited action might engender. The semantic meaning of the utterance is 'inability of object Z to perform function X'. The interpersonal discourse function of the utterance is again two-layered. On the one hand, it challenges the addressee's assumption that the action has no negative effect on the object. On the other, it functions as part of a prohibition, a challenge to the addressee's action.

3.3. *Reportive uses*

In the 'reportive use' category, *néng* appears in utterances which impart information without personal affect. Reportive *néng* does not actively index the speaker's stance in interpersonal communication. It may be used in an utterance that supplements another (but is not necessarily grammatically subordinate to it), e.g. by providing a reason or motivation for it, as shown in (12):

(12) C2: (no longer wants a lego, is about to throw it to C3)

zhèi	*bù*	***néng***	*yòng*	*le .*	*gěi*	*nǐ*	*ba .*
this	not	can	use	PERF	give	you	PRTCL

'This cannot be used any more. (I) give it to you.'

Here the speaker is not trying to change the addressee's belief with the *néng* utterance. The utterance simply provides a rationale for her action. In this use, the speaker does not present the situation as a potential conflict, since she simply throws the lego to the other child without waiting for response. Reportive *néng* can occur in questions, answers, and statements. The basic criterion is that *néng* does not privilege an interpersonal message.

As a summary of the discussion on the physical meaning uses of *néng*, I present the breakdown of the frequency of each subcategory for each age group in Table 4.

From Table 4, we see that the majority of *néng* utterances in the physical meaning category do not present the agent's ability or the physical characteristics of an object as a static entity. Instead, they present them primarily in contexts where an obstacle exists. Furthermore, this obstacle is derived from the child's assumptions about what the addressee believes, which constitutes

Table 4. *Breakdown of discourse functions of the physical meaning category of* néng *by age*

Age	Challenge to Assumptions	Justification for Prohibitions	Representational Uses	N
3	52%	8%	10%	92
5	42%	3%	-	74
7	38%	-	14%	90

Note: N is the total occurrences of *néng*, including social and epistemic meanings. Therefore, the percentages in each age group do not add up to 100%.

the force which the *néng* utterance is intended to counter at the interpersonal level. In other words, *néng* is used to overcome an assumed doubt (on the part of the addressee) about physical abilities and characteristics.

Essential to an understanding of the modal *néng* is an understanding of both its referential meaning and its interpersonal functions. In these *néng* utterances, the addressee, although unmentioned, is always implicitly present in the discourse interaction. To emphasize this presence at the discourse (interpersonal) level, I gloss the discourse function of this category as 'Don't assume X', which emphasizes that *néng* is highly social and transitive.

Maintaining the traditional distinction between semantic and pragmatic meanings, we can say that in its physical sense, *néng* refers semantically to physical ability, but pragmatically it indexes interpersonal challenge in an active and intentional manner.

4. The social meaning category

Unlike the physical meaning uses, the social meaning uses no longer convey 'social meaning' pragmatically, but express it directly. The physical ability meaning is no longer relevant. When a speaker tells an addressee that the latter cannot do X, it is obvious from the situation that the addressee has the ability to do X, and that this ability is either actualized or about to be actualized. The only meaning *néng* has here is social permission. Social meaning uses of *néng* are rare among 3 year olds, but very frequent among 5 year olds. The uses may be divided into four groups: (1) prohibitions; (2) permissions; (3) reportive uses; and (4) self regulations.

4.1. *Prohibitions*

Prohibition is the major social meaning use, especially among the 5 year olds. A typical example is shown in (13):

> (13) C1: *ni bù* ***néng*** *dă rén.*
> you not can beat people
> 'You can't beat people.'
> *bă rén tóu dă huài le, bă tā de tóu kăn xiàlái, gĕi rénjiā, duì ma?*
> '(if) her head is hurt, (then) his head will be chopped off and given to her. Right?'

The form of the utterance differs here from that of physical meanings. In social meanings, the subject is the second person and the sentence is negative. Utterances in this category are of a specific form: 'You cannot VP.' In contrast to the physical uses, for social uses, semantic meaning and discourse function are identical: preventing an action from taking place, which is glossed as 'Don't do X.' This identity between semantic meaning and discourse function may explain why uses of this category are referred to as discourse-oriented uses (Palmer, 1990). Since the 3 year olds seldom use *néng* with this social meaning while the 5 year olds do so quite frequently, we should regard this use category as a new development in the meaning of *néng* (see Table 2 for a breakdown).

4.2. *Permissions*

Seeking permissions is a marginal use in the current corpus; only a few *néng* utterances from the 7 year olds can be thus categorized.[11] An example of this use is shown in (14):

> (14) C2: (wants to get water from restroom for toy tea set. asks Guo)
> ***néng*** *jiē diăr shuĭ qù ma?*
> can get little water go Q
> 'Can (I) go get some water?'
> GU: *mm, bù néng jiē diănr shuĭ. dāi huĭr nòng shī le , jiù gāi.*
> 'mm, (you) cannot go get water. You'll get (the floor) wet.'

With this meaning, the *néng* utterance presupposes a social constraint or obstacle that will block the speaker's action, in this instance the children's understanding that once they start the play session, they are not allowed to leave the room without permission. The discourse function of *néng* utterances of this type is an attempt to remove the social constraint. Its semantic meaning refers to the same goal. But note that no interpersonal challenge is involved, since the child does not attempt to defeat the constraint, but simply inquires whether the authority will temporarily lift it.

4.3. *Reportive uses*

In reportive utterances, *néng* is clearly used in the sense of social permission, but it merely reports an event involving a social constraint without attempting to regulate the participants' behavior. In this category, *néng* is usually used in the descriptive part of utterances, as in (15):

(15) C3: (The teacher has told C1, C2, and C3 to stay in the classroom after the experiment session if the rest of the class is gone to outside. C3 sees the class leaving for outside)
ei ya , tāmen zǒu le.
'Oh uh, they are all leaving.'
zánmen wár wán bù ***néng*** *xià qù le ,*
we play finish not can down go PERF,
zěnme bàn ya?
how do Q?
'(When) we finish playing, we cannot go down any more. What should we do?'

A report of a third person's directive is shown in (16):

(16) C1: (pretends to kiss a doll)
wǒ gēn tā qīn zuī ne.
'We are kissing.'
C2: *lǎoshī shuō bù* ***néng*** *shuō qīn zuǐ de huà .*
teacher say not can say kiss mouth REL talk
'The teacher said that (we) cannot talk about kissing.'

From the context in (16), the illocutionary force of the *néng* utterance appears to be to criticize C1 or stop him from talking about kissing. It looks rather like prohibition uses. However, the prohibition is conveyed by reporting a norm, i.e. what the teacher said before. The modal *néng* is embedded in the quotation from the teacher, and thus does not privilege the interpersonal message from the speaker. For this reason, these utterances are categorized as reportive uses.

4.4. *Self regulations*

This category, too, is only used by the 7 year olds. Structurally, it is similar to the prohibition category, but differs in that the (explicit or implicit) subject of the *néng* sentence is the first-person speaker. The prohibition is self-directed. An example of this category is given in (17):

(17) C3: (gives C2 a toy, then changes her mind, shyly withdraws toy from C2)
bù, *bù* ***néng*** *gěi* *nǐ* *zhèige*.
no, not can give you this.
'No, (I) can't/shouldn't give you this.'

In this example, the child speaker has internalized the force dynamics (i.e. the two opposing forces come from the same person), which elsewhere is socially distributed. In other words, the social opposition that elsewhere exists between two people has here become a psychological opposition in which the self is split, representing two opposing forces simultaneously.

5. The ambiguous case category

Ambiguous cases include those *néng* utterances in which a physical-ability interpretation and a social-permission interpretation are equally reasonable. The physical-characteristics meaning of *néng* may in fact license the social permission meaning, or, conversely, social permission is presented as if it were part of the physical characteristics of the object in question. Thus the meaning in this category is intrinsically ambiguous.[12] There are four sub-categories of ambiguous utterances, which differ in their discourse functions: (1) challenge to prohibition; (2) permission seeking; (3) permission giving; and (4) prohibition.

5.1. *Challenge to prohibition*

The use of *néng* to challenge a prohibition typically occurs in explicit confrontations. The experimenter utters a prohibition or makes a comment about an inappropriate action, and the child responds with a challenge containing words like *gànmá* 'how come', *wèishénme* 'why', or the challenge question marker *ya* (roughly 'what you just said is highly questionable and totally against my expectation'). The following is an example:

(18) C2: (does not know how to open a cotton bundle, holds out bundle to Guo)
zhège zěnme dǎ kāi ya ?
'How to open this?'
GU: *zhège bù **néng** dǎ kāi.*
'This can't be opened.'
C2: *bù **néng** dǎ kāi gànmá ?*
not can make open how-come
'How come it can't be opened?'

In the physical-ability meaning category discussed earlier, the challenge is generally presupposed by the child and thus implicit. But in this category, the confrontation is on record and represents a head-on defiance of the addressee. In terms of semantic meaning, *néng* here is a direct copy of the previous adult use. In the adult use, the sentence structure OBJ+not+*néng*+V makes the physical-ability interpretation and the social-permission interpretation equally possible. It may refer to the physical characteristics of the object; thus, in (18) the cotton bundle cannot physically be opened. Or it may refer to the adult's authority, i.e. he doesn't allow it to be opened. This ambiguity cannot be resolved, since both interpretations are licit, and the physical condition is often the reason for the social prohibition.

5.2. *Permission seeking*

In this category, *néng* is used to ask for permissions to act. The sentence structure is again in the OBJ+*néng*+V+Q form. The focus is on the object, while the agent is backgrounded. Although from the context it appears that *néng* is basically concerned with social permission, the structure of the sentence closely associates the predicated meaning with the object, as if permission were part of the intrinsic characteristics of the object, similar to its physical characteristics. An example of this category is shown in (19):

(19) C1: (helps Guo put lego into the box during clean-up, picks up a lego car, asks)
zhè ***néng*** *fàng ma ?*
this can put Q
'Can this (be) put in?'
GU: *á? néng.*
'What? Yes, it can.'

This category is essentially the same as the permissions category, with a clear social meaning. The difference is that here *néng* is not completely dissociated from its source in the physical world.

5.3. *Permission giving (compliance)*

This category is a special type of assenting, consisting only in compliance with the addressee's previous request. Here the actor is the speaker, while in the general sense of permission giving, the actor will be the addressee or a third party. The following is an example of the compliance use of *néng*:

(20) GU: (toys dropped onto floor, Guo to C1)
néng *gěi jiǎn qǐ lái ma?*
'Can (you) pick it up (for me)?'
C1: ***néng*** *ya.*
can PRTCL(=of course)
'Sure, (I) can.'

In this use, although the speaker complies with the request, it is not clear whether *néng* refers to the physical ability which makes compliance possible or to the speaker's consent itself. The social permission meaning is not clearly differentiated from the physical meaning.

5.4. *Prohibition (focus on objects)*

This category has the same discourse function as the prohibition category discussed in 4.1., but the referential meaning of *néng* is ambiguous. A typical example of this category is given in (21):

(21) C2: (C1 plays daddy role. C2 takes C1's playdough)
gěi wǒ .
'Give (it) to me.'
C3: (to C2)
nèi shì bàba de dōngxi , bù ***néng*** *yào .*
that is daddy 's thing not can take
'That belongs to daddy and (it) can't (be) taken.'

From the sentence structure, we can see that *néng* is closely associated with the object rather than the agent, suggesting that the social convention whereby one should not take daddy's belongings is an inherent characteristic of the object rather than an inappropriate act. Since the social meaning is not clearly differentiated from the physical meaning, these utterances are classified as ambiguous.

6. The epistemic-like meaning category

This category is called epistemic-like because the epistemic meaning of *néng* in Mandarin is marginal. Tsang (1981) claims that *néng* cannot be used epistemically at all. However, Lü (1980), a more comprehensive and authoritative source, cites examples showing *néng* used in root possibility and epistemic possibility senses in questions and negative utterances. In the current corpus, the 7 year olds produced some *néng* utterances with an epistemic-like sense, all in the form of questions. *Néng* itself may be positive or negative, and the epistemic meaning is not clearly differentiated from root possibility or sometimes even from the general root meaning. Thus we cannot treat these as having full-fledged epistemic meaning. However, as will be clear in later discussion, *néng* does communicate the speaker's evaluation of conclusions in relation to evidence. Thus we are justified in speaking of epistemic uses. Since this meaning is only used by the 7 year olds, we will treat it as a new semantic development. A typical example is shown in (22):

(22) C2: (looks for pot and cannot find it)
zhèi guō méi le .
'This pot has disappeared.'
C3: (turns around to look for it, to C2)
bù ***néng*** *ba ?*
not can Q(=tentative)
'(That) can't be, (can it)?'

In this example, *néng* is used clearly in an epistemic sense. C2 makes an assertion, and C3 casts strong doubt on C2's conclusion. A more controversial example is (23):

(23) C2: (puts lego on board)
gǎngtíng , zhèige .
'This is the police station.'
C3: (turns to C2, challengingly)

gǎngtíng	***néng***	*zài*	*jiā*	*lǐ*	*ma ?*
police station	can	at	home	inside	Q ?

'Can a police station be in a home?'

In this example, *néng* can be interpreted as referring to a social convention, that is, whether police stations can be located in a home. However, in this use, C3 is not trying to argue that it is right or wrong to locate police stations in private homes; rather, she is questioning the correctness of C2's claim. The issue is not one of social appropriateness, but rather the validity of C2's assertion given C3's knowledge of the cultural convention at issue. Thus the discourse function of disvalidating the addressee's previous statement gives rise to the interpretation of the semantic meaning 'A police station cannot (possibly) be in a home'. As the examples in (22) and (23) show, epistemic uses of *néng* occur in a discourse frame of confrontational argumentation. Their discourse function of challenging the addressee's previous claims gives rise to the epistemic-like semantic meaning.

The question arises whether the challenge comes from the rhetorical question form or from the modal *néng*. Admittedly, a part of the challenge does come from the rhetorical question, since challenge is the primary illocutionary function of that sentence form in Mandarin. Rhetorical questions also include an important prosodic feature: sentence stress on the verb, or modal, if there is one. Thus, in (23) the main stress is on *néng*. It cannot be placed on other sentence constituents without changing the meaning. Since modals always receive the main stress in rhetorical questions like (23), and since rhetorical questions are typically used in arguments or challenges, the discourse function of challenge is carried over into the meaning of the modal. This hypothesis is particularly compelling for *néng* since it specializes in the challenge function in other meaning domains.

Thus, the argumentative sentence form and the interactional context together provide the semantic source for the epistemic meaning of *néng*. It is important to note, however, that this epistemic meaning is not always dependent on the rhetorical question form. In the context given in (22), C2 goes on to answer C3's challenge by asserting *néng ya* 'It can (be the case), of course', as shown in (24):

(24) C3: (turns around to look for it, to C2)
bù ***néng*** *ba ?*
not can Q (=tentative)
'(That) can't be, (can it)?'
C2: (matter of fact manner)
néng *ya !*
can PRTCL (=of course)
'Of course (it) can.'

Thus, although the epistemic meaning is elusive, it does not necessarily depend on a particular sentence form. What it depends on at this stage of development is considerable contextual framing, i.e. challenges and counter challenges in argumentation.

To conclude the discussion of the data, all the meanings and functions of the Mandarin modal *néng* are shown in Figure 1, And Table 5 gives a breakdown of the frequency of each subcategory across all three age groups.

Table 5. *Breakdown of frequencies for all subcategories of* néng *by age*

Age	*Physical Meaning*			*Ambiguous*				*Social Meaning*				*Epistemic*	N
	3.1	3.2	3.3	5.1	5.2	5.3	5.4	4.1	4.2	4.3	4.4	6.0	
3	52%	8%	10%	3%	5%	3%	7%	6%	-	4%	-	-	92
5	42%	3%	-	3%	-	3%	7%	39%	-	4%	-	-	74
7	38%	-	14%	1%	-	2%	8%	13%	2%	2%	7%	12%	90

Physical meaning category
3.1 Challenge to addressee's assumptions
3.2 Justification for prohibition
3.3 Reportive uses

Ambiguous case category
5.1 Challenge to prohibition
5.2 Permission seeking
5.3 Permission giving (compliance)
5.4 Prohibition (focus on object)

Social meaning category
4.1 Prohibition (focus on agent)
4.2 Permissions
4.3 Reportive uses
4.4 Self regulations

Epistemic-like meaning category
6.0 Epistemic-like uses

Physical meaning
- 3.1 Challenge to addressee's assumptions
  - Boasting
  - New discoveries
  - Problem reporting
- 3.2 Justification for prohibition
- 3.3 Reportive uses

Ambiguous meaning
- 4.1 Prohibition (focus on agent)
- 4.2 Permission seeking
- 4.3 Reportive uses
- 4.4 Self regulations

Social meaning
- 5.1 Challenge to prohibition
- 5.2 Permission seeking
- 5.3 Permission giving (compliance)
- 5.4 Prohibition (focus on object)

Epistemic-like meaning 6.0 Epistemic-like uses

Figure 1. *Summary of semantic and functional categories of* néng

7. Discussion

7.1. The first aim of this paper is to argue that the Mandarin modal *néng* not only has a set of referential meanings — ability, permission, and possibility —, but it also serves important interpersonal discourse functions. In the physical abilitative meaning, *néng* challenges what the speaker believes to be the addressee's assumptions about the speaker's abilities. In the social permission meaning, *néng* challenges the addressee's actions. And in the epistemic-like meaning, *néng* challenges the addressee's immediately preceding assertion. This interpretation of a common interpersonal function for the modals (i.e. challenge) differs from Perkins' formulation of the core semantic meaning of the English modals in terms of possibility and necessity as applied to the physical, social, and rational domains (Perkins 1983). Perkins focuses on the common features that can be extracted from the static semantic meaning of the English modals. But what I am arguing here is that a common denominator for the different semantic meanings of *néng*, — i.e. dynamic, deontic, and epistemic — arises from the interpersonal discourse function *néng* serves, namely that of *challenge*. Each of *néng*'s semantic meanings serves primarily to issue a challenge rather than to make a statement about abilities, permissions, and possibilities. Discourse analysis of *néng* prompts us to pose the broader question of what modals are and what they do in language. Why is there a grammatical category 'modal auxiliaries' that expresses possibility and necessity?

In order to answer this question, let us look at two of the many different ways of representing modal meanings. In English, physical ability can be expressed either by the modal auxiliary *can* or by the adjective *able*, as in *be able to*. Similarly, social permission can be expressed by *can* or *be permitted to*. In each case the two options are referentially equivalent. But they differ in grammatical status. Modal auxiliaries belong to a closed grammatical class, while adjectives and verbs belong to open lexical classes. Along the continuum between lexical words and grammatical morphemes, modal auxiliaries are more grammaticalized than adjectives and verbs. This grammatical difference has significant consequences with regard to the meanings expressed. With lexical forms such as *able* or *permitted*, the speaker presents a fact without any personal involvement. We interpret the utterance as 'I'm stating X to you'. But when modal auxiliaries are used, the resulting utterances are colored by speaker involvement in the form of opinion, affect, or personal dynamics. We interpret such utterances as 'I'm challenging/objecting to/arguing with you by stating X to you.' This division of labor fits Traugott's (1982) formulation of trends in grammaticalization. When a lexical form is grammaticalized, its meaning may also evolve from propositional to expressive/interpersonal. Similarly, when discussing the Tense, Aspect, and Mood system, Givón (1984:269) points out that "as *discourse-pragmatic* features, they play a crucial role ... in indicating their time/truth/certainty/probability modalities vis-a-vis *the speaker-hearer contract*" (emphasis mine). Child language research has shown that modals are employed by children to convey their different social stances in terms of interpersonal commitment in play with other children (Gerhardt 1985, 1990 for English; Shepherd, 1981 for Antiguan Creole). All this points to a special function for modals in expressing interpersonal meanings.

The claim that modals indicate the speaker's subjective evaluation of the modalized proposition is hardly novel (e.g. Lyons 1977; Halliday 1973). However, previous approaches have failed to recognize the crucial *interpersonal* function of speaker involvement. Concern has traditionally been with the relationship between speaker and proposition, rather than with that between speaker and addressee, with the proposition serving as a means of actualizing the latter relationship. Lyons (1977), for example, glosses the deontic modality meaning as 'let it be so', and the dynamic modality meaning as 'it is so'. Although the constitutive power of language that he attributes to deontic modality is social in nature, he fails to recognize that his gloss represents only part of the social interaction. Speakers are not simply playing with the creative power of language. Rather, they are participating in a social exchange, and the creative power of language is used to regulate the interpersonal relationship between the speaker and the addressee. In this sense, Palmer's (1990) characterization of deontic modality as 'discourse oriented' comes closest to the position argued in this paper. But his analysis still focuses on a single participant's involvement in the discourse. What's more, his analysis is limited to the deontic modals, which are generally regarded as having performative force. This paper argues, in contrast, that 'discourse orientation' is the fundamental property for modals in all the three domains — dynamic, deontic, and epistemic. Language has developed the grammatical category of modal auxiliaries to serve the function of regulating interpersonal relations in social interaction.

7.2. The second goal of this paper is to argue not only that our understanding of the discourse functions of modals is indispensable to our understanding of their meanings, but also that their discourse functions form an important source of semantic change. Semantic bleaching and abstraction, strengthening of inferential meanings, and metaphorical transfer have been recognized as the basic processes of semantic change involved in grammaticalization (e.g. Bybee 1988; Traugott 1988; Sweetser 1988). However, given their methodological limitations, historical studies have seldom investigated the role played by interpersonal discourse functions in semantic change. Studies of developmental change in child language can give us insightful revelations in this respect. In particular, the development of the social permission meaning in the 5 year olds' uses of *néng*, and of the epistemic-like meaning in the 7 year olds' uses of this modal, reflects a process of semanticization of the interpersonal-discourse function that is associated with earlier uses of *néng*. The discourse function of *néng* gradually saturates its semantic content, resulting in a new semantic meaning.

The change from the 3 year olds' abilitative meaning to the 5 year olds' social permission meaning is revealing. For the 3 year olds, the physical -meaning uses of *néng* all share a discourse function, roughly glossed as 'Don't assume X' (see Section 3).[13] In addition, the justification for prohibi-

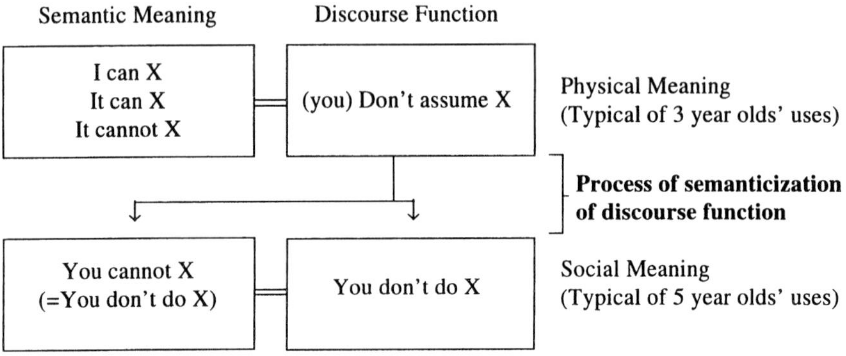

Figure 2. *Process of semanticization of discourse function*

tions category has the dual function of 'Don't assume X' and 'Don't do X'. For the 5 year olds, the newly developed prohibition meaning has 'Don't do X' as its semantic content and discourse function. What is the connection? I suggest that the interpersonal function of challenge has been semanticized, i.e., what began as a contextual meaning frequently associated with the form has become conventionalized and incorporated into the semantic content of that form.[14] This process of change is illustrated in Figure 2.

By this process, *néng*'s discourse function of challenge, pragmatically interpreted in the 3 year olds' uses, becomes its semantic content in the 5 year olds' uses. In this semantic change, a challenge to the addressee's assumption becomes a challenge to the addressee's action. Two crucial components of the challenge function are involved in the semanticization process. 'Don't' as in 'Don't assume X' contains both a social regulative meaning and a negative meaning. In the 3 year olds' physical-meaning uses of *néng*, the social regulative meaning is absent from the semantic content. Through semanticization, it ultimately becomes part of the semantic content of *néng*, and with it, the negative meaning comes to the surface.

Admittedly, longitudinal data are needed to reveal the step-by-step process of semanticization of a discourse-interactional function. But for the time being, this analysis seems more satisfactory than other possible explanations for this semantic change in children's use of *néng*.

7.3. There are at least two alternative explanations for this semantic change. The first is imitation of adult uses. But imitation cannot explain why children should wait until age 5 before starting to learn the adult social-permission meaning. The 3 year olds, it seems, hear as many social-permission uses from adults as do the 5 year olds.[15]

7.3.1. Delayed imitation cannot be explained by the social power differential between the 3 and 5 year olds either. Even in Chinese society where children are supposedly trained to be obedient and respectful of authority, they nevertheless seem to want power and control. This is especially true in play with peers, as in the current corpus. During the play sessions, the 3 year olds frequently tried to impose their will on the other children. When they wanted to thwart the others, they would simply take the toys. The children also knew how to act as if they had adult authority, offering lessons to other children. For example, when the children used *néng* in the physical meaning as justification for a prohibition, their intonation changed to a higher and leveled pitch, as if they were adults lecturing other children. Children also challenged the adults' prohibitions explicitly as shown in the challenge to prohibition uses. All this indicates that 3 year old Chinese children are hardly powerless and timid creatures.

Even if we accept the notion that 3 year olds do not use *néng* for prohibitions because they lack social power, we cannot explain why they fail to use it for permission seeking, which should fit their allegedly weak status. From Table 5, we see that permission-seeking uses are rare in the ambiguous category. In the unambiguous social-meaning category, even 7 year olds rarely use *néng* for seeking permissions. I suggest that this differential usage indicates that challenge is central to *néng*. If the general deontic modal meaning consists of prohibitions (permission denying), permission seeking, permission giving, and their reportive derivatives, then our developmental data show prohibition to be the first basic stage in children's acquisition of the general deontic modal meaning.

7.3.2. The second reason why the simple imitation explanation is unsatisfactory comes from the 5 year olds' use of prohibitions. A careful look at their sentence forms in the social-meaning category reveals that these differ from adult usage. Adults' prohibitive uses of *néng* appear consistently in sentences with no subject, as shown in (25):

(25) GU: *bù* **néng** *qiǎng.*
not can grab
'(you) can't grab (it).'

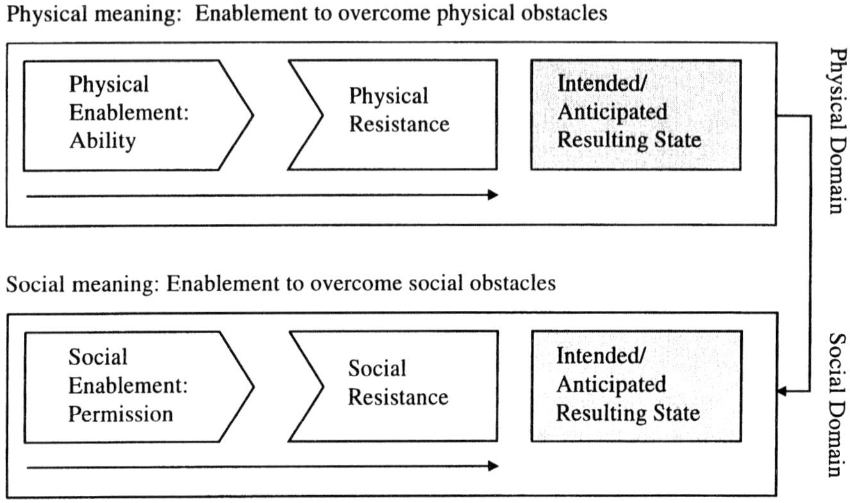

Figure 3. *Semantic structure transfer account*

But as illustrated earlier, many of the 5 year olds' social meaning uses of *néng* include a second-person subject, as shown in (26):

(26) C1: *nǐ bù* ***néng*** *dǎ rén.*
you not can hit people
'You can't hit people.'

Simple learning from adult uses cannot account for the addition of an explicit second-person subject by the 5 year olds.

7.4. The second alternative explanation is that the semantic change results from a transfer of the basic semantic structure from the physical to the social domain. According to the model put forth by Sweetser (1982) to explain the historical change in the English modals, this potential alternative account would look like Figure 3.

Néng, in its physical abilitative meaning, refers to a physical force which enables the actor to overcome physical obstacles. In its social meaning, *néng* refers to the social force which enables the actor to overcome social obstacles. In the change from the 3 year olds' abilitative uses of *néng* to the 5 year olds' social-meaning uses, the semantic structure of the earlier physical meaning is metaphorically extended to the social domain. However, this account again fails to explain why the new social deontic meaning in the 5 year olds' uses starts with the discourse function of prohibition, using the sentence form 'You cannot VERB'.

Since the predominant form in the 3 year olds' abilitative uses is 'I/It can X', the semantic-structure transfer explanation predicts that a social permission meaning will first surface in forms indicating social enablement, like 'I/you/he/she can do X', either as permission seeking or permission granting. Many transitional sentence forms and discourse contexts where the physical meaning and social meaning are not clearly differentiated should also appear, e.g., sentences such as 'You can read and talk, but you cannot get out of bed for a week' (said by a doctor to a patient who has just received a heart transplant), where the two *cans* have a physical as well as a social permission meaning. However, the majority of social-meaning uses by the 5 year olds are unambiguous prohibitions which take the surface form 'You cannot do X'. The semantic-structure transfer account cannot explain why physical enablement in the form of 'I can X' becomes social disenablement in the form 'You cannot X'.

7.5. In contrast to the two alternative explanations, my explanation of the semantic development, i.e. as involving semanticization of earlier discourse functions, explains why this semantic change takes the particular course it does. The discourse functions and sentence form of the social-permission meaning are consistent with the discourse function that *néng* serves in the earlier physical meaning, i.e. challenging the addressee's expectations. The sentence form of the prohibitive uses of *néng* is nothing but an explication of the challenge function pragmatically interpreted in the 3 year olds' uses. Thus, we are led to the conclusion that the *semanticization of challenge* is the crucial factor in the semantic development of *néng* that takes place between ages 3 and 5.

A similar argument explains the development of the epistemic-like meaning in the 7 year olds' uses. The epistemic meaning of *néng* by the 7 year olds is still quite elusive and context-dependent, allowing us to observe the ongoing process through which the context gives rise to a new meaning. Thus, in example (23), 'Can a police station be in a home?', *néng* is not emptied of its root meaning. A strong sense of root possibility is present, i.e. it is conventionally not the case that police stations are located in people's homes.

However, in the discourse context of an argument, the primary concern of the speaker focuses on refuting the addressee's previous assertion, in this case, the addressee's claim that the lego structure is a police station. Thus the root possibility meaning is backgrounded only to serve as the premise for the conclusion that it is not the case that the lego construction in question is a police station. It is the speaker's focus on the truth validity of the addressee's claim in the context of contradiction that shifts the meaning of *néng* from cultural-conventional appropriateness to logical possibilities, providing the structural basis for the epistemic modality, i.e. arriving conclusions on the basis of given premise. From the perspective of ontogeny, the apparently individual-based psychological process of reasoning emerges from highly social and interpersonal contexts.

7.6. Although I have emphasized in this paper the dynamic interpersonal functions *néng* serves, I do not claim that it is never used for reportive purposes. *Néng* does, in fact, get used in reportive ways, with both its physical abilitative meaning and its social-permission meaning. However, the main claim of this paper is that, from the developmental perspective, *the primary function of modals is to convey interpersonal meaning*. Reportive usage should be viewed as secondary to, and derivative from, the discourse functions. This proposal was first made by Lyons, who offers a profound insight into the understanding of modality when he says:

> Languages are learned and used in contexts which are in part determined by the variable assumptions and presuppositions of the people who use them; and these assumptions and presuppositions are not necessarily representable in terms of a set of determinable propositions. The objectification of both epistemic and deontic modality is something that we have here taken to be secondary in the acquisition of language; and it may very well be that not all languages, but only those that have been long used in literate societies for the specialized purpose of academic discussion, provide the means for this kind of objectivization. [...] Modality, as it operates in a good deal of everyday language-behavior, cannot be understood, or properly analyzed, otherwise than in terms of the indexical and instrumental functions of language, to which its descriptive function is, at times if not always, subordinate. (Lyons 1977:849)

Lyons's wisdom of 25 year ago finds empirical confirmation today. I hope that this study is only the beginning of programmatic research into the functional origins of modality.

To conclude, let me recapitulate my main findings. Developmental data indicate that the meaning of the Mandarin modal *néng* cannot be fully understood unless we consider its interpersonal functions. In all meaning categories, *néng* is primarily used to convey a challenge to the addressee. This discourse function is the primary factor motivating the semantic change of *néng* from the 3 year olds' physical abilitative meaning through the 5 year olds' deontic meaning, to the 7 year olds' epistemic-like meaning. The process involved in this semantic change is hypothesized as semanticization of discourse function.

NOTES

* This paper was inspired by joint research on children's use of the English modal *can* carried out by Julie Gerhardt and the author. Many of the ideas originated in discussions related to that project. Thanks are due to Julie Gerhardt for detailed comments on the earlier versions of the paper, to Mary Erbaugh for comments on theoretical issues and insights into the Chinese language and culture, and to Suzanne Fleischman for her thorough and painstaking editing which has clarified and sharpened many crucial ideas and made this paper readable. I would also like to thank Dan Slobin, Eve Sweetser, and Leonard Talmy for reading an earlier version of the paper and helping me to clarify and sharpen the concepts and arguments. Susan Ervin-Tripp, Amy Kyratzis, and several of my fellow graduate students also gave helpful feedback, for which I am grateful. Of course I assume full responsibility for errors of fact or interpretation.

The data used in this study were originally collected for a research project on children's use of modals. International travel for data collection was generously supported by the Institute of East Asian Studies, UC Berkeley. Purchase of tapes was funded by a graduate student research grant by the Institute of Human Development, UC Berkeley. The research was supported by the Chancellor's Dissertation Year Fellowship, UC Berkeley, Ma Hsiang Fang Research Fellowship, and NSF grant No. NSF-BNS-8919569 to Susan Ervin-Tripp for research on pragmatic factors in syntax development at the Institute of Cognitive Studies, UC Berkeley, which also provided computer, copying, and videotape laboratory facilities.

1. The ideas of interpersonal challenge and contested ability were first proposed by Gerhardt (personal communication) in her analysis of children's use of English *can*. Her proposal was that the child-speaker contests what he or she assumes to be the addressee's belief that the child is unable to carry out the action predicated in the utterance. Thus *can* is used to challenge and fix a state of doubt about the ability in question. For example, when a child says *I can put the poncho on*, there is an expectation that putting on the poncho is a difficult task, and thus it is questionable that the child has the ability to do it. Evidence supporting this claim is also found in the use of the Spanish modal *poder*. Silva-Corvalán (this volume) reports that while both *saber* and *poder* may refer to ability, *saber* simply makes a neutral statement, while *poder* implies the existence of difficulty or an obstacle in accomplishing the predicated action. Thus the use of *saber* in contexts like *I can swim the butterfly stroke for hours* is ungrammatical.

2. However, Robin Lakoff (1972) offers extensive and interesting discussions on the pragmatics of modals. Unfortunately, Lakoff draws a sharp distinction between the pragmatics and the semantics of modal meanings, and fails to recognize their interplay. Bybee (this volume) illustrates the role contextual inferences play in diachronic changes of modal meanings. She proposes that the 'present' reading of the past forms of the English modals has resulted from the conventionalization of pragmatic inferences.

3. See Sweetser (1990:56-57) for a brief survey of traditional treatments of modality.

4. For more discussion on the grammatical and semantic status of *néng*, see Li & Thompson (1981) and Tsang (1981).

5. However, Sweetser (1982) notes that epistemic uses of *can* in English are also limited, with the affirmative form being rarely used. See also Palmer (1990) and Coates (1983).

6. For discussion on root possibility, see Coates (1983:93-99). I use the term *epistemic* as defined by Sweetser (1990), i.e. as reflecting our understanding of the world of reasoning in terms of premises and conclusions.

7. However, there is a dialectal difference between Beijing Mandarin and Taiwan Mandarin, in which *kěyǐ* can be used in the negative form.

8. The V-not-V question in Mandarin is similar to the English yes-no question. For more discussion, see Li & Thompson (1981:535-45).

9. PRTCL = Sentence-final Particles; PERF = Perfect Marker; PROG = Progressive Marker; REL = Relative Clause Marker; Q = Question Marker.

10. This idea of children's conception of adults' expectations of their abilities as manifested in child-adult discourse comes from Julie Gerhardt's analysis of children's use of English *can* (personal communication).

11. The marginality of the permission use of *néng* in the data is unrelated to the existence of a competing form *kěyǐ* (see Section 1), also a low-frequency form in the corpus.

12. This meaning category represents a relatively small proportion of the uses of *néng* for all age groups (see Table 2).

13. With the exception of the reportive uses, which make up only a marginal proportion.

14. Hopper (1982:16) uses the term *semanticizing* in discussing Russian aspectual functions; Traugott and König (1991) use the term *strengthening of informativeness* in a similar sense.

15. No studies have been done on the amount of input of modal auxiliaries children get in Mandarin. My estimate that 3 year olds and 5 year olds get essentially the same input is based on the frequency of modal usage by the adult experimenter, i.e. the author, in the current data corpus. Although this tells nothing about what the children hear at home or in school, it does suggest that adult use of modals in the different meanings may not vary according to the age of the addressee.

REFERENCES

Bybee, Joan. 1988. "Semantic Substance vs. Contrast in the Development of Grammatical Meaning". *Proceedings of the Berkeley Linguistics Society Meeting* 14: 247-64.

Bybee, Joan. This volume. "The Semantic Development of Past Tense Modals in English."

Coates, Jennifer. 1983. *The Semantics of the Modal Auxiliaries.* London: Croom Helm.

Gerhardt, Julie. 1985. "On the Use of *Will* and *Gonna*: Toward a Description of Activity-types for Child Language". *Discourse Processes* 8: 143-75.

Gerhardt, Julie. 1990. "The Relation of Language to Context in Children's Speech: The Role of *hafta* Statements in Structuring 3-year-old's Discourse". *IPrA Papers in Pragmatics* 4:1/2: 1-57.

Givón, T. 1984. *Syntax: A Functional Typological Introduction, Vol. 1.* Amsterdam: John Benjamins.

Halliday, M.A.K. 1973. *Explorations in the Functions of Language.* London: Edward Arnold.

Hopper, Paul. 1982. "Introduction". *Tense-Aspect: Between Semantics and Pragmatics.* Amsterdam: John Benjamins.

Lakoff, Robin. 1972. "The Pragmatics of Modality". *Papers from the Eighth Regional Meeting of the Chicago Linguistics Society* 8: 229-46.

Li, Charles & Sandra Thompson. 1981. *Mandarin Chinese: A Functional Reference Grammar.* Berkeley, CA: University of California Press.

Lyons, John. 1977. *Semantics,* 2 vol. Cambridge: Cambridge University Press.

Lü, Shuxiang. 1980. *Xiàndài hànyǔ bābǎi cí (*Eight Hundred Words in Modern Mandarin*).* Beijing: Shangwu yinshuguan (The Commercial Press).

Ogden, Charles & Ivor Richards. 1923. *The Meaning of Meaning: A Study of the Influence of Language upon Thought and of the Science of Symbolism.* London: Routledge & Kegan Paul.

Palmer, Frank. 1990. *Modality and the English Modals,* 2nd ed. London: Longman.

Perkins, Michael. 1983. *Modal Expressions in English.* London: Frances Pinter.

Shepherd, Susan. 1981. "Modals in Antiguan Creole, Child Language Acquisition, and History." Unpublished doctoral dissertation, Stanford University.

Silva-Corvalán, Carmen. This volume. "Contextual Conditions for the Interpretation of 'poder' and 'deber' in Spanish".

Sweetser, Eve. 1982. "Root and Epistemic Modals: Causality in Two Worlds". *Proceedings of the Berkeley Linguistics Society Meeting* 8: 484-507.

Sweetser, Eve. 1988. "Grammaticalization and Semantic Bleaching". *Proceedings of the Berkeley Linguistics Society Meeting* 14: 389-405.

Sweetser, Eve. 1990. *From Etymology to Pragmatics: Metaphorical and Cultural Aspects of Semantic Structure.* Cambridge: Cambridge University Press.

Talmy, Leonard. 1988. "Force Dynamics in Language and Cognition". *Cognitive Science* 12: 49-100.

Traugott, Elizabeth. 1982. "From Propositional to Textual and Expressive Meanings: Some Semantic-Pragmatic Aspects of Grammaticalization". *Perspectives on Historical Linguistics.* ed. by Winfred Lehmann & Yakov Malkiel. Amsterdam: John Benjamins.

Traugott, Elizabeth. 1988. "Pragmatic Strengthening and Grammaticalization". *Proceedings of the Berkeley Linguistics Society Meeting* 14: 406-16.
Traugott, Elizabeth & Ekkehard König. 1991. "The Semantics-Pragmatics of Grammaticalization Revisited". *Approaches to Grammaticalization, Vol. I.* ed.by Elizabeth Traugott & Bernd Heine. Amsterdam: John Benjamins.
Tsang, Chui-Lim. 1981. "A Semantic Study of Modal Auxiliary Verbs in Chinese." Unpublished Doctoral Dissertation, Stanford University.

The Discourse and Interactive Functions of Obligation Expressions

John Myhill
Laura A. Smith
University of Michigan

0. Introduction.

The field of functional-typological linguistics can be thought of as having two focuses: detailed functional descriptions of phenomena in individual languages and cross-linguistic generalizations based upon these descriptions.*

The latter endeavor is dependent upon the former, in that cross-linguistic generalizations must be based upon a cross-linguistic database. The importance of an extensive empirical base has been clearly illustrated by developments in the study of, e.g. word order; the large amount of empirical data on word order variation which appeared in the 1980's has fueled considerable theoretical speculation on the universal functions of word order variation (Givon 1983, Sun and Givon 1985, Myhill 1986, 1992, Payne 1987, Herring 1990). The same may be said about voice and aspect (Hopper 1979, Myhill 1984, Cooreman, Fox, and Givon 1984, Cooreman 1988, Thompson 1989).

No such base of empirical studies exists for many other linguistic phenomena, including modality marking. This is unfortunate, because a more detailed framework for describing modality would be useful for making typological generalizations. For example, if we consider the problem of grammaticalization, it has been observed (Bybee and Pagliuca 1987 among others) that some words associated with obligation meaning become markers of future tense (e.g. *shall*), others come to be used for inference (e.g. *must*), while still others develop both functions (e.g. the Spanish Synthetic Future, diachronically derived from a construction literally translating as 'have to').

We do not as yet know why some obligation markers develop in one direction and others develop in another. This may be simply arbitrary, but a more interesting possibility is that what we now call obligation subsumes a number of subfunctions, each associated with a distinct historical development. At present, however, we have no way of telling whether this is the case, because existing descriptions of the functions of obligation markers are insufficiently detailed.

The main purpose of the present paper is to begin to develop a framework for describing the discourse and interactive functions of obligation marking. In the short run, this will serve a useful descriptive purpose by providing a categorization of obligation constructions in different languages. In the long run, this categorization system will allow for more powerful cross-linguistic generalizations about universal form-function relationships.

We will consider and contrast the expression of obligation in four languages: English, Chinese, Hopi, and Biblical Hebrew. These were chosen because they are genetically unrelated, are available in text form, and are familiar to us. The main questions we want to address are: In what contexts do speakers of a given language choose to use an obligation marker? How do these contexts differ across languages? In a language with more than one obligation morpheme at the speaker's disposal, what factors motivate the choice of one or another of these morphemes? In English, for example, when do we prefer *have to* to *gotta*, or vice versa? Do speakers of Chinese use the same criteria to distinguish between, say, *dei* and *yao*? In addressing these questions, we will be working toward a typology of obligation contexts across languages.

Interestingly, the languages we will investigate differ not only in how they use obligation markers but also in how frequently they use them: English and Chinese have a number of commonly-occurring obligation markers, while Hopi has only one productive (and not particularly common) lexical marker of obligation. Biblical Hebrew, on the other hand, has none at all (we will suggest that word order serves a related function in this language). Both Hopi and Biblical Hebrew have a large number of clauses in which, from the English point of view, there is an 'implied' obligation, without there being an explicit marker.

Our approach in this study will be to analyze and categorize naturally occurring tokens associated with obligation. We will not give a dictionary-style 'definition' of obligation, because we do not believe that such a definition can be meaningfully or objectively applied to naturally occurring data. Instead, we will use a list of obligation markers as traditionally understood in each language. We will then take as the goal of our investigation a characterization of the circumstances under which these markers of obligation are used, that is, the discourse function of the expression of obligation. We will show that certain obligation markers are used in certain circumstances and others are used in other circumstances; thus, rather than 'defining' these markers, we will systematically characterize the circumstances in which they are used. This approach is consistent with the general methodology of functional linguistics; as noted above, research into such phenomena as word order, voice, and aspect has shown that the functions involved are too abstract to allow a dictionary-style definition, and characterization of usage offers the most objective account of function.

In section 1, we will discuss preliminary considerations. We will consider previous efforts to categorize types of obligation meaning. We will then briefly review research on grammaticalization, which will be relevant when we discuss which forms to include in our study. In section 2 we will turn to our empirical studies of English, Chinese, Hopi, and Biblical Hebrew.

1. Preliminary considerations.

1.1. *Previous categorizations of obligation meaning.*

Linguists have distinguished between strong and weak obligation. In English, *must* and *have* to are associated with 'strong' obligation while *should* and *ought* to are associated with 'weak' obligation. In distinguishing between 'strong' and 'weak' obligation, Palmer (1986:100) states that for 'weak' obligation

> the speaker admits the possibility that the event may not take place. This is seen in [the difference between] *He ought to/should come, but he won't* (and) **He must come, but he won't*. The second of these is most unlikely, if not anomalous; if the speaker thinks that the obligation may not be fulfilled, *ought to/should* would be used.

We have found it difficult to apply this criterion objectively to naturally occurring data. If we apply it strictly, we find practically no cases where the speaker can guarantee that the projected event will take place.

A speaker can say *You have to leave now*, realizing that the hearer may in fact not leave. Such is the case with the great majority of naturally-occurring tokens of 'strong' obligation markers such as *have to*. If we change the criterion to mean that the speaker is *acting* as though the action will definitely take place, then we have to find independent evidence that the speaker is acting this way. In the great majority of naturally-occurring cases, there is no evidence other than the presence of a morpheme which has been designated as marking 'strong' obligation; the argument for calling these 'strong' obligation markers is therefore circular.

Coates 1983 makes a distinction between obligation which can be paraphrased as 'it is obligatory/absolutely essential that...' and obligation paraphrasable as 'it is important that...', the first type being 'stronger'. However, as Coates notes (pg. 34), the parameters for distinguishing between these are 'indicative rather than definitive,' and 'between these two extremes there is considerable fuzziness.' For example, she suggests that (1) is paraphrasable with 'obligatory' and (2) is paraphrasable with 'important,' but it seems to us that the reverse is just as plausible:

(1) *They were told by the Chairman, Mr. Jos. D. Miller, "You must have respect for other people's property."*

(2) *If you commit murder, Charlotte, you must be punished.*

In attempting to apply Palmer's and Coates' tests for 'strong' and 'weak' obligation to naturally occurring data, we found too many cases for which there was no evidence of the strength of the obligation other than use of a 'strong' vs. 'weak' obligation marker. We therefore have not attempted to apply independent tests for the 'strength' of the obligation.

Another parameter used to distinguish between different types of obligation function is referred to variously as 'discourse orientation' (Palmer 1974), 'subjectivity' (Lyons 1977), and 'speaker involvement' (Coates 1983). Coates (p. 33) considers the important parameter distinguishing *must* and *have to* to be whether the "speaker is interested in getting (the) subject to perform the action." This distinction is consistent with our own intuitions about some of the English and Chinese data, but we were hard-pressed to code for it objectively. Often, we simply could not determine the degree to which the speaker was interested in having the action performed. Indeed, it is not clear why a speaker would mention an obligation to perform an action unless s/he had some interest in having that action carried out.

Palmer (1986:103) argues similarly that "The most natural distinguishing feature [between *must* and *have to*] is that with [...] *have to* the speaker is disassociating himself from the obligation [...], and, by implication therefore, associating himself with it in using *must* [...]". Here too, we found it frequently, if not usually, impossible to determine objectively the degree of speaker association with the obligations.[1] However, there were some functional subcategories for which something resembling this distinction could be objectively coded and was relevant to the choice of marker. We also found that we could include in our characterizations of certain types of obligation function something about the attitude of the speaker towards the obligation (although it is not clear how similar this is to what Coates calls `speaker involvement'); this will be described in Section 2 when we discuss the categories used in our analyses.

Coates (1983) notes a number of other criteria which can be useful in categorizing types of obligation constructions: person/animacy of the subject and speaker authority over the subject. We have found these parameters to be much more straightforward and objectively applicable than 'strong/weak' and 'involved/uninvolved', and we will make use of some of them in the discussion in Section 2.

1.2. *Grammaticalization.*

Cross-linguistic research on grammaticalization (Givon 1975; Ultan 1978; Bybee and Pagliuca 1987) has shown that the diachronic development from lexical to grammatical form follows certain routes. For example, markers of future tense (inflections or auxiliaries) often diachronically derive from verbs or constructions expressing desire (e.g. English *will*, Indonesian *mau*), motion (e.g. English *go*, Spanish *ir*), or obligation (e.g. English *shall*, the Spanish Synthetic Future). This research has also demonstrated that there are universal form/function relationships, such that lexical forms are associated with certain types of functions and grammatical forms are associated with different types of functions; those functions which are consistently associated with more grammatical form can be considered to be more 'grammatical' functions (see Bybee 1985). For example, the English auxiliaries used to be main verbs with more 'lexical' meanings such as obligation and desire, and in the course of becoming auxiliaries (developing structural properties which distinguish them from main verbs, e.g. contracting, not taking *do*-support) they also developed more 'grammatical' functions, such as future, inference, etc. The distinction between lexical and grammatical is of course not discrete for either forms or functions, but particular forms and functions may still be designated as more lexical or more grammatical. At any point in time, a form can have both more lexical and more grammatical functions.

Bybee and Pagliuca (1987) present evidence that functional changes in the course of grammaticalization are not random, but rather that a grammaticalizing morpheme develops functions similar to the functions it already has, e.g., *shall* as a future marker retains shades of its lexical meaning 'owe' in contexts such as *the lessee shall give notice at least 30 days in advance*. Once a morpheme has developed these functions, it can go on to develop other new related functions. Thus in the course of a grammaticalization process through which a lexical morpheme with an obligation meaning becomes a grammatical morpheme with, e.g. future meaning, the grammaticalized function differs from the earlier lexical function but is related to it in a non-arbitrary way. In other words, the more grammaticalized function retains some elements of an earlier lexical function. Bybee and Pagliuca (1987:115) note that, for example, "[...] the contemporary modal nuances of *shall* and *will* are direct continuations of their original lexical meanings, those of *shall* are all related to obligation and those of *will* are related to desire." They support this argument with data from Coates' 1983 empirical study of the use of modal auxiliaries in present-day British English.

Because obligation markers commonly develop other functions which are related to obligation, it is important to the study of grammaticalization to include those other, more grammaticalized functions. We will use the term *obligation* to refer to the set of obligation functions in the traditional sense, and we will use '*obligation*' (with scare quotes) to refer to this set of obligation functions and also its related, more grammatical functions (e.g. certain types of inference and future meaning) which morphemes associated with obligation commonly develop. In our usage in this paper, the future functions of, e.g. *shall* (in a dialect productively using this word) are considered a type of 'obligation' function, because they relate to the obligation functions which *shall* used to have; on the other hand, the future functions of *go* are not generally associated with 'obligation'.

1.3. *Delimitation of the database.*

In any text-based study, it is necessary to decide which data to include and which to exclude. We have stated that this paper will analyze obligation. What do we mean by obligation? One possible approach to this problem is to give a dictionary-style definition of obligation and include in our study every token in the languages investigated which meets this definition. However, after wrestling with this problem, we found little merit to this approach; any definition we used would necessitate another definition (e.g., if we say that an obligation is a requirement, responsibility, or necessity to do something, then we must define 'requirement,' 'responsibility,' or 'necessity').

Instead, we will delimit our database by designating certain morphemes in certain languages as obligation markers on the basis of a consistent translation relationship (in texts and bilingual dictionaries) with English morphemes commonly recognized as associated with obligation. Although reliance on translations is not an ideal solution to the problem, it appears to us to be better than using one or another abstract definition of obligation in general which might be controversial and which would definitely be difficult or impossible to apply objectively to naturally occurring data.

Delimiting the database is complicated by the fact that obligation markers commonly also have other functions. As noted above, obligation markers often develop inference or future meaning. Thus, English *must*, *have to*, *have got to*, and *should* can also have the meaning of inference (*That must be Joe knocking on the door*). However, in the great majority of our data, it is generally easy to distinguish those with obligation meaning from those with inference meaning, and we have excluded the latter from our analysis. The situation is more complicated for obligation markers with future meaning, where the two meanings often merge (Coates 1983, among others), with individual tokens showing both future and obligation meaning; in such cases, it is frequently difficult or impossible to say how much obligation meaning a token has. This creates a problem in analyzing the function of forms which have or have had both functions, such as *shall,*[2] the Spanish Synthetic Future, and Chinese *yao*. The only such form we will discuss is *yao*; we will describe our approach to this problem in Section 2.2.

In determining which data to include, we also need to consider the problem of cross-linguistic comparability. If we produce a list of the tokens of the Hopi obligation marker *nawus*, divided up into its different functions, and another list of tokens of English *have to*, divided up into its different functions, we have no way of telling whether the differences in frequency of these functions are artifacts of the respective texts. For example, we found that in our English texts *gotta* is used for biological needs (e.g. *I gotta take a leak*) but in our Hopi texts *nawus* is never used for this function; however, there was no context of this type in the Hopi texts, and we therefore cannot conclude that *nawus* lacks this function.

In order to limit the effect of this problem, i.e. that the distribution of morpheme functions is an artifact of the texts used, and to facilitate cross-linguistic comparison, we will make use of English translation data in our studies of Chinese, Hopi, and Biblical Hebrew. Translations are not an ideal source of data, but they are objective, as we have used someone else's translations rather than doing it ourselves. Translations sometimes retain more of the structure of the original than would be colloquial in the target language. Thus, our claims about obligation functions in English will be based on original English sources; the translation data serve only as a supplement for purposes of comparison, and it is important not to overestimate the similarities between expressions of obligation in two languages on the basis of translation. However, the tendency to retain the structure of the original in translation makes cases in which the structure of the original is *not* retained all the more striking as evidence for functional differences between the languages.

Biblical Hebrew presents a special problem for the study of obligation marking. In our database for this language, there is no commonly-occurring lexical marker of obligation, and so it is not immediately obvious which data to include.[3] As stated above, we will argue that something resembling 'obligation' function in this language is marked by word order alternation: the language is normally verb-initial, and non-verb-initial word order has as one of its functions something similar to 'obligation' marking. As this type of 'obligation' marking (if it can be called that) is grammatical rather than lexical, we would expect it to be associated not only with the more specific lexical types of obligation function considered in other languages but also with the more grammaticalized functions which obligation markers commonly develop. Therefore, in comparing Biblical Hebrew and English, we will consider not only more basic obligation functions such as the obligation meaning of *must* and *should*, but also more grammatical functions, such as inference and those associated with *shall*.

2. Empirical studies.

In this section, we will discuss the results of empirical studies we have done of obligation marking in English, Chinese, Hopi, and Biblical Hebrew. We have used original texts from each language (supplemented by English translations for the last three languages); these will be briefly discussed in the relevant sections. As will be seen from the following discussion, the situation regarding usage of the various obligation markers is extremely complicated; to keep confusion to a minimum, we will limit the data we analyze to one genre, dialogue in written texts; future work will of course have to investigate other genres.

2.1. *English.*

The English data were collected from three plays by the modern American playwright Lanford Wilson. The plays are *The Hot L Baltimore* (1973), *The mound builders* (1976), and *Burn this* (1987). Since coding of data was often highly context dependent, brief plot summaries are useful: *The Hot L Baltimore* is the story of downtrodden but often witty hotel residents whose decaying home is up for demolition. In *The mound builders*, archaeologists uncover a rare Indian burial site whose treasures are lost forever when the landowner's son, no longer able to sell the land, avenges his lost profits. *Burn this* portrays a group of New York artists who insightfully and often cynically reflect on their lives after the accidental death of a close friend. These plays have the advantage of using very colloquial language, which is especially important for gathering tokens of (*have*) *gotta*. We chose plays by a single author to avoid admitting author preference (rather than function) as a factor in morpheme choice; this will serve to minimize the number of complicating variables in this pilot study. For practical reasons, we narrowed down English obligation markers to five: *have to*, *gotta*, *should*, *oughtta*, and *supposed* to.[4] A total of 153 occurrences were found in the three plays.

For reasons described above, traditional distinctions such as strong vs. weak obligation are not useful to the study of naturally occurring data because they cannot be objectively applied; therefore, we have developed alternative means of categorization. After extensive analysis of the data, the criterion which most clearly suggested itself was whether or not someone is negatively affected by the action expressed in the verb phrase, and, if so, which person is negatively affected. We found that the English obligation expressions are often used to reflect the speaker's negative evaluation of an event. Consider, for example, the following clause about a friend of two accident victims:

(3) *He had to go out there and identify Dom and Robbie, notify their families.* (Wilson 1987:9)

Here the speaker uses *had* to to express the unpleasantness of the action. Without *had to*, there would be no explicit reflection of the speaker's negative evaluation of the action as unpleasant. Furthermore, if the action were something we typically think of as positive, then *have to* would imply something quite different, as shown in (4)-(5):

(4) *Ed had to go to this wonderful party, the lucky bastard.*
(5) *Ed* ***had to*** *go to this wonderful party, and no one could talk him out of it.*

In (4), the speaker uses *had to* to convey disappointment at missing out on some fun, while in (5) the speaker uses *had to* to convey annoyance at Ed's unbridled determination (i.e., Ed was hell-bent on going). Note that in (3) the unpleasantness is experienced by the subject, while in (4) and (5) it is experienced by the speaker. The use of *had to* in (5) could also imply that the subject is negatively affected (i.e., Ed went against his will), but this interpretation is inconsistent with the clause *no one could talk him out of it.* Such examples as (3)-(5) demonstrate that markers such as *have to*, traditionally labeled 'obligation' markers, do not simply report obligation; rather, they convey evaluations by the speaker of the effect of the event. An interesting non-obligation use of *have to* clearly illustrates this function of negative evaluation:

(6) *Why did he go out? Why didn't someone hear him... WHY DID HE HAVE TO HEAR NOISES IN THE NIGHT?* (caps in original) (Wilson 1976:146)

We can see that this is not an obligation usage because the subject has no control over the action, *hear*. Rather, *have to* expresses the speaker's negative evaluation of a grievous situation (her husband's disappearance). We have classified a number of different types of negative effect in Table 1 below (a-g), and will discuss each in turn, after which we will examine tokens with no clear negative effect (h-k). We note here that coding tokens is a difficult task with

Table 1. *Discourse functions of five English obligation markers supposed*

Functional category	*have to*	*had to*	*gotta*	*should*	*should have*	*supposed is/ are*	*supposed was/ were*	*oughtta*	TL
a. Negative effect on subject	18	8	4	0	0	0	0	0	30
b. Mitigated inconvenience to listener (1st pers. sj)	2	4	9	0	0	0	0	0	15
c. Negative effect on listener, speaker unsympathetic 2nd pers. sj.	6	0	3	0	0	0	0	0	9
d. Negative effect on speaker	0	0	0	0	0	0	0	0	0
e. Reprimand (2nd pers. sbj)	2	0	0	1	0	5	1	3	12
f. Counterfactual (non-2ndpers. sj.)	0	0	0	1	6	7	2	5	21
g. Help not needed	5	0	0	0	0	0	0	0	5
h. Facetious suggestion	0	0	1	2	0	0	0	3	6
i. Advisable action									
1st pers. subj.	0	0	0	7	0	0	0	0	7
2nd pers. sj	1	0	7	8	0	0	0	2	17
Generic subject	0	0	0	1	0	0	0	0	2
j. Procedures/routines	7	1	3	0	0	0	0	0	11
k. Biological/physical need	0	2	9	0	0	0	0	0	11
l. Uncodable	1	0	4	2	0	0	0	0	7
TOTAL	42	15	40	22	6	12	3	13	153

modals, which reflect a speaker's inner mental state. It is difficult to get at what a speaker is thinking, because people often say the opposite of what they mean; they can be sarcastic, facetious, or insincere. Interpretation of utterances can easily become quite subjective if care is not taken. Keeping this in mind, we have tried to code the data consistently, making liberal use of overall discourse context and extra-linguistic factors (stage cues/descriptions) to guide our interpretations. We will refer to these factors throughout the paper.

Since *have to*, *gotta*, and *should* are the most common obligation markers, comprising 78% of the data base, we will focus on these, commenting briefly on the others.

We have separated the *had to* tokens from the *have to* tokens because in the past tense the distinction between *have to* and *gotta* is neutralized (**I did gotta*, **I gotta-ed*), and *had to* is the past tense form for *gotta*. This particularly affects the categories 'Mitigated inconvenience' and 'Biological/physical need', which are normally represented with *gotta* rather than *have to* but which have a number of *had to* tokens. Hence, there is some evidence that *had to* occurs in functions not normally associated with *have to*.

When there is another auxiliary preceding, only *have to* and not *gotta* appears in our data (**He might gotta leave, *He's gonna gotta leave, *He'll gotta leave, *Does he gotta leave?*).[5] However, it is generally grammatically possible to substitute *gotta* alone for AUX+ *have to* (e.g. *You're gonna have to leave* vs. *You gotta leave*). On the basis of our data, it appears that in this situation the usual functional distinction between *have to* and *gotta* is maintained; in other words, the AUX+ *have to* tokens pattern like the AUXless *have to* tokens, not like the *gotta* tokens. For this reason, we include the AUX+ *have to* tokens with the other *have to* tokens in Table 1.

Turning now to discussion of the categories in Table 1, the 'Negative effect on subject' category includes those usages illustrated in examples (7)-(9) below, where the action expressed in the verb phrase is emotionally or physically unpleasant to the subject.[6] Table 1 shows that this function favors *have to* over *gotta* (18 vs. 4).

(7) *This glowering older brother had to go get my clothes...*
(Wilson 1987:22)

(8) *They're tearing down the whole building, so we all have to move.*
(Wilson 1973:48)

(9) *I gotta get Horse's things.*
(Wilson 1973:46)

We have evaluated 'negative effect' on the strength of various cues either in the utterance or in the broader context. In (7), for example, *glowering* signals the brother's view of the action as unpleasant (as perceived by the speaker, of course). As for (8), earlier comments (e.g. the speaker's refusal to help distribute eviction notices) reveal that the speaker is upset about the impending demolition. Lastly, in (9), a mother is resigned to moving her son's belongings out of the hotel after unsuccessfully imploring the manager to let him stay.

The second category listed in Table 1 is 'Mitigated inconvenience to listener.' All tokens of this type have 1st person subjects, and so the speaker is in effect excusing doing something against the interests of the listener by referring to an obligation requiring this action, as in (10):

(10) *I've got to talk money with some St. Louis real-estate men this evening. This isn't going to be much of a vacation for you, Jean.*
(Wilson 1976:13)

The speaker in (10) is apologizing to his assistant's wife, who will presumably see little of her husband during the excavation (her 'vacation'). We have no evidence that the speaker/subject himself is unhappy about talking money; in fact, he may well be enthusiastic about it.

The 'Mitigated inconvenience to listener' function is particularly common in ending (or avoiding entering into) conversations, as in (11):

(11) Dan: *Drink your beer.*
Chad: *I gotta get my ass home.* (Wilson 1976:76)

The obligation in such cases can easily be vague or invented, since the listener will not normally challenge its existence or importance. However, our database does contain two tokens where the listener does not accept the priority of the ostensible obligation:

(12) Paul: *I gotta be somewhere tomorrow.*
Jackie: *Come on, everyone's gotta be somewhere tomorrow.* (Wilson 1973:97)

(13) Anna: *Actually, I've got to get back to—*
Pale: *Actually, would you just hold it a second, okay?* (Wilson 1987:29)

Gotta is the preferred way to mark 'Mitigated inconvenience'; it occurs 9 times with this function. *Had to* occurs four times (presumably because gotta lacks a past tense form) while *have to* only occurs twice, including (14):

(14) *I have to work; you have work to do.* (Wilson 1987:81)

One possible explanation for the use of *have to* in (14) is that the speaker is already at wits' end with the listener and is more interested in getting rid of him than in veiling her disinterest. In fact, he has just done something which warrants little courtesy from her; he has picked up a second phone in her apartment and intimidated her boyfriend into hanging up. The distribution of tokens for this category thus suggests that *gotta* is the preferred morpheme for mitigating an inconvenience to one's listener, while *have to* in this context implies a reason rather than an apology.

In categories (a) and (b), 'Negative effect on speaker' and 'Mitigated inconvenience', we see a split in the functions of *have to* and *gotta*: *have to* is associated with cases where the subject evaluates (or could be expected to evaluate) the action negatively, while *gotta* is associated with cases where the subject (who is the speaker, since all tokens have 1st person subjects) implicitly apologizes for the negative effect the action has on the listener. There is an interesting illustration of this contrast in two excerpts from the narrative of a single speaker. In (15), she uses *gotta* to portray herself trying to weasel out of an invitation, while in (16), she uses *have to* to describe the unpleasant consequences of failing to do this.

(15) *His mother's on the bed with a washcloth on her forehead. I'm trying to tell them how I've got to get a bus back to civilization...* (Wilson 1987:20)

(16) *So then it's midnight and the last bus has left at ten, which they know, I'm sure, damn them, and I hadn't checked, like an idiot. So I have to spend the night in Robbie's little nephew's room in the attic.* (Wilson 1987:21)

Note that (15) is humorous precisely because it mixes the offensive phrase *back to civilization* with the courtesy of justifying a departure. *Have to* (historic present) in (16), on the other hand, is consistent with the subject/speaker's obviously negative view of the ordeal.

The third functional category in Table 1 is 'Negative effect on listener, speaker unsympathetic'. In the English data, there is only one subtype for this category, with 2nd person (or 1st person inclusive, which includes the listener) subjects. For this subtype, the listener is to perform the action and be negatively affected by it, and the speaker is unsympathetic or even hostile; this unsympathetic attitude distinguishes these tokens from tokens of 'Negative effect on subject' with 2nd person subjects (which are in any case very rare in the English database). This type is exemplified in (17)-(18):

(17) *It's a damn shame you're going to have to find yourself some other field of operation.* (Wilson 1976:128)

(18) *We gotta go when I need it, damnit.* (Wilson 1976:61)

In (17), the speaker owns some property which he intends to sell to a developer, while the listener is an anthropologist committed to protecting an excavation site on the property. In (18), the speaker is trying to persuade the listener to do as he requests, and the listener is resisting.

This type has 6 tokens of *have to* and three of *gotta*. It appears that an important factor distinguishing *have to* from *gotta* here is whether the speaker regards this unpleasant obligation as being imposed by factors beyond the immediate control of the interactants. When there is a legal or quasi-legal basis for the obligation, *have to* is used 5 of 6 times (this is related to the 'Procedures/routines' function of *have to*, which we will discuss below)[7]. Thus in (17) the speaker believes that negotiations have already been made to sell the land, and is under the mistaken impression that the anthropologist has no legal recourse to prevent the sale. On the other hand, when the basis for imposing the obligation is purely personal, as in (18), *gotta* is used two of three times.

As we have noted, the only subtype of 'Negative effect on listener' represented in the English data is the one with 2nd person subjects. Obligation markers can also be used in this category with 1st person subjects (*If you don't keep quiet, I'm gonna have to break your nose*) and 3rd person subjects (*He's gonna have to teach you a lesson*), but there are no tokens of this in the English database (we will see in Section 2.2 that there are such tokens in the Chinese database).

The fourth functional category is 'Negative effect on speaker'; this type is defined as having a non-1st person subject, which distinguishes it from 'Negative effect on subject' with 1st person subject. There are no tokens of this category in the English database, although such uses are possible, e.g. in *Why did he have to do that?* the obligation marker can indicate the speaker's disapproval (of course, it can also indicate that the subject could be expected to view the obligated action negatively). We will see in Section 2.2 that obligation markers are used in the Chinese database with this function.

The fifth functional category, 'Reprimands', also implies a negative effect on someone.[8] There are 12 tokens of this type, exemplified in (19) (20):

(19) *Hey. Paul. You're supposed to be doing this with me.*
(Wilson 1973:136)

(20) *You ought to be ashamed of yourself, robbing Mr. Morse.*
(Wilson 1973:102)

This type is most commonly represented in our data with *supposed to* (6 tokens) or *oughtta* (3 tokens). *Supposed* to implies a tacit understanding between the subject and a second party (e.g., compare *You're supposed to be meeting him tomorrow* with *You ought to be meeting him tomorrow*). In (19), the speaker is looking through hotel records to help Paul find his missing grandfather; the speaker assumes an understanding between herself and Paul that he will help in response to her gesture, but he has not done so. *Oughtta*, on the other hand, conveys the speaker's personal and often detached viewpoint, an on-the-spot opinion, negatively evaluating a situation. Hence, in (20), the speaker is disgusted with the listener's behavior, but hardly feels rebuffed. In this latter utterance, *supposed to* would be odd because it would imply that the speaker expected the listener to exhibit shame, and was somehow disappointed when the listener didn't; the reprimand would then appear to be not for the action committed, but for the failure to show remorse.[9] In all the utterances under this category, as with all the categories we have examined so far, the obligation morpheme expresses a negative evaluation of a situation.[10]

'Counterfactuals' (statements which are positive about events which do not occur, or statements which are negative about events which do occur) differ from 'Reprimands' in terms of subject differ from 'Reprimands' in terms of subject type, as noted above; the former are non-2nd person, while the latter are *only* 2nd person. We include counterfactuals among tokens implying a negative effect because the speaker, in noting an error, has presumably recognized some negative consequence of it.[11] As shown in Table 1, each of the 'weak' obligation markers is represented in the Counterfactual category — 9 *supposed to*, 7 *should* (*have*), and 5 *oughtta* — a total of 21 tokens. As with 'Reprimands', we find that *supposed to*, unlike the other markers, implies an understanding between the subject (or agent) and another party, while *oughtta* implies the speaker's on-the-spot viewpoint. Compare the following:

(21) *I'm supposed to be home with Frank 'cause he's on morphine and God knows what condition he might be in.* (Wilson 1973:12)

(22) *He ought to sleep with it (the window) open anyway; you can't talk to him about it.* (Wilson 1973:34)

In (21), *supposed to* implies some previous understanding (e.g. between speaker and doctor) which calls for the subject's presence at home; *oughtta* would imply that the obligation has just occurred to the speaker, and sounds oddly detached. In (22), on the other hand, *oughtta* characterizes the recommended action as advisable in the eyes of the speaker and evaluates the current situation negatively; *supposed to* would imply that the speaker presumes some previous arrangements between the subject and some party (e.g. the speaker herself).[12]

Although *should* is possible in (21) and (22), it is rare in our database in the 'Counterfactual' category (only one token). *Should have*, on the other hand, is quite common, and is exemplified in (23):

(23) *No, I should have come with you.* (Wilson 1987:20)

The 'Help not needed' category is made up of utterances using *You don't have to....* Here, the speaker is (ostensibly at least) relieving the subject of some burden:

(24) *No, that's okay, you don't have to do that.* (Wilson 1987:90)

(25) *You don't have to go through them, I'll go through them.* (Wilson 1973:65)

We have thus far looked at 7 categories (a-g in Table 1) in which an obligated action (or a failure to fulfill an obligation) has a negative effect on someone — listener, speaker, or third party. We will now turn to the remaining categories (h-k), where no such effect is clearly inferrable.

One of these is 'Facetious suggestions', which has only 6 tokens and hence will be illustrated briefly. In this category, the suggestions are not expected to be taken seriously:

(26) *Mr. Morse, you gotta throw away the mustard plaster and take something worthwhile to bed with you.* (Wilson 1973:27)

(27) *Hell, probably ought to celebrate.* (Wilson 1976:125)

We know from context that the speakers do not really expect their suggestions to be carried out. Mr. Morse is senile and hard-of-hearing; the comment is a joke. (27) is also a half-hearted proposition: the speaker has just learned that the married woman whom he has been pursuing is pregnant and as uninterested in him as ever, and he is hardly disposed to celebrate.

'Advisable action' tokens can be divided into three subtypes, depending upon the person of the subject. With 1st person subjects, there are 7 tokens, all using *should* and all couched in terms of personal opinion and/or uncertainty; four are in subordinate clauses under *I think*, one is a question, one is under *I decided,* and one follows *maybe*, so that all are in one way or another couched in terms of personal opinion and/or uncertainty. This type is exemplified in (28)-(29):

(28) *I think I should go straighten my room.* (to give the listeners some privacy) (Wilson 1987:83)

(29) *Should I set an alarm or something for him, so he doesn't miss work again?* (Wilson 1987:75)

Moving now to 'Advisable action' with 2nd person subjects, the most common markers used were *gotta* (7 tokens), e.g. (30), and *should* (8 tokens), e.g. (31):

(30) *You gotta get up to your girl.* (Wilson 1987:20)
(31) *There are some cost accountants and some professional architects down at Memphis you should talk to.* (Wilson 1976:129)

The difference here is probably at least partially due to the relatively colloquial nature of *gotta*. We also suspect that something such as 'speaker involvement' favors the use of *gotta*; however, this parameter is extremely difficult to measure, especially with few tokens.

There is one example of 'Advisable action, generic subject':

(32) *It's the night of nights! People should be up.* (Wilson 1976:79)

Our next category, 'Procedures/routines', consists of obligated actions which have no clear negative effect on anyone. As Table 1 shows, *have to* and *gotta* are used for this function, with *have to* favored (7 vs. 3).[13] In this category, actions are often habitual, as in (33)-(34)14:

(33) *She took her stuff — I have to take my own, though. That's the way we do it.* (Wilson 1973:116)
(34) *They had to hang around the house and tend the fields — sacrifice to the gods of harvest and whatnot.* (Wilson 1976:46)

There are only three instances of *gotta* in this category. It is not clear why *gotta* is sometimes used here, and we would need a larger database to demonstrate anything conclusive.

The last of our categories, 'Biological/physical need', is straightforward. In the present tense, it is only expressed with *gotta*; in the past, it is expressed twice with *had to*, presumably because *gotta* lacks a past tense form. Examples are (35)-(36):

(35) *I had to piss so bad — about Fifteenth Street and Eighth or Ninth Avenue...* (Wilson 1987:62)
(36) *I gotta have another beer.* (Wilson 1976:120)

Perhaps one factor favoring *gotta* in these contexts is informality: we are more inclined to express physical needs around people we know well and with whom we are more likely to use the more colloquial *gotta*.

To summarize, in our English data, we have divided tokens based on whether the action can be said to negatively affect anyone. The English obligation morphemes analyzed here are associated with negative effect in more than half (63%) of the utterances coded. *Have to* is preferred over *gotta* when the speaker is attempting to portray an event as having negative consequences for the subject and/or the speaker; it can even be used in this function in non-obligation utterances (not gathered here, e.g., *Why did he have to hear noises in the night?*), where the verb is non-volitional and the action is beyond the control of the subject. *Have to* is also preferred to *gotta* in routines and procedures. With the form *You don't have to...*, the speaker is either expressing a reprimand or (at least ostensibly) relieving the listener of an obligation. *Gotta*, on the other hand, is the choice when mitigating an imposition, where the speaker often portrays an intention as an obligation in order to avoid offending the listener. *Gotta* is also used in reference to biological/physical needs, and its use with this function may be motivated in part by the informality which makes such mentions acceptable in the first place.

The remaining obligation expressions — *should*, *supposed to*, and *oughtta* — are less frequent in our data and have a different set of functions. The major functions of *should* are to express the speaker's wish that something else had happened (counterfactuals), to frame cooperative suggestions, and to refer to actions which the speaker has thought about taking. *Supposed to* and *oughtta* are both most commonly used in reprimands and counterfactuals in our data. *Supposed to* suggests action obligated by previous agreement or by tacit understanding between the subject and another party; *oughtta* occurs in situations where the speaker expresses personal distaste for a situation, although s/he is often not directly affected by it.

As we have noted, informality undoubtedly plays a role in the choice of obligation marker, particularly with *gotta*. Having described the general functions of *gotta* in the present study, it will be easier for future studies using data with broader stylistic variation to identify deviations from these general functions which are motivated by stylistic considerations.

2.2. *Chinese.*

The Chinese data were gathered from dialogue in two plays by Cao Yu, *Beijingren* ("Peking Man," 1954) and *Leiyu* ("Thunderstorm," 1961)[15]. The first portrays a once-prosperous family in decline, the second a pair of ill-fated lovers from different social classes who turn out to be long-separated siblings. There were several reasons for selecting these plays. First, they are by the same author and hence keep author-preference and dialect variables constant.[16] Second, the plays are recent enough to contain dialogue fairly typical of modern colloquial Chinese; Cao Yu's works are recognized as representative of the new genre *huaju* (spoken drama), which contrasts sharply with the lyrical, highly formulaic style of traditional Chinese drama. Third, *Beijingren* is available in a reasonably idiomatic English translation and is long enough to yield a sufficient number of English tokens. This is important for Chinese-English comparison (at the end of this section).

We examined three Chinese obligation markers, the preverbal auxiliaries *dei, yao*, and *gai*.[17] We have gathered only their preverbal and (where there was an overt subject) post-subject occurrences, excluding tokens with nominal or sentential complements (e.g., *Zhe dei ta guan* 'this *dei* he handle'='This has to be handled by him').

All of these morphemes also have epistemic functions, which are excluded here. The morphemes are illustrated in the following examples:[18]

(37) *Ni qian le wo de, ni* ***dei*** *huan* (Cao 1954:369)
you owe ASP me PRT you pay-back
'You have to pay back what you owe me.'19

(38) *Yihou shenme dou* ***yao*** *gaosu ma!* (Cao 1954:395)
from-now-on something all tell Mother
'From now on you must tell your mother (=speaker) everything.'

(39) *Nimen ye* ***gai*** *gei nimen fuqin songxing na!*
you(pl) also to your(pl) father bid-farewell PRT
(Cao 1954:335)
'You two should also say goodbye to your father.'

The status of *dei* and *gai* as obligation markers is supported by descriptions in several grammars (e.g., Liu 1983:116, Chao 1968:741-42, Li and Thompson 1981:182-83). *Yao*, however, is problematic because it can also express desire/intention and prediction/future meanings, as exemplified in (40)-(41):

(40) *Ke ni daying le wo. Wo* ***yao*** *fang, wo* ***yao*** *fang!*
but you promise ASP me I fly I fly
(Cao 1954:296)
'But you promised! I want to fly it (the kite), I want to!'

(41)	*Tamen*	*shuo*	*Dujia*	*Laotaiye...*	*jiu*	***yao***	*duanqi...*
	they	say	Du-family	old-master	just		cease-breath

(Cao 1954:383)
'They say Old Master Du is going to die anytime now...'

Additionally, when preceded by the negative marker *bu*, *yao* has imperative function (i.e. *bu yao*+verb='don't+verb). The question is thus: Which *yao* usages should be counted as obligation? There are four possible strategies for addressing this problem. One is to include all *yao* occurrences; however, this would mean including a large number of utterances which do not appear to mark anything resembling obligation meaning (e.g., *Wo yao jiabei huan ni* 'I'll pay you back double'). Another strategy would be to exclude all *yao* tokens, but that would eliminate numerous examples where *yao* conveys a clear sense of obligation. A third strategy would be to include only those *yao* tokens which are translated as one of the English obligation morphemes. However, some *yao* utterances have more idiomatic translations, such as (42) (Cao 1954:423):

(42)	*Zenme*	*yang*	*de*	*rizi*	*dou*	*shi*	***yao***	*guo*	*de.*
	any	type	PRT	day	all	are		experience	PRT

(Cao 1954:423)
'Everything will be all right, no matter what happens.'

(42) is more literally translated as 'All kinds of days have to be experienced', i.e., one has to take the bad times with the good. If we used translations as a criterion for inclusion, we would be forced to exclude data such as (42); we could of course ignore the translation data under such circumstances, but we prefer to use more objective criteria for inclusion.

We ultimately decided upon the following strategy: we included or excluded tokens of *yao* based upon whether they fit into any of the categories of obligation meaning described in Section 2.1. We first gathered all non-negated occurrences of *yao* from *Beijingren*, which yielded 189 tokens (this was enough for our purposes, so we did not gather tokens of *yao* from *Leiyu*). Of these 189, we eliminated 15 in which *yao* is unequivocally a future-marker, that is, in which there is an inanimate subject and/or a non-agentive verb (e.g. (41) above). For the remaining 174 tokens, we categorized 68 as belonging to one of two general types, one (59 tokens) where someone is negatively affected by the action expressed in the verb phrase (i.e. types a-g described in section 2.1), and the other (9 tokens) comprised of the different subtypes of obligation function without negative effect (i.e. types h-k).

The remaining 106 *yao* tokens are typically either assertions of intended action (with 1st or 3rd person subjects), unsolicited promises (with 1st person subjects), or detached inquiries as to the listener's intentions (with 2nd person subjects); we set these tokens aside. The 68 *yao* tokens included in our database do not invariably translate into English with obligation morphemes, and in some cases such a translation is not even plausible. However, we do not regard this as a problem, because it is our ultimate goal to develop characterizations of types of obligation functions which are language-universal and not dependent upon whether one language or another happens to represent them with an obligation marker.

We should note that, by adopting this strategy, we are proposing not a solution, but an approach. Exactly what constitutes an obligation usage of *yao* is still an open question, partly because the morpheme conflates what from an English viewpoint are two distinct meanings, obligation and intention.

Our database of Chinese obligation markers thus consists of 29 tokens of *dei*, 68 tokens of *yao*, and 26 tokens of *gai*. *Dei* and *gai* tokens were gathered from both plays, *yao* tokens from only one. Table 2 compares the raw frequencies of the three morphemes by showing their distribution in the one play from which *yao* tokens were gathered:

Table 2. *Obligation* dei, yao *and* gai *in* 'Beijingren'

Dei	10	11%
Yao	68	73%
Gai	15	16%
Total	93	100%

Table 3 shows the distribution of these morphemes in terms of the functional categories described for English in section 2.1. Note that while some of the obligation functions represented in the English data are not represented in the Chinese data (and vice versa), the same functional categories are in general useful for both languages.

As in English, we distinguish between those functional categories for which we can infer that someone would be negatively affected (a-g), and those for which we cannot (h-k). In the former group are the bulk of *dei* and *yao* tokens, in the latter the bulk of *gai* tokens.

Table 3. *Functional categories for* dei, yao, *and* gai

	dei	*yao*	*gai*	Total
a. Negative effect on subject	7	14	0	21
b. Mitigated inconvenience to listener (1st pers. subj.)	5	4	0	9
c. Negative effect on listener, unsympathetic				
1st pers. subj.	0	8	0	8
2nd pers. subj.	10	0	0	10
3rd pers. subj.	0	7	0	7
d. Negative effect on speaker	1	24	0	25
e. Reprimand (2nd pers. subj.)	0	2	3	5
f. Counterfactual (non-2nd pers. subj.)	0	0	7	7
g. Help not needed	0	0	0	0
h. Facetious suggestion	0	0	0	0
i. Advisable action				
1st person subject	0	2	8	10
2nd pers. subj.	6	4	6	16
Generic subject	0	2	1	3
j. Procedures/routines	0	1	0	1
k. Biological/physical need	0	0	0	0
l. Uncodable	0	0	1	1
Total	29	68	26	123

To express 'Negative effect on subject', both *dei* and *yao* are used, as in (43)-(44):

(43) ...*chi renjia de qianliang, jiu* ***dei*** *shou*
eat somebody PRT money-grain then be-subject-to
renjia de guan. (Cao 1961:7)
somebody PRT discipline
'...if somebody's paying your wages you've got to take orders from them.'

(44) *Keshi tamen shuo zhe zhang xianzai* ***yao*** *fu...*
but they said this account now pay
(Cao 1954:277)
'But they said the bill had to be paid right now.'

The distinction between *dei* and *yao* in this category appears to be related to the nature of the obligation. Most of the *dei* tokens (6/7) deal with the subject's prescribed behavior toward another party (who is mentioned), and the behavior is obligated by virtue of their social relationship. These obligations include accepting the authority of one's employer (as in (43)), being filial to one's father-in-law, being mindful of one's family's needs, etc. Note that these *dei* obligations are constant to the extent that the social relationship holds; where the relationship is permanent, as in say, child-to-parent obligations, the obligations are permanent, and hence in some sense generic. In contrast, most of the *yao* tokens (13/15) refer to actions that are either marked as inherently unpleasant independent of social relationships (e.g., having to suffer in life, having to worry) or necessary under temporary circumstances (e.g., paying a bill, as in (44), or selling a prized possession)[20]. The second category, 'Mitigated inconvenience to listener', also occurs with both *dei* and *yao*, illustrated in (45)-(46):

(45) *Ma,* *nin* *bie* *shuo* *zhexie* *hua* *le,* *wo* *hai*
mother you-honorific not say these word ASP I still
dei *zou* *ne.* (Cao 1961:123)
go PRT
'Mother, please don't say these things now, I've got to get going.'[21]

(46) *Wo* ***yao*** *zou,* *wo* *yijing* *deng* *le* *liang* *nian* *le.*
I leave I already wait ASP two year ASP
(Cao 1954:362)
'I have to leave this place, I've already waited two years.'

As in the English data, utterances in this functional category have 1st person subjects; the speaker is acting against the wishes of the listener while mitigating the inconvenience in some way. The distinction between these *dei* and *yao* usages is as follows: In four out of five of the *dei* clauses, the speaker needs the cooperation of the listener to carry out the action. For example, in (45), the speaker is a son who cannot in good conscience leave without his mother's blessing. In contrast, three of the four *yao* usages occur when the speaker's action (e.g. leaving after declining an invitation to stay) is not contingent upon anyone else's permission. *Yao*'s function here is clearly related to its intention function, since the speaker can be expected to carry out the action without the listener's acquiescence. The intention to perform an act negatively affecting the listener is mitigated by other expressions in the clause; e.g., (46) above is preceded by a clause translating as 'I can't wait any longer', demonstrating that the speaker has no choice. Our next category,

'Negative effect on listener, speaker unsympathetic', is divided into three types depending upon the person of the subject. Clauses with 1st person subjects (47) are all threats using *yao*, while clauses with 2nd person subjects (48) are all hostile commands using *dei*:

(47) *Kai men! Wo* ***yao*** *shao fangzi la!* (Cao 1954:367)
open door I burn house ASP
'If you don't open the door, I'll burn the house down!'

(48) *Zhe shi ni qian wo de qian, ni* ***dei*** *huan...*
this is you owe me PRT money you pay-back
(Cao 1954:369)
'...that's what you owe me, and that's what you're going to pay me back for.'

In examples with 3rd person subjects, the speaker characterizes intentions carried out independent of and presumably against the listener's wishes; there are 7 tokens of this type in the database and all 7 use *yao*. For example, the listener in (49) is negatively affected by the obligation because he is in love with the subject and arrangements are being made for her to marry someone else:

(49) *Renjia* ***yao*** *jiaren...* (Cao 1954:299)
she get-married
'She has to get married...'

Note that, in the English data discussed in 2.1, there are also utterances with 2nd person subjects in the 'Negative effect on listener, speaker unsympathetic' category; these are hostile predictions or commands. There are, however, no tokens in this category with 1st or 3rd person subjects. It is our impression that such cases are rarely expressed with obligation markers in English; `I have to burn the house down' is not a plausible translation of (47), and the listener-affected interpretation of the translation of (49) is impossible in English (indeed, the translation `She has to get married' gives the impression that it is `she' and not the listener who is negatively affected by the obligation, which is not the sense of the original). To be sure, it is possible in English to use an obligation marker in this functional category with a 1st person subject — always, it seems, in combination with a future marker (e.g. *I'm gonna have to burn the house down*). However, no such examples occur in our English database, and there is a clear tendency in English to emphasize *either* the intentional meaning (with *will* or *gonna* and no obligation marker), *or* the 'Mitigated inconvenience' meaning, where the obligation marker 'absolves' the speaker of responsibility (e.g. *I'm sorry I have to do this*). In Chinese, on the other hand, *yao* conflates the intention and obligation meanings and is commonly used when the listener is negatively affected, with or without mitigation on the part of the speaker.

Yau is the preferred morpheme in our next functional category, 'Negative effect on speaker', occurring in 96% (24/25) of the cases. This category includes only cases where the subject is non-1st person, as in (50) below, which distinguishes it from 'Negative effect on subject' with 1st person subjects:

(50) *Lin* *zou,* *lin* *zou,* *hai* ***yao*** *exiongxiongdi* *dui*
about-to leave about-to leave still fiercely to
wo *fa* *yi* *dun* *piqi.* (Cao 1954:300)
me emit one CL anger
'Here he is getting ready to leave and he's ranting and raving at me like this.'

10 of the 25 tokens of this type are questions (generally with 2nd person subjects) in which the speaker questions the motivation of the subject, as in (51)-(52):

(51) *Suyi,* *ni* *weishenme* ***yao*** *gaosu* *Yuanjia* *Popo* *ne?*
Suyi you why tell Yuan-family uncle PRT
(Cao 1954:363)
'Auntie Su, why did you have to tell Uncle Yuan about it?'

(52) *Ni* ***yao*** *gan* *shenme?* (Cao 1954:363)
you do what
'What are you doing?' (i.e. 'What do you think you're doing?')

In all of these cases, the action has a negative effect on the speaker (this is not obvious from the English translation of (52), but it is clear from the context in Chinese, hence our alternative English translation 'What do you think you're doing?').

There are no tokens of 'Negative effect on speaker' with obligation markers in the English database, although this usage is certainly possible, as in the translation of (51), or (6) (*Why did he have to hear noises in the night?*).

Table 4 Functions of *dei* and *yau*

dei	*yao*
Negative effect on subject ('X has to do/be Y toward Z') under circumstance Z')	Negative effect on subject ('X has to do (awful thing) Y
Mitigated inconvenience to listener ('Please, I've got to X')	Mitigated inconvenience to listener ('Sorry, I'm gonna have to X')
Negative effect on listener, unsympathetic, 2nd pers. subj. (e.g. 'You have to X, and you won't like it')	Negative effect on listener, unsympathetic, 1st or 3rd pers. subj. (e.g. 'I'm/he's gonna have to X, and you won't like it')
	Negative effect on speaker ('Why did you have to X?')

For reasons which are not clear, English does not use an obligation marker when there is a question word other than *why*. For example, *What do you have to do?* does not occur when the obligation marker indicates the speaker's disapproval of the action (parallel to the speaker-affected interpretation of *Why do you have to do that?*); rather, the obligation marker depicts the action as having a negative effect on the subject. Although obligation markers are sometimes possible with 'Negative effect on speaker' in English, this usage is obviously less common than with *yao*. The functions discussed thus far have been represented in the data by *dei* or *yao*, but not *gai*, and in this respect differ from the remaining functions, which generally favor *gai*. We summarize the functions of *dei* and *yao* discussed thus far (categories a-d) in Table 4 (the parenthetical English examples capture the gist of the Chinese contexts).

The contrast between *dei* and *yao* is clear from Tables 5-6, which show (on the x-axis) the subject type, and (on the y-axis) the negatively affected party, for the functional categories discussed so far (a-d). Most of the *dei* clauses in our data (16/23, or 70%) have the listener negatively affected. These are exclusively 1st person subjects (mitigated discourtesies) or 2nd person subjects (hostile commands). With *yao*, on the other hand, listener-affected clauses comprise only 35% (20/57) of the tokens, while speaker-affected clauses comprise 58% (33/57). Furthermore, with *yao*, the subjects of these clauses are often 3rd person.

Table 5. dei—*subject type (x-axis) and negatively affected party (y-axis)*

	Speaker	Listener	3rd party	Generic	Total
1st pers.	2	5	0	0	7
2nd pers.	0	11	0	0	11
3rd pers.	1	0	4	0	5
Generic	0	0	0	0	0
Total	3	16	4	0	23

Let us now look at the remaining obligation functions in which a negative effect on someone can be inferred.

Among these are 'Reprimands' and 'Counterfactuals'; like English, Chinese uses obligation morphemes to express both meanings. 'Reprimands' here have 2nd person subjects, which distinguishes them from 'Counterfactuals'.

In our data, there are five reprimands, two with *yao* and three with *gai*. In the former (unnegated) category, the speaker expresses dissatisfaction with the listener's failure to do something, as in (53), while in the latter (all three negated), the speaker reprimands the listener for having taken action deemed wrong, as in (54):

(53) *Yihou shenme dou* ***yao*** *gaosu ma!* (Cao 1954:395)
from-now-on what all tell mother
'From now on you must tell your mother (=speaker) everything!'

(54) *Feng, ni yiwei wo zheme zisizili ma? Ni bu*
F. you think I this selfish PRT you not
gai *zhenme kan wo.* (Cao 1961:40)
thus view me
'Now, Feng! You don't imagine I'm that selfish, do you? You mustn't think I'm that sort.'

'Counterfactual' meaning in our data is represented only with *gai*, usually with negation (5/7 tokens), as in (55):

(55) *Wo zao jiu* ***gai*** *xue naxie xinpai de*
I long-ago then learn-from those modern PRT
taitaimen... (Cao 1954:290)
wives
'I should have learned from those modern wives a long time ago...'

Table 6. yao—*subject type and negatively affected party*

	Speaker	Listener	3rd party	Generic	Total
1st pers.	9	12	0	0	21
2nd pers.	10	1	0	0	11
3rd pers.	14	7	2	0	23
Generic	0	0	0	2	2
Total	33	20	2	2	57

We will now turn to Chinese usages in which the action of the verb suggests no clear negative effect on anyone. The first two such categories ('Help not needed' and 'Facetious suggestion') are not represented in our data by the Chinese morphemes studied here.

We will next discuss the 'Advisable action' category. With 1st person subjects, *gai* is usually used here (8/10 times), as in (56):

(56) *Wo shuo ye* ***gai*** *wenwen Su biaomei de yijian ba.*
I say also ask Su cousin PRT idea PRT
(Cao 1954:407)
'...I think that we should talk to Cousin Su about it first.'

With 2nd person subjects, on the other hand, 'advisable actions' are expressed using all three obligation markers (6 *dei*, 4 *yao*, 6 *gai*). *Dei* is used when the speaker cannot be assumed to have authority over the listener; indeed, in 4 of the 6 *dei* clauses here, there is independent evidence that the speaker is showing deference. In (57), deference is indicated by the polite form of the 2nd person pronoun; the speaker is a servant, consoling a bereaved houseguest.

(57) *Zhe shi meifazi de shi, —keshi nin* ***dei***
this is no-way PRT matter but you (honorific)
kuku... (Cao 1961:133)
have-a-cry
'...there's nothing you can do now — now come on, you must have a cry.'

In contrast to *dei*, all four *yao* clauses in this category are uttered by an authority figure (e.g. parent, elder), as in (58), where a woman is admonishing her pregnant niece:

(58) *Ni* **yao** *dui* *wo* *shuo* *shihua.* (Cao1954:317)
you to me tell truthful-word
'(You've got to) tell me the truth.'

With both *dei* and *yao*, the speaker is strongly interested in seeing the action performed, usually out of commitment to the listener's well-being, or because of some personal agenda, or both.

Unlike the *dei* and *yao* tokens in this category, the 6 *gai* tokens have subjects showing neither deference nor authority. Consider (59), where the speaker appears to make a friendly suggestion to two would-be lovers (one of whom is her husband):

(59) *Lin* *zou* *le,* *ye* **gai** *liu* *dian* *jinian.* (Cao 1954: 310)
about-to leave ASP also keep a-bit remembrance
'Now that he's leaving, you should have something to remember each other by.'

There are also three tokens of 'Advisable action' with generic subjects, two using *yao*, as in (60), and one using *gai*:[22]

(60) *wo* *shuo* *yige* *ren* **yao** *you* *dian* *liangxin.* (Cao 1954:330)
I say a person have a-little conscience
'I say a person should have a little conscience.'

Gai is typically translated as 'should', the 'weak' obligation marker in English, and in our data it shares several features with that morpheme. Over half of the *gai* tokens (15/26) occur in the 'Advisable action' category, so that its use with this function is much more common than *dei* (6/29) or *yao* (8/68). Similarly, most of the tokens of *should* (16/22) occur in this category, but very few tokens of *have to* (1/42) or *gotta* (7/40) do. As in English *should* clauses, many of the *gai* tokens in this category (6/15) occur with a hedge, e.g. with the particle *ba* meaning 'Don't you think so?'[23] or with something translating as 'I think'. Such hedges (see (60) above) never occur with *dei* or *yao* in these categories.

The last two functional categories, 'Procedures/routines' and 'Biological/physical need' are only minimally represented in our Chinese data, and hence will not be discussed here. Returning now to categories e-k in Table 3, we can summarize the 'No negative effect' functions of *dei*, *yao*, and *gai* as in Table 7 (again, the English examples are intended to convey the gist of the categories).

Table 7. *Functions of* dei, yau, *and* gai

dei	*yao*	*gai*
	Reprimand ('You must X, but you haven't yet.')	Reprimand ('You shouldn't have Xed but you did.')
		Counterfactual ('X should(n't) have Yed.')
Advisable action	Advisable action ('Maybe I/we should X.')	Advisable action
('With all due respect, you've got to X.)	('You've got to X; I know what's best for you.') ('People should X.')	('Maybe you should X.')

The only noteworthy overlap of the three morphemes is with 'Advisable action, 2nd pers. subj.', and here the distinction is linked to the relationship between speaker and listener: In general, *dei* marks deference, *yao* marks authority, and *gai* is neutral. *Gai*, like English should, tends to have hedges in this category, and is the only morpheme used in counterfactuals.

To compare obligation usages in English and Chinese, we tabulated obligation morphemes in *Beijingren* against an English translation.[24] For this purpose, we included from each text all clauses which had a (non-epistemic) obligation marker in Chinese, English, or both. For *yao* clauses, this included the 68 tokens discussed above, plus an additional four which translated with an English obligation morpheme. Since *gotta*, *supposed* to, and *oughtta* are all extremely rare in the translation (only five tokens), we will exclude them here.

The translation correlations are shown in Table 8. Where only one language has an obligation marker, we indicate whether the other has a productive alternative way of encoding obligation meaning ('other oblig. marker'), or whether the clause is unmarked for obligation ('no marker'). This is especially relevant for clauses translated with *should*, where the Chinese has several means of expression other than a preverbal modal (e.g., clause-final particle *ba*, meaning roughly 'Why don't....').[25]

The data in Table 8 suggest that, of the three Chinese morphemes, *yao* occurs in places where English is least likely to use an obligation morpheme; most 'non-obligation' translations in the English (41/47) take *yao* in the Chinese. This is not surprising, given *yao*'s intentional meaning; about a third of these *yao* clauses (14/41) translate with *gonna*, *will*, or *want*, while nearly

Table 8. *Chinese-English comparison (*Beijingren+*English translation)*

	must	*have/ had to*	*should*	other marker	no marker	TL
dei	0	1	3	2	4	10
yao	2	22	5	2	41	72
gai	1	0	11	1	2	15
other oblig	2	1	13	X	X	16
no marker	1	20	8	X	X	29
TL	6	44	40	5	47	142

X=no data gathered

another third (12/41) use the Present Progressive form to express unilateral action already underway (e.g., *...and he's ranting and raving at me*). We only included tokens of *yao* corresponding to one or another of our categories of obligation function, generally having a negative effect on someone;[26] this negative effect frequently makes it at least possible to translate *yao* tokens into English with obligation markers, but the data in table 8 show that this is relatively uncommon.

Of the English morphemes, *have to/had* to marks the contexts least likely to take an obligation expression in Chinese. 20 of the 29 'non-obligation' contexts in Chinese take *have to* in the English, and 14 of these 20 fall into two categories: they refer either to past events, and translate as *had* to or *did have to* (6 tokens), or to habitual actions or states (8 tokens), usually with a time adverbial like *meitian* 'every day'. In our *Beijingren* data, Chinese morphemes which generally share the functions of *have to* — *dei* and *yao* — occur almost exclusively in either future or present contexts: *dei* never translates with any past tense English form, while *yao* does so only 10% of the time (7/72 times). It appears that past obligations in Chinese are rarely expressed with either *dei* or *yao*. As for habitual actions or states, English seems more likely than Chinese to explicitly mark a negative evaluation by using an obligation marker. In (61), for example, *have to* makes it clear that the speaker does not perform her routine willingly, while the Chinese translation uses no obligation marker:

(61) *...lian wo bu shi ye xia chufang bangzhe*
even I not be also go-down-to kitchen help
Zhang Shun... (Cao 1954:295)
'Even I have to help Zhang Shun (=servant) in the kitchen.'

In many of these clauses, *have to* reinforces the speaker's negative evaluation, even when the unpleasantness of the action is quite obvious (e.g. with the verb *suffer*). We suspect that in English, this function is important in habituals because a repeated action might otherwise imply the speaker's willingness.

In cases where a Chinese obligation marker is translated into English with an obligation marker, there is a strong tendency for *yao* to be translated with the 'strong' obligation marker 'have to' and *gai* with the 'weak' marker should; this is consistent with the patterns in the original data. There are, however, a few cases where *yao* is translated with 'should'. These are generally cases where some kind of abstract morality is being discussed, as in 60 ('I say a man should have a little conscience'). In English, the use of a weak obligation marker here suggests that if the subject fulfills this obligation it is because s/he is a good person rather than because it is an absolute obligation; strong obligation markers do not seem appropriate here.

2.3. *Hopi.*

Hopi has only one word which we can consider to be a productive marker of obligation, *nawus*.[27] Basic word order in Hopi is SOV, and *nawus* normally comes between the subject and the object or complement PPs. Unlike the obligation markers in English and Chinese, which have syntactic and/or phonological properties of auxiliaries, *nawus* is a free, fully lexical form, which has the syntactic distribution of an adverb. Although it is the only productive way of marking obligation in Hopi, it is relatively uncommon; *must*, *have to*, *should*, and *be to* each occur more frequently in the English translation than *nawus* occurs in the Hopi.

Our Hopi data are taken from Malotki and Lomatuway'ma (1987a and 1987b), and Geertz and Lomatuway'ma (1987), collections of Hopi texts with English translations. The texts consist of personal narratives as well as traditional stories about the god Maasaw and his interactions with Hopis and various anthropomorphized animals. As in the other languages, we include only data from conversational (as opposed to narrative) parts of the texts. *Nawus* occurs 27 times in the conversations in these texts, always with an obligation function (even in two cases where it is not translated into English with a typical obligation form).

For the purposes of delimiting our database and comparing Hopi and English, it is necessary to determine when a type of obligation meaning can be

Table 9. *Obligation expressions in Hopi and English*

	Nawus	No *nawus*
Have to	12	29
Must	8	33
No choice (but to)	4	0
Need (to)	1	7
Should	0	29
Be to	0	26
Supposed to	0	9
Better	0	3
Got to	0	1
No obligation word	2	X
Total	27	137

inferred from the text even if it is not marked with *nawus*. The strategy employed in Section 2.2 in selecting tokens of *yao* to include in the data base, namely, including tokens which correspond to an obligation category described in Section 2.1, is not feasible in Hopi. As we will see, the categories are not really appropriate for the Hopi data, and additionally we would have to apply them to every single clause in the data, with *nawus* or without, which would be prohibitively time-consuming. Under these circumstances, the only realistic course of action is to use the English translations as our criteria for inclusion. Thus we include in our database for this section all sentences which have *nawus* in the Hopi and/or a word expressing obligation in the English translation. As mentioned in Section 2.2, this strategy has the disadvantage of excluding tokens where some kind of obligation meaning appears to be present but an obligation marker is not used in the English translation; however, the alternative approaches have stronger disadvantages. The translation relationships in the database are shown in Table 9.[28]

The first observation which we can make from Table 9 is that *nawus* appears to be associated specifically with 'strong' obligation, as it is only translated with the 'strong' obligation forms *must, have to*, and *no choice*, but never with the 'weak' markers *should, be to, supposed to*, or *better*. For reasons noted above, it is problematic to develop independent criteria to test the 'strong/weak' distinction. However, it is worth mentioning that in all but one of the 27 cases, the obligation is fulfilled; in the one exception, a child disobeys his parents' command, but it is clear that the parents intended a command rather than a recommendation. This pattern is consistent enough to support the view that *nawus* is specifically associated with 'strong' obligation.

We will now turn to the problem of characterizing the functions of *nawus*. One strategy for doing this is to apply the categories for obligation types used in Sections 2.1 and 2.2, which could be applied to the English and Chinese data in a more or less straightforward fashion. However, when we attempted to do this with the Hopi data (or even the English translations), we found that very frequently these data did not fit neatly into the categories.

In the English database, there is relatively little difficulty distinguishing between obligation constructions involving 'Negative effect on subject' (which almost never have 2nd person subjects), 'Negative effect on listener', 'Advisable action' with 2nd person subjects (which are basically for the good of the 2nd person), and 'Procedure/routine'. There is rarely overlap between these categories.

In Hopi, on the other hand, this categorization system generally does not work. Many of the tokens in the obligation-function database involve people in a superior position stating things which have to be done by people in an inferior position (a rare situation in our English database, where there is a more egalitarian relationship between the characters). It is often unclear whether to categorize such cases as 'Procedure/routine'; when the basis of the instructions seems to be more ritualistic the initial temptation is to code them as 'Procedures', whereas when the leader seems to think out and improvise a course of action on the basis of the specifics of the situation, these might be coded as something else (e.g. 'Negative effect on subject', 'Advisable action'). However, this essentially amounts to categorizing the instructions of a Hopi leader on the basis of whether or not they can be rationally explained in a Western frame of reference. For example, it is not clear how to categorize instructions on conducting a raindance. While there are some general rules, there is also considerable scope for improvisation, and so this sort of situation lies somewhere in between 'Advisable action' and 'Procedures'.

Another difficulty with applying the categories of Section 2.1 to the Hopi data lies in defining 'Negative effect' and determining who is negatively affected. In the Hopi data, subjects are often required to perform unpleasant tasks necessary for the good of their social group. These actions may be 'negative' for the subject but are at the same time 'Advisable actions', since the listener, as a member of the group, will in some sense benefit (if only in the long run); commanding such actions might even be considered hostile, since the speaker is essentially imposing an unpleasant task on the listener. Tokens of this type are common and difficult to code. In the English data, on the other hand, this problem essentially does not come up; if the speaker imposes or

Table 10. *Use of* nawus

	Nawus	No *nawus*
Decision at moment of crisis	6	1
Subject explicitly shows disinclination	11	5
Subject has been doing opposite	3	0
Specific word showing unpleasantness	6	3
Permanent separation	1	2
Other	0	126

suggests an obligation to the listener, it is almost invariably either clearly hostile and against the interests of the listener, or else clearly cooperative and supportive of the interests of the listener.

For these reasons, we felt that the categories used in the descriptions of English and Chinese were inappropriate for description of the Hopi data; there were simply too many cases where it was not clear how to apply them. We have therefore developed other categories of obligation function to use in analyzing the Hopi data. The database will be the same as that used in table 9, consisting of all sentences in dialogues which have *nawus* in the Hopi and/or an obligation marker in the English translation. Table 10 summarizes the frequency of *nawus* for the different types of obligation functions.

We will describe and exemplify these functions below, drawing parallels where appropriate with some of the categories used in Sections 2.1 and 2.2.

The first category is 'Decision at moment of crisis'. *Nawus* is used in this situation 6/7 times. This often corresponds to 'Advisable action, 2nd pers. subj.'; there is no clear evidence that the action is viewed as negative. This generally occurs at the beginning of a story when a crisis comes up and the people have to change their normal way of life to deal with it. For example, at the beginning of one story about a boy and his mother, winter is coming on, they are running out of firewood, and, unlike previous years, no one has volunteered to get firewood for them. The mother uses *nawus* twice in telling her son that they must take action:

(62) *um as nawus itamungem komoktoni. Itam hapi son*
you for-us get-wood-FUT we really not
nawus *kohot qa na'sastani* (Malotki and Lomatuway'ma 1987a:12)
wood not prepare-FUT
'You must go gather some firewood for us. We really have to stock up with wood...'

In this case, as in others, once a course of action is decided upon, *nawus* is not used again. The boy immediately agrees to go, and the mother then gives him a series of instructions without using *nawus*. The English translation also tends to avoid expressions of obligation in favor of imperatives, but there is one use of the obligation marker *need* (*You need only cut it into pieces about this long* (Malotki and Lomatuway'ma 1987a:15)). Later, talking to someone else, the boy says 'because there is no one to bring wood for us, I have had to come here myself' (Malotki and Lomatuway'ma 1987a:15); here again, the Hopi does not use *nawus*. Similarly, in another story, a group of Hopis learn that they are about to be attacked by a group of Paiutes. Immediately, one of them states: *Pay itam tur nawus itaatumalay haak maatatve*, 'We will have to let go our work for the time being (to prepare for war)', using *nawus* (Malotki and Lomatuway'ma 1987a:54). Once this decision has been made, various leaders give instructions on how to deal with the conflict, but now that they have embarked upon a course of action, *nawus* is not used again.

This pattern is consistent with the discussion of the distinction between obligation and imperative function in Palmer 1986. Palmer hypothesizes that imperatives present commands in a semantically neutral way, while obligation expressions are used in social contexts where giving commands is marked behavior. Thus imperatives are appropriate when the speaker is in a position of authority (e.g. officer to private) and/or the speaker and hearer have temporarily determined to enter into a cooperative relationship (e.g. preparing for a battle). Expressions of obligation with 2nd person subjects, on the other hand, are most strongly associated with situations in which the speaker wishes to give a command to the listener but no such command relationship can be presupposed.[29] The use of *nawus* is therefore associated with a moment of crisis, when the subject must be convinced to reorder priorities. Once this has been done, the obligation is presupposed rather than asserted, and *nawus* is no longer used.

The next functional category for Hopi is 'Subject explicitly shows disinclination' to do the proposed action. *Nawus* is used 11 times in 16 tokens in this situation (which often corresponds to 'Negative effect on subject', 'Advisable action, 2nd pers. subj.', or 'Help not needed'). In one case, a man is putting a repulsive mask on his daughter-in-law for ceremonial purposes. The English translation of the relevant section is 'As he was about to place the mask over her head, however, she shrank back from him', and then he says to her (Malotki and Lomatuway'ma 1987a:234):

(63) *Ta'ay, pay um son* ***nawus*** *it qa ang pakini*
come PRT you not PRT not on put
'Come, you'll have to put this on.'

In another story, a Hopi leader has sent some men to make an offering to the god Maasaw, but when they see how disgusting he looks, they run back without making the offering. Their leader tells them *Is ohiy, pay uma son nawus qa piw awyani* 'Too bad, you'll have to go back', with *nawus* (Malotki and Lomatuway'ma 1987b:50). This category has some resemblance to the first in that both are used specifically when the speaker is attempting to convince the listener that an action must be undertaken.

In the third category, 'Subject has been doing opposite of what the speaker wants', the subject is instructed to change his/her behavior; here *nawus* is used three out of three times. This type is generally similar to 'Advisable action, 2nd pers. subj.'. In one case a man is performing a ceremonial dance in an egotistical fashion, believing that the dance will succeed specifically because of him. Others realize this and tell him that he must confess to it (confession being required by Hopi ethics in this case). One says to him:

(64) *Um oovi* ***nawus*** *itam umi nahostani*
you so us to confess
(Geertz and Lomatuway'ma 1987:348)
'You must confess to us'

This usage of *nawus* is similar to the one exemplified in (63). The next category is 'Specific word showing unpleasantness'; this was only counted if the 'unpleasant' word is in the same clause (this category often corresponds to 'Negative effect on subject'). *Nawus* is used 6/9 times for tokens of this type. For example, the god Maasaw informs a man:

(65) *Noq oovi um hiitawit uutiw'ayay, maanat, pas aw*
PRT so you one your-niece girl very to
unangway'taqey put um ***nawus*** *tavini*
beloved her you sacrifice
(Malotki and Lomatuway'ma 1987b:94)
'You'll have to sacrifice the niece who is most dear to you (to obtain fat to keep the sun burning)'

Here the unpleasantness of this obligation is emphasized with the term *unangway'taqey* 'beloved', and *nawus* is used. Similarly, *nawus* is used in the following sentence: *Noq oovi itam yang utuhu'puva nawus qa oo'onakyangw yang tutskwava hiita noonovaniqey put a'aniwnaya* 'For this reason we Hopis must suffer through hot weather and by toiling hard raise the crops in the fields' (Malotki and Lomatuway'ma 1987a:132). Here there are also specific words emphasizing the unpleasantness of the obligation (*utuhu'puva* 'hot' and *oo'onakyangw* 'get tired').

In the fifth category, 'Permanent separation,' the speaker informs the listener of the necessity of a death or other permanent separation. In this situation, *nawus* is used in one of three tokens. This type generally corresponds to 'Negative effect on subject'. For example, the god Maasaw informs the Hopi that they cannot all live in the same place and says, using *nawus*:

(66) *Uma son* ***nawus*** *qa naanahoyyani*
you not not go-in-different-ways
(Malotki and Lomatuway'ma 1987b:61)
'You'll have to migrate in different directions'

To summarize, we have seen that *nawus* is basically limited in its uses to a subset of the uses of the English obligation markers. These can be grouped into two types:

(i) At the moment of speech, there is a conflict between what the subject has been doing or wants to do and the exigencies of the situation. The speaker states the obligation to motivate the subject (which may be 1st person plural) to change his/her priorities. This includes the first three types discussed above.

(ii) The action undertaken is particularly unpleasant (or is at least represented as such), but must be done anyway. This includes the last two types discussed above. The great majority of the tokens with obligation markers in the English translation do not fit either of these types; in such cases, *nawus* is never used.

2.4. *Biblical Hebrew.*

Thus far, we have discussed markers in English, Chinese, and Hopi with a variety of functions which can be considered to represent types of obligation. Our analysis of Biblical Hebrew differs in that we will not attempt to categorize different types of obligation functions but rather to demonstrate that these and related functions can be expressed through purely grammatical rather than lexical means.

As argued in Section 1.2, obligation markers can develop functions which are more grammatical, such as inference and future meaning, and we would expect these more grammatical functions to be related to the more lexical obligation functions in a non-arbitrary way. There will then be a network of related functions consisting of different types of obligation function and also certain types of more grammatical functions like inference and future. We will refer to this network of related functions as 'obligation' (with scare quotes). Note that 'obligation' does not include *all* types of inference/ future functions, but only those related to obligation and likely to develop from an erstwhile obligation marker.

This view of 'obligation' as representing a network of related functions (ranging from strongly lexical to highly grammaticalized) is supported in an interesting fashion by data from Biblical Hebrew. This language has no lexical marker of obligation similar to English *have to*, Chinese *dei*, or Hopi *nawus*. However, something resembling 'obligation' meaning is expressed through word order alternation. Biblical Hebrew generally has verb-initial order (69% of the time in our database), and the use of non-verb-initial order has as one of its functions the expression of something resembling 'obligation'.

Before demonstrating this, we should note that we are **not** claiming that 'obligation' meaning is expressed through non-verb-initial order in Biblical Hebrew. It is more accurate to say that the use of non-verb-initial order expresses an abstract function which, in certain contexts, resembles 'obligation', and which, from the English point of view, is interpreted as 'obligation'. For this reason, sentences using non-verb-initial order in these contexts are consistently rendered in languages such as English with 'obligation' markers.

We have gathered data from all the conversations in the first 30 books of Genesis and an English translation (Plaut 1981). Our database includes all clauses with functions which might be considered future, subjunctive, optative, imperative, and/or modal, a total of 450 Hebrew clauses and their translations. We then coded the data according to the Hebrew word order pattern and the English translation.

Because Hebrew lacks a lexical obligation morpheme, our strategy for analyzing must be different from that used for the other languages in this

Table 11. *Hebrew word order and English 'obligation' markers*

	Non-verb-initial	Verb-initial	Non-verb-initial%
Shall	46	27	63%
Should	5	0	100%
Be to	4	1	80%
Must	2	1	67%
Total 'obligation'	57	29	66%
Other	81	283	22%

Chi-square=63.42 p<.001

study. Attempting to apply an abstractly defined, universal meaning of 'obligation', or even more specific meanings such as those used in Sections 2.1 and 2.2, to a Biblical Hebrew text results in too many indeterminate cases where the Hebrew does not unequivocally tell us whether 'obligation' function is present. The alternative is to use translation data. English has a number of words associated with 'obligation' function, and consistent use of these words in translations of a construction indicates that that there is a connection between that construction and 'obligation' function. Of course, the degree of consistency will vary depending on which translation is used; however, as will be seen, the pattern is so strong that we believe that it would appear no matter which translation was used. Our results are shown in table 11.[30]

We include here *should*, *must*, and *be to*, which mark obligation function (*must* and *should* also have related functions such as inference), and *shall*, which previously marked obligation and which now has future function while retaining some of its old obligation meaning (Bybee and Pagliuca 1987); *have to* and *gotta* did not occur in the translation. All of these words represent 'obligation' functions (functions associated with lexical obligation markers and the related functions which these later develop). The coding of the translation data was entirely on the basis of the lexical form used in the English translation; no distinction was made between different usages of *shall*, *should*, *be to*, and *must*.

Table 11 shows that non-verb-initial order is three times as common when an 'obligation' marker is present in the English translation as when the English has no obligation marker (66% vs. 22%). There is thus evidence of a strong relationship between non-verb-initial order and 'obligation' meaning. This relationship is by no means categorical; 22% (81/364) of the non-'obligation' clauses are non-verb-initial and 34% (29/86) of the 'obligation' clauses are verb-initial. However, a large number of these exceptions can be explained as due to other functions of word order alternation in Hebrew and auxiliary usage in English. Non-verb-initial order in Hebrew is associated not only with 'obligation' but also with clauses with contrastive topicalization or focusing (Fox 1983), as in (67)-(68) (these and following translations are from Plaut 1981):

(67) *ten-li hanefesh vharxush qakh-lax.* (Genesis 14:21)
give-me the-persons and-the-possessions take-for-yourself
'"Give me the persons, and take the possessions for yourself."'

(68) *shvu-laxem poh 'im-hakhamor va?ani vhana'ar*
stay here with-the-ass and-I and-the-boy
nelxah 'ad-koh. (Genesis 22:5)
go up-there
'"You stay here with the ass. The boy and I will go up there."'

In such contrastive pairs, non-verb-initial order is normally only used for the second contrastive clause, not the first (Myhill and Xing 1992); these clauses account for a large number of non-verb-initial constructions not translated as 'obligation' markers. In presenting these examples, we are not, of course, implying that there is any tendency to avoid 'obligation' markers in English in sentences with contrastive function, but rather that contrast provides another motivation for using non-verb-initial order in Hebrew; this accounts for many of the 81 non-verb-initial constructions in our data which are not translated with 'obligation' markers.

We turn now to another exception to the correlation of non-verb-initial clauses in Hebrew and 'obligation' markers in English. Of the 29 exceptional clauses using verb-initial order and translating with an 'obligation' auxiliary, 22 share the following three features:

(a) God is talking;
(b) There is a 2nd or 3rd person subject;
(c) The clause does not occur in a plausible context for using the imperative.[31]

When these three features are present, there is an overwhelming tendency for the English translation to use 'obligation' markers (particularly *shall*) regardless of the word order in Hebrew: out of 63 tokens with these three features, 56 use *shall*, 3 use *be to*, 1 uses *must*, 2 use *will*, and 1 uses *can*; in similar cases which are plausible contexts for imperatives, of course, the translation simply uses an imperative (e.g. 'Go from your land...'). It appears that the translators are following a stylistic convention of using *shall* in God's speech about someone else's future actions (excluding imperatives); this occurs 89% of the time. The most likely explanation for this is that *shall* has acquired an archaicizing function independent of its 'obligation' function and so is particularly suitable for conveying God's prognostications and pronouncements about the fate of humans.[32]

Of the remaining 7 tokens (out of 29) of verb-initial constructions exceptionally translated with English 'obligation' markers, all follow the equivalent of *if* or *when* clauses in Hebrew, e.g. (69):

(69) *v?im-lo?* *to?veh* *ha?ishah* *lalexet* *akhareixa*
and-if-not willing the-woman to-go after-you
vniqatah *mishvu'ati.* (Genesis 24:8)
you-will-be-free from-my-oath
'And if the woman is not willing to go with you, you will be free from my oath.'

Such apodosis clauses are invariably verb-initial in our Biblical Hebrew database (in 25 tokens), regardless of whether they translate with 'obligation' words. We have shown, then, that one function of non-verb-initial order in Biblical Hebrew is related to 'obligation'. Since this is not the only function of this order (it also marks contrast), we are not claiming a categorical correlation between this order and translation with 'obligation' markers, but 'obligation' is a major function of this order. The use of word-order alternation to mark 'obligation' function presumably compensates to some extent for the fact that the language does not have a lexical obligation marker.

It is not at this stage entirely clear why Biblical Hebrew should mark 'obligation' function with word order. Cross-linguistic research will be necessary to determine whether the relationship between non-verb-initial order and 'obligation' is widespread and based on general cognitive principles or simply restricted to Biblical Hebrew and more or less coincidental. We might tentatively hypothesize that this relationship may be related to the notion of **continuity**.[33]

Givón (1977) and others have argued that in narrative discourse, the unmarked order of presentation is 'iconic sequence' (the order of clauses mirrors the order in which the events reported in these clauses took place); more specifically, temporally sequenced clauses are continuous and unsequenced clauses are discontinuous. Givón shows that in Biblical Hebrew, verb-initial order is associated with continuous (temporally sequenced) clauses, while non-verb-initial order is associated with clauses which are discontinuous (unsequenced) clauses (Myhill 1992 argues that this pattern is in fact universal in languages with predominant VS word order).

The continuous/discontinuous dichotomy applies only to narrative portions of a text, where past actions are reported; however, a related distinction emerges in other types of text. For example, we can say that apodosis clauses, as in (69), are 'continuous' because they have a similar function in irrealis time (chronologically following the protasis) as sequenced clauses have in past time. The fact that apodosis clauses are categorically verb-initial in Biblical Hebrew is then consistent with the general pattern of verb-initial clauses being continuous in this language. Clauses involving contrast (as in (67), on the other hand, are not verb-initial and can be construed as discontinuous, because they interrupt a narrative or a chain of logical reasoning for the purpose of making a comparison between two entities.

If we apply the concept of continuity to conversations about future time, we can associate it with **cooperation**, while discontinuity is associated with 'obligation'. We hypothesize that the unmarked assumption in a conversation about the future is that the interlocutors will talk about it cooperatively. Myhill 1993 provides quantitative data showing that verb-initial order in future clauses in Biblical Hebrew is associated with situations involving some type of cooperation, e.g., the speaker proposes a course of action to the listener, one event enables another (a purpose clause), or the speaker hopes that something good will happen to the listener. On the other hand, 'obligation' meaning and non-verb-initial order are associated with contexts lacking 'cooperation' of this type, e.g., the speaker predicts something bad for the listener, or the speaker makes a unilateral statement about the future which does not consider the actions and feelings of the listener.

The distinction between cooperation and 'obligation' also appears to be expressed by the contrast between verb-initial and non-verb-initial order in commands. When the speaker can presuppose the listener's cooperation (because the speaker is in a higher-ranking position or because the interlocutors have already agreed upon a plan), the Imperative form is used, and it is almost always verb-initial (Myhill 1993). On the other hand, when the speaker cannot presuppose the listener's cooperation (because the speaker is not in a position to command the listener), non-verb-initial order is usual, as in (70):

(70) *?elay* *tavo?*. (Genesis 30:16)
to-me you-come
'"You are to sleep with me."'

The speaker here is Leah addressing her husband Jacob. She has just bought him for the night from her sister, his other wife Rachel. Normally, wives do not command their husbands in this text, so the social context for presupposing the right to command is not present here. Thus, the Hebrew uses a non-verb-initial construction with the Imperfect form of the verb (rather than the Imperative) and the English translation uses an obligation expression. This distinction between imperative and 'obligation' function is in line with Palmer's (1986) argument (mentioned in Section 2.3) that imperatives are semantically neutral, used in situations where the speaker is in a position to command the listener, while obligation marking is appropriate for commands when the speaker is not in a position to give orders. Stating the obligation is thus a justification for giving the command; this is presumably also related to the morphologically unmarked status of imperatives as opposed to obligation expressions.

This account of why non-verb-initial order is associated with 'obligation' function in Biblical Hebrew is of course speculative, and the matter will have to be researched in other languages with a high incidence of verb-initial order. For the moment, it seems to be at least a reasonable way to approach the question of why Biblical Hebrew should have a means of expressing obligation so radically different from that of the other languages discussed in this paper.

3. Conclusion.

The main purpose of this study has been to develop a framework for the cross-linguistic description and comparison of obligation functions in natural usage. We have discussed and exemplified types of obligation functions in four languages and correlated these with obligation markers in particular languages. We have gone to some length to describe and exemplify the functions identified in our database so that linguists working in other languages might test them against their data. The functions generally correlate with particular markers in the languages we have investigated, and when a given function occurs commonly with more than one marker we have attempted to divide it into subfunctions which might account for the distribution of markers. Given the relatively small size of our database, we cannot expect to have entirely determined the factors governing the choice of forms, nor do we expect our list of obligation functions to be exhaustive.

It is important to note here what we have **not** attempted to do. We have not attempted to define exactly what obligation means in general. After analyzing a large number of expressions of obligation in the languages investigated here, it is clear to us that obligation expressions do not simply report objectively necessary actions. Rather, they are devices used by speakers to evaluate and justify actions, so that the only way to analyze their function is in terms of usage rather than 'meaning'. We have of course used an intuitive notion of obligation to delimit our database, but this has been done purely for convenience; neither our functional categories nor the morphemes we have chosen to analyze are intended to exhaustively represent or define obligation.

We have also not attempted to organize the categories of obligation function into 'core' and 'peripheral' types, along the lines of Coates 1983. It would of course be possible to choose one or another function as 'core' obligation and rank the others according to the number of shared semantic features. However, there appears to be no objective basis for choosing one function over another as 'core', nor any obvious motivation for organizing the data in this fashion.

It is probably the case that some of obligation functions are more lexical while others are more grammatical. Research such as Bybee 1985 has demonstrated that some functions are consistently associated with more lexical representation while other functions are consistently associated with more grammatical representation, and it is clear that the future and inference functions which obligation markers can develop are more grammatical than the obligation functions we discuss here. However, among the obligation functions we identify here, it is not clear which are more lexical and which more grammatical. To determine this, it would be necessary to gather data from a wide variety of languages and to look for cases in which some of the functions are expressed through more lexical forms and others through more grammatical forms. Alternatively, we might study in detail the diachronic development of a single marker in a single language to see how this marker has progressed from one function to another. If there is a change in terms of the predominant functions of the marker, we might hypothesize that the earlier functions are more lexical and the later functions more grammatical.[34] This line of research is likely to produce interesting results; however, it is premature at this stage to speculate on what they might be.

We have not developed a single list of obligation functions which can be applied to all texts from all languages; the obligation functions which we used for the English and Chinese texts turned out not to be the most appropriate or revealing ones for the Hopi and Biblical Hebrew texts. The use of obligation markers is obviously closely connected to the organization of a society, and the societies associated with these languages differ in a number of ways. This does not invalidate the search for a 'universal' list of obligation functions. However, such a task is beyond the scope of a single paper; additionally, making such a list would require data from more than four languages. Rather than attempt such an ambitious project here, we have analyzed the data from each language in a way which seemed most appropriate to that language. This study has therefore not resulted in a comprehensive list of obligation functions perfectly suited to texts in all languages, but rather has identified a variety of functions which may or may not prove useful in the (long-term) goal of constructing such a list.

We suspect, however, that even if such a comprehensive list of obligation functions were to be constructed, it would not necessarily solve the problem of cross-linguistic comparability. For example, on the basis of the Hopi data, we could make a category like 'Instructions for performing a ritual spiritually beneficial to the community as a whole', which might be objectively applica ble to data from any language. However, this context would occur rarely if ever in original texts in languages such as English and Chinese. This difficulty can be alleviated somewhat through the use of translation data (e.g. English translations of Hopi texts); additionally, we might look for data from certain sections of a society where this context would be most likely to come up. This may sound like a formidable task, but it seems to us the only way to compare obligation functions in widely differing languages in an empirically responsible fashion. The alternative would be to have a vague understanding of obligation as a general universal concept, and to say that speakers of individual languages interpret this concept in accordance with their social structures and world view; however, it seems to us that this approach will not lead to much in the way of solid empirical findings either in descriptions of individual languages or in cross-linguistic comparisons.

The present paper, then, has sought to show that obligation function can be productively analyzed with quantitative methods. Largely due to historical accident, quantitative discourse-oriented research has focused primarily on word order and voice alternations, and it is important that linguists working in this field expand the range of phenomena under investigation. Quantitative methods produce results which cannot be obtained from introspection alone, and they force the researcher to think in terms of objectively defineable criteria. We do not deny the value of introspective research; however, we see few if any linguistic phenomena which cannot benefit from quantitative as well as introspective investigation.

NOTES

* We thank Joan Bybee and Suzanne Fleischman for their extensiveand helpful comments on an earlier draft of this paper.

1 Both Palmer (1979:91) and Coates (1983:33) admit that it is often difficult to categorize tokens according to the criterion of speaker involvement.

2 *Shall* is very rare in the original English texts we used and in the English translations of the Hopi and Chinese texts. It is, on the other hand, quite common in the translation we used of the Biblical Hebrew text. However, this is not a problem, because in Biblical Hebrew we are analyzing 'obligation' function (including the more grammaticalized functions which obligation markers develop) rather than obligation function, so there is no need to distinguish the obligative *shall* from its future-oriented uses.

3 Lambdin (1971:129) notes that the expression '*al* + NP + *l* + infinitive is used to express obligation or responsibility, but there were no tokens of this construction in our database.

4 Except where otherwise indicated, *gotta* will include *have got to*, *got to*, and *gotta*, and *oughtta* will include *ought to* . *Must* occurs only once in Wilson's dialogue, *need to* only four times. Hence, we have not included them in this study.

5 *Does* (subj) *gotta*? is acceptable to some speakers, but it does not occur in our data. We use the asterisk to indicate non-occurrence in our data base, not to indicate that we or the playwright would reject a form as ungrammatical (although in some cases we would).

6 In one token, the subject is actually avoiding something emotionally or physically unpleasant (*No, you do that 'cause you got to, 'cause you'd be embarrassed not to* (Wilson 1976:117)).

7 This speaker-external source of authority is probably related to the low 'speaker involvement' or low 'subjectivity' associated with *have to* (see Section 1.1).

8 Conceptually, of course, reprimands are a type of counterfactual, e.g., *You shouldn't have done that* is counterfactual because the auxiliary is negated but the addressee must have done the action. We distinguished these categories in our coding by including as reprimands only counterfactual clauses with 2nd person subjects.

9 Two of the *supposed* to tokens may also be partly motivated by negation (*...you aren't supposed to be here* rather than *you ought not be here*) and/or past tense; we get neither **ought not* nor **didn't ought* in our data.

10 Our *oughtta* reprimands are somewhat borderline obligation usages, since their verbs are stative (*be ashamed, be used to*). You cannot oblige someone to 'perform' a state; on the other hand, you can oblige someone to perform an action that avoids or effects a state, and on this reasoning, we have included such tokens.

11 This discussion of counterfactuals is not intended to be exhaustive; a much larger database is needed for a thorough and systematic analysis of natural usage.

12 The association of *supposed* to with arrangements by unmentioned agents is likely due to its origin as a passive construction (we thank Joan Bybee for suggesting this).

13 One *have to* token is negated with *don't*, which may explain the speaker's not using *gotta*.

14 Coates (1983:54) observes that, in its 'root' or obligation meaning, *have got to* is never habitual while *have to* can be. She cites the distinction between *I have to get up at 7 a.m. every day* and **I've got to get up at 7 a.m. every day.*

15 *Beijingren* was written in 1940 and slightly revised by the author in 1954; in the text, we cite it as Cao 1954. *Leiyu* was written in 1934 and revised twice by the author before its 1961 printing, and we cite it as Cao 1961.

16 This is important because *dei* is commonly recognized as a Beijing colloquialism. As a Tianjin native (see Rand et al 1980), Cao Yu is not a representative speaker of the Beijing dialect. It would be interesting to compare the *dei* vs. *yao* distinction in Cao's work to that of a Beijing native, where some of the *yao* functions described here would presumably be filled by *dei*.

17 All of these can also be used as main verbs, often translating as 'take, require', 'want', and 'owe', respectively. Under *gai* we have included 7 tokens of *yinggai*, the latter often described as a more formal variant. Though there are no doubt some differences in their functions, we will not attempt to distinguish them here.

18 Our abbreviations are: ASP=aspect, PRT=particle, FUT=future, CL=classifier.

19 Unless otherwise indicated, translations of *Beijingren* examples are from Lo 1986 and translations of *Leiyu* examples are from Wang and Barnes 1954.

20 The two exceptions refer to obligations to father-in-law and family, respectively. But even these obligations are to some extent also specific to the circumstances: The speaker's husband, who usually assumed part of this responsibility, has left.

Another feature distinguishing *dei* and *yao* tokens in the 'Negative effect on subject' category is word order. In our data, most transitive verbs with *yao* (10/12, or 83%) have preverbal patients (see (44)). This is significant given that none of the four transitive *dei* constructions in this category have preverbal patients, and *yao* constructions with preverbal patients using are rare (less than 10%) in our other functional categories and in the language overall (Myhill and Xing 1992). It is not clear why *yao* utterances which are 'Negative effect on subject' should have this unusual word order pattern, but we did notice that patient-verb order is always used in the 8 instances where the action is not marked as inherently negative. It may be that the patient-verb order is used here to emphasize that the subject is obligated to do the action and to discourage the intentional reading.

21 This is our translation; Wang and Barnes 1958 omit this sentence in their translation.

22 This translation is our own and directly reflects the structure of the Chinese. The translation in Lo 1986 is much looser: 'Shouldn't we listen to our consciences?'

23 See Li and Thompson 1981:307 for a description of the function of this particle.

24 Unfortunately, the translators appear to have had a stylistic bias against *(have) got to*; they used it only once, in contrast with Wilson, who uses it frequently.

25 We have excluded 'Don't have to' clauses from this table, since these are not expressed with any of the Chinese morphemes studied here.

26 Except for the four other tokens translated into English with an obligation morpheme.

27 We have decided to analyze only *nawus* after extensive study of Hopi texts and Albert and Shaul's 1985 Hopi-English lexicon. We investigated several other words as possible obligation markers. Albert and Shaul translate *paapu* as 'admonition (modal), should do it (reminder)', but in the texts we consulted, the English translations of sentences with *paapu* almost never have a word with obligation meaning. Albert and Shaul list 'should do' as one of the functions of *as*, but this is an extremely common discourse particle with a wide variety of functions, and only a fraction of the tokens using it have any obligation meaning. They refer to *naapas* as a 'modal of disapprobation' ('you shouldn't do that'); *naapas* is used with this function in our database, but there are only three tokens of it. *Sonqa* sometimes appears to function as a marker of obligation. However, it really means 'definitely' (it is composed of *son* and *qa*, both negative markers). It translates considerably more often as some non-modal marker of certainty than as an obligation marker. It is of course an interesting question why certain markers which are not basically obligation markers occur consistently (though infrequently) in sentences translating into English with explicit obligation; this is relevant to the present study, but beyond its scope.

28 We include here only the obligation meanings of these English words. This contrasts with the translation data from Biblical Hebrew, where we include the usages of the English words associated with obligation, whether or not the particular token appears to represent obligation. The motivation for this distinction, as discussed in Section 1.2, is that in Hopi we are dealing with a lexical, literal expression of obligation (*nawus*), which we want to compare with literal obligation in English, while in Biblical Hebrew, as we will see, we are dealing with a grammatical expression of obligation (signaled by a word order alternation). We therefore want to include both concrete (literal) expressions of obligation in English and the more abstract (grammatical) meanings related to obligation which words associated with the expression of obligation later develop.

There are two tokens of *nawus* which we have marked as being translated with 'no obligation word'. One is translated as 'It will take you several days to reach your goal' (Malotki and Lomatuway'ma 1987a:116), more literally 'You will have to arrive at your goal in several days'. The other is translated as 'It's Maasaw only who rests during the day and goes around at night' (Malotki and Lomatuway'ma 1987b:89); this is a reprimand to someone who is sleeping too late, and it is more literally translated as 'It should be only Maasaw who...' Both of these clearly convey some type of obligation meaning. However, the fact that they are represented with an obligation form in Hopi but not English shows that it is not totally accurate to say that *nawus* marks a subset of the functions marked by English obligation markers.

29 It is of course the case that mothers are generally in a social position which sanctions giving commands to their children; thus mother-to-child commands are generally relatively unmarked. However, in the Hopi texts even this type of relationship calls for *nawus* when the speaker is trying to orient the listener towards a new goal in order to deal with a crisis which has arisen.

30 The data here also include subjects possessed by humans (e.g. 'His soul shall be cut off from his people'). They exclude sentences with negatives and question words (which are obligatorily clause-initial) and subordinate clauses (which have subordinators in initial position).

31 Implausible imperative contexts are:

(a) The listener can't control the action because the verb doesn't take a volitional subject (e.g. 'You shall be the father of many nations').
(b) The listener can't control the action because it is addressed to him and his descendents (e.g. 'You shall keep my covenant').
(c) The listener can't control the action because it is addressed to other people not present (e.g. 'You shall come into the ark, you and your sons and your wife and your sons' wives with you.').
(d) The listener can control the action, but it is contingent on another action which the listener cannot control (e.g. 'Your wife Sarah shall bear you a son, and you shall call his name Isaac').

32 It appears that a number of the non-imperative constructions with (a) God speaking; (b) a 2nd or 3rd person subject; (c) non-verb-initial order in Hebrew; and (d) *shall* in the English translation are cases in which the Hebrew text portrays God as speaking in a more cooperative, human fashion (which is not uncommon), but the English translation nevertheless represents God in a transcendent manner. Examples are 'you shall be buried at a ripe old age' (Genesis 15:15), where God makes a personal statement about Abraham's future, and 'your descendants shall seize the gates of their foes' (Genesis 22:17), where God is rewarding Abraham for his willingness to sacrifice his son Isaac, and so there is an element of cooperation. This may be compared with the more typical case, where God simply makes a promise independent of any particular human action, and non-verb-initial order is normal (e.g. 'Kings shall come from her' (Genesis 17:16)). Scholars such as Heschel (1975) and Rosenberg and Bloom (1990) have argued, for completely different reasons, that there is no evidence for a purely transcendent conception of God in the Old Testament but that interpreters of the text influenced by Greek thinking have overemphasized the transcendent aspect in their translations and interpretations; this would account for tokens where *shall* is used to translate verb-initial clauses.

33 Another possible explanation is that the verbal form typically used in non-verb-initial constructions with 'obligation' function (the Imperfect) is historically derived from a modal marker of obligation plus a verb which subsequently fuss together. The Imperfect is characterized by personal prefixes agreeing with the subject — possibly derived from fusion of a pronoun + obligation marker which eventually became prefixed to the verb. This account is purelyspeculative, and we do not know of any historical evidence for it. Additionally, any such account would be complicated by the fact that the Imperfect is largely syncretic with two other forms, the Va-consecutive and the Jussive, which are invariably (for the Va-consecutive) or almost invariably (for the Jussive) verb-initial.

34 It is tempting to speculate that, since Hopi has the most restricted overt marking of obligation of the languages investigated, the functions associated with *nawus* are the most lexical, while other functions are more grammatical. This may turn out to be true. However, even if *nawus* does represent a more lexical type of obligation function, it does not necessarily represent the *only* such function; obligation markers are themselves diachronically derived from words with other meanings, and presumably the function of a given obligation marker will depend upon the meaning of its source.

DATA SOURCES

Cao, Yu. 1962 (1934, rev 1961). *Leiyu* ('Thunderstorm'). In: *Caoyu Xuanji* (Selected Plays by Caoyu). Beijing: People's Literary Press.

Cao, Yu. 1962 (1940, rev 1954). *Beijingren* ('Peking Man'). In: *Caoyu Xuanji* (Selected Plays by Caoyu). Beijing: People's Literary Press.

Geertz, Armin W. and Michael Lomatuyway'ma. 1987. *Children of cottonwood: Piety and ceremonialism in Hopi Indian puppetry. American Tribal Religions, vol. 12.* Lincoln: University of Nebraska Press.

Lo, Leslie Nai-Kwai (et al), transl. 1986. *Cao Yu Peking Man.* New York: Columbia University Press.

Malotki, Ekkehart, and Michael Lomatuway'ma. 1987a. *Stories of Maasaw, a Hopi god. American Tribal Religions, vol. 10.* Lincoln: University of Nebraska Press.

Malotki, Ekkehart, and Michael Lomatuway'ma. 1987b. *Maasaw: Profile of a Hopi god. American Tribal Religions, vol. 11.* Lincoln: University of Nebraska Press.

Plaut, W. Gunther. 1981. *The Torah: A modern commentary.* New York: Union of American Hebrew Congregations.

Wang, Tso Liang and A. C. Barnes, transl. 1958. *Thunderstorm* (Translation based on minor 1954 revisions). Beijing: Foreign Language Press.

Wilson, Lanford. 1973. *The Hot L Baltimore.* New York: Hill and Wang.

Wilson, Lanford. 1976. *The Mound Builders.* New York: Hill and Wang.

Wilson, Lanford. 1987. *Burn This.* New York: Hill and Wang.

REFERENTIES

Albert, Roy, and David Leedom Shaul. 1985. *A Concise Hopi and English Lexicon.* Amsterdam: John Benjamins.

Brown, Penelope, and Stephen C. Levinson. 1987. *Politeness: Some Universals in Language Usage.* Cambridge: Cambridge University Press.

Bybee, Joan. 1985. *Morphology: A Study of the Relation between Meaning and Form.* Amsterdam & Philadelphia: John Benjamins.

Bybee, Joan, and William Pagliuca. 1987. "The Evolution of Future Meaning." *Papers from the 7th International Conference on Historical Linguistics,* ed. by A.G. Ramat et al., 109-122. Amsterdam & Philadelphia: John Benjamins.

Chao, Yuen Ren. 1968. *A Grammar of Spoken Chinese*. Berkeley: University of California Press.
Coates, Jennifer. 1983. *The Semantics of the Modal Auxiliaries*. London: Croom Helm.
Cooreman, Ann. 1988. "Ergativity in Dyirbal Discourse." *Linguistics* 26.717-746.
Cooreman, Ann, Barbara Fox, and T. Givón. 1984. "The Discourse Definition of Ergativity." *Studies in Language* 6.343-374.
Fox, Andrew. 1975. "Topic continuity in Biblical Hebrew narrative." Givón 1983. 215-54.
Givón, T. 1975. "Serial Verbs and Syntactic Change: Niger-Congo." *Word Order and Word Order Change* ed. by Charles N. Li, 47-112. Austin: University of Texas Press.
Givón, T. 1977. "The Drift from VSO to SVO in Biblical Hebrew: The Pragmatics of Tense-Aspect." *Mechanisms of Syntactic Change* ed. by C.N. Li, 181-254. Austin: University of Texas Press.
Givón, T. (ed.). 1983. *Topic Continuity in Discourse*. Amsterdam & Philadelphia: John Benjamins.
Heschel, Abraham J. 1975. *The Prophets*, Vol. II. New York: Harper and Row.
Herring, Susan. 1990. "Topic and Focus Positions as a Consequence of Word Order Type: What is Universal?" Paper presented at the International Pragmatics Conference.
Hopper, Paul. 1979. "Aspect and Foregrounding in Discourse." *Discourse and Syntax* (*Syntax and semantics* 12), 213-241. New York: Academic Press.
Lambdin, Thomas O. 1971. *Introduction to Biblical Hebrew*. New York: Charles Scribner.
Li, Charles N. and Sandra A. Thompson. 1981. *Mandarin Chinese: A Functional Reference Grammar*. Berkeley: University of California Press.
Liu, Yuehua. 1983. *Shiyong Xiandai Hanyu Yufa* (Chinese Grammar). Beijing: Foreign Language Teaching and Research Press.
Lyons, John. 1977. *Semantics*. Cambridge: Cambridge University Press.
Myhill, John. 1984. "A Study of Aspect, Word Order, and Voice" University of Pennsylvania Ph.D. disseration.
Myhill, John. 1986. "The Two VS Constructions in Rumanian." *Linguistics* 24.331-350.
Myhill, John. 1992. "Word Order and Temporal Sequencing." *The Pragmatics of Word Order Flexibility* ed. by Doris Payne, 265-278 Amsterdam & Philadelphia: John Benjamins.
Myhill, John. 1993. A Verb Position in Future Clauses in Biblical Hebrew. *Language Variation and Change 4.289-309.*
Myhill, John, and Zhiqun Xing. 1992. "Towards an Objective Definition of Contrast." University of Michigan manuscript.
Palmer, Frank. 1974. *The English Verb*. London: Longman.
Palmer, Frank. 1979. *Modality and the English Modals*. London: Longman.
Palmer, Frank. 1986. *Mood and Modality*. Cambridge: Cambridge University Press.
Payne, Doris. 1987. "Information Structuring in Papago Narrative Discourse." *Language* 63.783-804.
Rand, Christopher C. and Joseph S. M. Lau, transl. 1980. *The Wilderness* (Yuan-Yeh), by Cao Yu. Bloomington: Indiana University Press.
Rosenberg, David, and Harold Bloom. 1990. *The Book of J*. New York: Grove Weidenfeld.

Sun, Chao-Fen, and T. Givón. 1985. "On the So-Called SOV Word Order in Mandarin Chinese." *Language* 61.2.329-51.

Thompson, Chad. 1989. *Voice and Obviation in Athabaskan and other Languages*. University of Oregon Ph.D. dissertation.

Ultan, Russell. 1978. "The Nature of Future Tenses." Universals of Human Language, vol. 3, ed. by J. Greenberg. 83-123, Stanford: Stanford University Press.

Apprehensional Epistemics

Frantisek Lichtenberk
University of Auckland

1. Introduction[1]

Epistemic modality, one type of which is the focus of this study, is characterised by subjectivity, by pragmatic force. It has to do with "belief, knowledge, truth, etc. in relation to proposition" (Palmer 1986:96), and with "the degree of commitment by the speaker to what he says" (Palmer 1986:51).

Many languages exhibit a historical relation between epistemic modality on the one hand and other types of modality on the other. Bybee and Pagliuca (1985:63) refer to the latter group collectively as 'agent oriented modalities', including the notions of ability, obligation, desire, and intention. The results of their extensive study suggest a unidirectional process of development of agent-oriented modalities into epistemic modalities (Bybee and Pagliuca 1985:66). Developments in the opposite direction do not occur. To say that agent-oriented modalities develop into epistemic modalities rather than vice versa is, of course, not to say that epistemic modalities can only develop from agent-oriented modalities. It remains an empirical matter to determine what other sources of epistemic modalities there are; the type of epistemic modality to be discussed here does not (typically) develop from agent-oriented modalities.

This study is concerned with a type of modality that is both epistemic and attitudinal: it has to do with the speaker's degree of certainty about the factual status of a proposition and also with his or her attitude concerning the desirability of the situation encoded in the clause. This is a case not of polysemy but of mixed modality (von Wright 1951): both types of modality are present simultaneously. For reasons that will become apparent later, I will refer to this mixed modality as 'apprehensional-epistemic'.

The development of apprehensional-epistemic modality is of relevance to the study of semantic/functional change, specifically to the issue of the directionality of change in terms of degrees of subjectivity and pragmatic strength. Traugott (1989 and elsewhere (see Section 5 for references)) has suggested that semantic change is characterized by an increase rather than a decrease in subjectivity, by pragmatic strengthening rather than weakening. This is true of semantic change in lexemes and also of the early stages of grammaticalization. Although the data discussed here by and large support Traugott's hypothesis, they at the same time suggest a refinement.

I will start by discussing in some detail data from To'aba'ita, an Austronesian language spoken in the Solomon Islands. Although the information on the present-day uses of the element in question is reasonably detailed, there is no direct historical evidence concerning the development of the modality. To overcome this problem, I will first consider some indirect, structural and historico-comparative evidence, and, following that, data from several other languages where similar independent developments have taken place. In the case of two of those languages, there is some direct historical evidence bearing on the issue. From the various kinds of evidence available, a general pattern in the development of the modality emerges even though there are some differences of detail among the languages.

2. Apprehensional-epistemic modality in To'aba'ita

To'aba'ita has a modality marker of the form *ada*, which is formally a complementizer. As demonstrated in examples (1), (3), (5), and (6), *ada* is used to signal relative uncertainty on the part of the speaker about the factual status of the proposition; in other words, *ada* functions as an epistemic downtoner. For convenience, I will gloss *ada* and similarly functioning forms in other languages as 'LEST'; this does not, however, mean that the uses of these elements are necessarily exactly the same as those of English *lest*.

(1) *Ada* *'oko* *mata'i.*[2]
LEST you(SG):SEQ be sick
'You may be sick.'

Compare:

(2) *'Oe* *'o* *mata'i.*
you(SG) you(SG):FACT be sick
'You are sick.'

(3) *Ada* *dani* *ka* *'aru.*
LEST rain it:SEQ fall
'It may rain.'

Compare:

(4) *Dani* *kai* *'aru.*
rain it:NONFACT fall
'It will rain.'

(5) *Ada* *keka* *fanga* *sui* *na'a.*
LEST they:SEQ eat COMPL PERF
'They may have finished eating.'

(6) *Ada* *bii* *na'i ka* *a'i* *si*
LEST food in stone oven this it:SEQ NEG.VB it:NEG
'ako *ba -na.*
be cooked LIM-its
'The food in the stone oven may not be done yet.'

While *ada* functions as an epistemic downtoner in the examples above, this is not its only function there. Besides signaling less-than-full certainty on the part of the speaker about the factual status of the proposition, *ada* also signifies that the possible situation is in some way undesirable. Following Dixon (1977), I will refer to this function as 'apprehensional': there is apprehension — typically on the part of the speaker — that a potential (undesirable) situation may turn out to be so. The undesirability of the situation encoded in (1) is obvious; (3) could be used to express fear about being caught in the rain; (5) might be used if, for example, the speaker was worried about not getting any food; and (6) could be used as a warning against premature opening of a stone oven (both the closing and the opening of a stone oven are laborious processes).

In the examples above, *ada* is a mixed-modality marker: it has an epistemic function, as a downtoner, and it has, what, following Palmer (1986), one may call a 'volitive-modality' function, more specifically an apprehensional function: there is fear that an undesirable state of affairs may obtain.[3] As will be seen later, *ada* has some other uses besides apprehensional-epistemic. Apprehensional-epistemic modality is highly 'subjective' in the sense of Traugott 1989: it reflects the speaker's uncertainty about whether a state of affairs does, did, or will obtain, together with his/her own evaluation of that state of affairs as undesirable (for example, rain is not necessarily undesirable, as after a period of drought).

The examples above demonstrate that *ada* can be used with propositions of any temporal status: present (1), future (3), or past (5). Nevertheless, the subject/tense marker is always the same: Sequential. The Sequential subject/tense markers are used elsewhere to indicate temporal sequence: the situation encoded by a verb with a Sequential subject/tense marker follows the situation encoded in the preceding clause:

(7) *Buriana kera oli Siriaoa ka lae mai*
after they:FACT return S. it:SEQ go hither
ka dau i maa-na 'aba tha Bari'i.
it:SEQ alight on eye-its arm ART B.
'After they [people] had gone back, Siriaoa [a bird] alighted on Bari'i's wrist.'

Since *ada* sentences require Sequential, rather than other (Factative or Nonfactative), subject/tense markers, the temporal status of the proposition being expressed is not overtly signaled; thus (1) could be used to express not only 'You may be sick' but also 'You may have been sick' and 'You may get sick'.[4]

Ada is used not only with an apprehensional-epistemic function, as in the examples above. It is also used as a complementizer with clauses embedded under a verb of fearing; there the apprehension about an undesirable situation is expressed by the higher verb:

(8) *Nau ku ma'u 'asia na'a ada laalae to'a baa*
I I:FACT be.afraid very LEST later people that
ki keka lae mai keka thaungi kulu.
PL they:SEQ go hither they:SEQ kill us(INCL)
'I am scared the people might come and kill us.'/'I am scared lest the people should come and kill us.'

I will refer to the use of *ada* (and the LEST elements in other languages) with clauses embedded under predicates of fearing as the 'fear' function. In the fear function also, the embedded clause introduced by *ada* must have a Sequential subject/tense marker, regardless of the temporal status of its proposition vis-à-vis the temporal status of the proposition of the higher clause. In (9) the situation encoded in the *ada* clause necessarily precedes the time of fearing:

(9) *Nau ku ma'u 'asia na'a ada to'a na'i ki*
I I:FACT be.afraid very LEST people this PL
keka lae mai keka thaungi kulu.
they:SEQ go hither they:SEQ kill us(INCL)
'I am scared the people may have come to kill us.'

Compare the parallel example (8) above, where the situation encoded in the *ada* clause is subsequent to the time of fearing; in both cases the subject/tense marker in the *ada* clause is sequential.

Even though *ada* clauses require the Sequential/subject tense markers, regardless of the temporal status of the situation encoded in the clause, there is an important distinction between present-time and past-time situations on the one hand and future-time situations on the other (including future in the past). The distinction has to do with the possibility of precautions against a possible undesirable state of affairs, whether in the sense of averting it altogether, or in the sense of somehow alleviating its (anticipated) effects. One cannot take precautions against past and present situations, but one can take at least some precautions against possible future situations. In some cases, one may be able to avert a potential future situation; one may, for example, hide in order not to be seen:

(10) *Ada wane 'eri ka riki nau.*
LEST man that he:SEQ see me
'[I fear] the man might see me.'

Even if a future situation cannot be averted, one may be able to take measures to alleviate its effects, for example, by taking an umbrella when it looks like rain:

(11) *Ada dani ka 'arungi kulu.*
LEST rain it:SEQ fall on us(INCL)
'We might get caught in the rain.'/'We might get rained on.'

A distinction can then be made between a 'precautionary situation' and an 'apprehension-causing situation': a precautionary situation is (to be) brought about because of the possibility of an apprehension-causing situation.

This brings us to the third and last use of *ada*, which is to connect a clause encoding an apprehension-causing situation to a preceding clause encoding a precautionary situation. Sentences (10) and (11) above express only apprehension-causing situations. In the corresponding sentences (12) and (13) respectively, both the apprehension-causing and the precautionary situations are expressed:

(12)

Nau	*ku*	*agwa*	*'i*	*buira*	*fau*	*ada*	*wane*	*'eri*
I	I:FACT	hide	at	behind	rock	LEST	man	that
ka	*riki*	*nau.*						
he:SEQ	see	me						

'I hid behind a rock so that the man might not see me.'/'I hid behind a rock lest the man see me.'

(13)

Kulu	*ngali-a*	*kaufa*	*ada*	*dani*	*ka*
we(INCL)	take -them	umbrella	LEST	rain	it:SEQ
'arungi	*kulu.*				
fall on	us(INCL)				

'Let's take umbrellas in case we get caught in the rain.'/'Let's take umbrellas lest we should get caught in the rain.'

There are two basic kinds of relation between an apprehension-causing situation and a precautionary situation. In one, there is a direct causal link between the two: if no precaution is taken, the apprehension-causing situation will take place: if not X, then Y. In other words, the precautionary situation serves to avert the apprehension-causing situation: X in order that not Y. I will refer to the use of a LEST element under these circumstances as 'avertive'. In the other type, there is no causal link; whether an apprehension-causing situation takes place or not is independent of the precautions being taken.[5] The precautions are taken *in case* the apprehension-causing situation should occur: X in case Y. I will refer to the use of a LEST element under these circumstances as 'in-case'.

The question to be considered is whether or not the avertive (negative-purpose) and the in-case uses of *ada* (and of the LEST elements in other languages) represent two distinct functions. In other words, is this a case of polysemy or (perhaps fuzzy) monosemy?

There is something to be said for the monosemy thesis. It could be argued that although two uses — avertive and in-case — are distinguishable, they nonetheless do not represent distinct functional categories. Rather, *ada* could be said to have a fairly general function, something like signaling that there is a possibility, likelihood of an undesirable situation coming about, on account of which a precautionary situation is brought about. Whether the interpretation is avertive or in-case depends on extralinguistic, pragmatic factors, specifically on the presence or absence of a causal link between the two situations. If the apprehension-causing situation cannot be averted by the precautionary situation, only the in-case meaning is possible. If the apprehension-causing situation can be averted, both meanings may be possible (see note 5). The following sentence may be given both an avertive (a) and an in-case (b) interpretation:

(14)

... *wane*	*kai*	*too*	*i*	*laala*	*kai*	*lio*
man	he:NONFACT	stay	at	inside	he:NONFACT	look

ma'asi	*-a*	*maelimae*	*ada*	*ka*	*lae*	*mai*
wait.for	-him	enemy	LEST	he:SEQ	go	hither

ma	*ka*	*ili -a*	*ta -si*	*doo.*
and	he:SEQ	do -it	some-CLASS	thing

a. '... the man would stay inside and look out for the enemy so that he [the enemy] might not come and do something.'

b. '... the man would stay inside and look out for the enemy in case he came and did something.'

A proponent of the monosemy approach would have to argue that (14) exhibits pragmatic rather semantic ambiguity, depending on whether the man's looking out was supposed to *prevent* the enemy (coming and) doing something. (For the concept of 'pragmatic ambiguity' see Horn 1989 and references therein.) On the other hand, a proponent of the polysemy thesis can argue that since in many sentences only one interpretation (either avertive or in-case) is possible, this suggests that two distinct — though obviously related — semantic categories are involved.

There are other, stronger arguments in favor of the polysemy approach. *Ada* is not the only means of signaling negative purpose in To'aba'ita. Besides *ada*, To'aba'ita also has a Purpose marker *fasi*, which, however, is used to encode not only negative but also, predominantly, positive purpose. When *fasi* encodes positive purpose, the purpose clause is grammatically positive;

when it encodes negative purpose, the purpose clause is negative. See examples (15) and (16), respectively:

(15) *Fale-a ta -si fanga 'ana wela na'i*
give-it some-CLASS food to child this
fasi(-a) ka bona.
PURP(-it) he:SEQ be quiet
'Give some food to the child so that he is quiet.'

(*Fasi*, which ultimately derives from a transitive verb 'leave, forsake' (see further below), optionally indexes the purpose clause by the object marker *-a*.)

(16) *Nau ku agwa 'i buira fau fasi-a wane 'eri*
I I:FACT hide at behind rock PURP-it man that
'e a'i si riki nau.
it:FACT NEG.VB he:NEG see me
'I hid behind a rock so that the man might not see me.'

Although both *fasi* and *ada* can mark negative purpose (compare 16 and 12), *ada* is preferred in this function. However, unlike *ada*, *fasi* does not have the in-case function. The following examples demonstrate the similarities as well as the differences between *ada* and *fasi*. Examples (17) and (18) demonstrate the avertive, negative-purpose uses:

(17) *Ngali -a kaleko 'aa'ako fasi 'osi*
take -them clothes warm PURP you(SG):NEG
gwagwari 'a-fa rodo.
be cold at-CLASS night
'Take warm clothes so that you are not cold at night.'

(18) *Ngali -a kaleko 'aa'ako ada 'oko gwagwari*
take -them clothes warm LEST you(SG):SEQ be cold
'a-fa rodo.
at-CLASS night
'Take warm clothes so that you are not cold at night.'

It is even possible for *fasi* and *ada* to be used jointly to mark negative purpose (although this is not common), in which case it is *ada*, not *fasi*, that determines the structure of the clause encoding the situation to be averted (the clause is grammatically positive). Compare in this regard (19) below with

(17) and (18) above:

(19)

Ngali -a		*kaleko*	*'aa'ako*	*fasi(-a)*	*ada*
take	-them	clothes	warm	PURP(-it)	LEST
'oko		*gwagwari*	*'a-fa*	*rodo.*	
you(SG):SEQ		be cold	at-CLASS	night	

'Take warm clothes so that you are not cold at night.'

Since *fasi*, unlike *ada*, has only an avertive function, a sentence like (20) is incongruous (indicated by '#'), while (21) with *ada* is fine:

(20)

#Ngali	*-a*	*kaleko*	*'aa'ako*	*fasi-a*	*fanu*	*'eri*	
take	-them	clothes	warm	PURP-it	place	that	
'e	*a'i*	*si*	*gwagwarila*	*ba -na*	*'a-fa*	*rodo.*	
it:FACT	NEG.VB	it:NEG	be cold	LIM-its	at-CLASS	night	

#'Take warm clothes so that it may not be cold at night.'

(21)

Ngali -a		*kaleko*	*'aa'ako*	*ada*	*fanu*	*'eri*	*ka*
take	-them	clothes	warm	LEST	place	that	it:SEQ
gwagwarila	*ba*	*-na*	*'a-fa*	*rodo.*			
be cold	LIM	-its	at-CLASS	night			

'Take warm clothes in case it's cold at night.'

Taking warm clothes may avert the person's feeling cold, but it cannot prevent the weather being cold. (When presented with (20), my consultant said the sentence was nonsensical.)

Ada appears to be the only element with a simultaneously apprehensional and epistemic-downtoning function. To'aba'ita has a variety of other means of epistemic downtoning, but they do not *necessarily* have an apprehensional connotation. Compare the following two examples, the first with *ada* and a necessarily apprehensional force, the second with another epistemic downtoner which has no evaluative force:

(22) = (5)

Ada	*keka*	*fanga*	*sui*	*na'a.*
LEST	they:SEQ	eat	COMPL	PERF

'[I fear] they may have finished eating.'

(23)

Mad-e		*a'i*	*kera*	*fanga*	*sui*	*na'a.*
or	-it:FACT	NEG.VB	they:FACT	eat	COMPL	PERF

'They may have finished eating.'

In (23) epistemic downtoning is signaled by *mad-e a'i*, literally 'or it is not'. Whether the situation encoded in (23) is undesirable depends on the context.

What was said above about the replaceability of the To'aba'ita LEST element by the purpose marker is true also of English *lest*, which likewise has an avertive and an in-case function. As consideration of the glosses of (17) and (20) above will show, *so that ... not* is semantically equivalent to *lest* when the latter has a negative-purpose function but not when it has an in-case function. Czech has a LEST element used with an apprehensional-epistemic function and a fear function. The same etymon also functions as a purpose marker regardless of positive/negative polarity, but it is not used with an in-case function. And in Martuthunira (Australia), there is an overt formal difference between LEST clauses of purpose and in-case LEST clauses. (English, Czech, and Martuthunira will be discussed in Section 3.)

The various states of affairs mentioned above — (a) that an element used to encode negative purpose need not have an in-case function; (b) that there is a formal difference between negative-purpose and in-case clauses in at least one language; and (c) that there are differences in paraphrase possibilities between negative-purpose and in-case clauses — serve as evidence that the avertive and the in-case functions are conceptually distinct from each other. Consequently, the use of one element in both functions is a case of polysemy, not monosemy. (This means that sentence (14) above is semantically rather than pragmatically ambiguous.) However, even though the avertive and the in-case functions are distinct, they are nonetheless related. I will use the cover term 'precautioning function(s)' for both when there is no need to distinguish between them.[6]

To'aba'ita *ada*, then, has three basic functions: precautioning (avertive and in-case), fear, and apprehensional-epistemic. As will be seen in Section 3, this kind of polysemy is not at all unusual cross-linguistically, and at this stage it is useful to compare and contrast the three functions. When a LEST element is used with a precautioning function, there are two clauses in a complex sentence, a LEST clause encoding an apprehension-causing situation and a clause encoding a precautionary situation (as in examples 12 and 13 above). Both situations are prominent; both are encoded. When a LEST element is used with a fear function, the LEST clause, encoding an undesirable situation, is embedded under a predicate of fearing (as in 8). Apprehension is signaled explicitly by the higher predicate. When a LEST element is used with an apprehensional-epistemic function, it itself expresses the meanings of possibility as well as apprehension, and the clause can function as an independent sentence (as in 1). However, even though the semantic/pragmatic distinctions among the three functions are reasonably clear in principle, the task of determining which function a given LEST element fulfills in a particular sentence is not always clearcut, depending as it does on certain other considerations; see the discussion of the Martuthunira data in Section 3.

The question to be addressed next is the development of the polysemy of To'aba'ita *ada*. In order to find an answer, we have to move outside of To'aba'ita and look at some closely related languages. In To'aba'ita, *ada* functions only as a grammatical element, but in at least some of its close relatives the etymon is found functioning lexically, as a verb: Kwaio *aga* 'look (at)', *agasi* 'see' (Keesing 1975), Kwai *ada* 'see' (Tryon & Hackman 1983), and Lau *ada* 'open the eyes, use the eyes, see, look, wake (intr.)', *adasi* 'look at, watch, expect, wait to see' (Fox 1974). In Kwaio, the etymon appears to be used only in the verbal function. The information on the Kwai form comes from a word list, and it is unclear whether the form has any other functions. Of the three languages with cognates of *ada*, Lau is genetically closest to To'aba'ita (Tryon & Hackman 1983:27, note 1). And in Lau, *ada* is used not only as a verb, but also grammatically. Although the relevant information on Lau is rather limited, it is evident that Lau *ada* can be used grammatically (at least) with the avertive function. The following examples from South Lau illustrate the lexical as well as the grammatical uses of *ada*:

(24) *Alifii -laa ada wela ka ada.*
be noisy -NOMI LEST child SEQ wake up
'Quiet, (or) the child will wake up.'
(Lit.: 'being noisy, the child will wake up')

(25) *Ada suli 'oe ada 'oe ka 'asia.*
Look after you(SG) LEST you(SG) SEQ fall
'Look out, or you'll fall down!.'

In what follows, I will sketch out the likely development of the apprehensional-epistemic function of To'aba'ita *ada*. Because of the lack of historical records, there is no direct evidence of the steps to be postulated, but there are several kinds of indirect evidence all pointing in the same direction. There is structural evidence permitting some internal reconstruction, comparative evidence from closely related languages, and the existence of similar semantic shifts in other, unrelated languages.

At an early stage, the etymon functioned as a verb meaning 'see, look at, watch'. Later the verb acquired a 'warning' meaning, 'look out, watch out'; see the South Lau example (25) above. The use of verbs meaning 'see, look at, watch' with a warning meaning is not unusual crosslinguistically. It is found in, for example, English (*look out, watch out*), Basque (*begira* 'look at', *begira gero!* 'be careful!' (*gero* 'later')), Zulu (*beka* 'look, look at, watch, take precautions against, be careful'), and also in present-day To'aba'ita (compare the uses of *riki* in (27) and (28) below). Sweetser (1990) points out a common type of polysemy in Indo-European languages that unites meanings having to do with vision and meanings having to do with guarding, keeping control, and monitoring (although this kind of polysemy can apparently arise in either direction).

Ada was used as a verb of warning against possible future undesirable situations: **ada* + clause 'look out, Y might/will happen', 'look out so that Y may not happen'. The use, in present-day To'aba'ita, of the sequential subject/tense markers in *ada* clauses embedded under verbs of fearing and in independent *ada* sentences regardless of the temporal status of the proposition encoded in the *ada* clause is evidence that when *ada* was used as a verb of warning it was so used with reference to situations subsequent to the act of warning. Most likely, *ada* was used in this function in exhortations and commands ('Look out, ...!'), which in To'aba'ita are normally expressed by a simple verb, without a subject/tense marker, as in (26) (and in 28 below):

(26) *'Ono 'i ninima-ku!*
sit at beside-my
'Sit (down) beside me!'

At this stage, negative purpose was most likely marked by the element **fa'asi*, of which To'aba'ita *fasi* is a descendant. Positive purpose was marked by a different element, **uri*. It was only later that **fa'asi/fasi* acquired a positive-purpose marking function. (For more detailed discussion see Lichtenberk 1991.)

At some stage in the history of To'aba'ita, *ada* ceased to be a verb; today *ada* cannot form a predicate and cannot occur with a subject/tense marker. To express the concepts of 'seeing' and 'looking at', the verb *riki* is used:

(27) ... *ma keka riki-a ba'u 'eri...*
and they:SEQ see-it banana that
'... and they saw the banana tree ...'

And just as once was the case with *ada*, *riki* also has the meaning 'look out, watch out'. It can thus cooccur with *ada*:

(28) *Riki -a ada 'oko dekwe -a kwade'e kuki 'ena.*
see -it LEST you(SG):SEQ break -it empty pot that
'Look out; you might break the empty pot.'/'Mind you don't break the empty pot.'

When *ada* still functioned as a verb, it was used to encode a general precautionary event: 'look out, watch out'; the specific nature of the precautionary event depended on the situation. After ceasing to function as a verb, *ada* continued as a grammatical element with a warning function signaling that a precaution was to be taken in view of a possible adverse future situation. In this function, *ada* began to encroach on the territory previously occupied by the negative-purpose marker, present-day *fasi*. As a result, *fasi* has to a large degree ceded negative-purpose marking to *ada*; today it is used primarily to signal positive purpose. The details of the historical process whereby *ada* has nearly displaced *fasi* in marking negative purpose may be unrecoverable, but the fact that *fasi* and *ada* may cooccur in present-day To'aba'ita (see 19 above) can be taken as evidence of the process.

The apprehensional-epistemic function of *ada* is a later development from the precautioning function, most likely through an intermediate stage of the fear function. An undesirable future situation is likely to be feared. Through this metonymy, *ada* clauses began to be embedded under predicates of fearing. When one fears a situation, one fears a *potential* situation: 'I am afraid that Y might happen/have happened/be happening'. In a discussion of LEST clauses subordinated to predicates of fearing in Ngiyambaa (Australian), Donaldson (1980:286) says that such sentences express "'fear of the *possibility* of [e.g.] falling', not 'fear of [e.g.] falling' as such" (original emphasis).

That the fear function is a later development, postdating the warning and precautioning functions is suggested by the use of the sequential subject/tense markers in *ada* clauses embedded under verbs of fearing even if the situation encoded in the *ada* clause is not posterior to the time of fearing, as in (9) above. It is conceivable that at an earlier stage *ada* was used to express warning only about potential situations against which precautions could be taken, i.e. situations subsequent to the act of warning, and that by the time *ada* developed the fear function, the subject markers had become devoid of the sequentiality-marking function there.

The final step (thus far at least) in the history of *ada* is the development of the apprehensional-epistemic function. At the 'fear' stage, apprehension was signaled by the predicate dominating the *ada* clause; the *ada* clause encoded a possible situation. Later, through metonymy the notion of apprehension came to be associated with *ada*. That is, since *ada* was used to introduce clauses that encoded apprehension-causing situations (as signaled by the higher verb), it acquired the connotation of apprehension. After this had happened, a predicate of fearing was no longer necessary. The notions of possibility and apprehension were both signaled by *ada*; as an apprehensional-epistemic complementizer, *ada* could now introduce independent sentences.

3. Apprehensional epistemics in other languages

Polysemy uniting an apprehensional-epistemic function with fear and precautioning functions is not unique to To'aba'ita; and in at least one language a further development has taken place beyond the apprehensional-epistemic stage.

LEST forms appear to be common in Australian languages, Diyari being one of them. Austin (1981:225) says this about LEST clauses in Diyari:

> 'Lest' clauses basically serve to indicate some situation which the speaker considers to be unpleasant and which should be avoided. They are most commonly used as admonitions or threats but they are also used in giving warnings ...

The LEST element is a verbal suffix *-yaṯi*. *-yaṯi* has a precautioning function, both avertive (29) and in-case (30):

(29) *ŋapu -ri -ya -mayi ŋaṯu yiṉa ṉanda-yaṯi*
quiet -INCH -IMP-EMPH I:SUBJ you(SG):DO hit -LEST
'Be quiet or I'll hit you.' (Austin 1981:225)

(30) *makita paḍaka -Ø -mayi wanku yundu*
gun:ABS take -IMP-EMPH snake:ABS you(SG):SUBJ
waḻa ṉayi -yaṯi
soon see -LEST
'Carry a gun in case you see a snake.' (Austin 1981:225)

LEST clauses can also be embedded under a predicate of fearing:

(31) *ŋaṉi* *yapa-li* *ŋana -yi* *ŋaṉa* *ṯuṯu -yali*
I:SUBJ fear -ERG be -PRES I:DO reptile-ERG
maṯamaṯa-ṯadi-yaṯi
bite:RED -DUR -LEST
'I'm afraid that some reptile might bite me.'(Austin 1981:227)

And the LEST suffix can also be used in independent sentences with an apprehensional-epistemic function:

(32) *ṉulu* *-ka* *kiṉṯala-li* *yinaṉa* *maṯa-yaṯi*
it(NONFEM):SUBJ-TOKEN dog -ERG you(SG):DO bite-LEST
'This dog might bite you.' (Austin 1981:229)

According to Austin, "in all the examples of this type of construction it is clear from the context that an 'understood' imperative, warning or suggestion is implicit", and such sentences "may be regarded as structurally subordinate because it is always *possible* to add a main clause before them, although context may make it unnecessary" (Austin 1981:229, original emphasis). In the situation encoded in (32), "the context would be clear and make it unnecessary to say 'Look out!' or 'Be careful!' and so on" (ibid.). But there is no reason to appeal to an 'understood' main clause; this is precisely what the apprehensional-epistemic function of LEST elements is all about: there is a possibility of a situation coming about, and there is apprehension about that possibility.

Another Australian language, Martuthunira, has a LEST form, which is used with precautioning — avertive and in-case — functions and possibly also with an apprehensional-epistemic function (Dench 1988). (Dench gives no examples of the LEST element with a fear function.) What is interesting about Martuthunira is that it makes an overt distinction between those cases where an apprehension-causing situation directly results from lack of precaution and those cases where there is no such causal link. In other words, there is a formal distinction between the avertive and the in-case functions. The LEST element is a suffix on the verb; in addition, the verb may carry a nominal inflectional suffix, either accusative or locative. If the apprehension-causing situation results from the absence of a precautionary situation, the verb carries accusative marking:

(33) *Mir.ta wantha-rninyji murla-a yakarrangu-la*
NEG leave -FUT meat -ACC sun -LOC
puwa -npa -wirri -i.
rotten-INCH -LEST -ACC
'Don't leave the meat in the sun or it'll go rotten.'
(Dench 1988:109)

When there is no implication of a causal link between the absence of a precautionary situation and an apprehension-causing situation, the verb in the LEST clause carries either locative marking, as in (34), or no nominal marking, as in (35).

(34) *Kartu wankuma-lalha paju, walyi -lalha ngurnu*
you(SG):NOM check -PAST very uncover -PAST that:ACC
punkurrimarnu-u purntura-a wanti -lha -a wayil
blanket -ACC rolled -ACC lie -PAST-ACC maybe
wii nhartu -ngara, parralhara-ngara wii, wayil wii
if what -PL centipede -PL if maybe if
wanti -wirri-la mirtungkura -la punkurrimarnu -la?
lie -LEST -LOC underneath -LOC blanket -LOC
'Did you check carefully and undo that rolled up blanket in case there was anything, perhaps a centipede, lying underneath it?'
(Dench 1988:109-10)

Dench says that in Martuthunira a LEST clause may function as a main clause. This would suggest an apprehensional-epistemic function of the LEST element; however, in both examples of LEST sentences that Dench gives, the LEST sentence is preceded by another sentence that encodes a precautionary situation, as in (35):

(35) *Mir.ta thaawu -rninyji. Pawulu puni -wirri kayulu-la -rru*
NEG let go -FUT child go -LEST water -LOC-NOW
nyuni -lu -rru.
drown -PURP:SS -NOW
'Don't let (him) go. The child might go in the water and drown.'
(Dench 1988:110)

Taking the LEST sentence in isolation, the LEST element may be said to have an apprehensional-epistemic function: '[I fear] the child might go in the water and drown'. However, if one takes the preceding sentence into consideration as well, the LEST element can be said to have a precautioning function. Similarly, in the following (made-up) example the LEST element could be seen as having not just a fear function but also an avertive function: 'Don't let him go. I fear lest he should go in the water and drown.' Although the distinctions among the precautioning, fear, and apprehension-epistemic functions are clear in principle, in some cases the identification of the function of a LEST element depends on whether or not one takes wider, extrasentential context into consideration.

Note the absence of nominal (accusative or locative) marking on the verb 'go' in (35). According to Dench (1988:110-111),

> the speaker apparently chooses not to imply that the unpleasant situation will come about as a consequence of the addressee's actions or inaction. The marking options — accusative, locative, or unmarked — allow a range of interpretations about the responsibility on the part of the participants for the situation described by the lest clause.

An apprehensional-epistemic construction is also found in Hua (Papuan); the same construction is also used with precautioning — avertive and in-case — functions (Haiman 1980). From the examples given, it is not clear whether or not the construction is also used with a fear function.

Apprehensional epistemics are not restricted to languages where the marker in question can only signal negative, not positive, purpose. Czech has a Purpose marker *aby*, used to express both positive and negative purpose. The following examples are from colloquial Czech, but the same is true, *mutatis mutandis*, of standard Czech. *Aby* carries a suffix indexing the subject of its own clause. When the purpose is positive, the purpose clause is grammatically positive:

(36) *Spěchal sem domů aby -ch zastih televizní noviny.*
I.hurried AUX home PURP-1SG I.caught T.V. news:ACC
'I hurried home to catch the T.V. news.'

When the purpose is negative, the purpose clause is grammatically negative:

(37) *Spěchal sem domů aby -ch ne -propás televizní*
I.hurried AUX home PURP-1SG NEG-I.missed T.V.
noviny.
news:ACC
'I hurried home so I wouldn't miss the T.V. news.'

Aby can be used to express negative purpose, but it cannot be used with an in-case function. For that reason, (38) is incongruous:

(38)

#Vem	*si*	*deštník*	*aby*
you(SG).take:IMP	MID:DAT	umbrella:ACC	PURP:3SG

ti	*ne -pršelo*	*na*	*cestu.*
you(SG):DAT	NEG -it.rained	on	road:ACC

#'Take an umbrella so that it does not rain while you're on the road.'

(38) cannot be used to mean 'Take an umbrella in case it rains while you're on the road.'[7]

While *aby* is decidedly anomalous in (38), it can be used to introduce parallel clauses that are embedded under a predicate of fearing or that are independent; see (39) and (41) below.

Negative clauses introduced by *aby* may be embedded under predicates of fearing:

(39)

Bojím	*se*	*aby*	*nám*	*ne -pršelo*	*na*
I.am.afraid	MID:ACC	LEST:3SG	US:DAT	NEG -it.rained	on

cestu.
road:ACC
'I'm afraid it might rain while we're on the road.'

The feared situation need not be subsequent to the time of fearing:

(40)

Bojím	*se*	*aby*	*ne -byl*	*nemocnej.*
I.am.afraid	MID:ACC	LEST:3SG	NEG-he.was	sick

'I'm afraid he might be sick.'

Finally, *aby*, introducing a negative clause, may also be used with an apprehensional-epistemic function to encode a possible undesirable situation, future or not:

(41)

Aby	*nám*	*ne -pršelo*	*na*	*cestu.*
LEST:3SG	US:DAT	NEG-it.rained	on	road:ACC

'[I fear] it might rain while we're on the road.'

(42)

Aby	*ne -byl*	*nemocnej.*
LEST:3SG	NEG-he.was	sick

'[I fear] he might be sick.'

Aby has an avertive, negative-purpose use, but not an in-case use. Nevertheless, in the fear and the apprehension-epistemic functions *aby* can be used in encoding situations that cannot be averted, either because they are of the non-avertible type (39, 41) or because they may exist already (40, 42). This suggests that the apprehensional-epistemic function developed from the fear function rather than directly from the avertive, negative-purpose use.

Another example of the development of the apprehensional-epistemic function comes from Classical Greek. The LEST element had the form *mé:*. An early function of *mé:* was that of a negator used in certain contexts. (There was another negator *ou*, used elsewhere.) *Mé:* was used in prohibitions, which can be thought of as a kind of avertive function: a prohibition is issued in order to avert an undesirable situation. Unlike the cases considered thus far, in Greek prohibitions the precautioning situation is not encoded in a clause of its own; instead, it consists of the speech act of issuing a prohibition:

(43) *mé: poié:se:is* *toûto*
NEG you(SG).do:IMP this:ACC
'do not do this' (Goodwin 1929:89)

Another use of *mé:* in independent clauses was to express "apprehension, coupled with a desire to avert the object of fear, both ideas being inherent in the construction" (Goodwin 1929:90):

(44) Homer, Iliad XVI. 128:
mè: dè: nê:as hélo:si ...
LEST indeed ships:ACC they.seize:SUBJUNCT
'may they not (as I fear they may) seize the ships ...'
(Goodwin 1929:90)

This apprehensional-avertive use of *mé:* is characteristic of Homeric Greek (Goodwin 1929).

At a later stage, apprehensional-avertive clauses introduced by *mé:* came to be used under predicates of fearing:

(45) Xenophon, Anabasis III. 2, 25:
dédoika mè: epilathó:metha tê:s oíkade hodoû
I.fear LEST we.forget:SUBJUNCT ART:GEN homeward road:GEN
'I fear lest we may forget the road home'(Goodwin 1929:24)

The feared situation is typically, though not necessarily, posterior to the time of fearing.

Mé: also acquired the function of marking negative purpose, another type of avertive use. At an earlier stage, to express negative purpose one of several purpose markers had been used, with *mé:* as a negator in the purpose clause:

(46) *apérchetai, hína mè: toûto íde:i*
he.departs PURP NEG this:ACC he.see:SUBJUNCT
'he is departing that he may not see this' (Goodwin 1929:106)

Later, the original purpose markers may be dropped, and *mé:* becomes a "connective" expressing negative purpose (Goodwin 1929:108, 109):

(47) *machoúmetha mè: nê:as hélo:si*
we.will.fight LEST ships:ACC they.seize:SUBJUNCT
'we will fight that they may not seize the ships'
(Goodwin 1929:90-91)

Mé: had other uses that are not of direct concern to this study. However, there is one function of *mé:* that is relevant. At a later stage still, *mé:* came to be used to express "cautious assertions", expressing "a suspicion that something *may be* (or *may prove to be*) true" (Goodwin 1929:92, original emphasis):

(48) Plato, Gorgias 462 E:
mè: agroikóteron ê:i tò ale:thès eipeîn
LEST rude thing it.is:SUBJUNCT ART:ACC truth:ACC say
'I am afraid the truth may be too rude a thing to tell'
(Goodwin 1929:92)

As Goodwin (1929:92) puts it:

> In these cautious assertions and negations, although no desire of the speaker to avert an object of fear is implied, there is always a tacit allusion to such a desire on the part of some person who is addressed or referred to, or else an ironical pretence of such a desire of the speaker himself.

What Goodwin says about "ironical pretence" of a desire of the speaker to avert the undesirable situation suggests that this construction was used even when the undesirable situation was not under anybody's control, when there was no question of it being averted. In other words, this use of *mé:* is apprehensional-epistemic, not precautioning. That this was indeed the case is shown by the fact that the cautious-assertion use of *mé:* is not restricted to future situations. *Mé:* may be used with possible present or past situations (in which case the verb is in the appropriate indicative rather than the subjunctive):

(49) Aristotle, Ethics X. 1, 3:

mé:	*pote*	*dè*	*ou kalô:s*	*légetai*
LEST	at some time	but	NEG well	it.is.said:IND

'but it may be that this is not well said' (Goodwin 1929:93)

The next set of examples comes from English. English has thc form *lest*, which is usually said to have two functions, which the OED identifies as follows: First, it is used "as a negative particle of intention or purpose, introducing a clause expressive of something to be prevented or guarded against". This is a precautioning function, avertive, as in (50), and in-case, as in (51):

(50) *He was put in a cell with no clothes and shoes lest he injure himself.* (Collins COBUILD English Grammar, p.355)

(51) *He remained inside the fortress lest the enemy should arrive in great numbers.*

The following sentence is ambiguous between an avertive and an in-case interpretation of the LEST clause, depending on whether the medicine is to prevent the illness or cure it:

(52) *When you go to Africa, take this medicine with you lest you (should) get ill.*

The following sentence also is open to both an avertive and an 'in-case' interpretation; in fact, the two interpretations are not mutually exclusive — an instance of what Coates (1983) calls 'merger':

(53) Hole, C., English Shrines and Sanctuaries:
And lest future generations should wonder why St. Withburga herself is not enshrined here, a tablet informs the visitors that the monks stole the relics. (Scheurweghs 1959:381)

The tablet is there *in case* the visitors should wonder why St. Withburga is not enshrined there (absence of the tablet would not necessarily bring about the visitors' wondering), and its presence does remove the visitors' (further) wondering.

Second, *lest* is used "after verbs of fearing, or phrases indicating apprehension or danger, to introduce a clause expressing the event that is feared" (OED):

(54) *I trembled lest they should see us.* (Jespersen 1933:349)

The feared situation need not be subsequent to the time of fearing:

(55) *I fear lest he may have deceived me.*

Historically, *lest* derives from an Old English comparative construction *þȳ lǣs þe*, earlier *þȳ lǣs*, 'by that/which (i.e. whereby) less' (*þȳ*, also spelled *þi*, *þe*, 'by which', *lǣs* 'less', *þe* Relative particle). Later, *þȳ* dropped out, and *læs þe* became *les te* and then *lest* (OED).

Both of the main functions of *lest*, precautioning (56) and fear (57), are found in Old English:

(56) Beowulf, XXVII.1917-19:
sǣlde tō sande sīdfæþme scip oncerbendum fæst, þȳ læs hym ȳþa ðrym wudu wynsuman forwrecan meahte
'He tethered to the beach the roomy ship, held fast with anchor-ropes, lest the waves' force should drive the joyous craft away from them.'(Klaeber 1950; translation from Hall 1950)

(57) King Alfred, Pastoral Care 461.30:
Ac him is ðonne micel ðearf ðæt he hine hrædlice selfne gewundige mid ðy ege ðæt he him ondræde ðylæs he weorðe upahæfen for his wordum.
'But there is then to him a great need to feel the pangs of terror, fearing lest he should become arrogant on account of his own words.' (Mitchell 1985:16)

Although both functions are attested in Old English, it appears that the precautioning function historically preceded the fear function. According to Mitchell (1985:16), although *þy læs* could be used to introduce clauses embedded under verbs of fearing, such clauses were usually introduced by *þæt*. Secondly, Mitchell (1985:495), following Shearin (1909), speaks of the development of *þy læs (þe)* "final" clauses, i.e. LEST clauses with a precautioning function, into "object" or "noun" clauses, i.e. clauses that functioned as complements of verbs of fearing. In both main functions that have been identified, *lest* introduces dependent clauses. However, *lest* may also be used to introduce an independent sentence:

(58) *Sir, — To those of Yugoslav origin who keep urging New Zealand involvement in the affairs of their homeland, I would like to remind them of the terrible cost to the world, and New Zealand, the last time someone acted violently in Sarajevo. Lest we forget.*(A letter to the editor, New Zealand Herald, 11/20/1991.)

In (58) *lest* has an apprehensional-epistemic function: '[I fear] we might forget'. It is *lest* itself that expresses the apprehension about a potential undesirable event.

Lest is not common in modern English; a recent grammar characterises it as formal, old-fashioned (Collins COBUILD English Grammar). Given the relative obsolescence of *lest*, it is unlikely that its apprehensional-epistemic use will ever become well established. (The few examples that I have come across of *lest* introducing an independent sentence all contain the verb *forget*. This usage is most likely ultimately modeled on Rudyard Kipling's use of *lest* in his poem Recessional: *Lord God of Hosts, be with us yet, Lest we forget — lest we forget ... Judge of the Nations, spare us yet, Lest we forget — lest we forget.*)

The last set of examples comes from Fijian, an Austronesian language, but only relatively distantly related to To'aba'ita; there is no reason to assume that the developments in the two languages are related to each other.[8] What is interesting about Fijian is that a further development of the LEST element has taken place there, beyond the apprehensional-epistemic stage. The examples below come from Standard Fijian (essentially the Bauan dialect) and from the Boumaa dialect; the LEST element appears in several different forms, depending on the dialect, on its linguistic environment, and on the source of the data: *dē* or *de* in Standard Fijian and *dee* in Boumaa.

The LEST element is used with a precautioning function:

(59) Standard Fijian

kua	*ni*	*driva*	*vakatotolo*	*de -o*	*na*	*qāī*
PROH	COMP	drive	fast	LEST-you(SG)	FUT	SEQ

coqa
run into s.t.
'don't drive fast lest you run into something' (Schütz 1985:442)

A LEST clause can be embedded under a predicate of fearing:

(60) Standard Fijian

sā rere ko koya de kasa na waqa
PERF be afraid ART he LEST:it run aground ART canoe
'he is afraid lest the canoe should run aground'
(Churchward 1941:24)

The LEST element may also be used with an apprehensional-epistemic downtoning force:

(61) Standard Fijian

de sega beka ni dina
LEST NEG perhaps COMP be true
'it may not perhaps be true' (Churchward 1941:24)

(62) Standard Fijian

āū nanu -m -a sara gā dē ko na sega
I think -TRANS -it INT LIM LEST you(SG) FUT NEG
ni māi wā -raki āū
COMP hither wait for -TRANS me
'I thought that you might not wait for me'(Schütz 1985:443)

Even though as an epistemic downtoner *dē* is typically used with an apprehensional force, it may in fact be used as a neutral downtoner, without any connotation of apprehension. In (63) below, *dē* introduces a clause embedded under the verb 'think', and according to Schütz (1985:443), "there seems to be no afflictive meaning to the situation represented by the *dē* phrase". (Compare (62) above, where also the LEST clause is embedded under 'think'.) In private communication (November, 1991) Schütz has confirmed that, given the broader context, the interpretation of the LEST clause in (63) is indeed non-afflictive:

(63) Standard Fijian

erāū nanu -m -a gā na vēitinani,
they(DU) think -TRANS -it LIM ART mother.and.child
dē sā vodo tiko māi ko Rejieli,
maybe:he PERF ride CONT hither ART R.
e na dua vēi ira
it ART one ABL them
'the two of them, mother and son, thought that Rejieli might be riding in one of them' (Schütz 1985:443)

According to Paul Geraghty (personal communication, December, 1991), the non-apprehensional epistemic-downtoning use of *dē* in Standard Fijian is "not at all rare". (64) is another example:

(64) *dē sā noqu na kalougata*
maybe:it PERF my ART luck
'maybe I'm the lucky one!' (Geraghty, p.c., Dec., 1991)

Similarly in the Boumaa dialect, where, according to Dixon, the *dee* clause [typically] refers to some unpleasant possibility, and the other clause to something that can be done either to avoid that possibility or to compensate for it, ... However, a *dee* clause *need* not refer to anything unpleasant. The other clause may describe something which, if accomplished, *might* yield a welcome result (referred [to] by the *dee* clause) (Dixon 1988:260, 261, original emphasis)

(65) Boumaa Fijian
au vaa'aasama -ta'ina ti'o dee o -na la'o
I think -TRANS CONT maybe you(SG) -FUT go
mai (se sega)
hither or NEG
'I've been thinking that you might come here (or you might not)' (Dixon 1988:269)

However, the Fijian element has a further function: in Boumaa, according to Dixon (1988:269, 270), *dee* is also used in "the most polite speech-style" to express requests, or "to make a strong point in a polite way" (Dixon 1988:269, 270). In saying (66), the speaker "adopted an extremely reverential tone" (Dixon 1988:269):

(66) Boumaa Fijian
au 'ere -a ti'o dee rawa ni o
I ask -TRANS CONT POLITE can COMP you(SG)
va'amacala -ta'ina a -ituvatuva ni veiqaravi
make clear -TRANS ART -order of presentation
va'avanua va'atuuraga
traditional chiefly
'I ask that it might be possible for you to explain the order of traditional, chiefly presentations' (Dixon 1988:269-270)

With (67), according to Dixon (1988:270), "what the speaker means (and is understood to mean) is 'I feel that the motion should be changed'":

(67) Boumaa Fijian
au *aa* *rai -ca* *dee* *rawa* *ni* *veisau -ta'i*
I PAST see-TRANS POLITE can COMP change-TRANS
a *moosoni* *yai*
ART motionthis
'I felt that the motion might possibly be changed'
(Dixon 1988:270)

The politeness function of the etymon is also found in Standard Fijian:

(68) Standard Fijian
dē *rawa* *ni* *tou* *cakacaka* *vata*
POLITE can COMP we(PAUC,INCL) work together
'perhaps we could work together' (Geraghty. p.c., July, 1993)

According to Geraghty (personal communication), (68) expresses a polite suggestion: the speaker desires to work together with the others.

What has happened in Standard and Boumaa Fijian is that the LEST element is losing the necessarily apprehensional connotation and is developing into a neutral epistemic downtoner; furthermore, on its way to becoming a neutral epistemic downtoner, the element has come to be used as a politeness marker.[9] Crosslinguistically, epistemic downtoning is a common feature of polite speech, a marker of deference (see Givón 1990:822 for some references).[10]

Since epistemic downtoning is one of the features of politeness, how can we be certain that the Fijian LEST element has acquired a *new* pragmatic function, that of a politeness marker? There are two pieces of evidence that this is the case. First, in polite speech, the element is (normally) followed by *rawa* 'can' (Dixon 1988:269, Geraghty, personal communication, July, 1993); this does not appear to be the case with the other uses. Second, and more importantly, in the polite-speech use there need not be any epistemic uncertainty: "*dee rawa* can be used to make *a strong point* in a polite way" (Dixon 1988:270; emphasis added): in (67) the speaker is expressing his belief (and is understood as such) that "the motion should be changed" (ibid). Similarly, in (68), according to Geraghty, the speaker makes a suggestion in a polite way. In one function, the element signals epistemic uncertainty without necessary politeness; in the other, in conjunction with *rawa*, it expresses politeness rather than uncertainty.

4. The development of apprehensional epistemics

A number of languages contain an element that has an apprehensional-epistemic downtoning function. (In some languages, e.g. Czech, the clause encoding the potential undesirable situation must be grammatically negative.) The same element may also be used with other functions: precautioning (in-case, avertive (negative-purpose)) and fear. Consideration of the data presented above suggests the following general historical development:

(69) precautioning > fear > apprehensional-epistemic

Of the three functions, the precautioning one is historically primary; it may (but, of course, need not) give rise to the fear function. In the precautioning function, LEST elements signal that there is a potential undesirable situation against which a precaution is to be taken. The implication of a situation being undesirable, or indeed feared, becomes explicit by virtue of clauses encoding such situations as subordinate to predicates of fearing. What one fears is a potential situation. This might suggest that it is the in-case variety of the precautioning function that motivates the development of the fear function. However, recall that in Czech the element that has a fear function (as well as an apprehensional-epistemic function) is used only with an avertive (negative-purpose) function, not with an in-case function. This can be taken as evidence that the rise of the fear function is motivated — metonymically — by the undesirability component of apprehension-causing situations. (This does not preclude the possibility of the in-case function acting as a contributory motivating factor.) Over time, through metonymy based on cooccurrence of linguistic forms, the notion of apprehension comes to be associated with the LEST element, and the predicates of fearing become expendable. When LEST clauses come to be used without being embedded under predicates of fearing, the LEST element becomes an apprehensional epistemic. It signals both the possibility of an undesirable situation and apprehension.

For two languages in the sample (Martuthunira and Hua), the sources of the data give examples of the precautionary and the apprehensional-epistemic functions, but no examples of the fear function. At this stage it is not clear whether these are merely lacunae in the data or whether the apprehensional-epistemic function may indeed develop directly from the precautioning function.

Crosslinguistically, apprehensional epistemics are used typically with respect to future situations, but non-future uses are possible as well, at least in some languages. (This is also true of the fear uses of the LEST elements.) The typically future use of apprehensional epistemics is to be ascribed to 'persistence' (Hopper 1991) from the avertive, negative-purpose use (purpose being necessarily future-oriented).[11]

An apprehensional epistemic may lose the connotation of apprehension and thus become a neutral epistemic downtoner, even though the apprehensional connotation may still be the typical case. This kind of development has taken place in Standard and Boumaa Fijian.

The category of the precautioning function subsumes the avertive and the in-case functions. At this stage, because of lack of relevant data, it is impossible to tell whether there is a general unidirectional historical process whereby one of the two functions develops from the other, avertive from in-case, or in-case from avertive. Example (53) above suggests that the development of one function from the other proceeds through a state where both meanings may be present or available simultaneously in a sentence (see also 52).

As far as the sources of the precautioning function, as a category, are concerned, little can be said at present. In To'aba'ita, the precautioning function derives from a verbal warning meaning, 'look out, watch out', itself from 'see, look at, watch'. English *lest* derives from a comparative construction, 'by which less', while the Classical Greek apprehensional epistemic can be traced back to a negator. I do not have relevant information on any of the other LEST elements discussed above. Wayan Fijian has a LEST element with avertive, in-case, and fear functions, but apparently not an apprehensional-epistemic function (Pawley and Sayaba, forthcoming; Pawley, personal communication, October, 1992). The Wayan LEST element (unrelated to the Standard and Boumaa Fijian and the To'aba'ita LEST elements) derives from a verb meaning 'survey, watch, see s.t., take a close look at s.t., examine or look carefully at s.t.'; this is reminiscent of the development of the To'aba'ita LEST element. Central Siberian Eskimo has a Volitive-of-Fear mood, which expresses the notions of 'for fear that Y', 'lest Y'. According to de Reuse (1991), the mood marker (a suffix on verbs) derives from the verb 'think'; there is no mention of an apprehensional-epistemic function.

At present there is no evidence that apprehensional epistemics (typically) derive from agent-oriented modalities (cf. Bybee and Pagliuca 1985, referred to in Section 1). In fact — judging from the small amount of historical evidence available — it is the notions of apprehension and precaution that are the main motivating factors in the development of LEST elements, with the epistemic-downtoning function arising as a by-product.

5. Directionality in semantic/functional change

In a number of studies of semantic/functional change, Traugott has argued that there is a general unidirectional process whereby meanings become more, rather than less, subjective, and that semantic, relatively objective meanings develop into pragmatic, relatively subjective meanings/functions rather than vice versa (see, for example, Traugott 1982, 1989, 1990, and also Traugott & König 1991). Traugott (1989:34, 35) identifies three unidirectional tendencies (T) in semantic/pragmatic change:

(70) T1: Meanings based in the external described situation > meanings based in the internal (evaluative/perceptual/cognitive) described situation.
T2: Meanings based in the external or internal described situation > meanings based in the textual and metalinguistic situation.
T3: Meanings tend to become increasingly based in the speaker's subjective belief state/attitude toward the proposition.

T1 can feed T2 and either one can feed T3.

T1 and T3 have to do with the subjectification of meaning; T2 is concerned with the development of textual cohesive functions and functions having to do with performing speech acts. Semantic/pragmatic change in grammaticalization, at least in the early stages, is characterized not by semantic weakening, bleaching, but by a change in the nature of the meaning: from relatively more objective meanings to relatively more subjective meanings/functions, and from (relatively) objective meanings to textual and speech-act functions.

As for the factors motivating the kinds of semantic/pragmatic change characterized by the three tendencies, Traugott (1989) suggests that a distinction needs to be made between the development of epistemic meanings, which are subject to T3, on the one hand, and the development of other, non-epistemic meanings, which are subject to T1 and T2, on the other. The development of non-epistemic meanings is typically metaphor-based, while the development of epistemic meanings is based on metonymy, in particular on the conventionalization of conversational implicatures/invited inferences.

Now, assuming that the scenario concerning the development of apprehensional epistemics presented above is essentially correct, it is evident that — where relevant — the developments in question do in many respects follow the three tendencies identified by Traugott. The change in the meaning of To'aba'ita *ada* from 'see, look at, watch' to 'look out, watch out' exemplifies both T1 and T2. The change is from a relatively objective meaning to a relatively subjective meaning, and the lexeme comes to be used to perform a speech act: a situation is interpreted by the speaker as undesirable, and the lexeme is used to issue a warning. It is the speaker's own interpretation of a situation as one calling for a warning (others need not interpret the same situation in this way).

In the absence of historical evidence, the details of the development cannot be determined, but it is not implausible to assume that after *ada* acquired the warning function, *ada* clauses began to be preceded by clauses encoding precautionary situations, and *ada* eventually became a conjunction with new, precautioning — avertive and in-case — functions. What we get is development of a textual element from a speech-act element.[12] When *ada* clauses began to appear embedded under predicates of fearing, *ada* acquired a new textual function, that of a complementizer. Finally, the development of the apprehensional-epistemic function from the fear function is an instance of T3: *ada* comes to signal both apprehension and less-than-full certainty.[13]

Traugott (1989:35) says that "meanings tend to become more subjective". While it is true that changes from less to more subjective meanings can be observed in the developments of the apprehensional epistemics, there are also developments that do not fit this pattern. First, although it is true that the development of apprehensional epistemics involves pragmatic strengthening (the LEST element coming to signal uncertainty and apprehension), this is not necessarily the end of the process of semantic/pragmatic change. As we have seen in the case of Fijian, a LEST element may lose its necessarily apprehensional force and come to be used as a neutral epistemic downtoner. When an erstwhile apprehensional epistemic comes to be used without the apprehensional force, the result is pragmatic weakening.

Second, in Standard and Boumaa Fijian the (neutral) epistemic element has acquired a new function, that of a politeness marker. What we get is a shift from one pragmatic function — epistemic — to another pragmatic function — politeness marking. One would be hard put to argue whether this involves pragmatic strengthening or weakening

Clearly, not every instance of semantic/functional change in grammaticalization results in greater subjectivity, in pragmatic strengthening; grammatical functions do not keep on becoming more and more subjective, bearing more and more pragmatic significance. One finds both pragmatic strengthening and weakening, and also shifts from one type of pragmatic function to another. Traugott and König (1991:212) say that it is the early stages of grammaticalization processes that are characterized by pragmatic strengthening, by a change from less to more informativeness (see also Traugott 1982). But this raises the problem of defining the *early* stages of a grammaticalization process: when does 'early' stop and 'late' begin?.

On the basis of studies of pragmatic shifts in grammaticalization, including the present one, the following principle of directionality of semantic/pragmatic change in grammaticalization can be formulated:

(71) In a grammaticalization chain, pragmatic strengthening standardly precedes pragmatic weakening, not vice versa.

The principle does not claim that in every single chain of grammaticalization processes both pragmatic strengthening and weakening are manifested (they are not likely to be both manifested if the chain is relatively young), but it does claim that if both are manifested the changes that involve weakening are more likely to follow rather than precede the changes that involve strengthening. The principle also subsumes shifts from one type of pragmatic function to another.

Although the evidence concerning the empirical status of the principle of directionality of semantic/pragmatic change in grammaticalization is encouraging, there is clearly need for many more case studies of semantic/functional change to test the validity of the principle.

ABBREVIATIONS

ABL	- ablative	MID	- middle
ABS	- absolutive	NEG	- negative, negator
ACC	- accusative	NOM	- nominative
ART	- article	NOMI	- nominalizer
AUX	- auxiliary	NONFACT	- nonfactative
CLASS	- classifier	NONFEM	- non -feminine
COMP	- complementizer	NOW	- now
COMPL	- completive	PAST	- past
CONT	- continuative	PAUC	- paucal
DAT	- dative	PERF	- perfect
DO	- direct object	PL	- plural
DU	- dual	POLITE	- politeness
DUR	- durative	PRES	- present
EMPH	- emphatic	PROH	- prohibitive
ERG	- ergative	PURP	- purpose
FACT	- factative	RED	- reduplication
FUT	- future	SEQ	- sequencer, sequential
GEN	- genitive	SG	- singular
IMP	- imperative	SS	- same subject
INCH	- inchoative	SUBJ	- subject
INCL	- inclusive	SUBJUNCT	- subjunctive
IND	- indicative	TOKEN	- token
INT	- intensifier	TRANS	- transitive
LIM	- limiter	VB	- verb
LOC	- locative	s.t.	- something.

NOTES

1. I am grateful to Reuel Riianoa and Lawrence Foanaota for the To'aba'ita data, to Athanasius Faifu for the South Lau data, to Paul Geraghty and Albert Schütz for data and information on Standard Fijian, to Andrew Pawley for information on Wayan Fijian, and to Frantiska Lichtenbergová for her help with the Czech data. In revising this paper, I have greatly profited from discussions at the Mood and Modality Symposium and from detailed comments by Suzanne Fleischman.

2. The other conventions and abbreviations used in glossing the examples are given above.

3. Besides fear, Palmer includes hopes and wishes under volitive modality, "fear [being] essentially the counterpart of hope (not of wish)" (Palmer 1986:119).

4. Besides Sequential subject/tense markers, To'aba'ita has 'Factative' subject/tense markers, used to encode past and certain non-past situations (see *kera* in 7), and 'Non-factative' subject/tense markers, used to encode future and certain non-future situations (see *kai* in 14).

5. It is, of course, possible for an apprehension-causing situation not to be connected by a causal link to certain precautions but to be so connected to certain other precautions.

6. Note that the term 'precautioning' identifies types of function of LEST elements (avertive and in-case), while the term 'precautionary' has to do with situations (the precautions (to be) taken in view of an apprehension-causing situation).

7. The notion of 'in case' can be expressed by, for example, *v případě že/kdyby* 'in case that/if' and *kdyby náhodou* 'if by chance', in which case the clause encoding the potential situation is grammatically positive. The potential situation is not necessarily undesirable.

8. LEST elements are common in the Oceanic subgroup of Austronesian, of which To'aba'ita and Fijian are members. A LEST element is also found in Melanesian Pidgin, where its presence is most likely due to Oceanic-substrate influence. The Pidgin LEST element has the form *nogut*, from English *no good*.

9. In another Fijian dialect, Nabukelevu, the cognate of the Standard and Boumaa Fijian LEST elements has (at least) an avertive and an in-case function; there is no mention of a fear, an apprehensional-epistemic, or a politeness-marking function in Pawley's (1982) brief sketch of Nabukelevu grammar.

10. Givón speaks of 'epistemic deference'.

11. Although Hopper uses the term 'persistence' specifically with reference to changes from lexical meanings to grammatical functions, basically the same phenomenon is found in changes from one grammatical function to another. Of course, a component of the source grammatical function may itself be due to persistence of a component of the still earlier lexical meaning.

12. It remains to be seen whether this development in To'aba'ita is accidental or whether there is a general tendency for speech-act functions to give rise to textual functions rather than the other way around.

13. Sweetser (1990) gives a number of examples of polysemy uniting content-expressing, epistemic, and speech-act meanings/functions in English. The development of To'aba'ita *ada* from the content-expressing meaning 'see, look at, watch' to the speech-act, warning function 'look out, watch out' and ultimately to the apprehension-epistemic function is a diachronic counterpart of this kind of synchronic polysemy.

REFERENCES

Adamson, Sylvia, Vivien Law, Nigel Vincent & Susan Wright, eds. 1990. *Papers from the 5th International Conference on English Historical Linguistics, Cambridge, 6-9 April 1987*. Amsterdam/Philadelphia: John Benjamins.

Aronoff, Mark, ed. 1991. *Proceedings of the LSA Arizona Institute Workshop on Morphology*. SUNY Press.

Austin, Peter. 1981. *A Grammar of Diyari, South Australia. Cambridge Studies in Linguistics* 32. Cambridge: Cambridge University Press.
Austin, Peter, ed. 1988. *Complex Sentence Constructions in Australian Languages.* Amsterdam/Philadelphia: John Benjamins.
Bybee, Joan L. & William Pagliuca. 1985. "Cross-Linguistic Comparison and the Development of Grammatical Meaning." Fisiak 1985. 59-83.
Capell, A. 1973. *A New Fijian Dictionary* (4th ed.). Suva, Fiji: Government Press.
Churchward, C. Maxwell. 1941. *A New Fijian Grammar.* Suva, Fiji: Government Press.
Coates, Jennifer. 1983. *The Semantics of the Modal Auxiliaries.* London and Canberra: Croom Helm.
Collins COBUILD English Grammar. 1990. London and Glasgow: Collins.
Dench, Alan. 1988. "Complex Sentences in Martuthunira." Austin 1988. 97-139.
Dixon, R. M. W. 1977. *A Grammar of Yidiɲ.* (Cambridge Studies in Linguistics, 19.) Cambridge: Cambridge University Press.
Dixon, R. M. W. 1988. *A Grammar of Boumaa Fijian.* Chicago and London: University of Chicago Press.
Donaldson, Tamsin. 1980. *Ngiyambaa: The Language of the Wangaaybuwan.* (*Cambridge Studies in Linguistics,* 29.) Cambridge: Cambridge University Press.
Fisiak, Jacek, ed. 1985. *Historical Semantics: Historical Word-Formation.* Berlin: Mouton.
Fox, Charles E. 1974. *Lau Dictionary. Pacific Linguistics* C-25. Canberra: Australian National University.
Givón, T. 1990. *Syntax: A Functional-Typological Introduction,* Vol. II. Amsterdam/Philadelphia: John Benjamins.
Goodwin, William W. 1929. *Syntax of the Moods and Tenses of the Greek Verb.* London: Macmillan and Co.
Haiman, John. 1980. *Hua: A Papuan Language of the Eastern Highlands of New Guinea.* (*Studies in Language Companion Series* 5.) Amsterdam: John Benjamins.
Hall, John R. C. 1950. *Beowulf and the Finnesburg Fragment* (new ed.). London: George Allen & Unwin.
Hopper, Paul J. 1991. "On Some Principles of Grammaticization." Traugott & Heine 1991. 17-35.
Horn, Laurence R. 1989. *A Natural History of Negation.* Chicago and London: University of Chicago Press.
Jespersen, Otto. 1933. *Essentials of English Grammar.* London: George Allen & Unwin.
Keesing, R. M. 1975. *Kwaio Dictionary. Pacific Linguistics* C-35. Canberra: Australian National University.
Klaeber, Fr. 1950. *Beowulf and the Fight at Finnsburg* (3rd ed.). Boston: D. C. Heath.
Lehmann Winfred P. and Yakov Malkiel, eds. 1982. *Perspectives on Historical Linguistics.* Amsterdam: John Benjamins.
Lichtenberk, Frantisek. 1991. "On the Gradualness of Grammaticalization." Traugott & Heine 1991. 37-80.
Mitchell, Bruce. 1985. *Old English Syntax* (Vol. II). Oxford: Clarendon Press.
Oxford English Dictionary (2nd ed.). 1989. Oxford: Clarendon Press.
Palmer, F. R. 1986. *Mood and Modality.* Cambridge: Cambridge University Press.

Pawley, Andrew. 1982. "A Sketch Grammar of the Nabukelevu Language of Kadavu." *Te Reo* 25.35-93.
Pawley, Andrew and Timoci Sayaba. Forthcoming. *Wayan Dictionary: Describing the Wayan Dialect of the Western Fijian Language.* (Pacific Linguistics.) Canberra: Australian National University.
de Reuse, Willem J. 1991. "The Role of Internal Syntax in the Historical Morphology of Eskimo". Aronoff 1991.
Scheurweghs, G. 1959. *Present-Day English Syntax: A Survey of Sentence Patterns.* London: Longmans.
Schütz, Albert J. 1985. *The Fijian Language.* Honolulu: University of Hawaii Press.
Shearin, Hubert G. 1909. "The Expression of Purpose in Old English Poetry." *Anglia* 32:235-252.
Sweetser, Eve. 1990. *From Etymology to Pragmatics: Metaphorical and Cultural Aspects of Semantic Structure. (Cambridge Studies in Linguistics* 54.) Cambridge: Cambridge University Press.
Traugott, Elizabeth Closs. 1982. "From Propositional to Textual and Expressive Meanings; Some Semantic-Pragmatic Aspects of Grammaticalization." Lehmann & Malkiel 1982. 245-271.
Traugott, Elizabeth Closs. 1989. "On the Rise of Epistemic Meanings in English: An Example of Subjectification in Semantic Change." *Language* 65.31-55.
Traugott, Elizabeth Closs. 1990. "From Less to More Situated in Language: The Unidirectionality of Semantic Change." Adamson et al. 1990. 497-517.
Traugott, Elizabeth Closs & Bernd Heine, eds. 1991. *Approaches to Grammaticalization,* Vol. I: *Theoretical and Methodological Issues.* Amsterdam/Philadelphia: John Benjamins.
Traugott, Elizabeth Closs & Ekkehard König. 1991b. "The Semantics and Pragmatics of Grammaticalization Revisited." Traugott & Heine 1991. 189-218.
Tryon, D. T. & B. D. Hackman. 1983. *Solomon Islands Languages: An Internal Classification. Pacific Linguistics* C-72. Canberra: Australian National University.
von Wright, Georg H. 1951. *An Essay in Modal Logic.* Amsterdam: North-Holland.

Moods and MetaMessages. Alienation as a Mood

John Haiman
Macalester College

0. Introduction

Many discussions of mood as a motivated general category describe it as "the grammaticalization of the speaker's attitude to the propositional content of his message" (cf. Palmer 1986: 16, 51, 96). Belief in its truth is indicative; suspended judgment as to its validity, subjunctive; the wish for its realization, imperative or optative; ignorance as to its truth, coupled with curiosity, is interrogative; fear of its realization, avolitional or apprehensive. But there are many other propositional attitudes which are not so universally codified even as words, to say nothing of grammatical mood markers.

In this paper, I want to describe some of these sub-canonical moods: the quasi-modal marker I will deal with is that of negation or rejection, which, like the modalities of ability and obligation, has deontic, epistemic, and *de dicto* meanings. I will focus neither on the deontic (= "I don't want this"), nor the epistemic (= "This is not the case"), but on the *de dicto* or metalinguistic meaning of negation (= "I reject these words"). At the end of an unsystematic survey of some markers of metalinguistic negation, primarily in English, I want to offer a guess as to why — with one significant exception — they have never achieved ritual grammatical canonization as grammaticalized mood markers in any language I have ever heard or read about.

1. The sarcastive

One might (for example) call the *sarcastive* that modality (or, more plausibly, that collection of related modalities) which expresses the speaker's belief that the content of the ostensible message is not only false, but ridiculous. Like many other propositional attitudes, sarcasm is easily recognized, and we have a folklore about sarcasm and an extensive vocabulary for talking about it. But there is no spoken language familiar to me in which the sarcastive modality is marked with a clearly recognized and stable separate morpheme of the sort that gets written up in sober grammatical descriptions.

There are a small number of very widespread and iconically motivated suprasegmental markers of disgust (e.g. nasalization), non-commitment (e.g. monotone), contemptuous mimicry (e.g. falsetto) and alienation (e.g. sing-song) which signal lack of belief, identification, or enthusiasm in one's message. I have described some of these in greater detail elsewhere (Haiman 1989, 1990, 1991).

But there are segmental (and, in the written language, orthographical) realizations of these attitudes as well. Here are a couple of segmentally realized sarcastive modality markers which are current in colloquial American English (current, at least, as I write these words):

1.1 *Like*

In the examples of (1), the whole utterance following *like* (or its predictable synonym *as if*) is in the scope of this marker. The hearer is warned that what follows *like* is what the speaker may be expected to believe, but does not.

(1) a. *Like I care.* (= I don't care.)
b. *Like there's any difference.* (=There's no difference.)
c. *Like I haven't heard that one before.* (=I've heard that one before.)
d. *As if TV advertising weren't intrusive enough already.* (= TV advertising is too intrusive already.)

Possible equivalents with invariably sarcastic meaning in French and Russian are *si tu crois que* "if you think that" and *mozhno podumat'* "(it is) possible to think":

(2) a. *Si tu crois que je l'ai regardé!*
'Like I was looking at him.'
b. *Mozhno podumat' ja bespokojus'.*
'Like I care'

1.2 *....not*

This utterance deflater signals that the preceding utterance (often a compliment) was meant facetiously. Until it is uttered, the hearer may believe that the prior utterance was sincere.

(3) a. *He's a snappy dresser.....not!*
b. *Guess I'll hit the books in time for that quiz.....not!*
c. *Real Life with Jane Pauley... not.*
d. *Bush will kill that program. Not.*
e. *That's a fabulous science fair project. Not!*

According to Larry Horn (e-mail circular of December 21, 1991), this prototypically generation X (Wayne's World) locution surfaced not on the TV show *Saturday Night Live* about three years ago (as is commonly supposed), nor even (pace William Safire) ten years before that, in 1978, when Steve Martin, on the same show, uttered (3e), but at least a couple of generations before then. Horn credits his correspondent Richard Piepenbrock with unearthing a Little Nemo cartoon of 1910 in which this locution appears (McCay 1990), and notes, I think quite correctly, that it is highly unlikely to have been an innovation there. Clearly, this totally motivated construction has come around often in American speech — without ever becoming firmly established. A British English equivalent with a longer history is — *I don't think*, now almost entirely obsolete (Suzanne Kemmer, pc.).

Sarcastive retroactive *..not* is clearly an example of what Horn (1985) has called metalinguistic negation, and it differs from garden-variety epistemic or deontic negation only in position. It is interesting that the formal relationship between *de dicto* negation and the ordinary *de re* negation is parallel to the difference that Horn extensively discusses in cases like

(4) a. *I'm not happy: in fact, I'm downright miserable.*
b. *I'm not "happy" : I'm ecstatic.*

The latter is metalinguistic. And it is the metalinguistic *not* which cannot appear as a derivational prefix:

(5) a. I'm unhappy: in fact, I'm downright miserable.
b. *I'm unhappy: I'm ecstatic.

In each case, the "metalinguistic" negator contrasts with its garden variety *de re* opposite number in that it is *further separated* from the constituent or the utterance which it negates. I've argued that separation from its embedding context is one of the ways in which a speaker marks the peculiar other-worldly status of quoted or mentioned material (Haiman 1989): perhaps the external position of the negator in iself serves as a kind of iconically framing quotation mark.

1.3 ..... *or anything*

The clause introducer *not that* is generally used to signal that the speaker's interest in what follows is minimal:

(6) a. *Not that I value my sanity so highly.*
b. *Not that I care about the money.*

The motivation is clear. A reconstituted "full" paraphrase would be something like:

(7) a. *It's not that I value my sanity so highly.* (What terrifies me are screams of my fellow lunatics, the curses of my keepers, and the clanging of the chains.) (with apologies to Pushkin)
b. *It's not that I care about the money.* (What I *do* care about is the principle of the thing.)

Like many other things, however, a meaning can be mocked through ostensible exaggeration or emphasis. (It seems to me that this is the essence of all caricature.) When strengthened by the tag *or anything*, the belittling constituent *not that* is apparently strengthened: but in practice, the speaker's ostensible act of trivialization is *mocked.*

(8) a. *Not that I care about the money or anything.* (=I care passionately about the money.)
b. *Not that it's cold out or anything.* (= It's real cold out.)
c. *Not that you annoyed me or anything.* (=You annoyed the hell out of me.)

But for the fact I have a teenager in the family, I wouldn't have heard this marker.

1.4 *Quote*

This is of course a spoken rendition of the orthographic quote sign. Although in dictation *quote...unquote* is a discontinuous constituent with arbitrarily long strings within its scope, as a sarcastive *quote (unquote)* is continuous and only the following word (or, at most, short phrase) is within its scope.

(9) *Your quote (unquote) principles are nothing but snobbism.*

Quote is the only sarcastive morpheme which has lasted for any continuous length of time in English. It is also the only one which has grammaticalized congeners that I have been able to find in other languages.

The *quotative* is an evidential category in a large number of the world's languages (cf. Chafe & Nichols, 1986). In at least two of these, its meaning has been extended to convey irony as it does in English. Thus, Turkish:

(10)	*Her*	*gün*	*koş-*	*uyor-*	*muş*
	every	day	run	PROG	evid 3SG

'He reportedly runs every say'

"can convey not only hearsay, but doubting scorn when predicated of a well-known exercise hater" (Aksu-Koç & Slobin 1986:162; the authors also cite Kononov (1956:232) who notes that the evidential in Turkish conveys "an ironical attitude toward the carrying out of an action").
Similarly, the Albanian admirative, which is 'traditionally
defined as the mood expressing surprise' is 'also used to express irony, doubt, and reportedness' (Friedman 1986:180):

(11)	*E*	*na*	*i*	*dashka*	*bullgaret..*	*ai e ..*
	and	to-us	them	loves(adm.)	Bulgarians	he ha!
	e	*pse*	*keshtu*	*u pritka*	*nje*	*Bullgar?*
	and	why	thus	is-met	a	Bulgarian

'And he 'likes' Bulgarians. Him? Hah! After all, is that how you treat a Bulgarian?'

Friedman (ibid. 183) notes that in this sentence, the speech event "I like Bulgarians" is *mocked* (rather than simply reported). In the written translation, the quotation marks seem to capture the admirative perfectly.

In Rumanian, lexical equivalents of the quotative morpheme are the sentential adverbs *parca* 'seemingly' and *adica* 'that is to say, in other words', as in (Mallinson 1986:6).

(12) a. *parca noi am furat maşina?*
seemingly we have stolen car
'I suppose that you're now going to say *we* stole the car?'
b. *adica, sa fiu eu cel care a murit?*
i.e. SUBJ am I DEM=MS who HAS=3SG died
'I suppose you're going to say I'm the one that died?'

Note that Mallinson's felicitous English translation of the sarcastive as 'I suppose you're going to say' is also a periphrastic quotative.

Another possible congener is Japanese post-utterance *datte* 'said', but only if it is separated from the preceding quotation by a slight — framing — pause (Adachi, ms.):

(13) a. *"Watashi wa ii mono shika kawanai kara" datte.* (sincere)
b. *"Watashi wa ii mono shika kawanai kara" ...datte.* (sarcastic)
I (TOP) good things only not buy because says
'"I only buy good quality things" (...) she says.'

Natural as the extension from quoting to mocking mimicry may seem to us, it is by no means universal. Robert Oswalt, for example (p.c.), emphasizes that in Kashaya neither the quotative evidential, nor the actual direct quote followed by /nihcedu/ 'say' can ever be used to signal irony, sarcasm, or doubt of the veracity of the source; nor does this seem to be possible in Pomo generally. I would speculate that those languages in which the quotative cannot be sarcastic may be among those fabled languages and cultures immortalized by Douglas Q. Adams in *The Hitchhikers' Guide to the Galaxy* where, as in Betelgeuse, "they don't have sarcasm" at all.

2. The guiltive

In the following pages, I will discuss a more elusive (though instantly recognizable) related propositional attitude which I'll call the *guiltive*, for which not even an adequate pretheoretical folk vocabulary exists. Consider the following three examples from Philip Roth's *Portnoy's Complaint*:

(14) *"Don't ask what kind of day I had with him yesterday." So I don't. "Alex",* sotto voce *still, "when he has a day like that you don't know what a difference a call from you would make." I nod. "And, Alex" — and I'm nodding away, you know — it doesn't cost anything, and it may even get me through— "Next week is his birthday.*
That Mother's Day came and went without a card, plus my birthday, those things don't bother me." (39)

(15) *...my father carries himself to the kitchen table, his head sunk low, as though he has just taken a hand grenade in his stomach. Which he has. Which I know.*
"You can wear rags for all I care, you can dress like a peddler, you can shame and embarrass me all you want, curse me, Alexander, defy me, hit me, hate me —" (70)

(16) *Yes, she* will *give me the food out of her mouth, that's a proven fact! And still I will not stay five full minutes by her bedside. "Run", says my mother, while Mrs. Re-ver-ed, who in no time at all has managed to make herself my enemy, and for the rest of my life, Mrs. Re-ver-ed says, "Soon Mother will be home, soon everything will be just like ordinary...*
"Sure, run, run, th ey all run these days," says the kind and understanding lady — oh, they are all so kind and understanding, I want to strangle them! — **"walking they never heard of, God bless them."** (75)

The sarcastive attitude is recognized — is meant to be recognized — when the speaker's ostensible message is accompanied by a derived meta-message "this message is bogus". All it takes to be sarcastic is a single speaker, who produces both the message and the denigrating commentary on it.

The guiltive, however, is a cooperative venture, a linguistic *pas de deux* in that essentially the *same derived metamessage* ("this message is bogus") is not produced by the speaker but is rather left to be supplied by the addressee, who is thereby made to feel like a worm.

As I have tried to show, the sarcastive is overtly marked. Cues for the sarcastive meta-message (literally 'I don't mean this message') include 'spitting it out with a sneer', nasalization, deadpan monotone, sing-song, caricatured courtesy, formality, and sympathy, such indices of *fakery* as mark rhetorical questions and commands (e.g. "Don't ask me what kind of day I had with him yesterday"), and a small repertoire of the indices of *mimicry*, including most obviously (written, gestured, or pause-marked) quotation marks. Colloquial English includes as well a handful of segmental signs. All of these signs more or less iconically convey the framing metamessage 'This message is counterfactual' or 'I don't mean this', *whence the inference* follows that 'this message is bogus'.

The guiltive speech act is entirely different, in that, in order to properly trash her interlocutor, the guilter (typically but not always the stereotyped Jewish mother) has to sound perfectly sincere (and hence cannot be heard to broadcast the metamessage 'I don't mean this', which must therefore be covert). This suggests a kinship between the guiltive and *polite* language, in which the speaker also suppresses his/her own emotions, is known to be suppressing them, and still sounds "sincere".

Nevertheless, it is instantly obvious that the bolded passages from *Portnoy's Complaint* above are in the guiltive mood, rather than polite: while the illocutionary force of politeness is (presumably) to avoid aggression, the illocutionary force of guiltive utterances is clearly a kind of passive-aggressive one-upsmanship whose purpose is to make the hearer feel bad. How is this clear? How do the passages above do this work, and how do they contrast with the same passages uttered with genuine politeness or with genuine sincerity, assuming that such a sincerity is even possible?

Some obvious suggestions that Dear Abby might provide for a non-guilt-producing illocution include the following:

(14') *Don't exaggerate your selflessness. (If you want to be sincere, say:* " Of course *it bothered me that you forgot Mother's Day and my birthday." If you want to be polite, don't mention the incident at all.)*

(15') *Don't exaggerate your pain. (If you want to be sincere, say: "It really hurts my feelings that you won't dress up for synagogue." If you want to be polite, don't show you're upset at all.)*

(16') *Don't exaggerate your forbearance. (Sincerity might impel you to say: "You wretched little beast, running off to play baseball!" Politeness, once again, would impel you to keep quiet.)*

What's common to all of the ostensibly benign messages from Portnoy's elders is that the speaker's ludicrously *exaggerated* selflessness, hurt, and generosity, all express the explicit meta-message that "I the utterer of this message am a saint/martyr".

This metamessage, then, is not so much a commentary on the message itself, as on the nature of the person who can utter it sincerely. Implicit for Portnoy to elucidate are the derived metamessage "this message is therefore objectively bogus", and the accompanying inference that "you, Portnoy, are a heartless swine".

3. The mass-productive

I have already suggested that emphasis may have contradictory effects: ostensibly it increases the import of a message, while in practice it undermines it. The same is true of repetition, the simplest kind of emphasis imaginable. Paradoxically, replication (both of objects and of signs) validates in some cases, invalidates in others: see for example Moravcsik's exemplary cross-linguistic discussion of reduplication (Moravcsik 1978).

3.1 *Replication validates*

3.1.1 The "big lie" repeated is believed. This much is a truism, but it entails an equally plausible corollary: not even the truth is believed if uttered only once in the context of a culture of incessant repetition. If, on TV, we saw George Bush streaking through Washington *just once*, and the clip were never repeated, we would soon tend to think we had only imagined it. Incessant repetition breeds a kind of if-it's-true-I'll-get-a-chance-to-see-it-again-later philosophy. In other words: replication is a prerequisite for truth.

3.1.2. Replication produces wealth, visibility, and glamour for mass media stars. It confers "seriousness" on political candidates. The validating power of the prototypical replicating medium, TV, is so much a given, that the humour of the Calvin and Hobbes cartoon included here as Figure 1 lies not in the recognition that "TV validates existence" (a point for me as a plodding linguist, but a self-evident cliché for the cartoonist) but in the pomposity of the kid's diction, and in the irony that Calvin and Hobbes have themselves achieved the status of "cultural icons" precisely through the replicating medium of the comics.

Figure 1

3.2 *Replication invalidates*

History repeats itself: the first time as tragedy, the second (and all subsequent) times as farce.

3.2.1. Irrespective of its source (whether hand-made or mass produced) any individual object loses its value in a context of mass produced items: any single thing can be replaced by something nearly identical.

3.2.2. The philosophically once problematic notion of similarity becomes more and more natural, familiar and plausible. Forever obsolete are unconvincing homespun similes based on identities from nature: "like two peas in a pod". Universal Categories become objectively, as well as psychologically, real. Possibly, no two peas, no two dogs, no two people are completely alike: but two identical cans of Campbell soup, two Fords, two copies of a paperback, two pieces of china, two sofas, two cameras, two suits, are much less of a problem. Borges' nominalist Funes complained that we had the same word, not only for dogs in general, but for the same animal, viewed head on at 3:14, and in profile at 3:15 (Borges 1963). Mass production suggests Funes had it wrong, and that Andy Warhol was right: the artificial universe is populated with mass produced articles which, as far as the human eye and ear can judge, are as nearly identical as electrons, certainly as alike as photocopies of the same original. Your Campbell Soup can is indistinguishable from the Platonic

Campbell Soup Can laid up in Heaven. Each of the glamorous zombies in the videos of Robert Palmer is conceptually and perceptually identical with all the others.

3.2.3. It becomes necessary to express personality and originality (in dress; in a living room) primarily through idiosyncratic *combinations* of mass produced items: through collage (as in art) or sampling (as in rap music), rather than through original production. (We may observe a parallel to the phenomenon of double articulation: individual items, by virtue of their mass production, are on the way to becoming as meaningless as phonemes.)

3.3. *Repetition as a diachronic paradigm*

3.3.1. The meaning of a morpheme, or of an utterance, is determined not only by the extralinguistic circumstances under which it is uttered, all the other utterances with which it contrasts (synchronic paradigmatic context), and by the utterances which precede and follow it (synchronic syntagmatic context). It may also be determined, or at least affected, by speakers' awareness of the sheer number of times it has been uttered before (by themselves or by others).

Jingles, clichés, hackneyed platitudes, sayings, tags, maxims, aphorisms, slogans, mottoes, proverbs, saws, adages, boilerplate —whatever we reproduce as "blah, blah blah" (Ong 1971.303) —are the Campbell Soup cans of discourse, and mean something different from freshly minted expressions. The William Tell Overture, the injunction "Don't leave home without it", the question "Who you gonna call?", the exclamation "I love what you do for me" and hundreds of others are both enriched or impoverished through being recognized as mass produced.

A speaker consciously quoting "X" is taking a different stance towards his ostensible message than one who utters "X" (or believes himself to be uttering it) for the first time. (My favorite example of the resultant ambiguity of any text is Borges' profound short story "Pierre Menard, Author of the Quixote", whose hero undertakes to write portions of the Quixote, but with the mindset of a twentieth Century French symbolist poet rather than a sixteenth century Spanish veteran. The different context in which the same words are uttered invests the text with totally unfamiliar meanings). For a more homely example, consider the act of *reclamation*, whereby oppressed minorities preempt pejorative epithets generally hurled against them for ironical use amongst themselves: "nigger", "bitch", "dyke" and "fag" can be terms

Indeed, the Republican establishment denounces Duke at every turn —Bush has called him "an insincere charlatan." But Democrats gleefully keep putting Duke at the Republican doorstep and GOP officials often have difficulty drawing the line between Duke's carefully chosen rhetoric and established party positions, such as opposition to racial quotas.

Republicans praised Kirk Fordice when he was elected governor of Mississippi last year. His campaign themes included criticism of affirmative action programs, warnings against racial quotas in hiring and welfare overhaul. Duke is raising those issues too.

Republican Party Chairman Clayton Yeutter concedes that much of what Duke says is similar to what Fordice and Bush say. "The fundamental economic views of these two gentlemen and the president of the United States are similar," Yeutter said. "The difference comes in the types of human beings who are involved. David Duke is a charlatan and a fraud."

Figure 2

of jocular endearment. For another example of a related phenomenon, consider the difference between received perceptions of identical racist sentiments uttered by George Bush and David Duke, reproduced as figure 2.

The self-conscious quoter's stance may be *positive*: affectionate, an attempt at asserting a phatic bond with others who recognize the quote; or it may be *negative*: an expression of mockery or boredom, and of a lack of personal commitment. It may be both.

3.3.2 *Grammaticalization*

The *form* of an utterance is also affected by these three variables. When both form and meaning are affected by repetition, grammaticalization has occurred. The most familiar semantic aspect of grammaticalization is the erosion of meaning. But repetition may flat-out *destroy* meaning:

Brian: *You are all individuals!*
Multitudes (in unison): *"We are all individuals."*
(Monty Python's *Life of Brian*)

Consider a commercial invitation which many of us have heard more than once: to "buy one, and get another one free". This familiar offer was recently (*Minneapolis Star Tribune* Dec.11, 1991) ruled false advertising in Minneapolis, where one company, Pearle Vision, had been using it to advertise their eyeglasses . Precisely because the offer had stood for awhile, the Better Business Bureau correctly reasoned, *the regular price had in fact been halved.* Here — literally — a true statement became false through repetition. There are in general two ways in which this may happen.

Any word like "sale", "individual", or "special" which has "unique" or "unusual" somewhere in its definition or its presuppositions becomes *literally* false (by definition) simply by virtue of being repeated. This is what happened with the Pearle Vision come-on, and this is what happens when the messiah instructs the multitudes to chant in unison "we are all individuals" in *Life of Brian.* Something like this has happened with the reflexive pronoun in English, which is still homophonous with the emphatic pronoun. (In fact, we now signal suprising coreference through the oblique non-reflexive pronoun, as in "the prosecuting attorney believed me, and *I* believed me." cf. Haiman ms.)

More generally, any text becomes pale — if not false —through repetition. We tend to become aware of this only when we realize that the words of a familiar unattended ritual have become practically a practically meaningless formula. The word *dear* in salutations, when applied not only to strangers, but to anonymous committees, is a good example of this trend. And, of course, this has happened to the closing salutation also:

> For a while, we simply closed all letters, "Love". It didn't matter if we were writing to parents, lover, friend, or dentist [...] Finally, we wore the word out. (Richard 1992)

This brings me finally to the point of this section. If the utterance of a repeated expression may express the speaker's lack of commitment to it, then *whatever formally marks an utterance as a repetition can count as a sort of mood marker.* Given how often what we say is recycled, it is amazing how undeveloped are our means for labelling our clichés or standard routines as such, thereby safely distancing ourselves from them (if that is what we want to do). For example, it is entirely clear what the quotation marks are signalling in the

Doonesbury / By Garry Trudeau

Figure 3

wonderful Doonesbury cartoon of Figure 3, but it is by no means clear how they are to be pronounced.

The most codified of the self-conscious repetition marking devices in English (but I have also noted it in Russian, Turkish, and Oromo) is a weary descending singsong chant (with stylized intonation and rhythm), often prefaced by "I know: ", prefaced or followed by "Yeah, right: ", uttered on the same descending melody. This melody typically occurs where the speaker is ironically quoting an interlocutor or the wisdom of the silly ancestors.

(17) a *I know.* 'The check is in the mail.'
b *Yeah, yeah.* 'Read my lips.'
c *Sure, sure.* 'Look both ways before you cross the street.'
d *He's retiring.* (Yeah, sure). (*Time* June 18,1990, in an article on the "Joe Isuzu" character.)

Another is the hen-pecked husband's eternally weary pre-interrogative *now*, or post-interrogative marker *this time*, both heavily stressed, as in:

(18) a. ***Now** what have I done?*
b. *What is it **this time**?*

In indicating that he has asked the question many times before, the Henpecked Husband is signalling his lack of the concern or curiosity which attend a normal question.

Another way of indicating that an utterance has been often repeated is to repeat it yourself. While it is generally true that repetition serves the vaguely iconic function of "emphasis" (cf. Wierzbicka 1991:262), it is nevertheless true that repetition may directly signal weariness, boredom, and alienation (cf. Haiman 1991). It is (I think) no accident that the weary sarcasm of the bored repeater of other people's threadbare clichés is preceded by an almost obligatory repetition — "yeah, yeah", "sure, sure" or the like.

Japanese does this also. *Ume* 'good' is appreciative; but *umai, umai, umai* is almost invariably sarcastic (Adachi, ms.).

Larry Gorbet points out that Yiddish "schmo reduplication" has much the same kind of pejorative function: *justice-schmustice*, in reduplicating, but also distorting, the word, conveys the speaker's attempt to trivialize the concept the word represents.

In a cryptic passage on reduplication in Ewe, Ansre (1963:132) suggests that reduplication of an entire sentence in this language has the same kind of pragmatic function: the repeated sentence is usually " [an] *alleged saying*, giving notions *that need to be corrected* " or, possibly, notions which are treated as "cheap talk":

(19) *maalee maalee,* *Di wodOna*
'(I shall bathe)'[2] makes one go to bed dirty

4. Proper names > common nouns

The Holy Roman Empire, as everyone knows, was neither holy, nor Roman, nor an Empire. Although many proper names originate as definite descriptions, once congealed as proper names, they are no longer required nor expected to mean what they say. Perhaps this could be viewed as a special case of grammaticalization. In any case, the device is self-consciously used as an artful disclaimer of commitment in at least one recent case of false advertising, *Ragu* foods vs. the Food and Drug Administration (*Advertising Age*, May 28, 1990). The company marketed "Ragu fresh Italian pasta sauces", and the FDA took exception to the word "fresh", which was inappropriate for processed tomatoes. After a nine-month suit, the company capitulated: they announced they were marketing "Ragu fresh Italian *brand* pasta sauces". The term "fresh" is now "part of the product's brand name, and not a product description".

Arguably, this example is one of a purely legalistic trick (and one that actually failed, as Larry Horn has informed me, his best efforts as hired gun for *Ragu* notwithstanding). But personal experience offers many parallels, particularly in the transformation of descriptive nicknames into proper names. A fat boy I knew (in Onondaga Camp, 1952) was called *Fatso* as an insult, but once everyone called him that as a matter of course, the insult dissipated. I still recall my amazement as a six-year old ESL student overhearing the question "What's the matter, Fatso?" voiced by another kid in the unself-conscious accents of genuine solicitude and concern.

A visible change which probably originates through repetition is the conversion of definite descriptions into common nouns: a *gentleman* (with compound stress) is not necessarily a *gentle man* (with nuclear stress), and an *oldboy* literally cannot be an **old boy*. But there is no case I know of where a speaker has ever used this structural property to signal lack of commitment to the words s/he utters.

Conclusion

My major question in this discussion is: why have virtually none of these devices for signalling lack of speaker's commitment achieved the grammatical status of the subjunctive or the interrogative? (The only ones that come close are *quote* and stylized intonation, both of which have other, more central functions.)

I suspect that this has not happened because the indices of sarcasm, like those of anger and other personal emotions, belong to the same realm: they are not really signs but symptoms of these emotions. Raising one's voice is probably a symptom of anger in whatever language that one chooses to speak: nevertheless, no language has grammaticalized increased amplitude as a sign of anger. Why? Maybe because it's too universal, too natural, and too self-evident. Signs don't get codified until they're at least a little bit arbitrary.

And maybe sarcasm has failed as yet to get grammaticalized (this sounds paradoxical, speaking of sarcasm), because — being a symptom — it's too *sincere*. I regard it as an essential defining property of a sign that we can choose to use it, and thus be able to use it insincerely. We have at our disposal a number of metalinguistic devices for signalling insincerity of the first order: "this message is bogus". But perhaps as humans at the present stage of our evolution we are limited by a purely performance-like constraint (similar to that on center-embedding) which inhibits us from signalling insincerity of the second or higher orders: * "this (meta)metamessage is bogus", which we could utter once the symptomatic "this message is bogus" was harnessed as a sign, is simply not sayable by your normal average human, even in postmodern America.

ACKNOWLEDGEMENTS

I'am very grateful to Larry Horn, Suzanne Fleischman and Michele Emanatian for their comments and suggestions on this paper.

REFERENCES

Adachi, T. ms. "Sarcasm in Japanese". Macalester College.
Aksu-Koç, A. and D. Slobin. 1986. "Developments in the Use of Evidentials in Turkish." Chafe and Nichols 1986: 159-67.
Ansre, G. 1963. "Reduplication in Ewe". *Journal of African Languages*, vol. 2, part 2: 128-32.
Borges, J. 1963. "Funes the memorious". in his *Labyrinths*. New York: New Directions.
Chafe, W. and J. Nichols, (eds) 1986. *Evidentiality: The Linguistic Coding of Epistemology*. Norwood, NJ: Ablex.
Friedman, V. 1986. "Evidentiality in the Balkans: Bulgarian, Macedonian, and Albanian." Chafe and Nichols 1986: 168-87.
Haiman, J. 1989. "Alienation in Grammar." *Studies in Language* 13.121-70.
Haiman, J. 1990. "Sarcasm as Theater." *Cognitive Linguistics* 1.181-206.
Haiman, J. 1991. "The Bureaucratisation of Language." Wolfart 1991: 45-70.
Haiman, J. ms. "Grammatical Signs of the Divided self."
Horn, L. 1985. "Metalinguistic Negations and Pragmatic Ambiguity". *Language* 61. 121-74.
Kononov, A.N. 1956. *Grammatika Sovremennogo Turetskogo Literaturnogo Jazyka*. (=Grammar of contemporary literary Turkish). Leningrad: Akademia Nauk.
Mallinson, G. 1986. *Rumanian*. London: Croom Helm.
McCay, W. 1990. *The Complete Little Nemo in Slumberland*. Vol. 4. Richard Marschall, ed. New York: Remco Worldservice books.
Moravcsik, E. 1978. "Reduplicative Constructions". In *Universals of Human Language*, vol. 3: *Word Structure*, ed. J. Greenberg et al., Stanford: Stanford University Press, 297-334.
Ong, W. 1971. *Rhetoric, Romance, and Technology*. Ithaca: Cornell University Press.
Palmer, F. 1986. *Mood and Modality*. Cambridge: Cambridge University Press.
Richard, J. 1992. "The Distance from '67 to '92: Would You Hug a Stranger?" *Baltimore Sun* April 28, 1992.
Roth, P. 1970. *Portnoy's Complaint*. New York: Dell.
Wierzbicka, A. 1991. *Cross-Cultural Pragmatics*. The Hague: Mouton.
Wolfart, H. ed. 1991. *Linguistic Studies Presented to John Finlay*. Winnipeg: Algonkian and Iroquoian Linguistics Memoirs.

III
Irrealis Modality and Subjunctive

The Realis-Irrealis Distinction in Caddo, the Northern Iroquoian Languages, and English

Wallace Chafe
University of California, Santa Barbara

0. Introduction

There are many ways in which language sheds light on the nature of the mind, and conversely ways in which an understanding of mental phenomena can further our understanding of language. The realis-irrealis distinction illustrates the usefulness of combining linguistic and cognitive insights in ways that will contribute to an improved understanding of both. In Chafe (1994) I explored various paths by which ideas enter consciousness, among them the direct perception of current states and events, the remembering of previously experienced states and events, and the imagining of states and events that are judged not to accord with current objective reality. Of interest here is the evidence languages provide for a cognitive distinction between what may be called realis and irrealis ideas, and how recognizing such a distinction can help us understand what we find in languages.

I will begin with a discussion of the Caddo language, which obligatorily expresses reality or irreality in all its verbs. Caddo also suggests one of many diachronic paths by which the distinction may come to be grammaticized, and helps us understand how, in the course of such a development, there may develop inconsistencies. I will then turn to the Northern Iroquoian languages, whose morphology reflects a three-way reality distinction. Finally, I will mention the fact that English, which does not mark reality overtly, nevertheless shows its influence indirectly in the semantics of specificity.

Realis expressions are typified by the following, where I have included constructed English examples for easy comparison:

(1)	past states	*I had a toothache.*
	past perfective events	*I got the car fixed.*
	present states	*I've got a toothache.*
	present imperfective events	*The car's getting fixed.*

We can suppose that states and events like these are believed by the invented speaker to accord with objective reality. The first two examples express memories of a state or event that was directly experienced by the speaker at an earlier time. The third expresses a state that is being experienced at the time of speaking. The fourth expresses a somewhat more inferential kind of knowledge (the speaker may not be directly perceiving the relevant events at the moment of speaking), but memory combined with normal expectations have led this speaker to believe that the event accords with reality.

Realis expressions like those in (1) contrast with irrealis expressions like the following, illustrated with a constructed event (the idea of getting the car fixed) that in each case is imagined rather than directly perceived or remembered:

(2)	yes-no questions	*Did you get the car fixed?*
	negations	*I didn't get the car fixed.*
	futures	*I'm going to get the car fixed.*
	necessities	*I need to get the car fixed.*
	possibilities	*I might get the car fixed.*
	imperatives	*Get the car fixed.*
	prohibitions	*Don't get the car fixed.*
	conditions	*If I get the car fixed...*

There is nothing in the overt grammar of English that unites expressions like those exemplified in (2) and opposes them to expressions like those in (1). This lack of overt marking in some languages along with the apparent inconsistency of marking in others has led some investigators to doubt whether the realis-irrealis distinction has any general validity at all. Trask (1993:147), for example, in his dictionary of grammatical terms defines *irrealis* dismissively as "a label often applied in a somewhat *ad hoc* manner to some distinctive grammatical form, most often a verbal inflection, occurring in some particular language and having some kind of connection with unreality. Palmer (1986) recommends that this term should be avoided in linguistic theory on the ground that it corresponds to no consistent linguistic content."[1] Bybee, Perkins and Pagliuca (1994) express similar qualms. These reservations are understandable, given the diverse and often inconsistent ways in which reality and irreality manifest themselves. As we will see, however, it is fair to imagine that if linguistics in its present guise had been developed by the Caddo and not by speakers of the languages of Europe, the reality distinction would be regarded as having a central importance to language and thought. Bybee, Perkins, and Pagliuca specifically question the functional basis of the distinction, they are troubled by its seemingly heterogeneous manifestations in languages, and they find it unhelpful in understanding diachronic developments. Rather than responding immediately to each of these areas of doubt, largely repeating points made in Givòn (1994), I will proceed to a description of the manifestations of reality in Caddo, the Northern Iroquoian languages, and English, returning in the end to the general issue of whether and how reality is relevant to an understanding of language and the mind.

1. Caddo

The Caddo people once lived in a large number of towns that were spread over what is now eastern Texas, northern Louisiana, and southern Arkansas. European encroachment into that area, which began with the De Soto expedition in 1541, was devastating, and after a series of tragedies and removals, the few remaining Caddo settled in southwestern Oklahoma in the nineteenth century. In spite of four and a half centuries of subservience to other languages, the Caddo language is still spoken, although only by a rapidly diminishing number of elderly people. I would hope that one of the lessons of the following discussion would be the urgent need to learn as much as we can from such rapidly dying languages during the few years in which they will still be with us.

Caddo is a prototypically polysynthetic language, and one of the prominent features of its verbs is the inclusion of a prefix that refers to one or more of the participants in an event or state. Such a "pronominal prefix" distinguishes person, case, and -- of most interest here -- reality. (Number is marked elsewhere in the verb.) Persons include 1st, 2nd, 3rd, and, in addition, what I have called a Defocusing person which functions rather like German *man* or French *on* (Chafe 1992). Case includes Agent, Patient, and Beneficiary. Reality includes Realis and Irrealis. The reality distinction is an obligatory, clearly marked, and unambiguous feature of every pronominal prefix (with one minor exception), and thus of every verb. Realis and Irrealis can be thought of as contrasting semantic components that combine with the four persons and the three cases in a three-dimensional array that establishes the semantics of the pronominal prefix system.

The Realis and Irrealis prefixes have the following underlying forms:

Realis Prefixes:

	Agent	Patient	Beneficiary
1st person	*ci-*	*ku-*	*ku-*
2nd person	*yahʔ-*	*si-*	*si-*
3rd person	---	---	*nu-*
Defocusing	*yi-*	*ya-*	*yu-*

Irrealis Prefixes:

	Agent	Patient	Beneficiary
1st person	*t'a-/t'i-*	*ba-*	*ba-*
2nd person	*sahʔ-*	*saʔa-*	*saʔu-*
3rd person	*sa-*	*sa-*	*ʔu-*
Defocusing	*ʔa-*	*ʔaʔa-*	*ʔaʔu-*

Several points are worth noting. It can be seen that 3rd person participants are not always marked. Specifically, they are missing for Realis Agents and Patients, which are actually the most frequently occurring of all 3rd person referents. They *are* marked, however, when they function as Realis Beneficiaries or when they are Irrealis, regardless of case. Thus, even though there is not always an overt 3rd person marker, it is always clear whether a 3rd person verb is Realis or Irrealis. It can also be seen that the Realis and Irrealis forms have virtually nothing in common. Realis *ci-* contrasts with Irrealis *t'a-* or *t'i-*, Realis *ku-* with Irrealis *ba-*, and so on. There is thus no reason to think that the Irrealis forms had their origins in modifications of the Realis forms. The historical origins of the two sets appear to be distinct.

In addition to the prefixes listed above, there are also various combinations of 1st and 2nd person Agents with 1st and 2nd person Patients and Beneficiaries:

Realis Prefixes:

1st person Agent with 2nd person Patient	*t'a-*
1st person Agent with 2nd person Beneficiary	*t'u-*
2nd person Agent with 1st person Patient	*yahku-*
2nd person Agent with 1st person Beneficiary	*yahku-*

Irrealis Prefixes:

1st person Agent with 2nd person Patient	*t'a-*
1st person Agent with 2nd person Beneficiary	*t'aˀu-*
2nd person Agent with 1st person Patient	*sahku-*
2nd person Agent with 1st person Beneficiary	*sahku-*

Here it can be seen that the combination of a 1st person Agent with a 2nd person Patient is the only environment in which the Realis-Irrealis distinction is neutralized. The fact that this single form, *t'a-*, is also homophonous with one form of the Irrealis 1st person Agent prefix (see above) appears to be only a coincidence.

While person and case are properties of the *referent* expressed by the pronominal prefix, the domain of reality is not the referent, but rather the state or event expressed by the entire clause (a clause being typically coextensive with a verb). One may wonder why the expression of a clause-level meaning should ride along on a pronominal prefix, but we may never know the circumstances under which the language developed this way of doing things.

There are a variety of contexts that condition the use of the Irrealis prefixes. All but one of them involves the simultaneous presence of a so-called prepronominal prefix: a verb-initial prefix whose function is compatible with irreality. The fact that these prepronominal prefixes participate less than fully in the complex phonology of the verb suggests that some if not all of them were, at an earlier stage of the language, separate particles, and that they have become attached to verbs more recently.

1.1 *Yes-No Questions.*

The one environment in which an Irrealis prefix is used without an accompanying prepronominal prefix is the yes-no question. In Caddo, then, a yes-no question can be regarded as the unmarked use of the Irrealis. Because the boundaries of Caddo morphemes have been obscured through numerous sound changes, it is useful to cite examples in an interlinear format whose second line provides reconstructed forms in which morpheme boundaries are more clearly evident.[2] In the third line each morpheme is glossed, and the fourth line provides a translation of the entire word.

(3) *sàyybáwnah*
sahʔ-yi=bahw-nah
2ND.AGENT.IRREALIS-see-PERFECT
'have you seen him?'

Unlike yes-no questions, question-word questions are expressed with Realis prefixes. For example:

(4) *dikadàyybáwnah*
dikat-yahʔ-yi=bahw-nah
WHAT?-2ND.AGENT.REALIS-see-PERFECT
'what have you seen?'

It is easy to interpret the difference between (3) and (4) as motivated by the fact that a yes-no question implies a lack of knowledge as to whether the event actually occurred (you may not have seen him), whereas a question-word question presupposes the event and asks only about the identity of a participant. Thus, (4) presupposes that you have seen something, and the speaker wants only to know what it was.

The fact that all the remaining uses of the Irrealis pronominal prefixes involve the attachment of a prepronominal prefix to a form which, by itself, expresses a yes-no question suggests a way in which the marking of irreality may have entered the language. It may well be that the Irrealis forms of the pronominal prefixes arose first as a way of marking questions, to which the prefixes described below, perhaps in their earlier incarnation as particles, came to be attached. If this was indeed the path of development, it would have amounted to a tacit recognition by speakers that all these uses share a common property of irreality.

1.2 *Negations.*

An obvious site for irreality is negation (but see Mithun in press). Simple negations in Caddo are expressed with the Negative prepronominal prefix *kúy-* 'not':

(5) *kúyt'áybah*
kúy-t'a-yi=bahw
NEGATIVE-1ST.AGENT.IRREALIS-see
'I don't see him'

Simple negations may be modified in various ways. For example, the Negative prefix may be immediately followed by *-c'í-* to indicate an event that is not real at the present time, but might be expected to become real in the future. In other words, the combination *kúy-c'í-* means 'not yet':

(6) *kúyc'ít'áybah*
kúy-c'í-t'a-yi=bahw
NEGATIVE-YET-1ST.AGENT.IRREALIS-see
'I haven't seen it yet'

Or the Negative prefix may be followed by *-ˀní-* to express the idea of an event that happened in the past, but is not happening now. In other words, the combination *kúy-ˀní-* means 'not any more'. It is followed by the alternative 1st person Irrealis Agent form *t'i-* rather than the *t'a-*:

(7) *kúyˀnít'íibah*
kúy-ˀní-t'i-yi=bahw
NEGATIVE-ANY.MORE-1ST.AGENT.IRREALIS-see
'I don't see it any more'

An additional possibility is to supplement the combination just described with the morpheme *-káy-* 'anything':

(8) *kúyˀníkáyt'áybah*
kúy-ˀní-káy-t'a-yi=bahw
NEGATIVE-ANY.MORE-ANYTHING-1ST.AGENT.IRREALIS-see
'I don't see anything any more'

An alternative to the simple Negative prefix *kúy-* is the Temporal Negative prefix *nus-* 'not for a long time'. It too is followed by the 1st person Irrealis Agent form *t'i-*:

(9) *nust'íibah*
nus-t'i-yi=bahw
TEMPORAL.NEGATIVE-1ST.AGENT.IRREALIS-see
'I haven't seen it for a long time'

All of these negative options condition an Irrealis pronominal prefix.

1.3 *Prohibitions.*

Prohibitions, or negative imperatives, also condition an Irrealis pronominal prefix. They are expressed with the prepronominal prefix *kaš-*:

(10) *kaššáyʔbah*
kaš-sahʔ-yi=bahw
PROHIBITIVE-2ND.AGENT.IRREALIS-see
'don't look at it'

1.4 *Obligations.*

The expression of an obligation with the prepronominal prefix *kas-* 'should, be supposed to' also requires the Irrealis form:

(11) *kassánáyʔaw*
kas-sa-náy=ʔaw
OBLIGATIVE-3RD.AGENT.IRREALIS-sing
'he should/is supposed to sing'

1.5 *Conditions.*

Conditions are also Irrealis. There are two prepronominal prefixes that express conditionality. One of them is the Particular Conditional prefix *hí-* 'if', indicating the possibility of a particular event:

(12) *hít'áybah*
hí-t'a-yi=bahw
CONDITIONAL-1ST.AGENT.IRREALIS-see
'if I see it'

The other is the Generic Conditional prefix *nas-* 'if, whenever', used with generic events:

(13) *nast'áybah*
nas-t'a-yi=bahw
GENERIC.CONDITIONAL-1ST.AGENT.IRREALIS-see
'if, whenever I see it'

Such events are often predicted for the future:

(14) *nast'áybáwˀaˀ*
nas-t'a-yi=bahw-ˀaˀ
GENERIC.CONDITIONAL-1ST.AGENT.IRREALIS-see-FUTURE
'if, whenever I see it (future)'

Negative Future conditions are expressed with *nadús-* 'if not':

(15) *nadúst'áybáwˀaˀ*
nadús-t'a-yi=bahw-ˀaˀ
NEGATIVE.CONDITIONAL-1ST.AGENT.IRREALIS-see-FUTURE
'if I don't see it (future)'

1.6 *Other Irrealis Options.*

There are several other prepronominal prefixes that condition Irrealis pronominal prefixes. One of them is the Simulative prefix *dúy-* 'as if':

(16) *dúyt'áybah*
dúy-t'a-yi=bahw
SIMULATIVE-1ST.AGENT.IRREALIS-see
'as if I saw it'

Another is the Infrequentative prefix *wás-* 'seldom':

(17) *wást'áybah*
wás-t'a-yi=bahw
INFREQUENTATIVE-1ST.AGENT.IRREALIS-see
'I seldom see it'

Of special interest is the Admirative prefix *hús-*, expressing surprise:

(18) *húsbaasáyˀk'awihsaˀ*
hús-ba-ˀa=sa-yi=k'awih-saˀ
ADMIRATIVE-1ST.BENEFICIARY.IRREALIS-name-know-PROGRESSIVE
'my goodness he knows my name!'

This last usage is perhaps itself surprising. It would seem that, although the event or state itself is real enough (in this example he does know my name), the fact that it is contrary to the speaker's expectation — a negation of normality — is what is responsible for the use of the Irrealis. It is as if the speaker were saying, "It's unreal that he knows my name!" (an interpretation suggested to me by Alan Taylor).

Although the types of expressions listed above — yes-no questions, negations, obligations, conditions, simulatives, infrequentatives, and admiratives — can be seen as functionally motivated members of the Irrealis category, the occurrence of *Realis* pronominal prefixes with imperatives might be seen as an inconsistency:

(19) *dáyˀbah*
yahˀ-yi=bahw
1ST.AGENT.REALIS-see
'look at it!'

More problematic, perhaps, is the use of Realis prefixes with futures, especially in view of the fact that future is so fundamental to the expression of irreality in Papuan languages (Roberts ms.):

(20) *cíibáwˀaˀ*
ci-yi=bahw-ˀaˀ
1ST.AGENT.REALIS-see-FUTURE
'I'll look at it'

(21) *cíibáwčah*
ci-yi=bahw-čah
1ST.AGENT.REALIS-see-FUTURE.INTENTION
'I'm going to look at it'

Both imperatives and futures convey ideas of events that have not yet happened, having entered the speaker's consciousness through imagination. Why, then, should Caddo treat them as realis? Two quite different answers can be suggested. One is that reality is not a binary but a gradient dimension in which imperatives and futures express ideas that are judged to be relatively more in accord with reality than, say, yes-no questions or negations. Speakers may have a relatively stronger expectation that commands will be obeyed or that predicted events will take place. When we turn to the Northern Iroquoian languages we will find, in fact, that futures (and their use as imperatives) have been grammaticized with a status intermediate between the extremes of realis and irrealis.

But the exemption of Caddo imperatives and futures from the irrealis category could have a different explanation. It is likely that ways of expressing imperatives and futures were established in the language well before the negative and other particles came to be attached to what were originally interrogative verbs, as suggested above. Imperatives and futures, that is, may stem from a more ancient layer of Caddo morphology. Already entrenched in the language, they would then have failed to participate in the more recent grammaticization of irreality in the pronominal prefixes. It is difficult to decide which of these explanations is correct (perhaps both are), but either is plausible, and either serves to demonstrate how irreality (like other semantic functions) may come through time to be represented in ways that may appear synchronically to be inconsistent.

2. The Northern Iroquoian languages

Spoken in New York, Ontario, and Quebec, the languages that constitute the northern branch of the Iroquoian family include Mohawk, Oneida, Onondaga, Cayuga, Seneca, and Tuscarora, as well as other languages now extinct. All of these languages behave in a similar fashion with respect to the matters to be discussed here, and I will discuss them as a single entity.

When Northern Iroquoian verbs are inflected for the Punctual (perfective) aspect, they obligatorily contain one of a set of three prefixes that segment a continuum of reality. The occurrence of these prefixes with other aspects — the Stative (perfect) and Habitual (both imperfective and generic) — is optional, and is marked with a special added suffix. At one end of this reality continuum is the Factual prefix (reconstructable in most environments as **waˀ-*), expressing the speaker's belief in the reality of the event or state. At the other end is the Optative prefix (reconstructable in most environments as **aa-*), expressing either obligation or possibility. In some contexts the Optative is best translated 'should', in others 'might'. Intermediate between these extremes lies the Future prefix (reconstructable as **ę-*), used for a state or event the speaker expects to materialize but is not certain of. Verbs with the Future prefix are also often used as imperatives, a fact which suggests that the exemption of both imperatives and futures from irrealis marking in Caddo, as discussed above, may indeed have a functional basis. In short, whereas the

Caddo system divides this dimension simply into Realis and Irrealis, the Northern Iroquoian system shows a three-way division. The examples below are taken from the Seneca language:

(22) *oʔgeegęʔ*
waʔ-ke-kę-ʔ
FACTUAL-1ST.AGENT-see-PUNCTUAL
'I see/saw it' (direct perception or memory)

(23) *ęgeegęʔ*
ę-ke-kę-ʔ
FUTURE-1ST.AGENT-see-PUNCTUAL
'I'll see it' (prediction)

(24) *aageegęʔ*
aa-ke-kę-ʔ
OPTATIVE-1ST.AGENT-see-PUNCTUAL
'I should/might see it' (obligation or possibility)

This Northern Iroquoian continuum interacts with yes-no questions, negations, and other irrealis contexts in complex ways. I will limit the discussion here to questions and negations. Yes-no questions are expressed with both an intonation contour and a phrase-final particle in most of the languages, but in Seneca with intonation alone. Such questions are expressed in ways that are independent of the reality dimension. That is, they may be marked as Factual, Future, or Optative, or (with aspects other than the Punctual) they may have no reality marking at all.

The difference between Caddo, where all yes-no questions are Irrealis, and Northern Iroquoian, where such questions may show any degree of reality or none at all, also invites two possible explanations. One might suppose that interrogation lies outside the scope of reality, so that, for example:

(25) *ęhseegęʔ*
ę-hse-kę-ʔ
FUTURE-2ND.AGENT-see-PUNCTUAL
'will you see it?'

with a yes-no question intonation has a meaning that could be paraphrased "Is it or is it not the case that you will see it?" whereas the corresponding Caddo word:

(26) *sàyybáwʔaʔ*
sahʔ-yi=bahw-ʔaʔ
2ND.AGENT.IRREALIS-see-FUTURE
'will you see it?'

might be paraphrased "Will you see it or won't you see it?"

An alternative possibility, not inconsistent with the first, is that Northern Iroquoian questions are actually requests for confirmation. Thus, (25) might correspond more closely to English "You'll see it?" with a question intonation, a translation that mirrors the Seneca surface form (regarding confirmative questions in English see Chafe 1970a:333-337 and, in Onondaga, Chafe 1970b:24). A confirmative question allows any degree of reality in the proposition for which confirmation is requested. This explanation can be combined with that in terms of scope, in the sense that confirmation lies outside the degree of reality. For present purposes it is enough to point out that the different treatment of yes-no questions by Caddo and the Northern Iroquoian languages can have a functional motivation.

Negation presents a different picture. A detailed discussion of negative forms and their cooccurrences in the Northern Iroquoian languages would take us too far afield, but we can note that the Negative prefix in these languages (allowing for a few special exceptions) does not cooccur with any of the reality prefixes. Negative past meanings are expressed with a Stative (perfect) form of the verb, which does not require a reality prefix:

(27) *daʔageegęęh*
teʔ-wake-kę-ęh
NEGATIVE-1ST.PATIENT-see-STATIVE
'I haven't seen it'

Negative Futures are expressed with the so-called contrastive prefix (which involves an element of surprise), together with the Optative prefix and a verb that ends in the same way as an imperative (Chafe 1967: 32):

(28) *thaageegęh*
th-aa-ke-kę-h
CONTRASTIVE-OPTATIVE-1ST.AGENT-see-IMPERATIVE
'I won't see it'

This unusual morphologized construction combines the three irrealis features of negation, surprise, and the imperative to express idiomatically the Negative Future meaning.

It was noted above that the reality prefixes are obligatory with the Punctual aspect. They may occur with other aspects, but when they do, the special nature of their occurrence is marked with an additional suffix. In effect, reality is an obligatory category with verbs inflected as perfective, but is optional and marked with verbs inflected as perfect, imperfective, and generic. These languages thus suggest a special attachment between degrees of reality and events that are regarded as particular. It would be interesting to know whether this affinity appears in other languages.

3. English

In English the realis-irrealis dimension fails to receive the unmistakable overt marking we find in Caddo and, distributed differently, in the Northern Iroquoian languages. It nevertheless shows itself in a more subtle but no less valid manner in its determination of the distinction between specific and nonspecific referents (e.g. Chafe 1970a:199; Jackendoff 1972, Chapter 7; Givòn 1989, Chapter 5). This distinction is recognizable in the context of certain verbs such as *look for*:

(29) *I looked for a book.*

where there is ambiguity as to whether or not the speaker has a specific book in mind, as opposed to:

(30) *I bought a book.*

where only the specific meaning is at home. Of interest is the fact that the nonspecific meaning is correlated with contexts that are typically irrealis:

(31)	yes-no questions	*Did you buy a book?*
	negations	*I didn't buy a book.*
	futures	*I'm going to buy a book.*
	obligations	*I need to buy a book.*
	possibilities	*I might buy a book.*
	imperatives	*Buy a book.*
	prohibitions	*Don't buy a book.*
	conditions	*If I buy a book...*

Imagine, for example, that you and I are walking past an airport bookstore and I say, "I need to buy a book." With the specific meaning, I might continue "It's one I read a review of yesterday". With the nonspecific meaning, I might go on to say "So I'll have something to read on the plane." It appears that in irrealis contexts English allows and even encourages the interpretation of a direct object referent as nonspecific. The contexts in (31) are just those that are overtly marked as Irrealis in Caddo, except for the fact that they include *Future*, thus confirming the natural inclusion of future in the Irrealis category. It is possible that this relation between irreality and nonspecificity of reference is widespread if not universal, thus confirming the widespread or universal relevance of the irrealis category. But that remains to be seen.

4. Conclusion

The realis-irrealis distinction reflects judgments that certain ideas stem from direct perception, memory, or expectations of what is normal, while others have their source in imagining. This distinction can be thought of as a covert semantic pressure that emerges in different languages in different ways. It emerges in Caddo in a clear and ubiquitous formal distinction, every verb being marked for either reality or irreality. The Caddo assignment of specific functions to these two categories is motivated and coherent, with yes-no questions, negations of various sorts, prohibitions, obligations, conditions, simulations, and surprises in the irrealis category. Neither futures nor imperatives are marked as Irrealis, however, either because Caddo draws the line at this point in the realis-irrealis continuum, and/or because ways of expressing futures and imperatives were morphologized in the language prior to the marking of irreality.

The distinction emerges differently in the Northern Iroquoian languages, which show a three-way rather than a binary contrast with perceived and remembered reality at one extreme, obligation and possibility at the other, and between them the future (with an imperative use as well). Unlike Caddo, the Northern Iroquoian languages do not treat yes-no questions as irrealis, perhaps because the scope of questioning is external to reality, perhaps also because Iroquoian questions are more confirmative in nature than the more clearly disjunctive questions of Caddo. The Negative and Factual prefixes are, as might be expected, incompatible in the Northern Iroquoian languages, and negative futurity is expressed with a grammaticized combination of surprise and possibility, along with an imperative ending. The three-way reality distinction is obligatory with perfective verbs, but it is optional and marked with perfects, imperfectives, and generics.

Reality fails to be overtly marked in English, but its force is nevertheless felt through the irrealis creation of an environment in which referents may be interpreted as nonspecific. The contexts that produce this effect line up well with the Caddo Irrealis contexts, except for the inclusion of future.

I hope to have shown (1) that the realis-irrealis dimension has a consistent functional basis in people's judgments concerning the degree to which their ideas accord with what they believe to be objective reality; (2) that the apparent inconsistency with which such judgments are manifested in different languages can be explained sometimes in terms of a gradient rather than a binary dimension of reality, sometimes in terms of layers of morphologization, and sometimes in terms of scope; and (3) that recognition of the pressures exerted by the reality dimension is ultimately essential to an understanding of certain aspects of language change.

We are left with the question of the ontological status of the reality dimension as it relates to the several moods and modalities. The extent to which ideas are judged to accord with objective reality leads to a categorization of specific moods and modalities, in combination with specific tenses and aspects, into two or three overarching categories. The categories themselves may surface as realis and irrealis semantic components of morphemes as in Caddo, as complete morphemes as in the Northern Iroquoian languages, or as indirect influences on the specific-nonspecific referential distinction as in English. Realis and irrealis can thus be seen as comparable to broader categories such as tense or aspect, or for that matter mood and modality, within each of which several values are available. They are most closely related to moods and modalities in the sense that they reflect a speaker's attitude toward the idea being expressed, but their effect is to combine the more specific moods and modalities into larger groupings.

FOOTNOTES

1 Curiously, a search of Palmer's book does not reveal any such recommendation.

2 In the first, and sometimes the second lines the acute accent mark indicates a high pitched vowel, the grave accent a pitch that falls from high to low. Long consonants and vowels are shown with doubled letters. Caddo stems usually consist of a lexicalized combination of two or more historically distinct morphemes, which are joined in the

second line with an equals sign. The separate meaning of each of these stem-internal morphemes is often obscure, and here I have simply given an English gloss for the stem as a whole.

REFERENCES

Bybee, Joan, Revere Perkins & William Pagliuca. 1994. *The Evolution of Grammar: Tense, Aspect, and Modality in the Languages of the World.* Chicago: University of Chicago Press.

Chafe, Wallace. 1967. *Seneca Morphology and Dictionary.* (Smithsonian Contributions to Anthropology, Volume 4.) Washington, DC: Smithsonian Press.

Chafe, Wallace. 1970a. *Meaning and the Structure of Language.* Chicago: University of Chicago Press.

Chafe, Wallace. 1970b. *A Semantically Based Sketch of Onondaga.* Indiana University Publications in Anthropology and Linguistics, Memoir 25.

Chafe, Wallace. 1992. "Uses of the Defocusing Pronominal Prefixes in Caddo." *Anthropological Linguistics* 32:57-68.

Chafe, Wallace. 1994. *Discourse, Consciousness, and Time: The Flow and Displacement of Conscious Experience in Speaking and Writing.* Chicago: University of Chicago Press.

Givón, Talmy. 1989. *Mind, Code and Context: Essays in Pragmatics.* Hillsdale, NJ: Lawrence Erlbaum.

Givón, Talmy. 1994. "Irrealis and the Subjunctive." *Studies in Language* 18:265-337.

Jackendoff, Ray S. 1972. *Semantic Interpretation in Generative Grammar.* Cambridge, MA: The MIT Press.

Mithun, Marianne. "On the Relativity of Irreality." This volume.

Palmer, Frank R. 1986. *Mood and Modality.* Cambridge: Cambridge University Press.

Roberts, John R. Ms. The Category 'Irrealis' in Papuan Medial Verbs.

On the Relativity of Irreality

Marianne Mithun
University of California, Santa Barbara

0. Introduction

A modality distinction reported in languages in a number of parts of the world is that between Irrealis and Realis. The terminology has been applied to constructions in languages of Australia (Comrie 1985; Palmer 1986), Austronesia (Dempwolff 1939, Chung & Timberlake 1985), Papua New Guinea (Foley 1986; Roberts 1990), Africa (Givón 1994), Europe (Chung & Timberlake 1985; Givón 1994), South America (Wise 1986, Payne & Payne 1990), Mesoamerica (Craig 1977; Givón 1994), North America (Buckley 1988; Miller 1990) and to various creole languages (Romaine this volume) to mention only a few. It has been used widely in both grammars of individual languages and general discussions of modality.

As pointed out by Bybee, Perkins & Pagliuca (1994), however, the grammatical categories referred to by the terms are far from uniform cross-linguistically. Construction types marked as Irrealis in one language may be marked as Realis in the next. In some languages Imperatives are classified as Irrealis, in others as Realis; futures, questions, and negatives also show some variation. The formal expression of the distinction varies cross-linguistically as well. In some languages, only the Irrealis category is expressed overtly, in others both Irrealis and Realis are expressed, and in still others one or the other is expressed by multiple markers. The distinction may be indicated in various areas of the grammar: by particles, by clausal clitics, by verbal inflection, and perhaps even by verbal derivation (Eatough ms on Nisenan). In many languages it is carried as a feature of markers that also express other functions, such as tense or aspect, clause linking, or pronouns, as in Caddo

(Chafe this volume) and Amele (Roberts 1990). Irrealis/Realis distinctions may even appear in several different parts of the grammar of a single language. Buckley (1988) describes pairs of Completive and Inchoative suffixes in Alsea; one member of each pair is Irrealis, the other Realis. In addition, an Irrealis/Realis distinction is carried in this language by complementizers: *sís* introduces Irrealis clauses, *mís* Realis clauses. Jamul Diegueño contains both an inflectional Irrealis suffix *-x* and an Irrealis/Realis distinction carried on the switch reference suffixes marking dependent clauses (Miller 1990).

Given this variation, the utility of the labels 'Irrealis' and 'Realis' for cross-linguistic comparison is open to question. If there is no common semantic or pragmatic basis for the terminology, its application to such diverse phenomena could lead to unnecessary confusion. In what follows, the Irrealis and Realis categories of several languages will be compared. It will be suggested that despite the apparent heterogeneity of the categories to which the distinction is applied, indeed perhaps because of it, the Irrealis/Realis terminology can prompt fruitful cross-linguistic comparisons with potential for furthering our understanding of certain processes of grammaticization.

1. Central Pomo

Languages of the Pomoan family, spoken in northern California, contain several pairs of verb-final markers that link clauses. The markers distinguish Irrealis and Realis moods. Their forms are listed in (1).

(1) Central Pomo clause linkers

		SAME	DIFFERENT
1. Irrealis	'while', 'and', 'then'	*-hi*	*=hla*
2. Realis			
- Simultaneous	'and', 'while', 'as'	*-in*	*=da*
- Sequential	'and', 'then'	*-ba*	*=li*

The Irrealis markers in the top row (*-hi*, *=hla*) are used to link clauses expressing actions or states that the speaker portrays as purely within the realm of thought. Such constructions convey ideas known through imagination rather than direct perception (Chafe, this volume). The Realis markers in the bottom two rows (*-in*, *=da*, *-ba*, *=li*) link clauses expressing events portrayed as actualized, having occurred or actually occurring. The choice of markers within each of these categories reflects further distinctions: whether the linked actions or states are presented as components of a single event (SAME) or as distinct events (DIFFERENT), and, if they are Realis, whether the linked activities or states are simultaneous (overlapping in time) or consecutive (occurring in sequence).

The uses of each marker are described below. Except where otherwise specified, examples cited here are drawn from spontaneous speech, generally conversation or narrative embedded within conversation. Speakers quoted here are Mrs. Frances Jack and Mrs. Kate Daniels of the Hopland rancheria, Mrs. Salome Alcantra and Mrs. Florence Paoli of the Yokaya rancheria, and Mrs. Eileen Oropeza of the Point Arena rancheria. All material was transcribed and translated with the help of Mrs. Jack.*

1.1 *The Central Pomo Irrealis Clause Linkers*

The markers identifying Irrealis dependent clauses are *-hi* and *=hla*. The first, *-hi*, links clauses expressing what are portrayed as components of the same event.

(2) Irrealis same event linker: FJ
*Mé·n=ʔti mí=· lálil čá-·n-ma-**hi*** kay
so=but that=at back run-IMPFV-COOPERATION-SAME.**IRREALIS** too
'But we could drive back there **and**
ya mu·l da ʔ=mí=·=li hlá-qač̓=ʔle.
1.AGENT that road COP=that=at=with go.PL-up-=CONDITIONAL
go up that road.'

The second Irrealis marker, *=hla*, links clauses expressing what are portrayed as different events.

(3) Irrealis different event linker: FP
*Ma čalél qów=ʔ-ne=**hla***
2.AGENT just out=by.gravity-set=DIFF.**IRREALIS**
'**If** you just threw it out

ṭ· mu·l bá-č̓=iʔle.
feel that big-INCHOATIVE.PFV=CONDITIONAL
I guess it would grow.'

The clauses bearing the linkers are grammatically dependent, since they cannot stand alone as independent sentences, but they are not necessarily subordinate semantically. In (2), for example, 'We could go back up there and drive up that road', the Irrealis marker links two semantically and pragmatically equivalent constituents of a larger sentence expressing root possibility. (The free translations were provided by Mrs. Jack, who was present at all conversations and aware of both the linguistic and extra-linguistic context.) Irrealis linkers appear in a wide variety of constructions that express events portrayed as non-actualized.

(4) Irrealis linker in counterfactual construction: KD
Me·n *mí=**hla*** *mu·l*
so say=DIFF.**IRREALIS** that
'**If** she'd said that

ʔa· *ʔč^{h}á·=ʔle* *ʔa·.*
1.AGENT sit=CONDITIONAL 1.AGENT
I'd stay longer.' [But she said ...]

(5) Irrealis linker in conditional construction: FJ
*Wá-q-**hi*** *ʔe*
go-level-SAME.**IRREALIS** COP
'**If** I go

ló·-h-du-w=ʔk^{h}e.
help-IMPFV-IMPFV-PFV=FUTURE
I'll be helping out.'

(6) Irrealis linker in deontic construction: FJ
čá-w=hṯow *ʔé·y=yo-**hi***
house-LOC=from away=go-SAME.**IRREALIS**
'He should leave home *and*

táwhal *da-čé·=ʔle.*
work handling-catch=CONDITIONAL
get a job.'

(7) Irrealis linker in future construction: FJ
Té·nta=lil *wá-·n-**hi***
town=to go-IMPFV-SAME.**IRREALIS**
'I'll bring it back

ʔa· *qó=be-w=ʔk^{h}e.*
1.AGENT toward=carry-PFV=FUTURE
on my way to town.' ('I'll go to town and bring it back.')

(8) Irrealis linker in hortative construction: FJ
Ya=ka *háy* *š-dí-č-ma-**hi***
1.PL.AGT=INF wood drag-carry-INCH-CO-SAME.**IRREALIS**
'Let's get some wood **and**
qʰá=kay *š-dí-č-ma-w=ʔkʰe.*
water=too dragging-carry-INCHOATIVE-CO-PFV=FUTURE
haul in some water.'

(9) Irrealis linker in imperative construction: EO
Qʰá *čʰní·=ʔel* *dó-č-**hi**,*
water bread=the make-SEMELFACTIVE-SAME.**IRREALIS**
'Make the water bread *and*

mú·tu-ya-l *qa·-wá·-č̓-ka-m.*
3-PL-PATIENT biting-go-IMPFV.PL-CAUSATIVE-IMPERATIVE
invite them to eat it.'

1.2. Central Pomo Realis clause linkers

There are two pair of Realis dependent markers. They link past or present events. (There are no past or present tense markers.) One pair, *-in* and *=da* 'while', link simultaneous actions or states. The actions or states need not be simultaneous for their full duration, but simply overlapping at some point. The first marker, *-(i)n*, links what are portrayed as components of the same event.

(10) Simultaneous Realis, same event: EO
ʔa· *Edna=to* *čá=·l* *yó-·h-du-**n**.*
1.AGENT =PATIENT house=to go-PFV-IMPFV-SAME.SIM-**REALIS**
'I go to Edna's house **and**

híntil=ʔel *ča·nó-·d-an=ya* *mú·tu.*
Indian=the talk-IMPFV-IMPFV=EVID 3.PATIENT
talk Indian to her.'

The other, *=da*, links what are portrayed as distinct events.

(11) Simultaneous Realis, different events: SA
Mu·l *ʔoč̓* *qašóy=**da***
that still alive=DIFF.SIM.**REALIS**
'**While** he was still alive,

me·n=da *ʔ=mu·l* *to·* *qʰaʔá-n* *ʔe* *mu·l*
such=at COP=that 1.PATIENT dream-IMPFV COP that
I dreamed that

to· *ʔ-t̓á-w* *he* *čanó-č̓.*
1.PATIENT with.fingers-sense-PFV and/or talk-SEMELFACTIVE.PFV
he touched me and said something.'

The second Realis pair, *-ba*/*=li* 'and then', link clauses expressing consecutive events.

(12) Sequential Realis, same event: SA
*Mu·l šó·-č-**ba*** *qamát̓* *t̓á·-ʔ-du-w.*
that hear-SML-SAME.SEQ.**REALIS** angry sense-RFL-IMPFV-PFV
'I heard that **and** got mad.' or '**When** I heard that, I got mad.'

(13) Sequential Realis, different events: FP
to· *meṭ̓* *ʔ-né-·ya-w=**li***
1.PATIENT such gravity-set-DEFOCUS-PFV=DIFF.SEQ.**REALIS**
'I was nominated **and**

míya· *mé* *dá-·ʔ-du-w* *č̓ʰó-w.*
3.POSS father like-RFL-IMPFV-PFV not-PFV
his father didn't like it.'
(or '**When** I was nominated, his father didn't like it.')

Clauses expressing habitual and past habitual events are also linked with Realis markers.

(14) Central Pomo past habitual: FP
Behé·m ...
pepperwood
'Pepperwood,

méṭ̓=li *mu·l* *qʰá-·* *qó·m-ad-an*
that.kind=with that water-LOC bathe-IMPFV-IMPFV
'he would bathe with that

*qasíl=**da*** *šé·maʔwi.*
be.cold=DIFF.SIM.**REALIS** early.morning
early in the morning **when** it was cold.'

Multiple markers can appear within a sentence. In (15), 'grab' and 'pull out' are joined by *-ba*, both of which are in turn linked by *=da* to the verb 'cut'.

(15) Central Pomo linked dependent clauses: SA
*tʰaná=ʔel da-čé-**ba***
hand=the handling-seize-SAME.SEQ.**REALIS**
'**When** they grabbed his hand **and**

*š-ṭʰí-č-na-w=**da**,*
drawing-open-SEMELFACTIVE-AWAY-PFV=DIFF.SEQ.**REALIS**
pulled it (a knife) out,

šʔún mu·l ča-qʰá-č̓-ka-m=ma.
self that sawing-cut-RFL-CAUS-PFV=FACTUAL
he cut himself.'

1.3 *The classification of questions*

Questions show the same Irrealis/realis classification as their declarative counterparts. The future question in (16) contains an Irrealis linker.

(16) Irrealis question: FP
ʔí=wa ma ša-čó-t=ʔkʰe
be=Q 2.AGENT swinging-whip-MULTIPLE.EVENT=FUTURE
'Are you gonna whip us

*ya-l ča=·l dé-m-ma-**hi**?*
1.PL-PATIENT house=to lead.PL-M.E.-CO-SAME.**IRREALIS**
when you take us home?'

The question about the past in (17) contains a Realis marker.

(17) Realis question: FJ
*Tʰaná da·-sé-·č̓-**ba***=wa
hand pulling-wash-RFL-SAME.SEQ.**REALIS**=Q
'Did you wash your hands **and**

ma ʔé· čʰʔól-č̓i-w?
2.AGENT hair comb-RFL-PFV
comb your hair?'

1.4 *The classification of negatives*

Similarly, negatives show the same Irrealis/Realis categorization as their positive counterparts. The negative counterfactual construction in (18) contains an Irrealis linker, as would its positive counterpart.

(18) Irrealis negative counterfactual: FJ

Mu·l	*ˀa·*	*mu·l*	*yhé-·n*	*č^{h}ó-w=**hla***
that	1.AGENT	that	do-IMPFV	not-PFV=DIFF.**IRREALIS**

'**If** I hadn't done that

sí·n	*p^{h}ta·*	*ya*	*šṭ'ó,*	*bel*	*mačí,*	*nap^{h}ó=ˀle.*
how	wonder	1.PL	now	this	day	sit.PL=CONDITIONAL

I wonder where we'd be today.'

The negative conditional construction in (19) contains an Irrealis linker, as would its positive counterpart.

(19) Irrealis negative conditional: SA

Ma	*me·n*	*ˀí-w*	*č^{h}ó-w=**hla**,*
2.AGENT	such	do-PFV	not-PFV=DIFF.**IRREALIS**

'**If** you don't do that,

ma	*bé=da*	*ma·*	*baséṭ'*	*ṭ^{h}abá·ˀč'i-w*	*p^h-wí-w=ˀk e.*
2.AGT	this=at	things	bad	lie-INCH-PFV	vis-perceive-PFV-FUT

you're going to see some bad things happening around here.'

The negative imperative in (20) contains an Irrealis linker, just like positive imperatives.

(20) Irrealis negative command: FJ

Dá=·wi	*ˀč^{h}á·č-**hi***
road=on	stop-SAME.**IRREALIS**

'Don't stop **and**

k^{h}yá	*swé·l-an=ˀk^{h}e*	*t^{h}ín*	*ˀe*	*ma.*
game	play-IMPFV=FUTURE	not-IMPV	COP	2.AGENT

play on the way home.'

The negative statement about the past in (21) contains a Realis linker, just like positive statements about past events.

(21) Realis negative past: FP

Ranch	*=ˀel*	*q̓dí*	*yhé-t-ač̓*	*čʰó-w*	*ˀí-**n***
	=the	good	do-M.E-IMPFV.PL	not-PFV	be-SAME.SIM.**REALIS**

'*Because* they didn't keep up the rancheria,

ya-l	*qó=·l*	*mčá-w*	*dá-·ˀ-č̓i-w.*
1.PL.PATIENT	out=to	throw.PL-PFV	WANT-RFL-IMPFV.PL-PFV

they wanted to throw us out.'

The Central Pomo Irrealis/Realis distinction is strikingly similar to those in a large number of other unrelated languages. In the Papuan language Amele, for example, described in Roberts (1990), dependent clauses are also identified by markers that carry an Irrealis/Realis distinction. Counterfactual, conditional, obligatory, future, hortatory, and imperative constructions appear with Irrealis markers, essentially the same construction types as in Central Pomo. Past, present, and habitual actions are linked with Realis markers. The Realis markers further distinguish simultaneous and sequential events. Questions and negatives show the same Irrealis/Realis classification as would their positive declarative counterparts. It is not difficult to discern a motivation behind the choice of terms 'Irrealis' and 'Realis' for this distinction. Statements categorized as Irrealis portray events as still within the realm of thought alone, while those categorized as Realis are portrayed as actualized, actually occurring or having occurred.

Categories identified as 'Irrealis' and 'Realis' are not uniform across all languages, however. While many languages show patterns strikingly similar to those in Central Pomo and Amele, some show minor differences, and a few show substantial ones. The variation suggests that either the distinction underlying the categories is not in fact comparable across languages, or that the distinction is constant, but its application differs. If the basic distinction varies, then the common terminology could be misleading. If the distinction is the same, and differences are confined to its application, the variation might be explicable in terms of the diachronic developments of grammatical categories in individual languages.

2. Some cross-linguistic differences

Some kinds of constructions, such as counterfactuals and conditionals, are generally classified as Irrealis in all languages with a grammaticized Irrealis/Realis distinction. Several constructions show somewhat more variation across languages than these, however, in particular imperatives, futures, questions, and negatives. In what follows, suggestions will be made for kinds of diachronic explanations that might underlie the variation.

2.1 *Imperatives*

In Central Pomo and Amele, commands are classified as Irrealis, as in (9) above. The classification seems motivated, in that commands can easily be conceived of as expressing thoughts of actions rather than the realization or actualization of them. In some languages, however, imperatives are classified as Realis. In Maricopa, for example, a language of the Yuman family in Arizona, reality is indicated by verbal suffixes. Gordon reports that the Irrealis suffix *-h(a)* "is used typically in cases in which no part of the action or state expressed by the verb is realized [...] It can be used to mark simple future, though it is far more usual for it to be used to signal an exhortive or contrary-to-fact sense [...] *-h(a)* is also used in Irrealis (future, possible, or obligation) nominalizations" (1986:109).

(22) Maricopa Irrealis: (Gordon 1986:27, 109)

a. *ny-aay-**ha***
1/2-give-IRREALIS
'I will give it to you.'

b. *haat* *nyi-ttpooy-nt-**ha***
dog.PL PL.OBJ-kill-PL.ACTION-too-IRREALIS
'It might kill dogs too.'

c. *aanylyviim* *m-vaa-kis* *ʔnym-yuu-**ha***
yesterday 2-come-COND 2/1-see-IRREALIS
'If you had come yesterday, you would have seen me.'

Realis suffixes indicate that 'the speaker is presenting the information as fact, not as possibility, inference, or preference. A verb marked with [a Realis suffix] expresses an action, event, or state which is taking place in the present or has taken place in the past' (1986:24).

(23) Maricopa Realis: (Gordon 1986:24)

a. *aham-**m***
hit-**REALIS**
'He hit him.'

b. *hot-hot-**m***
good-good-**REALIS**
'It is very good.'

Imperatives appear with Realis suffixes.

(24) Maricopa imperative: (Gordon 1968:25)
*k-tpuy-**m***
IMP-kill-**REALIS**
'Kill it!'

Several kinds of diachronic developments could lead to a categorization of imperatives as Realis. One possible explanation could come from the order in which an emerging Irrealis form might be applied to new contexts over time. The distinction might first be made only in indicative clauses, then spread only later into other contexts, among them the imperative. Systems in which imperatives are not classified as Irrealis could represent the intermediate stage in such a development. A second possible explanation could come from differing expectations of actuation. While counterfactual propositions are expected not to occur or have occurred at all, imperatives could be seen to imply reasonable expectations of compliance: in some societies, for example the utterance of a command might be taken conventionally to entail immediate and certain performance of an action. A third possible explanation could come from ways in which speakers might exploit the option of overtly marking expectation. Speakers might intentionally mark commands as Realis to imply strong certainty of their immediate actualization. In fact, many languages contain two options: a polite imperative, classified as Irrealis, and a strong imperative, classified as Realis.

Jamul Diegueño, a Yuman language of southern California, contains an Irrealis suffix *-x* that is cognate with the Maricopa *-h(a)*. Miller (1990:119) reports that the suffix appears with counterfactuals, conditionals, potentials, obligations, warnings, desideratives, and futures, as well as in adversative, purpose, and hypothetical relative clauses and nominalizations. It marks action that is 'desired, potential, or otherwise unrealized'. Realis constructions show no *-x*. Jamul contains two kinds of Imperative constructions: a

Polite Imperative, containing the basic second person Subject Prefix and an Irrealis Suffix, and a Basic Imperative, containing a special Second Person imperative Prefix and no Irrealis Suffix.

(25) Jamul Diegueño Imperatives (Miller 1990:119),
a. *nya-m-mápa-pu* *m-rar-**x**-s*
INDEF-2-NOM.want-DEM 2-do-**IRREALIS**-EMPH
'Do whatever you want (polite imperative)'

b. *k-naw*
2-run
'Run! (basic imperative)'

Roberts (1990:390) notes that Alamblak, an East Sepik language of Papua New Guinea, shows a similar choice. Polite Imperatives are categorized as Irrealis, and strong imperatives as Realis. Roberts points out the parallel with English commands: *Would you be seated* versus *Sit down!*. The presence of both Irrealis and Realis imperatives in these languages shows that both options are semantically possible.

2.2 *Futures*

Future events are often classified as Irrealis cross-linguistically, in languages that have such a catogory, since they have not (yet) occurred (Comrie 1985:45; Givón 1994). In a few languages, however, including Caddo (Chafe this volume), future events are classified as Realis.

One possible explanation for the existence of Realis futures is parallel to one of those proposed for Realis imperatives. Futures can vary in their probability of occurrence. Speakers could exploit the Irrealis/Realis distinction to mark their expectation of actuation. The Central Pomo Irrealis/Realis distinction is in fact used for this very purpose. While most Futures are categorized by speakers as Irrealis, as in (5), (7), and (16) above, some are categorized as Realis. Discussing how they would spend the Fourth of July, Mrs. Paoli remarked that they would go to the annual community picnic, then continued with (26).

(26) Central Pomo Realis Future: FP
*Maʔá qa·-wá-·č̓-**in***
food biting-go-IMPFV.PL-SAME.SIM.**REALIS**
'We'll go around

hlá-·ʔw-ač̓=kʰe.
walk.PL-around-IMPFV.PL=FUTURE
eating.'

On another occasion, Mrs. Jack related what her mother had told her as a child.

(27) Central Pomo Realis Future: FJ
šé· *ʔul* *ma,*
long.time already 2.AGENT
'In the future,

*yém-aq̓=**da**,*
old-INCHOATIVE.PFV=DIFF.SIM.**REALIS**
when you are older,

ʔa· *čʰó-w=**da**,*
1.AGENT not-PFV=DIFF.SIM.**REALIS**
when I am no longer here,

ma *ʔyá-·q-an-ka-w=ʔkʰe.* ...
2.AGENT know-INCHOATIVE-IMPFV-CAUS-PFV=FUTURE
you will remember. ...

ʔa· *čʰó-w=**da**,*
1.agent not-PFV=DIFF.SIM.**REALIS**
After I am gone,

má *ʔbá-·n-či̓-w=ʔkʰe.* ...
2.AGENT suffer-DUR-REFL-PFV=FUTURE
you will suffer.'

The use of the Realis linkers with futures was not a mistake. The choice was significant. Mrs. Jack produced the sentence in (28) as an elicited translation.

(28) Central Pomo: FJ
Ma-báya *čá-·l* *yó-w=**da***
POSS-man house=to go-PFV=DIFF.SIM.**REALIS**
'**When** her husband gets home,

ʔe *mu·l* *maʔá* *čʰú-w=ʔkʰe.*
COP that food eat-PFV=FUT
she'll eat.'

When asked about the use of *=da* in this context, she replied, 'With *=da* he'll get home for sure.' The Irrealis counterpart *=hla* would suggest some uncertainty. The Realis futures cited in (26) and (27) above were used for events the speaker portrayed as certain to occur: eating at the picnic, getting older, and dying.

The Central Pomo option of categorizing futures as either Irrealis (frequent) or Realis (rarer) shows that both are semantically coherent combinations. A system in which futures were systematically categorized as Realis could conceivably arise because the Irrealis form was so highly marked semantically that speakers used it sparingly with futures. Such a scenario is certainly not the only way in which such a pattern could develop. Chafe (this volume) describes a possible path of development of a different sort for Caddo, in which structural characteristics of the markers shape the system.

2.3 *Questions and negatives*

In many languages, including Central Pomo and Amele, interrogation and negation have no effect on the reality marking of clauses. Questions about hypothetical situations are generally categorized as Irrealis, while questions about actualized events are generally categorized as Realis, just like their declarative counterparts. Similarly, negative constructions show the same Irrealis or Realis categorization as their positive counterparts. The situation is quite different in Caddo, however, where questions and negatives are systematically categorized as Irrealis.

In fact the differences between the two systems are not as chaotic as they may first appear. They reflect a contrast in the semantic scope of the reality markers on the one side and the interrogative and negative markers on the other. In Central Pomo, basic propositions are categorized as Irrealis or Realis, independently of their status as statements or questions.

(29) Central Pomo Questions

QUESTION (REALIS (PROPOSITION))

In (30), cited earlier as (16), the basic proposition is categorized as Irrealis on the basis of its futurity. The Irrealis proposition is then questioned.

(30) Central Pomo questioned Irrealis: FP
*ˀí=wa ma šačót=ˀkʰe yal ča·l démma-**hi**ˀ*
be=Q you whip=FUT us home take-when.**IRREALIS**
'Are you gonna whip us when you take us home?'

QUESTION (- REALIS (you will whip us))

In (31), cited earlier as (17), the basic proposition is categorized as Realis on the basis of its past perfective status. The complete Realis past perfective event is then questioned.

(31) Central Pomo questioned Realis: FJ
*Tʰaná da·sé·č̓-**ba**=wa ma ˀé· čʰˀólč̓iw?*
hand wash-**SAME.SEQ.REALIS=Q** you hair comb.PFV
'Did you wash your hands and comb your hair?'

QUESTION (+ REALIS (you washed your hands and combed your hair))

Caddo questions show the opposite scope relations. Reality marking is sensitive to the status of sentences as questions.

(32) Caddo Questions

- REALIS (QUESTION (PROPOSITION))

All Caddo questions are categorized as Irrealis: questioned propositions are not asserted to have occurred.

(33) Caddo Irrealis question: Chafe this volume
süyybáwnah
***sah**ˀ-yibahw-nah*
2.AGENT.**IRREALIS**-see-PERFECT
'Have you seen him?'

- REALIS (QUESTION (you saw him))

Similar semantic scope differences can be seen by comparing the negative constructions in Central Pomo and Caddo. In Central Pomo, propositions are categorized as Irrealis or Realis independently of negation.

(34) Central Pomo Negatives

NEGATION (REALIS (PROPOSITION))

In (35), cited earlier in (19), the proposition is categorized as Irrealis on the basis of its conditional status. The Irrealis conditional clause is then negated.

(35) Central Pomo negated Irrealis: SA
*Ma me·n ˀíw č^{h}ów=**hla*** . . .
you such do.PFV not.PFV=if.**IRREALIS**
'**If** you don't do that, [you're going to see some bad things happening].'

NEGATIVE (- REALIS (you will do that)

In (36), cited earlier in (21), the proposition is categorized as Realis because it expresses a past perfective event. This Realis construction is then negated.

(36) Central Pomo negated Realis: FP
*Ranch= ˀel q̓dí yhétač̓ č^{h}ów ˀí-**n*** ...
the good do not-PFV not be.**REALIS**
'*Because* they didn't keep up the rancheria, [they wanted to throw us out].'

NEGATIVE (+ REALIS (they kept up the rancheria))

The opposite scope relations can be seen in Caddo. Reality categorization is sensitive to negation.

(37) Caddo negation

- REALIS (NEGATIVE (PROPOSITION))

All negative statements are categorized as Irrealis in Caddo, since they report non-actualized events or states.

(38) Caddo Irrealis negative (Chafe this volume)
kút'áybah
*kúy-**t'a**-*yibahw
NEG-1.AGENT.**IRREALIS**-see
'I don't see him.'

- REALIS (NEGATIVE (I see him))

Such cross-linguistic differences in semantic scope are not unusual. English and German show a similar contrast in *must not* ('it is necessary that one not ...') versus *muss nicht* ('it is not necessary that one ...').

The scope relations described here for Central Pomo and Caddo correctly predict the categorization of negative commands, or prohibitives in each language. In Central Pomo, prohibitives are systematically categorized as Irrealis on the basis of their imperative status.

(39) Central Pomo scope relations: imperatives
commands: - REALIS (IMPERATIVE)
prohibitions: NEGATIVE (-REALIS (IMPERATIVE)).

(40) Central Pomo prohibitive: FJ

Dá·wi	*ʔč^há·č-**hi***	*k^hyá*	*swé·lanʔkhe*	*t̥^hín*	*ʔe*	*ma.*
road.on	stop-SAME.IRREALIS	game	play	not	it.is	you

'Don't stop **and** play on the way home!'

NEGATION (- REALIS (IMPERATIVE (you stop and play on the way home)))

In Caddo, prohibitions are systematically categorized as Irrealis as well but on the basis of their negativity.

(41) Caddo scope relations: Imperatives
commands: + REALIS (IMPERATIVE)
prohibitions: - REALIS (NEGATIVE (IMPERATIVE))

(42) Caddo Prohibitive: (Chafe this volume)
kaššáyʔbah
*kaš-**sah**ʔ-yibahw*
NEG-2.AGT.**IRREALIS**-see
'Don't look at it!'

- REALIS (NEGATIVE (IMPERATIVE (you look at it)

Such scope differences could arise in a number of ways. A simple hypothesis would be that scope differences might result from differences in the order in which the distinctions are grammaticized. Their paths of development can be much more complex, however. Scope relations may even shift within the history of a single language.

Mesa Grande Diegueño, a Yuman language of southern California closely related to Jamul, contains an Irrealis suffix *-x* cognate with the Jamul Irrealis suffix of the same form (Langdon 1970:158-9). The suffixes appear in all of the same contexts except for one: in Mesa Grande, negated clauses obligatorily carry the Irrealis suffix, but in Jamul they do not.

In Mesa Grande, negation is indicated by an inflected negative auxiliary verb. In the sentence in (43), the verb 'for me to go' carries the Irrealis suffix as the hypothetical complement of want, but the verb 'they want it' carries the Irrealis suffix only because the sentence is negated.

(43) Mesa Grande negative (Langdon 1970:159)

ʔənya·	*puy*	*ʔəxap-x-vu*	*əwa·p-**x***	*uma·w.*
I	there	I.go.in-IRREALIS-SPEC	they.want.it-**IRREALIS**	they.not

'They didn't want me to go there.'

In Jamul, negation is indicated by a clause final negative word, such as *xemaaw* in (44) below. The negative sentence contains no Irrealis suffix unless required for some other reason, such as a conditional context.

(44) Jamul negative (Miller 1990:113)

nya'wach	*yu'ip*	*xemaaw.*
we.SUBJ	hear.PL	NEG

'We didn't hear.'

An examination of the forms of the Jamul Negative words indicates that there has been a shift within Jamul. All three negatives, *xemaaw* 'not', *xchan* 'almost, but not', and *xmir* 'not yet', begin with *x*. The Irrealis suffix which originally appeared on the verb immediately preceding the negative has been reanalyzed as part of the negative marker itself. Miller (1990:203-5) reports that the negative words, which she terms 'expiring auxiliaries', have lost characteristics of auxiliaries, and no longer bear inflectional prefixes for person of subject.

3. Conclusion

The comparison of the Irrealis/Realis distinctions described here suggests some fruitful directions for the investigation of grammaticization patterns. In Central Pomo, as in many other languages, counterfactual, conditional, deontic, future, hortative, and imperative constructions all contain Irrealis markers. Some of these types, such as counterfactual and conditional constructions, are widely categorized as Irrealis cross-linguistically. They are in fact often cited as the best evidence for the appropriateness of the label 'Irrealis' for a marker. Counterfactual and conditional constructions convey ideas that are most clearly within the realm of thought (imagination) rather than actualized reality (perception).

Imperatives are classified as Irrealis in many languages, but not all. Several kinds of diachronic explanations might underlie the discrepancy. An emerging Irrealis distinction might first be applied within a small grammatical context in a language, such as statements, before expanding to other construction types such as commands. An alternative explanation might come from the fact that imperatives could be viewed as closer to potential actuation than counterfactuals or conditionals. The utterance of a command might imply an expectation of immediate compliance. A third kind of explanation could involve speakers' exploitation of the distinction for expressive purposes. Speakers might choose to use Realis imperatives to reinforce the implied expectation that the act is certain to be carried out, soon to be actualized. The possibility of such a scenario is strengthened by the existence in a number of languages of two options: a polite imperative classified as Irrealis, and a strong imperative classified as Realis.

Futures are classified as Irrealis in most languages; they represent events that have not yet occurred, events still within the realm of thought. On occasion, however, they are marked as Realis. Again, several possible paths of diachronic development might lead to this cross-linguistic variation. Chafe (this volume) shows how the presence of a future suffix in Caddo may have obviated the need for the development of a new construction based on newly emerging Irrealis forms. Alternatively, Realis futures might result from conditions similar to those hypothesized to underlie Realis imperatives. Futures might be seen to assert imminent actuation. Speakers might choose to exploit the Irrealis/Realis distinction to express varying expectations of actuation. In fact in Central Pomo, futures may be classified as either Irrealis or Realis, depending on the speaker's portrayal of the event in question as merely probable or certain to occur.

Interrogation and negation have no effect on reality classification in many languages. In Central Pomo, for example, questioned or negated futures are Irrealis, just like their positive declarative counterparts, while questioned or negated past perfectives are Realis. In other languages, however, such as Caddo, questions and/or negatives are systematically classified as Irrealis. These differences are not as obviously attributable to varying expectations of actuation. They may instead reflect a difference in the relative semantic scope of the markers within the languages. In languages like Central Pomo, reality categorization has narrower scope than interrogation and negation. Propositions are categorized as Irrealis or Realis independently of their status as questions or negatives. In languages like Caddo, the scope relations are reversed. Question formation and negation have narrower scope than reality categorization. The Irrealis/Realis classification is thus sensitive to the status of constructions as questions or negatives. A number of diachronic paths could lead to such differences in semantic scope. One might be a difference in the order of grammaticization of the individual constructions within a language. Others might be more complex, such as the Jamul formal reanalysis of the negative construction.

The comparison of these seemingly disparate systems shows complete accord in the nature of the basic Irrealis/realis distinction that underlies them. In all of the languages, events and states classified as nonactualized, those that remain within the realm of thought and imagination, are overtly distinguished from those portrayed as actualized, having occurred or currently occurring. The differences among the systems lie in the application of the distinction to various contexts, the categorization of individual grammatical constructions within each language. Some differences may result from special uses of the distinction for expressive purposes, such as the classification of Imperatives as Realis to indicate certainty of immediate actualization. Some may stem from differences in the degree of probability deemed necessary for Irrealis marking, as in the case of futures. Some may mirror differences in the relative semantic scope of the Irrealis/Realis distinction and other grammatical distinctions, such as interrogative or negative. Such scope differences could arise in many ways, only a few of which have been explored here.

If the 'Irrealis/Realis' terminology were not used, the cross-linguistic convergences in the semantic nature of the distinction, and the contrasts in its application, might go unnoticed. Of course special care should be taken in cross-linguistic comparisons of these categories, as with any modal categories, to ensure that the distinctions on which they are based are indeed comparable. Grammarians describing particular languages can help to prevent misunderstandings if they provide sufficient evidence that a particular marker does indeed represent the nonactualization of Irrealis mood in a variety of contexts, for example, rather than the temporal deixis of future tense. With such care, this area of modality will give us much to discover about processes of grammaticization that lead to the convergence and divergence of grammatical systems.

ABBREVIATIONS

CO	COOPERATIVE	SEQ	SEQUENTIAL
DIFF	DIFFERENT EVENT	SIM	SIMULTANEOUS
INF	INFERENTIAL	SPEC	SPECIFIC
M.E.	MULTIPLE.EVENT		

NOTE

* Edith Bavin, Joan Bybee, and Suzanne Fleischman provided helpful comments on an earlier draft of this paper.

REFERENCES

Buckley, Eugene 1988. "Temporal Boundaries in Alsea." *Proceedings of the Berkeley Linguistics Society*, 14.10-22.

Bybee, Joan, William Pagliuca & Revere Perkins. 1994. *The Evolution of Grammar: Tense, Aspect and Modality in the Languages of the World.* Chicago: University of Chicago Press.

Capell, Arthur. 1971. "The Austronesian Languages of Australian New Guinea." *Current Trends in Linguistics 8: Oceania* ed. by Thomas A. Sebeok, 240-340. The Hague: Mouton.

Chafe, Wallace 1993. "Real and Unreal in Caddo." This volume.

Chung, Sandra & Alan Timberlake. 1985. "Tense, Aspect and Mood." *Language Typology and Syntactic Descrition III*, ed. by Timothy Shopen, 202-258. Cambridge: Cambridge University Press.

Comrie, Bernard. 1985. *Tense.* Cambridge: Cambridge University Press.

Craig, Colette G. 1977. *The Structure of Jacaltec.* Austin: University of Texas Press.

Dempwolff, O. 1939. *Grammatik der Jaben Sprache auf Neuguinea.* Hamburg: Friederichsen de Gruyter.

Eatough, Andrew ms. Central Hill Nisenan: Grammar, Wordlist, and Texts. Santa Cruz: University of California.

Foley, William A. 1986. *The Papuan Languages of New Guinea.* Cambridge: Cambridge University Press.

Givón, Talmy 1994. "Irrealis and the Subjunctive." *Studies in Language* 18.2.

Gordon, Lynn 1986. *Maricopa Morphology and Syntax. (University of California Publications in Linguistics* 108.) Berkeley: University of California Press.

Langdon, Margaret 1970. A Grammar of Diegueño: The Mesa Grande Dialect. *University of California Publications in Linguistics* 66. Berkeley: University of California Press.

Miller, Amy 1990. A Grammar of Jamul Diegueño. Ph.D. dissertation, University of California, San Diego.
Palmer, Frank R. 1986. *Mood and Modality*. Cambridge: Cambridge University Press.
Payne, Doris L. & Thomas E. Payne. 1990. Yagua. *Handbook of Amazonian Languages*, ed. by Desmond C. Derbyshire & Geoffrey K. Pullum, 2.249-474. Berlin: Mouton de Gruyter.
Roberts, John R. 1990. "Modality in Amele and other Papuan Languages." *Journal of Linguistics* 26: 363-401.
Romaine, Suzanne 1993. "The Grammaticalization of Irrealis in Tok Pisin." This volume.

The Grammaticalization of Irrealis in Tok Pisin

Suzanne Romaine
Merton College, University of Oxford

0. Introduction*

In this paper I will address a case of semantic and syntactic change involving the grammaticalization of irrealis marking in Tok Pisin, an English-based pidgin/creole spoken in Papua New Guinea. Modality, and in particular, the marking of so-called irrealis, has figured prominently in discussions of tense-mood-aspect (hereafter TMA) systems in pidgins and creoles since Bickerton's claims about the universality of a creole prototype consisting of a three member inventory of preverbal particles marking the same semantic functions. These elements all contrast with the unmarked form of the verb. In most creoles the irrealis marker is rather transparently derived from verbs or auxiliaries such as *go* or *sa* (<*shall*) in English-based creoles. In others such as Tok Pisin, however, a temporal adverbial has been recruited for this function (compare Portuguese-based creoles *lo* from *logo* 'next' with Tok Pisin *baimbai* from 'by and by').

Bickerton (1981:80) identifies three stages in a gradual process which leads to the incorporation of these particles from a clause-external syntactic position to the status of preverbal auxiliaries. Some examples are given in 1 to 3 to illustrate these proposed stages with reference to the grammaticalization of *baimbai* in Tok Pisin.

(1) *Baimbai mi go*
'By and by I'll go.'
(2) *Bai mi go*
'I'll go.'
(3) *Mi bai go*
'I'll go.'

In the first stage *baimbai* and other similar elements appear optionally clause-finally or clause-initially. In the second, they are incorporated into the auxiliary but cannot combine with any Aux constituents, while in the third they display combinatorial capacities. Tok Pisin is not quite in step with Bickerton's stages since in (2) we see a phonologically reduced and unstressed form of *bai* still in clause-external position rather than incorporated within Aux. The third example shows *bai* in preverbal position, but does not specify whether there are any restrictions on its co-occurrence with other Aux constituents. Nevertheless, in many respects Tok Pisin represents an excellent case for examining this alleged sequence of grammaticalization since all three stages currently co-exist. In other ways, however, Tok Pisin's development is atypical, both with respect to what has happened in other pidgins and creoles, as well as with respect to the grammaticalization paths chosen by other languages.

This general sequence of grammaticalization of TMA markers is also taken by many others to be a significant hallmark of creolization. Labov (1977:29), for example, says:

> It is not at all obvious that a pidgin will develop obligatory tense markers when it becomes a native language. Yet this has happened in case after case. When pidgins become creoles, the system of optional adverbs gives way to an obligatory tense marker next to the verb.

More recently, Markey (1982) and Mühlhäusler (1986:156-7) have cited the use of sentence-external propositional qualifiers as a major typological characteristic of pidgins (see also Kay and Sankoff 1974:64). Sankoff and Laberge (1980) argued on the basis of research done in the late 60s and early 70s that the Tok Pisin temporal adverb *baimbai* is becoming a marker of future tense. Moreover, they link this change to "the passage of Tok Pisin from a second language lingua franca to the first language of a generation of urban New Guineans". I will say more about the extent to which such developments are triggered by creolization and exclusive to creoles in Sections 3., 4.3 and 5.

In 2. I situate my use of the term 'irrealis' within the context of modality and explain its relevance to the Tok Pisin case.

Bickerton's claims have been based largely on his analysis of data from Hawai'i Creole English (HCE), partly in the conviction that "data of any kind on the antecedent pidgins of any creole but HCE are simply non-existent" (1981:79). The latter assertion is unwarranted. In this paper I will make use of new historical data on Pidgin English in the Pacific together with synchronic Tok Pisin data I collected during 1986 and 1987 in Papua New Guinea.

1. Brief description of corpus

The spoken data were recorded over a two year period in 1986 and 1987 as part of a study of rural and urban Tok Pisin in two provinces in Papua New Guinea (see Romaine 1992 for further details). The two provinces, Madang and Morobe, lie on the New Guinea Coast. The number of Tok Pisin speakers has been steadily increasing there, though it is difficult to give precise figures. In the 1966 and 1971 Censuses, which covered only 10% of the village population, respondents were asked to say which members of the household over the age of 10 were able to speak Tok Pisin. In Madang Province there has been an increase in the number of reported speakers of Tok Pisin between the years 1966 and 1971 from 62% to 69%, while in Morobe Province it has increased from 47% to 59%.

1.1 *Spoken Data*

The spoken corpus to be dealt with here consists of tape-recorded material comprising some 700,000 words from nearly 500 children and adults. The majority of the speakers fall between the ages of 5 and 17 and were drawn from 11 areas. I have indicated in Table 1 the nine areas which I will discuss here; in those marked urban, the children are largely first language speakers, while in rural areas the children are mainly second language speakers. Adults are not included in the numbers given here, although I will discuss some data collected from adults in one of the rural areas, Indagen. The Unitech sample is a longitudinal mini-sample within the larger survey. These children were first contacted and interviewed at a school in Lae. Their parents live on the campus of the Papua New Guinea University of Technology and they took part in regular after-school recording sessions over a period of two years. The data for these children consist of narratives, free play and video story retellings. In other areas such as Indagen and Bulolo there are some longitudinal data too since some of the same speakers were interviewed in 1986 and 1987.

1.2 *The Written Corpus*

At the same time as the analysis of the spoken material is being carried out, I have been compiling a corpus of written texts (both contemporary and historical) for comparison. Table 2 gives brief details of that part of the corpus I will be referring to here and further information about the texts can be found in Romaine (1992). *Nupela Testamen* (the 1966 translation of the New Testament) and the weekly newspaper in pidgin, *Wantok*, played important roles in the standardization of Tok Pisin. The other two main sources which were used to make up the written corpus are *Save Na Mekim* (Understanding and Doing;

Table 1. *Details of Sample of Spoken Data*

Province	Date	Location	Setting	N. children	No.words
Morobe	1986	Lae/Taraka	urban	74	70782
	1986	Lae/Unitech		12	30619
	1986	Bulolo	urban	18	16092
	1986/7	Indagen	rural	79	108572
	1987	Geraoun	rural	33	14768
	1987	Waritsian	rural	32	51113
Madang	1987	Kusbau	urban	104	178472
	1987	Rempi	rural	42	67815
	1987	Erima	rural	40	60497
	1987	Bahor	rural	48	106391
TOTAL				482	705121

Table 2. *The written corpus*

Text	Date	No. words
Nupela Testamen	1966	3720
Wantok	1982	9838
Save Na Mekim	1982	4825
Konstitusen	1986	3453
personal letters	1986/7	1294
TOTAL		23130

Bergman 1982) and *Konstitusen Bilong Independen Kantri Papua Niugini* (The Constitution of the Independent Country Papua New Guinea; Mihalic 1986a). In each case samples were taken from these texts for analysis. The total corpus amounts to some 23,000 words.

The written corpus also includes a small sample of 7 personal letters sent to me by various speakers. These were written by a houseboy in Lae (N = 2); two women in Indagen (N= 3); 2 women in Madang who run a mobile pre-school unit (N = 1); the headman of Musep village, near Indagen (N = 1). There is also one official letter written by the assistant secretary to Morobe Province advising various community governments about the research I was doing.

2. *Baimbai, bai* and the marking of irrealis

It is not entirely clear from the historical record when *baimbai* began giving way to *bai*. My guess is that this happened sometime in the 1950s and 1960s, but I will have more to say about that in 3. All three stages are represented in the data from Bulolo, Unitech (Lae), Erima and Indagen, as can be seen in examples (4) to (8). The same is true incidentally for the speech of adults.

(4) *Baimbai yu kaikai.* [BL1F4]. [1]
'Then [after you've cooked], you'll eat.'

(5) *Mi droim maunten, na bihain bai mi wokim wara wantaim.* [BL1M5].
'I'll draw the mountain, and then I'll do the water that goes with it.'

(6) *Em i go insait nau, bai ol kaikai* [IND1F1]
'He went inside and then they ate.'

(7) *Yu stretim ston insait long hul ia orait ston bai stap nau bai yu stretim hul ok yu putim disla kaikai ia* [BL M5]
'You arrange the stones inside the pit, and once the stones are there, you arrange the pit and you put the food in.'

(8) *Ol man bai bihainim em ol bai kisim em.* [IND1F1]
'The men then followed him and they caught him.'

Example (4) is one of ten examples of *baimbai* I have found so far in the children's corpus. The speaker is a fourth grade girl in Bulolo, who is a second language speaker of Tok Pisin from Irian Jaya. She also uses *bai* in both clause-initial and preverbal position, as can be seen in (9). The only other instances of *baimbai* are from one of the Unitech girls and the children in Erima.

(9) *Nau wanpla longlong man ia draipla kanu blem, nau disla longlong ia em sa kaikai ol man nau. Longlong man ia kam luk ol manki na em tok, "Yupla sa waswas long ia, mi kisim yupla go, bai mi lusim yupla na yu bai waswas long disla". Na em kisim ol go.* [BL1F4].
'There was a crazy man who had a canoe, and he ate people. This crazy man saw the boys and said, "You boys wash over here and I'll catch you, now I'll leave and you'll wash over there." Then he got them.'

Thus, even today all three stages of this process of grammaticalization can be represented synchronically in the speech of one speaker. It is evident, however, that even at the time when Sankoff and Laberge obtained their data, *baimbai* was a recessive feature. In a corpus of 395 examples of *bai* in the speech of 18 people (9 children and adolescents between the ages of 5 and 17, and 9 adults between the ages of 25-45) recorded near Lae, they found only five instances of *baimbai*. These were phonetically already somewhat reduced, i.e. [bəm'bai] or [bə'bai] and were found in the speech of three of the nine adults. There were no instances of *baimbai* in the speech of the children they interviewed (see Romaine and Wright (1987) on morphophonological condensation in children's speech). Nevertheless, it is clear from my data that the use of *baimbai* is not entirely exclusive to rural and/or second language speakers, or adults.

As far as the meaning of *baimbai* and *bai* is concerned, it will be obvious even from the few examples I have given here that *bai* is a highly redundant marker which signals more than time relations. It often occurs with other adverbs indicating relations of time or the sequence of events. For example, in 5, the connectives *na bihain* 'and then/afterwards' make it clear that the activity of the second clause takes place after that reported in the first. In this context *bai* is clearly redundant, and functions not so much as a tense marker but merely as a sequence marker in discourse. This use of *bai* is in line with its historical origin as a temporal adverb. In some texts it appears almost with every clause. This can be seen in (10).

(10) *Krokodail tok olsem, "Nau bai mi go long wara na bai mi painim ol dok na ol dok bai sindaun, bai mi kisim em go long aus bilong em. Em bai wokabaut bilong mi.", em tok, krokodail olsem. Krokodail tok olsem, "Bai mi go long wara na painim dok". Na em go long wara na em lukim bikpla ston na dok sindaun i stap.* [IND1F6].
'The crocodile said, "I'll go down to the river and look for dogs. Dogs will be sitting there and I'll get one and take him back to his house. Then he'll come to mine", the crocodile said. The crocodile said, "I'll go down to the river and look for the dog." He went to the river and saw a big stone and the dog was sitting there.'

Generally speaking, there is no obligatory marking of tense in Tok Pisin. In this extract from a narrative in (10), the context makes it clear that the events referred to take place in the past. The crocodile is of course making statements here about what he will do in the future and uses *bai* to do so. In this respect *bai* marks an intention, but it can also be understood in some respects as a prediction about what will happen at some later point in time. It is this meaning of prediction which is central to the notion of future according to Bybee et al. (1991). I will return to this point in 4.3. Once the direct discourse of the crocodile is finished, we are back into the frame of narrative time, i.e. past events. That is why we find the unmarked verb form *lukim* 'he saw', which is the usual form for reporting past events. The latter is cited by Bickerton (1981) as a general characteristic of creole tense systems; namely, the zero form of the verb encodes past tense for verbs of action. As might be expected from the nature of reported speech, a great many occurrences of *bai* are found in conjunction with it. At this stage I want to introduce the notion of 'irrealis' into the discussion and to claim that *bai* could be regarded either as an irrealis or as a future marker. The paths leading to the grammaticalization of futures and modality intersect at certain points because events in the future are by definition hypothetical and there is some uncertainty about them. In this sense we might say that the common demoninator of irrealis modality is futurity or uncertainty (see Givón 1984:318).

Many linguists have noted the confusing and often overlapping ways in which the terms 'aspect', 'tense', 'mood' and 'modality' have been used. In their discussion of mood and modality Bybee et al. (1994: Ch 6, section 12) comment, in particular, on some of the problems surrounding the use of the term 'irrealis,' especially in discussions of non-Indo-European languages.

The concept of irrealis is clearly central to a consideration of futurity, which is often treated as a matter of tense. Givón (1984:285), for instance, writes that "the future is a clear irrealis tense, dealing with hypothetical, possible, uncertain states or events that have not yet occurred. Roberts (1990:363) includes within the category of irrealis future tense, imperative mood and counterfactual mood, while for Bickerton (1981) irrealis consists of futures and conditionals. These labels refer to meanings which traditionally have been associated with and discussed under the heading of modality. Synchronically, Bybee (1985:156-9) has cited many instances of languages whose future markers have primarily a modal function. Moreover, the diachronic connection between irrealis modality and futurity is clearly indicated in Bybee et al. (1991).

Some such as Roberts (1990:370) have also observed that the English future tense is really a modality because it is expressed with a form which has a modal function. Thus, in Old English, for example, *will* indicated modality, but it has since come to be used as a future auxiliary. He (1990:369) also points out that in many Papuan languages future tense is a modality.

Indeed, in many languages the distinction between realis and irrealis is alleged to be central. Givón (1984:309), for instance, says that many Austronesian languages make their major morphological distinction between realis and irrealis in TMA systems. Roberts (1990) and Foley (1986) have claimed that for many of the Papuan languages the basic distinction is between realis and irrealis. The centrality of the realis/irrealis opposition in both these language families is not without relevance to a discussion of Tok Pisin since they form its substratum in its most comprehensive sense. All of Roberts' principal examples from the Papuan family are spoken in Madang Province, where some of the varieties of Tok Pisin to be discussed here were investigated, but the general patterns he observes have a wider areal distribution, extending into Morobe Province, where the other spoken varieties of Tok Pisin I discuss here were recorded.

In attempting to dismiss the realis/irrealis distinction as ill-founded, Bybee et al. (1994) query whether it is possible for the past habitual to be categorized as irrealis in some languages when it is more generally taken to be a prototypical case of realis in others. Personally, I do no find this problematic (if indeed it is correct) since I believe there are cultural prerequisites to grammatical analysis. In any event, I would suggest instead that it is perhaps more often the case for languages to use the same morpheme to mark both past tense and unreal or hypothetical events and states. As Steele (1975) and others have noted, the basic connection between the past tense and irrealis is their sharing of the characteristic of being distant from present reality. Consider, for instance, the use of the past in hypotheticals such as *I wish I had a new car* (see the discussion in James 1982 and 1991). Verbs in the protases of contrary-to-fact or unreal conditionals referring to the future are also inflected with *-ed* in English, e.g. *If you travelled to Hawai'i, you'd like it there.*

Not surprisingly, *bai* is also used in similar kinds of conditionals in Tok Pisin. This can be seen particularly when *bai* occurs in construction with *sapos* (from 'suppose') in a kind of *if/then* construction as in (11). It can also be used on its own, as in (12), where both the antecedent or cause clause and the result clause are introduced by *bai*. It is semantically equivalent to an *if/then* construction, even though there is no overt marking as such. The extension from temporality to causality in this kind of construction is a natural one in the sense that what is caused is later in time than the event or state which precedes it. As I will show in 4., an understanding of the semantics of *bai* is crucial to interpreting the significance of the syntactic developments I will look at next.

(11) *Sapos fesbon em fesbon meri, bai ol ol kolim Asan.* [BL1F6]
'If the first born child is a girl, then they will call her Asan.'

(12) *Bifo long mipela em ol sa wokim olsem. Man i gat laik long yu na yu no laik. Orait, em man. Em bai makim yu, bai yu no laik long en, bai em bai bagarapim yu disla kain olsem ... Bifo taim bilong tumbuna em kilim meri indai. Em tu bai indai bifo. Nau lo i strong tru. Orait bihainim lo tasol.* [IND1EM].
'Before our custom used to be like this. If a man liked you and you didn't like him. Ok, he's a man. He would mark you. If you didn't like him, then he'd rape you like this. In the old days he would kill a woman and she would die then. Now, however, our laws are powerful and they just have to follow law.'

2.1 *The syntactic distribution of* bai *in nine areas*

I will now look at the syntactic position of *bai* in the nine areas in more detail. My analysis revealed that 56% of the occurrences of *bai* are preverbal, while 44% are clause-initial. The data also show that although *bai* can either precede or follow noun phrases, there is a tendency for noun phrase subjects to occur with preverbal *bai* (see further in Sankoff and Laberge 1980:207). The third person singular pronoun *em* strongly favors the occurrence of preverbal *bai*. The shift to preverbal position appears to begin in the third person singular and then spreads throughout the pronominal paradigm.

My findings on the position of *bai* in the nine individual areas can be compared with those of Sankoff and Laberge shown in Table 3. If we are dealing with on-going change, as they claim, then their data appear to have intersected the change at a point just before *bai* shifts to preverbal position since most of their occurrences of *bai* are still clause-initial. In my data the balance has shifted in favor of preverbal positioning of *bai*. Interestingly, they found no significant differences between the adults and children with respect to the ordering of *bai*.

More specifically, it can be seen that the situation in Bulolo and Rempi more closely parallels that reported by Sankoff and Laberge (1980), who worked in Lae. That is, the shift from clause-initial to preverbal positioning of *bai* is underway, but clause-initial position is at least marginally still the most frequent. It is really only in Indagen that the shift is well advanced, and possibly nearing completion, whereas it is only just beginning in Bulolo and Rempi. The other areas, both rural and urban, represent an intermediate stage. In general, apart from Bulolo and Waritsian, the areas in Morobe Province are ahead of those in Madang. The Taraka children in Lae are most directly comparable to the urban children interviewed by Sankoff and Laberge nearly 20 years ago and it would appear that change has progressed remarkably quickly in that time span in this area.

Judging from past sociolinguistic studies of the role of social factors in linguistic change, we might reasonably expect both sex differentiation and significant age-grading, if change is taking place. Recall that Sankoff and Laberge found no differences between children and adults. However, their data base is too small to show the effect of age grading either between the adult and younger population, or within these groups. Moreover, they do not take into account the possibility of regional differences. My study found no significant gender distinctions in the use of *bai*.

If it is the case that preverbal *bai* represents a change in progress, we would probably find differences between both children and adults as well as within the younger group of speakers. More specifically, we should find that adults and older children showed a predominantly clause-initial pattern and

Table 3. *The distribution of bai in nine areas (compared with Sankoff and Laberge; figures are percent)*

	% Clause-initial	% Preverbal
[Sankoff/Laberge	59	41]
Rempi	58	42
Bulolo	56	44
Kusbau	50	50
Bahor	50	50
Waritsian	47	53
Erima	45	55
Geraoun	39	61
Lae (Taraka)	36	64
(Unitech)	32	68
Indagen	25	75

younger children showed increasing use of preverbal *bai*. There are some indications that this is true, though there is not always a regular age-by-age increment in certain areas. Age grading is particularly apparent for some of the individual areas more so than others. For instance, there is no significant age grading in Bahor, Erima or Geraoun. However, the oldest children in Geraoun use mainly clause-initial *bai*, while the younger ones all use more preverbal *bai*. In Unitech, there is significant age grading between younger and older speakers, which happens to coincide with sex differentiation because the girls are all younger than the boys. All the Indagen children use more preverbal *bai*, though the oldest age group, namely, 16 year-olds use predominantly clause-initial *bai*. The Indagen adults who use 44% clause-initial *bai* are thus behind the younger generation with respect to this change. Age-grading is, however, particularly apparent in the two areas where the shift appears not to be implemented yet, namely Rempi and Bulolo.

Thus, the change appears rather sporadic in its transition and is not clearly progressing in some areas like Erima, Kusbau and Bahor in a regular way which is tied solely to increasing age, but there is still more to be said about the differences between children and adults in my corpus. It is obvious that whatever changes were taking place in the status of *bai* were well underway prior to the existence of a large number of native speakers. If stabilization and nativization are prerequisites for this kind of grammaticalization, then it is surprising that Sankoff and Laberge did not find the change further along in Lae 20 years ago. In fact, they claim (1980:208-9) that not only do native speakers appear to be carrying further tendencies which were

Table 4. *Incidence of bai among first (i.e. urban) and second (i.e. rural) language speakers (figures are normalized to distribution per 1000 words)*

		Normalized	N *bai*	N words
children:	urban	8.0	2374	295965
	rural	7.0	2878	409156
			5252	705121
adults	rural	11.5	498	43221

already present in the language, but also that fluent speakers show no difference from native speakers with respect to use of *bai*. Sankoff and Laberge (1980:205) say that '*bai* seems to be redundant and obligatory for both adults and children', with no observable differences between them. They record almost equal numbers of *bai* for both groups (children = 192; adults = 203).

Certainly at the moment in other areas of the grammar and lexis, those innovations which are associated with town speakers are the ones most likely to be picked up by others (see Romaine, 1989b and 1993). It may be that the reason why Indagen and Geraoun show such a high rate of preverbal usage is that influence from Lae has spread out first to these areas and they have now overgeneralized or accelerated the change, though if that is the case, it is surprising that Bulolo does not follow Lae too. Bulolo is connected to Lae by a relatively good road while Indagen, though closer to Lae (some 25 miles in the mountains to the northeast), is connected by air only. Geraoun is connected only by bush track to Indagen and surrounding areas.

However, by comparing Table 3 with Table 4, we can see statistically significant differences between both rural and urban children as well as between children and adults. Although first language speakers of Tok Pisin clearly use *bai* more frequently overall than second language or rural speakers, it is the second language speakers in rural areas who lead in the introduction of preverbal *bai*. While it would appear that children rather than adults are ahead in introducing preverbal *bai* as the canonical way of marking irrealis, it is the rural adults who show the highest rate of *bai* usage.

To interpret these findings more fully, I turn now to a consideration of the syntactic developments in comparative and historical perspective, and then I will look at the semantic aspects of this change. At that stage I will also return to the question of age grading.

3. Discussion of syntactic developments in historical and comparative perspective

There are at least three issues which need to be discussed in order to clarify the sequence of steps identified by Sankoff and Laberge as part of the grammaticalization process. Firstly, do these stages reflect true diachronic ordering? Secondly, what is the connection between syntactic positioning and phonological reduction? Thirdly, is this sequence coincident with creolization? To take the last question first, I have already indicated that it does not appear to be, despite the fact that Sankoff and Laberge (1980:195) link this change in *bai* to 'the passage of Tok Pisin from a second language lingua franca to the first language of a generation of urban New Guineans'. In order to illuminate all three questions, however, I will need to consider further diachronic and comparative evidence.

Evidence from the formative stages of Tok Pisin's development is very sketchy. Earlier sources mention *baimbai* but not *bai*. This is true even of Mihalic's (1957) first edition of the Tok Pisin grammar and dictionary. Murphy (1966:59), however, lists it in his dictionary and it can be found in print in Tok Pisin newspapers, e.g. *Nius bilong Yumi* published fortnightly by the colonial administration, from the 1960s onwards. In the 1971 edition of his dictionary and grammar, Mihalic (1971:63) lists *bai* with *baimbai* and says that it is derived from English 'by and by', and has the same range of meanings.

It seems likely that *bai* is a result of phonological reduction of *baimbai*, as Sankoff and Laberge claim, even though the two forms have apparently co-existed for some time. Further support for this can be found in Solomon Islands Pijin, a near relative of Tok Pisin. The form *bambae* and its reduced variants *babae* and *bae* are all currently in use and have been for some time. Older speakers (36+) tend to be conservative and use mainly *bambae* and *babae*. The younger generation tend to use *bae* (Jourdan 1985). In Bislama, a variety of Melanesian pidgin spoken in Vanuatu also closely related to Tok Pisin, similar variants are in use, though Crowley (1990:262) reports that *bae* is now more widespread than *bambae* in the modern language. Whatever the precise historical details are, it seems clear that *baimbai* has become very marginal in ordinary conversational use in Tok Pisin, and indeed, much more so than in Bislama and Solomon Islands Pijin.

With regard to the positioning of *bai*, the historical sources which have been discussed by other scholars such as Sankoff and Laberge indicate that clause-initial positioning is the earlier. All of the 11 instances of *baimbai* cited by Churchill (1911:37) are clause- or sentence-initial. Four of these occur before a noun phrase, and the others before pronouns. Mihalic (1957:43) lists *baimbai* with a group of adverbs which he claims are found only at the beginning of a sentence. In his later edition he says only that it is one of a set of adverbs found usually at the beginning of a sentence.

It is striking that none of the earlier historical sources mentions the possibility of preverbal *baimbai*, and Sankoff and Laberge have overlooked it too. I have, however, collected a number of attestations of it both diachronically and synchronically in speech and writing, as can be seen in examples (13) through (42). I will now use them to argue that the question of syntactic positioning of *bai* and phonological reduction must be seen as separate issues. Their conflation by Sankoff and Laberge (and Labov) fails to accommodate a number of competing developments which have made the grammaticalization process less straightforward than it appears. The existence of these examples indicates that the incorporation of the full form *baimbai* within the verb phrase probably existed as a grammatical option long before phonological reduction or creolization, or indeed, the existence of a community of fluent second language speakers.

Examples (13), (14) and (15) are from the earliest textual records from the jargon stage. The first two attestations for pidgin English in New South Wales and Queensland predate the labor trade. Crowley (1990:252) notes there is evidence that the clause-initial future marker also began to appear occasionally in post-subject position in the early 1880s. It is also attested in Samoan Plantation Pidgin, as in (16). Examples (17) through (21) are recorded from the German colonial period. [2]

(13) *me bye and by come back.* [New South Wales, 1844, Troy 1985]
'I'll come back'.

(14) *Suppose you no kill piccaninnies, that fellow by and by jump up kipper.* [Queensland, 1858, Praed 1885]
'If you don't kill the children, they will grow up into adolescents and kill you.'

(15) *Brother belong-a-me by and by he dead.* [reported in Beche-la-mar by E.L. Lazard 1880 in Noumea, New Caledonia to Schuchardt 1883]
'My brother will die soon.' [3]

(16) *Brata bilong mi baimbai dai.* [Samoan Plantation Pidgin, Mühlhäusler 1978:103)
'My brother will die.'
(17) *me think German by and by come and raus em alltogether English.* [Detzner 1920:226]
'Perhaps the Germans will come and get rid of the English completely.'
(18) *German by and by strong belong English.* [Detzner 1921:131].
'The Germans will be strong against the English.'
(19) *Master, I think fight by and by finished, Germans now strong belong English.* [Detzner 1921:177]
'Master, I think the fight will be finished, the Germans are strong against the English.' [4]
(20) *Tripela de baembai i pinis.* [Borchardt 1930]
'Three days will have passed.'[5]
(21) *Now bymby dry* [Vogel 1911:212, Pak Island, Bismarck Archipelago]
'Now the coat will become dry'.

Examples (22), (23) and (24) are all from adult speakers of contemporary varieties of Melanesian Pidgin, namely Solomon Islands Pijin, and Vanuatu Bislama.

(22) *Solomon bambai pinis kaikai.* [PM, Solomon Islander in Samoa, 1975]
'Solomon will finish eating.'
(23) *ou, lotu ia baebae kam i spoel-em devol blong iumi.*
[DA, Talise, Guadalcanal, SI, Keesing 1988:186]
'If this church comes, it will destroy our ancestral spirits'.
(24) *Olsem we yumi save finis, sua nao se gavman bambae i no save tekem tufala lanwis blong Inglis mo Franis i kam wanples.*
[Ligo 1987:83, Bislama]
'As we already know, it is certain that the government will not bring together the two languages English and French.'

Examples (25) through (30) are contemporary spoken instances from adult Tok Pisin speakers. Examples (26) and (27) are from a 71 year-old man, one of the oldest men in Indagen village, while (28) through (30) are from a 52 year-old man, who speaks Boiken, a Papuan language spoken near Wewak in

East Sepik Province. He is a former schoolteacher and government interpreter, who was partly educated in Australia. The Indagen adults produced 8 instances of *baimbai*, half of which were preverbal. Examples (31) through (34) are from children in Erima, who produced a total of 4 instances of *baimbai*, all of which were preverbal.

(25) *Na Zaria i tok, em baimbai kilim yu.* [J. Z'Graggen. Daria A Narratives, Madang Province]
'And Zaria said, he would kill you.' [6]

(26) *Em yet baimbai olim em.* [IND87MISC1BW]
'He himself will hold him.'

(27) *Ol i baimbai i go.* [IND87MISC1BW]
'They will go.'

(28-30) *Mi tok olsem pisin baimbai i karamapim tasol long bihain Inglis bai i karamapim na dispela kantri baimbai trupela tok bilong mampapa bilongen long ples bilong em tru baimbai i pinis.*
[Recording made by J. Fingelton, legal consultant to East Sepik government in 1987].
'I say that pidgin will replace [them i.e. local languages], but later English will replace it and the real language of the older generation of the village will be finished.'

(31) *Em baimbai kam lo kaikai yu.* [ERM1FKW]
'He'll come to eat you.'

(32) *Planti papa empla baimbai koros.* [ERM4MWA]
'Many men will be angry.'

(33) *Moning yumi go, baimbai dikim weisan.* [ERM5FMM]
'In the morning we'll go and dig some sand.'

(34) *Strongpela wot baimbai kisim disla meri.* [ERM5FMM]
'Strong words will get this woman.'

The rest of the examples in (35) to (42) are written, most of them from Bible translations, especially *Nupela Testamen*, but occurrences of preverbal *baimbai* go back to some of the earliest mission texts such as in (35-36). Example (41) is from the newspaper *Nius bilong Yumi* and (42) is from modern written Tok Pisin.

(35-36) *Em baimbai i bringim tok bilong Ridimer, em baimbai i mekim stret ol man.*
[Hall 1955:141, citation from *Liklik Katolik Baibel* 1934]

'He will bring the word of the redeemer, and he will make all men straight.'

(37) *Long las de bilong dispela graun bambai i olsem tasol.*
[*Nupela Testamen*, 1966. Mt. 13:49].
'And on the last day of the world this is the way it will be.'

(38) *Em bambai i kam bek gen wankain.*
[*Nupela Testamen*, 1966. Ap.1:11.]
'He will come back again.'

(39) *Em bambai i save as bilong dispela tok mi autim.*
[*Nupela Testamen*, John 7:17]
'He will know the reason for what I am saying.'

(40) *Skai wantaim graun baimbai i pinis.*
[*Nupela Testamen*, Mk 13:31.]
'Heaven and earth will pass away.'

(41) *Ol dispela man baimbai i stap long Australia inap olsem wan mun. Oli baimbai i stap wantaim arapela kain kain taun kaunsel long Victoria na Tasmania. As bilong limlimbur bilong ol em long baimbai long lukim Australia taun kaunsel wok olsem wanem.* [*Nius bilong Yumi* 15 April 1966. Vol. 8 no.6., p.2].
'These men will stay in Australia for a month. They will visit other kinds of town councils in Victoria and Tasmania. The reason for their extended stay is so that they will be able to see how Australian town councils work.'

(42) *Dispela buk long Tok Pisin i bambai helpim planti pipol long Papua Niugini save long nupela na gutpela we long mekim gut sindaun long ples bilong ol.* [Preface to *Save na Mekim*, 1982. Michael Somare, former Prime Minister]
'This book in Tok Pisin will help plenty of people in PNG to know about new and good ways of making a good life in their villages.'

My examples are important for a number of reasons. They demonstrate the option of using preverbal *baimbai* has apparently been available in the language for at least a century, if we accept examples like (13) through (21) as accurate renditions, and it still exists today in the speech and writing of fluent users. They show that phonological reduction is neither a necessary nor sufficient precondition for preverbal placement of the marker. Example (43) may also provide evidence for the possibility of yet another variant, namely, a clause-initial reduced form of *baimbai.*

(43) *bam yu go stap*? [ERM5FMM]
'Will you go and stay there?'

This means that there is good reason to question the strict chronicity and implicational relationships among the three stages proposed by Sankoff and Laberge. The existence of preverbal *bai* today may derive from reduction of preverbal *baimbai* in situ rather than by movement, and therefore, their stages do not correspond to discrete points in time. Thus, the use of clause-initial *bai* need not represent an intermediate stage in the grammaticalization. It is possible of course that the synchronic examples are not survivals in any direct sense of the earlier attestations, and are therefore not genuine reflexes of this construction. They may be simply analogical reformations patterned on preverbal *bai*. In fact, Sankoff and Laberge (1980:201) note a personal communication from Anne Chowning, who claims that "in areas of New Britain in the 1950s, *bai* was the exclusively used form, with *baimbai* appearing later as a novel introduction". It is dangerous to assume, although it is commonly done, that older speakers preserve an earlier stage of the language and do not change their speech over the course of their lifetimes.

It would likewise be a mistake to assume too much continuity in the life cycle of a pidgin. It should not be surprising that the same structural innovations arise at different stages in the development of a language and either spread or fade away. The possiblity of convergent etymology as an important factor in determining lexicalization in pidgin and creole languages (see Romaine 1988) is now widely acknowledged, and it seems plausible to assume that structures compete for grammaticalization too. The more potential sources for grammaticalization of a construction, the more likely that construction is to be incorporated, though different speakers may pull the language in different directions.

There is also another structural possibility which could have paved the way for the grammaticalization of *bai* in preverbal position. A number of the children and adults use the form *em bai*, as in (44) and (45). Here the third person pronoun *em* is not syntactically integrated as a clause argument. It is easy to see how speakers might have regarded this as a short form of *baimbai* if we return to example (12), where we have a case in which *bai* appears on both sides of the third person singular pronoun *em*, i.e. *bai em bai bagarapim yu disla kain olsem*. In rapid speech the sequence of *bai em bai* is almost identical with *baimbai*. It is easy to see how the full form *baimbai* might have been first reanalyzed in this position to the sequence *bai em bai*, which would then have set the precedent for the reduced form *bai* to occur both clause-initially and preverbally. This also fits in with the finding that it is the third person pronoun which provides the point of departure for the diffusion of preverbal *bai* throughout the pronominal paradigm. If this is true, then phonological reduction of *baimbai* is not the only source for the short form *bai*.

(44) *em bai tupela sindaun.* [NDMISC87FA]
'The two of them will sit down'.

(45) *i go pas tumas, em bai skin bilong en kamap hatpela tumas.* [IND86MISCSB]
'If it [airplane] goes very fast, the outside becomes very hot.'

There are also many examples where *bai* appears both preverbally and clause-initially with a repetition of the same verb, as in the cases in (46-48). There are also cases where preverbal and clause-initial uses are juxtaposed within the same utterance, which suggests that for some speakers the two are optional variants, possibly with some stylistic or pragmatic significance.

(46) *Nau bai kau bai go.*
'Now the cow will go.'[UT1F5]

(47) *Bai bed ia bai bruk. Bed ia bai bruk.*
'The bed will break. [UT1F1]

(48) *Ol bai katim ol karot ia bai ol katim ol karot.*
'They will cut the carrots.'[UT1F]

As far as developments in the written language are concerned, most of the contemporary written texts I have looked at show predominantly clause-initial *bai*. For example, *Nupela Testamen* (1966) has 80% and *Save na Mekim* (1982), 81%, as can be seen in Table 5. The Tok Pisin version of the New Testament is now noticeably archaic in aspects of its syntax, such as predicate marking and the use of *bai*, as well as in lexicon, but it has set an important standard for the written language (see Romaine 1989a). The weekly newspaper *Wantok*, however, has predominantly (63%) preverbal *bai* and is thus more in line with what appears to be the long term trend in the spoken language, however laggard the actual transition appears to be in some areas.

We can see that all of the written texts, except *Wantok* and the personal letters, are characterized by more frequent use of clause-initial *bai*. This is especially true for Nupela *Testamen* and *Save na Mekim*, as opposed to the *Konstitusen*, which shows a pattern very similar to Bulolo and Rempi.

Table 5. *Distribution of* bai *in the written corpus*

Text	% Clause-initial	% Preverbal
Save Na Mekim	81	19
Nupela Testamen	80	20
Konstitusen	55	45
Wantok	37	63
personal letters	27	73

Keesing (1988:184) argues for substratum influence in the form of a common Oceanic pattern for incorporation of the future marker within the verb phrase. The early attestations in New South Wales Pidgin English (see examples (13) and (14)) and Chinese Pidgin English (see note 4) make superstrate influence more likely since the Australian and Chinese substratum would have been different from each other and each would have been different from the Oceanic substrate. However, since his primary aim is to argue for early stabilization of Melenesian Pidgin, i.e. prior to separation into regional dialects, he (1988:187) also claims that by the late nineteenth century *bambae* seems to be a grammaticalized form and not simply an adverb temporally framing the clause. He (1988:182) notes that what happened to *bambae* is "theoretically important because [...] the transformation of what was until recent decades a temporal adverb in sentence- (or clause-initial) position to a grammaticalized preverbal particle is supposed to reflect a late phase in Melanesian pidgin development, particularly associated with incipient creolization." This indicates that for him syntactic position of the marker is the criterion for deciding whether we are dealing with a grammaticalized form. Sankoff and Laberge and Labov, on the other hand, rely on both position and reduction. If we separate the issues of position and reduction from semantic development for the moment, what is crucial is to determine at what stage we are dealing with a form which is no longer a temporal adverb (see Romaine 1990). This is of course not an easy matter. A number of scholars of grammaticalization have cited category shift and semantic bleaching as concomitant processes of grammaticalization. Some comments made by an Indagen speaker in (49) when questioned about the variation between clause-initial and preverbal *bai* are interesting because he mentions preverbal *baimbai* as a possible variant. However, he does not attach any important difference in meaning to the variants.

(49) *Baimbai, nogat, em nau liklik. Baimbai em i go, baimbai i kam. Em baimbai i kam. Baimbai em. klostu bai. I gat kainkain mining i stap. Bai baimbai ating wankain olsem.* [IND87MISC9P].
'You only hear *baimbai* a little bit now, as in *baimbai em i go, baimbai i kam, em baimbai i kam.* That's *baimbai.* It's just about the same as *bai.* They have a similar sort of meaning. *Bai* and *baimbai* are almost the same thing.'

Only a careful semantic analysis of the meanings encoded by *baimbai* and *bai* in clause-initial and preverbal position from the earliest Pacific Jargon English records to the present day will shed light on what has happened. I will do this with reference to more general claims made by Bybee et al. (1991) about the grammaticalization of future markers in language to see to what extent the changes postulated for Tok Pisin fit their predictions.

4. Semantic development of *bai*

Bybee et al. (1991) make two strong claims relating to the development of futures:

(1) Futures in all languages develop from a small set of lexical sources and all future morphemes from a given source go through similar stages of development.

(2) The semantic change is accompanied by formal reduction.

With regard to the first point, they make a more general distinction between aspectual and non-aspectual futures because they say that these two groups develop in entirely different ways. Tok Pisin *bai* is an example of a non-aspectual future. [7] However, they identify four routes of development, one of which can be applied to the case of *bai* in Tok Pisin; namely, cases where temporal adverbs indicating a time after the moment of speech or a reference to time come to encode the future. Since the other three routes are more commonly attested in the sample which Bybee et al. (1991) looked at, they do not exemplify the fourth one or discuss it in detail. Thus, the extent to which Tok Pisin matches their claims in all the precise details will have to await investigation of other languages in which temporal adverbs have developed into tense markers, such as the case of the Kru languages studied by Marchese (1986).

Whether the second claim is substantiated by the developments in Tok Pisin depends on the extent to which it is possible to determine what meanings are encoded by *baimbai*, both synchronically and diachronically, particularly when it appears in preverbal position. It is clear from the data that the reduced form *bai* has become primarily an irrealis marker in preverbal position. To demonstrate this, I will first look at the semantic development of *baimbai* and *bai* in more detail.

4.1 *Degree of semantic grammaticalization*

Bybee et al. (1991:20) identify prediction as the protypical and defining use for future grams, although more than half of the future grams in their data base also had other uses. Examples (10) through (12) in Tok Pisin have shown a similar range of uses other than prediction as components of the meaning of *bai*. Bybee et al. (1991) take these as clues to the semantic development of futures, telling us where the grams come from and how far they have advanced in their development. Other meanings such as imperative are typical of later stages. The original meaning of a gram also determines the range of use it will have at later stages.

There is evidence to suggest that in Pacific Jargon English and its immediate descendents that *baimbai* already encoded an irrealis distinction. A small corpus of 48 examples of *baimbai* collected from an on-going survey of 19th century textual records on Pacific Pidgin English was examined to see what meanings were expressed. Out of a total of 48, only 8 were preverbal and these all encoded the meaning of later, or remote future, or prediction in the sense of Bybee et al. (1991), as in (13). Of the cases of clause-initial *baimbai*, most of these (N = 24) too encoded remote futures, but others encoded results or later sequences of events, some of which can be understood as warnings and threats, as they still do in modern Tok Pisin, as in (50).

(50) *Bai i go antap tru tumach, baimbai em i blek, olsem blek.* [IND87MISC1]
'If it goes too far on top, it gets black, like black.

The existence of preverbal *baimbai* with future meaning indicates that the preverbal slot was already becoming specialized for grammatical markers some time ago. Eventually, the preferred option was for *bai* to be used in preverbal position with phonological reduction when it expressed certain particular meanings. I will show now in more detail how this was accomplished.

Bybee et al. (1991:19) note that future marking is found primarily in main rather than subordinate clauses because prediction is a type of assertion. The same is true in Tok Pisin, as can be seen in examples like (51) and (52). Sankoff and Laberge (1980:204-5) found that independent clauses in conditional constructions appear to take *bai* obligatorily, which agrees with the claim made by Bybee et al. (1991). Only after a long period of development do futures come to be used obligatorily in subordinate clauses. There are, however, some examples where *bai* does occur in subordinate clauses, as in (53). In (54) both clauses take *bai*, although there is no explicit marking of subordination.

(51) *Bed ia bai bruk na em bai kam gen.* [UT1F1]
'The bed will break and he will come again'.

(52) *Sapos neks yia yutupla kam bek, mipla bai kam lukim yutupla.* [IND86MISCBW]
If you both return next year, we will come to see you.'

(53) *Sapos draipla wulf ia bai kam brukim haus blol em no inap bruk.* [UT1M3]
'If the big wolf comes to break down their house, it won't break.'

(54) *Nais tru, b'ol singim, b'ol man krai.* [KUS6FMK]
'It's very nice. Whenever they sing it [the Australian national anthem], everyone cries.'

There are always more cases where *bai* is preverbal in main clauses than it is clause-initial (with the exception of Rempi), as can be seen in the data in Table 6. This adds support to the idea that preverbal *bai* is a marker of future.

The implication of these calculations is that *(bam)bai* was not originally a 'future', or rather, a tense/aspect marker, but developed its future meaning in

Table 6. *Number of preverbal and clause-initial bai in subordinate vs. main clauses*

	Bahor		Kusbau		Rempi		Erima		Lae		Indagen	
	PV	CI	PV	CI	PV	CI	PV	CI	PV	CI	PV	CI
main	66	34	55	45	47	53	62	38	63	37	79	21
subord	47	53	40	60	40	60	60	40	66	34	76	24

main clauses. The data in Table 7, which I will discuss shortly, support this too, in that the most frequent meanings in the preverbal slot in main clauses are the tense/aspect ones of future, habitual and sequence.

Before looking at Table 7 in more detail, however, we need to look more closely at the meanings encoded by *bai* in preverbal and clause-initial positions. The relevant semantic categories appear to be the following: habitual (aspect), sequence, result, imperative/suggestion and intention/purpose. I noted earlier that some linguists such as Roberts (1990) categorize imperatives as irrealis. Habituals also fall within the scope of irrealis for Givón (1984) since they make reference to generics rather than specifics and are in this sense non-referential. The merger between, or use of the same marker, for habituals and irrealis apparently occurs in a number of creoles (see Taylor 1971). Bybee et al. (1991) observe a connection between futurity and imperatives which arises from situations in which a speaker makes a prediction about the addressee, e.g. *you're going to wash to hands before dinner.*

Bybee et al. (1991:26) also say that developing grams often retain traces of their earlier lexical meaning. Certainly, *bai* has retained traces of the earlier meanings of *baimbai*. It has other uses too, such as imperative. This supports their proposal that the use of future for imperative develops out of the prediction sense and is therefore a late use (Bybee et al. 1991:28). I have already given some examples of the other modal and aspectual meanings of *bai* in (10) to (12). Some additional examples of *bai* used to encode result/sequence/habitual in the past are in (55) to (56). Notice that both preverbal and clause-initial *bai* can encode the past habitual. Example (57) shows the use of *bai* in sequencing (cf. also (5)), while (58) shows its use in suggestions or imperatives. Example (59) illustrates the intention/prediction meaning of *bai*.

Table 7. *Meanings encoded by preverbal and clause-initial* bai *in main and subordinate clauses (F/H/S = future, habitual, sequence; R = result; I/It/S =imperative/intention/suggestion)*

		Kusbau		Rempi		Erima		Lae		Indagen	
		PV	CI	PV	CI	PV	CI	PV	CI	PV	CI
M	F/H/S	88	12	77	23	89	11	91	9	94	6
A	R	33	67	33	67	25	75	25	75	100	0
I	I/It/S	18	82	1	99	23	77	27	73	55	45
N											
S	F/H/S	38	62	47	53	65	35	79	21	84	16
U	R	53	45	33	67	32	68	51	49	69	31
B	I/It/S	19	81	20	80	34	66	18	82	48	52

(55) *Tasol man em putim kain hat olsem ol meri bai respectim ol moa yet. Em pasin bilong tumbuna.* [IND86MISC1]
'However, if men wore this kind of hat, the women respected them even more. That was the custom of our ancestors'

(56) *Ol mipla save ron shutim ol sampla fis ol bai slip antap lo rif.* [REM4MAM]
'We habitually catch the fish that sleep on the reef.'

(57) *Bihain bai pepa bai i kam insait long ... komuniti gavman na bai mipela lukim wanem tok bai i kam insait.* [IND87MISC1]
'Then the document will come to the community and we will look to see what it says.'

(58) *Desla mangi ia tok: "Bai yumi go long bus".* [REM2FBA]
'This boy said: "Let's go to the bush'.

(59) *Ating bai mi go long maket nau.* [REM1MFM]
'I think I will go to the market now.'

Clauses which express imperatives, suggestions, hypothetical results and intentions/purposes show the greatest clause-initial use of *bai*, while clauses with future, habitual and sequence show the strongest tendency toward preverbal *bai*. Thus, preverbal *bai* tends to be used where there is a good chance of realization of the activity of the main verb modified by *bai*, whilc clause-initial *bai* is preferred for cases where there is a dependency on some condition or state, e.g. in clauses introduced by *sapos*. Contrast, for instance, the hypothetical or irrealis condition in (60), where *bai* is clause-initial, with (12), where the events have a greater likelihood of occurrence and *bai* expresses predictions and intentions.

(60) *I no olsem Lae na bai yutupla tingting planti* [*raskol*]. *Em peles, i no gat raskol, bai sidaun isi. Sapos long taun, yes, bai yutupla wari.* [IND87MISC2]
'It isn't like Lae where you both would think there would be a lot of rascals [gangs of thieves]. This is the village, there aren't rascals, you can rest easy. If you were in town, yes, you'd have to worry.'

It is by now evident that semantic factors are more important than syntactic ones in determining the position of *bai*. Different varieties are at different stages of development with regard to the shift towards preverbal *bai* being used to encode the future. It is instructive to look at variation in one syntactic environment, namely, *long* clauses. In example (61) from Bahor *bai* is clause-initial in a subordinate clause introduced by *long*, whereas in (62) from Indagen both instances of *bai* are preverbal. In (62) the first use of *bai* encodes a prediction or future result, whereas the second one expresses purpose or intention, as does (61). Both of these meanings now tend to be expressed increasingly by preverbal *bai* in Indagen. In the other areas clause-initial *bai* is still used. In (63), also from Bahor, we see a case of preverbal *bai* used in a *long* clause because here the meaning is habitual result.

(61) *Em tokim pikini bilong en lo* [a reduced form of *long*] *tumoro b'ol go chekim pig*. [BAH5FSK]
'He told his son that tomorrow they would go to check on the pig.'

(62) *Sapos sios i kamap bikpela, em bai gim graun long ol bai sanapim aus lotu*. [IND86MISCSN]
'If the church [membership] gets big, it will give land for them to build a church.'

(63) *Olgeta taim em sa singaut long mani long ol man bai helpim em*. [BAH1FBS]
'He is always crying out for money for people to help him'.

The children from Kusbau, Bahor, Rempi, Erima, Lae and the Indagen adults all generally use the same system. The Indagen children, who are the most advanced in their use of preverbal *bai*, behave differently. In cases where the other children have primarily clause-initial *bai*, Indagen usage is split roughly 50/50 between clause-initial and preverbal *bai*. Thus, there are no environments where clause-initial *bai* is favored. Clauses expressing intention are on the point of becoming environments for preverbal *bai*. This indicates the existence of a hierarchy of environments for change, as in Figure 1. The change begins in main clauses and is less advanced in subordinate ones.

Table 8 shows the differences among four areas in more detail with reference to the age grading dimension. The results show that Indagen clearly leads the other areas in its use of preverbal *bai* in marking futures as well as other modalities such as intentions, suggestions, etc. There is also age-grading such that younger speakers are introducing more preverbal *bai*. The difference between the Indagen younger (Grades 1-4) and older (Grade 5+) speakers is considerable with respect to the use of preverbal *bai* in the marking of suggestions, intentions, etc. The adults and older children (i.e. from Grade 5

Direction of change towards more preverbal ⟶

Area:	Bahor	Kusbau	Rempi	Erima	Lae	Indagen
PREVERBAL	F/H/S	F/H/S	F/H/S	F/H/S	F/H/S/R	F/H/S/R/I
CLAUSE-INITIAL	I/It	I/It	I/It	I/It	I/It	It

Figure 1. *Hierarchy of change from clause-initial to preverbal bai in main clauses (F = future; H = habitual; S = sequence; R = result; I = imperative; It = intention)*

Table 8. *Regional differences in the use of* bai

Percent of cases where *bai* encodes future/habitual/result										
Grade/Age	1-2		3-4		5-6		30 yrs		70 yrs	
	PV	CI	PV	CI	PV	CI	PV	CI	PV	CI
Indagen	91	9	89	11	84	16	94	6	72	28
Lae	75	25	91	9	81	19				
Erima	72	28	71	29	77	23				
Rempi	65	35	51	49	53	47				
Percent of cases where *bai* encodes intention, suggestion, etc.										
	PV	CI	PV	CI	PV	CI	PV	CI	PV	CI
Indagen	62	38	54	46	44	56	5	95	20	80
Lae	29	71	18	82	16	84				
Erima	23	77	42	58	15	85				
Rempi	19	81	8	92	6	94				

onward) in Indagen have the older system which is more like Lae in that the meanings of suggestion, imperative and intention are still encoded primarily by clause-initial *bai*. It is the youngest children in Grades 1-4 whose usage is most advanced. [8]

I now return to the predictions Bybee et al. make about the development of futures. They (1991:29) classify future grams into four semantic ages based on the uses they have in addition to their future use, as shown in Table 9. They classify grams which develop from temporal adverbs in the same schema as movement-derived futures. They put all the non-aspectual future grams into this schema since they illustrate a different path of development from the aspectual futures. It is also clear from Table 9 that some of the postulated meanings for FUTAGE 1 and 4 overlap with those of modality, i.e. possibility, obligation, desire, probability, etc. Table 9 can also be compared with Figures 1, 2 and 3 in Bybee et al. (1994: Ch. 6), which implicate the future in grammaticalization paths towards various modalities.

Table 9. *Meaning components for each FUTAGE* (from Bybee et al. 1991:33, Table 2)

FUTAGE 1	FUTAGE 2	FUTAGE 3	FUTAGE 4
obligation	intention	future	probability
desire	root poss		possibility
ability	andative		imperative
	venitive		use in complements
	immediate future		use in protases

Bybee et al. (1991:57) explicitly list *baimbai* in their sample of future grams and categorize it as a FUTAGE 3 (relying on Hall's 1943 texts). Although they do not mention *bai*, presumbly it would belong to FUTAGE 4, on the assumption that it is a later development from *baimbai*, and it encodes, as I have shown, the meanings of possibility, imperative, etc. However, it still preserves the meaning of intention and immediate future, so it has not completely lost these meanings, which Bybee et al. (1991) classify as belonging to Stage 2, and therefore younger (see further in 4.3.).

4.2 *Degree of grammaticalization and position*

Bybee et al. (1991) also make some predictions about the form and positioning of grams in relation to the degree of grammaticalization they have undergone. They (1991:33) note that positioning of affixes is governed by the source constructions from which the affixes arose diachronically, which in turn is governed by general typological features of the language. They predict a form/meaning correlation reflecting degree of grammaticalization. Grams that are older and have undergone more development tend to be closer to the stem, more fused and shorter or more reduced in segmental material (Bybee et al. 1991:33). Bickerton (1981) and others (e.g. Givón 1982) have made much of the tendency for creoles to encode tense, mood and aspect by means of preverbal particles. Bickerton's claim is that there is a creole prototype. The use of particles rather than bound morphology clearly reflects the influence of typology since pidgins and creoles generally dispense with morphology.

As far as Tok Pisin is concerned, the preverbal slot is not the only one reserved for grammatical markers. The tense, mood and aspect markers, *save*, *laik*, *ken*, *bin*, etc. all occur preverbally, but the completive marker *pinis* is almost always postverbal. By comparison, in Torres Strait Creole, for instance, all grammatical markers precede the verb.

Bybee et al. (1991:34) also propose three measures of the extent of grammaticalization of form: fusion, dependence and shortness. If we assume that preverbal *bai* is closer to the verb stem and thus more fused, then by these criteria, preverbal *bai* is the more recent form, while clause-initial *bai* then would be less so. Thus, preverbal *bai* should be more grammaticalized than clause-initial *bai*. Without going into the details of their measures, I will note briefly how Tok Pisin *bai* and *baimbai* compare on the three parameters. The results are shown in Table 10.

Using five measures of the degree of fusion between a gram and the verb, Bybee et al. (1991) calculate for each gram a value ranging from 0 to 9 by assigning numerical values to these five variables. Higher scores indicate a greater degree of grammaticalization. Only preverbal *bai* shows any degree of grammaticalization. It is less grammaticalized than English *-ed*, for example, as in *walked*, which receives a score of 8, but more than *will*, which receives 0.

The dependence scale, also ranging from 0 to 9, measures the extent to which the gram is losing its autonomy independently of whether it is fusing with the verb. They believe that lack of fusion is usually due to the gram's position. This applies to *bai* since in clause-initial position, it is losing its autonomy, but not fusing with the verb. The four criteria depend on the assumption that as a gram becomes more dependent, it develops more phonological and morphological allomorphy and loses stress.

As is evident from examples like (61), there are a number of allomorphs of *bai*, e.g. *bai*, *b'* and *ba*, but these are phonetically conditioned. There is also loss of stress, but it is not obligatory. Only the preverbal and clause initial *bai* show any degree of grammaticalization on this scale. By comparison, English *-ed* has a score of 7, and *will*, a score of 6.

The shortness scale measures the extent of segmental reduction of a gram by starting with a score of 10 and subtracting points for each segment of the gram. A consonant has a value of -1, a vowel, -2 and a long vowel, -3. I have counted diphthongs as long vowels on the assumption that [e:], for instance is equivalent to [ee]. Thus, *baimbai* scores 3, and *bai*, 8. Again,

Table 10. *Degree of grammaticalization of* baimbai *and* bai

			fusion	dependence	shortness	total
FUTAGE	1	*baimbai*	0	0	3	3
	2	*bai* CI	0	1	8	9
	3	*bai* PV	1	1	8	10

comparing these scores to those for English grams, *bai* has the same score as *will* for shortness, but both score less than *-ed.*

By correlating the scores achieved on these three measures of fusion, dependence and shortness, Bybee et al. (1991:39) predict that forms with higher FUTAGEs will have significantly higher values and they argue for a reliable trend in their data towards higher measures of formal grammaticalization as one moves from FUTAGE 1 through FUTAGE 4. It is somewhat problematic to apply these measures to a language with little morphology since the measures are best suited to cases which display highly developed phonological and morphological conditioning of allomorphs. Nevertheless, we can see in Table 10 that preverbal *bai* has the greatest degree of grammaticalization. This is consistent with the fact that preverbal *bai* is attested only in recent decades.

Bybee et al. (1991:41) conclude that there is a significant correlation between the semantic properties hypothesized to belong to older grams and the formal properties which accompany grammaticalization. There are several biases in their method, which I have no space to comment on here. One, however, which they recognize and attempt to rectify, is that typology may interfere with the correlations. This affects Tok Pisin since it is a young language by comparison with languages like English. Older languages may be expected to have a greater number of older and therefore more highly fused grams than languages with shorter time depth. Inflecting languages on the whole may be expected to show more fusion, but this fusion may not indicate a greater age of grams.

4.3 *Evaluation of the claims made by Bybee et al. (1991) in relation to* baimbai *and* bai

Having now traced both the syntactic and semantic development from *baimbai* to *bai* in Tok Pisin, I can now evaluate the relevance of the claims made by Bybee et al. (1991) about the evolution of futures. I have no reason to doubt their statement that all futures develop from a limited set of lexical sources and go through similar stages of development. However, in the case of Tok Pisin, it is clear that formal reduction was not an absolute prerequisite for the development of future meaning. In fact, Bybee et al. (1991:42) found a deviation in FUTAGE 4 for both the measures of dependence and shortness. Upon examining their correlations in Table 3 and 4 more closely, it appears that as far as shortness is concerned, FUTAGE 2 shows a slightly lower score than FUTAGE 1, and FUTAGE 3, a lower score than FUTAGE 4 (see Bybee et al. 1991:40). Thus, shortness is the least reliable of their measures of degree of formal grammaticalization. If the case of Tok Pisin is indicative of other cases, where several forms overlap in terms of their range of uses, it is not surprising to find this result. While there is evidence of a long term trend to specialize preverbal *bai* for the meanings typical of FUTAGEs 3 and 4, at the moment grammaticalization is very much in progress and 'old' uses of *baimbai* still survive. As far as Sankoff and Laberge's hypothesis of a three stage development is concerned, it would seem that there is no evidence for reduction in situ of preverbal *baimbai*. By dint of the methods used by Bybee et al. (1991), in particular, their reliance on published sources rather than detailed semantic analyses of a large corpus of data from the languages concerned, it is inevitable that their results are static rather than dynamic and reflect the products of grammaticalization rather than the on-going process.

Thus, as I indicated earlier, there is reason to believe that the FUTAGE assigned to *baimbai* is inaccurate. Bybee et al. (1991:27) say that FUTAGE 3 contains "all those grams that have future as their only meaning. This stage represents the period during which all agent-oriented uses have been eroded, and no further uses have yet developed". They do note, however, that their classification may be inaccurate since they relied on reference grammars which may have been incomplete. Within their schema we cannot reconstruct an earlier stage of meaning for *baimbai*. It is clear, however, from the examples I have given and my discussion of the uses of *baimbai* in Pacific Jargon English as well as in modern Tok Pisin that its meaning is not restricted to the future understood in the narrow sense of a marker indicating time relations.

I would like to propose the schema in Table 11 for classifying clause-initial and preverbal *baimbai* and *bai* with reference to the FUTAGES proposed by Bybee et al. (1991). The semantic scope of *baimbai* covers at least FUTAGES 2 and 3, while *bai* extends from FUTAGE 2 through 4. The differences among these options are quantitative, with preverbal *bai* tending to be the more grammaticalized.

We can now make some further observations about the connection between irrealis and futurity and their grammaticalization channels. To begin with, it is clear that the view of grammatical categories adopted by Bybee et al. (1991) is one in which notions such as tense, mood and aspect are viewed

Table 11. *FUTAGES for* baimbai *and* bai

FUTAGE 1	FUTAGE 2	FUTAGE 3	FUTAGE 4
obligation	intention	future	probability
desire	root poss		possibility
ability	andative		imperative
	venitive		use in complements
	immediate future		use in protases
	← CI *BAIMBAI* PV ⟶		?
	←CI *BAI* PV ⟶		

as sets of diachronically related functions. I find this perspective insightful and would add to it the principle that there will be some overlap between functions. Bybee et al. (1991:26) believe that the use of modalities to state intentions is an important link in the chain of developments leading to the grammaticalization of futures. Once the intention use becomes established, a further inference can be made to the effect that one can predict the subject will do what he/she intends to do (compare example (10) discussed earlier). Some of the more modern uses of preverbal *baimbai* in Tok Pisin are of this character and they may have provided the transition to the use of reduced forms in preverbal position. Compare some of the examples I cited earlier from *Nupela Testamen* (37-40), and (42). Bybee et al. (1994: Ch. 6:54) comment that while intention can develop into prediction, which is the criterial use for futures, and from there come to be used for purpose clauses, it is apparently not necessary for the future to serve as an intermediate step between intention and purpose.

It is also clear from the examples I have given that *bai* has evolved beyond FUTAGE 3 because it expresses imperatives, and can also be used in subordinate clauses, e.g. in complement clauses (i.e. *long* complements) and in the protases of conditional sentences. While formal reduction doesn't seem to be a prerequisite for Stage 3, it isn't clear that it is essential for FUTAGE 4 either. Compare (41), where *baimbai* appears in a long complement clause.

I don't have any spoken examples of *baimbai* in *long* clauses, which is why I have put a question mark under FUTAGE 4 for *baimbai*, and (41) is odd in certain respects. Note, for instance, the repetition of *long*. It could be that this development is restricted to media Tok Pisin. The newspaper also uses preverbal *bai* in complement clauses, as can be seen in (64). While some issues appear to use mainly *bai*, both preverbally and clause-initially, other issues use mainly *baimbai*. I am currently doing a diachronic study of *bai* and other syntactic features in media Tok Pisin, which I hope will shed light on this usage.

(64) *Bihain oli mekim pinis general survey o lukluk raun oli tingting bilong mekim ol rot bai olsem bilong bung wantaim long ol ples balus na bris bilong mekim isis moa wakabaut long olgeta hap long Territory.* (*Nius bilong Yumi.* October 1962, Vol. 4. No. 12, p. 4). 'After they complete the general survey they are thinking of making the roads connect with the airports and bridges in order to facilitate travel within all parts of the Territory.'

Another problem which may be specific to the Tok Pisin data or have more general relevance for the predictions made by Bybee et al. (1991) once we have more data from other cases where temporal adverbs have become future markers is the classification of imperatives under FUTAGE 4. A strict chronological progression from FUTAGE 1 to 4 would imply that more cases of preverbal than clause-initial *bai* should be used with the meaning of imperative. As I showed above, however, clauses which express imperatives, suggestions, hypothetical results and intentions/purposes show the greatest clause-initial use of *bai*.

5. Conclusion

From a cross-linguistic perspective it is obvious that neither the process nor specific chain of grammaticalization transforming a sentence-initial temporal adverb into a preverbal tense particle is unique or necessary to pidgin and creole languages. Marchese (1986:254-7), for instance, notes the development of tense auxiliaries from time adverbs in Kru languages. Some Kru tense markers are clearly reduced forms of time adverbs and now have the distributional properties of auxiliaries rather than adverbs and can even cooccur in the same clause with the corresponding adverb, e.g. a general past tense is derived from the corresponding adverb meaning 'yesterday' by semantic extension. This case bears further examination within the framework developed by Bybee et al.

Creoles, however, appear to be no different from 'natural' languages with respect to the routes of development they follow in the grammaticalization of futures. The most common source for futures in pidgins and creoles is to use a verb of movement, e.g. *go* in most English-based pidgins and creoles. Notable exceptions occur among some of the Portuguese and Spanish-based Atlantic Creoles such as Papiamentu and Cape Verde Creole, which use *lo* [<Spanish/ Portuguese *luego/logo* 'later']. In Kristang (Malacca Creole Portuguese), which has *logu*, the future marker can occur both within and outside the verb phrase.

Although I have already demonstrated that creolization is not a trigger for the grammaticalization of *bai* as a future or irrealis marker in Tok Pisin, I return now to this issue in my concluding remarks as it was my point of departure. I have already argued that creolization per se, in so far as it is mainly an urban phenomenon, does not appear to be responsible for the shift of *bai* to preverbal position.

There are some further relevant parallels when we examine comparative evidence from other pidgins and creoles, which weaken the link between creolization and the grammaticalization of preverbal tense particles. The most interesting and relevant case is that of Solomon Islands Pidgin. There nativization does not seem to have affected the positioning of *bae*. Jourdan (1985) found that rural adults had the highest incidence of preverbal *bae*; however, these accounted for only 11% of the occurrences of *bae*. Thus, preverbal *bae* is not by any means as frequent a variant for younger speakers of Solomons Island Pijin as it is for those of Tok Pisin. Monolingual speakers hardly ever use preverbal *bae*. Thus, for both younger and older speakers in all areas, clause-initial *bae* is still the most frequent variant. Although Crowley (1990:496;270) suggests that Bislama in Vanuatu was probably acquiring native speakers in small numbers for most of its history, he says that the placement of *bae* probably parallels more closely the pattern found in Solomon Islands Pijin than that in Tok Pisin.

Another relevant case from the Pacific is Hawai'i English Creole. In the pidgin stage, temporal adverbs occur sentence-externally, either initially or finally. When the creole developed, neither *bambai* nor *pau* (compare Tok Pisin *pinis*), the completive marker, underwent any change of meaning, nor were they incorporated into the auxiliary. A closer comparison of Tok Pisin with Hawai'i Pidgin/Creole English, however, reveals a difference in outcome which is probably due to the longer time period for stabilization in Tok Pisin and in the Melanesian Pidgins in general by comparison to creolization in Hawai'i, which was more abrupt. Although Hawai'i Pidgin English and the

Melanesian Pidgins have both *baimbai* and *go*, in Hawai'i, *bambai* never became regularized as a future tense marker.

Further evidence to support the lack of connection between creolization and grammaticalization of preverbal tense markers is found in Sango. Despite the fact that there is now a second generation of creole speakers, the future marker *fade* (identical to the adverb *fade* 'right now') always occurs first or early in the sentence and is never phonologically reduced (Samarin 1975). Nor has its use become obligatory. An example is given in (65).

(65) *fade tongana kete nginza ti mo ake, mo goe vo a-Nivaquine quoi*
If small money of you is, you go buy Nivaquine.
'If you should have a little money, you ought to buy some Nivaquine (anti-malarial medicine).'

In conclusion then, I have argued that there is no evidence to indicate that creolization and/or urbanization is associated with the incorporation of tense markers into the verb phrase in preverbal position in Tok Pisin. The existence of preverbal *baimbai* with future meaning shows that the preverbal slot was available for tense markers long before phonological reduction or the existence of a community of native speakers. I have also shown that the grammaticalization process follows in many respects the universal paths of development for futures predicted by Bybee et al. (1991) at the same time as it intersects with many of the key routes leading to modality.

FOOTNOTES:

* I would like to thank Joan Bybee and Gillian Sankoff for their helpful comments on an earlier version of this article. I would also like to thank the directors of the Max-Planck-Institut-für-Psycholinguistik, W.J.M. Levelt and Wolfgang Klein, for their support and encouragement, and also Fiona Wright and Rod Mitchell, who assisted in the research at various stages. I am also very grateful to the Papua New Guinea University of Technology for providing a research base and to the Provincial Government of Morobe and Madang Provinces for permission to conduct research. I am also grateful to Susan Hockey of the Oxford University Computing Service for assistance with the Oxford Concordance Programme used in the analysis of the data.

1. The coding system is to read as follows: BL1 = Bulolo 1986; IND1 = Indagen 1986; UT1 = Unitech 1986, etc. F = female; M = male. The number indicates the grade. Where initials appear and no grade is given, the speaker is an adult.

2. I am grateful to Philip Baker for providing me with some of the examples from German New Guinea and Australia.

3. Schuchardt (1883) also notes the occurrence of *by and by* in Chinese Pidgin English and quotes the following example, which interestingly contains a preverbal usage: *my by'mby catchee he* 'I will get it.' Although Baker (1987:179) has attested this feature for Chinese Pidgin English and other Pacific Pidgin Englishes he does not note any preverbal occurrences. He dismisses one instance recorded by Leland (1876:110) as unauthentic because the author never visited the Far East and composed all his examples in London, e.g. *he fedders by'mby stlate all-same nother hin* 'Its feathers will become straight like those of any other hen.'

4. Detzner claims to have lived among bush speakers of Tok Pisin for several years. He continued fighting the war in the remote bush withough surrendering for four years after Rabaul was firmly in the hands of Britain and Australia. He quotes numerous examples of Tok Pisin as used by the police force. However, the use of the copula *be* and several other unexpected non-standard features suggests that we are dealing with a somewhat suspect literary form of Tok Pisin. After Detzner was repatriated, he published a disclaimer of his book, *Vier Jarhen unter Kannibalen.* He said (1932:307-8) said the book contained a number of misrepresentations concerning his journeys in New Guinea. His travels were scientific in part only and were to be taken as primarily a fictional account (see Biskup 1968).

5. Borchardt was a Catholic missionary on Manus Island. His language is clearly influenced by the Rabaul tradition. His examples are fabricated; most other examples have clause-initial *baimbai*. His Guidance for learning the Tok Boi was translated from the German original in 1930.

6. I owe this example to John Z'graggen.

7. Grams that have 'future' as one of their meanings may also more typically develop from auxiliary constructions which have the meanings of 'desire', 'obligation' or 'movement towards a goal'. These routes are also illustrated by other ways of expressing future in Tok Pisin, e.g. *laik* 'want/desire', *go* 'to go', and *ken* 'to be able'. Bybee et al. (1991:55) classify *laik* as a FUTAGE 1 gram expressing an agent-oriented modality.

8. There may also be a developmental aspect to the progression of this change from clause-initial to preverbal *bai*. The data partly reflect the fact that older children and adults use more clauses expressing the meanings of intention, etc. and thus, have more environments for clause-initial *bai* to occur than do the younger speakers. The higher rates of preverbal *bai* usage could indicate that the temporal meanings of *bai* are learned earlier than the others, at least in some areas. The youngest children in both Lae and Indagen in fact use fewer modal clauses than the younger children in other areas. However, this tendency appears at odds with claims made about the priority of aspect over tense in language acquisition more generally (see Romaine 1988:Chapter 7 for an evaluation of these claims in relation to creoles).

REFERENCES

Baker, P. 1987. "The Historical Developments in Chinese Pidgin English and the Nature of the Relationships between the Various Pidgin Englishes of the Pacific Region". *Journal of Pidgin and Creole Languages* 2.149-62.

Bergmann, U., ed. 1982. *Save Na Mekim*. Lae: Liklik Buk Information Centre.

Bickerton, D. 1981. *Roots of Language*. Ann Arbor: Karoma.

Biskup, P. 1968. "Hermann Detzner: New Guinea's First Coast Watcher". *Journal of the Papua and New Guinea Society* 2.5-21.

Borchardt, K. 1930. *Anleitung zur Erlernung des Tok-Boi, mit Wörterbuch*. Manus, mimeo.

Bybee, J., Pagliuca, W. and Perkins, R.D. 1991. "Back to the Future". *Approaches to Grammaticalization*. ed. by E.C. Traugott and B. Heine. Vol. II, 17-58. Amsterdam: John Benjamins.

Bybee, J.L., Pagliuca, W. and Perkins, R.D. 1994. *The Evolution of Grammar: Tense, Aspect and Modality in the Languages of the World*. Ch. 6: Mood and Modality. Chicago: University of Chicago.

Churchill, W. 1911. *Beach-la-Mar, the Jargon or Trade Speech of the Western Pacific*. Washington,D.C.: Carnegie Institution.

Crowley, T. 1990. *Beach-La-Mar to Bislama: The Emergence of a National Language in Vanuatu*. Oxford: Oxford University Press.

Detzner, H. 1921. *Vier Jahren unter Kannibalen*. Berlin: A.Scherl.

Detzner, H. 1932. *Zeitschrift der Gesellschaft für Erdkunde* 1932.307-8.

Foley, W.A. 1986. *The Papuan Languages of New Guinea*. Cambridge: Cambridge University Press.

Givón, T. 1982. "Tense-Aspect-Modality: The Creole Prototype and Beyond". *Tense-Aspect. Between Semantics and Pragmatics*. ed. by P. Hopper, 114-63. Amsterdam: John Benjamins.

Givón, T. 1984. *Syntax. A Functional-Typological Approach. Introduction*. Vol. 1. Amsterdam: John Benjamins.

Hall, R.A. 1943. *Melanesian Pidgin English: Grammar, Texts, Vocabulary*. Baltimore: Linguistic Society of America.

Hall, R.A. 1955. *Hands Off Pidgin English*. Sydney: Sydney and Melbourne Publishing Company Pty, Ltd.

James, D. 1982. "Past Tense and the Hypothetical: a Cross-Linguistic Study". *Studies in Language* 6. 375-403.

James, D. 1991. "Preterit Forms in Moose Cree as Markers of Tense, Aspect, and Modality". *International Journal of American Linguistics* 57.281-297.

Jourdan, C. 1985. *Sapos Iumi Mitim Iumi. Urbanization and Creolization in the Solomon Islands*. Ph.D. dissertation. Australian National University.

Kay, P. and Sankoff, G. 1974. "A Language Universals Approach to Pidgins and Creoles". *Pidgins and Creoles: Current Trends and Prospects*. ed. by D. De Camp and I. Hancock, 61-72. Washington,D.C.: Georgetown University Press.

Keesing, R. 1988. *Melanesian Pidgin and the Oceanic Substrate*. Stanford: Stanford University Press.

Labov, W. 1977. "On the Adequacy of Natural Languages: The Development of Tense". Linguistic Agency University of Trier Paper No. 23. Series B.
Leland, C.G. 1876. *Pidgin-English Sing Song*. London: Trübner and Co.
Ligo, G. 1987. *Lanwis long nyus. Introdaksen long Stadi blong Bislama: Buk Blong Ridim*. ed. by T. Crowley, 81-4. Suva, Fiji: Ekstensen Sevis, Yunivesiti blong Saot Pasifik.
Liklik Katolik Baibel. 1934. Alexishafen: Catholic Mission Press.
Marchese, L. 1986. *Tense/Aspect and the Development of Auxiliaries in Kru Languages*. SIL Publications in Linguistics, 78. Dallas: Summer Institute of Linguistics.
Markey, T.L. 1982. "Afrikaans: Creole or Non-Creole?" *Zeitschrift für Dialektologie und Linguistik* IL.169-207.
Mihalic, F. 1957. *Grammar and Dictionary of Neo-Melanesian Pidgin*. Westmead, NSW: The Mission Press.
Mihalic, F. 1971. *The Jacaranda Dictionary and Grammar of Melanesian Pidgin*. Port Moresby: The Jacaranda Press.
Mihalic, F. 1986a. *Konstitusen Bilong Independen Kantri Papua Niugini*. Boroko, PNG: Word Publishing Company.
Mihalic, F. 1986b. *Stail Buk bilong Wantok Niuspepa*. [reprint].
Mühlhäusler, P. 1978. "Samoan Plantation Pidgin English and the Origin of New Guinea Pidgin". *Papers in Pidgin and Creole Linguistics No.1*. Pacific Linguistics. Series A-24.67-119. Canberra: Australian National University.
Mühlhäusler, P. 1986. *Pidgin and Creole Linguistics*. Oxford: Blackwell.
Murphy, J. 1966. *The Book of Pidgin English*. Brisbane: W.R. Smith and Paterson Pty.
Nupela Testamen bilong Bikpela Jisas Krais na Buk bilong Ol Sam. 1966. Port Moresby: The Bible Society of Papua New Guinea.
Praed, Mrs. Campbell 1885. *Australian Life: Black and White*. London: Chapman and Hall.
Roberts, J.R. (1990). "Modality in Amele and other Papuan Languages". *Journal of Linguistics* 26: 363-401.
Romaine, S. 1988. *Pidgin and Creole Languages*. London: Longman.
Romaine, S. 1989a. "Some Differences Between Spoken and Written Tok Pisin". *English World Wide* 9.243-69.
Romaine, S. 1989b. "Change and Variation in the Lexicon of Tok Pisin in Papua New Guinea". *Synchronic and Diachronic Approaches to Linguistic Variation and Change*. ed. by T. Walsh, 268-80. Washington,DC: Georgetown University Press.
Romaine, S. 1990. "Substratum, Stabilization and Grammaticalization in Melanesian Pidgin English". *Pacific Studies* 14: 79-85.
Romaine, S. 1993. "The Decline of Predicate Marking in Tok Pisin". *The Atlantic Meets the Pacific*. ed. by F. Byrne and J. Holm, pp. 251-61. Amsterdam: John Benjamins.
Romaine, S. 1992. *Language, Education and Development: Urban and Rural Tok Pisin in Papua New Guinea*. Oxford: Oxford University Press.
Romaine, S. and Wright, F. 1987. "Short Forms in Tok Pisin". *Journal of Pidgin and Creole Languages* 2.64-7.
Samarin, W.J. 1975. "Historical, Ephemeral and Inevitable Verbal Categories". Paper presented at the International Conference on Pidgins and Creoles, Honolulu, Hawai'i.

Sankoff, G. and Laberge, S. 1980. "On the Acquisition of Native Speakers by a Language". *The Social Life of Language*. G. Sankoff. 195-211. Philadelphia: University of Pennsylvania Press. [Reprinted from *Kivung* (1973) 6.32-47].

Schuchardt, H. 1883. "Kreolische Studien V: Über das Melaneso-englische". *Sitzungsberichte der kaiserlichen Akademie der Wissenschaften zu Wien, Philosophisch-historische Klasse*, 105.151-61.

Steele, S. 1975. "Past and Irrealis: Just What Does it All Mean?" *International Journal of American Linguistics* 41.200-217.

Taylor, D. 1971. "Grammatical and Lexical Affinities of Creoles". *Pidginization and Creolization of Languages*. 293-6 ed. by D. Hymes. Cambridge: Cambridge University Press.

Troy, J. 1985. *Australian Aboriginal Contact with the English Language in New South Wales: 1788-1845*. B.A. thesis. University of Sydney.

Vogel, H. 1911. *Forschungsreise im Bismarckarchipel*. Hamburg.

The Evaluative Function of the Spanish Subjunctive

Patricia V. Lunn
Michigan State University

1. Introduction

Whether or not mood encodes realis/irrealis is surely an unanswerable question in language universal terms (but see Chafe, Mithun, Romaine, this volume and Roberts, ms, on language-specific cases), given the impossibility of satisfactorily defining 'reality' and the interference of internally motivated diachronic change. But the fact remains that speaker judgment and mood are more overtly linked than are speaker judgment and tense, aspect or voice (though such links can, of course, be inferred). Fleischman (1989) suggests that evaluation strategies in epic narration carried out by tense-aspect can provide a window onto world view and cultural presuppositions of narrators, and I think that the same can be said for the window that the Subjunctive provides onto the world view of speakers of Spanish.

This paper argues that, in contemporary Spanish, the mood system is a device through which speakers can evaluate the information value of clauses. Further, because speakers may take an evaluative stance with respect to any proposition, the identification of the Subjunctive with syntactic subordination is breaking down. This process is fed by metalinguistic use of the Subjunctive in certain registers, by usage that reflects the indicative history of the *-ra* form of the Past Subjunctive, and by the identification of the highly non-assertive-*se* form of the Past Subjunctive with the auxiliary verb *haber*, an identification which allows the *-se* form to appear wherever *haber* is used.

The Spanish Subjunctive is primarily expressive of epistemic modality.[1] Numerous studies, following Bolinger (1968) and Terrell and Hooper (1974), have shown that the best synchronic description of the Spanish mood system links choice of the Indicative (I) to assertion and choice of the Subjunctive (S) to non-assertion. A proposition may be unworthy of assertion because the speaker has doubts about its veracity:

(1) *Dudo que sea (S) buena idea.*
'I doubt that's a good idea'

or because the proposition is unrealized:

(2) *Necesito que me devuelvas (S) ese libro.*
'I need you to return that book to me.'

or because the proposition is presupposed:

(3) *Me alegra que sepas (S) la verdad.*
'I'm glad that you know the truth.'

Assertion and non-assertion are not the only options, however. Klein (1980) has shown that the territory between assertion and non-assertion is occupied by a cline of speaker attitudes, with choice of the Subjunctive becoming more likely as speakers report diminished degrees of certainty with respect to propositions.

Lunn (1989) has shown that Subjunctive-marked propositions, whether true or false, share the semantic quality of low-information value. Low-information value is an instantiation of what Sperber and Wilson (1986) term low relevance. Sperber and Wilson argue that the expectation that communicated propositions will modify and improve existing information is the motive force in discourse comprehension: "Every act of ostensive communication communicates the presumption of its own optimal relevance" (1986:158). In Spanish, propositions that are less than optimally relevant, either because they add nothing new to existing information or because they add nothing true to existing information, are marked with the Subjunctive.

Subjunctivizable information can be characterized as not possessing certain qualities, a suggestive characterization in view of the language-universal link between negation and irrealis modalities.[2] Potentially assertable information must have two qualities: in the speaker's opinion, it must be both reliable as to truth value and informative as to news value. Information that is believed to be flawed in truth value or flawed in news value is unlikely to be asserted.

This description accounts both for grammaticized uses of the morphology, like those exemplified above, and for ungrammaticized uses. Clearly, speakers of Spanish are making judgments about information quality when they use the Subjunctive, and this means that they have broad power to use the Subjunctive electively. This, in turn, results in an increasingly confusing syntactic pattern of mood usage.

2. Complementary theme/rheme analyses

Gsell and Wandruszka (1986:84-87) use the theme/rheme framework to show that presupposed information in comment sentences (like (3) above, in which the main clause is a comment on a presupposed proposition) is thematic. Thematicity is related not only to mood marking, but also to word order.

Variation in mood choice after *el hecho de que* 'the fact that' is illustrative of the complexity of mood choice in Spanish. It is well known that either Subjunctive or Indicative can be used after *el hecho de que*, though discussions of this structure are often based on decontextualized or invented sentences (Lipski 1978; Woehr 1975). In an effort to monitor the context from which data were taken, Krakusin and Cedeño (1992), studied mood choice after *el hecho de que* in a ten-year series of magazine columns written by the political analyst and columnist Mariano Grondona. Their study confirmed that mood choice was directly linked to information value. When information had already been introduced in the column or when it was of such moment that it could be assumed to be common knowledge, it was marked with the Subjunctive. In contrast, propositions neither previously discussed nor universally known were marked with the Indicative.

Moreover, a word-order generalization that can be linked to a theme/rheme analysis emerged from the data. Subjunctive-marked clauses appeared in initial position, i.e., before the main verb. The use of the Past Subjunctive (PS) in (4) is an example.

(4) *El hecho de que en los cuatro el régimen democrático se impusiera (PS) facilitaba la tarea.*
'The fact that in all four the democratic regime was imposed made the task easier.' (Krakusin and Cedeño 1992:1290)

Clauses marked with the Indicative, in contrast, appeared after the main verb.

(5) *Lang soslaya el hecho mayor de que las ciencias físicas están (I) penetradas de visiones filosóficas del universo y de todo lo que se encuentra en él.*
'Lang overlooks the major fact that the physical sciences are shot through with philosophical visions of the universe and of all that is in it.' (Krakusin and Cedeño 1992:1291)

With respect to the linear distribution of theme and rheme, Contreras (1976:26) established that "the highest ranking rheme occurs in final position". Clearly, the information value of these factive clauses determines both their mood marking and their position in the sentence. Guitart (1991) has suggested a similar approach to the Spanish Subjunctive by distinguishing between pragmatic presupposition, based on speaker assumptions about hearer knowledge, and semantic presupposition, based on sentence-level truth conditions.

3. Journalistic uses of the Subjunctive

In journalistic discourse, there are subgenres that are characterized by very heavy Subjunctive use. In particular, the specialized press which addresses a knowledgeable readership (e.g. gossip magazines, sports pages and bullfighting news) uses the Past Subjunctive to mark information which can be assumed to be known to assiduous readers. These publications have an enormous readership, which means that these uses of the Subjunctive are widely disseminated. Many native speakers, in response to questions about such usage, say that it "sounds like something you'd hear on the news", which reveals that this kind of Subjunctive marking of known information forms part of the input for native speakers' grammars. The use of the Subjunctive discussed below serves the discourse function of backgrounding old information and the metalinguistic function of identifying certain styles of writing as journalistic.

(6) *Casi once años después de que el Bayern de Munich alcanzara (PS) su tercera y última Copa de Europa, los vigentes campeones de la RFA y España van a volver a enfrentarse en un encuentro oficial.* (*La Vanguardia*, 8.4.87)

'Almost eleven years after Munich Bayern won its third and last European Cup, the current champions of the FRG and Spain are going to meet one another in an official match.'

(7) *La pareja, que se hiciera (PS) famosa por interpretar el papel de marido y mujer en "El pájaro espino", es en la vida real un matrimonio feliz.* (*Hola*, 6.7.85)
'The couple, who became famous for their role as husband and wife in "The Thorn Birds", is happily married in real life.'

In this kind of writing, judgments about information value are based on a very broad definition of discourse context. The discourse contexts in which the subjunctivized propositions of (6) and (7) are judged to constitute old information include previous editions and may span a fairly long period of time.

The Subjunctive in (7) appears in a non-restrictive relative clause, where the grammars say that it should not appear at all (Solé and Solé 1977:187-94). Given that non-restrictive relative clauses facilitate the introduction of additional information, it is surprising that the non-assertive Subjunctive should appear in them. This anomaly can be explained in relevance terms: journalistic information is marked for low relevance if it is considered to be known to a faithful readership. The flagging of known information serves to communicate the additional message that writers assume readers to be knowledgeable; this use of the Subjunctive serves not just to classify information but to create solidarity between a publication and its readers.

In some cases, all that is necessary in order for a proposition to be presupposed is prior appearance in a headline. Then, when reiterated in the following text, the information is marked with the Subjunctive.

(8) a. Headline: *La bandera que besó es la que, en su día, también besó (I) el Rey don Juan Carlos, y bordó (I) su tatarabuela la Reina doña María Cristina.* (*Hola*, 26.10.85)
'The flag that he kissed is the one that one day King Juan Carlos also kissed and his great-great-grandmother Queen María Cristina embroidered.'

b. Text: *Y, al final, besó la bandera roja y gualda que hace treinta años besara (PS) su padre el Rey y que un día bordara (PS) su tatarabuela la Reina doña María Cristina.*
'And, at the end, he kissed the red and gold flag that his father the King had kissed thirty years ago, and that his great-great-grandmother Queen María Cristina had once embroidered.'

Another example of the link between mood choice and old/new information appeared in a recent newspaper report on a notorious murder. Under the headline *Una maleta con un niño muerto* 'Suitcase with dead child inside' appeared the following sentence.

(9) *Nadie en la ciudad, ni la policía, ni los vecinos, encontraron los motivos por los que una mujer ... pudo (I) matar al menor de los hijos de su vecina ... y enviara (PS) después el cuerpo a Madrid dentro de una maleta.* (*El País*, 22.5.92)
'No one in the city, on the police force, or in the neighborhood understood the reasons why a woman could kill her neighbor's youngest child and then send his body to Madrid in a suitcase.'

The first subordinate verb, *pudo*, is in the Indicative mood, while the verb *enviara*, in the clause which repeats the headline information, is in the Subjunctive. The uniquely gruesome disposal of the body was talked about all over Spain, so it is impossible—and unnecessary—to decide whether the factor controlling mood choice here is the global discourse context or the format of the article in which the verb appeared. In the terms of category theory, this is a case of multiple motivation for the explanation of the extension of a category. As Lakoff (1987:86) says, "where motivation is concerned, the more kinds of motivation, the better."

The discourse context that governs mood choice in the journalistic data cited in this section and in Section 2 can be as narrow as one article, or as broad as a chronologically extended series of references to one topic. The use of the Subjunctive to mark known information serves as acknowledgment of the shared context of propositions, and in this sense it serves an interpersonal discourse function.

4. Dialect variation

In many Latin American dialects, when a conditional *si* clause is introduced by *no sé* 'I don't know', the following verb appears in the Subjunctive, e.g. *No sé si pueda (S)* 'I don't know if I can'. Continental speakers find this usage odd, but it is widespread in America. Denial of knowledge in combination with the conditional conjunction tips the semantic balance in favor of the non-assertive Subjunctive.

For many Latin American speakers, starting a sentence with *no sé* apparently licenses use of the Subjunctive even in clauses in which it would not normally appear. There are prosodic and syntactic differences in Spanish between the complementizer *que* 'that' and the interrogative pronoun *qué* 'what', yet even embedded questions can contain a Subjunctive verb if they are introduced by *no sé*. I recently heard a Latin American speaker say (10).

(10) *No sé qué tal sea* (S).
'I don't know what it's like.'

The standard form of this sentence is *No sé qué tal es (I)*. In sentences like (10), a semantic factor, speaker uncertainty about a proposition, determines use of the Subjunctive.

The use of the Past Subjunctive to make a polite request for hearer participation is current in Chile, to judge from dialogue in the short story "Santelices" by the contemporary writer José Donoso.

(11) *El departamento es lindo, de lujo, viera (PS) qué moderno.* (Donoso 1965:190)
'The apartment is pretty, deluxe, you should see how modern.'

I have also heard, in Ecuador, the verb *conocer* 'to get to know' used in this way:

(12) *Conocieras la quinta de mis suegros*
'You should visit my in-laws' farm.'

Note that *viera* and *conocieras* are not in subordinate clauses, nor are they modal verbs (which are conventionally used in the Past Subjunctive to form polite commands, as in ex. (20)).

In Guatemala, I have heard the tags *¿cómo te dijera/explicara (PS)?* 'how can I tell you/explain to you', which are uttered when the speaker is searching for words. In most dialects, the Present Indicative form of these verbs would be used. Again, these Subjunctives appear outside of the expected subordinate-clause context.

In Mexico, speakers telescope the meaning of *parecer* 'to seem' and the low assertiveness of the Past Subjunctive to yield *pareciera*, which is used in main clauses in the following way.

(13) *Pareciera (PS) agotado, destruido físicamente.*
'It seemed as if he were worn out, physically destroyed.'
(Taibo 1976:142)

There are many other Indicative/Subjunctive contrasts cited in Kany's *American-Spanish Syntax* (1951:170-185) which attest to a general pattern of the form Politeness:Subjunctive::Assertion:Indicative, and also to the heightened politeness or non-assertiveness of the Past versus the Present Subjunctive. This pattern is the semantic source of the main-clause uses of the Subjunctive discussed in this section.

5. Other sources of instability in the mood system

The Subjunctive is associated with modesty because of its non-assertive meaning, and this meaning sometimes overrides the syntactic parameters of Subjunctive usage. In adverb clauses, the Subjunctive can have the force of downplaying the importance of a clause. For example, Camilo José Cela made the following remark after being awarded the Nobel Prize for literature.

(14) *El mundo no va a dejar de girar porque me hayan (S) dado el Nobel.*
'The world's not going to stop turning because they've given me the Nobel Prize.'

Subjunctive adjective clauses usually modify unknown or nonexistent nouns, as in *No conozco a nadie que hable catalán* 'I don't know anybody who speaks Catalan'. In (15), though, the modified noun is real and known.

(15) *Sólo he conocido a dos personas que tuvieran (PS) tanto o más miedo que yo a los automóviles.* (*El País*, 18.12.86)
'I've only known two people who were as afraid or more afraid than I am of automobiles.'

The force of the Subjunctive here is to minimize the importance of these few people. The semantically minimizing use of the Subjunctive has no clear syntactic limits.

Another source of confusion is the Indicative Pluperfect origin of the *-ra* Past Subjunctive form. Via a process discussed by Klein-Andreu (1991) and Lunn and Cravens (1991), the functions of the Latin Pluperfect Indicative were taken over by the Romance analytic pluperfect, leaving to the Latin form the backgrounding functions that are associated with the subjunctive mood. This is the source of the modern Spanish Past Subjunctive in *-ra*. (A similar process now going on in Mandarin is described by Guo, this volume.) Parallel to the dominant *-ra* form is a form in *-se*, which comes from a Latin Pluperfect (Romance Imperfect) Subjunctive.

Evidence of the original usage of the *-ra* form was still extant in the Romantic period in Spain (mid-nineteenth century), and intentional usage of the form with pluperfect meaning is one of the precious characteristics of Romantic prose (Wright 1932). In modern Spanish, such usage continues to characterize highly formal or archaizing prose, such as the following clauses from a much longer sentence in the short story "Syllabus" by the Spanish author Juan Benet.

(16) *Aquellas herméticas sentencias, cuyos secretos sentidos tantas veces escaparan (PS) a la concurrencia, volverían a aclararse por obra de su propia ironía,...* (Benet 1981:285)
'Those hermetic aphorisms, whose secret meanings had so many times escaped the audience, would once again become clear by dint of his own irony,...'

The *-ra* form is so thoroughly identified with the subjunctive mood that its marginally productive use as an indicative pluperfect has been generalized to the unquestionably Subjunctive *-se* form.

(17) *El conductor se encuentra atrapado en el interior de su coche después de que éste se precipitase (PS) a un riachuelo.* (*Hola*, 21.5.87)
'The driver is seen trapped inside his car after it had run into a stream.'

The Subjunctive must be used after *antes de que* 'before', and it is possible that the appearance of the Subjunctive in cases like (17) is partly due to the conceptual pairing of the opposites *antes de que* and *después de que*, as happens also in French. The use of the Past Subjunctive after *desde que* 'since' raises the same issues.

(18) *Varios meses han transcurrido desde que Carmen Harto y Gonzalo de Borbón decidiesen (PS) separarse tras un fugaz y sorprendente matrimonio.* (*Hola*, 9.4.85)
'Several months have passed since Carmen Harto and Gonzalo de Borbón decided to separate after a brief and surprising marriage.'

In some cases, as in the one above, the Subjunctive may be triggered as well by the journalistic assumption that a previous notorious event is well known to the readership.

Sometimes, confirmation of the known status of a Subjunctive-marked proposition is present in the text, as in (19).

(19) *Al día siguiente de que Isabel Preysler iniciase (PS) su veraneo, según informamos en la página 44 de este número,...* (*Hola*, 17.8.85)
'The day after Isabel Preysler had begun her summer vacation, as we reported on page 44 of this issue...'

Clearly, it is not possible to separate the individual strands of motivation for the use of Subjunctive morphology. Pragmatic and discourse motivation exist alongside semantic motivation and lexical analogy.

6. The two forms of the Past Subjunctive in Spanish

Because of its indicative history, the *-ra* Past Subjunctive is used in ways that the *-se* form usually is not. It is quite conventional to use the *-ra* form of certain modal verbs in main clauses in order to make polite requests and suggestions.

(20) *Quisiera hacerle una pregunta.*
'I would like to ask you a question, if I may.'

The *-se* form sounds obsequious and pompous in this formula, and few speakers report having heard it. It is crucial, however, that it is the exaggerated politeness of the *-se* form that is objectionable here. The *-ra* form is fully identified with the Subjunctive mood, and the alternate Past Subjunctive *-se* form is, at least in theory, substitutable for it.

The *-ra* form is also likely to be chosen for the 'old information' journalistic uses discussed in Section 5 above. The *-se* form is occasionally used in this way, however, which shows that the criterion for substitutability is morphological: speakers identify both the *-ra* and the *-se* forms as Subjunctives. Examples (18) and (19) above illustrate the old information use of the *-se* form.

If main-clause and pluperfect uses of the *-ra* form are classified as non-Subjunctive, as most traditional grammars would have it, the difference between the *-ra* and the *-se* forms is hard to describe. Gili y Gaya, for example, says that "both forms are interchangeable as long as they are Subjunctive" (1964:179). If, however, all of the *-ra* uses are considered Subjunctive, then it is possible to make the generalization that the *-se* form encodes less assertion than the *-ra* form both because it rarely appears in the main clause and quasi-pluperfect environments of the *-ra* form, and because of contrasts like that between (21) and (22).

(21) *Quisiera que usted me aclarase (PS) algunas cosas.* (Vázquez Montalbán 1977:41)
'I'd like you to clear up a few things for me.'

(22) *Quisiera que recordaras (PS) primero si ha sido cliente tuyo o si puedes preguntárselo a alguna colega.* (Vázquez Montalbán 1977:23)
'I'd like you to remember first if he's been a client of yours or if you can ask a colleague about him.'

In these sentences (from dialogue in the novel *La soledad del manager*), the *-se* form appears with the formal second-person pronoun *usted*, while the *-ra* form appears with the familiar second-person pronoun *tú*.

The Past Subjunctive can be used in place of the Conditional (especially with the verb *haber*, to be discussed in Section 7 below). It is usually the *-ra* form that is so used, as exemplified in *hubiera sido* 'would have been' in this advertisement.

(23) *Esos sí que fueron tiempos difíciles. Noé necesitó un vehículo de gran capacidad, aguantador, fuerte y sobre todo confiable. Y se lo tuvo que fabricar él. Ahora hubiera (PS) sido diferente. ¡Pobre Noé! En realidad nunca tuvo otra alternativa. Seguramente si hubiese (PS) podido elegir, Volkswagen habría sido su otra opción.*
'Those were sure hard times. Noah needed a large-capacity vehicle that was durable, strong and above all reliable. And he had to make it himself. Now things would have been different. Poor Noah! He really didn't have any alternative. Surely, if he had been able to choose, Volkswagen would have been his other option.'

In this text, the *-se* form is used in the protasis of a conditional sentence: *si hubiese podido* 'if he had been able'. The contrastive value of the *-se* form is thus exploited by having it appear in a subordinate clause with past time reference, while the *-ra* form appears in a main clause with present time reference. This chain effect is often to be observed when, in a given context, there are a number of syntactic slots for which degrees of modality may be selected. Klein-Andreu (1986) explains the various possibilities in detail. Lunn (1988) discusses other data which show the *-se* form to be a less assertive variant of the *-ra* form.

7. Dialect variation in the use of the *-se* Past Subjunctive

The *-se* form is the minority form in all dialects, though its frequency varies a great deal from dialect to dialect. In this section, *-se* usage in modern novels from Peru, Argentina and Spain is examined. The novels were chosen because their authors are famous for their ability to write prose that evokes the spoken language.

Listening to Peruvian Spanish, one gets the impression that the *-se* form is virtually unused in that dialect. This impression is borne out by the novel *Un mundo para Julius*, written in 1970 by the Peruvian novelist Alfredo Bryce Echenique. In this book, the *-se* form appears only 21 times in nearly 500 pages, which amounts to slightly less that 2% of all Past Subjunctives. None of these *-se* forms appears in the Lima speech of the characters. The verb *hubiese*, from the auxiliary *haber* 'to have', accounts for 10 of the 21 cases, or 48% of all *-se* verbs. Only one of the verbs in the *-se* form is a transitive verb. Also, 8 of the *-se* forms, 38%, appear in negative clauses. In *Un mundo para Julius*, residual *-se* usage can be described as linked with—but not triggered by—negation and *haber*.

In the novel, the *-se* form is often used in the description of highly unlikely or fanciful situations, which may or may not be marked with an introductory irrealis conjunction.

(24) *Muchas veces tropezó la chola con los mayordomos o con el jardinero que yacían muertos alrededor de la carroza, para que Julius, Jesse James o Gary Cooper según el día, pudiese (PS) partir tranquilo a bañarse.* (Bryce Echenique 1991:13)
'Often the Indian girl tripped over the servants or the gardener who were lying dead around the coach, so that Julius, Jesse James or Gary Cooper, whoever he was that day, could go off quietly to his bath.'

(25) *Ni más ni menos que si estuviese (PS) reinventando el mundo.* (Bryce Echenique 1991:327)
'As if he were reinventing the world, no less.'

It is interesting to note that although as many as 75 pages may go by without a *-se* form, on five occasions the form is used once and then again on a directly or closely following page, giving the impression that use of the form activates some schema which licenses its reuse, but which once forgotten may lie dormant.

For Argentine Spanish, DeMello (1993:240) reports that *-se* usage is relatively high in uneducated speech. In Manuel Puig's 1976 novel, *El beso de la mujer araña*, 27% of all Past Subjunctive verbs are in the *-se* form. Most of the novel takes the form of dialogue, from which it may be inferred that the form appears in the popular Buenos Aires dialect of the characters. Apparently, it appears even in highly spontaneous language.

(26) *Ay, ayyy...mirá, son unas puntadas tan fuertes...como si me agujereasen (PS).* (Puig 1976:118)
'Oh, ohhh...see, they're such strong pains...as if they were making holes in me.'

What motivates the use of the *-se* form here is the counterfactual *como si* 'as if'; 38% of *-se* Subjunctives are found in contrary-to-fact clauses.

As in the Peruvian dialect, auxiliary *haber* accounts for a high percentage of the verbs appearing in the *-se* form: 50%. The *-se* form is used in main clauses several times, each time as a form of *haber*.

(27) *Me hubieses (PS) despertado antes, Molina.* (Puig 1976:96)
'You should have woken me up sooner, Molina.'

The modality expressed here is agent-oriented; once Past Subjunctives appear in main clauses, the low assertiveness that they convey and the assertiveness inherent in the main clause combine to license the inference 'should have happened but didn't'. There is even a case of main-clause *-se* in the Peruvian data, also in the form of *hubiese*. Clearly, this verb licenses the widest usage of the form.

-Se usage in the Spanish novel *Si te dicen que caí* by Juan Marsé (1973) falls between the poles of the virtual non-use of the form in the Peruvian text and its frequent use in the Argentine text. The *-se* form appears in dialogue in

the Spanish text, which suggests its continued usage in the Madrid dialect of the characters. However, the *-se* form accounts for only 13% of all Past Subjunctive verb forms in the book, about half of the Argentine figure. As in the Peruvian and the Argentine texts, the *-se* form appears most often with the auxiliary *haber*, here in 55% of all cases.

In this text, as in the Peruvian text, there is an alternation of extended non-use of the *-se* form and closely spaced occurrences of it. Such evidence shows how a form is sporadically used even as it falls out of use. As speakers produce longer and longer periods of non-use, the form disappears from learners' input.

As in the Argentine text, a significant percentage (39%) of the *-se* forms in *Si te dicen que caí* are introduced by a counterfactual conjunction. However, it is not the case in any of the texts examined for this paper that the *-se* form must appear in counterfactual clauses; the *-ra* form may appear there as well. That a high percentage of the minority *-se* forms should appear in contrary-to-fact clauses is logical; in this highly non-assertive environment, a form that encodes a high degree of non-assertion should be used.

Klein-Andreu (1991) traces the genesis of the Subjunctive use of the originally indicative *-ra* form to its early backgrounding functions. In her data, use of the *-ra* form in a fourteenth-century text correlated significantly with the 'low focus' factors of negation and the use of the copular and auxiliary verbs *ser*, *estar* and *haber*. It is striking that, in the modern language, use of the most non-assertive of the Subjunctive forms continues to be linked with these factors.

In Table 1, the first number shows the percentage of Past Subjunctive forms that carry *-se* morphology. Note that, despite the differences in absolute *-se* usage, the co-occurrence of *-se* morphology and auxiliary *haber* is remark-

Table 1. *Percentage of use of* -se *Subjunctive forms in these dialects.*

	% of PS	*HUBIESE*	w/NEG	C to F	in MC
Peru	2%	48	38	33	5
Spain	13	55	23	39	13
Argentina	27	50	20	38	15

NEG = negative clauses
C to F = contrary to fact
MC = main clauses

ably similar. The number on the right shows the percentage of *-se* forms that appear in main clauses. Fully 100% of these main-clause uses, in all three dialects, are realized as *hubiese*; *-se* morphology can travel with *haber* to the main clause, even though the semantic value of the morphology would seem to exclude it from this locus of assertion.

I have done the same analysis on other novels by the same authors, and found that the percentage of Past Subjunctives realized as *-se* varies from book to book, as authors adopt the point of view of very different narrators, and as the authors themselves live for long periods away from their native countries. The ranking, however, from least to greatest use of *-se*, does not change.[3]

8. Textual patterns of Subjunctive use

Even grammaticized uses of the Subjunctive can be avoided simply by providing each proposition with its own main clause. Sentences (1)-(3), for example, can be recast as (28)-(30), in which modality in the sense of speaker attitude towards a proposition is expressed, but the Subjunctive mood is absent.

(28) Será una buena idea, pero lo dudo.[4]
'It might be a good idea, but I doubt it.'

(29) ¿Sabes ese libro? Lo necesito.
'You know that book? I need it.'

(30) Sabes la verdad. Me alegro.
'You know the truth. I'm glad.'

The model of the active speaker of Spanish who manipulates mood choice in order to structure discourse is particularly well described by Lavandera (1983). Such use of mood marking suggests Traugott's identification of a intermediate tendency in semantic change for meanings based in extralinguistic reality to develop into meanings grounded in text-making (1989:35).

If indeed non-assertion is a chosen stance, one might expect that frequency of Subjunctive use should correlate with certain narratively non-assertive stages in conventionally structured texts. In order to find out if this was so, I looked at Subjunctive use in a recent mystery novel, *El balneario* (1986) by the Spanish author Manuel Vázquez Montalbán.

Writers of mystery novels play a conventionalized game with their readers in which clues to the ultimate solution are hidden in narrative digressions; these digressions serve both to entertain and to mislead the reader. In order to see how Subjunctive use correlated with the structure of the plot, the average number of Subjunctives per page was figured for each chapter, and this crude measure was used to identify high-use and low-use chapters. What was revealed by this analysis is that the Subjunctive is most used in those chapters where information is withheld or implied, and is least used in those chapters in which the dénouement is foretold or explained.

In *El balneario*, which is about a series of murders which take place in a Spanish spa, use of the Subjunctive reaches its high point in a segment in which the spa's patrons attempt to convince the investigating officer that they each should be allowed to leave because they are important people with important connections. The term 'veiled threat' comes to have a new iconic meaning here. The other high-Subjunctive chapters contain theorizing about the meaning of clues gathered up to that point, and a description of a hunger-motivated attack on the spa's kitchen. In typical mystery novel style, these chapters in which nothing new seems to be added to the reader's stock of knowledge about the crime end with the introduction of information which moves the plot along. Just as the reader is being lulled by hypothesis or amused by clowning—and by the non-assertive message of the high-Subjunctive text—something happens.

The most limited use of the Subjunctive comes in an early chapter in which the detective visits the site where, as it turns out, the key to the mystery lies. The high-Indicative text telegraphs the conclusion. The other low-Subjunctive sections come at the end of the novel, in which the dark history of the spa is revealed. In these sections, the reader is modally invited to attend to highly informative text material.

"The syntax of the text," in which plots are regarded as sentence-like structures, is a European structuralist concept. It is not necessary, however, to subscribe to all of the assumptions of such analyses in order to acknowledge that highly conventionalized narrative forms—like mystery novels—are likely to evidence patterning at the text level. One kind of macro-pattern may be evidenced in frequency of occurrence of certain morphological forms. It is this kind of pattern of Subjunctive usage that can be seen in *El balneario*.

9. Conclusions

It has been shown that choice of the Subjunctive in Spanish is sensitive to semantic, textual and analogic factors. Though Subjunctive morphology continues to appear primarily in subordinate clauses, the Subjunctive can appear in non-restrictive relative clauses (as in (7)), in embedded questions (as in (10)), and in main clauses (as in (11), (12),(13), (23) and (27)) as the expression of a wide range of speaker attitudes and intentions. Some main-clause uses of the Subjunctive are the reflex of the indicative history of the *-ra* form, while the identification of the *-se* form with the auxiliary verb *haber* has allowed that form—the most non-assertive—to migrate to main clauses as well.

Silva-Corvalán, following Bolinger (1956), has argued that, of a series of syntactically and semantically related forms, the one that will be lost is "the form which is farthest away from the speaker, in the sense that it refers to objects or events which are farthest from him in his objective (e.g., actual distance) or subjective (e.g., possibility of actualization) world" (1985:565). The *-se* form is clearly the most remote modal form, both objectively and subjectively; it is past tense and strongly non-assertive. Moreover, the *-se* form of the Past Subjunctive is closely identified with *haber*, the auxiliary used to form the temporally remote Pluperfect. This is so even in dialects where the form is still frequently used.

In this discussion of the loss of Subjunctive forms, it is significant that in the Quito dialect of Spanish, the Present Subjunctive is colloquially used in the subordinate clause of past tense sentences. I have heard many sentences like this one: *Tenía vocación de pintor, pero sus padres nunca permitieron que pinte* 'Painting was his vocation, but his parents never let him paint'. In most dialects, the "sequence of tenses" would require the Past Subjunctive (*pintara*) rather than the present Subjunctive (*pinte*). In *quiteño*, in which the *-se* Subjunctive is little used, the *-ra* Subjunctive is the "outermost" form and therefore the one, on this analysis, most vulnerable to loss. Indeed, some of its uses are disappearing in this dialect.

The *-se* form of the Past Subjunctive is going out of the language via the same path on which the *-ra* form came in: that of the temporally remote pluperfect. That *-se* morphology is identified with a specific verb (rather than with a specific syntax) means that the form can be used in main clauses as well as subordinate clauses (as in (27) above), thus further muddying the syntactic identification of Subjunctive morphology and subordination.

Heine (this volume) has discovered that, for the German modal verbs, "the highest values of agent-oriented and the lowest values of epistemic modality are found with items associated with high verbality". This is suggestive in view of the fact that, in Spanish, the copulas and auxiliaries—which lack some of the characteristics of full verbs—have a special behavior with respect to modality. In the texts examined, the low-assertiveness *-se* form appears preferentially with copular and auxiliary verbs. The next form up in assertiveness, the *-ra* form, appears freely in main clauses only as *hubiera*, from *haber*. The verbs that appear in Participle form with this auxiliary are usually non-action verbs. The list *deseado* 'desired,' *esperado*' hoped,' *pensado* 'thought,' *querido* 'wanted' (all mental act verbs) and *sido* 'been,' covers the majority of the possibilities. The one case of a second-person subject has already been discussed as (27); here, significantly, the modality is agent-oriented.

Finally, there is a hard-to-define but very real performance factor at work in all of this. In modern Spanish, the mood system is a tremendously sophisticated rhetorical device, and individual speakers are more or less competent with respect to using it in a sophisticated way. There are native speakers of Spanish who are masterful manipulators of the mood system, and there are native speakers who are clumsy at using mood to produce rhetorical effects. These varying degrees of rhetorical—as opposed to grammatical—competence constitute input for learners of the language, and this loop serves to further subjectify the system.

Recent work in categorization has shown that the structure of categories varies depending on what the goal of categorization is. According to Barsalou, "it appears that people use a variety of differences between exemplars when judging typicality" (1987:104); with respect to mood in Spanish, speakers are presented with syntactic, semantic, discourse and metalinguistic differences from which to judge what constitutes a typical Subjunctive. Concepts are temporary constructs in working memory which typically "vary widely as a function of goals, current context, and recent experience" (1987:135). The data presented in this paper exemplify some of the goals and contexts which influence choice of the Spanish Subjunctive. The grammar of mood in Spanish "emerges" (Hopper 1988) from the complex interaction of many factors.

NOTES

1. The use of the Subjunctive to express agent-oriented modality is limited in Spanish. In addition to cases like (27), to be discussed below, there is the archaic and formulaic *quién* +PS, e.g. *quién pudiera escribir* 'would that/if only I could write.' Agent-oriented modality is usually expressed by lexical morphemes, as predicted by Bybee (1985:166).

2. Except for the affirmative singular and plural forms, the Imperative shows Subjunctive morphology. The use of the unmarked verb form (third person, singular, present tense) for the affirmative *tú* command follows a common pattern (Bybee 1985:172). The use of the Subjunctive forms with all negative commands again suggests a correlation between negation and irrealis. And the use of the Subjunctive for all formal commands is surely due to the non-assertive (and therefore polite) value of the morphology.

3. The figures cited here for overall *-se* usage in Lima and Madrid are strikingly similar to those found by DeMello (1993) in a study based on a corpus of educated oral speech. The percentage for Lima was exactly the same (2%), and that for Madrid only slightly higher (16%). Educated Buenos Aires speech, however, showed significantly lower *-se* usage at 6%. The use of a popular dialect in the novel accounts for this disparity, as *-se* usage is reportedly heavy in uneducated Argentine speech. Among the dialects studied by DeMello, the highest *-se* usage was found in San Juan, Puerto Rico.

4. Example (28) shows how the Future tense may carry modal meanings; *será* is the Future form of the verb *ser* 'to be'. This use of the Future has been widely commented on (see e.g. Bybee, Pagliuca and Perkins (1994), and Klein (1980)). If the Synthetic Future (as opposed to the analytic 'going to' future) develops into a kind of morphological modal, as suggested in Fleischman (1982), it will be one more case in which mood marking has moved into the main clause in Spanish. Niño-Murcia (1992) documents a development along these lines in the Spanish of Andean Ecuador, where the Synthetic Future is being used as a kind of polite command.

REFERENCES

Barsalou, L. W. 1987. "The Instability of Graded Structure". *Concepts and Conceptual Development: Ecological and Intellectual Factors in Categorization*, ed. by Ulrich Neisser, 101-140. Cambridge: University Press.

Benet, Juan. 1981. *Una tumba y otros relatos*. Madrid: Taurus Ediciones.

Bolinger, Dwight L. 1956. "Subjunctive *-ra* and *-se*: 'Free Variation'?" *Hispania* 39.345-49.

Bolinger, Dwight L. 1968. "Postposed Main Phrases: An English Rule for the Romance Subjunctive". *Canadian Journal of Linguistics* 14.3-30.

Bryce Echenique, Alfredo. 1991. *Un mundo para Julius*. Barcelona: Plaza & Janés.

Bybee, Joan L. 1985. *Morphology: A Study of the Relation between Form and Meaning* (=*Typological Studies in Language*, 9) Amsterdam & Philadelphia: John Benjamins.

Bybee, Joan L., William Pagliuca, & Revere D. Perkins. 1994. *The Evolution of Grammar: Tense, Aspect and Modality in the Languages of the World*. Chicago: University of Chicago Press.

Chafe, Wallace. This volume. "The Realis-Irrealis Distinction in Caddo, the Northern Iroquoian Languages, and English".
Contreras, Heles. 1976. *A Theory of Word Order with Special Reference to Spanish*. Amsterdam: North-Holland.
DeMello, George. 1993. "*-Ra* Vs. *-Se* Subjunctive: A New Look at an Old Topic". *Hispania* 76.235-44.
Donoso, José. 1965. *Los mejores cuentos de José Donoso*. Santiago de Chile: Editora Zig-Zag.
Fleischman, Suzanne. 1982. *The Future in Thought and Language: Diachronic Evidence from Romance*. Cambridge: University Press.
Fleischman, Suzanne. 1989. "Temporal Distance: A Basic Linguistic Metaphor". *Studies in Language* 13.1-50.
Gili y Gaya, Samuel. 1964. *Curso superior de sintaxis española* (9a ed.). Barcelona: Bibliograf.
Gsell, Otto & Ulrich Wandruszka. 1986. *Der Romanische Konjunctiv*. Tübingen: Niemeyer.
Guitart, Jorge M. 1991. "Aspectos pragmáticos del modo en los complementos de predicados de conocimiento y de adquisición de conocimiento en español". *Indicative y subjuntivo* ed. by Ignacio Bosque, 315-29. Madrid: Taurus Universitaria.
Guo, Jiansheng. Tis volume. "The International Structuring of Meaning: Children's Use and Development of the Manderin Model *Neng* (Can)".
Harris, Martin. B. 1986. "The Historical Development of *si*-clauses in Romance". *On Conditionals* ed. by E. C. Traugott, A. ter Meulen, J. S. Reilly & C. A. Ferguson, 265-84. Cambridge: University Press.
Heine, Bernd. This volume. "Agent-Oriented vs. Epistemic Modality: Some Observations on German Modals".
Hopper, Paul. 1988. "Emergent Grammar and the A Priori Grammar Postulate". *Linguistics in Context: Connecting Observation and Understanding* ed. by Deborah Tannen, 117-34. Norwood, NJ: Ablex.
James, Deborah. 1982. "Past Tense and the Hypothetical: A Cross-Linguistic Study". *Studies in Language* VI. 375-403.
Kany, C. E. 1951. *American-Spanish Syntax* (2nd ed.). Chicago:University Press.
Klein, Flora. 1980. "Experimental Verification of Semantic Hypotheses Applied to Mood in Spanish". *Georgetown University Papers in Language and Linguistics* 17.15-34.
Klein-Andreu, Flora. 1986. "Speaker-Based and Reference-Based Factors in Language: Non-Past Conditional Sentences in Spanish". *Studies in Romance Linguistics* ed. by Carmen Silva-Corvalán & Osvaldo Jaeggli, 99-119. Dordrecht: Foris.
Klein-Andreu, Flora. 1991. "Losing Ground". *Discourse Pragmatics and the Verb* ed. by Suzanne Fleischman & Linda Waugh, 164-178. London: Croom Helm.
Krakusin, Margarita and Cedeño, Aristófanes. 1992. "Selección del modo después de *el hecho de que*". *Hispania* 75.1289-1293.
Lakoff, George. 1987. "Cognitive Models and Prototype Theory". *Concepts and Conceptual Development: Ecological and Intellectual Factors in Categorization* ed. by Ulrich Neisser, 63-100. Cambridge: University Press.
Lavandera, Beatriz R. 1983. "Shifting Moods in Spanish Discourse". *Discourse Perspectives on Syntax* ed. by Flora Klein- Andreu, 209-31. New York: Academic Press.

Lipski, John. 1978. "Subjunctive as Fact?". *Hispania* 61.931-934.
Lunn, Patricia V. 1989. "The Spanish Subjunctive and 'Relevance'". *Studies in Romance Linguistics* ed. by Carl Kirschner & Janet A. DeCesaris, 249-60. Amsterdam & Philadelphia: John Benjamins.
Lunn, Patricia V. 1988. "Some Stops on the Modality Line". *New Analyses in Romance Linguistics* ed. by Dieter Wanner and Douglas A. Kibbee, 221-33. Amsterdam & Philadelphia: John Benjamins.
Lunn, Patricia V. 1989. "Spanish Mood and the Prototype of Assertability". *Linguistics* 27.687-702.
Lunn, Patricia V., and Thomas D. Cravens. 1991. "A Contextual Reconsideration of the Spanish *-ra* 'Indicative'". *Discourse Pragmatics and the Verb* ed. by Suzanne Fleischman & Linda Waugh, 147-63. London: Croom Helm.
Marsé, Juan. 1978. *Si te dicen que caí.* Barcelona: Seix Barral.
Mithun, Marianne. This volume. "On the Relativity of Irreality".
Niño-Murcia, Mercedes. 1992. "El futuro sintético en el español norandino: Caso de mandato atenuado". *Hispania* 75.705-13.
Puig, Manuel. 1976. *El beso de la mujer araña.* Barcelona: Seix Barral.
Roberts, John R. ms. "The Category 'Irrealis' in Papuan Medical Verbs".
Romaine, Suzanne. This volume. "The Modal Function of *bai* in Tok Pisin".
Silva-Corvalán, Carmen. 1985. "Modality and Semantic Change". *Historical Semantics, Historical Word Formation*, ed. by Jacek Fisiak, 547-542. Berlin: Mouton.
Solé, Carlos A. and Solé, Yolanda R. 1977. *Modern Spanish Syntax.* Lexington MA: D. C. Heath.
Sperber, Dan and Wilson, Deirdre. 1986. *Relevance: Communication and Cognition.* Cambridge MA: Harvard University Press.
Taibo, Paco Ignacio II. 1976. *Días de combate.* México: Editorial Patria.
Taylor, John. 1989. *Linguistic Categorization: Prototypes in Linguistic Theory.* Oxford: Clarendon Press.
Terrell, Tracy & Hooper, Joan B. 1974. "A Semantically Based Analysis of Mood in Spanish". *Hispania* 57.484-94.
Traugott, Elizabeth C. 1989. "On the Rise of Epistemic Meanings in English: An Example of Subjectification in Semantic Change". *Language* 65.31-55.
Vázquez Montalbán, Manuel. 1977. *La soledad del manager.* Barcelona: Editorial Planeta.
Vázquez Montalbán, Manuel. 1986. *El balneario.* Barcelona: Editorial Planeta.
Woehr, Richard. 1975. "Grammar of the Factive Nominal in Spanish". *Language Sciences* 36.13-19.
Wright, L. O. 1932. *The -ra Verb Form in Spain.* (=*University of California Publications in Modern Philology* 15.1). Berkeley: University of California Press.

IV
Modality and Other Categories of Grammar

Negation and the Modals of Possibility and Necessity

F.R. Palmer
University of Reading

Introduction

Even a brief look at the forms used for modality accompanied by negation in a few languages will show that there is a great deal of irregularity, in the sense of lack of regular correspondence between form and meaning. This paper investigates the negative modal forms of a number of diverse languages within a simple typological paradigm, and shows that several kinds of suppletion are used and that there is a strong tendency for some terms in this paradigm to be regular and other forms to be irregular.

1. The nature of the irregularity

The irregularity takes two forms:

(i) There is a simple lack of one-to-one correlation, between form and meaning, so that it is not possible to predict for a given form what will be its meaning, or, vice versa, what will be the form to express a particular modal meaning. This is simply illustrated from both French and Italian:

(1)	French	*Il faut*	*partir*		
		it is.necessary	to.go		
		'(We) must go'			
		Il ne	*faut*	*pas*	*partir*
		it NEG	is.necessary	NEG	to.go
		'(We) mustn't go'			

Italian	*Deve*	*venire*
	must+3SG	to.come
	'You must come' (polite form)	
	Non deve	*venire*
	NEG must+3SG	to.come
	'You mustn't come'	

Since in both cases the negative marker is formally placed with the modal, it might be expected that it would be the modality, the meaning of 'must', that of obligation, that is negated, with the resultant meaning 'there is no obligation' (English: 'needn't'); in fact, the meaning is 'there is obligation not to' (English 'mustn't'). (The Italian sentence can also be interpreted in terms of 'no obligation', but that does not invalidate the point being made; for examples from other languages see Section 5).

Since form and meaning are to be compared and contrasted, the choice of terminology is important. The terms 'modal' and 'full verb' will be used for the formal, grammatical, elements, while for meaning, the terms used will be 'modality' and 'proposition;' provided these distinctions are clearly made, the terms 'negated', 'negation' etc., can be used for both form and meaning. Any lack of correspondence between negation of the modal and negation of the modality or between negation of the full verb and negation of the proposition is considered to be an irregularity.

In the examples above, then, while the modal is formally negated, semantically it is the proposition, not the modality, that is negated. This irregularity may be described in terms of the negation being 'misplaced.' It may be added, however, that this kind of misplacement of the negative is not confined to modals: it is also to be found in e.g. *I don't think he'll come* (= 'I think he won't come').

(ii) A second type of irregularity is found where there are gaps in the paradigm, especially where these gaps appear to be filled by suppletion from other modal forms in the language. This can be illustrated from English:

(2) *You must go*
You musn't go
You needn't go

Obligation to act and obligation not to act are expressed by forms of *must*, but for no obligation to act the negative form of another verb, *need*, is required.

No less important, though possibly less immediately obvious, is the kind of suppletion found in:

(3) *He must be in his office*
He can't be in his office
He may not be in his office

The first may be roughly paraphrased 'I firmly conclude that he is in his office', but the notions 'I firmly conclude that he is not in his office' and 'I do not firmly conclude that he is in his office' are not usually expressed by a form of *must*. Instead, the forms that may be used to express these meanings are those of *may* and *can*, modals expressing a 'possible' conclusion ('It is possible that ...'); an explanation for this is discussed in Sections 2 and 7.

2. The modals of possibility and necessity

As the title of this paper indicates, it is concerned only with the modals of possibility and necessity, and, moreover, only with epistemic and deontic modality, deontic possibility and necessity being interpreted in terms of the modals for permission (English *may/can*) and obligation (English *must*) respectively. The *can* of ability (dynamic possibility) is not included for two related reasons, that it is less modal and more like verbs such as *wish, intend* etc., and it does not raise the same kind of problems with negation as the other forms.

There are three reasons for this delimitation of the area of discussion:

(i) It is comparatively easy to identify such modals across languages, though it must be allowed that there are some differences of meaning. In particular, in some languages it would seem that there is no distinction between 'mustn't come' and 'oughtn't to come', while a Hebrew speaker felt that the form he gave me for 'He must be in his office', might be better translated as 'Of course he is in his office.' But problems of this kind beset any kind of cross-linguistic comparison.

(ii) It is possible to paraphrase them in terms of such expressions as 'It is possible/necessary that ...', and thereby to indicate where the negation is semantically located (its scope) — 'It is not possible/necessary that ...' and 'It is possible/necessary that ... not ....' This is important, because it is assumed that in the ideal or regular situation the grammatical placement of the negative indicates the scope of the negation. If the modal is negated, the expected paraphrase will be 'It is not possible/necessary that ...', while if the full verb is negated, the paraphrase will be 'It is possible/necessary that ... not ....' One concern of this paper is the way in which modal systems diverge from this ideal and the forms are, in this sense, irregular.

(iii) Possibility and necessity are related logically in terms of negation, and these relations are to some degree mirrored in language. This is clearly seen from English. Consider:

(4) *He may be in his office*
He can't be in his office
He may not be in his office

These express 'possible that', 'not possible that' and 'possible that not' respectively. (There is suppletion of *can* for *may*, but both are essentially modals of possibility). However, as noted in Section 1 (ii), the second and third examples can be seen as the negative forms of *He must be in his office* ('necessary that', indicating a firm conclusion). This can be explained in terms of the logical equivalence Not Possible ≡ Necessary Not and Possible Not ≡ Not Necessary.

Because of irregularity, the lack of correspondence between form and meaning, it is essential to distinguish between the characterization (in terms of negation and possibility/necessity) of the forms and the meanings of the modals. This can be achieved by using quotation marks for the meanings, but not for the forms; thus it can be said of the examples above that the not-possible form (*can't*) is used to express 'necessary-not' and the possible-not form (*may not*) is used to express 'not-necessary' (but see Section 7 for the problem with *may not*).

In my analysis there are twelve different categories (see Palmer 1990: 39). These are, with the relevant English forms:

(5)	Epistemic	'possible'	*may*
		'not-possible'	*can't*
		'possible-not'	*may not*
		'necessary'	*must*
		'not-necessary'	*(may not)*
		'necessary-not'	*(can't)*

Deontic	'possible'	*can/may*
	'not-possible'	*can't/may not*
	'possible-not'	*(needn't)*
	'necessary'	*must*
	'not-necessary'	*needn't*
	'necessary-not'	*mustn't*

(The forms in brackets indicate the suppletive forms used in English that are dependent on the necessity/possibility equivalences).

It is not suggested that all the modal forms fit precisely into the logical system, although this seems to be true of the epistemic modals in English, where the negative necessity forms are provided by the logical equivalences. With the deontic modals, however, there are forms that appear to be logically equivalent, yet do not have identical functions in the language. Thus denial of permission with *can't* can be interpreted as 'not-possible', and obligation not to act with *musn't* as 'necessary-not', yet they are clearly not identical in meaning, even though they share the feature of precluding action; here language and logic do not wholly coincide. Yet, in contrast to this, there is only one form to express both permission not to and no obligation — the not-necessary form *needn't*; here language is consistent with logic.

3. The language material

Twenty-two languages were investigated. Most of the material was provided by interviewing native speakers, many of them Ph.D students in the Department of Linguistic Science in the University of Reading. They were asked to provide the most natural equivalents of English sentences and no attempt was made to check the material against published grammars; in any case, that would probably have been a futile exercise, since most grammars contain little or nothing on the topic. The Tigrinya material comes from personal research. Only two written sources were consulted, Davidsen-Nielsen (1990) and Thiagaran (1980), both written by scholars fully aware of the issues. This sample may not be sufficient to draw any firm general conclusions, but it is successful in pointing out features likely to be of typological interest.

There were two problems with this material:

(i) Not surprisingly, several of the languages investigated provided few relevant forms, and can be seen as having very little modal system. Thus for Oromo (N. Kenya) the only apparent negative form was that for epistemic 'possible-not' (which was regular):

(6) *inni afisa isa keesa jira fa*
he office his inside be possible
'He may be in his office'

inni afisa isa keesa hinjiru fa
he office his inside NEG+be possible
'He may not be in his office'

For the 'not-possible' 'He can't be in his office' the speaker offered only 'He isn't', and for the epistemic necessity only forms with an emphatic particle on 'office', while for the deontic forms he offered only imperatives.

Of course, there may be forms in the language that the speaker had not thought of, but that does not necessarily invalidate my remarks, for my interest lies primarily in establishing the most natural forms, rather than attempting to establish a neat system. I am positive about the existence of gaps in Tigrinya, on which I worked in detail many years ago, but have now been able to check with both my original assistant and his daughter. There is no modal expression for epistemic 'not-possible', the negative declarative being used instead, while for deontic 'not-necessary' the only form they could suggest was:

(7) *bə-ḥayle 'aytəbəlla'*
by-force eat+NEG+IMP
(Lit. 'Don't eat by force') 'You needn't (don't have to) eat'

There are, almost certainly, languages that have no system in terms of negation and possibility/necessity, e.g., those with an evidential system (see Palmer 1986: 66-76).

(ii) It was not always easy or even possible to decide which were the relevant modal forms. Thus for French, it seemed at first that the forms to be considered were the verbs *pouvoir* and *devoir* plus the infinitive, but, from a consensus of a number of French scholars, it appears that, in practice, epistemic possibility is expressed by *il se peut que*, and the impersonal *il faut* is more commonly used for deontic necessity. There was a different problem with Welsh. One speaker (a professional linguist) provided me with an almost perfectly regular set of forms using the verb *gallu* for possibility and the impersonal *rhaid* for necessity. A second speaker (with no knowledge of linguistics) assured me that *gallu* could only be used to expressed ability, and came up with non-modal forms of the type 'It is possible that ...' for epistemic possibility and forms of the verb *cael* 'get' for deontic possibility; he offered a regular form for epistemic 'necessary-not' and regular forms for deontic 'not-possible' and 'not-necessary', but none of the other negatives (see Section 5).

4. Regular and irregular systems

I did not discover a language with a perfectly regular system. The closest to it was found in Modern Greek, where only one form, that for deontic 'not-necessary', was irregular. The regular forms were:

(8) *bori na ine sto γrafio tus* (epistemic possibility)
it.can that they.are in.the office theirs
'They must be in their office'

δen bori na ine . (not-possible)
not can that they.are ...
'They can't be ...'

bori na min ine ... (possible-not)
it.can that not they.are ...
'They may not be ...'

prepi na ine sto γrafio tus (epistemic necessity)
it.must that they.are in.the office theirs
'They must be in their office'

δen prepi na ine ... (not-necessary)
not it.must that they.are ...
'They may not be ...'

prepi na min ine ... (necessary-not)
it.must that not they.are ...
'They can't not be ...'

boris na fiγis (deontic possibility)
you.can that you.leave
'You can (may) leave'

δen boris na fiγis (not possible)
not you.can that you.leave
'You can't (may not) leave'

boris na mi fiγis (possible-not)
you.can that not you.leave
'You needn't leave'

prepi na fiγis (deontic necessity)
it.must that you.leave
'You can (may) leave'

prepi na mi fiγis (necessary-not)
it.must that not you.leave
'You mustn't leave'

For the irregular 'not-necessary', two forms were suggested:

(9) *ðen ine anangi na fiγis*
not is necessary that you.leave
'You needn't leave'

ðen xriazete na fiγis
not is.needed that you.leave
'You needn't leave'

A relevant observation about the Greek system is that there is a finite subordinate clause introduced by a 'that' conjunction. It is this, undoubtedly, that influences the regularity. Such regularity was found in several other languages for epistemic modality where that type of modality alone employs a finite subordinate clause, e.g., in one set of forms in French (see Section 3 above):

(10) *Il se peut qu'il soit ...*
it REFL can that.he is ...
'He may be ...'

Il ne se peut pas qu'il soit ...
It not REFL can not that.he is ...
'He can't be ...'

Il	*se*	*peut*	*qu'il*	*ne*	*soit*	*pas ...*
it	REFL	can	that.he	not	is	not ...

'He may not be ...'

Where the 'ideal' situation is not to be found, i.e., where the scope of the negation is not reflected in the grammatical placement of the negative, there are several possibilities:

(i) The simplest is that another verb is used. Two examples of this are found in English: the use of *can* in place of epistemic *may* for 'not-possible' (*can't*) and the use of *need* in place of deontic *must* for 'not-necessary' (*needn't*).

(ii) The logically equivalent form is used. An example is the use of ('not- possible') *can't* in English as the form for epistemic 'necessary-not' corresponding to *must* (see (2) and, for other examples, Section 5).

(iii) The negative is 'misplaced', placed on the 'wrong' verb. This was found commonly and almost exclusively with 'necessary-not' (mostly with deontic modality); this was signalled grammatically by the not-necessary form. This too was illustrated, from French and Italian, in Section 1, and there are further examples in Section 5.

(iv) There is a rather different construction, but using the relevant modal. Thus for Latvian, the form proposed for deontic 'possible-not' (permission not to) was literally 'You can come in, or not':

(11)	*tu*	*drīksti*	*nākt*	*ieksa*	*vai*	*ne*
	you	can	come	in	or	not

'You needn't come in'

(v) The form used is not related grammatically to the modal system.

5. Logical suppletion

One of the most interesting points is the suppletion in terms of the logical equivalences. For most of the languages, suppletive forms of this kind were offered for at least one place in the paradigm, but there is a problem with some languages, in that there were gaps in the paradigm and no suppletive forms were offered. Yet it cannot be said with any certainty that suppletive forms could not have been used, for it is possible the native speaker simply did not immediately think of them (and I carefully refrained from suggesting them).

There was only one language with no suppletive forms of this type — Modern Greek, where all the forms except that for deontic 'not-necessary' were regular (see Section 4).

Where suppletive forms were offered, they followed two main patterns:

(i) Suppletive forms are used for both types of negation of necessity (both 'not-necessary' and 'necessary-not'), possibility forms being used for both. This is especially common with epistemic modality, as already illustrated for English by (3) which is repeated here:

(3) *He must be in his office*
He can't be in his office
He may not be in his office

Similar forms were found for Assamese, Italian and one variety of Welsh. Examples from the first two are:

(12) Assamese

ɔfis-ot	*t^hakibɔ*	*lage*	
office-in	to.be	he.must	

'He must be in the office'

ɔfis-ot	*na*	*t^hakibɔ*	*pare*	(possible-not →'not necessary')
office-in	not	to.be	he.may	

'He may not be in the office'

ɔfis-ot	*t^hakibɔ*	*nɷare*	(not-possible →'necessary-not')
office-in	to.be	he.NEG+may	

'He can't be in the office'

Italian

Deve	*essere*	*nell'*	*ufficio*
He.must	be	in.the	office

'He must be in the office'

Può	*non*	*essere*	*nell'*	*ufficio*	(possible-not →
He.can	not	be	in.the	office	'not-necessary')

'He may not be in the office'

Non	*può*	*essere*	*nell'*	*ufficio*	(not-possible →
Not	he.can	be	in.the	office	'necessary-not')

'He can't be in the office'

However, for Italian, the not-necessary form was suggested as an alternative for the last:

(13)

Non	*deve*	*essere*	*nell'*	*ufficio*
Not	he.must	be	in.the	office

'He can't be in the office'

(Although this uses the 'must' verb, the negation is misplaced, the not-necessary form being used for 'necessary-not', as it is also used with deontic necessity in Italian — see Sections 1 and 5).

Japanese, alone of the languages investigated, appeared to use suppletion for both types of deontic necessity. Surprisingly, perhaps, even the positive necessity form was suppleted, using a double negative ('can't not');

(14)

tabe	*naku*	*te wa*	*ikenai*	(not-possible-not →'necessary')
eat	not		may.not	

'You must eat'

tabe	*te wa*	*ikenai*	(not-possible →'necessary-not')
eat		may.not	

'You mustn't eat'

tabe	*naku*	*temo ii*	(possible-not →'not-necessary')
eat	not	may	

'You needn't eat'

(ii) Suppletive forms were used for negation of the proposition alone ('possible-not' and 'necessary-not'), the forms negating the modality being regular and used to provide the suppletive forms (the not-necessary and not-possible forms respectively).

This pattern is found in Danish for the epistemic modals only. Thus Davidsen Nielsen (1990: 78-87) recognizes only two forms that negate epistemic modality:

(15)

Det	*kan*	*ikke*	*være*	*sandt*	(not-possible)
that	can	not	be	true	

'That can't be true'

Det behøver ikke være sandt (not-necessary)
that mustnot be true
'That may not be true'

These are treated as the two negatives of both:

(16) *Det kan være sandt*
that can be true
'That may be true'

Det må være sandt
that must be true
'That must be true'

If in Danish the negative formally negates the modal (see Section 7), these forms are regular when used to negate the modality (to express 'not-possible' and 'not-necessary'), but are used suppletively for the forms that negate the proposition (as 'necessary-not' and 'possible-not' respectively).

There was a similar situation with deontic modals for one version of Welsh: only the modals are negated, and these negate the modality, so that the forms negating the proposition are suppletive:

(17) *Mi gewch chi ddod yfory*
You get you to.come tomorrow
'You may come tomorrow'

(Ni) chewch chi ddim ddod yfory ('not-possible/
(not) get you not to.come tomorrow 'necessary-not')
'You can't come tomorrow' (or 'You mustn't ...')

(Mae'n) rhaid i chi ddod yfory
(It.is) necessary to you to.come tomorrow
'You must come tomorrow'

('d oes) ddim rhaid i chi ddod yfory
('not necessary'/'possible-not')
(it.is.not) not necessary to you to.come tomorrow
'You needn't come tomorrow'

However, Welsh has another means of expressing 'necessary-not' — see Section 6.

6. Deontic 'not-possible' and 'necessary-not'

The most striking result of this exercise lies in the comparison of the forms for deontic 'not-possible' (denial of permission) and 'necessary-not' (obligation not to). In every one of the languages except Oromo, which, as was noted earlier, barely has any system, and Tamil, the 'not-possible' form was regular in that negation was formally marked on the modal. Some examples are:

(18) Tigrinya

lətə'atto	*'aytəkə'ələn*	*'ika*
that.you.come.in	you.not.being.able	you.are

'You cannot/may not come in'

Latvian

tu	*ne*	*drīksti*	*nākt*	*ieksa*
you	not	can	come	in

'You cannot/may not come in'

By contrast, in all the languages except two, the form used for 'necessary-not' was irregular. The possibilities were:

(i) In ten of them, Arabic, Assamese, Danish, English, Farsi, French, Italian, Kinyarwanda, Tamil and Tigrinya, it is the modal that was formally negated, i.e., there was misplacement of the negative (although in Italian and Tamil the same form was used for 'not-necessary', while in Farsi the regular form with negation on the full verb was also possible — and see Section 6 for a discussion of Danish and English). Examples are (see also (1) for Italian):

(19) Arabic

la:zim	*jizi*
must	you.come.in

'You must come in'

ma:/mu	*la:zim*	*jizi*
not	must	you.come.in

'You mustn't come in'

Kinyarwanda

agomba	*kwinjira*
he.must	to.come.in

'He must come in'

ntagomba *kwinjira*
NEG+he.must come.in
'He mustn't come in'

The form used for expressing 'not-necessary' in these languages varied. While Italian and Tamil (see above) used the same form, Kinyarwanda and Assamese used rather different constructions, while Arabic, Danish, English and Farsi employed a different verb and the others had no form that was clearly modal.

(ii) The form given in five languages, Bahasa Malaysia, Chinese, Hebrew, Kikuyu and Japanese, was the suppletive not-possible form, and this was also given as an alternative to the form with misplaced negative for Italian and Tamil. In all of these languages except Chinese and Japanese, negation on the necessity modal had the regular 'not-necessary' sense (Chinese and Japanese had no necessity forms with negation, and used the suppletive 'possible-not' for 'not-necessary'). Examples are:

(20) Bahasa Malaysia
dia *mesti/perlu* *masuk*
he/she must come.in
'He/she must come in'

dia *tak* *mesti/perlu* *masuk*
he/she not must come.in
'He/she needn't come in'

dia *tak* *boleh* *masuk*
he/she not can come.in
'He/she mustn't (can't/may not) come in'

Chinese
ta *míŋ tjen* *bi* *ʃy lé*
he tomorrow must come
'He must come tomorrow'

ta *míŋ tjen* *kŏe i* *bu* *ʃy lé*
he tomorrow can/may not come
'He needn't come tomorrow'

ta *míŋ tjen* *bu* *kŏe i* *ʃy lé*
he tomorrow not can/may come
'He mustn't come tomorrow'

There is probably also similar suppletion in German (but see Section 7):

(21) *Du musst herein kommen*
You must in.here come
'You must come in'

Du musst nicht herein kommen
You must not in.here come
'You needn't come in'

Du darfst nicht herein kommen
You can/may not in.here come
'You mustn't come in'

The point here is that the verb *dürfen* (*darfst*) is probably best seen as a possibility verb (though translated 'need' as well as 'can' by dictionaries), used both in positive forms and as the lexically suppletive verb for *mögen* (although *können* is also used):

(22) *Du magst herein kommen*
You can/may in.here come
'You can (may) come in'

Du darfst nicht herein kommen
Du kannst nicht herein kommen
You can/may not in.here come
'You can't (may not) come in'

This shows that the possibility verb *dürfen* is used suppletively to express necessity, in place of *müssen* (not-possible to express 'necessary-not').

Welsh has another alternative. Instead of the suppletive 'not-possible' form given in (17), the 'necessary' form may be used if followed by the negative verb *peidio*, which is, slightly misleadingly perhaps, glossed as 'refrain' below:

(23) *Rhaid i chi beidio â ddod yfory*
Must to you refrain from to.come tomorrow'
'You mustn't come tomorrow'

The two languages in which negation is regular, with the negation of the full verb giving the 'necessary-not' interpretation were Modern Greek and one version of Welsh. The Greek example has already been given and discussed. What is surprising is that it is the form used for 'not-necessary', rather than the form for 'necessary-not', that is irregular in Greek. This is expressed not by negation on the modal, but by a different, probably non-modal, verb, as illustrated in (9), which is repeated here:

(9) *ðen ine anangi na fiγis*
not is necessary that you.leave
'You needn't leave'

ðen xriazete na fiγis
not is.needed that you.leave
'You needn't leave'

7. Function of the negative

There is a problem with some of the Germanic languages in that it is not at all certain that it can be determined whether it is the modal or the full verb that is negated. In English, it is to be assumed that the negative is formally associated with the modal, since it is generally cliticised. In that case, there is misplacement of the negative in *You mustn't' come*. If this were regular, it would have the 'non-necessity' meaning, which is, in fact, expressed by *needn't.* The position in Danish and German is less obvious. In Danish *skulle* is commonly used for obligation (as well as *mätte*), but the negative forms, with *behøve* used suppletively, are (Davidsen-Nielsen 1990: 200-1):

(24) *Du skal ikke svare*
you must not reply
'You mustn't reply'

Du behøver ikke svare
you must not come
'You needn't come'

The first of these should be compared with the German *Du musst nicht herein kommen* in (21). The difference in meaning is surprising. If it is assumed that, as in English, the negatives *ikke* and *nicht* are formally associated with the modal, Danish is irregular, but German is regular. Conversely, of course, if the negatives were assumed to negate the full verb, Danish would be regular and German irregular. Since, however, these negative markers are placed between the modal and the full verb, it may be that there is no way of determining which of these two they formally negate.

In Danish, however, there is some evidence to suggest that the negative belongs formally with the modal: in certain subordinate clauses it precedes the modal. Examples are (Davidsen-Nielsen personal communication):

(25) *Jeg mener at man ikke skal/behøver dømme*
]I think that one not must pass judgment on
nogen så hurtigt
someone so quickly
'I think one mustn't/needn't pass judgment on someone that quickly'

I know of no similar evidence to decide the issue in German. Since, however, negatives normally follow other verbs in German, it is not unreasonable to associate the negative formally with the modal.

There is, perhaps, a problem with English epistemic *may not*: this is not normally cliticized, so that the negative is not so clearly associated formally with the modal. Consistency with the other modals, however, would suggest that it is the modal that is negated. In that case, however, the form is irregular, since it is a not-possible form expressing 'possible-not;' moreover, it is the only example from all the languages considered in which there is displacement of the negation with this meaning. It is tempting to suggest that it is precisely because it has this meaning that the form is not cliticized, and so suggests negation of the full verb (and regular negation of the proposition). However, if that is so, one might expect (falsely) that deontic *must + not* should also not permit cliticization, and so similarly indicate negation of the full verb and of the proposition.

One solution is to say that in these languages it is not possible to signal the contrast of negation of the modality and negation of the proposition by differential placement of the negative (negating the modal and negating the full verb): the negative formally belongs to the whole verbal complex, as in English with other auxiliaries — with *isn't coming* and *hasn't come*. Moreover, the contrast is almost always made by the use of suppletion (e.g., English *must/need*, German *müssen/dürfen*, Danish *skulle/behøve* etc.; it may be precisely because negative placement cannot signal the contrast that suppletion is used. However, these languages can still be included within the general typological framework, because, if the modality is taken to negate the whole verbal phrase, the most natural interpretation would be 'It is not the case that it is possible/necessary ...;' this would be the same as with the regular marking of negation of the modal. Judgments about regularity (and about suppletion) are, then, still possible: it can still be said that the German *must nicht*, expressing 'not-necessary', is regular, while the corresponding forms in English and Danish (*mustn't, skal ikke*), expressing 'necessary-not' are irregular.

8. Possible explanations

Is there any explanation for the features discussed in Sections 6 and 7? The issue of suppletion is, perhaps, easy to account for: economy is achieved by using the logical equivalences. They are particularly appropriate with epistemic modality, where logic and language appear to coincide, but less appropriate with deontic modality, where, for instance, 'not-possible' (denial of permission) and 'necessary-not' (obligation not to) are not identical in meaning, even though both preclude action.

The comparative irregularity of the 'necessary-not' form is probably due to two factors. The first is that this is a very commonly used form, and, in particular, much more common than 'not-necessary.' The second is that elsewhere in language the scope of negation is not accurately indicated by the grammar, as shown by the example noted in Section 1, *I don't think he'll come* (= 'I think he won't come'). It is, perhaps, not wholly surprising if the form that negates the modal is used for this purpose; it would emphasize the essentially negative aspect of the prohibition. This is especially so if there is only one formal way of associating the modal verb with negation, as in English. By contrast, the 'not-possible' form is usually regular, but this too may be accounted for by its frequent use, in that there would be no reason not to use the most obviously available form.

REFERENCES

Davidsen-Nielsen, N. 1990. *Tense and Mood in English; A comparison with Danish.* Berlin & New York: Mouton de Gruyter.

Palmer, F.R. 1986. *Mood and Modality.* Cambridge: Cambridge University Press.

Palmer, F.R. 1990. *Modality and the English Modals.* London: Longman.

Thiagaran, K. 1980. Modal systems of English and Tamil. Ph.D. thesis, University of Madras.

APPENDIX

The table below indicates the type of form offered for each modal type in the languages investigated. The symbols used are:

- √ Regular
- S Suppletive in terms of the possible/necessary equivalences
- M Negation misplaced
- D Different modal form
- C Construction different, but modal form used
- \- No form offered or form not in the modal system

	Epistemic				Deontic			
	Not-Pos	Pos-Not	Not-Nec	Nec-Not	Not-Pos	Pos-Not	Not-Nec	Nec-Not
Arabic (Hijazi)	-	√	√	√	√	√	D	M
Assamee	√	√	S	S	√	-	-	M
Bahasa Malaysia	√	√	√	√	√	S	√	S
Chinese	√	√	S	S	√	√	S	S
Danish	√	S	√	S	√	S	√	M
English	D	R	S	S	√	S?	D	M
Farsi	√	√	-	√/R	√	-	D	√/M
French	√	√	S	S	√	√	-	M
German	√	S	√/D	S	√	-	√	S
Greek	√	√	√	√	√	√	D	√
Hebrew	√	√	-	√	√	√	√	S
Italian	√	√	S	R/S	√	√	√	M/S
Japanes	D	√	S	S/√	√	√	S	S
Kikuyu	√	S	√	S	√	S	√	S
Kinyarwanda	√	√	-	-	√	√	C	R
Latvian	√	√	-	-	√	C	√	-
Luo	√	D	-	-	√	-	√	-
Oromo	-	√	-	-	-	-	-	-
Serbo-Croatian	D	√	√	S	√	S	√	D
Tamil	√	S	D	D	S	D	√	M/S
Tigrinya	-	√	√	-	√	-	-	M
Welsh (i)	√	√	S	S	√	S	√	√
(ii)	-	-	-	√	√	S	√	S

A Functional Theory of Complementizers*

Zygmunt Frajzyngier
Dept. of Linguistics, University of Colorado

1. Introduction

My main goal in this paper is to present a functional theory of complementizers. The category of complementizers, an important component of complex and simple sentence structure, remains undefined, as documented further in the paper. A secondary goal is to show the interconnectedness of elements of the same functional domain in a grammatical system. More specifically, I show that presence of one or more complementizers, treated as a parametric variation within the GB framework, is closely linked to the synchronic or diachronic presence or absence of devices encoding various kinds of modalities, and to the place these markers occupy in the clause. Applying the proposed theory I describe (1) the motivations and conditions contributing to the absence of complementizers in the matrix clause, and (2) the occurrence of two complementizers in a sequence. The results of the present study fully support postulating mood as a component of a sentence. Since this work addresses substantial issues in the structure of language, its results should be of interest to functional theories and to formal theories such as GB and GPSG, which postulate the existence of COMP as a component of a sentence. Some of the properties that have been ascribed to the category COMP in various works can be explained by its semantic function of encoding modality, while other properties may turn out to be artifacts of analyses.

2. The notion of complementizer

The non-lexical category COMP, first introduced in Bresnan (1970) plays an important role in several contemporary theories. Within GB theory COMP interacts with the theory of Government, Case theory, and Binding theory, and is an important element with respect to movement rules (cf. Chomsky 1986a; 1986b; 1992; Rizzi 1990). COMP may be empty or may be filled by such elements as the English 'that', 'for', etc. It may also be filled by WH-words as a result of WH-movement. In English there cannot be both a complementizer and a WH-word (i.e., the COMP position cannot be filled by two words). There are, however, languages in which there may be two or more complementizers in a sequence, as is the case in Dutch (cf. Koster 1987:206ff). Within GB theory such cases are treated as resulting from movement rules usually involving WH-movement, (e.g., Bouchard 1984; Wachowicz 1974; Cichocki 1983; Comorovski 1986; Rudin 1986; and Rizzi 1990). In other theoretical approaches two complementizers in a sequence are either explicitly allowed (e.g., Kac 1978:76) or implicitly allowed (e.g., Givón 1980, 1990).

While there is some consensus among linguists when it comes to identifying a morpheme as a complementizer, there is considerable divergence as to which morphemes should or should not be included in the set of complementizers. This divergence is due to the fact that the term itself is rather poorly defined. The term 'complementizer' includes the old term 'subordinating particle' that 'marks' sentential subjects and objects, but also includes some morphemes, such as interrogative markers occurring in the matrix clause. Often the identity of this category is taken for granted, (e.g., Lefevbre 1980; Bickerton 1981; Dasgupta 1983; Borsley 1985; Joseph 1985; Lawal 1986; Dimmendaal 1989; Heine et al. 1991). In many works, an example or a list of examples is given in lieu of a precise definition. Chomsky (1986:161), for example, states that in English COMP may be 'that, for or null'. The complementizer may also be defined by analogy, e.g., as the morpheme that corresponds to the English 'that' (Lefevbre 1980). It is through the examples of complementizers that we may be able to detect what the underlying and largely tacit assumptions are with respect to this category.

A random selection from some recent attempts to define complementizers indicates that they are most often treated as morphemes signaling that the following clause is a complement. Thus Noonan (1985:44-45) states that 'Complement types often have associated with them a word, particle, clitic, or affix whose function is to identify the entity as a complement. Such forms are known as complementizers'. He further (p.47) lists among English complementizers 'that', 'if', and 'to'. Palmer (1986) in an extensive discussion of types of complement clauses, uses the term 'conjunction' for what other linguists call 'complementizers'. He does not define the term, but in discussing conjunctions in various languages he ascribes to them modal functions. Ransom (1986:87-88) defines complementizers as 'semi-lexical forms that occur within the complement, setting it off from the main clause and, at the same time, signaling its modality'. She lists among English complementizers 'that', 'whether', 'for-to', and 'whether-to'. Givón (1990:552ff) refers to the morphemes in question as 'subordinating —"separating"—morphemes', but also uses the term 'complementizer' (p. 554) and describes their function as participating 'in the coding of the event-integration scale'. The underlying principle in these studies appears to be that for a morpheme to be classified as complementizer, it has to occur in a specific syntactic position, viz. before the embedded clause (cf. Bickerton 1981:109), regardless of the relative order of the two clauses.

In the present paper I discuss morphemes that are usually analyzed, or likely to be analyzed, as complementizers. I show that complementizers are lexically separate modality markers that happen to occur in a specific syntactic position. As such they are just one of the means by which languages encode modality.

Descriptions that take separating the main and the embedded clauses to be the main function of complementizers cannot explain the occurrence of the same morphemes in simple sentences or in the main clauses of complex sentences, i.e., in syntactic environments that do not require or allow the function of 'separation'. The analyses that postulate separation as the main function of complementizers face the additional problem of motivating the existence of a morpheme whose function is to 'separate' clauses, since there is no possibility of clauses ever overlapping in time. It is not therefore clear what the metaphor of 'separation' stands for. One could argue that the function of complementizers is to mark a clause as a complement, but even that function is not well justified in view of the fact that that there are many types of complement clauses that do not require or even allow a complementizer, even in languages that have complementizers. A third problem with such descriptions is that they do not account for morphemes that occur in positions other than at the beginning of the embedded clause. These morphemes are, as will be shown, in complementary distribution with complementizers, and hence belong to the same set. And finally, if the separation of the main and the embedded clauses, or the marking of a clause as a complement, are the functions of complementizers, why should a language have two or three complementizers in a sequence when one morpheme should be enough?

While early transformational grammar was concerned with the choice of particular complementizers (cf. Rosenbaum 1967), GB theory so far has not shared the same concern. Functionalist approaches are very much interested in the function of specific complementizers. The works dealing with particular complementizers in English and other languages are much too numerous to be listed in this article. For a selection of such works see (Bolinger 1968, Kirsner and Thompson 1976, Ransom 1985, Frajzyngier 1991a, Frajzyngier and Jasperson 1991) and the references there. None of these works answers the following questions: Why are there complementizers in some main clauses but not in others? Why is it that in some languages there may be only one complementizer in the embedded clause, but in other languages there may be two and possibly more complementizers in the embedded clause? I claim that the answer to these questions lies in the function of complementizers. I also discuss phenomena linked with the presence of complementizers that affect other components of a sentence.

3. Hypothesis

The main hypothesis of the present paper is that complementizers constitute a part of the system of modality markers, more specifically, that they encode deontic, epistemic, and other types of modality. As such, they may mark either the main or the embedded clause. The term modality is understood in the present work as it is in Palmer (1986), viz. as the speaker's attitude toward the proposition, but it also includes the agent-oriented and the speaker-oriented distinction of modalities (see Bybee et al., 1994). I consider interrogative also to be a part of epistemic modality, as it is either an inquiry about the truth of the proposition ('yes/no questions'), an inquiry about a specific element of the proposition ('WH-questions'), or an inquiry about the truth of an assumption ('tag questions'). The hypothesis affirms the function of complementizers envisioned to a certain degree in Palmer (1986) and covers an area left untouched in Bybee et al. (1994). It is possible that in some languages complementizers eventually assumed the role of 'separating' two clauses, or of 'introducing' an embedded clause. In the present paper, this last stage in the development of complementizers, even if it is true, will not be discussed.

There are several ways in which this hypothesis can be supported. One is by examining the meaning of complementizers, more specifically by contrasting sentences with a complementizer with those without, or by contrasting sentences with different complementizers. There are many studies of individual languages whose results support the hypothesis, though these studies were published before the hypothesis was postulated (see Bolinger (1968), Kirsner and Thompson (1976), Frajzyngier and Jasperson (1991) for English, and Bickerton (1981) for various Creole languages).

But the hypothesis may also be supported in another way which I will pursue in this paper. If the hypothesis is true, one should expect complementary distribution between complementizers and other modality markers essentially along the following lines: If there is a complementizer marking an α modality there should not be other α modality markers in the clause, and if there is an α modality marker already present in a clause there should not be a complementizer encoding the α modality. If an epistemic or a deontic modality is not marked in the embedded clause it may be marked by a complementizer. If an α modality is marked within the embedded clause it will not be marked by a complementizer.

Another important support for the main hypothesis comes from its ability to explain a number of cross-language syntactic phenomena. These phenomena are: (1) Lack of complementizers in one major type of simple or main clause; (2) presence of two complementizers associated with one embedded clause; (3) presence of one complementizer in the embedded clause (this falls out naturally from the discussion of (2)); and (4) relationship between complementizers and inversion in English.

4. The 'null' COMP in the main clause

Even in theories which postulate that every sentence has a COMP, it is recognized that the COMP position may remain empty. Bresnan (1970), who first proposed the rule S' —> COMP S, attempted to explain the empty COMP by postulating that complementizers are also a part of the underlying structure of simple sentences but that they are deleted in the surface structure. She associated declaratives with the deleted 'that' and interrogatives with the deleted 'WH' (Bresnan 1970:301). For an analysis that does not postulate COMP deletion in the simple sentence see Emonds (1985:318), who identifies S' and P' as COMP and P. In the main clause the underlying P is empty.

I explain the absence of complementizers in simple sentences by postulating two factors, both of which agree with the proposed hypothesis. One is that indicative sentences convey what the speaker intends to be taken as his belief. In other words, indicative sentences have an inherently defined epistemic modality. I do not defend this hypothesis here as I have argued for it extensively elsewhere (Frajzyngier 1985 and 1987; but cf. Palmer 1987). With respect to the deontic modality, I propose, that the indicative clause is the unmarked case, i.e., it indicates neither obligation nor wish. The main support for this analysis comes from the fact that obligation, wish, and all other types of deontic modalities have to be marked by inflectional markers, modal verbs, modal adverbs, or other devices that a language may have.

The reason why even non-indicative main clauses sometimes lack complementizers is that their modalities are coded by syntactic devices such as word order, by morphological changes on the verb, or by phonological devices such as intonation, vowel or consonant length. Thus the Gothic verb-final *-u,* which marks the interrogative modality, would most probably not be considered a complementizer, e.g.:

(1) *skuld-u ist kaisaragild giban kaisara*
'is it lawful to give tribute money to Caesar?' (Visser 1969, 3:1547)

The following examples illustrate the complementary distribution of complementizers with other devices marking modality in the main clause. As indicated earlier, the interrogative 'whether' is considered by most authors a complementizer in English:

(2) I asked whether she came
(3) I don't know whether she came

Polish *czy* is also a complementizer, as shown by the following examples:

(4) *Spytałem* *czy* *przyszła*
ask:1SG:PERF:PAST COMP come:3F:SG:PERF:PAST
'I asked whether she came'

(5) *Nie* *wiem* *czy* *przyszła*
NEG know COMP come:3F:SG:PERF:PAST
'I don't know whether she came'

Unlike contemporary English 'whether', but similar to its Old English equivalent, Polish *czy* may also occur in main interrogative clauses inquiring about the truth, e.g.:

(6) *Czy* *przyszła*
COMP come:3F:SG:PERF
'Did she come?

The complementizer *czy* has an interesting distribution with respect to the interrogative intonation. The sentence (6) may, but does not have to, have the interrogative intonation marked by heavy stress on the penultimate vowel of the verb *przyszła*. But an interrogative sentence may also be produced without the complementizer *czy*. In such a case, however, the verb *przyszła* must have the interrogative intonation, viz.:

(6) *a.* *Przýszła*
come-3F-SG-PERF
'Did she come?'

The absence of deontic complementizers in the simple/main clause in many languages can be explained in a way similar to the absence of epistemic complementizers, viz. by the complementary distribution of various means to encode the same modality. I will illustrate the problem using examples from Polish and French.

In Polish the wish, a component of mood of obligation, for first and third person is marked by a complementizer, as in the following examples:

(7) *a-by* *tylko* *przyszła*
COMP-COMP only come:3F:PERF
'I wish she would come'

(8) *niech* *by* *(tylko)* *przyszła*
COMP COMP (only) come:3F:PERF
'I wish she would come' (chances are she won't)
'I dare her to come'

In Old French obligation or wish was marked by an inflectional device, the subjunctive mood:

(9) Dex te desfande, chevaliers, de mesaventure
'may God protect you, knight, against bad luck' (Jensen 1990:356)

The subjunctive in French was also used, however, for functions other than encoding the mood of obligation. Bourciez (1967:709) states that from the end of the 17th century *que,* which is identical with the complementizer, becomes an obligatory marker before the subjunctive, indicating a wish or an order.

(10) *que les dieus nous aient en lor garde*
'may the gods keep watch over us' (Medieval French, Jensen 1990:356)
Que son nom soit béni!
'May his name be blessed'
Qu'il périsse!
'May he perish!' (Bourciez 1967:709)

Therefore what on the surface may appear to contradict my earlier claim about the complementary distribution of devices coding the same modality is in fact a confirmation of this principle. The subjunctive in contemporary French is no longer primarily a marker of the mood of obligation.

The facts with respect to the main clause may be summarized as follows: The main clause does not have a complementizer if one of the following two conditions is met: (1) The clause is indicative, and hence is inherently marked for epistemic value expressing the speaker's belief in the truth of the proposition and is unmarked for the deontic value, i.e., it does not express a wish, an order, or an obligation; or (2) there exist clause-internal, mainly inflectional, devices to encode the modality of the clause.

5. Two complementizers in a sequence

Theoretically, a situation could arise in which the simple clause is marked for more than one modality, and each of the modalities is encoded by a separate morpheme. The previously cited examples (7) and (8) from Polish could be considered instances of two complementizers occurring in a simple clause. In example (7) the sequence of complementizers is *a-by* and in example (8) *niech by*. The first complementizer encodes obligation and the second a hypothetical mood. Compare also the following example where the sequence is *o-by*:[1]

(11) *o-by przyszła*
COMP-COMP come:3F:PERF:PAST
'I wish she would come'

As for the occurrence of two complementizers in a complex sentence, in addition to the markers of deontic and epistemic modalities already outlined for the simple clause, there may be a complementizer marking the embedded clause as being in the de dicto or in the de re domain (both domains being types of epistemic modality). This is especially true for sentential complements of verbs of saying and verbs of perception (see Frajzyngier 1991a; Frajzyngier and Jasperson 1991). In many languages de dicto complementizers have been extended in function to serve as markers of indirect evidence, as described in Frajzyngier (1991a). The potential composition of the embedded clause modality markers, whether clause-internal or -external (these are usually referred to as 'complementizers'), is therefore as follows: (1) De dicto/de re - (2) epistemic - (3) deontic (I make no claims with respect to the order of these elements). In this representation 'epistemic' indicates any epistemic distinction other than the de dicto/de re. The possibilities are as follows: One, two, or all three types of modalities may be overtly coded. It is also possible that the clause may be characterized by one modality only, and that that modality is an inherent property of the clause, i.e., there is no overt modality marker. The evidence for the hypothesis that complementizers are just one of the means of coding modality consists in showing that the presence of a particular complementizer is linked with the absence of clause-internal markers of modality, and that the absence of a particular type of complementizer is linked with the presence of clause-internal markers of modality.

6. Two disjoint complementizers

Whether two complementizers occur in a sequence or are separated by some other material depends crucially on the position of the second complementizer within the embedded clause (and of course on the presence of other devices coding the same modality as would have been coded by a complementizer). This dependence will be illustrated by deontic complementizers in three languages: Polish, which does not have inflectional devices to mark obligation with respect to first and third person but has two complementizers; French, which has the subjunctive mood and a complementizer; and Guider

(Central Chadic), which does not have inflectional devices and whose marker of obligation does not occur at the beginning of the embedded clause. In all three languages, complements of volitional verbs and volitional expressions do not have markers of obligation if the subjects of the main and the embedded clauses are the same, e.g.:

(12) *chce-my* *jeść*
want-1PL eat:INF
'we want to eat' (Polish)

(13) *chce* *jeść*
want:3SG eat-INF
'he/she wants to eat'(Polish)

(14) *Je* *veux* *le savoir*
1SG want it know
'I want to know it' (French)

In Guider, one of the equivalents of the verb 'to want' is a periphrastic construction with the literal meaning 'x's mouth is on . . . '. Such an expression may be followed by an NP to realize the equivalent of 'X wants an NP', e.g.:

(15) *má-w* *á* *kà* *mbáɣ lá*
mouth-1SG PREP on drink
'I want a drink'

Such an expression may be also followed by a clause, to realize the equivalent of 'X wants S', e.g.:

(16) *má w* *á* *kà* *zəmà*
mouth-1SG PREP on eat
'I want to eat'

(17) *má-w* *á* *kà* *zəm* *hlùá*
mouth-1SG PREP on eat meat
'I want to eat meat'

In Polish, if the subjects of the main and the embedded clauses are different, then the embedded clause is marked for the deontic modality of obligation. The marker is composed of the free complementizer *że* and the enclitic *by*, which has a hypothetical function, e.g.:

(18)

chcemy	*że-by-ś*	*jad-ł*	*owoc-e*
want:1PL	COMP-COMP-2SG	eat-PERF	fruit-PL:ACC

'we want you to eat fruit'

(19)

chce	*że-by-m*	*jadł*	*owoc-e*
want:3SG	COMP-COMP-1SG	eat-PERF	fruit-PL:ACC

'He wants me to eat fruit'

In Guider the marker of obligation *gə́nì* (*gə́n* in non-pausal position) occurs after the verb of the simple sentence, e.g.:

(20)

mə́	*l*	*gə́nì*
1PL	go	OBLIG

'let us go'

(21)

mə́	*mbát*	*gə́nì*
1PL	depart	OBLIG

'let us leave'

(22)

kə̀	*də̀*	*sə́*	*wə̀*	*gə́n*	*wàyá*
2SG	cook:-OPT	BEN	1SG	OBLIG	food

'you should cook for me'

The marker of obligation *gə́nì* occurs in the embedded clause when the subjects of the main and the embedded clauses are different. Moreover, the marker remains in clause-final position and hence there is no complementizer as it is traditionally understood, i.e. there is no marker at the beginning of the embedded clause, e.g.:

(23)

mà-w	*à*	*kà*	*də̀*	*zó-ŋ*	*gə́nì*
mouth-1SG	LOC	on	3	come-PL	OBLIG

'I want them to come'

In French when the subjects of the main clause and the embedded clause are different, the embedded clause is in the subjunctive mood and is introduced by the complementizer *que*, an automatic consequence of the mood of obligation, e.g.:

(24)

Je	*veux*	*qu'il*	*le*	*sache*
1SG	want	COMP-3M	it	know:SUBJ

'I want him to know it'

7. Two complementizers in Lele

7.1 *The system*

Lele (East Chadic) codes obligation for first and third person and the imperative for second person through a suffix on the verb. Consequently, as predicted by the hypotheses presented in this paper, the language should not have complementizers marking these specific deontic functions. The prediction is borne out by the facts. In the following sentences the modality of obligation in the embedded clause is coded by the imperative form of the verb *ír* 'go'. Note that the sentences have a de dicto complementizer *ná* since the main verb is a verb of saying:

(25)	*ŋ̀-yá*	*bé-gè*	*ná*	*gé*	*ír-à*
	1SG-tell	BEN-3PL	COMP	3PL	go-IMPER

'I told them to go'

(26)	*yà-dí*	*bú-dú*	*ná*	*ír-à*
	say-3M	BEN-3F	COMP	go-IMPER

'he told her to go'

The doubt in truth marker *sàŋ*, a marker of epistemic modality, occurs in clause-final position and therefore there is no sequence of two modality markers, or complementizers, e.g.:

(27)	*ná-ì*	*nè*	*báy*	*gō*	*ségrè*	*sàŋ*
	COMP-3M	COP	person	DEM	hunter	DOUBT

'he$_i$ said that he$_i$ is a hunter' (it may be that he only pretends to be one)[2]

cf.

(28)	*cánígè*	*ná-ì*	*nè*	*báy*	*gō*	*ségrè*
	Canige	COMP-3M	COP	person	DEM	hunter

'Canige$_i$ said that he$_i$ is a hunter'

Lele does not, however, have an inflectional form of the verb that indicates hypothetical or irrealis mood, which in Indo-European languages often conveys hearsay information. According to our prediction, in the absence of inflectional markers, if such a mood were to be marked, a complementizer would be one of the ways to realize it. In what follows I show that Lele indeed has a complementizer whose function is to mark less than direct evidence.

7.2 *Complementizer gō*

This complementizer is used with verbs of perception. It has the epistemic function of indicating direct perception on the part of the subject of the main clause. The complementizer occurs at the beginning of the embedded clause, hence the structure of a sentence with this complementizer is as follows: Subject V (Object) gō S, e.g.:

(29)

ŋ̀-ɗéŋlí	*kúlbá*	*lám-dò*	*gō*	*gè*	*jè*	*wál-dù*
1SG-hear	cow	noise-3F	COMP	INDEF	PROGR	slaughter-3F

'I heard the cow being slaughtered'

(30)

ŋ̀-ɗéŋlí	*lám-dì*	*gō*	*jè*	*èjé*
1SG-hear	noise-3M	COMP	PROGR	come

'I heard him coming'

(31)

ŋ̀-gòl-í	*gō*	*jè*	*wàl-dí*	*kúlbà*
1SG-see-3M	COMP	PROGR	slaughter-3M	cow

'I saw him slaughter a cow'

(32)

ŋ̀-gòl-dù	*gō*	*jè*	*wàl-dú*	*kúlbà*
1SG-see-3F	COMP	PROGR	slaughter-3F	cow

'I saw her slaughter a cow'

The importance, for the proposed hypothesis, of the complementizer *gō* as the marker of direct perception is that it codes de re modality. English, for the same kind of modality, uses either infinitive clauses or '-ing' complements, as illustrated by translations of the examples given above and as described in Frajzyngier and Jasperson (1991), and to a certain extent in Bolinger (1968).

The complementizer *gō* is identical with the relative clause marker and a subordinator introducing purpose clauses, e.g.:

(33)

báíŋdí	*gō*	*éjè*	*ná*	*ín-ìŋ*	*káŋ*	*nè*	*bùgán-íŋ*
man	REL	come	CONJ	ASSOC-1SG	here	COP	friend-1SG

'the man who brought me here is my friend'

(34)

jènè-dú	*kányà lé*	*gō*	*kìlé*	*cáanì*	*kùsùgù-ní*
prepare 3F	food	PURP	trade	away	market-AT

'she prepares food to sell it on the market'

(35)	*ŋ́-jè*	*né*	*kìré*	*gō*	*ódé*	
	1SG-PROG	look	means	PURP	go	

‘I am looking for the means to go’

Given the fact that relative clause markers and complementizers in many Chadic and other languages often derive from demonstratives, it is more than likely that the de re complementizer *gō* and the relative clause marker derive from the same source, probably a demonstrative whose traces can be found in the pronominal system as well.

7.3 *Complementizer ná*

The complementizer *ná* (sometimes realized with mid rather than high tone, cf. Palayer 1981) occurs after verbs of saying and thinking and indicates that what follows is in the domain de dicto, e.g.:

(36)	*cánígè*	*ná*	*dá-ì*	*kólòŋ*	*nè*	*báy*	*gō*	*ségrè*
	canige	COMP	3M	there	COP	man	DEM	hunt

‘Canige said that he [one over there] is a hunter’

(37)	*kìrbí-dí*	*ná-ì*	*nè*	*báy*	*gō*	*ségrè*
	think-3M	COMP-3M	COP	man	DEM	hunt

‘he$_i$ thinks that he$_i$ is a hunter’

Embedded interrogative clauses that follow the main verb *tón* ‘ask’ are also introduced by the complementizer *ná*, e.g.:

(38)	*ŋ̀-tón*	*ná*	*é-jé*	*gè*	*wán*	*gà*
	1SG-ask	COMP	come-PERF	3PL	nevertheless	INTERR

‘I asked whether they nevertheless came’

(39)	*ŋ̀-tón*	*ná*	*ɓálè*	*dí*	*gō*	*òje´-ŋ*	*gà*
	1SG-ask	COMP	be able	3M	COMP	help-1SG	INTERR

‘I asked whether he could help me’

(40)	*ŋ̀-tón*	*gí*	*ná*	*gí*	*ɓál*	*gō*	*òje´-ŋ*	*gà*
	1SG-ask	2M	COMP	2M	be able	COMP	help-1SG	INTERR

‘I asked you whether you could help me’

(41)	*ŋ̀-tòn*	*ná*	*wéì*	*bà*	*ɓál*	*gō*	*òje´-ŋ*	*gà*
	1SG-ask	COMP	who	be	able	COMP	help-1SG	INTERR

‘I asked who could help me’

As is the case with de dicto complementizers in other languages (cf. Kirsner and Thompson 1976; Frajzyngier 1993, 1991a, and Frajzyngier and Jasperson 1991), *ná* indicates indirect evidence when it occurs after verbs of perception:

(42) *ŋ̀-gòl ná wàl-dí kúlbà*
1SG-see COMP slaughter-3M cow
'I saw that he slaughtered a cow'

(43) *cánígè déŋlí ná gírbí-dú jè kòjò kò-rò*
Canige hear COMP forget-3F PERF hoe POSS-3F
'Canige heard that she forgot her hoe'

Another piece of evidence that *ná* is a de dicto complementizer is provided by causative constructions. In one construction, the main clause has the verb *jíbé* 'push', 'cause', followed by a nominal or a pronominal object, followed by a clause with an infinitival verb, i.e., a verb without any subject affixes. The construction has the meaning: 'make X do Y', e.g.:

(44) *jìb-íŋ-dí jè dà káŋ*
cause-1SG-3M come LOC here
'he made me come here'

(45) *jìb-íŋ-dí jè e'jè nà*
cause-1SG-3M come there
'he made me go there (close to him)'

If the VP with the verb *jíbé* is followed by the complementizer *ná* and then by a clause with an overt subject whose verb is in the imperative form, the construction has the meaning 'tell X to do Y', e.g.:

(46) *ŋ́-jìb-dù ná nà kányà lé*
1SG-cause-3F COMP cook:IMPER thing eating
'I told her to cook some food'

(47) *jìb-íŋ-dí ná ŋ-'údà*
push-1SG-3M COMP 1SG-go:IMPER
'he told me to go'

(48) *ŋ́-jìbí-ì ná dí údà*
1SG-push-3M COMP 3M go
'I told him to go'

(49) *dàdú jíb-gè ná kùjà-gé kúnì kùlèn-dí*
3F cause-3PL COMP clean:IMPER-3PL house belly-3M
'she told them to clean the inside of the house'

As indicated by the translations, the sentences above do not entail that the action of the embedded clause has taken place. But the crucial evidence comes from the fact that the above sentences may be followed by a negative proposition denying the accomplishment of the action of the embedded clause, e.g.:

(50) *jìb-íŋ-dí ná ŋ-'údà bá ŋ'é ɗé béì*
push-1SG-3M COMP 1SG-go:IMPER CONJ 1SG-go NEG ?
'he told me to go but I didn't '

Hence the function of the complementizer *ná* is to transfer the potential reality into the de dicto domain.

An additional piece of evidence for the de dicto/de re distinction between *gō* and *ná* is provided by complements after the verb *nàrí* 'refuse' and the phrase *nàrí... kìré* 'forbid', where the element *kìré* is an independent lexical item with the meaning 'way', 'road', 'means'. The structure of the sentence with an embedded clause is as follows: (Nominal Subject) *nàrí* Object (Pronominal Subject) *kìré gō* S. Note that the pronoun occurring after the verb *nàrí* is an object pronoun rather than a benefactive. Since *kìré* must be considered an object, the main clause in fact has two objects, e.g.:

(51) *nàrî-ì-dú kírè gō kílé bú-dù gúrbálò*
refuse-3M-3F way COMP buy BEN-3F cloth
'she forbade him to buy her a cloth'

If the verb *nàrí* is not followed by the noun *kìré* then it is treated as a verbum dicendi and has the complementizer *ná*, and the verb of the embedded clause occurs in the imperative form, e.g.:

(52) *ŋ́-nàrí-ì ná ír-à*
1SG -refuse-3M COMP go-IMPER
'I forbade him to go'

7.4 *Complementizers after the verb sèn 'to know'*

The verb *sèn* 'to know' may be followed by the single complementizer *gō*, e.g.:

(53) *ŋ-sèn gō ngú gírbí kòjò kú-ŋgù*
1SG-know COMP 2PL forget hoe POSS-2PL
'I know that you(pl) forgot your hoes'

It may also be followed by two complementizers in a sequence whose order must be *gō ná,* e.g.:

(54) *ŋ-sèn gō ná gírbí-gè kòjò kè-gè*
1SG-know COMP COMP forget-3PL hoe POSS -3PL
'I know that they forgot their hoes'

When *gō* is the only complementizer it indicates that the source of knowledge is the speaker's personal experience. The evidence for this hypothesis is provided by the fact that a sentence with *gō* as the only complementizer may be followed by a clause corresponding to 'because I have seen it' and may not be followed by a clause corresponding to 'because I was told so', e.g.:

(55) *ŋ-sèn gō gì gírbí jè kòjò kòm bè kōlō ŋ-gól*
1SG-know COMP 2M forget PERF hoe 2M:POSS give cause 1SG-see
'I know that you forgot your hoe, because I have seen [you forgetting the hoe]'

(56) *ŋ-sèn gō mé gírbí kòjò kèrè *bè kōlō*
1SG-know COMP 2F forget hoe 2F POSS give cause
gé yá-ŋ
INDEF tell-1SG
for 'I know that you forgot your hoe, because I was told so'

If the verb *sèn* is followed by the two complementizers *gō* and *ná* then the sentence means that the source of knowledge is hearsay. The evidence for this function is provided by the fact that a sentence with the two complementizers may be followed by a clause corresponding to 'because I have been told so' and may not be followed by a clause corresponding to 'because I have seen it', e.g.:

(57) *ŋ-sèn gō ná gì gírbí jè kòjò kòm bè*
1SG-know COMP COMP 2M forget DIST hoe 2M.POSS give
kōlō gé yá-ŋ
cause INDEF tell-1SG
'I know that you forgot your hoe, because I was told so'

(58) **ŋ-sèn* *gō* *ná* *gì* *gírbí* *jè* *kòjò* *kòm*
1SG-know COMP COMP 2M forget DIST hoe 2M:POSS
bè *kōlō* *ŋ-gòl*
give cause 1SG-see
'I know that you forgot your hoe, because I saw it'

Another piece of evidence that the function of *ná* is to indicate hearsay as the source of knowledge is provided by the fact that in an imperative sentence with the verb 'know', i.e., in a sentence where the complement is obligatorily a fragment of speech rather than a fragment of reality, the complementizer is *ná* rather than *gō* e.g.:

(59) *sínà* *ná . . .*
know COMP
'know that . . . '

The last piece of evidence I present here for the functions of *ná* and *gō* is the fact that one cannot use both complementizers after a verb of perception. Thus the following sentences are ungrammatical:

(60) **ŋ̀-gòl-í* *gō* *ná* *wàl-dí* *kúlbà*
1SG-see-3M COMP COMP slaughter-3M cow
for 'I saw him slaughter a cow'

(61) **ŋ̀-gòl-i* *ná* *gō* *wàl-dí* *kúlbà*
1SG-see-3M COMP COMP slaughter-3M cow
for 'I saw him slaughter a cow'

The ungrammaticality stems from the fact that the main verb of perception is followed by the direct perception marker *gō* and also by the indirect perception marker *ná*, creating an internal contradiction within the clause.

8. Two complementizers in Mupun

The importance of the data from Mupun lies in the fact that the language has a clause-internal epistemic marker coding doubt in the truth of the proposition, and inflectional markers coding imperative and obligation. According to the proposed hypothesis, neither doubt in truth nor obligation should be realized by complementizers. The prediction is fully borne out by the data. The language also has two other modality markers, both occurring at the beginning of the clause: a prohibitive marker and an interrogative marker. According to our predictions, such a marker may be preceded by a de dicto complementizer, resulting in a sequence of two complementizers. The data support this prediction as well. A discussion of the four cases follows.

8.1 *Epistemic marker*

The epistemic modality marker *páa,* which encodes a hypothetical mood, occurs after the subject of the embedded clause. This marker and its theoretical implications have been described in Frajzyngier (1985). As predicted by the proposed hypothesis, there is no other complementizer in Mupun coding the hypothetical function.

The verba dicendi complementizer is *nə́* (described in Frajzyngier 1991b, 1993). There is a productive construction with a verb of saying followed by an embedded clause with the doubt in truth marker *páa* (in the examples to follow, L stands for 'logophoric'):

(62) *a sat nə wu paa mbə yo muan*
2M say COMP 3M DOUBT FUT go trip
'you said that he will go on a trip (but he may or may not go)'

cf.

(63) *a sat nə wu mbə yo muan*
2M say COMP 3M FUT go trip
'you said that he will go on a trip'

(64) *wu sat nə ɗin paa ɗi cin hankuri*
3M say COMP 3M.L DOUBT 3M.L make patience
'he said that he was patient (but I have my doubts)'

There is a shift in the function of *páa* from doubt in truth marker to hypothetical when the subject of the embedded clause is first or second person, as illustrated by the following examples, where the embedded clause expresses a state that may occur only if the subject consents to the request:

(65) *wu sat nə ha paa a cin hankuri*
3M say COMP 2M DOUBT 2M do patience
'he asked you to be patient (if you please)'

(66) *wu sat nə wa paa a cin hankuri*
3M say COMP 2M:EMPHATIC DOUBT 2M do patience
'he asked you to be patient (if you please)'

8.2 *Deontic modality*

The optative and imperative in Mupun are marked by low tone on subject pronouns in both main and embedded clauses, e.g. (only tones on pronouns are marked):

(67) *mó grəp pupwap*
3PL cut:PL fish
'they cut a fish into pieces'

(68) *mò grəp*
3PL cut:PL
'they should cut it into pieces'

Since the mood of obligation is marked by inflectional devices, there is, in accord with our prediction, no complementizer marking the mood of obligation. The embedded clause may occur without a complementizer or be preceded by a de dicto complementizer *nə*, e.g.:

(69) *dəm à sat mò grəp*
go 2M tell 3PL cut:PL
'go and tell them to cut it into pieces'

(70) *mo sat nə yì cin ɗik*
3PL say COMP 2F do marriage
'they said that you should marry'

cf.

(71) *mo sat nə yí cin ɗik*
3PL say COMP 2F do marriage
'they said that you got married'

(72) *mo sat nə à la mat*
3PL say COMP 2M take wife
'they said that you should marry'

cf.

(73)

mo	*sat*	*nə*	*á*	*la*	*mat*
3PL	say	COMP	2M	take	wife

they said that you married'

8.3 *Prohibitive marker*

Unlike the mood of obligation, which is coded by inflectional devices, the prohibitive mood is marked by a separate lexical item *táajì*, occurring at the beginning of the clause, e.g.:

(74)

taaji	*yi*	*dam*	*pee*	*n-an*
COMP	2F	bother	place	PREP-1SG

'don't bother me'

In a complex sentence the de dicto complementizer *nə* may be followed by the complementizer *táajì*. When this combination occurs, the distribution of functions between the two complementizers is as follows: The first complementizer indicates that what follows is in the de dicto domain, which is an epistemic function. The second complementizer functions as a marker of the deontic modality of the embedded clause. Thus each of the complementizers encodes a different modal function, e.g.:

(75)

n-sat	*n-wur*	*nə*	*taaji*	*gwar*	*dam*	*pee*	*n-an*
1SG-tell	PREP-3M	COMP	COMP	3M:ADR	bother	place	PREP-1SG

'I told him not to bother me'

(76)

mo	*sat*	*puo*	*n-an*	*nə*	*taaji*	*n-dəm*	*n-jos*	*kas*
3PL	say	word	PREP-1SG	COMP	COMP	1SG-go	PREP-Jos	NEG

'they warned me not to go to Jos'

8.4 *Interrogatives*

Mupun has a rich system of clause-final interrogative markers for yes/no questions. Some of these are *-a*, *-wo*, *a ri* , *-on*, and *-e*. Presumably these would not be considered complementizers because they do not occur between the main and the embedded clauses, e.g.:

(77) *n-kak na get mu sin makaranta ndaŋ*
1SG-think COMP PAST 1PL make school follow
together-INTERR
siak-e
'I think we went to school following each other, didn't we?'

(78) *n-tal pə wur a nə a gwar a miskoom-e*
1SG-ask PREP 3M COP 3PL COP 3M:ADR COP chief-INTERR
'I asked him whether he was a chief'

The difference between embedded interrogatives and main clause interrogatives can be seen in yes/no questions. Embedded yes/no questions, which may end with any of the interrogative markers listed above, also have an interrogative complementizer *két*. Since the verb of the main clause is a verb of saying, the embedded clause may also be preceded by the verba dicendi complementizer *nə* or by *ko*, giving the double complementizer construction *nə két* or *ko két*. There is even a triple complementizer construction when *ko két* occurs after the complementizer *nə*, e.g.:

(79) *mo tal pə an nə ko ket n-man war-a*
3PL ask PREP 1SG COMP COMP COMP 1SG-know 3F-INTERR
'they asked me if I knew her'

(80) *mo tal pə an nə ko ket n-man war-wo*
3PL ask PREP 1SG COMP COMP COMP 1SG-know 3F-INTERR
'they asked me if I knew her'

(81) *mo tal pə war nə ket pa man an-a*
3PL ask PREP 3F COMP COMP 3F.L know 1SG-INTERR
'they asked her$_i$ whether she$_i$ knew me'

The verba dicendi complementizer *nə* is optional even if the main clause verb is a verb of saying, e.g.:

(82) *n-tal pə wur(nə) ko ket wur kə kes akaranta*
1SG-ask PREP 3M (COMP) COMP COMP 3M PERF finish school
'I asked him$_i$ if he$_i$ has finished school'

If the embedded clause is fronted, then *két* is the only complementizer before the embedded clause, e.g.:

(83) *ket* *mo* *wul* *n-tulu* *ɓe* *ba* *n-man* *kas*
COMP 3PL arrive PREP-home CONS NEG 1SG-know NEG
'I don't know if they arrived home'

It may be argued that the presence of the interrogative complementizer *két* and a clause-final interrogative marker contradicts the principle stated earlier that there should not be two markers coding the same modality. In fact there is no contradiction here, as the function the marker *két* is to delimit the scope of the question, from the whole sentence to just the embedded clause.

9. Two complementizers in Polish

The importance of the discussion of the Polish data is as follows: There are no clause-internal markers of epistemic modality nor of deontic modality for the first and third person. In accordance with the hypothesis of the present paper one can expect that such a modality may be expressed through modal verbs, adverbs, or a complementizer. If the modality is expressed through a complementizer one can expect that after verba dicendi, and possibly after verba sentiendi, a sequence of at least two complementizers may occur, of which one is a complementizer of verbs of saying and the other codes another epistemic or deontic modality.

The Polish enclitic *by*, mentioned earlier in the paper, indicates a hypothetical or irrealis mood. It is clearly a modality marker and can be attached to verbs, nouns, pronouns, adjectives, complementizers, adverbial clause markers, and exclamations, e.g.:

(84) *był* *by-m* *w* *Warszawie* *gdy-by . . .*
be-PERF HYP-1SG in Warsaw when-HYP
'I would have been in Warsaw if . . .'

The enclitic *by* can be added to the morpheme *ni* to express the epistemic modality of doubt in truth of the proposition; while *by* added to the morpheme *o* encodes the deontic modality expressing wish. The resulting structures *ni-by* and *o-by* occur in clause-initial position, i.e., in the position of complementizers such as the interrogative *czy*, e.g.:

(85) *Ni-by* *był* *w* *Warszawie*
COMP be:3M:SG:PERF PREP Warsaw:DAT
'Apparently he was in Warsaw'

(86)

O-by	*był*	*w*	*Warszawie*	*w*	*lipcu*
COMP-COMP	be:3M:SG:PERF	PREP	Warsaw:DAT	PREP	July

'I wish he were in Warsaw in July'

The de dicto complementizer in Polish is *że,* e.g.:

(87)

Powiedziałem	*że*	*byłem*	*w*	*Warszawie*
say:PERF:PAST:1SG	COMP	be:PAST:1SG	PREP	Warsaw:DAT

'I said that I was in Warsaw'

As in many other languages, the de dicto complementizer in Polish can be used after verbs of perception to indicate indirect evidence, e.g.:

(88)

widziałem	*że*	*był*	*w*	*dom-u*
see:PERF:PAST-1SG	COMP	be:PAST:3SG.M	PREP	home-GEN

'I saw that he was at home'

Given the fact that hypothetical markers in Polish occur at the beginning of the clause, one can expect that after verba dicendi there will be two complementizers between the main and the embedded clause. This is indeed the case. The following example illustrates the occurrence of an epistemic complementizer after the de dicto complementizer:

(89)

Powiedział	*że*	*ni-by*	*był*	*w*	*Warszawie*
say:PERF:PAST:3SG	COMP	COMP	be:PAST:3SG	PREP	Warsaw:DAT

'He said that he was in Warsaw' (I have my doubts about it)

The sequence *że oby* is ungrammatical. Instead the particle *by* can be added directly to the de dicto complementizer *że* with the resulting meaning of the mood of obligation, e.g.:

(90)

Powiedziałem	*że-by*	*przyjechał*
say:PERF:PAST:1SG	COMP-COMP	come:PAST:3SG
do	*Warszawy*	
PREP	Warsaw:GEN	

'I told him to come to Warsaw'

(91)

Powiedział	*że-by-m*	*spalił*	*papier-y*
say:PERF:PAST:3SG	COMP-COMP-1SG	burn:PERF	paper-PL

'He said that I should burn the papers'

Thus it is possible to have in Polish a sequence of two or three complementizers, each performing a different modal function.

10. Complementizers and inversion in English

I am not aware of any attempts to explain the lack of subject-auxiliary inversion in embedded interrogative clauses, such as:

(92) *I asked whether should he go
(93) I asked whether he should go

and the presence of inversion in the simple clause, e.g.:

(94) Should he go?
(95) He should go

The hypothesis proposed in the present paper explains the lack of inversion in a principled way. If we assume that subject-auxiliary inversion encodes the interrogative modality (cf. Quirk and Greenbaum 1975), and that the complementizer 'whether' encodes the same interrogative modality, then the two devices should not occur together in the same clause. And this is indeed the case. In Old English, the inversion was a much more widespread device than it is today because it included not only subject-auxiliary but also subject-verb inversion. Unlike in contemporary English, the interrogative main clause in Old English could be marked by the particle *hwaeðer*, corresponding to contemporary 'whether' (cf. Closs Traugott 1972:73). The interesting fact about this particle is that when 'whether' was used in the main clause there was no subject-auxiliary or subject-verb inversion. Similarly in contemporary English, there is no inversion in embedded interrogative clauses, e.g.:

(96) *Hwaeðer ge nu secan gold on treowum?*
'Whether you now seek gold in trees?
'Do you now seek gold in trees?' (Closs Traugott 1972:73)

This fact is fully predictable from the proposed hypothesis. 'Whether' marks interrogative modality, the same modality that is marked by subject-auxiliary or subject-verb inversion. Therefore, since the use of the two markers would be redundant, only one device coding interrogative function is used in the interrogative clause.

What remains to be explained is why there is inversion in simple 'WH' interrogative clauses, but no inversion when these clauses are embedded in another clause.

(97) Which books have you lent him?
When will you come back?
How did you mend it? (Quirk and Greenbaum 1975:197)

(98) I asked which books *have you lent him
I asked when *will you come back
I asked how *did you mend it

cf.

(99) I asked which books you have lent him
I asked when you will come back
I asked how you mend it

Here is an explanation for the presence of inversion in specific interrogatives in the main clause and the lack of inversion when these clauses are embedded. I have proposed elsewhere for Chadic languages (Frajzyngier 1985) that the Chadic equivalents of 'WH' interrogatives were actually not interrogative markers but rather indicators of what the question is about. The interrogative modality in Chadic is usually coded by clause-final interrogative particles and by intonation (cf. Leben 1989). I propose that the situation in English reflects to some degree an older system which in many features resembled the system postulated for Chadic. In Indo-European languages interrogative pronouns are identical with the indefinite pronouns roughly corresponding to 'someone' and 'something'. The contemporary 'what', 'who' and 'which' also derive most probably from Old English indefinite pronouns *hwaet* 'whatever', *hwa* 'whoever' and *hwilc* 'any'. Closs Traugott illustrates this function with a contemporary example:

(100) Who pays the piper calls the tune (Closs Traugott 1972:153)

I propose that the WH-words in main clauses in contemporary spoken English are not markers of interrogative modality but rather indicate what component of the clause the question is about. The interrogative modality is provided by at least two other devices: subject-auxiliary inversion (with auxiliary 'do' provided according to familiar rules) and by interrogative intonation. Without the two devices the clause does not carry the interrogative meaning. I propose that in the complex sentence the WH-word of the embedded clause becomes a complementizer, making the subject-auxiliary inversion a second, and hence, superfluous, device to mark interrogative modality.

11 Conclusions

I have shown in this paper that morphemes labeled complementizers constitute a device to code the modality of a clause, and as such they are related to other markers of modality such as modal verbs, modal adverbs, inflectional modality markers, devices to code interrogative function, etc. The absence of complementizers in indicative main clauses in some languages is explained by the fact that such clauses are inherently marked as conveying a speaker's belief in the truth of the proposition. Such clauses are also unmarked with respect to deontic modality. It is possible that in some languages complementizers may acquire a purely formal function and became obligatory markers of embedded clauses with different modal characteristics. It is also possible that complementizers may lose their function of coding modality completely.

The explanation provided in this paper may be useful also to those formal theories that postulate the existence of COMP as a component of some types of clauses, on the condition that COMP is understood as representing modality of the clause. Whether these theories will accept this reinterpretation of COMP is an entirely different matter.

ABBREVIATIONS

BEN	Benefactive
COMP	Complementizer
CONJ	Conjuction
COP	Copula
DAT	Dative
DEM	Demonstrative
DOUBT	Doubt in truth marker
F	Femine
FUT	Future
GEN	Genitive
HYP	Hypothetical
IMPER	Imperative
INDEF	Indefinite
INTERR	Interrogative
LOC	Locative
M	Masculine
NEG	Negation
OBLIG	Marker of obligation
PAST	Past tense
PERF	Perfective
PL	Plural
POSS	Possessive marker
	Possessive pronoun
PROGR	Progressive
PURP	Purpose marker
REL	Relative marker
SG	Singular
SUBJ	Subjunctive

NOTES

* Work on this paper was supported by a grant from the National Endowment for the Humanities, No. RT-21151-90. I would like to acknowledge the generous help of colleagues, through conversations and correspondence. For the French data I am grateful to Anne Abeille, Philippe Alcouffe, and Sylvie Bruno; for information on Quebecois French and some bibliographic pointers I am grateful to Gary Coen, and for Dutch data (not used in the present paper) and references I am grateful to Jan Odijk, J. Zwart, and Gerrit Dimmendaal. I would like to thank Eric Atwell, University of Leeds, for checking the LOB corpus for me for the occurrence of two complementizers in a sequence in English (none were found, but cf. Caroll 1983). I gathered data on Lele, an East Chadic language spoken in Chad, during fieldwork in North Cameroon in the summer of 1990. I gathered data on Guider, a central Chadic language spoken in North Cameroon, in the summers of 1990 and 1991. Data on Mupun, collected over a period of many years, are taken from Frajzyngier 1991b and 1993.

I would like to thank Immanuel Barshi, Karen Ebert, Bernd Heine, Elizabeth O'Dowd, David Pesetsky, Erin Shay and participants of the Symposium on Mood and Modality, especially John Haiman, Gillian Sankoff, Eve Sweetser, and Werner Abraham, for questions raised and comments on various aspects of the present paper. None of them is, however, responsible for any shortcomings of this paper.

1 For a discussion of *by* in Russian see Brecht 1977.

2 In Lele, as in many Chadic languages, the verb 'to say' is often omitted. The only trace of its presence is the complementizer.

REFERENCES

Bickerton, Derek. 1981. *Roots of Language*. Ann Arbor: Karoma.

Bolinger, Dwight. 1968. "Entailment and the Meaning of Structures." *Glossa* 2.2.119-127.

Bolinger, Dwight. 1972. *That's That*. The Hague: Mouton.

Bouchard, Dennis. 1984. *On the Content of Empty Categories*. Dordrecht: Foris.

Bourciez, Edouard. 1967. *Eléments de Linguistique Romane*. Paris: Klincksieck.

Borsley, Robert D. 1986. "Prepositional Complementizers in Welsh". *Journal of Linguistics* 22.67-84.

Brecht, Richard. 1977. "Ctoby or cto and by". *Folia Slavica* 1.1.33-41.

Bresnan, Joan W. 1970. "On Complementizers: Toward a Syntactic Theory of Complement Types". *Foundations of Language* 6.3.297-321.

Bybee, Joan with Revere Perkins and William Pagliuca. (1994) *The Grammaticization of Tense, Aspect and Modality in the Languages of the World*. Chigago: University of Chigago Press

Caroll, Susanne. 1983. "Remarks on For-To Infinitives". *Linguistic Analysis* 12.4.415-451.

Chomsky 1986a. *Barriers*. Cambridge, Mass.:MIT Press.

Chomsky 1986b. *Knowledge of Language*. New York: Praeger.

Chomsky, Noam. 1992. *A Minimalist Program for Linguistic Theory*. (*MIT Occasional Papers in Linguistics 1.)* MIT: Cambridge, MA.

Cichocki, W. 1983. "Multiple Wh-Questions in Polish: A Two COMP Analysis". *Toronto Working Papers in Linguistics*, 4.53-71

Comorovski, Ileana. 1986. "Multiple Wh-Movement in Rumanian". *Linguistic Inquiry* 17.1 171-177.

Dasgupta, Probal. 1983. "Bangla Equatives, Complementizers, Final Foci, and Root". *Linguistic Analysis* 11.2.103-137.

Dimmendaal, Gerrit F. 1989. "Complementizers in Hausa". *Current Progress in Chadic Linguistics* ed. by Z. Frajzyngier. 87-110. Amsterdam: Benjamins.

Emonds, Joseph E. 1985. *A Unified Theory of Syntactic Categories*. Dordrecht: Foris.

Frajzyngier, Zygmunt. 1985. "Truth and the Indicative Sentence". *Studies in Language* 9.243-254.

Frajzyngier, Zygmunt. 1987. "Truth and the Compositionality Principle: A Reply to Palmer". *Studies in Language* 11.211-217.

Frajzyngier, Zygmunt. 1991a. "De Dicto Domain in Language". *Approaches to Grammaticalization*. Ed. by Traugott, Elizabeth C. and Bernd Heine. Volume 1. Amsterdam: Benjamins, 219-252.

Frajzyngier, Zygmunt. 1991b. "Typology of Complex Sentence in Mupun". *Phrase complexe dans les langues tchadique*. ed. by Herrmann Jungraithmayr and Henry Tourneux, 27-72. Paris: Geuthner.

Frajzyngier, Zygmunt. 1993. *A Grammar of Mupun*. Berlin: Reimer.

Frajzyngier, Zygmunt. in press. "Two Complementizers of Lele". *Studia Chadica and Hamito-Semitica*. ed. by Rudolf Leger and Dymitr Ibriszimow.

Frajzyngier, Zygmunt and Robert Jasperson. 1991. "That Clauses and Other Complements". *Lingua* 83.133-153.

Givón, Talmy. 1980. "The Binding Hierarchy and the Typology of Complements". *Studies in Language* 4.333-377.

Givón, Talmy. 1990. Syntax. *A Functional Typological Introduction*. Vol. 2. Amsterdam: Benjamins.

Heine, Bernd; Ulrike Claudi and Friederike Hünnemeyer. 1991. *Grammaticalization. A Conceptual Framework*. Chicago: University of Chicago Press.

Jensen, Frede. 1990. *Old French and Comparative Gallo-Romance Syntax*. Tübingen: Niemeyer.

Joseph, Brian D. 1985. "Complementizers, Particles, and Finiteness in Greek and the Balkans". *Folia Slavica* 7.3.390-411.

Kac, Michael. 1978. *Corepresentation of Grammatical Structures*. University of Minnesota Press.

Kirsner, Robert, and Sandra A. Thompson. 1976. "The Role of Pragmatic Inference in Semantics: A Study of Sensory Verb Complements in English". *Glossa* 10:2, 200-240.

Koster, Jan. 1987. *Domains and Dynasties*. Dordrecht:Foris.

Lawal, Nike S. 1986. "A Note on Yoruba Subordinator 'ti'". *Journal of West African Languages* 16.2. 27-33.

Leben, William. 1989. "Intonation in Chadic: An Overview". *Current Progress in Chadic linguistics* ed. by Z. Frajzyngier.199-218. Amsterdam: Benjamins.

Lefevbre, Claire. 1980. "Cases of Lexical Complementizers in Cuzco Quechua and the Theory of COMP". *Journal of Linguistic Research* 1.2.91-112.

Noonan, Michael. 1985. "Complementation". Shopen 1985:42-140.
Palayer, Pierre. 1981. "Notes de grammaire." *Livre de lecture lele*. Ed. by Martine Garrigues Cresswell avec la participation de Christophe Weibegue. Sarh, Tchad: Centre d'Études Linguistiques, Collège Charles Lwanga.
Palmer, F. R. 1986. *Mood and Modality*. Cambridge: Cambridge University Press.
Palmer, F.R. 1987. Truth Indicative? *Studies in Language* 11.1-2, 206-210.
Quirk, Randolph and Sidney Greenbaum. 1975. *A Concise Grammar of Contemporary English*. New York: Harcourt, Brace, Jovanovich.
Ransom, Evelyn N. 1986. *Complementation: Its Meaning and Forms*. Amsterdam: John Benjamins.
Rizzi, Luigi. 1990. *Relativized Minimality*. Cambridge, Mass.: MIT Press.
Rosenbaum, P. 1967. *The Grammar of English Predicate Complement Constructions*. Cambridge, Mass.: MIT press.
Rudin, Catherine. 1986. *Aspects of Bulgarian Syntax: Complementizers and WH-constructions*. Columbus, Ohio: Slavica Publishers.
Shopen, Timothy, (ed). 1985. *Language Typology and Syntactic Description*. Cambridge: Cambridge University Press.
Traugott, Elizabeth Closs . 1972. *A history of English Syntax*. New York: Holt, Rinehart and Winston.
Visser, F. Th. 1969. *An historical Syntax of the English Language*. Leiden: Brill.
Wachowicz, Krystyna A. 1974. "Against the Universality of a Single WH-Question movement". *Foundations of Language* 11.155-166.

The Semantic Development of Past Tense Modals in English

Joan L. Bybee
University of New Mexico

The English modal auxiliaries, *would, should, might,* and *could* are historically the Past Tense forms of *will, shall, may* and *can* respectively.[1] However, their meaning and usage in Modern English are not derivable from the combination of past meaning with the meaning of the Present modals. Rather the uses of the Past Tense modals may be divided into three types: (i) hypothetical uses; (ii) present tense uses; and (iii) past tense uses.

In Modern English the hypothetical uses are the most common according to the analysis of spoken and written texts done by Coates (1983). They are most obvious in the *then*-clauses of hypothetical conditional sentences. In some cases the hypothetical meaning occurs along with what is sometimes called the 'root' meaning of the modal. For instance in (1) *would* indicates 'hypothetical willingness' (Coates 1983: 211), while in (2) *could* indicates 'hypothetical ability':

(1) *If you had that job lined up,* ***would*** *Fulbright then pay up?*
(2) *If you helped me, I* ***could*** *finish this in an hour.*

In the example in (3), no additional root meaning is present, and the modal conveys only the hypothetical conditional sense (Coates 1983:214):

(3) *I mean we all want be to millionaires, but if we were of course money* ***wouldn't*** *be worth anything.*

The present tense uses of originally Past modals are illustrated in examples (4) and (5) (from Coates 1983: 58, 152).

(4) *You* ***should*** *walk round the ramparts of the old city too.*

(5) *I think it unlikely actually, but he* ***might*** *do it today.*

Much less common are uses of the Past modals in past contexts, although they do occur, as the examples in (6) and (7) show (Coates 1983: 211, 111):

(6) *He believed Mr. Weaver* ***would*** *perform "outstanding service" in the post.*

(7) *"I just cannot remember a time when I* ***couldn't*** *swim," she told me.*

The ambiguity of *could* can be seen in the following bit of wisdom, expressed on a bumber sticker:

(8) *George Bush* ***couldn't*** *run a laundromat.*

This statement could be taken to mean that he tried and failed (the past tense reading), or that even if he tried, he would fail (the hypothetical reading).

Even though these modals are Past in form, the past uses of most of them are the least frequent of their uses, and for *should*, one could argue that there are no past uses at all.

This situation, especially with regard to the hypothetical uses, is paralleled in other languages, for it is common for the Conditional Mood to consist formally of the Past tense of the Future, as in Spanish and French, or the Past of another modal form, as for instance in Nahuatl (Andrews 1975) or Sierra Miwok (Freeland 1951). Such facts suggest that there may be something predictable about the diachronic development of the Past tense forms of modal verbs and that it may be fruitful to investigate the question of how and why past tense modals develop hypothetical and present tense uses, and whether there is any relation between these two developments.

In the following I will trace the semantic development of *would* and *should* only, but I expect the general findings to apply to *might* and *could* as well.

1. *Should* and *would* in Old and Middle English.

That *should* and *would* are originally past tense in meaning is clear from their uses in Old English texts, such as *Beowulf.* There we find many clear instances of *should* signalling destiny, duty or obligation of the subject in the past, corresponding to *sceal*, which has the same meaning in the present. Consider the examples (9) through (11) and their translations, based on Gordon 1926.

(9) *Næs þæt forma sið / þæt hit ellen-weorc æfnan* ***scolde***. (1464)
'That was not the first time that it (a sword) had to perform a deed of valor.'

(10) *þe he wið þam wyrme gewegan* ***sceolde***. (2400)
'when he had to fight the dragon.'

(11) *þæt þæt ðeodnes bearn geþeon* ***scolde***. (910)
'that the king's son was destined to prosper.'

Similarly, *wolde* is used almost exclusively to signal volition of the subject in the past, just as *wylle* was used to express volition in the present. Consider the examples in (12) through (14). Example (13) refers to a time that is past with reference to the time of the narrative, which is also past.

(12) ***wolde*** *self cyning symbel þicgan.* (1010)
'The king himself wished to join in the banquet.'

(13) *ðonne sweorda gelac sunu Healfdenes efnan* ***wolde***; (1040-41)
'when the son of Healfdene wanted to practice sword-play.'

(14) ***wolde*** *wig-fruma Wealhþeo secan, cwen to gebeddan.* (664-5)
'the war-leader wanted to look for the queen to bed down with.'

By the Middle English period, however, both *should* and *would* had made their way into present contexts, especially with first and second person. Consider first *wolde*, which is especially prominent in present usage in *Sir Gawain and the Green Knight*, where it can express present volition or willingness. Consider the following examples:

(15) "*I* ***wolde*** *yowre wylnyng worche at my myȝt...*" (1546)
'"I am willing to do your desire as far as I can..."'

(16) "*'Wher is', he sayd, "The gouernour of this gyng? Gladly I* ***wolde*** *Se that segg in syȝt, and with hymself speke raysoun.*" (224-6)
''Where is', he said, "The lord of this company? I would gladly See that knight and speak reason with him."'

To explain the present uses of Past forms, we must refer to the special properties of modal verbs. Modal verbs, whether they express desire, obligation, necessity, intention or ability, have in common the semantic property that they do not imply the completion of the action or event expressed by the infinitive with which they occur. (This property is in contrast with other complement-taking verbs such as *finish* and *manage*, which do imply completion [Givón 1973].) In the present tense, however, these modal verbs do imply a close relation between the agent and the main predicate, which may imply or predict a future completion of the event or activity of the main predicate. Especially in first person, present tense modal verbs such as Modern English *I wanna, I'm gonna, I hafta* or *I can* are used to state intentions, make offers and promises which our interlocutors can expect to be carried out. The same verbs in the third person are used to report intentions, offers and promises. Similarly, *I will* and *I shall* in the Gawain text are used to make promises, state intentions and resolutions, which one trusts will be carried out.

The situation with these same modal verbs in the past tense is quite different, however. The relation between the agent and the main predicate is much more tenuous. *He/I wanted to* for instance may be used both in contexts in which the desire was carried out and in contexts in which the desire was not carried out. As stative verbs, the past forms of modals assert that a state existed before the moment of speech, but they do not say whether that state still exists in the present or not. Thus past modals offer two areas of vagueness: (i) whether or not the predicate event was completed; and (ii) whether or not the modality remains in effect.

A modal in past time, then, leaves open the possibility that some conditions on the completion of the main event were not met, and therefore the modality may still be in effect. That is why when we say, for example,

(17) *I wanted to help you.*

in a situation where I didn't, it means that there were some conditions that were not met: something was standing in my way. Interestingly, we can also say *I wanted to help you* in a situation in which you still need help, but I do not intend to help you because something IS standing in my way. In other words, the existence of PAST blocking conditions is generalized to include the existence of PRESENT blocking conditions.

Note that the use of a Past Tense in a conditional sentence results in a hypothetical conditional. The hypothetical conditional is contrasted with the reality conditional which uses Present tense or a Future auxiliary:

(18) Hypothetical conditional:
If she saw Judy, she would tell her the news.

(19) Reality conditional:
If I see Judy, I will tell her the news.

The difference between the two is that the hypothetical conditional implies that it is considerably less likely that the condition will still be met. The difference in likelihood originates from the tense distinction in the following way: The past in both clauses of the hypothetical conditional sentence signals that the conditional relation held in past time. The modality in the *then*-clause signals that the relation is still in effect. (Cf. *If Mike saw her, he told her the news.*) On the other hand, the reality condition with Present tense means that the conditional relation begins in present time and projects into the future. The reason that the one framed in the past seems more hypothetical is that the conditional relation has existed in the past but the condition has not yet been met, suggesting that it may never be met.

This description of the origins of hypotheticality for past tense modals predicts that the uses of hypothetical conditionals that span past and present time are more basic and historically prior to those that are set in the future. As Suzanne Fleischman (personal communication) has pointed out, a hypothetical conditional may also refer to the future: *If in the next year the interests rates went down again, I would definitely consider refinancing.* No uses of this sort are found in the texts examined in the study reported below, suggesting that this use is a less common extension of the hypothetical use derived in the way described above.

The *if*-clause of a hypothetical conditional always contains a past form, and the past modals show up here as well. However, it is their use in the main clause that is more important for explaining how they come to be used in present contexts.

It is interesting that the *then*-clause of the hypothetical may take other modal verbs besides *would*, such as those shown in (20), even though some of them are not very highly grammaticized:

(20) *If I saw Judy,* { *I wanted to* / *I was gonna* / *I was supposed to* / *I intended to* / *I might* } *tell her the news.*

The Past tenses of all these modal verbs behave in a similar manner: They allow the interpretation that the modality is still in effect, and the predicate action will be carried out if the right conditions are met.

For this reason it seems appropriate to interpret Modern English *wanted to* as an analogue to *wolde* in the Late Old English and Middle English period.

I am suggesting that the use of *wanted to* in present time in Modern English is possible because it implies that certain conditions on carrying out the desired predicate may not be met. The so-called polite or remote uses of past tense as in

(21) *I wanted to ask you a question.*

arise in the same way. That is, (21) implies that there might be conditions that are unmet. Among these implied conditions is the question of whether the addressee wants to be asked a question — thus the deferential use of the past (see Fleischman 1989).

Note that under this analysis, the polite use of the Past tense depends upon the presence of a modal verb; it is not possible to get a polite reading of just any verb with the Past tense. Thus *He asked you a question* is no more polite than *He is asking you a question.* Some of the verbs that commonly have polite readings in past tense across languages are 'be obliged' (English *should*, Spanish *debía*), 'want' (English *would*, Spanish *quería*), 'be able' (English *could*, Spanish *podía*), and also mental or emotional state verbs, such as 'think'. All of these verbs have in common the fact that they are stative and that their past tense meaning leaves open the possibility that the past state continues into the present.

The difference between *I wyl* and *I wolde* in Gawain illustrates the conditional nature of the Past form nicely. *I wyl* is used to state intentions or willingness and may be taken as making a promise or resolution. Compare the use of *wyl* in (22) and (23) to that of *wolde* illustrated in (15) above.

(22) *Quoth Gawayn, "I schunt onez,*
And so ***wyl I*** *no more"* (2280-1)
'Gawain said, "I flinched once,
But I won't do it again."'

(23) *"For sothe," quoth that other freke, "so felly thou spekez,*
I wyl *no lenger on lyte lette thin ernde riȝt nowe."* (2302-3)
'"Truly," said the other (the green knight), "so fiercely you speak,
I will no longer delay your errand (right now)."'

These statements with *wyl* are waiting on no conditions. The first is a knight's resolution, which is apparently not conditional, and the second is followed by action.

Wolde also occurs with the conditions made explicit, as in the examples in (24) and (25):[2]

(24) *And I* ***wolde*** *loke on that lede, if God me let* ***wolde***. (1063)
'And I want to see that knight, if God would let me.'
(25) *Bot* ***wolde*** *ȝe, lady louely, then leve me grante...* (1218)
I ***wolde*** *boȝe of this bed, and busk me better;* (1220)
'But if you would, lovely lady, grant me leave...
I would get out of bed and dress myself better.'

The conclusion, then, is that the hypothetical and the present uses of Past modals are basically the same in semantic content. With the present uses of *wolde*, however, the conditions are not stated, they are only implied.

Turning now to *schulde* in Middle English we find a similar situation. *Shall* refers to what is to be. The deontic source may vary: it may be divine destiny, social obligation or mutual arrangement. *Schulde* refers to what was to be and carries the same vagueness of implication as the other modalities: the action may or may not have been completed; the modality may or may not still be in effect. In Middle English we find many uses of *schulde* to refer to what was to take place, without any implication that it did take place:

(26) *þere watz much derue doel driuen in the sale*
That so worthé, as Wawan ***schulde*** *wende on that ernde...*(558-9)
'There was great lamenting made in the hall
That so worthy as Gawain was to go on that errand.'
(27) *And went on his way with his wyȝe one,*
þat ***schulde*** *teche hym to tourne to þat tene place...*(2074-5)
'And (he) went on his way with the man
That was to show him how to get to that perilous place.'

As with *wolde*, all the conditions necessary for the completion of the main predicate may not be met, so the use of *schulde* is appropriate in a hypothetical conditional.

(28) '*For were I worth all þe wone of wymmen alyue...* (1269)
þer ***schulde*** *no freke vpon folde bifore yow be chosen.*' (1275)
'"For if I were worth all the host of women alive...
No man upon earth would be chosen before you."'

The fact that a hypothetical conditional relation still holds in the present makes the few present uses of *schulde* found in *Gawain* possible. In (29) I assume the condition to be 'if I looked for you.'

(29) *"Where* **schulde** *I wale þe," quoth Gauan, "where is þy place?"* (398)
'"Where shall I find thee," said Gawain, "where is thy place?"'

(30) *And quy þe pentangel apendez to þat prynce noble*
I am in tent yow to telle, þof tary hyt me **schulde**: (623-4) (Author speaking)
'And why the pentangle belongs to that noble prince
I intend to tell you, though it (should) slow my tale.'

(31) *"þaȝ I hade noȝt of yourez,*
ȝet **schulde** *ȝe haue of myne."* (1815-6)
'"Though I have nothing of yours,
Yet you should have something of mine."'

One very interesting example, (32), refers to an obligation established in the past, which is being met in the present. This example shows clearly that the use of a Past modal may imply the continuation of the modality into present time.

(32) *"At þis tyme twelmonyth þou toke þat þe falled,*
And I **schulde** *at þis Nwe ȝere ȝeply þe quyte."* (2243-4)
'"At this time a year ago you took what fell your lot,
And I am/was obliged at this New Year to promptly repay you."'

In an embedded or hypothetical context, the original lexical meaning of obligation or destiny has weakened considerably even in Middle English, so that it contributes little additional meaning:

(33) *Quat! hit clatered in þe clyff, as hit cleue* **schulde**. (2201)
'Quat! It (a noise) clattered on the cliff as if it would cleave it.'

(34) *And he asoyled hym surely and sette hym so clene*
As domezday **schulde** *haf been diȝt on the morn.* (1883-4)
'And he absolved him surely and made him so clean
As (if) doomsday should have been the following morn.'

A very interesting point to note about the distribution of *schulde* in the *Gawain* text is that all of the past uses save one are in embedded clauses — in complements, relative clauses, *as if*, or *if* clauses — where the main clause is marked for Past tense. The one exception is where *schulde* occurs in a main clause in the main past narrative line, but in this case it has *haf* with it:

(35) *And he schunt for þe scharp, and* **schulde haf** *arered;*
A rach rapes hym to, ryȝt er he myȝt,
And ryȝt bifore þe hors fete þay fel on hym alle, (1902-5).
'And he (the fox) swerved for the sharp blade, and should have retreated,
A hound hurries to him, just before he could,
And right before the horses' feet they all fell on him.'

In this Middle English text, *schulde* never has to convey a past sense by itself. It was compatible with a past context, but to convey pastness, it had to be bolstered with *have*.

2. *Should* and *would* in Shakespeare

If we continue to follow *should* and *would* into Early Modern English, and consider a Shakespearean play such as *The Merchant of Venice*, we find that the trend toward using *should* and *would* in present and hypothetical contexts has continued to the point where both modals appear in these contexts almost to the exclusion of past contexts.[3] Consider Table 1.

The present uses continue to be much the same for *would* although they grow in frequency. They occur mainly in the first person singular and mean 'I want' or 'I would like'. The present uses of *should* include the first singular question, as in (36), the second singular statement of obligation, as in (37), and a new development, the occurrence of *should* in complement clauses where no past time is signalled or implied, as in (38).

(36) *What* **should** *I say to you?* **Should** *I not say*
"Hath a dog money? ..." (I.2.115-6)

Table 1. *Uses of* should *and* would *in Middle and Modern English.*

	hypothetical	past	present	other	total
should					
Gawain	17%(6)	62%(21)	15%(5)	5%(2)	(34)
Merchant	58%(30)	6%(3)	21%(11)	14%(7)	(51)
Would					
Gawain	35%(12)	38%(13)	17%(6)	8%(3)	(34)[4]
Merchant	38%(20)	4%(2)	42%(22)	15%(8)[5]	(52)

(37) *You* ***should*** *in all sense be much bound to him.* (V.1.136)
(38) *You teach me how a beggar* ***should*** *be answer'd.* (IV.1.436)

It will be recalled that the hypothetical uses of modals may involve a retention of some of their lexical meaning, such as hypothetical obligation and hypothetical willingness. Thus in *Gawain* we find examples of *would* which signal hypothetical or conditional willingness, as examples (15) and (24). There is also an example in *Gawain* which is devoid of any volitional meaning and might be characterized as a conditional prediction:

(39) *Bot who-so knew the costes that knit ar therinne,*
He ***wolde*** *hit prayse at more prys, parauenture;* (1849-50)
'But whoever knew the qualities that are knit into it,
He would value it more highly, perhaps.'

In such examples, *would* is a pure conditional, since it contributes no other meaning to the clause.

In *The Merchant of Venice* such uses are common, but only for third person. *Would* occurs rarely with first person in *then*-clauses, and when it does, it signals volition. Compare (40) and (41) with third person, where *would* is conditional, to (42) where it is volitional.

(40) *Believe me sir, had I such venture forth,*
The better part of my affections ***would***
Be with my hopes abroad. (I.1.15-17)
(41) *For if they could, Cupid himself* ***would*** *blush*
To see me transformed to a boy.
(42) *If every ducat in six thousand ducats*
Were in six parts, and every part a ducat,
I ***would*** *not draw them, I* ***would*** *have my bond.*

Should complements *would* by occurring with a pure conditional sense in first person, and rarely in second or third person *then*-clauses.

(43) *If I could bid the fifth welcome with so good a heart as I can bid the other four farewell, I* ***should*** *be glad of his approach.* (I.2.121-3)

Another difference between *would* and *should* is that *should* appears frequently in *if*-clauses with only hypothetical meaning, while *would* appears rarely in *if*-clauses and then only with volitional meaning. Thus *should* has come to signal pure conditional or hypothetical in conditional sentences, while *would* maintains some of its volitional content in first person and *if*-clauses.

The difference between Elizabethan and Modern English with regard to these modals is that *would* is replacing *should* in the first person in *then*-clauses, and has in fact already done so in American English, and *would* is now appearing in *if*-clauses with only hypothetical meaning, where formerly it conveyed willingness.[6]

As for the present uses, my proposal is that the Past modals come to be used in the present via the hypothetical conditional: originally the present uses are hypothetical *then*-clauses without the conditions stated explicitly. As *should* illustrates, however, the conditional sense can be lost. The resulting present tense modal expresses obligation, as *shall* and *should* originally did, but in a weakened sense. The hypothetical meaning has had the effect of weakening the force of the obligation, through the implication that there are outstanding conditions. Thus modern *should* expresses weak obligation. This may be seen by comparing it to the stronger *have to*, in examples (44).

(44) *I should mail this today.* vs. *I have to mail this today.*

The other English Past tense modals, *could* and *might*, when used in a present context, also express a meaning that is weaker than their Present tense counterparts, *can* and *may.*[7] If Past modals evolve universally into present uses in the way proposed here, they will always express a meaning that is similar to their Present counterparts, but weakened by hypotheticality.

3. Implications

These facts about the gradual development of the hypothetical and present senses of Past modals and their loss of past meaning have a number of implications for the synchronic and diachronic analysis of Past tense modals. In particular, we have seen that it is the combination of the modal sense and the past sense that produces the hypothetical reading, and not past alone, nor the modality alone. Moreover, the hypothetical sense replaces the past sense over time. Therefore a synchronic analysis of Modern English such as the classical Chomskyan one (Chomsky 1957), which derives *would* and *should* by combining Past Tense with *will* and *shall* cannot be justified. The case for *should* is the clearest, since *should* no longer has any past readings at all and has needed *have* added to it to attain a past reading ever since the Middle English period.[8]

A case can also be made for *would* not containing any past sense, except for its past habitual use.[9] Note that the past uses of *would* in the corpus of spoken Modern British English examined by Coates represent only 16% of the total, with 82% of the uses being hypothetical. Furthermore, the small percentage of past uses occur in past contexts in which *would* does not on its own signal past time. I would argue, then, that *would* agrees with or is compatible with a past context, but does not contain as part of its own semantics a reference to past time. The gradual semantic changes that take place among the English Past tense modals are similar, but do not affect all the modals at the same time. Despite having some syntactic properties demonstrating classhood, each modal verb follows its own path and timetable of development (Bybee 1986).

There are also consequences for the analysis of the meaning of past tense morphemes. It has been suggested, for instance by Steele (1975), Waugh (1975), Langacker (1978) and James (1982) that in languages in which a past tense is used as a hypothetical that the past tense actually means 'remote from present reality' rather than 'preceding the moment of speech'. James points out a problem with this approach, which is that in normal contexts, the past tense, say in English or French, continues to mean 'before the moment of speech' and cannot be interpreted as merely 'remote' or 'distal'. That is, there is no justification for claiming that the normal sense of a past morpheme has become more general and no longer refers to past time just because in some contexts it means hypothetical.

What all of these authors have failed to stress is that it is not the past tense alone that is contributing the hypothetical meaning, but rather the past in combination with a modal verb, a subjunctive mood, a hypothetical marker (such as *if*), or, in some cases, the imperfective aspect (Fleischman, this volume). Moreover, I have argued that the diachronic progression shows that it is not the 'remoteness' of the past that leads to the hypothetical sense, but rather the fact that past combined with modality leaves open the possibility that certain conditions on the completion of the predicate have not been met. Thus there is no justification for claiming that the meaning of past tense in some languages is 'removed from present reality'.

Another issue concerns whether or not a 'Conditional Mood' should be viewed as the 'future of the past'. Since in *would* and *should*, as well as in the conditional mood in other languages, such as Spanish or French, we can see that formally the 'conditional' consists of the Past tense of the Future marker, it is tempting to claim that conditional meaning is the combination of past and future meaning and is historically derived from the future-of-the-past. Fleischman (1982) makes this claim for the Romance conditional, arguing that sentences such as (45) show that *would* may be conditional and future of the past at the same time.

(45) *Peter said he would come (if he got the money).*

For the Romance conditional she claims that "the conditional use was a secondary development contingent upon the earlier use of this form as a future for past time" (p. 66), though she presents no direct historical evidence for this position.

There are a number of reasons for rejecting this particular explanation of the relation between future and conditional, at least for English, and perhaps generally. First, in the English data, we have seen that the conditional uses of *would* and *should* developed while these two modals and their Present tense counterparts still signalled their original lexical meaning of 'desire or volition' and 'obligation or destiny'. Not only did they not wait until *will* and *shall* had become futures, they also did not wait until they had lost their original modal semantics. That is, I have claimed that it is the particular combination of these modalities with past time that creates the conditional, not the combination of past with future. If this hypothesis is correct, then we would expect to find languages in which a past modal has developed into a conditional without its present tense counterpart developing into a future. Indeed such cases exist. For instance in Classical Nahuatl, the form used in 'then'-clauses of conditional sentences (with the condition implied or explicit) is the Imperfect form of the verb meaning 'to want' (Andrews 1975). However, the future is not formed from the Present of this verb, it is a completely independent suffixal formation. Similarly, in the east central subdialect of Sierra Miwok, the Andative (be going to) marker *–y:i:* modified by the Distant Past marker is used to form a conditional. However, the Present Andative is not used as a future in that dialect, although it is so used in a reduced form in the southern dialect. The evidence that this is not a case of the 'future of the past' is that the conditional meaning is expressed by the unreduced form of the Andative, while in the dialect in which the Andative is used as a future, it is reduced to *yi* (Freeland 1951).

Finally, a more general conclusion is that we must expect grammaticizing semantic elements to merge in some cases, especially if they are always expressed together, and despite the fact that they may involve different grammatical categories, such as tense and modality. Our overzealous tendency as linguists to analyze every element down into minimal components often obscures rather than illuminates the diachronic tendencies for some types of grammatical meaning to merge.

NOTES

1. An earlier version of this paper was presented at the Eighth International Conference on Historical Linguistics in Lille, France, August 1987, and appeared in the Buffalo Working Papers in Linguistics, A special issue for Paul Garvin, 1990, 13-30. Special thanks are due to Suzanne Fleischman, William Pagliuca and the participants in the Mood and Modality Symposium for discussion of ideas contained herein. This work was supported by a fellowship from the John Simon Guggenheim Memorial Foundation.

2. *Wolde* also occurs in the if-clauses in these examples. Here it means 'want' or 'be willing' in the past.

3. *The Merchant of Venice* is written partly in poetry and partly in prose, making it more appropriate than one of the plays written entirely in verse. Of course, we cannot assume that Shakespeare's texts give a true representation of spoken Early Modern English. At the time, however, they apparently sounded natural enough for audiences to accept them, and moreover, they are the best evidence we have concerning spoken English of that period.

4. For the *Gawain* text, the numbers for *wolde* include *nolde* (*ne* + *wolde*).

5. The other uses of *would* in *The Merchant of Venice* are three generic uses in phrases such as 'as one would say' and four uses to mean 'I wish', in which the complement clause has a different subject than the main clause.

6. In American English, examples such as the following, where *would* is purely hypothetical and conveys no sense of willingness, are frequently heard in colloquial speech:

   (i) *If I would see her, I would tell her.*

7. *Must* is also considered Past tense in some analyses. However, its strong meaning suggests that it might derive from the Second Singular Present form, *moste.*

8. In American English *was supposed to* conveys past obligation (*I was supposed to go yesterday)* and *should* does not (**I should go yesterday*). Even *should* with *have* has specialized to counter-factual obligation (*I should have gone yesterday*).

9. The past habitual uses of *would* date from the Old English period and develop independently of the hypothetical uses.

REFERENCES

Andrews, J. R. 1975. *Introduction to Classical Nahuatl*. Austin: University of Texas Press.

Bybee, Joan L. 1986. "On the Nature of Grammatical Categories: A Diachronic Perspective." *Proceedings of the Second Eastern States Conference on Linguistics*, ed. by Soonja Choi 17-34.

Chomsky, N. 1957. *Syntactic Structures*. The Hague: Mouton.

Coates, J. 1983. *The Semantics of the Modal Auxiliaries*. London: Croom Helm.

Fleischman, S. 1982. *The Future in Thought and Language*. Cambridge: Cambridge University Press.

Fleischman, S. 1989. "Temporal Distance: A Basic Linguistic Metaphor". *Studies in Language* 13.1.

Freeland, L. S. 1951. *The Language of the Sierra Miwok. (Memoirs of IJAL* or *Indiana Publications in Anthropology and Linguistics* VI.) Bloomington: Indiana University.

Givón, T. 1973. "The Time-Axis Phenomenon". *Language* 49.800-825.

Gordon, R. K. 1926. *Anglo-Saxon Poetry*. London: Dent.

James, D. 1982. "Past Tense and the Hypothetical: A Cross-Linguistic Study". *Studies in Language* 4.375-403.

Langacker, R. W. 1978. "The Form and Meaning of the English Auxiliary". *Language* 54.853-82.

Steele, S. 1975. "Past and Irrealis: Just What Does it All Mean?". *IJAL*.41.

Waugh, L. 1975. "A Semantic Analysis of the French Tense System". *Orbis* 24.436-85.

Imperfective and Irrealis*

Suzanne Fleischman
University of California, Berkely

1. Introduction

In many languages of the world we encounter a more than chance connection between the aspectual category imperfective and irrealis modality. The connection manifests itself both synchronically and to a degree diachronically, and involves the use of verb forms marked for imperfective aspect, particularly but not exclusively where combined with past tense, to express a spectrum of meanings and functions subsumable under the modal heading of irrealis.

Synchronically, for example, we find imperfective pasts (including progressives) pressed into service in the negotiation of roles and settings that typically serves as a prelude to children's make-believe games, as in (1):

(1) J: ... *Pretend I* ***was moving*** *this up and down and up and down* [moves appendage on a doll]....
Z: *And pretend somebody* ***was iceskating*** *on the rink*[1]

Imperfectives appear likewise in the narration of dreams and other less-than-fully-conscious states, as in the example in (2), from a novel about the American west, in which the semi-conscious narrator ponders a statement made by the character Winder:

(2) *Now Winder* ***was wanting to know*** *what the hell the stage was doing on the pass at night anyway.* (Walter Van Tilburg Clark, *The Ox-Bow Incident*, p.126).[2]

A marked use of the imperfective past occurs in French — and conceivably other languages as well — in a style of hypocoristic discourse used by adults to address small children and pets, as in (3):

(3) *Comme il **était*** [IMP] *sage*! 'Now aren't you a good boy!'

And across languages, we find imperfective verbs used in styles of indirect quotation, including so-called free indirect discourse.

Diachronically, imperfective indicative forms have come to be used in a variety of hypothetical contexts, notably in conditionals. And in many languages, imperfective verbs and verbal periphrases have become grammaticalized, or further grammaticalized[3], as futures, conditionals, and subjunctives.

The examples cited above will be taken up again in the sections that follow, where the usages they illustrate will be analyzed in more detail. For the moment they should suffice to give readers an idea of the thrust of this inquiry, which grew out of some 'loose ends' left over from previous research.

In a 1989 paper on temporal distance as a metaphorical template for the expression of other kinds of distance that languages see fit to express, I pointed out that past-tense verb forms were often used to carry out a number of non-temporal functions, including those illustrated in (1) and (3) above. The time reference of these examples, it will be noted, is not past; thus the past-tense verbs must be doing some alternative work in the discourse.[4] The focus of my 1989 paper, however, was on pastness, with merely an acknowledgment that the verbs in question were also predominantly imperfective.

In my recent work on narrative, especially Fleischman (1990) and (1991), I looked at the tense-aspect categories used by fiction writers to report the speech and thought of their characters, notably in the quotation styles known as interior monologue and free indirect discourse, which privilege, respectively, the present tense and imperfective forms of the past. Yet here too, I merely speculated on why the verb forms chosen as the grammatical vehicles for these quotation styles are invariably imperfective. In the present inquiry I take up these dangling threads, weaving them together into an investigation focused specifically on the connection between imperfective aspect and irrealis modality,[5] and one that seeks to explain why imperfective forms so frequently gravitate toward irrealis meanings and contexts. The data I cite here are drawn primarily from Romance languages and from English, with occasional references to parallel — or nonconforming — phenomena in other languages.

2. Defining the categories

Before proceeding with my analysis, and in light of the fuzziness that comes to surround grammatical categories once we start comparing them across languages, let me propose some working definitions of the macro-categories at issue here, imperfective and irrealis.

2.1. Experts on aspect will presumably agree that imperfective aspect — which in some languages receives explicit coding only in past contexts[6] presents a situation[7] as *unbounded*, i.e., without endpoints. Though the situation may well have endpoints in the world to which the utterance refers, by choosing a verb with imperfective aspect, the speaker opts to leave these endpoints out of consideration.

A metaphor often called upon to contrast perfective and imperfective aspects is that of a camera lens focusing on a situation as if it were a visualizable object. Thus Lunn (1985:52) remarks, apropos of this aspectual opposition in Spanish:

> When a speaker's perspective on a time span permits [... a] situation to be viewed in its entirety and *in focus*, the speaker will refer to it in the preterit [= perfective past]. When a speaker's perspective *precludes such focus*, the situation will be referred to in the imperfect [= imperfective past]. (my emphasis)

As we shall see, the visual notion of focus provides an important key to understanding the relationship between imperfective aspect and irrealis modality.

Of the two endpoints of a situation, initial and terminal, it is the latter that tends to be of greater linguistic consequence in discourse. Accordingly, imperfective aspect is also commonly said to present a situation as non-completed. Thus Le Goffic (1986:57) observes, apropos of French, that insofar as the Present and the *Imparfait* can be used to express non-temporal meanings — unlike the *Passé Simple*, which cannot —, this is by virtue of their shared property of aspectual *non-completion*.

One additional point concerning imperfective aspect: following Comrie (1976) and Bybee & Pagliuca (1985), I include under the umbrella of 'imperfective' its aspectual subcategories continuous, habitual/iterative, and progressive, even though certain of these subcategories, in certain languages, may be subject to constraints not shared by the generalized imperfective (cf. n.7).

2.2 As a cross-language category of grammar, irrealis constitutes a decidedly untidy can of worms, given the extent to which languages differ over what they classify as realis and what they classify as irrealis. In fact, several papers in this volume that deal with irrealis (notably those by Chafe and Mithun) move this theoretical problem right up to center stage.

In his *Dictionary of Grammatical Terms in Linguistics*, Trask (1993) characterizes irrealis as "a label often applied in a somewhat *ad hoc* manner to some distinctive grammatical form, most often a verbal inflection, occurring in some particular language and having some kind of connection with unreality." This definition clearly won't get us very far. But precisely because of its failure to sharpen our understanding of the modality in question, it underscores the extent to which defining irrealis as a cross-language category has become a vexed question.[8] Though some investigators, for this reason, favor jettisoning irrealis altogether from the arsenal of linguistic metalanguage — the position Trask ascribes to Palmer —, I find myself more in agreement with Mithun's position (this volume, p. xx) that "despite the apparent heterogeneity of the categories to which the distinction is applied, indeed perhaps because of it, the irrealis/realis terminology can prompt fruitful cross-linguistic comparisons with potential for furthering our understanding of certain processes of grammatic[al]ization." It is in the spirit of this statement — with a crucial codocil to the effect that irrealis, like any linguistic category one seeks to compare across languages, should be understood as having a prototype structure — that I undertake the present investigation into the widespread cross-language tendency for imperfectively -marked verbs to be pressed into service to express a range of modal meanings that in different ways signal:

(4) a speaker's *lack of belief in* or *lack of commitment to* (a) the reality, realization, or referentiality of an event or sequence of events predicated in an utterance; (b) the realization of an agent's wishes, hopes, or intentions, as expressed in the proposition of an utterance; (c) the authenticity of an utterance or chunk of discourse (i.e. a sequence of utterances); or (d) what for lack of a better term I will call the 'canonicity' or normalcy of a discourse or of a communicative situation.

These various avatars of irrealis will become clearer as they are illustrated in the paragraphs that follow. But before proceeding to the analysis, a point of clarification is in order concerning the basis for my classification of a context or usage as irrealis.

As used here, irrealis refers solely to *meaning*, with no requirement that this meaning be expressed formally by a 'dedicated' irrealis morpheme. This caveat is necessary *a fortiori* given the limited degree to which irrealis receives explicit morphological coding in the languages best represented here.

3. Imperfective aspect in conditional sentences

The imperfective-irrealis connection most frequently discussed in the litera ture involves bi-clausal conditionals of the type referred to as unreal, hypothetical, or counterfactual. Without entering into the terminological debates over the synonymy (or hyperonymy) of these labels, suffice it to say that conditionals of this type are used to refer to events about which the speaker expresses some kind of negative belief (Palmer 1986:189). Examples from standard French and Spanish are given in (5) and (6). The examples in (5) involve present and future (i.e. nonpast) unreality:

(5) Nonpast conditionals
Fr. *Si j'avais le temps, je t'écrirais*
[IMP] [COND][9]
Sp. *Si tuviera tiempo, te escribiría*
[IMP SUBJ] [COND][10]
'If I had time, I would write to you'

For past unreality, the general rule is simply to add a past tense marker in some way, retaining the imperfective aspect (Dahl Forthcoming). For the Romance constructions illustrated in (6), this involves use of a conditional form of the 'have' auxiliary plus a past participle:

(6) Past conditionals
Fr. *Si j'avais eu le temps, je t'aurais écrit*
[PLUPERF] [PAST COND]
Sp. *Si hubiera tenido tiempo, te habría escrito*
[PLUPERF SUBJ] [PAST COND]
'If I had had time, I would have written to you'

Other languages using imperfective forms in unreal conditionals include Latin, Greek, German, Old Irish, Cree, various Balkan languages (Palmer 1986:192; James 1982:399; Galton 1987), and doubtless others as well.

The standard French and Spanish conditional constructions given in (5) and (6) use imperfective forms in the apodosis (main clause), and in French in the protasis (subordinate clause) as well. In Spanish the forms used in the protasis are subjunctive; albeit referred to as the Imperfect Subjunctive,[10] the verb form used in the protasis of (5) is imperfective in name only, given that the perfective/imperfective opposition is neutralized in Spanish in the past subjunctive. In colloquial and/or regional varieties of Romance it is not uncommon to find 'modal harmony' in unreal conditionals, involving either double Imperfects — indicative (Portuguese, Italian) or subjunctive (Spanish) — or double Conditionals (French, Spanish, Italian) (see Harris 1978:234-246). But again, the crucial fact for our purpose is that these forms are virtually all — nominally and/or historically — imperfective.

An alternative construction for past unreality, likewise documented in several varieties of Romance, substitutes the imperfect indicative for the past conditional, as exemplified in (7) and (8) from French and Italian:

(7) Fr. *Un simple coup de téléphone, **je venais*** [IMP] *tout de suite*
'All you had to do was call, I ***would have come*** right away'
It. *Perchè non me l'hai detto? **Veniva*** [IMP] *di sicuro*
'Why didn't you tell me? Of course I ***would have come***'

(8) Fr. *Une minute de plus (et) le train **déraillait*** [IMP]
It. *Ancora un attimo, e il treno **deragliava*** [IMP]
'One more second (and) the train ***would have derailled***'
(examples from Le Goffic 1986, Bertinetto 1986)

The attraction of imperfective aspect for unreal conditionals is discussed further in Section 10.

4. Motion-derived futures

A second context illustrating the migration of imperfectives into irrealis territory involves grammaticalization of the motion verbs 'come' and 'go' as auxiliaries in future and future-of-the-past constructions, as illustrated in the (semantically equivalent) sentences in (9), again from English and Romance:

(9) Eng. *I'm going* [PRES PROG]/*was going* [PAST PROG] *to do it myself*
Sp. *Voy* [PRES]/*iba* [IMP] *a hacerlo yo (mismo)*

Fr. *Je vais* [PRES]/*j'allais* [IMP] *le faire moi-même*
Ptg. *Vou* [PRES] *ía* [IMP] *fazé-lo eu mesmo*

How is it, one might ask, that in so many languages deictic verbs of spatial motion come to be used to locate situations in a timespan that is unrealized at reference time? Bybee & Pagliuca (1987:116) observe that 'come' and 'go' are likely candidates for future meaning (including future-of-the-past) *when they occur in the imperfective aspect.* For the languages documented above — and there are many others one could cite with motion-derived futures[11] — the auxiliaries are either (a) in the simple present tense, which in most languages is imperfective or neutral with respect to the perfective/imperfective distinction, but in any case not perfective (Comrie 1976:66); (b) in the imperfective past, or, (c) in the progressive, an imperfective subtype. Note that if perfective verbs are substituted for the imperfectives in the examples in (9), only a 'motion' reading is possible, no longer 'future-of-the-past':

(10) Eng. *I went to do it myself*
Sp. *Fui a hacerlo yo (mismo)*
Fr. *Je suis allé le faire moi-même*
Ptg. *Fui fazé-lo eu mesmo*

Bybee & Pagliuca (1987:116-17) contend that the movement (in time or space) conveyed by the construction in (9) should be understood as "already in progress" at the temporal or spatial reference point; specifically, they trace the futurate meaning back to an original meaning according to which "the subject is on a path toward a goal (which may be an event, state, or activity)." It is this 'in progress' meaning, then, that correlates with, and calls for, the imperfective aspect.

5. The 'pre-ludic' imperfect

In Fleischman (1989) I discuss in some detail the imperfective usage illustrated in (1), repeated for convenience as (11a), which Warnant (1966) has labeled the 'pre-ludic' imperfect, inasmuch as it occurs characteristically — and exclusively — in the negotiation of roles and settings that serves as a preface to children's make-believe games. Additional examples from Spanish and French are given in (11b)-(11c):

(11) a. J: ... *Pretend I* ***was moving*** *this up and down and up and down* [moves appendage on a doll] [...]
Z: *And pretend somebody* ***was iceskating*** *on the rink*
a. Sp. *Yo* ***era*** [IMP] *el jefe de la banda y tu* ***eras*** [IMP] *el hermano* '(Pretend) I was the leader of the gang and you were my brother'
c. Fr. *Moi, j'****étais*** [IMP] *le gendarme, et tu me* ***volais*** [IMP] *mon vélo* '(Pretend) I was the policeman and you were stealing my bike'

The key word here is 'make-believe': for in effect, the imperfective verbs serve to locate the situations they refer to in the realm of fantasy, of fictional activity.[12] Interesting to note in this connection is a link various investigators (Le Goffic 1986, Cappello 1986, Adam 1992) have posited between the French *Imparfait* and fictionality, particularly as this form is used in the protasis of unreal conditionals.

In a thought-provoking discussion, Adam (1992) proposes that the *Imparfait* should be viewed not so much as a tense of the past but as an "operator of fictionality." He bases this proposal on the modal uses of imperfective pasts that are of concern in the present inquiry.[13] Cappello (1986) refers similarly to the *Imparfait* as "the fictional analogue of the Present Indicative,"[14] a tense which is likewise pressed into service to express non-temporal meanings, including meanings that come under the heading of conditional or imaginary. (The present, we recall, is commonly found in the protasis of real, or open, conditions and is also the tense most frequently used across languages for generic or gnomic statements.) Seeking out a common property that will explain why the Present and the *Imparfait* in French can express non-temporal (i.e., modal) meanings, whereas the *Passé Simple* cannot, Le Goffic (1986) points to their shared imperfective — or as he calls it, non-completive — aspect.[15] It is this property, he argues, that explains, moreover, why the imperfective past (the *Imparfait*) and not its perfective counterpart (the *Passé Simple*) is chosen as the vehicle for free indirect discourse (see Section 9).

6. Politeness forms

Another category of utterances discussed in Fleischman (1989), which I subsume here under the irrealis rubric, includes politeness forms, in particular attenuated requests of the type exemplified in (12)-(15):

(12) Sp. ***Quería*** [IMP] *pedirle un pequeño favor*
Querría [COND] *pedirle un pequeño favor*
Quisiera [IMP SUBJ] *pedirle un pequeño favor*
Fr. *Je **voulais*** [IMP] *vous demander un petit service*
*Je **voudrais*** [COND] *vous demander un petit service*
J'aurais voulu [PAST COND] *vous demander un petit service*
It. ***Volevo*** [IMP] *chiederle un piccolo favore*
Vorrei [COND] *chiederle un piccolo favore*
'I wanted to ask you a little favor'

(13) a. ***I was hoping*** [PAST PROG] *we might get together for dinner. What do you say?*
b. ?? ***I hoped*** [SIMPLE PAST] *we might get together for dinner. What do you say?*

(14) a. ***I was thinking about*** [PAST PROG] *going to Italy in the summer. Are you interested?*
b. ?? ***I thought about*** [SIMPLE PAST] *going to Italy in the summer. Are you interested?*

(15) a. ***I was wondering*** [PAST PROG] *if you could tell me what time it is.*
b. ?? ***I wondered*** [SIMPLE PAST] *if you could tell me what time it is.*

The Romance examples in (12) all translate rougly as 'I wanted to ask you a little favor', with the different forms of the modal 'want' — all imperfective[16] — conveying different degrees of deference. (The fact that the English gloss uses the Simple Past is due to a language-particular constraint on the use of statives with progressive aspect.)

Bybee (this volume) emphasizes that utterances of this type typically involve modal auxiliaries, which as a class "do not imply completion of the action or event expressed by the infinitive with which they occur."[17] Inasmuch as Bybee includes under the modal umbrella mental-activity verbs (e.g., 'hope', 'think about' and 'wonder', as in (13)-(15)), her claim strikes me as well founded, *provided these verbs are combined with imperfective aspect.* I.e., inasmuch as they do not predicate the completion of the mental situations they refer to, by implicature they allow for the possibility that these mental activities are still going on, thereby leaving the addressee an opportunity to respond. This explains why the Past Progressive versions of the English examples in (13)-(15) are more natural than their Simple Past counterparts, which are all more or less pragmatically odd. But what remains to be explained is why I classify these polite request forms under the semantic rubric of irrealis.[18]

Indirect speech-acts of this type operate by camouflaging the illocutionary force of assertive and potentially face-threatening speech acts, such as requests, by clothing them in the form of simple declarative statements about the speaker's intentions or desires *in the past*. Statements of desire or intention in the past are generally used when the intended actions turn out to be unrealized,[19] and as Hale (1969) has observed, unrealized intentions constitute "a specific sort of irrealis."[20] What specifically marks these past intentions as unrealized, I would argue, is the imperfective aspect of the mental-activity verb. Whence the oddity of (13b) and (14b), where the closure effected by the perfective Simple Past (I am no longer hoping that/thinking about ...) clashes with the present time reference of the questions that follow. (15b) seems less awkward, for reasons not entirely clear to me; my intuition, however, is that speakers would be less likely to produce (15b) spontaneously than they would the corresponding utterances with Simple or Progressive Present verbs, as in (15c) below, which are less assertive and involve less potential loss of face than the present-tense counterparts of (13) and (14).

(15) c. ***I wonder/I'm wondering*** *if you could tell me what time it is.*

7. The 'hypocoristic' Imperfect

Several interpretations have been proposed for the so-called hypocoristic Imperfect, illustrated by the French examples given in (3) (repeated here as (16)) and in (17):

(16) *Comme il* ***était*** [IMP] *sage*! 'Now aren't you a good boy!'
(17) *Il* ***avait*** [IMP] *fort mal à son petit doigt, mon bonhomme?*
'Does my little man have a big 'hurt' on his little finger?'

This usage occurs exclusively in an endearing form of address (whence the label 'hypocoristic') used by adults — mainly women[21] — in speaking to young children and pets. Though the temporal reference is to the present of the speech situation, statements of this type are characterized by use of the *Imparfait* together with reference to the addressee in the third person.

Of the various explanations proposed for this phenomenon, the most compelling in my view is that of Gougenheim (1970). In using the hypocoristic Imperfect, Gougenheim argues:

> the speaker refuses to take seriously the words she utters. She says, in effect, for the benefit of an adult who is or might be listening — or for her own benefit, out of basic human self-respect: "Pay attention! What I'm saying is not serious. This is a game; this is fiction."[22]

Through this usage, then, the adult speaker distances herself from the words of her own utterance, acknowledging that they are not cast in the conventional adult forms. She marks the utterance in question as an inauthentic token of adult discourse. In line with Gougenheim's statement, Wilmet (1968-69:105) points out that the hypocoristic Imperfect is always a 'fiduciary' form: its use rests on an understood linguistic contract among speakers, from which young children — and, obviously, animals — are excluded inasmuch as they do not qualify as full-fledged interlocutors. In sum, the hypocoristic imperfect operates as a kind of metalinguistic evidential signaling the non-authenticity or non-canonicity of the speech situation itself — a usage I include under the last category of irrealis meaning given in (4).

Commenting on the hypocoristic Imperfect, Martin (1971:102) describes it as creating a world "centered around the child or pet addressee," "a reality in which the [adult] speaker is not really immersed." This brings us to the use of imperfective aspect to signal the irrealis status of represented worlds.

8. Imperfective aspect and irrealis worlds

As I have argued at various points in my work on narrative, notably in Fleischman (1990), adult speakers, as part of their linguistic competence, possess a typology of narrative genres, one of the most basic divisions of which seems to be realis vs. irrealis, i.e., a distinction between reports of events construed by the speaker and addressee(s) as real vs. reports of events construed as hypothetical, or as fictional vs. non-fictional. Moreover, there appear to be grammatical features, including tense-aspect categories, that correlate predictably with these narrative primes. Narration in the perfective past, which I take to be the unmarked tense of narration, correlates with stories that are, or purport to be, realis — including conventional fiction, which purports to be someone's experience; whereas genres which choose a basic reporting tense other than the perfective past are often irrealis. Jokes, for example, which are referentially irrealis — thus instantiating the first category of the definition of irrealis given in (4) —, are routinely told in the present tense. Any speaker of English immediately recognizes a story that starts out "This guy *walks* into a bar and *says* to the bartender..." as a joke, whereas the same information reported in the past tense might be construed, initially at least, as a narration of realis events. Both the imperfect and the present are selected across languages as the basic reporting tense of genres that refer to a legendary or mythical past, e.g. the Sanskrit *Rgvedas*, the Tamil Puranic stories, and epic universally (see Fleischman 1990:123-24).

The imperfective aspect of the present and the imperfect[23]enables these tenses to represent past experience as if it were in the process of occurring, unmediated by the post-hoc reflective consciousness of a reporting speaker.[24] Thus in many languages (e.g., Spanish, French, Italian, Rumanian, Dutch) these two tenses are used to report the contents of dreams, hallucinations, and other semi-conscious states, as seen in (2) above, repeated for convenience as (18):

(18) *Now Winder* ***was wanting to know*** *what the hell the stage was doing on the pass at night anyway.* (Walter Van Tilburg Clark, *The Ox-Bow Incident*, p.126)

This statement occurs at a point in the story just after the (first-person) narrator has been shot by a stagecoach guard. As Chafe (1994:242) observes, Winder's statement would normally have been perceived as a punctual event, but it entered the narrator's impaired consciousness "as if he were tuning in on part of a speech event that was diffuse and out of focus." What is captured by the imperfective aspect of the main-clause predicate is the semi-conscious state of the narrator, specifically his inability of focus in on particular events.

In the best known of medieval French epics, *The Song of Roland*, the very few Imperfects that occur at all are concentrated in the dream visions.[25] The passages given in (19) and (20), though taken from literary fiction, are representative of the reporting style used to narrate the contents of dreams and fantasies. The passage in (19), from a Spanish novel of the 19th century, reports a dream of one of the characters:

(19) ***Oía*** [IMP] *el reloj de la catedral dando las nueve;* ***veía*** [IMP] *con júbilo a la criada anciana durmiendo con beatífico sueño,* ***salía*** [IMP] *del cuarto muy despacito para no hacer ruido;* ***bajaba*** [IMP] ***la escalera*** *tan suavemente que* ***no movía un pié*** [IMP] *hasta no estar segura de poder evitar el más ligero ruido.* ***Salía*** [IMP] *a la*

huerta, deteniéndose un momento para mirar al cielo que ***estaba tachonado*** [IMP] *de estrellas*. (Benito Pérez Galdos, *Doña Perfecta*, p. 478)

'She **heard** [IMP] the cathedral clock striking nine; jubilant, she **saw** [IMP] the old housemaid deep in a beatific sleep. She **walked out** [IMP] of the room ever so slowly so as not to make a noise; she **went down** [IMP] **the stairs** so quietly that she **didn't lift her foot** [IMP] until she was sure not to make the slightest sound; she **walked out** [IMP] to the garden, stopping for a moment to observe the sky, which **was studded** [IMP] with stars.'

In the passage in (20), from a *fin-de-siècle* Italian novel, the protagonist fantasizes about his father's dying (at the time of the fantasy the father is still alive):

(20) *Subitamente, gli si formò* [PRET] *nello spirito l'imagine del padre agonizzante:* ***strammazzava*** [IMP] *come fulminato, a terra, di schianto;* ***sussultava*** [IMP], *non anche morto, livido, muto, contraffatto, con l'occhio pieno dell'orrore di morire;* ***rimaneva*** [IMP] *immobile, come sotto il secondo colpo d'un maglio invisibile, carne inerte* [...] *La madre gli disse* [PRET] [...] (Gabriele D'Annunzio, *Trionfo della Morte*; as cited in Bertinetto 1986:370)

'Suddenly, an image formed itself [PRET] in his mind of his father in the throes of dying: **collapsing**[26] [IMP] suddenly to the ground, as if struck by lightening; **convulsing** [IMP], as yet not dead but deathly pale, speechless, deformed, eyes filled with the horror of dying; he **remained** [IMP] immobile, as if struck by the second blow of an invisible hammer, his flesh inert, [...] His [the protagonist's] mother said [PRET] to him [...]'

It will be observed from these passages that the contents of dreams and fantasies tend to be packaged *not* in the form of punctual, bounded events, which are normally encoded by perfective pasts, but as situations in the process of being visualized, their endpoints out of focus; whence the choice of imperfective pasts. Accordingly, what we often find in reports of this type is a neutralization of the conventional discourse contrast between perfective and imperfective aspect for reporting eventive vs. non-eventive material. If the passage in (19) were a conventional narration, all predicates except *estaba tachonado* ('was studded') in the last clause would be reported as narrative events in the Preterit (= perfective past). As Lunn (1985:55) observes, "disoriented characters make strange aspectual choices: they find it impossible to place themselves at a vantage point from which events could most conventionally (i.e. coherently) be described."[27]

9. Speech and thought quotation

The hierarchy given in (21) below, adapted from Haiman (1989), lists several strategies for reporting speech, ordered according to their ostensible degree of fidelity to the original speaker's utterance,[28] a parameter which lends itself to interpretation along a realis/irrealis cline.

(21) Speech and thought reports: hierarchy of attenuation

a. DIRECT QUOTATION: *She said/thought: "What the hell are you doing here in my hotel room?"*

b. SEMI-INDIRECT QUOTATION (including free indirect discourse): *What the hell was he doing here in her hotel room?*

c. INDIRECT QUOTATION: *She wondered what he was doing in her hotel room.*

d. EVIDENTIALS (including quotatives): *He is said to have been/ was reportedly found in her hotel room* (adapted from Haiman 1989:149; examples mine)

These are not the only categories of speech and thought representation, but they will suffice for our purpose.[29]

9.1. The 'framework'[30] of the original speaker is best represented (i.e., the representation is maximally realis) in the case of direct speech, where, according to the quotation convention (see n.32), the original speaker's words, at least, are reproduced verbatim. As we move down the hierarchy, the quoted speaker's framework becomes progressively more attenuated, i.e. more removed from the reality of the original utterance, until finally, in the case of quotative evidentials, the original speaker's very identity becomes immaterial (Haiman 1989:149). The quotative evidential examples given in (22), from newspaper journalism in French, use forms of the Conditional, which is formally and historically imperfective:

(22) *Paul VI* ***envisagerait*** [COND] *de faire le tour du monde* (*Figaro*, Jan. 11, 1966) '[Pope] Paul VI is reportedly contemplating making a world tour'
L'association de l'Angleterre au Marché Commun ***serait proposée*** [PASSIVE COND] *par l'Allemagne* (*France Soir*, Nov. 30, 1967) 'Germany is said to have proposed the entry of England into the Common Market'

In journalistic discourse the source and accuracy of reported information are crucial, given the legal consequences of libel laws. Whence this quotative has acquired in French grammar the name 'conditionnel de presse' from the variety of discourse in which it most frequently occurs.

9.2. If direct quotation purports to reproduce an utterance verbatim,[31] indirect quotation — in languages that allow this style of speech report (see n.36) — provides only a semantic equivalent of the original utterance, i.e., it reproduces the propositional content of the original statement, integrated into the framing utterance of the quoter. Several investigators (Haiman 1989, Maingueneau 1990) have referred to indirect quotation as a type of 'translation' — from the original speaker's framework into that of the quoting speaker. This can be seen by comparing the examples of direct and indirect quotation given in (21a) and (21c) respectively. Chafe (1994: 222-23) sees indirect speech as constituting an acknowledgment of "the inability of a remembering consciousness to replicate distal language verbatim."[32]

9.3. The quotation style illustrated in (21b) has been variously labeled '*style indirect libre*', '*erlebte Rede*', 'represented speech and thought', 'narrated monologue', 'semi-indirect quotation', or 'free indirect discourse'. Additional examples are given in (23) and (24), from French and Italian respectively (sentences of free indirect discourse are bolded):

(23) *Jamais Frédéric n'avait été* [PLUPERF] *plus loin du mariage.* ***D'ailleurs, Mlle Roques lui semblait*** [IMP] ***une petite personne assez ridicule. Quelle différence avec une femme comme Mme Dambreuse! Un bien autre avenir lui était réservé!*** [IMP] ***Il en avait*** [IMP] *la certitude aujourd'hui.* (Flaubert, *Sentimental Education*, Part 3, Chapter 2, p. 350)

'Frédéric's thoughts had never been [PLUPERF] further from marriage. **Besides, Mademoiselle Roques struck** [IMP] **him as a somewhat ridiculous little thing. What a difference with a woman like Madame Dambreuse! A very different future was awaiting** [IMP] **him! He was** [IMP] **certain of that now.**'

(24) *Domenico gli disse* [PRET] *di non poter accettare su due piedi l'invito a trasferirsi.* ***Qui aveva*** [IMP] ***una rete di conoscenze, frequentava*** [IMP] ***ambienti che lo interessavano*** [IMP], ***otteneva*** [IMP] ***riconoscimenti; laggiù, chissà? Ma potevano*** [IMP] ***riparlarne l'indomani, quando veniva*** [IMP] ***a cena da loro.*** (cited by Bertinetto 1986:392)
'Domenico told [PRET] him not to accept right away the offer to move. **Here he had** [IMP] **a network of acquaintences, he frequented** [IMP] **milieus that interested** [IMP] **him, he received** [IMP] **recognition; there, who knows? But they could** [IMP] **talk about it again tomorrow when he came** [IMP] **to their place for dinner.'**

In a nutshell, what typically demarcates utterances of free indirect discourse is the presence of *features of direct quotation* — direct questions, exclamations, fragments, repetitions, deictics, emotive and conative words, colloquialisms — *reported in the style of indirect quotation*, i.e., using the deictic system of the narrative frame (notably with regard to tense and person) but normally *without* the inquit formulas characteristic of indirect quotation (e.g. *s/he said/ thought that..., wondered why...*, etc.).[33] I hasten to add that this description oversimplifies considerably a complex topic that has produced volumes of scholarly debate, for the most part among literary narratologists, since it is widely believed — and for epistemologically valid reasons — that this particular style of quotation is confined to fiction.[34]

As noted above, the utterances bolded in (23) and (24) are utterances of free indirect discourse, which is one linguistic strategy (though not the only one) for representing the contents of another mind, the subjectivity of the other. In the passage in (23) the bolded utterances correspond to the thoughts of Flaubert's protagonist Frédéric Moreau, in (24) to the advice of the reported speaker Domenico, 'translated' in both cases into the language of an unpersonified narrator. The narrator's language imposes on these words and thoughts, produced originally by a first-person subjectivity, the third-person pronouns and imperfective past tenses (imperfect, pluperfect, and conditional) of so-called 'speakerless' narration.

As Banfield (1982:108) notes, free indirect discourse is neither an *interpretation* of the character's speech or thought, which implies an evaluating speaker; nor a *direct imitation* of the quoted individual's voice; rather, the words or thoughts of the represented self retain all their expressivity without suggesting that their grammatical form was that originally uttered, aloud or silently.

9.4. The point of this somewhat protracted discussion of quotation styles is this: if we take direct quotation to be the the most realis representation of speech and thought — the prototype quotation strategy, as it were,[35] with respect to parameter (c) of the characterization of irrealis given in (4) —, then the remaining styles represent varying degrees of irrealis. Thus it is not coincidental, I submit, that in languages with a perfective/imperfective opposition in the past, irrealis quotation styles consistently privilege imperfective past tenses.

9.5. Several investigators have claimed that in languages with established written traditions of narrative fiction, free indirect discourse or analogous forms of semi-indirect quotation are only possible in literary fiction,[36] whereas in other languages this kind of mixed-perspective discourse that "wears its hybrid status on its sleeve" (Haiman 1989:149) can be found in natural narration. Let me suggest, however, that semi-indirect discourse can occur in natural narration even in languages like English or the standard Romance languages that have long established belle-lettristic traditions. And one of the features that marks this mixed quotation style, I submit, is the presence of inquit formulas in *imperfective* tenses.

Consider in this regard the natural-narrative examples given in (25)-(26), which introduce quotation with Progressive inquit formulas (all *verba dicendi* are bolded):

(25) [...] *an' I was about two blocks from my house when a cop got behind me and started following me*
and ***I was going*** <Q *Oh God, I know he's gonna, he's gonna pull me over for the [license] plate.* Q>[37]

(26) [...] *an'* ***I was saying*** <Q *Well, you can't just try, You hafta, you hafta — we can't hang up without you guaranteeing me that you or somebody's gonna show up here within two hours* Q>
and... so she ***said*** <Q *OK* Q>
an' we hung up [...]

Direct quotations normally represent semelfactive speech events, and are accordingly introduced by perfective verbs, e.g. *said* in the second-to-last line of (26). But elsewhere in (25) and (26) what is 'marketed' as direct quotation is not something the quoted speaker actually said, but something he was thinking or something he, as narrator, imagines he was thinking at the time, along the lines of the free indirect discourse of narrative fiction. (The fact that this is a first-person narration, i.e. one in which the narrator is also a character in the story and says 'I', makes the case slightly less compelling, since first-person narrators *are* in a position to have had access to the consciousness of their character-selves in the past (cf. n.35), which is not the case in non-personal — what is traditionally referred to as 'third-person' — narration.[38]) In any event, what matters here is that these forays into the consciousness of a quoted speaker or thinker appear to be signalled by the imperfective aspect of the introduction-to-discourse verbs.

I puzzled for some time over these imperfective *verba dicendi* — 'S/he was going...', 'I was telling John...', 'I was thinking...' — and their analogues in Romance (see Bertinetto 1986:399-401 for examples from Italian). From the contexts it was clear that the speech-events they referred to were not iterative/habitual, though they gave the impression of being so because of the imperfective aspect of the *verbum dicendi.*[39] Ultimately, I concluded that in a manner similar to the colloquial English quotative *like*, so cherished by every teenager in America (see Romaine & Lange 1991), imperfective *verba dicendi* in narrative signal that what follows *is not a direct-speech quote*, though it may have all the formal trappings of the direct-quotation style. Rather, it is a verbalization of something the quoted speaker was turning over in his or her mind. On this reading, it would be the 'ruminative' quality of the quoted material in irrealis quotations of this type that motivates the imperfective — and specifically iterative/habitual — aspect of the speech and thought tags.

Bybee (p.c.) has suggested an alternative interpretation of these imperfective inquit formulas which privileges not the iterative/habitual meaning associated with imperfectivity, as proposed here, but rather the ongoing/continuous meaning (on these two meanings as the major subcategories of imperfective aspect, see Comrie 1976:25). According to the latter view, an imperfective *verbum dicendi* gives the sense that a quoted utterance is 'in progress' and perhaps also backgrounded, given that what it reports is an ongoing mental attitude. An imperfective inquit formula will be chosen not when the speaker is reporting a sequence of events (where perfective verbs are called for), but when what is being reported on is rather how the speaker feels about something. Imperfective *verba dicendi* formally release the quoting speaker from a commitment to the exact replication of what the original speaker said — this is in line with category (c) of the characterization of irrealis given in (4) — and provides instead "a characterization that reflects the quoted speaker's feelings" (Bybee, p.c.).

Both of the above interpretations of imperfective inquit formulas (habitual and continous) are plausible. And both motivate the use of verbs with imperfective aspect to mark this style of quotation as irrealis, in the sense of being an inexact representation of a quoted speaker's utterance(s).

10. Habitual and irrealis

Several investigators have looked cross-linguistically at the classification of habitual as realis or irrealis (Givón 1984; Willett 1989; Dahl Forthcoming). Givón regards habitual as mixed.[40] On the one hand, it represents "a clear *strong assertion of facts*" (p. 285), which would account for the realis classification of habituals in Sherpa (Woodbury 1986:190-93), Bikol (Givón 1984:309), and no doubt elsewhere as well. But on the other hand, habitual does not refer to unique events — whence Banfield's (1985) reference to the French *Imparfait* as a 'mass' tense (in opposition to the perfective *Passé Simple*, which is a 'count' tense)[41] —, but is rather the aspect of generic, non-referring expressions, which fall under our irrealis heading (4a). This would explain why Bargam (a Papuan language), for example, treats past habitual as Irrealis (Roberts 1990). In Givón's examples, reproduced in (27):

(27) a. *Joe always cuts logs*
(27) b. *Every day Joe cuts a log, then...*

'log(s)' does not refer to any individual log or unique group of logs.[42] Rather, these are generic, non-referential statements. It is in this sense, Givón argues (p.285), that habitual resembles irrealis.

The link between irrealis and habitual (or iterative) is underscored by the fact that in many languages habitual — or the generalized imperfective, if the language lacks a distinct habitual — and conditional are formally identical. The best context for comparison is the apodosis (main clause) of unreal conditionals of the type illustrated in (5).

Commenting on Bulgarian forms that can mark either the modal Conditional or the aspectual Iterative, Aronson (1977:15) sees the connection as so close and so widespread as to constitute a potential universal. In support of this position he offers the semantically equivalent pairs of sentences given in (28), from English, Serbocroatian, and Hebrew respectively:

(28) a. Eng. *He **would play golf** every day **when*** [ITER] / ***if*** [COND] *he lived in Chicago*

b. Serbobcr. *Svakog **bi** dana **igrao** golf **dokje*** [ITER] / ***kadbi*** [COND] *živevo u Čikagu*

c. Heb. *Hu **haya msoxek** golf yom-yom **kaašer*** [ITER] / ***ilu*** [COND] *gar bŠikago*

For each pair of examples, the main clause is identical; only the particle in the subordinate clause tells us whether the sentence is iterative/habitual or conditional (cf. also Galton 1987).

Lazard (1975) cites parallel evidence from a spectrum of ancient and modern Indo-European languages in which a single morpheme expresses both past habitual and irrealis/conditional (and in certain cases also future-of-the past, analogous to Eng. *would*)[43]. He points out (pp.225f.) that where a generalized imperfect is used to express certain irrealis meanings, it is the habitual meaning, among the various possible meanings a durative past can be used to express, that specifically correlates with irrealis. He sees this affinity as particularly striking in that it is realized by a diverse range of morphological structures (the data he cites have nothing in common from the standpoint of form, their only commonality being their shared functions). Even in genetically related languages, the respective developments are apparently independent of one another — what Sapir referred to as 'drift'. Seeking to explain this affinity, Chung & Timberlake (1985:221) observe that if habitual subevents are indefinite both in number and in time (cf. n.42 above), they can also be viewed as extending over *possible* worlds.

In the grammatical environment under consideration here, the apodosis of unreal conditionals, a number of investigators (Lazard 1975, James 1982, Restan 1989, Dahl Forthcoming) have noted that in languages that distinguish perfective and imperfective aspect, what we invariably find is the imperfective past or one of its subtypes (progressive or, in particular, habitual), and not the perfective form that the context would predict (given that the main-clause verb most commonly denotes a single completed act). On the basis of broad cross-language investigation, Dahl speculates about a general tendency to use imperfective aspect in counterfactual constructions.

11. Imperfective and irrealis: why the attraction?

Seeking to account for why many languages use past tenses — specifically imperfective pasts — to express the hypothetical, James (1982) points to the shared semantic feature of non-completion. That is, imperfective and hypothetical both present predicated situations as unrealized or not fully realized at the time of reference.[44] An alternative explanation, not incompatible with the non-completion hypothesis, involves the discourse notion of backgrounding.

The correlation between imperfective aspect and backgrounding, first proposed by Weinrich (1964/1973) as an alternative to traditional interpretations of the *Imparfait/Passé Simple* opposition in French, became popularized among linguists through several papers by Hopper from the late '70s and early '80s (notably Hopper 1979, 1981). By now it has become a commonplace in the discourse literature. Background information, Hopper (1981:238) observes, involves a reduced assertion of the finite reality of an event. It is not involved in "the asserting of events in the story line, but makes statements that are CONTINGENT [his emphasis] and dependent on story line events. Typically, therefore, one finds in backgrounding those forms associated with a lower degree of assertiveness *and even forms designated as irrealis*" (1981:215, my emphasis). So if imperfective aspect is indeed associated in discourse with a reduced degree of assertiveness, then, as James observes, this would provide a natural explanation for why many languages choose it over perfective aspect to encode the hypothetical, since hypothetical statements likewise do not assert the truth of their propositions. Or, as Bybee, Perkins, and Pagliuca (1994:239) argue, mood is not about truth values, but about the speaker's choice between assertion and contrasting functions.

The foregrounding and backgrounding of information in discourse likewise correlates with the visual notion of focus, which, as I suggested in the introduction, provides a well motivated link between imperfective and irrealis. Simply put, information a speaker chooses to foreground is presented as in focus, background information as defocused, or out of focus.[45] In a now classic paper on transitivity, Hopper & Thompson (1980) make the case for a language-universal correlation between aspect and focus.[46] Their findings have subsequently been confirmed by a number of studies on narrative showing the focus and non-focus roles of perfective and imperfective aspects respectively.

In an illuminating paper contrasting the Preterit and Imperfect in Spanish, Lunn (1985) distinguishes these two categories of the Spanish past system in terms of the conferring vs. witholding of focus. There are two points of view, she notes, from which things are not in focus. On the one hand, if an observer is at a point from which foreground is in focus, then that observer is too far away for background to be in focus. This would explain the conventional connection between imperfective aspect and background. On the other hand, imperfective forms are also used to describe situations that are too close — physically and/or psychologically — to be sharply in focus. Thus Lunn explains novelist Juan Rulfo's use of the Imperfect to render the obsessive fantasy life of his protagonist Pedro Páramo, offering examples analogous to those cited in (18)-(20) above. The same out-of-focus perspective is strikingly conveyed in the passage in (29) below from Robbe-Grillet's novel *Jealousy*, which relies on a series of Present tenses (bolded in the example) to report the disjunctive perceptions of a jealous husband as he peers through the venetian blinds at his wife and her surroundings:

(29) ***C'est*** *à une distance de moins d'un mètre seulement qu'* ***apparaissent*** *dans les intervalles successifs, en bandes parallèles que* ***séparent*** *les bandes plus larges de bois gris, les éléments d'un paysage discontinu: les balustres en bois tourné, le fauteuil vide, la table basse où un verre plein* ***repose*** *à côté d'un plateau portant les deux bouteilles, enfin le haut de la chevelure noire, qui* ***pivote*** *à cet instant vers la droite, où* ***entre en scène*** *au-dessus de la table un avant-bras nu, de couleur brun foncé, terminé par une main plus pâle tenant le seau à glace. La voix de A...* ***remercie*** *le boy. La main brune* ***disparaît****. Le seau de métal étincelant, qui* ***se couvre*** *bientôt de buée,* ***reste posé*** *sur le plateau à côté des deux bouteilles.*
Le chignon de A... vu de si près, par derrière, ***semble*** *d'une grande complication.* ***Il est très difficile d'y suivre*** *dans leurs emmêlements les différentes mèches: plusieurs solutions* ***conviennent****, par endroit, et ailleurs aucune* (pp. 51-2).

> 'It **is** only at a distance of less than a yard that the elements of a discontinuous landscape **appear** in the successive intervals, parallel chinks separated by the wider slats of grey wood: the turned wood balusters, the empty chair, the low table where a full glass **is standing** beside the tray holding the two bottles, and then the top part of the head of black hair, which at this moment **turns** toward the right, where above the table **turns** a bare forearm, dark brown in color, and its paler hand holding the ice bucket. A...'s voice **thanks** the boy. The brown hand **disappears**. The shiny metal bucket, [which **is**] immediately **frosted over**, **remains** where it has been set on the tray beside the two bottles.
>
> The knot of A...'s hair, seen at such close range from behind, **seems** to be extremely complicated. **It is difficult to follow** the convolutions of different strands: several solutions **seem possible** at some places, and in others none.'

Scrutinized at such close range, the figure of the wife can only appear fragmented: a hand, a forearm, a knot of hair, its individual strands. A voice, not a character, thanks the serving boy. Verbalizing his perceptions as he watches, in the imperfective Present tense, the observer is unable to gain perspective on focalized objects, his vision severely distorted by the lack of distance betwen himself and what he observes and by the slats of the blinds. As Lunn points out (p.59), the lack of definition which such characters' aspectual choices impute to the situations they describe is precisely what an observer sees who is 'too close' to a scene.

A point of view *internal to a situation* also precludes focus on the part of an observer, and therefore results in the choice of imperfective forms when the observer undertakes to describe that situation (Lunn, p.57). This occurs, for example, when a narrator's consciousness rather than a situation external to the narrator becomes the focus of a story — which is often the case in modern fiction. The situations in which that narrator takes part are encoded in a non-focus way. This, Lunn claims, accounts for the sense of reverie evoked by the use of the Imperfect in Spanish to describe situations that could have been described objectively using the Preterit. It also accounts, I have argued (Fleischman 1990, 1991), for the use of the present tense in interior-monologue novels and related forms of fiction which undertake to verbalize the contents of a character's mind unmediated by a narrator's language.

The concept of focus, then, provides us with a fruitful metaphor linking aspect and perception. Generalizing this observation, Lunn argues that "the existence and comprehensibility of metaphors linking aspect and perception are meant to be taken as evidence that the aspect-perception link is real. That is, metaphors are held to be verbalizations of legitimate comparisons" (52f.). They capture truths about conceptualization, thus providing a solid cognitive ground on which to chart observed pathways of grammatical change.

12. Conclusion

What I have undertaken to present here is a spectrum of irrealis contexts, conforming to the typology set forth in (4), in which we find verb forms marked for imperfective aspect. These include hypothetical conditionals, motion-derived futures, politeness forms, the prefatory negotiation of children's make-believe games, hypocoristic baby-talk, the narration of dreams and other semi-conscious states, and various indirect forms of speech and thought quotation. There are no doubt additional contexts which have not come to my attention that likewise use imperfective forms to express irrealis meanings[48] — readers are encouraged to take note of such contexts —, just as there are languages in which we don't find imperfective aspect markers in certain of the irrealis contexts discussed here, or where we instead find perfectives.

One piece of apparent counterevidence involving aspect and evidentials is Nichols' proposal, based on evidence from Chinese Pidgin Russian, Turkish, Tibetan, and Sherpa, of a universal co-variance between perfective aspect and inference vs. imperfective aspect and "immediateness" or directness of evidence (Nichols 1986:254f.). Potential counterevidence is also available from Slavic, depending on how one interprets it.

In Bulgarian, for example, it is Perfective not Imperfective verbs that are acquiring a meaning more modal (i.e. conditional) than aspectual; however, the Perfective verbs in question are those built on the present stem, i.e. the Nonpast and, notably, the **Imperfect**. Moreover, the meanings of these categories, which Bulgarian classifies formally as Perfective, seem to correspond to meanings which in other languages come under the heading of imperfective (Aronson 1977). Macedonian presents a similar situation (Hacking 1993),[49] and references abound in the Slavic literature on the ability of the Russian

Perfective Nonpast to carry modal (specifically future) meaning, a characterization which Hacking extends to conditional contexts, "to make explicit the connection between the perfective nonpast and hypothetical meaning" (194).

Though here and there we encounter developments that fail to support or appear to contradict the macro-correlation proposed here between imperfective aspect and irrealis modality, such counterevidence seems neither sufficient nor of such nature as to undermine the overall well-foundedness of the correlation. The weight of evidence in support of the correlation, from a broad spectrum of related and unrelated languages, seems sufficient to establish this meaning shift as a widely documented pathway of linguistic development, leading in some instances to the grammaticalization of new expressions of evidentiality and/or epistemic modality.[410]

NOTES

* Abbreviated sections of this paper were presented at a symposium on Tense-Aspect (Cortona, Italy, October 10-13, 1993). The present version has benefitted from observations, data, and references offered by several colleagues present at that symposium, notably Carl Bache, Jacques Boulle, Oesten Dahl, Ekkehard König, and Co Vet. Acknowledgement is also due to Grace Fielder, and especially Jane Hacking, for guiding my foray into the arcane regions of Slavic aspectuality and conditionals, and to Wally Chafe, John Haiman, Sophie Marnette, Linda Waugh, and especially Joan Bybee for comments and critique of an earlier version.

1 Data from an exchange between two 4-year-old girls recorded by Amy Kyratzis.

2 My thanks to Wally Chafe for this example, reported on in Chafe (1994).

3 This statement assumes a view of grammaticalization that is not limited to the development of lexical items into grammatical morphemes, but includes also the "expansion" (Heine & Reh 1984) of items already operative in the 'service sector' of the language beyond their original function into other areas of grammar (see also Heine, Claudi & Hünneneyer 1991, chapter 6).

4 This in accord with a principle of linguistic recycling which Lass (1990) has labeled 'exaptation'.

5 For the record, this connection has not passed unnoticed. It has been alluded to, in diverse contexts, by Aronson (1977), James (1982), Le Goffic (1986), Cappello (1986), Bertinetto (1986), Bazzanella (1987), Adam (1992), Bybee (this volume), and no doubt elsewhere. However, none of the studies mentioned specifically targets the aspect-modality connection, as I propose to do here, bringing together a diverse range of phenomena under a single grammaticalization umbrella.

In a paper frequently cited as a paradigmatic case study of the interrelationship of grammatical categories, Slobin & Aksu (1986) offer compelling evidence that although tense, aspect, and modality are clearly distinct categories at the theoretical level, in practice (i.e., in actual usage) they cannot always be teased apart and studied in isolation from one another.

6 In languages that contrast perfective and imperfective aspect, this opposition may not be overtly expressed across the tense spectrum (in languages that have tense). Where this is the case, the opposition is explicitly (i.e., morphologically) expressed most often in the past. Thus Dahl (1985:92) observes that whereas progressives tend to appear in all tenses (in a language that has tense), general imperfectives tend to be limited to past tenses.

7 'Situation' will be used here as a cover term for the predicate classes traditionally referred to as events, processes, and states, or, according to the now familiar typology originally proposed by Vendler (1967), as states, activities, achievements, and accomplishments.

8 Trask adds (p. 147) that Palmer, in *Mood and Modality* (1986), recommends avoiding the term irrealis altogether in linguistic theory on grounds that it corresponds to "no consistent linguistic content." Like Chafe (this volume), I have searched *Mood and Modality* to corroborate this statement but was unable to locate it.

9 The French and Spanish Conditional forms (which double as Futures-of-the-Past) evolved from a Latin periphrasis combining Past Imperfective forms of 'have' with an infinitive: *scribere habeba(m)* (lit. to-write I-had [IMP]) > Fr. *écrirais*/Sp. *escribiría*. Standard Italian *scriverei* departs from this common Romance pattern in having chosen the Perfective form of the 'have' auxiliary, though both northern and especially southern Italian dialects show forms traceable to the Imperfective periphrasis as well as hybrid paradigms containing forms historically Imperfective alongside forms historically Perfective (see Rohlfs 1968:§§593-599).

10 Historically, this form began life as a Pluperfect Indicative. On this frequently analyzed development, see Lunn & Cravens (1991), Klein-Andreu (1991).

11 Among many commentaries on these constructions, see Givón (1973), Fleischman (1982), Bybee & Pagliuca (1987), Lichtenberk (1991), Bourdin (1992) and Forthcoming.

12 An alternative explanation, suggested by Oesten Dahl (p.c.), is that the verb form children select in this context will be whatever form their language happens to use in the protasis of unreal conditionals, e.g., the Conditional in Finnish, the Subjunctive in German, etc. This usage, in other words, would represent a special type of truncated, mono-clausal conditional. Undermining this explanation, however, is the situation in Spanish. Standard Spanish uses the Imperfect Subjunctive in the protasis of unreal conditionals, as in (5), yet Spanish children use the Imperfect Indicative in 'pre-ludic' contexts.

13 A less radical statement of this position, formulated with respect to Italian, is that of Bertinetto (1986:390), who argues that in the modal uses of the *Imperfetto* the meaning of temporal pastness is, if not neutralized, at least attentuated to the point of conveying 'non-actuality' or simply 'virtuality'. Cf. also Bazzanella (1987).

14 In his words, "comme le conditionnel, qui prend souvent des valeurs de 'futur fictionnel' (ou hypothéthique), l'imparfait de l'indicatif semble pouvoir assumer dans certains emplois non temporels une valeur de présent fictionnel" (38f.).

15 Commenting on hypotheticality in Slavic, Restan (1989) similarly suggests 'incompleteness' as the common feature linking this modality to imperfective past forms in many

languages. However, Restan does not systematically distinguish between imperfective and imperfect, the latter of which can, in certain Slavic languages (Bulgarian, Macedonian), be aspectually perfective (Jane Hacking, p.c.).

16 Save for the standard Italian Conditional, which, as explained in n.10, is historically perfective.

17 Martin (1971:101) claims, similarly, that polite requests in French always involve an auxiliary construction, e.g. with *venir* 'come' or *vouloir* 'want' (*Je venais/voulais vous proposer de venir dîner à la maison* 'I wanted to ask you to come for dinner'). As for the irrealis meaning, he refers to a paper by Valin (1964), who interprets the psychological mechanism involved as a projection of the predicated situation back into a fictitious past in which the speaker adopts a subordinate stance vis-à-vis the addressee. By shifting the main verb (i.e., the auxiliary) back into this fictitious past, the speaker makes the realization of the subordinate situation (expressed by the infinitive) appear to be contingent upon the good will of the addressee. A similar explanation is proposed by Bertinetto (1986:373) for this usage in Italian, though not all his examples involve a modal auxiliary, e.g. *Dove andavi* [IMP] *così di fretta?* 'Where are [lit. were] you going in such a hurry?' (uttered while the speaker is walking alongside the addressee).

18 Mithun (this volume) reports on several languages that, in a similar fashion, classify *polite* imperatives as irrealis, while stronger imperatives are treated as realis (though aspect is not involved in the contrast). She interprets the latter situation, i.e. classification of an unrealized situation as realis, as reflecting a high degree of speaker confidence — approaching certainty — that the situation will be realized.

19 If they had been realized, the utterance would presumably have been formulated differently, per Grice's maxim of quantity.

20 Hale (1969:22), as cited in Steele (1975).

21 Whether this usage represents a characteristic phenomenon of so-called women's language, or alternatively, is simply an epiphenomenon of the fact that childcare has been traditionally the responsibility of women, is a question which, albeit interesting, falls outside the scope of the present inquiry.

22 In Gougenheim's words: "...on ne veut pas prendre au sérieux les paroles qu'on prononce. On dit en somme, à l'adresse de l'adulte qui entend ou pourrait entendre ces propos (où vis-à-vis de soi-même, par respect humain): Attention, je ne parle pas sérieusement, je suis dans le jeu, dans le fictif" (p. 154).

23 Excluded from discussion here are languages in which the imperfect is not *ipso eo* imperfective, e.g. Bulgarian and Macedonian, which operate with two aspectual oppositions, Perfective/Imperfective and Aorist/Imperfect. The modal extensions of these and other Slavic aspectual categories will be taken up briefly in §§10 and 12.

24 Argumentation supporting this claim is presented at various points in Fleischman (1990).

25 Verses 719-20, 726, 2556-60 of the Oxford version.

26 For a more idiomatic translation capturing the vividness of the character's vision, I have rendered certain of the Italian Imperfects (*stramazzava*, *sussultava*) as nonfinite present participles ('collapsing', 'convulsing').

27 For additional literary examples, see Lunn (1985:55f), Fleischman (1990:248f; 1991).

28 I say 'ostensible' because fidelity to an original speaker's utterance turns out to be a complex business involving more than simply a mechanical reproduction of the propositional content of that utterance and, in the case of direct quotation, also its form (cf. n.32). The various pragmatic factors that come into play (e.g., intentionality, non-literal meaning, opaque reference, point of view) are sufficient — and sufficiently complex (messy?) — to have spawned a vast literature on the topic of speech-and-thought representation that has, over the years, engaged numerous linguists, literary analysts, and philosophers of language.

29 For a more finely grained typology, and one of the more illuminating presentations of the topic, see Leech & Short (1981, chapter 10); also Chafe (1994, chapters 16-17).

30 Haiman's term 'speaker's framework' provides an umbrella for the range of meanings, at various levels of linguistic functioning, that an utterance communicates.

31 Various investigators have argued and offered evidence for the 'constructed' nature of directly quoted speech (Tannen 1986, 1989:110-119; Mayes 1990:333-334; Chafe 1994, chapter 16). However, the issue of whether a quote is *in fact* a verbatim report is often not what matters most — except to journalists and their editors, at risk of costly libel suits, and to the individuals they (mis)quote. What matters is rather the *illocutionary and perlocutionary force* of direct quotation, i.e. what the speaker purports to — and effectively does — accomplish by reporting what someone said or wrote in a form that is conventionally understood to preserve maximum representational authenticity. Mayes speculates — correctly, I believe — that the assumption that direct quotes are more authentic than indirect quotes may have originated in *literate* cultures, where direct quotation is by convention exact (359). The fact that many direct quotes are inventions of the speaker suggests strongly that speakers use direct quotation for specific pragmatic purposes (Mayes, p. 330; see also Chafe, chapter 16).

32 Similarly Tannen (1986). I agree with this statement in theory. Nonetheless, and as Chafe acknowledges, speakers often use the direct-speech format to report language they know was not uttered in precisely the form in which they quote it, as evidenced by the following example, from a natural narrative, where the direct quote is preceded by an explicitly hedged inquit formula: ***I was saying things like**: "Well, could we stop by my house so that I can tell my family that I have to go to jail haha an' I can't make the funeral?"* That speakers act as if they *can* remember distal speech accurately and reproduce it verbatim is also suggested by the following utterance, from the same natural narrative (reference in n.38): *I remember him saying: "Son, you're under arrest, you have to go to jail"*.

33 For a more detailed analysis of the formal features and constraints of free indirect discourse, see Banfield (1978/1993). Like many analysts, Banfield identifies utterances of free indirect discourse on the basis of clause-level formal features. For a compelling challenge to this position, relevant in particular to languages like English that lack a distinctive imperfective aspect, see Ehrlich (1991), which establishes important discourse-based criteria for identifying this style of quotation.

34 A distinctive feature of fictional narrative that sets its apart from nonfiction is the cognitive access the narrator has to the mental states of other individuals; only in constructed narratives (i.e. fiction) which are true in constructed worlds can one individual enter — and represent through language — the consciousness of another. When conversational narrators appear to do this — and we often do — the thought quotation must technically be viewed as an inference, not an assertion.

35 Echoing Kuno (1972), Wierzbicka (1974:271) insists that "direct speech is in some important and intuitively clear way more basic than indirect speech. To see this it is sufficient to think of all those languages which do not have indirect discourse at all (whereas the existence of direct discourse seems to be universal), and also of the historical priority of direct discourse in those languages in which the gradual development of the indirect discourse is historically attested."

36 The most vehement advocate of this position is Banfield (1982, 1985, and elsewhere in her writings), who insists on the chronological coincidence of free indirect discourse with the emergence of the modern novel in the 19th century. For discussion, see Fleischman (1990, 230ff.), (Haiman 1989).

37 From "Jeff goes to jail," a narrative tape-recorded and transcribed by Annie Jaisser. In the transcribing of an oral narration editorial decisions inevitably have to be made, e.g., about punctuation, capitalization, and — most important for our purpose — conventions for quotation (cf. Chafe 1988). The quotation conventions chosen will, of course, reflect the transcriber's interpretation of the style(s) of quotation used. In (25) and (26) I have changed the transcriber's double quote marks to the stylistically neutral convention <Q ... Q>.

38 In Fleischman (1990, Chap. 7) I discuss the influence of the grammatical person of a narration (first vs. 'third') on what are here referred to as irrealis quotation styles.

39 An alternative reading of the imperfective aspect of these inquit formulas is presented below.

40 This should occasion no surprise. As shown in the papers in this volume by Mithun and Chafe, grammatical categories (e.g. future, imperative) or constructions (questions, negation) are not uniformly classified as realis or irrealis across languages, nor even at times within the same language (e.g. imperatives in Jamul Diegueño and Alamblak, as reported by Mithun).

41 This explains why the *Imparfait* will be chosen when the past events in question are construed collectively, whereas the *Passé Simple* (or *Passé Composé* in speech) will be chosen when they are construed individually. The collective construal corresponds to what is here referred to as habitual, the individual construal to what is here referred to as iterative. Hacking (1993:158) offers a particularly nice formulation of this distinction (with reference to Slavic, but easily generalizable), observing that imperfective aspect is consistent with a "global, stative overview of a series of repeated events," i.e. habitual, while perfective is called for if the focus is on "the individual quality of the subevents," i.e. iterative. Though there are languages that formally distinguish iterative from habitual (e.g. Old Persian, per Lazard 1975), for our purpose it is unnecessary to insist on the distinction. For the record, in Old Persian it is the Habitual marker *-i* that is also used to express irrealis meanings, notably in unreal conditionals of the type illustrated in (5).

42 Givón (1984:285) notes that the most common test for realis/irrealis involves the referentiality of indefinite arguments under the scope of these modalities.

43 Regarding Eng. *would*, Bybee, Perkins, & Pagliuca (1994:239) point out that historically the habitual and irrealis (conditional) uses are "entirely independent developments." Whereas for Macedonian, Galton (1987:365) opines that "the two probably developed alongside each other."

44 As James observes, "Imperfective aspect is usually held to have as its essential feature the fact that it indicates that an action or state is not being viewed as a complete whole, but rather as something going on in time and not yet completed. But likewise, if an action or state is hypothetical, then it is unrealized and in that sense is not an actual complete action or state. Thus, imperfective aspect and the hypothetical share a semantic feature in that they both indicate something which is in some way not fully realized" (1982:p. 399).

45 One difficulty with the backgrounding hypothesis, pointed out to me by Ekkehard König, is that background information tends to be presupposed, i.e., it is presented as being not subject to challenge. It would thus seem more likely to correlate with realis than with irrealis.

46 At issue here is 'focus' in the visual, perceptual sense, not as a category of information structure contrasting with 'topic'.

47 Chafe (1994 and p.c.) suggests that these various contexts, or the irrealis meanings they instantiate, have as a common denominator the marking of an event as *imagined* rather than directly experienced. This distinction figures as the last of a hierarchy of oppositions he sets up, according to which experiences are divided into those that are immediate and those that are displaced, and within the latter category, those that are remembered and those that are imagined, though he acknowledges the fuzziness of this last distinction.

48 Like Bulgarian, Macedonian has a dual aspectual system in the past involving two oppositions: Perfective/Imperfective and Aorist/Imperfect, though the status of the latter opposition — tense or aspect — remains controversial (see Fielder 1993, §§2.4.7-8). According to Aronson (1977), the latter opposition has remained fundamentally aspectual, while the former, superordinate opposition has become more modal, with the (suffixally derived) Imperfectives giving rise to the new "Simple Conditional" forms (cf. also Galton 1987, Hacking 1993, Fielder 1993).

49 Though these two categories of the linguistic metalanguage are differentiated at the theoretical level, in practice (i.e. when applied to real-language data) the distinction often blurs (see Willett 1988).

REFERENCES

Adam, Jean-Michel. 1992. "Si hypothétique et l'imparfait: une approche linguistique de la fictionnalité." *Etudes Littéraires* 25,1/2.147-166.

Aronson, Howard I. 1977. "Interrelationships between Aspect and Mood in Bulgarian." *Folia Slavica* 1,1.9-32.

Banfield, Ann. 1978. "Where Epistemology, Style, and Grammar Meet Literary History." *New Literary History* 9,3.415-54. Abridged version repr. in *Reflexive Language. Reported Speech and Metapragmatics* ed. by John Lucy, 339-364. Cambridge: Cambridge University Press, 1993.

Banfield, Ann. 1982. *Unspeakable Sentences. Narration and Representation in the Language of Fiction.* London: Routledge.

Banfield, Ann. 1985. "Grammar and Memory." *Berkeley Linguistics Society* 11.387-397.

Bazzanella, Carla. 1987. "I modi dell'imperfetto." *Italiano e oltre* 1.18-22.
Bertinetto, Pier-Marco. 1986. *Tempo, aspetto e azione nel verbo italiano. Il sistema dell'indicativo.* Florence: Accademia della Crusca.
Bourdin, Philippe. 1992. "Constance et inconstances de la déicticité: la resémantisation des marqueurs andatifs et ventifs." *La Déixis: Colloque en Sorbonne, 8-9 juin 1990* ed. by M-A. Morel & L. Danon-Boileau, 287-307. Paris: Presses Universitaires de France.
Bourdin, Philippe. Forthcoming. *'Aller' et 'venir' en linguistique générale: Pour une typologie des filières de la resémantisation.* Toronto: Editions du G.R.E.F.
Bybee, Joan L. This volume. The Semantic development of Past Tense Modals in English.
Bybee, Joan L. & William Pagliuca. 1985. "Cross-Linguistic Comparison and the Development of Grammatical Meaning." *Historical Semantics: Historical Word Formation* ed. by Jacek Fisiak, 59-83. Berlin: Mouton.
Bybee, Joan L. & William Pagliuca1987. "The Evolution of Future Meaning." *Papers from the 7th International Conference on Historical Linguistics* ed. by A. Giacalone Ramat et al., 109-123. Amsterdam: Benjamins.
Bybee, Joan L., Revere D. Perkins, & William Pagliuca. 1994. *The Evolution of Grammar: Tense, Aspect, and Modality in the Languages of the World.* Chicago: University of Chicago Press.
Cappello, S. 1986. "L'imparfait de fiction." In: Le Goffic, ed., 31-41.
Chafe, Wallace. 1988. "Punctuation and the Prosody of Written Language." *Written Communication* 5,4.396-426.
Chafe, Wallace. 1994. *Discourse, Consciousness, and Time.* Chicago: University of Chicago Press.
Chafe, Wallace & Johanna Nichols, eds. 1986. *Evidentiality: The Linguistic Coding of Epistemology.* (= *Advances in Discourse Processes*, 20). Norwood, NJ: Ablex.
Chung, Sandra & Alan Timberlake. 1985. "Tense, Aspect, and Mood." *Language Typology and Syntactic Description*, Vol. 3: *Grammatical Categories and the Lexicon* ed. by Tim Shopen, 202-258. Cambridge: Cambridge University Press.
Comrie, Bernard. 1976. *Aspect.* Cambridge: Cambridge University Press.
Comrie, Bernard. 1985. *Tense.* Cambridge: Cambridge University Press.
Dahl, Oesten. 1985. *Tense and Aspect Systems.* Oxford: Blackwell.
Dahl, Oesten. Forthcoming. "The relation between Past Time Reference and Counterfactuality: A New Look." *On Conditionals Again (Proceedings from the 1994 Workshop "Conditionals and Co.", Duisberg, Germany)* ed. by A. Athanasiadou & R. Dirven.
Ehrlich, Susan. 1991. *Point of View. A Linguistic Analysis of Literary Style.* London & New York: Routledge.
Fielder, Grace. 1993. *The Semantics and Pragmatics of Verbal Categories in Bulgarian.* Lewiston, NY: Edwin Mellen Press.
Fleischman, Suzanne. 1982. "The Past and the Future: Are they 'Coming' or 'Going'?" *BLS* 8.322-34.
Fleischman, Suzanne. 1989. "Temporal Distance: A Basic Linguistic Metaphor" *Studies in Language* 13,1.1-51.
Fleischman, Suzanne. 1990. *Tense and Narrativity. From Medieval Performance to Modern Fiction.* Austin: University of Texas Press/ London & New York: Routledge.
Fleischman, Suzanne. 1991. "Verb Tense and Point of View in Narrative." Fleischman & Waugh, 1991, 26-54.

Fleischman, Suzanne & Linda R. Waugh, eds. 1991. *Discourse Pragmatics and the Verb: The Evidence from Romance*. London & New York: Routledge.
Galton, Herbert. 1987. "Unreal Hypothetical Periods in South Slavic and Greek and Related Features." *In Honor of Ilse Lehiste* ed. by R. Channon & L. Shockey, 357-368. Dordrecht: Foris.
Givón, T. 1973. "The Time-Axis Phenomenon." *Language* 49.890-925.
Givón, T. 1984. *Syntax. A Functional-Typological Introduction*. Vol. 1. Amsterdam: Benjamins.
Gougenheim, Georges. 1970. "La valeur psychologique des temps dans le 'Monologue de Figaro'." *Etudes de grammaire et de vocabulaire français*, 149-54. Paris: Picard.
Hacking, Jane F. 1993. A Comparative Typology of Conditionals in Russian and Macedonian. Unpublished dissertation, University of Toronto.
Haiman, John. 1989. "Alienation in Grammar." *Studies in Language* 13,1.129-170.
Hale, Kenneth. 1969. "Papago/či-m." Cambridge, MA: MIT (mimeo).
Harris, Martin B. 1978. *The Evolution of French Syntax. A Comparative Approach*. London: Longman.
Heine, Bernd & Mechthild Reh. 1984. *Grammaticalization and Reanalysis in African Languages*. Hamburg: Buske.
Heine, Bernd, Ulrike Claudi & Friederike Hünnemeyer. 1991. *Grammaticalization*. Chicago: University of Chicago Press.
Hopper, Paul J. 1979. "Some Observations on the Typology of Focus and Aspect in Narrative Language." *Studies in Language* 3,1.37-64.
Hopper, Paul J. 1981. "Aspect and Foregrounding in Discourse." *Discourse and Syntax* (= *Syntax and Semantics*, 12) ed. by T. Givón, 213-41. New York: Academic Press.
Hopper, Paul J. & Sandra A. Thompson. 1980. "Transitivity in Grammar and Discourse." *Language* 56,2.251-99.
James, Deborah. 1982. "Past Tense and the Hypothetical: A Cross-Linguistic Study." *Studies in Language* 6,3.375-403.
Klein-Andreu, Flora. 1991. "Losing Ground: A Discourse-Pragmatic Solution to the History of *-ra* in Spanish." Fleischamn & Waugh, 1991. 164-178.
Kuno, Susumo. 1972. "Pronominalization, Reflexivization, and Direct Discourse." *Linguistic Inquiry* 3,2.161-195.
Lass, Roger. 1990. "How To Do Things With Junk: Exaptation in Language Evolution." *Journal of Linguistics* 26,1:79-102.
Lazard, Gilbert. 1975. "La catégorie de l'éventuel." *Mélanges linguistiques offerts à Emile Benveniste*, 221-232. Louvain: Peeters.
Leech, Geoffrey N. & Michael H. Short. 1981. *Style in Fiction*. London: Longman.
Le Goffic, Pierre. 1986. "Que l'imparfait n'est pas un temps du passé." Le Goffic, 1986. 55-69.
Le Goffic, Pierre, ed. 1986. *Points de vue sur l'imparfait*. Caen: Université de Caen.
Lichtenberk, Frantisek. 1991. "Semantic Change and Heterosemy in Grammaticalization." *Language* 67.475-509.
Lunn, Patricia V. 1985. "The Aspectual Lens." *Hispanic Linguistics* 2.49-61.
Lunn, Patricia V. & Thomas Cravens. 1991. "A Contextual Reconsideration of the Spanish *-ra* 'Indicative'." Fleischman & Waugh, 1991. 147-163.

Maingueneau, Dominique. 1990. *Éléments de linguistique pour le texte littéraire*, 2d ed. Paris: Bordas.
Martin, Robert. 1971. *Temps et aspect*. Paris: Klincksieck.
Mayes, Patricia. 1990. "Quotation in English." *Studies in Language* 14:325-363.
Mithun, Marianne. This volume. "On the Relativity of Irreality."
Nichols, Johanna. 1986. "The Bottom Line: Chinese Pidgin Russian." Chafe & Nichols, 1986. 239-257.
Palmer, Frank R. 1986. *Mood and Modality*. Cambridge: Cambridge University Press.
Restan, Per. 1989. "Ne bylo, no moglo by but': O gipoteticheskoi modal'nosti." [There Wasn't But There Could Have Been: Concerning Hypothetical Modality] *Scando-Slavica* 35.203-210.
Roberts, John R. 1990. "Modality in Amele and Other Papuan Languages." *Journal of Linguistics* 26.363-401.
Rohlfs, Gerhard. 1968. *Grammatica Storica della Lingua Italiana e dei suoi Dialetti*. Vol. 2: *Morfologia*, trans. by Temistocle Franceschi. Turin: Einaudi.
Romaine, Suzanne & Deborah Lange. 1991. "The Use of *Like* as a Marker of Reported Speech and Thought: A Case of Grammaticalization in Progress." *American Speech* 66,3.227-279.
Slobin, Dan I. & Ayhan A. Aksu-Koç. 1986. "A Psychological Account of the Development and Use of Evidentials in Turkish." Chafe & Nichols, 1986. 159-167.
Steele, Susan. 1975. "Past and Irrealis: Just What Does It All Mean?" *International Journal of American Linguistics* 41.200-217.
Tannen, Deborah. 1986. "Introducing Constructed Dialogue in Greek and American Conversational and Literary Narrative." *Direct and Indirect Speech* ed. by F. Coulmas, 311-332. Berlin: Mouton de Gruyter.
Tannen, Deborah. 1989. *Talking Voices*. Cambridge: Cambridge University Press.
Trask, R.L. 1993. *A Dictionary of Grammatical Terms in Linguistics*. London & New York: Routledge.
Valin, Roch. 1964. *La méthode comparative en linguistique et psychomécanique du langage*. Québec: Presses de l'Université Laval.
Vendler, Zeno. 1967. *Linguistics in Philosophy*. Ithaca: Cornell University Press.
Warnant, Léon. 1966. "Moi, j'étais le papa... L'imparfait préludique et quelques remarques relatives à la recherche grammaticale." *Mélanges de grammaire française offerts à M. Maurice Grevisse pour le trentième anniversaire du Bon usage*, 343-66. Gembloux: Duculot.
Weinrich, Harald. 1973. *Le temps*. trans. by Michèle Lacoste. Paris: Seuil (originally published in German, 1964).
Wierzbicka, Anna. 1974. "The Semantics of Direct and Indirect Discourse." *Papers in Linguistics* 7.267-307.
Willett, Thomas. 1988. "A Cross-Linguistic Survey of the Grammaticalization of Evidentiality." *Studies in Language* 12.51-97.
Wilmet, Marc. 1968-69. "L'imparfait dit 'hypocoristique'." *Français Moderne* 36.298-312 & 37.54. Repr. in *Etudes de morphosyntaxe verbale*, 83-106. Paris: Klincksieck, 1976.
Woodbury, Anthony C. 1986. "Interactions of Tense and Evidentiality: A Study of Sherpa and English." Chafe & Nichols, 1986. 188-202.

Index of subjects

B

C

J

K

L

M

P

S

T

U

V

W

Index of languages

R

S

T

U

W

Y

Z

Author Index

C

D

E

F

W

X

Y

Z

Typological Studies in Language

A complete list of titles in this series can be found on the publishers' website, *www.benjamins.com*

71 **NEDJALKOV, Vladimir P. (ed.):** Reciprocal Constructions. With the assistance of Emma Š. Geniušienė and Zlatka Guentchéva. *Expected June 2007*

70 **ZÚÑIGA, Fernando:** Deixis and Alignment. Inverse systems in indigenous languages of the Americas. xii, 309 pp. *Expected November 2006*

69 **ARANOVICH, Raúl (ed.):** Split Auxiliary Systems. A cross-linguistic perspective. viii, 268 pp. + index. *Expected December 2006*

68 **ABRAHAM, Werner and Larisa LEISIÖ (eds.):** Passivization and Typology. Form and function. 2006. x, 553 pp.

67 **VESELINOVA, Ljuba N.:** Suppletion in Verb Paradigms. Bits and pieces of the puzzle. 2006. xviii, 236 pp.

66 **HICKMANN, Maya and Stéphane ROBERT (eds.):** Space in Languages. Linguistic Systems and Cognitive Categories. 2006. x, 362 pp.

65 **TSUNODA, Tasaku and Taro KAGEYAMA (eds.):** Voice and Grammatical Relations. In Honor of Masayoshi Shibatani. 2006. xviii, 342 pp.

64 **VOELTZ, F. K. Erhard (ed.):** Studies in African Linguistic Typology. 2006. xiv, 426 pp.

63 **FILIMONOVA, Elena (ed.):** Clusivity. Typology and case studies of the inclusive–exclusive distinction. 2005. xii, 436 pp.

62 **COUPER-KUHLEN, Elizabeth and Cecilia E. FORD (eds.):** Sound Patterns in Interaction. Cross-linguistic studies from conversation. 2004. viii, 406 pp.

61 **BHASKARARAO, Peri and Karumuri Venkata SUBBARAO (eds.):** Non-nominative Subjects. Volume 2. 2004. xii, 319 pp.

60 **BHASKARARAO, Peri and Karumuri Venkata SUBBARAO (eds.):** Non-nominative Subjects. Volume 1. 2004. xii, 325 pp.

59 **FISCHER, Olga, Muriel NORDE and Harry PERRIDON (eds.):** Up and down the Cline – The Nature of Grammaticalization. 2004. viii, 406 pp.

58 **HASPELMATH, Martin (ed.):** Coordinating Constructions. 2004. xcv, 578 pp.

57 **MATTISSEN, Johanna:** Dependent-Head Synthesis in Nivkh. A contribution to a typology of polysynthesis. 2003. x, 350 pp.

56 **SHAY, Erin and Uwe SEIBERT (eds.):** Motion, Direction and Location in Languages. In honor of Zygmunt Frajzyngier. 2003. xvi, 305 pp.

55 **FRAJZYNGIER, Zygmunt and Erin SHAY:** Explaining Language Structure through Systems Interaction. 2003. xviii, 309 pp.

54 **AIKHENVALD, Alexandra Y. and R.M.W. DIXON (eds.):** Studies in Evidentiality. 2003. xiv, 349 pp.

53 **GIVÓN, T. and Bertram F. MALLE (eds.):** The Evolution of Language out of Pre-language. 2002. x, 394 pp.

52 **GÜLDEMANN, Tom and Manfred von RONCADOR (eds.):** Reported Discourse. A meeting ground for different linguistic domains. 2002. xii, 425 pp.

51 **NEWMAN, John (ed.):** The Linguistics of Sitting, Standing and Lying. 2002. xii, 409 pp.

50 **FEIGENBAUM, Susanne and Dennis KURZON (eds.):** Prepositions in their Syntactic, Semantic and Pragmatic Context. 2002. vi, 304 pp.

49 **WISCHER, Ilse and Gabriele DIEWALD (eds.):** New Reflections on Grammaticalization. 2002. xiv, 437 pp.

48 **SHIBATANI, Masayoshi (ed.):** The Grammar of Causation and Interpersonal Manipulation. 2002. xviii, 551 pp.

47 **BARON, Irène, Michael HERSLUND and Finn SØRENSEN (eds.):** Dimensions of Possession. 2001. vi, 337 pp.

46 **AIKHENVALD, Alexandra Y., R.M.W. DIXON and Masayuki ONISHI (eds.):** Non-canonical Marking of Subjects and Objects. 2001. xii, 364 pp.

45 **BYBEE, Joan and Paul J. HOPPER (eds.):** Frequency and the Emergence of Linguistic Structure. 2001. vii, 492 pp.

44 **VOELTZ, F. K. Erhard and Christa KILIAN-HATZ (eds.):** Ideophones. 2001. x, 436 pp.

43 **GILDEA, Spike (ed.):** Reconstructing Grammar. Comparative Linguistics and Grammaticalization. 2000. xiv, 269 pp.

42 **DIESSEL, Holger:** Demonstratives. Form, function and grammaticalization. 1999. xii, 205 pp.

41 **FRAJZYNGIER, Zygmunt and Traci S. CURL (eds.):** Reciprocals. Forms and functions. Volume 2. 2000. xii, 201 pp.